R

D0959690

German Dictionary

Second Edition

German · English
English · German
Deutsch · Englisch
Englisch · Deutsch

Edited by
Jenni Karding Moulton

Under the General Editorship of
Professor William G. Moulton
PRINCETON UNIVERSITY

Revised by
Jennifer L. Hornor

RANDOM HOUSE
NEW YORK

392337724

*Random House Webster's Pocket German Dictionary,
Second Edition*

Visit the Random House Web site at http://www.randomhouse.com/

Typeset and printed in the United States of America.

1998 Random House Edition
0 9 8 7 6 5 4 3 2 1
ISBN: 0-375-70160-5

New York   Toronto   London   Sydney   Auckland

Concise Pronunciation Guide

Consonants

b   Usually like English *b*: **Bett, graben.** But when final or before *s* or *t*, like English *p*: **das Grab, des Grabs, er gräbt.**

c   In foreign words only. Before *a, o, u,* like English *k*: **Café'.** Before *ä, e, i* in words borrowed from Latin, like English *ts*: **Cicero;** otherwise usually with the foreign pronunciation.

ch   After *a, o, u, au,* a scraping sound like Scottish *ch* in *loch,* made between the back of the tongue and the roof of the mouth: **Dach, Loch, Buch, auch.** In other positions, much like English *h* in *hue*: **Dächer, Löcher, Bücher, ich, manch, welch, durch.** In words borrowed from Greek or Latin, initial *ch* before *a, o, u, l, r* is like English *k*: **Charak'ter, Chor, Christ.** In words borrowed from Frer ch it is like German *sch*: **Chance.**

chs   As a fixed combination, like English *ks*: **der Dachs,** *the badger.* But when the *s* is an ending, like German *ch* plus *s*: **des Dachs,** genitive of **das Dach,** *the roof.*

ck   As in English: **backen, Stock.**

d   Usually like English *d*: **Ding, Rede.** But when final or before *s,* like English *t*: **das Band, des Bands.**

dt   Like English *tt*: **Stadt** just like **statt.**

f   As in English: **Feuer, Ofen, Schaf.**

g   Usually like English *g* in *get*: **Geld, schlagen, Könige, reinigen.** But when final or before *s* or *t,* like English *k*: **der Schlag, des Schlags, er schlägt.** However, *ig* when final or before *s* or *t* is like German *ich*: **der König, des Königs, er reinigt.** In words borrowed from French, *g* before *e* is like English *z* in *azure*: **Loge.**

h   As in English: **hier.** But after vowels it is only a sign of vowel length, and is not pronounced: **gehen, Bahn, Kuh.**

j   Like English *y*: **Jahr.** In a few words borrowed from French, like English *z* in *azure*: **Journal'.**

k   As in English: **kennen, Haken, buk.**

l   Not the "dark *l*" of English *mill, bill,* but the "bright *l*" of English *million, billion*: **lang, fallen, hell.**

m   As in English: **mehr, kommen, dumm.**

n   As in English: **neu, kennen, kann.**

Consonants

ng	Always like English *ng* in *singer*, never like English *ng + g* in *finger*. German **Finger, Hunger.**
p	As in English: **Post, Rippe, Tip.**
pf	Like English *pf* in *cupful*: **Kopf, Apfel, Pfund.**
ph	As in English: **Philosophie'.**
qu	Like English *kv*: **Quelle, Aqua'rium.**
r	When followed by a vowel, either a gargled sound made between the back of the tongue and the roof of the mouth, or (less commonly) a quick flip of the tongue tip against the gum ridge: **Ring, Haare, bessere.** When not followed by a vowel, a sound much like the *ah* of English *yeah,* or the *a* of *sofa*: **Haar, besser.**
s	Usually like English *z* in *zebra*, or *s* in *rose*: **sie, Rose.** But when final or before a consonant, like English *s* in *this*: **das, Wespe, Liste, Maske.**
sch	Like English *sh* in *ship*, but with the lips rounded: **Schiff, waschen, Tisch.**
sp st }	At the beginning of a word, like *sch + p, sch + t*: **Spiel, Stahl.**
ss ß }	Like English *ss* in *miss*. *ss* is written only after a short vowel when another vowel follows: **müssen.** Otherwise ß is written: finally **muß**, before a consonant **mußte**, or after a long vowel **Muße.**
t	As in English: **tun, bitter, Blatt.**
th	Always like *t*: **Thea'ter;** never like English *th*.
tion	Pronounced *tsyohn*: **Nation', Aktion'.**
tsch	Like *t + sch*: **deutsch.**
tz	Like English *ts*: **sitzen, Platz.**
v	In German words, like English *f*: **Vater, Frevel.** In foreign words, like English *v*: **Novem'ber, Moti've;** but finally and before *s*, like *f* again: **das Motiv', des Motivs'.**
w	Like English *v*: **Wagen, Löwe.**
x	As in English: **Hexe.**
z	Always like English *ts*: **zehn, Kreuz, Salz.**

Short vowels

a	Satz	Between English *o* in *hot* and *u* in *hut*.
{ ä	Sätze }	Like English *e* in *set*.
{ e	setze }	
i	sitze	Like English *i* in *sit*.
o	Stock	Like English *o* in *gonna*, or the "New England short *o*" in *coat*, *road*; shorter than English *o* in *cost*.
ö	Stöcke	Tongue position as for short *e*, lips rounded as for short *o*.
u	Busch	Like English *u* in *bush*.
{ ü	Büsche }	Tongue position as for short *i*, lips rounded as for short *u*.
{ y	mystisch }	

Unaccented short e

e	beginne	Like English *e* in *begin*, *pocket*.

Long vowels

{ a	Tal }	
{ ah	Zahl }	Like English *a* in *father*.
{ aa	Saal }	
{ ä	Täler }	In elevated speech, like English *ai* in *fair*; otherwise just like German long *e*.
{ äh	zählen }	
{ e	wer }	
{ eh	mehr }	Like English *ey* in *they*, but with no glide toward a *y* sound.
{ ee	Meer }	
{ i	mir }	
{ ih	ihr }	Like English *i* in *machine*, but with no glide toward a *y* sound.
{ ie	Bier }	
{ o	Ton }	
{ oh	Sohn }	Like English *ow* in *slow*, but with no glide toward a *w* sound.
{ oo	Boot }	
{ ö	Töne }	Tongue position as for long *e*, lips rounded as for long *o*.
{ öh	Söhne }	

v

{ u	Hut }	Like English *u* in *rule*, but with no glide toward a *w*	
uh	Kuh }	sound.	
{ ü	Hüte }	Tongue position as for long *i*, lips rounded as for	
üh	Kühe }	long *u*.	
y	Typ }		

Diphthongs

{ ei	Seite }	Like English *i* in *side*. Also spelled *ey, ay* in names:
ai	Saite }	*Meyer, Bayern.*
au	Haut	Like English *ou* in *out*.
{ eu	heute }	Like English *oi* in *oil*.
äu	Häute }	

The spelling of vowel length	Short	Long
An accented vowel is always short when	schlaff	Schlaf
followed by a doubled consonant letter,	wenn	wen
but nearly always long when followed by a	still	Stil
single consonant letter.	offen	Ofen
	öffnen	Öfen
	Butter	Puter
Note that	dünne	Düne
ck counts as the doubled form of **k**:	hacken	Haken
tz counts as the doubled form of **z**:	putzen	duzen
ss counts as the doubled form of **ß**:	Masse	Maße
Vowels are always long when followed by a	wann	Wahn
(unpronounced) **h**:	stelle	stehle
	irre	ihre
	Wonne	wohne
	gönne	Söhne
	Rum	Ruhm
	dünn	kühn
Vowels are always long when they are written	Stadt	Staat
double:	Bett	Beet
	Gott	Boot
In this respect, **ie** counts as the doubled form	bitte	biete
of **i**:		

German Accentuation

Most German words are accented on the first syllable: **Mo'nate,
ar'beitete, Düsenkampfflugzeuge.** However, the prefixes be-, emp-,
ent-, er-, ge-, ver-, zer-, are never accented: **befeh'len, der Befehl',
empfan'gen, der Empfang',** etc. Other prefixes are usually accented
in nouns: **der Un'terricht,** but unaccented in verbs: **unterrich'ten.**
Foreign words are often accented on a syllable other than the first:
Hotel', Muse'um, Photographie'.

Note particularly the accentuation of such forms as **übertre'ten,
ich übertre'te** *I overstep,* where über is a prefix; but **ü'bertreten, ich
trete ... über** *I step over* where **über** is a separate word, despite the
fact that **ü'bertreten** is spelled without a space. These two types will
be distinguished in this dictionary by writing **übertre'ten** but **über•
treten.**

German spelling does not indicate the place of the accent. In this
dictionary, accent will be marked when it falls on a syllable other
than the first: **Befehl', unterrich'ten, Photographie'.** Where it is not
marked, the accent is on the first syllable: **Monate, arbeitete,
Düsenkampfflugzeuge, Unterricht, über•treten.**

Nouns

This listing ↓	means this ↓
Wagen,-	plural is **Wagen.**
Vater,-̈	plural is **Väter.**
Tisch,-e	plural is **Tische.**
Sohn,-̈e	plural is **Söhne.**
Bild,-er	plural is **Bilder.**
Haus,-̈er	plural is **Häuser.**
Auge,-n	plural is **Augen.**
Ohr,-en	plural is **Ohren.**
Hotel',-s	plural is **Hotels'.**
Muse'um,-e'en	plural is **Muse'en.**
Doktor,-o'ren	plural is **Dokto'ren.**
Kopie',-i'en	plural is **Kopi'en,** with three syllables.
Kuß,-̈sse	final ß changes to medial ss because the ü is short.
Fuß,-̈e	final ß kept in all forms because the ü is long.

Junge,-n,-n	nominative singular is **Junge,** all other forms are **Jungen.**
Name(n),-	declined like **Wagen** (above), except that nominative singular is **Name.**
Beamt'-	takes adjective endings: **ein Beamter, der Beamte, zwei Beamte, die zwei Beamten.**
Milch	has no plural.
Leute, *n.pl.*	has no singular.

From almost any German noun meaning some kind of man or boy, a noun meaning the corresponding woman or girl can be formed by adding **-in:** **der Arbeiter** *worker (man or boy),* **die Arbeiterin** *worker (woman or girl);* **der Russe** *Russian (man or boy),* **die Russin** *Russian (woman or girl).*

Adjectives

Most German adjectives can also be used, without ending, as adverbs: **schlecht** *bad, badly.* The few which never occur without ending as adverbs are listed with a following hyphen: **link-** *left,* **ober-** *upper,* **zweit-** *second.* (The corresponding adverbs are **links** *to the left,* **oben** *above,* **zweitens** *secondly.*)

Adjectives which take umlaut in the comparative and superlative are listed as follows: **lang (-),** i.e., the comparative and superlative are **länger, längst-.**

Limiting or determining adjectives are listed in the nominative singular masculine, with an indication of the nominative singular neuter and feminine: **der, das, die, dieser, -es, -e; ein, -, -e.**

Descriptive adjectives take the following endings:

	Strong endings				Weak endings			
	masc.	**neut.**	**fem.**	**pl.**	**masc.**	**neut.**	**fem.**	**pl.**
nom.	-er	-es	-e	-e	-e	-e	-e	-en
acc.	-en	-es	-e	-e	-en	-e	-e	-en
dat.	-em	-em	-er	-en	-en	-en	-en	-en
gen.	-en	-en	-er	-er	-en	-en	-en	-en

Weak endings are used if the adjective is preceded by an inflected form of a limiting (determining) adjective; strong endings are used otherwise.

Verbs

Regular weak verbs are listed simply in the infinitive: **machen**. If a verb is used with a separable prefix (accented adverb), this is indicated by a raised dot: **auf•machen** (i.e., the infinitive is **aufmachen**, the present **ich mache . . . auf**, the past **ich machte . . . auf**, the past participle **aufgemacht**). An asterisk after a verb refers to the following lists of irregular weak and strong verbs. The sign † means that a verb takes the auxiliary verb **sein**; the sign ‡ means that a verb can take either **sein** or **haben**.

Irregular weak verbs

Infinitive	3rd sg. present	Past	Subjunctive	Past participle
haben	hat	hatte	hätte	gehabt
bringen	bringt	brachte	brächte	gebracht
denken	denkt	dachte	dächte	gedacht
brennen	brennt	brannte	brennte	gebrannt
kennen	kennt	kannte	kennte	gekannt
nennen	nennt	nannte	nennte	genannt
†rennen	rennt	rannte	rennte	gerannt
senden	sendet	sandte	sendete	gesandt
wenden	wendet	wandte	wendete	gewandt
dürfen	darf	durfte	dürfte	gedurft
können	kann	konnte	könnte	gekonnt
mögen	mag	mochte	möchte	gemocht
müssen	muß	mußte	müßte	gemußt
sollen	soll	sollte	sollte	gesollt
wollen	will	wollte	wollte	gewollt
wissen	weiß	wußte	wüßte	gewußt

Strong verbs

If a derived or compound verb is not listed, its forms may be found by consulting the simple verb. The sign + means that a regular weak form is also used.

Infinitive	3rd sg. present	Past	Subjunctive	Past participle
backen	bäckt	+buk	+büke	gebacken
befehlen	befiehlt	befahl	beföhle	befohlen
beginnen	beginnt	begann	begönne, begänne	begonnen
beißen	beißt	biß	bisse	gebissen
bergen	birgt	barg	bärge	geborgen
†bersten	birst	barst	bärste	geborsten
bewegen	bewegt	bewog	bewöge	bewogen
‡biegen	biegt	bog	böge	gebogen
bieten	bietet	bot	böte	geboten
binden	bindet	band	bände	gebunden
bitten	bittet	bat	bäte	gebeten
blasen	bläst	blies	bliese	geblasen
†bleiben	bleibt	blieb	bliebe	geblieben
braten	brät	briet	briete	gebraten
brechen	bricht	brach	bräche	gebrochen
dingen	dingt	+dang	+dänge	+gedungen
dreschen	drischt	drosch	drösche	gedroschen
†dringen	dringt	drang	dränge	gedrungen
†erbleichen	erbleicht	+erblich	+erbliche	+erblichen
erlöschen	erlischt	erlosch	erlösche	erloschen
essen	ißt	aß	äße	gegessen
‡fahren	fährt	fuhr	führe	gefahren
†fallen	fällt	fiel	fiele	gefallen
fangen	fängt	fing	finge	gefangen
fechten	ficht	focht	föchte	gefochten
finden	findet	fand	fände	gefunden
flechten	flicht	flocht	flöchte	geflochten
‡fliegen	fliegt	flog	flöge	geflogen
†fliehen	flieht	floh	flöhe	geflohen
†fließen	fließt	floß	flösse	geflossen
fressen	frißt	fraß	fräße	gefressen
frieren	friert	fror	fröre	gefroren
gären	gärt	+gor	+göre	+gegoren
gebären	gebiert	gebar	gebäre	geboren
geben	gibt	gab	gäbe	gegeben
†gedeihen	gedeiht	gedieh	gediehe	gediehen
†gehen	geht	ging	ginge	gegangen
†gelingen	gelingt	gelang	gelänge	gelungen
gelten	gilt	galt	gölte, gälte	gegolten
†genesen	genest	genas	genäse	genesen
genießen	genießt	genoß	genösse	genossen
†geschehen	geschieht	geschah	geschähe	geschehen
gewinnen	gewinnt	gewann	gewönne, gewänne	gewonnen
gießen	gießt	goß	gösse	gegossen

x

Infinitive	3rd sg. present	Past	Subjunctive	Past participle
gleichen	gleicht	glich	gliche	geglichen
†gleiten	gleitet	glitt	glitte	geglitten
glimmen	glimmt	+glomm	+glömme	+geglommen
graben	gräbt	grub	grübe	gegraben
greifen	greift	griff	griffe	gegriffen
halten	hält	hielt	hielte	gehalten
hängen	hängt	hing	hinge	gehangen
hauen	haut	+hieb	+hiebe	gehauen
heben	hebt	hob	höbe	gehoben
heißen	heißt	hieß	hieße	geheißen
helfen	hilft	half	hülfe, hälfe	geholfen
klimmen	klimmt	+klomm	+klömme	+geklommen
klingen	klingt	klang	klänge	geklungen
kneifen	kneift	kniff	kniffe	gekniffen
†kommen	kommt	kam	käme	gekommen
†kriechen	kriecht	kroch	kröche	gekrochen
laden	lädst	lud	lüde	geladen
lassen	läßt	ließ	ließe	gelassen
†laufen	läuft	lief	liefe	gelaufen
leiden	leidet	litt	litte	gelitten
leihen	leiht	lieh	liehe	geliehen
lesen	liest	las	läse	gelesen
liegen	liegt	lag	läge	gelegen
lügen	lügt	log	löge	gelogen
meiden	meidet	mied	miede	gemieden
messen	mißt	maß	mäße	gemessen
mißlingen	mißlingt	mißlang	mißlänge	mißlungen
nehmen	nimmt	nahm	nähme	genommen
pfeifen	pfeift	pfiff	pfiffe	gepfiffen
preisen	preist	pries	priese	gepriesen
quellen	quillt	quoll	quölle	gequollen
raten	rät	riet	riete	geraten
reiben	reibt	rieb	riebe	gerieben
‡reißen	reißt	riß	risse	gerissen
‡reiten	reitet	ritt	ritte	geritten
riechen	riecht	roch	röche	gerochen
ringen	ringt	rang	ränge	gerungen
rinnen	rinnt	rann	rönne	geronnen
rufen	ruft	rief	riefe	gerufen
saufen	säuft	soff	söffe	gesoffen
saugen	saugt	+sog	+söge	+gesogen
schaffen	schafft	schuf	schüfe	geschaffen
schallen	schallt	+scholl	+schölle	geschallt
‡scheiden	scheidet	schied	schiede	geschieden
scheinen	scheint	schien	schiene	geschienen
schelten	schilt	schalt	schölte	gescholten

xi

Infinitive	3rd sg. present	Past	Subjunctive	Past participle
scheren	schert	+schor	+schöre	+geschoren
schieben	schiebt	schob	schöbe	geschoben
schießen	schießt	schoß	schösse	geschossen
schinden	schindet	schund	schünde	geschunden
schlafen	schläft	schlief	schliefe	geschlafen
schlagen	schlägt	schlug	schlüge	geschlagen
†schleichen	schleicht	schlich	schliche	geschlichen
schleifen	schleift	schliff	schliffe	geschliffen
schließen	schließt	schloß	schlösse	geschlossen
schlingen	schlingt	schlang	schlänge	geschlungen
schmeißen	schmeißt	schmiß	schmisse	geschmissen
schmelzen	schmilzt	schmolz	schmölze	geschmolzen
schneiden	schneidet	schnitt	schnitte	geschnitten
schrecken	schrickt	schrak	schräke	geschrocken
schreiben	schreibt	schrieb	schriebe	geschrieben
schreien	schreit	schrie	schriee	geschrie(e)n
†schreiten	schreitet	schritt	schritte	geschritten
schweigen	schweigt	schwieg	schwiege	geschwiegen
schwellen	schwillt	schwoll	schwölle	geschwollen
‡schwimmen	schwimmt	schwamm	schwömme	geschwommen
†schwinden	schwindet	schwand	schwände	geschwunden
schwingen	schwingt	schwang	schwänge	geschwungen
schwören	schwört	+schwur, schwor	+schwüre	+geschworen
sehen	sieht	sah	sähe	gesehen
†sein	ist	war	wäre	gewesen
sieden	siedet	+sott	+sötte	+gesotten
singen	singt	sang	sänge	gesungen
†sinken	sinkt	sank	sänke	gesunken
sinnen	sinnt	sann	sänne, sönne	gesonnen
sitzen	sitzt	saß	säße	gesessen
speien	speit	spie	spiee	gespie(e)n
spinnen	spinnt	spann	spönne, spänne	gesponnen
spleißen	spleißt	spliß	splisse	gesplissen
sprechen	spricht	sprach	spräche	gesprochen
sprießen	sprießt	sproß	sprösse	gesprossen
†springen	springt	sprang	spränge	gesprungen
stechen	sticht	stach	stäche	gestochen
stecken	steckt	+stak	+stäke	gesteckt
stehen	steht	stand	stände, stünde	gestanden
stehlen	stiehlt	stahl	stähle, stöhle	gestohlen
†steigen	steigt	stieg	stiege	gestiegen
†sterben	stirbt	starb	stürbe	gestorben

xii

Infinitive	3rd sg. present	Past	Subjunctive	Past participle
‡stieben	stiebt	+stob	+stöbe	+gestoben
stinken	stinkt	stank	stänke	gestunken
‡stoßen	stößt	stieß	stieße	gestoßen
streichen	streicht	strich	striche	gestrichen
streiten	streitet	stritt	stritte	gestritten
tragen	trägt	trug	trüge	getragen
treffen	trifft	traf	träfe	getroffen
‡treiben	treibt	trieb	triebe	getrieben
‡treten	tritt	trat	träte	getreten
trinken	trinkt	trank	tränke	getrunken
trügen	trügt	trog	tröge	getrogen
tun	tut	tat	täte	getan
verbleichen	verbleicht	verblich	verbliche	verblichen
verderben	verdirbt	verdarb	verdürbe	verdorben
verdrießen	verdrießt	verdroß	verdrösse	verdrossen
vergessen	vergißt	vergaß	vergäße	vergessen
verlieren	verliert	verlor	verlöre	verloren
†wachsen	wächst	wuchs	wüchse	gewachsen
wägen	wägt	wog	wöge	gewogen
waschen	wäscht	wusch	wüsche	gewaschen
weben	webt	+wob	+wöbe	+gewoben
weichen	weicht	wich	wiche	gewichen
weisen	weist	wies	wiese	gewiesen
werben	wirbt	warb	würbe	geworben
†werden	wird	wurde, (ward)	würde	geworden
werfen	wirft	warf	würfe	geworfen
wiegen	wiegt	wog	wöge	gewogen
winden	windet	wand	wände	gewunden
wringen	wringt	wrang	wränge	gewrungen
‡ziehen	zieht	zog	zöge	gezogen
zwingen	zwingt	zwang	zwänge	gezwungen

Abbreviations

abbr.	abbreviation	*intr.*	intransitive
adj.	adjective	*jur.*	juridical
adv.	adverb	*m.*	masculine
arch.	architecture	*math.*	mathematics
art.	article	*med.*	medicine
bot.	botany	*mil.*	military
chem.	chemistry	*n.*	noun
comm.	commercial	*naut.*	nautical
conj.	conjunction	*nt.*	neuter
cpds.	compounds	*num.*	number
eccles.	ecclesiastical	*pl.*	plural
econ.	economics	*pol.*	politics
elec.	electricity	*pred.*	predicate
f.	feminine	*prep.*	preposition
fam.	familiar	*pron.*	pronoun
fig.	figuratively	*sg.*	singular
geogr.	geography	*tech.*	technical
geom.	geometry	*tr.*	transitive
gov't.	government	*typogr.*	typography
gram.	grammar	*vb.*	verb
interj.	interjection	*zool.*	zoology

Aachen, *n.nt.* Aachen, Aix-la-Chapelle.

Aal, -e, *n.m.* eel.

ab, *adv.* down; off; (**ab Berlin**) leaving Berlin; (**ab heute**) from today on; (**ab und zu**) now and then; (**von jetzt ab**) from now on.

ab·ändern, *vb.* revise.

Abänderung, -en, *n.f.* variation, revision.

Abart, -en, *n.f.* variety, species.

Abbau, *n.m.* working; reduction; razing.

ab·bauen, *vb.* raze; mine.

Abbild, -er *n.nt.* image, effigy.

ab·blenden, *vb.* dim (headlights).

ab·brechen*, *vb.* break off; cease, stop.

Abbruch, ⸚e, *n.m.* breaking off; cessation; damage.

ab·danken, *vb.* abdicate.

Abdankung, -en, *n.f.* abdication.

Abdruck, -e, *n.m.* (printed) impression, copy.

Abdruck, ⸚e, *n.m.* impress, mark, cast.

Abend, -e, *n.m.* evening; (**zu A. essen***) dine, have dinner.

Abendbrot, *n.nt.* supper.

Abenddämmerung, -en, *n.f.* dusk.

Abendessen, -, *n.nt.* dinner, supper.

Abendland, *n.nt.* Occident.

abendländisch, *adj.* occidental.

abendlich, *adj.* evening.

Abendmahl, -e, *n.nt.* Holy Communion, Lord's Supper.

abends, *adv.* in the evening.

Abenteuer, -, *n.nt.* adventure.

abenteuerlich, *adj.* adventurous.

Abenteurer, -, *n.m.* adventurer.

aber, *conj.* but.

Aberglaube(n), -, *n.m.* superstition.

abergläubisch, *adj.* superstitious.

abermals, *adv.* once again.

Abessi'nien, *n.nt.* Abyssinia.

ab·fahren*, *vb.* leave, depart.

Abfahrt, -en, *n.f.* departure; descent (skiing).

Abfahrtszeit, *n.f.* departure time.

Abfall, ⸚e, *n.m.* trash, rubbish; slope; decrease; defection.

ab·fallen*, *vb.* fall off; decrease; revolt.

abfällig, *adj.* precipitous; derogatory.

ab·fangen*, *vb.* intercept.

ab·fassen, *vb.* draw up, compose.

ab·fertigen, *vb.* take care of, expedite.

ab·feuern, *vb.* discharge (gun).

ab·finden*, *vb.* (**sich a. mit**) put up with.

Abflug, *n.m.* departure (plane).

Abfluß, ⸚sse, *n.m.* drain(age), outlet.

ab·führen, *vb.* lead off.

Abführmittel, -, *n.nt.* laxative.

Abgabe, -n, *n.f.* levy.

Abgasbestimmungen, *n.f.pl.* emission controls.

Abgase, *n.pl.* exhaust fumes.

ab·geben*, *vb.* hand over; check (baggage); cast (vote).

abgebrüht, *adj.* hard-boiled.

abgedroschen, *adj.* trite.

abgelegen, *adj.* remote.

abgemacht, *adj.* settled, agreed.

abgeneigt, *adj.* averse, disinclined.

abgenutzt, *adj.* worn-out.

Abgeordnet-, *n.m.&f.* representative, deputy.

abgeschieden, *adj.* separated, secluded; departed.

abgesehen von, *prep.* aside from.

ab·gewinnen*, *vb.* gain from.

ab·gewöhnen, *vb.* give up (habit, smoking).

Abgott, -er, *n.m.* idol.

Abgötterei, -en, *n.f.* idolatry.

Abgrenzung, -en, *n.f.* demarcation.

Abgrund, ⸚e, *n.m.* abyss, precipice.

ab·halten*, *vb.* hold off, restrain, deter.

abhan'den, *adv.* missing; (**a. kommen***) get lost.

Abhandlung, -en, *n.f.* treatise.

Abhang, ⸚e, *n.m.* slope.

ab·hängen*, *vb.* depend.

abhängig, *adj.* dependent.

Abhängigkeit, -n, *n.f.* dependence.

ab·härten, *vb.* harden.

ab·helfen*, *vb.* remedy.

Abhilfe, -n, *n.f.* remedy, relief.

abhold, *adj.* averse, disinclined.

ab·holen, *vb.* go and get, pick up, call for.

ab·hören, *vb.* listen to, monitor.

Abitur', -e, *n.nt.* final examination at end of secondary school; high school diploma.

Abkehr, *n.f.* turning away.

Abkomme, -n, -n, *n.m.* descendant; offspring.

Abkommen, -, *n.nt.* convention; agreement.

Abkömmling, -e, *n.m.* offspring, descendant; derivative.

ab·kühlen, *vb.* cool off.

ab·kürzen, *vb.* abbreviate; abridge.

Abkürzung, -en, *n.f.* abbreviation; abridgment; short cut.

ab·laden*, *vb.* unload.

Ablage, -n, *n.f.* depot, place of deposit.

Ablaß, =sse, *n.m.* letting off, drainage; *(eccles.)* indulgence.

ab·lassen*, *vb.* let off, drain; desist.

Ablativ, -e, *n.m.* ablative.

Ablauf, *n.m.* running off, expiration.

ab·laufen*, *vb.* run off, expire.

Ablaut, -e, *n.m.* ablaut (vowel alteration, as in *singen, sang, gesungen).*

ab·legen, *vb.* discard, take off.

ab·lehnen, *vb.* decline, reject.

Ablehnung, -en, *n.f.* rejection.

ab·leiten, *vb.* derive.

Ableitung, -en, *n.f.* derivation.

ab·lenken, *vb.* divert, distract.

Ablenkung, -en, *n.f.* diversion, distraction.

ab·leugnen, *vb.* deny, disavow.

Ableugnung, -en, *n.f.* denial, disavowal.

ab·lichten, *vb.* photocopy.

Ablichtung, -en, *n.f.* photocopy.

ab·liefern, *vb.* deliver.

Ablieferung, -en, *n.f.* delivery.

ab·lösen, *vb.* relieve.

Ablösung, -en, *n.f.* relief.

Abmarsch, =e, *n.m.* marching off, departure.

ab·melden, *vb.* report the departure of.

ab·mühen, *vb.* (sich a.) toil.

Abnahme, -n, *n.f.* decrease; purchase (business).

abnehmbar, -n, *adj.* removable.

ab·nehmen*, *vb.* *(tr.)* take off, remove; *(intr.)* decrease, lose weight.

Abnehmer, -, *n.m.* purchaser.

Abneigung, -en, *n.f.* antipathy, dislike, aversion.

abnorm', -e, *adj.* abnormal.

ab·nötigen, *vb.* force from.

ab·nutzen, *vb.* wear (something) out.

Abnutzung, -n, *n.f.* wearing out.

Abonnement', -s, *n.nt.* subscription.

abonnie'ren, *vb.* subscribe.

Abordnung, -en, *n.f.* delegation.

Abort, -e, *n.m.* toilet.

Abort', -e, *n.m.* abortion.

ab·rackern, *vb.* (sich a.) drudge.

ab·raten*, *vb.* dissuade.

ab·räumen, *vb.* clear off.

ab·rechnen, *vb.* settle accounts.

Abrechnung, -en, *n.f.* settlement of accounts.

Abrede, -n, *n.f.* (in A. stellen) deny.

Abreise, -n, *n.f.* departure.

ab·reisen, *vb.* depart.

ab·reißen*, *vb.* tear off; demolish.

Abriß, -sse, *n.m.* outline, summary.

abrupt, *adj.* abrupt.

ab·rüsten, *vb.* disarm.

Abrüstung, -en, *n.f.* disarmament.

Absage, -n, *n.f.* refusal (of an invitation), calling off.

ab·sagen, *vb.* decline, revoke, cancel.

Absatz, =e, *n.m.* paragraph; heel; landing; sale, market.

ab·schaben, *vb.* scrape off, abrade.

ab·schaffen*, *vb.* abolish, get rid of.

Abschaffung, -en, *n.f.* abolition.

ab·schätzen, *vb.* appraise, estimate.

Abschätzung, -en, *n.f.* appraisal, estimate.

Abschaum, *n.m.* dregs.

Abscheu, -e, *n.m.* abhorrence, loathing.

abscheu'lich, *adj.* abominable, detestable.

Abschied, -e, *n.m.* departure, leave, farewell.

Abschlag, ⸚e, *n.m.* chips; repulse; refusal.

ab·schlagen*, *vb.* chip off; repel; refuse.

abschlägig, *adj.* negative, refusing.

ab·schleifen*, *vb.* grind off, abrade.

ab·schließen*, *vb.* lock up, close off; conclude.

Abschluß, -sse, *n.m.* conclusion.

Abschlußprüfung, -en, *n.f.* final exam.

Abschlußzeugnis, *n.nt.* diploma.

ab·schneiden*, *vb.* cut off.

Abschnitt, -e, *n.m.* section.

ab·schrecken, *vb.* frighten off.

abschreckend, *adj.* forbidding.

Abschreckung, *n.f.* deterrence.

Abschreckungsmittel, -, *n.nt.* deterrent.

ab·schreiben*, *vb.* copy.

Abschrift, -en, *n.f.* copy.

abschüssig, *adj.* precipitous.

ab·schweifen, *vb.* digress.

ab·schwören*, *vb.* abjure.

Abschwörung, -en, *n.f.* abjuration.

absehbar, *adj.* foreseeable.

ab·sehen*, *vb.* look away; see from; **(a. von)** give up; **(auf mich abgesehen)** aimed at me; **(ist abzusehen)** can be seen.

abseits, *adv.* aside, apart.

ab·senden*, *vb.* send off, mail.

Absender, -, *n.m.* sender.

Absendung, -en, *n.f.* dispatch.

Absicht, -en, *n.f.* intent, purpose; **(mit A.)** on purpose.

absichtlich, *adj.* intentional.

absolut', *adj.* absolute.

absolvie'ren, *vb.* absolve; complete; finish (school); pass (an examination).

abson'derlich, *adj.* peculiar.

ab·sondern, *vb.* separate, detach; secrete.

absorbie'ren, *vb.* absorb.

Absorbie'rungsmittel, -, *n.nt.* absorbent.

Absorption', -en, *n.f.* absorption.

ab·spannen, *vb.* loosen (tension), relax.

ab·spielen, *vb.* **(sich a.)** occur, take place.

ab·splittern, *vb.* chip.

Absprache, -n, *n.f.* agreement.

ab·sprechen*, *vb.* deny.

ab·springen*, *vb.* jump down, bail out (of a plane).

Absprung, ⸚e, *n.m.* jump down, parachute jump; digression.

ab·stammen, *vb.* be descended.

Abstammung, -en, *n.f.* descent, ancestry; derivation.

Abstand, ⸚e, *n.m.* distance, interval; **(von etwas A. nehmen*)** renounce.

ab·statten, *vb.* grant; **(einen Besuch a.)** pay a visit.

ab·stauben, *vb.* dust.

Abstecher, -, *n.m.* digression, side trip.

ab·stehen*, *vb.* stand off, stick out.

ab·steigen*, *vb.* descend, dismount; put up at (an inn).

ab·stellen*, *vb.* put away; turn off.

ab·stempeln, *vb.* stamp, cancel.

ab·sterben*, *vb.* die out.

Abstieg, -e, *n.m.* descent.

ab·stimmen, *vb.* vote.

Abstimmung, -en, *n.f.* vote, plebiscite.

abstinent', *adj.* abstinent.

Abstinenz', *n.f.* abstinence.

ab·stoßen*, *vb.* knock off, repel, repulse.

abstoßend, *adj.* repulsive.

abstrahie'ren, *vb.* abstract.

abstrakt', *adj.* abstract.

Abstraktion', -en, *n.f.* abstraction.

ab·streifen, *vb.* strip.

Abstufung, -en, *n.f.* gradation.

ab·stumpfen, vb. become dull, blunt; make dull, blunt.

Absturz, ̈e, n.m. fall, crash.

ab·stürzen, vb. fall, crash.

absurd', adj. absurd.

Abszeß', -sse, n.nt. abscess.

Abtei', -en, n.f. abbey.

Abteil', -e, n.nt. compartment.

Abtei'lung, -en, n.f. division, section.

ab·tragen*, vb. wear out.

ab·treiben*, vb. drive off; cause an abortion.

Abtreibung, -en, n.f. abortion.

ab·trennen, vb. detach.

ab·treten*, vb. cede.

Abtretung, -en, n.f. withdrawal, cession, surrender.

Abtritt, -e, n.m. departure; exit; latrine.

ab·trocknen, vb. dry.

ab·tun*, vb. put aside, settle.

ab·wägen*, vb. weigh out, consider.

ab·wandeln, vb. change, inflect.

ab·wandern, vb. depart, migrate.

ab·warten, vb. wait (to see what will happen), bide one's time.

abwärts, adv. downwards.

ab·waschen*, vb. wash off.

Abwaschung, -en, n.f. ablution.

ab·wechseln, vb. alternate, take turns.

abwechselnd, adj. alternate.

Abwechs(e)lung, -en, n.f. change, alternation.

Abweg, -e, n.m. wrong way, devious path; (**auf A.e gera'ten***) go astray.

abwegig, adj. errant.

Abwehr, n.f. warding off, defense.

Abwehrdienst, -e, n.m. counterintelligence service.

ab·wehren, vb. ward off, prevent.

Abwehrsystem, n.nt. immune system.

ab·weichen*, vb. deviate, depart.

Abweichung, -en, n.f. deviation, departure.

ab·weisen*, vb. send away, repulse.

ab·wenden*, vb. turn away, deflect, avert.

ab·werfen*, vb. throw down, shed.

ab·werten, vb. devaluate.

Abwertung, -en, n.f. devaluation.

abwesend, adj. absent.

Abwesend-, n.m.&f. absent person, absentee.

Abwesenheit, -en, n.f. absence.

ab·wickeln, vb. unwind.

ab·winken, vb. gesture "no."

ab·wischen, vb. wipe off.

Abwurf, ̈e, n.m. throwing down; thing thrown down; (bombs) dropping; (sports) throw-out.

ab·zahlen, vb. pay off.

ab·zählen, vb. count off.

ab·zapfen, vb. draw off, tap.

ab·zehren, vb. waste away, consume.

Abzeichen, -, n.nt. badge, medal, insignia.

ab·ziehen*, vb. (tr.) draw off, subtract, deduct; (intr.) march off.

Abzug, ̈e, n.m. marching off, departure; drawing off, subtraction, drain; print; trigger.

ab·zwingen*, vb. force away from, extort.

Acetylen', n.nt. acetylene.

ach, interj. oh.

Achat', -e, n.m. agate.

Achse, -n, n.f. axis, axle.

Achsel, -n, n.f. shoulder.

acht, num. eight.

acht-, adj. eighth.

Acht, n.f. attention, care; (**sich in A. nehmen***) watch out, be on one's guard; (**außer A. lassen***) pay no attention to, neglect.

Achtel, -, n.nt. eighth part; (**ein a.**) one-eighth.

achten, vb. respect; (**a. auf**) pay attention to.

ächten, vb. outlaw, ostracise.

achtern, adv. aft.

acht·geben*, vb. watch out, pay attention.

acht·haben*, vb. watch out, pay attention.

achtlos, adj. heedless.

achtsam, adj. attentive.

Achtung, n.f. attention, regard, esteem; (**A.!**) watch out! attention!

achtzehn, num. eighteen.

achtzehnt-, adj. eighteenth.

achtzig, *num.* eighty.
achtzigst-, *adj.* eightieth.
Achtzigstel, -, *n.nt.* eightieth part; **(ein a.)** one-eightieth.
ächzen, *vb.* groan, moan.
Acker, -̈, *n.m.* field.
Ackerbau, *n.m.* farming.
Adap'ter, -, *n.m.* adapter.
addie'ren, *vb.* add.
ade', *interj.* adieu.
Adel, *n.m.* nobility.
Ader, -n, *n.f.* vein.
adieu, *interj.* adieu.
Adjektiv, -e, *n.nt.* adjective.
adjekti'visch, *adj.* adjectival.
Adjutant', -en, -en, *n.m.* adjutant, aide, aide-de-camp.
Adler, -, *n.m.* eagle.
Adler-, *cpds.* aquiline.
adlig, *adj.* noble.
Adlig-, *n.m.&f.* nobleman, -woman.
Admiral', -e, *n.m.* admiral.
Admiralität', -en, *n.f.* admiralty.
adoptie'ren, *vb.* adopt.
Adoption', -en, *n.f.* adoption.
Adres'se, -n, *n.f.* address.
adressie'ren, *vb.* address.
adrett', *adj.* trim, smart.
Advent', -e, *n.m.* Advent.
Adverb', -ien, *n.nt.* adverb.
adverbial', *adj.* adverbial.
Advokat', -en, -en, *n.m.* lawyer.
Aeronau'tik, *n.f.* aeronautics.
Affä're, -n, *n.f.* affair, love affair.
Affe, -n, -n, *n.m.* ape, monkey.
Affekt', -e, *n.m.* affect.
affektiert', *adj.* affected.
Affektiert'heit, -en, *n.f.* affectation.
äffen, *vb.* ape, mock.
affig, *adj.* affected, vain.
Affix, -e, *n.nt.* affix.
Affront', -s, *n.m.* affront, snub.
Afrika, *n.nt.* Africa.
Afrika'ner, -, *n.m.* African.
afrika'nisch, *adj.* African.
AG, *abbr.* (= Aktiengesellschaft) company.
Agent', -en, -en, *n.m.* agent.
Agentur', -en, *n.f.* agency.
Aggression', -en, *n.f.* aggression.
aggressiv', *adj.* aggressive.
agie'ren, *vb.* act.
Agno'stiker, -, *n.m.* agnostic.

Agno'stikerin, -nen, *n.f.* agnostic.
agno'stisch, *adj.* agnostic.
Ägyp'ten, *n.nt.* Egypt.
Ägyp'ter, -, *n.m.* Egyptian.
ägyp'tisch, *adj.* Egyptian.
Ahn, -en, *n.m.* ancestor.
Ahne, -n, *n.f.* ancestress.
ähneln, *vb.* resemble.
ahnen, *vb.* have any idea (that something will happen); forebode.
ähnlich, *adj.* similar.
Ähnlichkeit, -en, *n.f.* similarity.
Ahnung, -en, *n.f.* foreboding; hunch; **(ich habe keine A.)** I have no idea.
ahnungslos, *adj.* unsuspecting.
ahnungsvoll, *adj.* ominous.
Ahorn, -e, *n.m.* maple tree.
Ähre, -n, *n.f.* ear (of grain).
Aids, *n.* (no article), AIDS.
Ajatol'lah, *n.m.* ayatollah.
Akademie', -i'en, *n.f.* academy.
akade'misch, *adj.* academic.
Aka'zie, -n, *n.f.* acacia.
Akkord', -e, *n.m.* chord.
akkreditie'ren, *vb.* accredit.
Akkumula'tor, -to'ren, *n.m.* battery.
Akkusativ, -e, *n.m.* accusative.
Akne, -n, *n.f.* acne.
Akrobat', -en, -en, *n.m.* acrobat.
Akt, -e, *n.m.* act; nude (drawing).
Akte, -n, *n.f.* document, dossier, file.
Aktenmappe, -n, *n.f.* brief case.
Aktentasche, -n, *n.f.* attache case.
Aktie, -n, *n.f.* share (of stock).
Aktiengesellschaft, -en, *n.f.* corporation, stock company.
Aktion', -en, *n.f.* action, undertaking.
Aktionär', -e, *n.m.* stockholder.
aktiv', *adj.* active.
aktivie'ren, *vb.* activate.
Aktivie'rung, -en, *n.f.* activation.
aktuell', *adj.* topical, current.
Akupunktur', -en, *n.f.* acupuncture.
Aku'stik, *n.f.* acoustics.
aku'stisch, *adj.* acoustic.
akut', *adj.* acute.
Akzent', -e, *n.m.* accent.

akzentuie'ren, vb. accentuate.

Alarm', -e, n.m. alarm, alert.

alarmie'ren, vb. alarm, alert.

Alaun', -e, n.m. alum.

albern, adj. silly.

Albi'no, -s, n.m. albino.

Album, -en, n.nt. album.

Alchimie', n.f. alchemy.

Alchimist', -en, -en, n.m. alchemist.

Alge, -n, n.f. alga.

Algebra, n.f. algebra.

algebra'isch, adj. algebraic.

alias, adv. alias.

Alibi, -s, n.nt. alibi.

Aliment', -e, n.nt. alimony.

Alka'li, -n, n.nt. alkali.

alka'lisch, adj. alkaline.

Alkohol, -e, n.m. alcohol.

Alkoho'liker, -, n.m. alcoholic.

alkoho'lisch, adj. alcoholic.

Alko'ven, -, n.m. alcove.

All, n.nt. universe.

all; aller, -es, -e, pron.&adj. all.

Allee', -e'en, n.f. avenue.

Allegorie', -i'en, n.f. allegory.

allein', 1. adj. alone. **2.** conj. but.

allei'nig, adj. sole, only.

allemal, adv. always; **(ein für a.)** once and for all.

allenfalls, adv. in any case.

allenthal'ben, adv. everywhere.

aller-, cpds. of all; **allerbest',** best of all; etc.

allerart, adv. all sorts of.

allerdings', adv. certainly, to be sure, indeed, admittedly.

Allergie', -i'en, n.f. allergy.

allerhand, adv. all sorts of; **(das ist ja a.)** that's tremendous, that's the limit.

allerlei, adv. all sorts of.

alles, pron. everything.

allesamt, adv. altogether.

allgemein, adj. general, common; **(im a. en)** generally, in general.

Allgemein'heit, -en, n.f. generality, general public.

Allianz', -en, n.f. alliance.

Alliga'tor, -o'ren, n.m. alligator.

alliie'ren, vb. ally.

Alliiert'-, n.m.&f. ally.

alljähr'lich, adj. annual.

allmäch'tig, adj. almighty, omnipotent.

allmäh'lich, adj. gradual.

allmo'natlich, adj. monthly.

allnächt'lich, adj. nightly.

Alltag, -e, n.m. weekday, tedium; everday life.

alltäg'lich, adj. daily, routine.

allzu, adv. all too.

Almanach, -e, n.m. almanac.

Almosen, -, n.nt. alms.

Alpdruck, -e, n.m. nightmare.

Alpen, n.pl. Alps.

Alphabet, -e, n.nt. alphabet.

alphabe'tisch, adj. alphabetical.

alphabetisie'ren, vb. alphabetize.

Alptraum, -e, n.m. nightmare.

als, conj. as, when; than.

alsbald', adv. immediately.

alsdann', adv. thereupon.

also, adv. so, thus, and so, hence, therefore.

alt, adj. old.

Alt, -e, n.m. alto.

Altar', -e, n.m. altar.

Altar'diener, -, n.m. acolyte.

Alter, -, n.nt. age.

altern, vb. age.

alternativ', adj. alternative.

Alterna'tive, -n, n.f. alternative.

Altersgrenze, -, n.f. age limit.

Altersheim, -e, n.nt. nursing home.

Altertum, -ümer, n.nt. antiquity.

altertümlich, adj. archaic.

Altertumskunde, n.f. archaeology.

Ältest-, n.m. elder.

alther'gebracht, adj. traditional.

Altjahrsa'bend, -e, n.m. New Year's Eve.

altklug, -, adj. precocious.

ältlich, adj. elderly.

altmodisch, adj. old-fashioned.

Altpapier, n.nt. waste paper (to be recycled).

Altruis'mus, n.m. altruism.

Altstimme, -n, n.f. alto.

Alumi'nium, n.nt. aluminum.

Amalgam', -e, n.nt. amalgam.

amalgamie'ren, vb. amalgamate.

Amateur', -e, n.m. amateur.

Amboß', -sse, n.m. anvil.

ambulant', adj. ambulatory.

Ameise, -n, n.f. ant.

Ame'rika, n.nt. America.

Amerika'ner, -, *n.m.* American.
Amerika'nerin, -nen, *n.f.* American.
amerika'nisch, *adj.* American.
Amethyst', -e, *n.m.* amethyst.
Ammoniak', *n.nt.* ammonia.
Amnestie', -i'en, *n.f.* amnesty.
Amö'be, -n, *n.f.* amoeba.
amoralisch', *adj.* amoral.
amortisie'ren, *vb.* amortize.
Ampere', -, *(pron.* **Ampär')** *n.nt.* ampere.
amphi'bisch, *adj.* amphibious.
amputie'ren, *vb.* amputate.
Amputiert'-, *n.m.&f.* amputee.
Amt, -̈er, *n.nt.* office.
amtie'ren, *vb.* officiate.
amtlich, *adj.* official.
Amtseinführung, -en, *n.f.* inauguration.
Amtsschimmel, *n.m.* red tape.
amüsie'ren, *vb.* amuse; **(sich a.)** have a good time.
an, *prep.* at, on, to.
Anachronis'mus, -men, *n.m.* anachronism.
analog', *adj.* analogous.
Analogie', -i'en, *n.f.* analogy.
analo'gisch, *adj.* analogical.
Analphabet', -en, -en, *n.m.* illiterate.
Analphabe'tentum, *n.nt.* illiteracy.
Analy'se, -n, *n.f.* analysis.
analysie'ren, *vb.* analyze.
Analy'tiker, -, *n.m.* analyst.
analy'tisch, *adj.* analytic(al).
Anarchie', -i'en, *n.f.* anarchy.
Anästhesie', -i'en, *n.f.* anesthesia.
Anatomie', -i'en, *n.f.* anatomy.
Anbau, -ten, *n.m.* cultivation; addition (to a house).
Anbeginn, *n.m.* origin.
anbei', *adv.* enclosed, herewith.
an-beten, *vb.* worship, adore.
Anbetracht, *n.m.* **(in A.)** in view of.
Anbetung', -en, *n.f.* adoration.
an-bieten*, *vb.* offer.
Anblick, -e, *n.m.* sight, view, appearance.
an-brechen*, *vb.* begin; break; **(der Tag bricht an)** day breaks, dawns.

Anbruch, -̈e, *n.m.* beginning, (day)break, (night)fall.
Andacht, -en, *n.f.* devotion.
andächtig, *adj.* devout.
andauernd, *adj.* continual.
Andenken, -, *n.nt.* memory, memorial, souvenir.
ander-, *adj.* other, different.
and(e)rerseits, *adv.* on the other hand.
ändern, *vb.* change, alter, **(sich ä.)** change, vary.
anders, *adv.* otherwise, else, different.
anderswie, *adv.* otherwise.
anderswo, *adv.* elsewhere.
anderthalb, *num.* one and a half.
Änderung, -en, *n.f.* change, alteration.
an-deuten, *vb.* indicate, imply.
Andeutung, -en, *n.f.* indication, implication.
Andrang, *n.m.* rush, crowd.
an-drehen, *vb.* turn on.
an-eignen, *vb.* **(sich a.)** seize, appropriate.
Aneignung, -en, *n.f.* seizure, appropriation.
aneinan'der, *adv.* to one another, together.
Anekdo'te, -n, *n.f.* anecdote.
an-ekeln, *vb.* disgust.
an-erkennen* *(or* **anerkennen***)*, vb.* acknowledge, recognize.
anerkennenswert, *adj.* creditable.
Anerkennung, -en, *n.f.* acknowledgment, recognition.
an-fahren*, *vb.* drive up against, collide with, hit; speak sharply to.
Anfall, -̈e, *n.m.* attack.
an-fallen*, *vb.* fall upon, attack.
Anfang, -̈e, *n.m.* beginning.
an-fangen*, *vb.* begin.
Anfänger, -, *n.m.* beginner.
Anfängerin, -nen, *n.f.* beginner.
anfänglich, *adj.* initial.
anfangs, *adv.* in the beginning.
an-fassen, *vb.* take hold of, grasp, touch.
an-fechten*, *vb.* assail.
an-fertigen, *vb.* prepare, manufacture.
an-feuchten, *vb.* moisten.
an-feuern, *vb.* fire, incite, inspire.

an·flehen, vb. beseech.

an·fliegen*, vb. fly at, approach.

Anflug, -̈e, n.m. approach flight, slight attack, touch.

an·fordern, vb. claim, demand.

Anfrage, -n, n.f. inquiry, application.

an·freunden, vb. (sich a. mit) befriend.

an·führen, vb. lead on; allege; cite; dupe.

Anführung, -en, n.f. leadership; quotation, allegation.

Anführungsstrich, -e, n.m. quotation mark.

Anführungszeichen, -, n.nt. quotation mark.

Angabe, -n, n.f. fact cited, statement, assertion; (pl.) data.

an·geben*, vb. cite as a fact, state, assert; brag, boast.

Angeber, -, n.m. boaster.

Angeberei', -en, n.f. boast, boastfulness.

angeberisch, adj. boastful.

angeblich, adj. as stated, alleged.

angeboren, adj. innate, congenital.

Angebot, -e, n.nt. bid, offer.

angebracht, adj. proper.

angeheiratet, adj. related by marriage.

angeheitert, adj. tipsy.

an·gehen*, vb. concern.

angehend, adj. beginning, incipient.

an·gehören, vb. belong to.

angehörig, adj. belonging to.

Angehörig-, n.m.&f. dependent.

Angeklagt-, n.m.&f. accused, defendant.

Angel, -n, n.f. hinge, axis; fishing tackle.

angelegen, adj. important, of concern.

Angelegenheit, -en, n.f. matter, concern, affair.

angelehnt, adj. leaned against, ajar.

angeln, vb. fish, angle.

angemessen, adj. adequate, appropriate, suitable.

angenehm, adj. pleasant, agreeable.

angesehen, adj. respected, respectable.

Angesicht, -er, n.nt. face.

angesichts, prep. in view of.

angespannt, adj. tense.

Angestellt-, n.m.&f. employee.

angetrunken, adj. tipsy.

angewandt, adj. applied.

angewiesen, adj. dependent.

an·gewöhnen, vb. accustom to, get used to.

Angewohnheit, -en, n.f. habit, custom.

an·gleichen*, vb. assimilate, adjust.

Angleichung, -en, n.f. assimilation.

Angler, -, n.m. fisherman.

an·gliedern, vb. affiliate.

Angliederung, -en, n.f. affiliation.

angreifbar, adj. assailable.

an·greifen*, vb. attack, assault.

Angreifer, -, n.m. attacker, aggressor.

an·grenzen, vb. abut, border on.

angrenzend, adj. contiguous.

Angriff, -e, n.m. attack, aggression.

Angriffslust, n.f. aggressiveness.

Angst, -̈e, n.f. fear; (A. haben*) be afraid.

ängstigen, vb. frighten.

ängstlich, adj. timid, anxious.

an·haben*, vb. have on, wear.

Anhalt, -e, n.m. hold; basis.

an·halten*, vb. (tr.) stop, arrest; (intr.) last, continue.

anhaltend, adj. lasting.

Anhaltspunkt, -e, n.m. point of reference, basis, clue.

Anhang, -̈e, n.m. appendix; adherents.

Anhänger, -, n.m. follower; pendant; trailer.

an·häufen, vb. amass, accumulate.

Anhäufung, -en, n.f. accumulation.

an·heften, vb. affix, attach.

anheim'·stellen, vb. submit.

Anhieb, -e, n.m. first stroke; (auf A.) right away, right off the bat.

an·hören, vb. listen to.

Anilin', n.nt. aniline.

An·kauf, -̈e, *n.m.* purchase.
an·kaufen, *vb.* buy.
Anker, -, *n.m.* anchor.
Ankerplatz, -̈e, *n.m.* anchorage.
an·ketten, *vb.* chain.
Anklage, -n, *n.f.* accusation, indictment, impeachment.
an·klagen, *vb.* accuse, indict, impeach.
Ankläger, -, *n.m.* accuser, plaintiff.
an·klammern, *vb.* fasten (with a clamp); **(sich a.)** cling.
an·klopfen, *vb.* knock.
an·kommen*, *vb.* arrive; **(a. auf)** depend upon.
an·kündigen, *vb.* announce.
Ankunft, -̈e, *n.f.* arrival.
an·kurbeln, *vb.* crank up, get started.
an·lächeln, *vb.* smile at.
Anlage, -n, *n.f.* arrangement, disposition, investment; enclosure; *(pl.)* grounds.
an·langen, *vb. (tr.)* concern; *(intr.)* arrive.
Anlaß, -̈sse, *n.m.* cause, motivating factor.
an·lassen*, *n.f.* leave on; start.
Anlasser, -, *n.m.* starter.
anläßlich, *prep.* on the occasion of.
Anlauf, -̈e, *n.m.* start, warmup; attack.
an·laufen*, *vb.* run at, make for; swell, rise.
an·legen, *vb.* put on; invest; land.
an·lehnen, *vb.* lean against, leave ajar.
Anleihe, -n, *n.f.* loan.
an·leiten, *vb.* lead to, instruct.
Anleitung, -en, *n.f.* instruction.
an·lernen, *vb.* train.
an·lügen, *vb.* lie to.
an·machen, *vb.* fix, attach, turn on.
Anmarsch, *n.m.* (military) approach, advance.
an·maßen, *vb.* assume, presume.
anmaßend, *adj.* arrogant, presumptuous.
Anmaßung, -en, *n.f.* arrogance, presumption.
an·melden, *vb.* announce; register.

Anmeldung, -en, *n.f.* announcement, report, registration.
an·merken, *vb.* note.
Anmerkung, -en, *n.f.* (foot)note.
an·messen*, *vb.* measure for, fit.
Anmut, *n.f.* grace, charm.
anmutig, *adj.* graceful.
an·nähern, *vb.* (sich a.) approach.
annähernd, *adj.* approximate.
Annäherung, -en, *n.f.* approach, approximation.
Annahme, -n, *n.f.* acceptance, adoption; assumption, supposition.
annehmbar, *adj.* acceptable.
an·nehmen*, *vb.* accept, assume, suppose, infer; adopt.
Annehmlichkeit, -en, *n.f.* pleasure, agreeableness.
Annon'ce, -n, *n.f.* advertisement.
annonci'ren, *vb.* advertise.
annullie'ren, *vb.* annul.
Anomalie', -i'en, *n.f.* anomaly.
anonym', *adj.* anonymous.
an·ordnen, *vb.* order, arrange.
Anordnung, -en, *n.f.* order, arrangement.
an·packen, *vb.* grab hold of, get started with.
an·passen, *vb.* adapt, fit, try on; **(sich a.)** conform.
Anpassung, -en, *n.f.* adaptation.
anpassungsfähig, *adj.* adaptable, adaptive.
an·pflanzen, *vb.* plant.
Anprall, -e, *n.m.* collision, impact.
an·preisen*, *vb.* praise, recommend.
Anprobe, -n, *n.f.* fitting.
Anrecht, -e, *n.nt.* right, claim.
Anrede, -n, *n.f.* address, speech.
an·reden, *vb.* speak to, accost.
an·regen, *vb.* stimulate, incite.
Anregung, -en, *n.f.* stimulation; suggestion.
Anreiz, -e, *n.m.* stimulus, incentive.
an·reizen, *vb.* incite.
Anruf, -e, *n.m.* appeal, (telephone) call.
an·rufen*, *vb.* appeal to, invoke; call up.
Anrufbeantworter, *n.m.* answering machine.
Anrufung, *n.f.* invocation.

an·rühren, *vb.* touch; (cooking) mix.

an·sagen, *vb.* announce.

Ansager, -, *n.m.* announcer.

an·sammeln, *vb.* amass; (**sich a.**) congregate, gather.

Ansammlung, **-en**, *n.f.* collection, backlog.

ansässig, *adj.* resident.

Ansatz, **-e**, *n.m.* start; estimate.

an·schaffen, *vb.* get, obtain; buy.

Anschaffung, **-en**, *n.f.* acquisition.

an·schauen, *vb.* look at.

anschaulich, *adj.* graphic, clear.

Anschauung, **-en**, *n.f.* view, opinion.

Anschein, **-e**, *n.m.* appearance.

anscheinend, *adj.* apparent.

Anschlag, **-e**, *n.m.* stroke; poster; estimate; plot.

an·schlagen*, *vb.* (*tr.*) strike, affix, fasten, post; estimate; (*intr.*) work, start to function.

an·schließen*, *vb.* fasten with a lock, adjoin; (**sich a.**) join; fit tight.

anschließend, *adj.* afterwards.

Anschluß, **-sse**, *n.m.* connection, annexation.

an·schnallen, *vb.* buckle on; (**sich a.**) fasten seatbelt.

an·schneiden*, *vb.* start cutting.

an·schreiben*, *vb.* write down, score, charge.

Anschrift, **-en**, *n.f.* address.

an·sehen*, *vb.* look at.

Ansehen, *n.nt.* reputation, repute.

ansehnlich, *adj.* handsome; considerable, notable.

an·setzen, *vb.* fix, affix; set, schedule; estimate.

Ansicht, **-en**, *n.f.* view, opinion.

an·siedeln, *vb.* settle, colonize.

an·spannen, *vb.* stretch, strain; harness.

Anspannung, **-en**, *n.f.* strain, tension.

an·spielen, *vb.* start to play; allude.

Anspielung, **-en**, *n.f.* allusion.

an·spornen, *vb.* spur on.

Ansprache, **-n**, *n.f.* pronunciation; talk.

an·sprechen*, *vb.* address, accost.

ansprechend, *adj.* attractive.

Anspruch, **-e**, *n.m.* claim; (**A. machen auf**) lay claim to; (**in A. nehmen***) require, take up.

anspruchslos, *adj.* unassuming.

anspruchsvoll, *adj.* pretentious.

an·stacheln, *vb.* goad, incite.

Anstalt, **-en**, *n.f.* arrangement, institution.

Anstand, *n.m.* propriety; objection.

anständig, *adj.* decent.

Anständigkeit, **-en**, *n.f.* decency.

an·starren, *vb.* stare at.

anstatt', *adv.* instead of.

an·stecken, *vb.* pin on, put on; light, set fire to; (**a. mit**) infect; (**sich a.**) catch.

ansteckend, *adj.* contagious.

Ansteckung, **-en**, *n.f.* contagion.

an·stehen*, *vb.* line up, stand in line.

an·steigen*, *vb.* rise.

anstel'le, *prep.* instead of.

an·stellen, *vb.* place; hire, employ.

Anstellung, **-en**, *n.f.* employment.

Anstieg, **-e**, *n.m.* rise.

an·stiften, *vb.* incite, instigate.

an·stimmen, *vb.* intone, tune up.

Anstoß, **-e**, *n.m.* shock; impetus; offense.

an·stoßen*, *vb.* knock, bump against, nudge; offend; clink glasses.

anstoßend, *adj.* adjoining.

anstößig, *adj.* offensive.

an·streben, *vb.* strive for.

an·streichen*, *vb.* paint; underline; mark.

an·strengen, *vb.* strain; (**sich a.**) exert oneself, try hard.

anstrengend, *adj.* strenuous.

Anstrengung, **-en**, *n.f.* effort, exertion.

Anstrich, **-e**, *n.m.* coat of paint; appearance; touch.

Ansturm, **-e**, *n.m.* assault, run (on a bank).

Antark'tis, *n.f.* Antarctica.

antark'tisch, *adj.* antarctic.

Anteil, **-e**, *n.m.* share.

Anten'ne, **-n**, *n.f.* antenna.

antik', *adj.* antique.

Anti'ke, *n.f.* antiquity, classical times.

Antilo'pe, -n, *n.f.* antelope.

Antimon', *n.nt.* antimony.

antinuklear', *adj.* antinuclear.

Antipathie' -i'en, *n.f.* antipathy.

Antiquar', -e, *n.m.* second-hand bookdealer, antique dealer.

Antiquariat', -e, *n.nt.* second-hand bookstore.

antiqua'risch, *adj.* second-hand.

Antiquitä'ten, *n.pl.* antiques.

Antisemitis'mus, *n.m.* anti-Semitism.

antisep'tisch, *adj.* antiseptic.

antisozial', *adj.* antisocial.

Antlitz, -e, *n.nt.* countenance.

Antrag, -̈e, *n.m.* offer, proposal, motion.

an·treffen*, *vb.* meet up with.

an·treiben*, *vb.* drive on, propel, incite.

an·treten*, *vb.* enter into (office), start out on, step forward.

Antrieb, -e, *n.m.* impulse, impetus, force.

Antritt, -e, *n.m.* entrance into, start.

an·tun*, *vb.* put on, inflict, cause.

Antwort, -en, *n.f.* answer.

antworten, *vb.* answer.

an·vertrauen, *vb.* entrust; (**sich a.**) confide.

an·wachsen*, *vb.* grow, increase.

Anwalt, -̈e, *n.m.* attorney, advocate.

Anwältin, -nen, *n.f.* attorney, advocate.

Anwärter, -, *n.m.* applicant, aspirant.

an·weisen*, *vb.* instruct, direct; assign.

Anweisung, -en, *n.f.* instruction, assignment; money order.

anwendbar, *adj.* applicable.

an·wenden*, *vb.* apply, use.

Anwendung, -en, *n.f.* application, use.

anwesend, *adj.* present.

Anwesenheit, -en, *n.f.* presence.

Anwurf, -̈e, *n.m.* slur.

Anzahl, *n.f.* quantity, number.

an·zahlen, *vb.* make a down payment.

Anzahlung, -en, *n.f.* down payment.

an·zapfen, *vb.* tap (wire).

Anzeichen, -, *n.nt.* sign, symptom.

an·zeichnen, *vb.* mark, note.

Anzeige, -n, *n.f.* notice, advertisement; denunciation.

an·zeigen, *vb.* announce, advertise; denounce, report to police.

Anzeiger, -, *n.m.* advertiser; informer.

an·ziehen*, *vb.* draw along, attract; put on, dress; rise.

anziehend, *adj.* attractive.

Anziehungskraft, -̈e, *n.f.* attraction; (**A. der Erde**) gravity.

Anzug, -̈e, *n.m.* suit; approach.

an·zünden, *vb.* ignite, light.

an·zweifeln, *vb.* doubt, question.

apart, *adj.* out of the ordinary.

Apart'heid, *n.f.* apartheid.

Apathie' -i'en, *n.f.* apathy.

apa'thisch, *adj.* apathetic.

Apfel, -̈, *n.m.* apple.

Apfelmus, *n.nt.* applesauce.

Apfelsi'ne, -n, *n.f.* orange.

apoplek'tisch, *adj.* apoplectic.

Apos'tel, -, *n.m.* apostle.

aposto'lisch, *adj.* apostolic.

Apostroph', -e, *n.m.* apostrophe.

Apothe'ke, -n, *n.f.* pharmacy.

Apothe'ker, -, *n.m.* pharmacist.

Apothe'kerin, -nen, *n.f.* pharmacist.

Apparat', -e, *n.m.* apparatus.

appellie'ren, *vb.* appeal.

Appetit', *n.m.* appetite.

appetit'lich, *adj.* appetizing, inviting.

applaudie'ren, *vb.* applaud.

Applaus', *n.m.* applause.

Apriko'se, -n, *n.f.* apricot.

April', *n.m.* April.

Aquarell', -e, *n.nt.* watercolor.

Aqua'rium, -ien, *n.nt.* aquarium.

Äqua'tor, *n.m.* equator.

äquatorial', *adj.* equatorial.

Araber, -, *n.m.* Arab.

Ara'berin, -nen, *n.f.* Arab.

ara'bisch, *adj.* Arabic, Arabian.

Arbeit, -en, *n.f.* work.

arbeiten, *vb.* work.

Arbeiter, -, *n.m.* worker, workman, laborer.

Arbeiterin, -nen, *n.f.* female worker.

Arbeiterschaft, *n.f.* labor.

Arbeitge'ber, -, *n.m.* employer.

Arbeiterklasse, *n.f.* working class.

Arbeitsamt, *n.nt.* employment office.

Arbeitserlaubnis, -se, *n.f.* work permit.

Arbeitsgenehmigung, -en, *n.f.* work permit.

arbeitslos, *adj.* unemployed.

Arbeitslosenunterstützung, *n.f.* unemployment support.

Arbeitslosigkeit, *n.f.* unemployment.

Arbeitsplatz, ¨e, *n.m.* job, place of work.

Arbeitszimmer, -, *n.nt.* study.

Archäologie', *n.f.* archaeology.

Archipel', -e, *n.m.* archipelago.

Architekt', -en, -en, *n.m.* architect.

Architek'tin, -nen, *n.f.* architect.

architekto'nisch, *adj.* architectural.

Architektur', -en, *n.f.* architecture.

Archiv', -e, *n.nt.* archives.

Are'na, -nen, *n.f.* arena.

arg, *adj.* bad.

Argenti'nien, *n.nt.* Argentina.

Ärger, *n.m.* anger, annoyance, bother.

ärgerlich, *adj.* angry, annoying.

ärgern, *vb.* annoy, make angry, bother; **(sich ä.)** be angry.

Ärgernis, -se, *n.nt.* nuisance.

Arglist, *n.f.* guile.

arglos, *adj.* harmless, unsuspecting.

Argument', -e, *n.nt.* argument.

argumentie'ren, *vb.* argue.

Argwohn, *n.m.* suspicion.

argwöhnisch, *adj.* suspicious.

Arie, -n, *n.f.* aria.

Aristokrat', -en, -en, *n.m.* aristocrat.

Aristokratie', -i'en, *n.f.* aristocracy.

Aristokra'tin, -nen, *n.f.* aristocrat.

aristokra'tisch, *adj.* aristocratic.

Arithmetik', *n.f.* arithmetic.

Arka'de, -n, *n.f.* arcade.

arktisch, *adj.* arctic.

arm (¨), *adj.* poor.

Arm, -e, *n.m.* arm.

Arm-, *n.m.&f.* pauper.

Armband, ¨er, *n.nt.* bracelet.

Armbanduhr, -en, *n.f.* wristwatch.

Armee', -me'en, *n.f.* army.

Ärmel, -, *n.m.* sleeve.

Armleuchter, -, *n.m.* candelabrum.

armselig, *adj.* beggarly, miserable.

Armut, *n.f.* poverty, destitution.

Aro'ma, -s, *n.nt.* aroma.

arrangie'ren, *vb.* arrange.

arrogant', *adj.* arrogant.

Arroganz', -en, *n.f.* arrogance.

Arsen', *n.nt.* arsenic.

Art, -en, *n.f.* kind, sort, species; way, manner; **(A. und Weise)** way.

Arterie, -n, *n.f.* artery.

Arthri'tis, *n.f.* arthritis.

artig, *adj.* good, well-behaved.

Arti'kel, -, *n.m.* item, article.

artikulie'ren, *vb.* articulate.

Artillerie', -i'en, *n.f.* artillery.

Artischo'cke, -n, *n.f.* artichoke.

Arzt, ¨e, *n.m.* physician, doctor; **(praktischer A.)** general practitioner.

Ärztin, -nen, *n.f.* physician, doctor.

ärztlich, *adj.* medical.

As, -se, *n.nt.* ace.

Asbest', -e, *n.m.* asbestos.

Asche, -n, *n.f.* ash; **(glühende A.)** embers.

Asch(en)becher, -, *n.m.* ashtray.

aschgrau, *adj.* ashen.

Asiat', -en, -en, *n.m.* Asian.

asia'tisch, *adj.* Asian.

Asien, *n.nt.* Asia.

Asket', -en, -en, *n.m.* ascetic.

aske'tisch, *adj.* ascetic.

Asphalt', *n.m.* asphalt.

Aspirin', *n.nt.* aspirin.

assimilie'ren, *vb.* assimilate.

Assistent', -en, -en, *n.m.* assistant.

Assisten'tin, -nen, *n.f.* assistant.

assoziie'ren, *vb.* associate.

Ast, ¨e, *n.m.* branch.

ästhe'tisch, *adj.* aesthetic.

Asthma, *n.nt.* asthma.

Astigmatis'mus, -men, *n.m.* astigmatism.

Astrologie', -i'en, *n.f.* astrology.

Astronaut', -en, -en, *n.m.* astronaut.

Astronau'tin, -nen, *n.f.* astronaut.

Astronomie', -i'en, *n.f.* astronomy.

Asyl', -e, *n.nt.* asylum.

Atelier', -s, *n.nt.* studio.

Atem, -, *n.m.* breath.

atemlos, *adj.* breathless.

Atempause, -n, *n.f.* respite.

Atheist', -en, -en, *n.m.* atheist.

Atheis'tin, -nen, *n.f.* atheist.

Äther, *n.m.* ether.

äthe'risch, *adj.* ethereal.

Athlet', -en, -en, *n.m.* athlete.

athle'tisch, *adj.* athletic.

Atlan'tik, *n.m.* Atlantic Ocean.

atlan'tisch, *adj.* Atlantic.

Atlas, -lan'ten, *n.m.* atlas.

atmen, *vb.* breathe.

Atmen, *n.nt.* breathing.

Atmosphä're, -n, *n.f.* atmosphere.

atmosphä'risch, *adj.* atmospheric.

Atmung, *n.f.* respiration.

Atom', -e, *n.nt.* atom.

atomar', *adj.* atomic.

atomisie'ren, *vb.* atomize.

Atom'müll, *n.m.* nuclear waste.

Atomsperr'vertrag, ̈-e, *n.m.* non-proliferation treaty.

Attaché', -s, *n.m.* attaché.

Attentat', -e, *n.nt.* attempt on someone's life, assassination attempt.

Attentä'ter, -, *n.m.* assassin.

Attest', -e, *n.nt.* certificate.

ätzen, *vb.* etch; *(med.)* cauterize.

au, *interj.* ouch.

auch, *adv.* also, too; **(a. nicht)** not . . . either; **(a. jetzt)** even now.

Audienz', -en, *n.f.* audience.

audiovisuell', *adj.* audiovisual.

Audito'rium, -rien, *n.nt.* auditorium.

auf, *prep.* on, onto.

auf•atmen, *vb.* breathe a sigh of relief.

Aufbau, *n.m.* erection, construction; structure.

auf•bauen, *vb.* erect.

auf•blasen*, *vb.* inflate.

auf•bleiben*, *vb.* stay up.

auf•brechen*, *vb.* break open; start out.

auf•brauchen, *vb.* use up.

auf•decken, *vb.* uncover, unearth.

auf•drängen, *vb.* obtrude; **(sich a.)** obtrude.

aufdringlich, *adj.* obtrusive, importunate.

aufeinan'derfolgend, *adj.* successive, consecutive.

Aufenthalt, *n.m.* stay.

auf•erlegen, *vb.* impose.

Auferstehung, *n.f.* resurrection.

auf•fallen*, *vb.* be conspicuous.

auffällig, *adj.* noticeable, conspicuous, flashy.

Auffälligkeit, -en, *n.f.* conspicuousness, flashiness.

auf•fangen*, *vb.* catch; intercept.

auf•fassen, *vb.* conceive, interpret.

Auffassung, -en, *n.f.* conception, interpretation.

auf•flammen, *vb.* flash, flare up.

auf•fordern, *vb.* ask, invite, summon.

Aufforderung, -en, *n.f.* invitation, summons.

auf•frischen, *vb.* refresh.

auf•führen, *vb.* list; (theater) perform.

Aufführung, -en, *n.f.* performance.

Aufgabe, -n, *n.f.* task, assignment; (school) lesson.

Aufgang, ̈-e, *n.m.* rise.

auf•geben*, *vb.* give up, abandon; (luggage) check through; (food) serve; *(jur.)* waive.

Aufgebot, -e, *n.nt.* public notice; notice of intended marriage.

aufgebracht, *adj.* angry, provoked.

aufgedunsen, *adj.* bloated.

auf•gehen*, *vb.* (sun etc.) rise; *(math.)* leave no remainder; *(fig.)* be absorbed in.

auf•halten*, *vb.* hold open; stop, detain; **(sich a.)** stay.

auf•hängen*, *vb.* suspend; hang.

auf•heben*, *vb.* revoke, nullify; (**zeitweilig a.**) suspend; save.

Aufheben, *n.nt.* ado, fuss.

Aufhebung, **-en**, *n.f.* revocation, abolition.

auf•heitern, *vb.* cheer up.

auf•hören, *vb.* stop, quit.

Aufhören, *n.nt.* cessation.

auf•klären, *vb.* enlighten; tell the facts of life; (**sich a.**) clear.

Aufklärung, *n.f.* enlightenment.

Aufkleber, **-**, *n.m.* sticker.

auf•kommen*, *vb.* come into use; (**a. für**) be responsible for.

Auflage, **-n**, *n.f.* printing, circulation.

Auflauf, **⁼e**, *n.m.* crowd, mob; soufflé.

auf•lösen, *vb.* dissolve; (**sich a.**) disperse, disappear.

Auflösung, **-en**, *n.f.* dissolution.

auf•machen, *vb.* open; (**sich a.**) set out for.

Aufmachung, **-en**, *n.f.* make-up.

aufmerksam, *adj.* attentive, polite; alert.

Aufmerksamkeit, **-en**, *n.f.* attention, attentiveness.

auf•muntern, *vb.* cheer up.

Aufnahme, **-n** *n.f.* reception; (photo) shot; (phonograph, tape) recording.

auf•nehmen*, *vb.* take in; (phonograph, tape) record; film, photograph.

auf•opfern, *vb.* (**sich a.**) sacrifice oneself.

auf•passen, *vb.* pay attention, look out for.

auf•raffen, *vb.* (**sich a.**) bestir oneself; pull oneself together.

auf•räumen, *vb.* put in order, pick up; (**mit etwas a.**) debunk.

aufrecht, *adj.* upright.

aufrecht•erhalten*, *vb.* maintain, uphold.

Aufrechterhaltung, *n.f.* maintenance.

auf•regen, *vb.* excite, agitate; (**sich a.**) get excited.

Aufregung, **-en**, *n.f.* excitement.

aufreibend, *adj.* exhausting.

auf•reihen, *vb.* string.

auf•reißen*, *vb.* tear open.

auf•richten, *vb.* erect.

aufrichtig, *adj.* sincere, heartfelt.

Aufruf, **-e**, *n.m.* proclamation.

Aufruhr, *n.m.* riot; (**in A. geraten***) riot.

aufrührerisch, *adj.* insurgent; inflammatory.

auf•sagen, *vb.* recite.

aufsässig, *adj.* rebellious.

Aufsatz, **⁼e**, *n.m.* essay.

auf•saugen, *vb.* suck up, absorb.

auf•schieben*, *vb.* postpone, delay, procrastinate.

Aufschlag, **⁼e**, *n.m.* surtax; (trousers, sleeve) cuff.

auf•schlagen*, *vb.* open; hit the ground.

auf•schließen*, *vb.* unlock.

Aufschluß, **⁼sse**, *n.m.* information.

aufschlußreich, *adj.* informative.

Aufschnitt, *n.m.* cut; (**kalter A.**) cold cuts.

Aufschrift, **-en**, *n.f.* inscription; address; label.

Aufschub, *n.m.* postponement, stay.

Aufschwung, *n.m.* upward swing, boost.

auf•sehen*, *vb.* look up.

Aufsehen, *n.nt.* sensation.

aufsehenerregend, *adj.* spectacular.

Aufseher, **-**, *n.m.* supervisor.

Aufseherin, **-nen**, *n.f.* supervisor.

auf•setzen, *vb.* put on.

Aufsicht, *n.f.* supervision.

auf•speichern, *vb.* store up.

auf•springen*, *vb.* leap up; fly open; (skin) chap.

Aufstand, **⁼e**, *n.m.* uprising, insurrection.

aufständisch, *adj.* insurgent.

Aufständisch-, *n.m.* insurgent.

auf•stapeln, *vb.* stack.

auf•stehen*, *vb.* get up, rise, arise.

auf•steigen*, *vb.* mount, ascend, rise.

auf•stellen, *vb.* put up; nominate.

Aufstieg, **-e**, *n.m.* ascent, advancement.

auf•suchen, *vb.* look up; seek.

auf•tauchen, *vb.* emerge.

auf•tauen, *vb.* thaw.

Auftrag, ⁼e, *n.m.* instruction, order.

auf•tragen*, *vb.* instruct, assign; lay on; wear out; (food) serve up.

auf•treiben*, *vb.* raise.

auf•trennen, *vb.* rip.

auf•treten*, *vb.* appear; act.

Auftreten, *n.nt.* appearance; (sicheres A.) poise.

auf•wachen, *vb.* awake.

Aufwand, *n.m.* expenditure, display.

auf•wärmen, *vb.* heat up, warm up; (sich a.) warm oneself up.

auf•warten, *vb.* wait upon; wait up.

aufwärts, *adv.* upward(s).

auf•wecken, *vb.* wake up (somebody else).

auf•wenden*, *vb.* expend.

auf•wiegen, *vb.* balance.

auf•zählen, *vb.* enumerate; itemize.

auf•zeichnen, *vb.* record.

auf•ziehen*, *vb.* draw open; (watch) wind; (knitting) unravel; (child) rear.

Aufzug, ⁼e, *n.m.* lift, hoist, elevator; procession; (theater) act.

auf•zwingen*, *vb.* force upon.

Auge, -n, *n.nt.* eye; (blaues A.) black eye.

Augenarzt, ⁼e, *n.m.* oculist.

Augenärztin, -nen, *n.f.* oculist.

Augenblick, -e, *n.m.* moment, instant.

augenblicklich, *adj.* momentary, instant.

Augenbraue, -n, *n.f.* eyebrow.

Augenglas, ⁼er, *n.nt.* eyeglass.

Augenhöhle, -n, *n.f.* eye socket.

Augenlid, -er, *n.nt.* eyelid.

Augenschein, *n.m.* evidence.

augenscheinlich, *adj.* ostensible.

Augensicht, *n.f.* eyesight.

Augenwimper, -n, *n.f.* eyelash.

August', *n.m.* August.

aus, *prep.* out of, from.

aus•arbeiten, *vb.* elaborate; (sich a.) work out.

aus•arten, *vb.* degenerate.

aus•atmen, *vb.* exhale.

aus•bessern, *vb.* repair, mend.

aus•beuten, *vb.* exploit.

aus•bilden, *vb.* educate, train.

aus•bleiben*, *vb.* stay out; fail to materialize.

Ausblick, -e, *n.m.* outlook; view.

aus•brechen*, *vb.* erupt.

aus•breiten, *vb.* spread, expand.

aus•brennen, *vb.* burn out; (med.) cauterize.

Ausbruch, ⁼e, *n.m.* outbreak, outburst, eruption.

aus•brüten, *vb.* hatch.

aus•buchten, *vb.* (sich a.) bulge.

Ausdauer, *n.f.* endurance, stamina.

ausdauernd, *adj.* enduring.

aus•dehnen, *vb.* expand, extend; prolong; (sich a.) distend, dilate.

Ausdehnung, -en, *n.f.* expanse, expansion.

aus•denken*, *vb.* think up, invent.

aus•drehen, *vb.* turn off.

Ausdruck, ⁼e, *n.m.* expression, term.

aus•drücken, *vb.* express, phrase.

ausdrücklich, *adj.* explicit.

ausdrucksvoll, *adj.* expressive.

auseinan'der, *adv.* apart, asunder.

auseinan'der•gehen*, *vb.* part; diverge.

auseinan'der•nehmen*, *vb.* take apart.

auseinan'der•reißen*, *vb.* tear apart, disrupt.

auserlesen, *adj.* choice.

aus•fallen*, *vb.* fall out, not take place.

Ausflug, ⁼, *n.m.* excursion, outing.

aus•fragen, *vb.* interrogate, quiz.

Ausfuhr, *n.f.* export.

aus•führen, *vb.* carry out, execute; export.

ausführend, *adj.* executive.

ausführlich, *adj.* detailed, explicit.

Ausführung, -en, *n.f.* execution; statement.

aus•füllen, *vb.* fill out.

Ausgabe, -n, *n.f.* expense, expenditure; issuance; edition; (computer) output.

Ausgang, ⁼e, *n.m.* exit; end.

aus•geben*, *vb.* give out; spend, expend; issue; (**sich a. für**) pose as.

ausgefallen, *adj.* rare; odd.

aus•gehen*, *vb.* go out; date.

ausgelassen, *adj.* hilarious.

ausgenommen, *adj.* except for.

ausgestorben, *adj.* extinct.

ausgesucht, *adj.* select.

ausgezeichnet, *adj.* excellent.

aus•gleichen*, *vb.* balance, adjust.

aus•gleiten*, *vb.* slip.

aus•graben*, *vb.* excavate, dig up.

Ausguß, -̈sse, *n.m.* sink.

aus•halten*, *vb.* hold out; bear.

aus•händigen, *vb.* hand out, over.

Aushilfe, -n, *n.f.* assistance; stopgap.

aus•hungern, *vb.* starve out.

aus•kennen, *vb.* (**sich a.**) know about something, know one's way around.

aus•kleiden, *vb.* (**sich a.**) undress.

aus•kommen*, *vb.* get along (with).

Auskommen, *n.nt.* livelihood.

Auskunft, -̈e, *n.f.* information.

aus•lachen, *vb.* laugh at.

aus•laden*, *vb.* unload.

Auslage, -n, *n.f.* outlay; display.

Ausland, *n.nt.* foreign country; (**im A.**) abroad.

Ausländer, -, *n.m.* foreigner, alien.

ausländisch, *adj.* foreign, alien.

aus•lassen*, *vb.* leave out; let out.

aus•legen, *vb.* lay out; interpret; (money) advance.

Auslegung, -en, *n.f.* interpretation.

Auslese, -n, *n.f.* selection.

aus•liefern, *vb.* extradite.

aus•löschen, *vb.* extinguish, efface.

aus•lösen, *vb.* release, unleash.

Ausmaß, -e, *n.nt.* dimension.

Ausnahme, -n, *n.f.* exception.

aus•nutzen, *vb.* utilize; exploit.

aus•packen, *vb.* unpack.

aus•pressen, *vb.* squeeze.

Auspuff, -e, *n.m.* exhaust.

aus•radieren, *vb.* erase, obliterate.

aus•rangieren, *vb.* scrap.

aus•rechnen, *vb.* figure out.

Ausrede, -n, *n.f.* excuse.

aus•reichen, *vb.* suffice.

aus•reißen*, *vb.* run away, bolt.

aus•renken, *vb.* dislocate.

aus•richten, *vb.* align; execute; deliver (a message).

aus•rotten, *vb.* exterminate, eradicate.

Ausruf, -e, *n.m.* exclamation.

aus•rufen*, *vb.* proclaim, exclaim.

Ausrufezeichen, -, *n.nt.* exclamation point.

aus•ruhen, *vb.* rest.

ausruhsam, *adj.* restful.

aus•rüsten, *vb.* equip.

Aussage, -n, *n.f.* statement; testimony.

aus•sagen, *vb.* testify.

Aussatz, *n.m.* leprosy.

aus•schalten, *vb.* eliminate; (*elec.*) disconnect; turn off.

Ausschalter, -, *n.m.* (*elec.*) cutout.

aus•scheiden*, *vb.* eliminate; (*med.*) secrete; (**sich a.**) retire, withdraw.

Ausscheidung, -en, *n.f.* elimination.

aus•schelten*, *vb.* berate.

aus•schimpfen, *vb.* scold, bawl out.

aus•schlafen*, *vb.* (**sich a.**) sleep as long as one wants to, sleep in.

Ausschlag, -̈e, *n.m.* (*med.*) rash; (**den A. geben***) clinch the matter.

aus•schließen*, *vb.* shut out, exclude.

ausschließlich, *adj.* exclusive.

Ausschluß, -̈sse, *n.m.* exclusion.

aus•schmücken, *vb.* embellish.

Ausschnitt, -e, *n.m.* section; clipping; neck (of dress).

aus•schöpfen, *vb.* bail out (water), exhaust.

Ausschuß, -̈sse, *n.m.* committee, board; waste.

aus•schweifen, *vb.* go far afield; dissipate.

aus•sehen*, *vb.* look, appear.

außen, *adv.* outside; (**nach a.**) outward.

Außenbezirk, -e, *n.m.* outskirts.

Außenseite, -n, *n.f.* outside.

Außenwelt, *n.f.* outside.

außer, *prep.* beside(s); except; out of; **(a. sich)** beside oneself.

äußer-, *adj.* exterior, external.

außerdem, *adv.* besides.

außergewöhnlich, *adj.* extraordinary.

äußerlich, *adj.* outward.

äußern, *vb.* utter.

außerordentlich, *adv.* exceedingly.

äußerst-, *adj.* extreme.

äußerst, *adv.* extremely.

Äußerst-, *n.nt.* extremity.

außerstan'de, *adv.* unable.

Äußerung, -en, *n.f.* utterance.

aus·setzen, *vb.* set out; expose, subject.

Aussetzung, -en, *n.f.* exposure.

Aussicht, -en, *n.f.* view; prospect.

aus·speien*, *vb.* disgorge.

Aussprache, -n, *n.f.* pronunciation.

aus·sprechen*, *vb.* enunciate, pronounce; **(falsch a.)** mispronounce.

aus·spucken, *vb.* spit (out).

aus·spülen, *vb.* rinse.

Ausstand, -̈e, *n.m.* strike.

aus·statten, *vb.* equip, endow.

Ausstattung, -en, *n.f.* equipment, décor.

aus·stehen*, *vb.* bear, stand.

aus·steigen*, *vb.* get out.

aus·stellen, *vb.* show, exhibit; issue.

Ausstellung, -en, *n.f.* exhibit, exhibition.

aus·sterben*, *vb.* die out.

Aussterben, *n.nt.* extinction.

aus·stoßen*, *vb.* expel.

aus·strahlen, *vb.* radiate.

Ausstrahlung, -en, *n.f.* radiation.

aus·streichen*, *vb.* delete.

aus·strömen, *vb.* emanate.

aus·suchen, *vb.* choose, select.

Austausch, *n.m.* exchange.

austauschbar, *adj.* exchangeable.

aus·tauschen, *vb.* exchange.

aus·teilen, *vb.* distribute.

Auster, -n, *n.f.* oyster.

aus·tilgen, *vb.* expunge.

aus·tragen*, *vb.* deliver.

Austra'lien, *n, nt* Australia.

Austra'lier, -, *n.m.* Australian.

Austra'lierin, -nen, *n.f.* Australian.

aus·treiben*, *vb.* drive out, exorcise.

aus·treten*, *vb.* step out; resign; secede.

aus·üben, *vb.* exercise, practice.

Ausübung, -en, *n.f.* exercise, practice.

Ausverkauf, *n.m.* sale.

Auswahl, -en, *n.f.* choice, selection, assortment.

aus·wählen, *vb.* select, pick.

aus·walzen, -e, *n.m.* roll out, laminate.

Auswanderer, -, *n.m.* emigrant.

aus·wandern, *vb.* emigrate.

auswärtig, *adj.* external.

Ausweg, -e, *n.m.* way out, escape.

aus·weichen*, *vb.* evade, dodge.

ausweichend, *adj.* evasive.

Ausweis, -e, *n.m.* pass, identification.

aus·weisen*, *vb.* evict; **(sich a.)** identify oneself.

Ausweisung, -en, *n.f.* eviction.

auswendig, *adj.* by heart; **(a. lernen)** memorize.

aus·werten, *vb.* evaluate; reclaim.

Auswertung, -en, *n.f.* evaluation; reclamation.

aus·wickeln, *vb.* unwrap.

aus·wirken, *vb.* work out; **(sich a.)** have an effect.

Auswirkung, -en, *n.f.* effect, impact.

aus·wischen, *vb.* wipe out.

Auswuchs, -̈e, *n.m.* protuberance, excrescence.

aus·zahlen, *vb.* pay out.

aus·zeichnen, *vb.* distinguish; **(sich a.)** excel.

aus·ziehen*, *vb.* move out; (clothes) take off; **(sich a.)** undress.

Auszug, -̈e, *n.m.* exodus; excerpt, extract.

authen'tisch, *adj.* authentic.

Auto, -s, *n.nt.* auto.

Autobahn, -en, *n.f.* superhighway.

Autobus, -se, *n.m.* bus.

Autogramm', -e, -en, *n.nt.* autograph.

Automat', -en, -en, *n.m.* automat; automaton.

Automation', *n.f.* automation.

automa'tisch, *adj.* automatic.

autonom', *adj.* autonomous.

Autonummer, *n.f.* license (plate) number.

Autor', -en, *n.m.* author.

Auto'rin, -nen, *n.f.* author.

autoritär', *adj.* authoritarian.

Autorität', -en, *n.f.* authority.

Autovermietung, *n.f.* car rental.

Autowaschanlage, *n.f.* car wash.

Axt, ̈e, *n.f.* axe.

azur'blau, *adj.* azure.

B

Baby, -s, *n.nt.* baby.

Bach, ̈e, *n.m.* brook.

Backe, -n, *n.f.* cheek, jowl.

backen*, *vb.* bake.

Bäcker, -, *n.m.* baker.

Bäckerin, -nen, *n.f.* baker.

Bäckerei, -en, *n.f.* bakery, pastry shop.

Backpflaume, -n, *n.f.* prune.

Backstein, -e, *n.m.* brick.

Bad, ̈er, *n.nt.* bath.

Badeanstalt, -en, *n.f.* public bath.

Badeanzug, ̈e, *n.m.* bathing suit.

Bademantel, -̈, *n.m.* bathrobe.

baden, *vb.* bathe.

Badeort, -e, *n.m.* bathing resort.

Badewanne, -n, *n.f.* bathtub.

Badezimmer, -, *n.nt.* bathroom.

Bahn, -en, *n.f.* path, course.

Bahnhof, ̈e, *n.m.* station.

Bahnsteig, -e, *n.m.* platform.

Bahre, -n, *n.f.* bier.

Bajonett', -e, *n.nt.* bayonet.

Bakte'rie, -n, *n.f.* germ.

Bakte'rium, -rien, *n.nt.* bacterium.

balancie'ren, *vb.* balance.

bald, *adv.* soon, shortly.

Balken, -, *n.m.* beam.

Balkon', -s *or* **-e,** *n.m.* balcony.

Ball, ̈e, *n.m.* ball.

ballen, *vb.* (fist) clench.

Ballett', *n.nt.* ballet.

Ballon', -s, *n.m.* balloon.

Balsam, -e, *n.m.* balsam, balm.

balsamie'ren, *vb.* embalm.

Bambus, -se, *n.m.* bamboo.

banal', *adj.* banal.

Bana'ne, -n, *n.f.* banana.

Band, -e, *n.nt.* bond, tie.

Band, ̈e, *n.m.* (book) volume.

Band, ̈er, *n.nt.* band, ribbon, tape.

Bande, -n, *n.f.* band, gang.

bändigen, *vb.* tame.

Bandit', -en, -en, *n.m.* bandit, desperado.

bang(e), *adj.* afraid.

Bank, ̈e, *n.f.* bench.

Bank, -en, *n.f.* bank.

Bankgeschäft, -e, *n.nt.* banking; banking firm.

Bankier', -s, *n.m.* banker.

Bankkonto, -s, *n.nt.* bank account.

bankrott', *adj.* bankrupt.

Bankrott', -e, *n.m.* bankruptcy.

Bann, -e, *n.m.* ban; *(eccles.)* excommunication.

bannen, *vb.* banish, outlaw.

Banner, -, *n.nt.* banner.

bar, *adj.* cash.

Bar, -s, *n.f.* bar.

Bär, -en, -en, *n.m.* bear; (Große B.) Big Dipper.

Barbar', -en, -en, *n.m.* barbarian.

Barbarei', -en, *n.f.* barbarism.

barba'risch, *adj.* barbarian, barbarous.

barfuß', *adj.* barefoot.

Bargeld, -er, *n.nt.* cash.

Bariton, -e, *n.m.* baritone.

Barium, *n.nt.* barium.

Barke, -n, *n.f.* bark.

barmher'zig, *adj.* merciful.

Barmixer, -, *n.m.* bartender.

barock', *adj.* baroque.

Barome'ter, -, *n.nt.* barometer.

barome'trisch, *adj.* barometric.

Baron', -e, *n.m.* baron.

Barones'se, -n, *n.f.* baroness.

Barrika'de, -n, *n.f.* barricade.
Bart, ̈-e, *n.m.* beard.
Barthaar, -e, *n.nt.* whisker.
bärtig, *adj.* bearded.
bartlos, *adj.* beardless.
Barzahlung, -en, *n.f.* cash payment.
basie'ren, *vb.* base.
Basis, -sen, *n.f.* basis.
Baß, -sse, *n.m.* bass.
Bastard, -e, *n.m.* bastard.
basteln, *vb.* make with one's hands.
Bataillon', -e, *n.nt.* battalion.
Batist', -e, *n.m.* cambric; batiste.
Batterie', -i'en, *n.f.* battery.
Bau, -ten, *n.m.* construction; building; structure.
Bauch, ̈-e, *n.m.* belly.
bauen, *vb.* build, construct.
Bauer, -n, *n.m.* farmer, peasant; (chess) pawn.
Bäuerin, -nen, *n.f.* farmer, farmer's wife.
Bauernhaus, ̈-er, *n.nt.* farmhouse.
Bauernhof, ̈-e, *n.m.* farmyard.
baufällig, *adj.* dilapidated.
Baukunst, *n.f.* architecture.
Baum, ̈-e, *n.m.* tree.
Baumeister, -, *n.m.* builder.
baumeln, *vb.* dangle; (**b. lassen***) dangle.
bäumen, *vb.* (**sich b.**) rear.
Baumstamm, ̈-e, *n.m.* log.
Baumwolle, *n.f.* cotton.
bauschig, *adj.* baggy.
Bauunternehmer, -, *n.m.* contractor.
Bazar', -e, *n.m.* bazaar.
Bazil'lus, -len, *n.m.* bacillus.
beab'sichtigen, *vb.* intend.
beach'ten, *vb.* notice, pay attention to.
beach'tenswert, *adj.* noteworthy.
beacht'lich, *adj.* remarkable.
Beach'tung, -en, *n.f.* notice, consideration.
Beamt'-, *n.m.* official.
bean'spruchen, *vb.* lay claim to.
bean'standen, *vb.* object to.
bean'tragen, *vb.* propose, move.
bean'tworten, *vb.* answer.

bear'beiten, *vb.* work; adapt; handle, process.
beauf'sichtigen, *vb.* supervise.
beauf'tragen, *vb.* commission.
Beauf'tragt-, *n.m.* commissioner.
bebau'en, *vb.* till; build on.
beben, *vb.* quake, tremble.
Becher, -, *n.m.* beaker, goblet, cup.
Becken, -, *n.nt.* basin; pelvis.
Bedacht', ̈-, *n.m.* deliberation, care.
bedäch'tig, *adj.* cautious, deliberate.
bedan'ken, *vb.* (**sich bei jemandem für etwas b.**) thank someone for something.
Bedarf', -, *n.m.* need, demand.
bedau'erlich, *adj.* regrettable.
bedau'ern, *vb.* regret.
Bedau'ern, *n.nt.* regret.
bede'cken, *vb.* cover over.
beden'ken*, *vb.* bear in mind.
Beden'ken, -, *n.nt.* compunction, misgiving.
bedeu'ten, *vb.* mean, signify.
bedeu'tend, *adj.* significant, important.
Bedeu'tung, -en, *n.f.* significance, meaning.
bedeu'tungslos, *adj.* insignificant.
bedie'nen, *vb.* serve, wait on; operate (machine); follow suit (cards); (**sich b.**) help oneself.
Bedie'ner, -, *n.m.* operator (of a machine).
Bedie'nerin, -nen, *n.f.* operator (of a machine).
Bedient'-, *n.m.&f.* servant, attendant.
Bedie'nung, -en, *n.f.* service.
bedingt', *adj.* conditional, qualified.
Bedin'gung, -en, *n.f.* condition.
bedin'gungslos, *adj.* unconditional.
bedrän'gen, *vb.* beset.
bedro'hen, *vb.* menace, threaten.
bedrü'cken, *vb.* oppress.
bedrü'ckend, *adj.* oppressive.
bedür'fen*, *vb.* have need of.
Bedürf'nis, -se, *n.nt.* need, requirement.

Bedürf'nisanstalt, -en, *n.f.* comfort station.
bedürf'tig, *adj.* indigent, needy; in need of.
beeh'ren, *vb.* honor.
beei'len, *vb.* **(sich b.)** hurry.
beein'drucken, *vb.* impress.
beein'flussen, *vb.* influence.
beein'trächtigen, *vb.* impair.
been'den, *vb.* end, finish.
been'digen, *vb.* end, finish.
beer'digen, *vb.* inter, bury.
Beer'digung, -en, *n.f.* funeral.
Beere, -n, *n.f.* berry.
befä'higen, *vb.* enable, qualify.
befahr'bar, *adj.* passable.
befal'len*, *vb.* fall upon, attack.
befan'gen, *adj.* embarrassed.
befas'sen, *vb.* touch; **(sich b. mit)** take up, attend to, deal with.
Befehl', -e, *n.m.* command, order.
befeh'len*, *vb.* command, order.
Befehls'haber, -, *n.m.* commander.
befes'tigen, *vb.* fasten, fortify, confirm.
befeuch'ten, *vb.* moisten.
befin'den*, *vb.* find, deem; **(sich b.)** be located, feel.
befle'cken, *vb.* stain.
beflei'ßigen, *vb.* **(sich b.)** endeavor, take pains.
befol'gen, *vb.* follow, observe, obey.
beför'dern, *vb.* advance, promote, transport.
Beför'derungsmittel, *n.nt.* conveyance.
befra'gen, *vb.* question, interrogate.
befrei'en, *vb.* liberate, exempt.
Befrei'ung, -en, *n.f.* liberation, release.
befrem'den, *vb.* appear strange to, alienate.
befreun'den, *vb.* befriend; **(sich b. mit)** make friends with.
befrie'digen, *vb.* satisfy.
befrie'digend, *adj.* satisfactory.
Befrie'digung, -en, *n.f.* satisfaction.
befruch'ten, *vb.* fertilize, fructify.
Befug'nis, -se, *n.f.* authority.
befugt', *adj.* authorized.

befüh'len, *vb.* feel, finger.
Befund', *vb.* finding(s).
befürch'ten, *vb.* fear.
befür'worten, *vb.* advocate, recommend.
begabt', *adj.* gifted.
Bega'bung, -en, *n.f.* talent.
bege'ben*, *vb.* **(sich b.)** betake oneself; occur.
begeg'nen, *vb.* meet, encounter.
Begeg'nung, -en, *n.f.* meeting, encounter.
bege'hen*, *vb.* commit.
begeh'ren, *vb.* desire, covet.
begeis'tern, *vb.* inspire.
begeis'tert, *adj.* enthusiastic.
Begeis'terung, *n.f.* enthusiasm.
Begier'de, -n, *n.f.* desire, lust.
begie'rig, *adj.* eager, desirous.
begie'ßen*, *vb.* water.
Beginn', *n.m.* beginning.
begin'nen*, *vb.* begin.
Begin'nen, *n.nt.* inception.
beglau'bigen, *vb.* certify, accredit.
Beglau'bigungsschreiben, -, *n.nt.* credentials.
beglei'chen*, *vb.* settle.
beglei'ten, *vb.* accompany.
beglei'tend, *adj.* concomitant.
Beglei'ter, -, *n.m.* companion, escort; accompanist.
Beglei'terin, -nen, *n.f.* companion; accompanist.
Beglei'tung, -en, *n.f.* accompaniment.
beglück'wünschen, *vb.* congratulate.
begna'digen, *vb.* pardon.
begnü'gen, *vb.* **(sich b. mit)** content oneself with.
begra'ben*, *vb.* bury.
Begräb'nis, -se, *n.nt.* burial, funeral.
begrei'fen*, *vb.* comprehend.
begreif'lich, *adj.* understandable.
begren'zen, *vb.* limit.
Begren'zung, -en, *n.f.* limitation.
Begriff', -e, *n.m.* concept; **(im B. sein*)** be about to.
begrün'den, *vb.* establish; justify.
begrü'ßen, *vb.* greet.
Begrü'ßung, -en, *n.f.* greeting, salutation.

begün'stigen, vb. favor, support.
Begün'stigung, -en, n.f. favoritism, encouragement.
behä'big, adj. portly.
beha'gen, vb. please.
Beha'gen, n.nt. comfort, pleasure.
behag'lich, adj. comfortable, pleasant.
behal'ten*, vb. keep.
Behäl'ter, -, n.m. container.
behan'deln, vb. treat.
Behand'lung, -en, n.f. treatment.
Behang', -e, n.m. drapery.
behar'ren, vb. persevere, insist.
beharr'lich, adj. constant, persistent.
Beharr'lichkeit, n.f. perseverance.
behaup'ten, vb. assert, maintain; allege.
Behaup'tung, -en, n.f. assertion.
behe'ben*, vb. remove.
Behelf', -e, n.m. expedient, makeshift.
behel'fen*, vb. (sich b. mit) make do with.
behel'ligen, vb. bother.
behen'd(e), adj. nimble, agile.
beher'bergen, vb. shelter, lodge.
beherr'schen, vb. rule, govern; control, master; dominate.
Beherr'schung, n.f. rule, mastery.
beher'zigen, vb. take to heart.
beherzt', adj. courageous, game.
behilf'lich, adj. helpful.
behin'dern, vb. impede.
behin'dert, adj. disabled, handicapped.
Behin'dert, -, n.m.&f. disabled person, handicapped person.
Behin'derung, -en, n.f. impediment.
Behör'de, -n, n.f. governing office, authority.
Behuf', -e, n.m. purpose; benefit.
behufs', prep. for the purpose of.
behü'ten, vb. guard, protect, keep from; (Gott behüte) God forbid.
behut'sam, adj. cautious.
bei, prep. at, near, by; in connection with; (b. mir) at my house, on my person.
bei•behalten*, vb. retain.

Beibehaltung, -en, n.f. retention.
Beiblatt, -er, n.nt. supplement.
bei•bringen*, vb. bring forward; (jemandem etwas b.) make something clear to someone, teach someone something.
Beichte, -n, n.f. confession.
beichten, vb. confess.
Beichtstuhl, -e, n.m. confessional.
Beichtvater, -, n.m. confessor.
beide, adj.&pron. both.
Beifall, -e, n.m. applause.
Beifallsruf, -e, n.m. cheer.
bei•fügen, vb. add, enclose, attach, include.
Beifügung, -en, n.f. attachment.
Beihilfe, -n, n.f. assistance.
bei•kommen*, vb. get at.
Beil, -e, n.nt. hatchet.
Beilage, -n, n.f. enclosure; supplement; side dish.
beiläufig, adj. incidental.
bei•legen, vb. add, attach to, enclose.
Beileid, n.nt. condolences.
bei•messen*, vb. attribute.
Beimessung, -en, n.f. attribution.
Beimischung, -en, n.f. admixture.
Bein, -e, n.nt. leg.
beinahe, adv. almost.
bei•ordnen, vb. adjoin, coordinate.
bei•pflichten, vb. agree with.
beir'ren, vb. confuse.
beisam'men, adv. together.
Beisein, n.nt. presence.
beiseite, adv. aside, apart.
Beispiel, -e, n.nt. example.
beispiellos, adj. unheard of.
beißen*, vb. bite.
beißend, adj. biting, acrid.
Beistand, -e, n.m. assistance.
bei•stehen*, vb. assist.
bei•stimmen, vb. agree.
Beitrag, -e, n.m. contribution.
bei•tragen*, vb. contribute.
Beiträger, -, n.m. contributor.
bei•treten*, vb. join.
Beitritt, -e, n.m. joining.
bei•wohnen, vb. attend, witness.
Beiwort, -e, n.nt. epithet.
Beize, n.f. corrosion, stain.

beizei′ten, *adv.* in good time.

beizen, *vb.* corrode, stain.

bejah′en, *vb.* affirm, say yes to.

bejah′end, *adj.* affirmative.

bejahrt′, *adj.* aged.

bejam′mern, *vb.* deplore.

bejam′mernswert, *adj.* deplorable.

bekäm′pfen, *vb.* combat.

bekannt′, *adj.* well-known; acquainted.

Bekannt′-, *n.m.&f.* acquaintance.

bekannt′-geben*, *vb.* make known, announce.

bekannt′lich, *adv.* as is well known.

bekannt′-machen, *vb.* acquaint, make known.

Bekannt′machung, -en, *n.f.* proclamation.

Bekannt′schaft, -en, *n.f.* acquaintance.

bekeh′ren, *vb.* convert.

beken′nen*, *vb.* confess.

Bekennt′nis, -se, *n.nt.* confession.

bekla′gen, *vb.* deplore, lament; **(sich b. über)** complain about.

bekla′genswert, *adj.* deplorable, lamentable.

Beklagt′-, *n.m.&f.* accused, defendant.

beklei′den, *vb.* clothe, cover; fill (a position).

Beklei′dung, -en, *n.f.* clothing, covering.

beklem′men*, *vb.* oppress.

Beklom′menheit, *n.f.* anxiety.

bekom′men*, *vb.* get, obtain, receive; agree with, suit.

bekös′tigen, *vb.* feed, board.

bekräf′tigen, *vb.* confirm, corroborate.

beküm′mern, *vb.* grieve, distress.

Beküm′mernis, -se, *n.f.* grief, distress.

bekun′den, *vb.* manifest.

bela′den*, *vb.* load, burden.

Belag′, -̈e, *n.m.* covering, surface; (food) spread.

bela′gern, *vb.* besiege.

Bela′gerung, -en, *n.f.* siege.

Belang′, -e, *n.m.* importance.

belan′gen, *vb.* concern; sue.

belang′los, *adj.* unimportant, irrelevant.

belang′reich, *adj.* important, relevant.

belas′ten, *vb.* load, burden, strain; incriminate.

beläs′tigen, *vb.* annoy, bother, molest.

Belas′tung, -en, *n.f.* strain; inconvenience; incrimination.

belau′fen*, *vb.* **(sich b. auf)** amount to.

bele′ben, *vb.* animate, enliven.

Beleg′, -e, *n.m.* proof, evidence, documentation.

bele′gen, *vb.* attest; reserve (seat); sign up for (academic subject).

belegt′, *adj.* **(belegtes Brot)** sandwich.

beleh′ren, *vb.* teach.

belei′digen, *vb.* insult.

Belei′digung, -en, *n.f.* insult.

beleuch′ten, *vb.* illuminate.

Beleuch′tung, -en, *n.f.* illumination.

Belgien, *n.nt.* Belgium.

Belgier, -, *n.m.* Belgian.

Belgierin, -nen, *n.f.* Belgian.

belgisch, *adj.* Belgian.

belich′ten, *vb.* expose.

Belich′tung, -en, *n.f.* exposure.

belie′ben, *vb.* please.

Belie′ben, *n.nt.* pleasure, discretion; **(nach B.)** as you please.

belie′big, *adj.* any (you wish); **(eine beliebige Zahl)** any number you want.

beliebt′, *adj.* popular.

Beliebt′heit, *n.f.* popularity.

bellen, *vb.* bark.

beloh′nen, *vb.* reward.

Beloh′nung, -en, *n.f.* reward.

belü′gen*, *vb.* lie to.

belus′tigen, *vb.* amuse, entertain.

bema′len, *vb.* paint.

beman′nen, *vb.* man.

bemerk′bar, *adj.* noticeable, perceptible.

bemer′ken, *vb.* notice; remark.

bemer′kenswert, *adj.* notable.

Bemer′kung, -en, *n.f.* remark.

bemit′leiden, *vb.* pity, feel sorry for.

bemü′hen, *vb.* trouble; **(sich b.)** take pains, try hard.

benach'bart, *adj.* neighboring.
benach'richtigen, *vb.* notify.
Benach'richtigung, -en, *n.f.* notification.
benach'teiligen, *vb.* put at a disadvantage, handicap.
beneh'men*, *vb.* take away; (**sich b.**) behave.
Beneh'men, *n.nt.* behavior.
benei'den, *vb.* envy.
benei'denswert, *adj.* enviable.
Bengel, **-**, *n.m.* rascal.
benom'men, *adj.* groggy, confused.
benö'tigen, *vb.* need.
benut'zen, *vb.* use.
Benut'zung, -en, *n.f.* use.
Benzin', *n.nt.* gas, gasoline.
beob'achten, *vb.* observe.
Beob'achtung, -en, *n.f.* observation.
bequem', *adj.* comfortable, convenient.
Bequem'lichkeit, -en, *n.f.* comfort.
bera'ten*, *vb.* advise; (**sich b.**) deliberate.
Bera'ter, **-**, *n.m.* adviser, consultant.
berau'ben, *vb.* rob, deprive of.
Berau'bung, -en, *n.f.* deprivation.
berau'schen, *vb.* intoxicate.
bere'chenbar, *adj.* calculable.
berech'nen, *vb.* calculate, compute.
berech'nend, *vb.* calculating.
Berech'nung, -en, *n.f.* calculation, computation.
berech'tigen, *vb.* justify, entitle.
Berech'tigung, -en, *n.f.* justification.
bere'den, *vb.* persuade.
Bered'samkeit, *n.f.* eloquence.
beredt', *adj.* eloquent.
Bereich', **-e**, *n.m.* domain, scope.
berei'chern, *vb.* enrich.
berei'sen, *vb.* tour.
bereit', *adj.* ready, prepared.
berei'ten, *vb.* make ready, prepare.
bereits', *adv.* already.
bereit'willig, *adj.* willing (to oblige).
bereu'en, *vb.* repent, regret.

Berg, **-e**, *n.m.* mountain.
bergab', *adv.* downhill.
bergan', *adv.* uphill.
Bergarbeiter, **-**, *n.m.* miner.
bergauf', *adv.* uphill.
Bergbau, *n.m.* mining.
bergen*, *vb.* save, rescue, recover.
Bergkette, -n, *n.f.* mountain range.
Bergrutsch, -e, *n.m.* land slide.
Bergsteiger, **-**, *n.m.* mountain climber.
Bergsteigerin, -nen, *h.f.* mountain climber.
Bergung, *n.f.* salvage.
Bergwerk, -e, *n.nt.* mine.
Bericht', **-e**, *n.m.* report.
berich'ten, *vb.* report.
Bericht'erstatter, **-**, *n.m.* reporter.
Bericht'erstatterin, -nen, *n.f.* reporter.
berich'tigen, *vb.* report.
Berich'tigung, -en, *n.f.* correction.
bersten*, *vb.* burst.
berüch'tigt, *adj.* notorious.
berück'sichtigen, *vb.* consider, take into consideration; allow for.
Beruf', **-e**, *n.m.* profession.
beru'fen*, *vb.* call, appoint; (**sich b. auf**) refer to, appeal to.
Berufs'beratung, *n.f.* career guidance.
berufs'mäßig, *adj.* professional.
Beru'fung, -en, *n.f.* summons, appointment; appeal.
beru'hen, *vb.* rest, be based.
beru'higen, *vb.* quiet, calm.
Beru'higungsmittel, **-**, *n.nt.* sedative.
berühmt', *adj.* famous.
Berühmt'heit, -en, *n.f.* celebrity, fame.
berüh'ren, *vb.* touch.
Berüh'rung, -en, *n.f.* touch.
besa'gen, *vb.* say, indicate, mean.
besagt', *adj.* (afore)said.
besänf'tigen, *vb.* soften, soothe.
Besatz', **-e**, *n.m.* border, trimming, facing.
Besat'zung, -en, *n.f.* occupying forces; crew.
beschä'digen, *vb.* damage.

Beschä'digung, -en, *n.f.* damage.

beschaf'fen, *vb.* get, obtain, procure; provide.

beschaf'fen, *adj.* constituted; (so **b.**) of such a nature.

Beschaf'fenheit, -en, *n.f.* nature, quality.

beschäf'tigen, *vb.* employ, occupy, keep busy.

beschäf'tigt, *adj.* busy, engaged.

Beschäf'tigung, -en, *n.f.* occupation, employment.

beschä'men, *vb.* shame.

beschämt', *adj.* ashamed.

beschat'ten, *vb.* shade.

beschau'en, *vb.* look at, contemplate.

beschau'lich, *adj.* contemplative.

Bescheid', -e, *n.m.* answer, decision; information; (**B. geben***) let know; (**B. wissen* über**) know all about.

beschei'den*, *vb.* allot, apportion; inform.

beschei'den, *adj.* modest.

Beschei'denheit, *n.f.* modesty.

beschei'nigen, *vb.* certify.

Beschei'nigung, -en, *n.f.* certificate, certification.

beschen'ken, *vb.* (**b. mit**) make a present of.

beschie'ßen*, *vb.* shoot at, shell, bombard.

Beschie'ßung, -en, *n.f.* bombardment.

beschimp'fen, *vb.* abuse, insult.

Beschim'pfung, -en, *n.f.* abuse, insult.

beschir'men, *vb.* protect.

Beschlag', -̈e, *n.m.* metal fitting, coating, condensation; (**in B. nehmen***) confiscate.

beschla'gen*, *vb.* cover with, coat, mount; (**sich b.**) become coated, tarnish.

beschla'gen, *adj.* experienced, proficient.

Beschlag'nahme, -n, *n.f.* seizure, confiscation.

beschlag'nahmen, *vb.* seize, confiscate.

beschleu'nigen, *vb.* quicken, accelerate.

beschlie'ßen*, *vb.* finish, conclude, decide, make up one's mind.

Beschluß', -̈sse, *n.m.* decision, conclusion.

beschmie'ren, *vb.* smear, spread on.

beschmut'zen, *vb.* make dirty, soil.

beschnei'den*, *vb.* cut off, clip, circumcise.

beschö'nigen, *vb.* make pretty; gloss over, excuse.

beschrän'ken, *vb.* limit.

beschränkt', *adj.* limited, of limited abilities.

Beschrän'kung, -en, *n.f.* limitation.

beschrei'ben*, *vb.* describe.

Beschrei'bung, -en, *n.f.* description.

beschul'digen, *vb.* blame, accuse, incriminate.

Beschul'digung, -en, *n.f.* incrimination.

beschüt'zen, *vb.* protect.

Beschwer'de, -n, *n.f.* complaint, burden, trouble.

beschwe'ren, *vb.* burden; (**sich bei jemandem über etwas b.**) complain to someone about something.

beschwer'lich, *adj.* burdensome.

beschwich'tigen, *vb.* appease, soothe.

Beschwich'tigung, -en, *n.f.* appeasement.

beschwipst', *adj.* tight, tipsy.

beschwö'ren*, *vb.* swear to; implore.

Beschwö'rung, -en, *n.f.* swearing by oath; entreaty; exorcism.

besei'tigen, *vb.* remove.

Besei'tigung, *n.f.* removal.

Besen, -, *n.m.* broom.

beses'sen, *adj.* mad, possessed.

beset'zen, *vb.* occupy, fill; trim.

besetzt', *adj.* occupied, taken; (telephone) busy.

Beset'zung, *n.f.* occupation.

besich'tigen, *vb.* view, inspect, look around in.

Besich'tigung, -en, *n.f.* view, inspection, sight-seeing.

besie'deln, *vb.* settle, colonize.

Besie'd(e)lung, -en, *n.f.* settlement, colonization.

besie'geln, *vb.* seal.

besie'gen, *vb.* defeat.

besin'nen*, *vb.* (**sich b.**) remember, think over; (**sich anders b.**) change one's mind.

Besin'nung, -en, *n.f.* consideration, recollection; senses, consciousness.

besin'nungslos, *adj.* senseless, unconscious.

Besitz', -, *n.m.* possession, property.

besit'zen*, *vb.* possess, own.

Besit'zer, -, *n.m.* proprietor.

besitz'gierig, *adj.* possessive.

Besit'zung, -en, *n.f.* possession.

besof'fen, *adj.* drunk.

besoh'len, *vb.* sole.

beson'der-, *adj.* special.

Beson'derheit, -en, *n.f.* peculiarity.

beson'ders, *adv.* especially.

beson'nen, *adj.* thoughtful, cautious.

besor'gen, *vb.* take care of, get, buy.

Besorg'nis, -se, *n.f.* apprehension, anxiety.

besorgt', *adj.* anxious, worried.

Besor'gung, -en, *n.f.* management, care; errand.

bespöt'teln, *vb.* ridicule.

bespre'chen*, *vb.* discuss, talk over.

Bespre'chung, -en, *n.f.* discussion, review, conference.

besprit'zen, *vb.* spatter.

besser, *adj.* better.

bessern, *vb.* make better, improve.

Besserung, -en, *n.f.* amelioration, improvement; (**gute B.!**) I hope you get well soon.

best-, *adj.* best.

Bestand', -e, *n.m.* duration, stability; supply, stock.

bestän'dig, *adj.* steady, stable, constant.

Bestand'teil, -e, *n.m.* constituent, ingredient.

bestär'ken, *vb.* strengthen.

bestä'tigen, *vb.* confirm, acknowledge, verify.

Bestä'tigung, -en, *n.f.* confirmation, verification.

bestat'ten, *vb.* bury.

Bestat'tung, -en, *n.f.* burial.

beste'chen*, *vb.* bribe.

beste'chend, *adj.* attractive, tempting.

Beste'chung, -en, *n.f.* bribery, graft, corruption.

Besteck', -e, *n.nt.* cutlery; knife, fork, and spoon.

beste'hen*, *vb.* exist; survive; (test) pass; (**b. auf**) insist on; (**b. aus**) consist of.

Beste'hen, *n.nt.* existence; insistence.

besteh'len*, *vb.* steal from, rob.

bestei'gen*, *vb.* climb up, ascend; mount; go on board.

bestel'len, *vb.* order; send for; give a message; appoint; till.

Bestel'lung, -en, *n.f.* order; message; appointment; cultivation.

Bestel'lungsnummer, *n.f.* order number.

Bestel'lungsschein, *n.m.* order form.

bestens, *adv.* very well.

besteu'ern, *vb.* tax.

Besteu'erung, -en, *n.f.* taxation.

Bestie, -n, *n.f.* beast.

bestimm'bar, *adj.* definable, ascertainable, assignable.

bestim'men, *vb.* determine, decide, specify, designate, destine, dispose.

bestimmt', *adj.* definite.

Bestim'mungsort, -e, *n.m.* destination.

bestra'fen, *vb.* punish.

bestrah'len, *vb.* irradiate, treat with rays.

Bestre'bung, -en, *n.f.* effort.

bestreit'bar, *adj.* disputable.

bestrei'ten*, *vb.* contest, dispute, deny.

bestri'cken, *vb.* entangle, ensnare, captivate, charm.

bestür'men, *vb.* storm, attack, implore.

bestürzt', *adj.* dismayed.

Bestür'zung, -en, *n.f.* dismay.

Besuch', -e, *n.m.* visit, call; visitor, company; attendance.

besu'chen, vb. visit, attend.
Besu'cher, -, n.m. visitor.
betagt', adj. aged.
betä'tigen, vb. operate; show; **(sich b.)** be active.
betäu'ben, vb. stun, deafen, stupefy.
betäu'bend, adj. stupefying; narcotic, anesthetic.
Bete, -n, n.f. beet.
betei'ligen, vb. cause to share in; **(sich b.)** take part.
Betei'ligung, -en, n.f. participation.
beten, vb. pray.
beteu'ern, vb. assert, swear.
Beteu'erung, -en, n.f. assertion.
beti'teln, vb. entitle.
Beton', **-s,** n.m. concrete.
beto'nen, vb. stress.
Beto'nung, -en, n.f. stress.
betö'ren, vb. infatuate.
Betracht', n.m. consideration.
betrach'ten, vb. look at, consider, observe, contemplate.
beträcht'lich, adj. considerable.
Betrach'tung, -en, n.f. consideration, contemplation.
Betrag', **-e,** n.m. amount, sum.
betra'gen*, vb. amount to; **(sich b.)** behave.
Betra'gen, n.nt. behavior.
betrau'ern, vb. mourn for, deplore.
Betreff', n.m. reference.
betref'fen*, vb. affect, concern.
betreffs', prep. in regard to.
betrei'ben*, vb. carry on.
betre'ten*, vb. step upon, enter.
betreu'en, vb. take care of.
Betrieb', -e, n.m. works, management, activity; **(in B.)** running.
Betriebs'anleitung, -en, n.f. operating instructions.
Betriebs'leitung, n.f. management.
betrin'ken*, vb. **(sich b.)** get drunk.
betrof'fen, adj. taken aback; affected.
betrü'ben, vb. grieve.
Betrüb'nis, -se, n.f. grief.
Betrug', n.m. deceit, deception, fraud.
betrü'gen*, vb. deceive, cheat.

betrü'gerisch, adj. deceitful, crooked.
betrun'ken, adj. drunk, drunken.
Bett, -en, n.nt. bed.
Bettdecke, -n, n.f. bedspread.
betteln, vb. beg.
Bettler, -, n.m. beggar.
Bettlerin, -nen, n.f. beggar.
Bettplatz, -e, n.m. berth.
Bettzeug, n.nt. bedding, bedclothes.
beugen, vb. bend.
Beugung, -en, n.f. bend; inflection.
Beule, -n, n.f. swelling, bump, lump.
beun'ruhigen, vb. disturb, agitate.
Beun'ruhigung, -en, n.f. alarm, agitation.
beur'kunden, vb. authenticate.
beur'lauben, vb. give leave (of absence) to.
beur'teilen, vb. judge.
Beute, -n, n.f. booty, loot.
Beutel, -, n.m. bag, purse, pouch.
Bevöl'kerung, -en, n.f. population.
bevoll'mächtigen, vb. authorize, give full power to.
Bevoll'mächtigung, -en, n.f. authorization.
bevor', conj. before.
bevor'•stehen*, vb. be about to happen, be in store for.
bevor'stehend, adj. imminent.
bevor'zugen, vb. favor.
bewa'chen, vb. guard, watch.
bewaff'nen, vb. arm.
Bewaff'nung, -en, n.f. armament.
bewah'ren, vb. keep, preserve.
bewäh'ren, vb. **(sich b.)** prove itself.
Bewah'rung, -en, n.f. conservation.
bewäl'tigen, vb. overcome, master.
bewan'dert, adj. **(b. in)** experienced in, conversant with.
bewe'gen*, vb. induce.
bewe'gen*, vb. move.
Beweg'grund, -e, n.m. motive.
beweg'lich, adj. movable, active.

Bewe'gung, -en, *n.f.* movement, motion, exercise.

bewe'gunglos, *adj.* motionless.

bewei'nen, *vb.* bewail, deplore.

Beweis', -e, *n.m.* proof, evidence.

bewei'sen*, *vb.* prove, demonstrate.

bewer'ben*, *vb.* (**sich b. um**) apply for.

Bewer'ber, -, *n.m.* applicant, contestant, competitor, suitor.

Bewer'berin,, -nen, *n.f.* applicant, contestant, competitor.

Bewer'bung, -en, *n.f.* application.

bewer'ten, *vb.* evaluate, grade.

bewil'ligen, *vb.* approve, appropriate.

Bewil'ligung, -en, *n.f.* approval, appropriation.

bewir'ken, *vb.* cause, effect.

bewir'ten, *vb.* be host to, entertain.

bewohn'bar, *adj.* habitable.

bewoh'nen, *vb.* inhabit.

Bewoh'ner, -, *n.m.* inhabitant, occupant.

bewölkt', *adj.* cloudy.

bewun'dern, *vb.* admire.

bewun'dernswert, *adj.* admirable.

Bewun'derung, *n.f.* admiration.

bewußt', *adj.* conscious, aware.

Bewußt'los, *adj.* unconscious.

Bewußt'sein, *n.nt.* consciousness; (**bei B.**) conscious.

bezah'len, *vb.* pay.

Bezah'lung, -en, *n.f.* pay, payment.

bezau'bern, *vb.* bewitch, enchant.

bezeich'nen, *vb.* mark, designate, signify.

bezeich'nend, *adj.* characteristic.

Bezeich'nung, -en, *n.f.* designation.

bezeu'gen, *vb.* testify, attest.

bezie'hen*, *vb.* cover with, upholster, put on clean sheets; move into; draw (pay); (**sich b.**) cloud over; (**sich b. auf**) refer to.

Bezie'hung, -en, *n.f.* reference, relation; pull, drag.

Bezirk', -e, *n.m.* district.

Bezug', -̈e, *n.m.* cover(ing); case; supply; reference.

Bezug'nahme, *n.f.* reference.

bezwe'cken, *vb.* have one's purpose, aim at.

bezwei'feln, *vb.* doubt.

BH, -s, *n.m.* bra.

Bibel, -n, *n.f.* Bible.

Biber, -, *n.m.* beaver.

Bibliothek', -en, *n.f.* library.

Bibliotheka'r, -e, *n.m.* librarian.

Bibliotheka'rin, -nen, *n.f.* librarian.

biblisch, *adj.* Biblical.

bieder, *adj.* upright, bourgeois.

biegen*, *vb.* bend; (**sich b.**) buckle.

biegsam, *adj.* flexible, pliable.

Biegung, -en, *n.f.* bend.

Biene, -n, *n.f.* bee.

Bier, -e, *n.nt.* beer.

Bierlokal, -e, *n.nt.* tavern, pub.

Biest, -er, *n.nt.* beast; brute.

bieten*, *vb.* bid, offer.

Bieter, -, *n.m.* bidder.

Bieterin, -nen, *n.f.* bidder.

bifokal', *adj.* bifocal.

Bigamie', *n.f.* bigamy.

bigott', *adj.* bigoted.

Bild, -er, *n.nt.* picture, painting.

bilden, *vb.* form.

bildend, *adj.* educational, formative.

Bildhauer, -, *n.m.* sculptor.

Bildhauerin, -nen, *n.f.* sculptor.

bildhauern, *vb.* sculpture.

bildlich, *adj.* figurative.

Bildung, *n.f.* learning, education, refinement.

Billard, *n.nt.* billiards.

Billett', -e, *n.nt.* ticket.

billig, *adj.* cheap; equitable.

billigen, *vb.* approve.

Billigkeit, -en, *n.f.* cheapness; justness.

Billion', -en, *n.f.* billion.

Binde, -n, *n.f.* bandage; (**Damenbinde**) sanitary napkin.

binden*, *vb.* tie; bind.

bindend, *adj.* binding.

Bindestrich, -e, *n.m.* hyphen.

Bindfaden, -̈, *n.m.* string.

Bindung, -en, *n.f.* tie, bond; (ski) binding; (*fig.*) obligation.

binnen, *prep.* within.

Binnenland, -̈er, *n.nt.* inland.

Biographie', -i'en, *n.f.* biography.

biogra'phisch, *adj.* biographical.

Biologie', -i'en, *n.f.* biology.

biolo'gisch, *adj.* biological.

Biosignalrück'gabe, -n, *n.f.* biofeedback.

Birke, -n, *n.f.* birch.

Birne, -n, *n.f.* pear.

bis, *adv.&prep.* till, until.

Bischof, -̈e, *n.m.* bishop.

bisher', *adv.* hitherto.

Biskuit', -e, *n.nt.* biscuit.

Bißchen, -, *n.nt.* bit; (**ein b.**) a bit, a little.

Bissen, -, *n.m.* bite, mouthful.

Bit, -s, *n.nt.* (computer) bit.

bitte, *interj.* please; you are welcome.

Bitte, -n, *n.f.* request, plea.

bitten*, *vb.* ask, request; beg.

bitter, *adj.* bitter.

bizarr', *adj.* bizarre, freak.

Bizeps, -e, *n.m.* biceps.

blähen, *vb.* bloat, puff up.

Blama'ge, -n, *n.f.* disgrace.

blamie'ren, *vb.* disgrace.

blank, *adj.* bright, shining; (without money) broke.

Blase, -n, *n.f.* bubble; bladder; blister.

Blasebalg, -̈e, *n.m.* bellows.

blasen*, *vb.* blow.

blaß, *adj.* pale.

Blässe, *n.f.* paleness.

Blatt, -̈er, *n.nt.* leaf; piece of paper.

Blattern, *n.pl.* smallpox.

blau, *adj.* blue; drunk.

Blaubeere, -n, *n.f.* blueberry.

Blech, *n.nt.* tin.

Blei, *n.nt.* lead.

bleiben*, *vb.* stay, remain.

bleich, *adj.* pale; (**b. werden**) blanch.

bleichen, *vb.* bleach.

bleiern, *adj.* leaden.

bleifrei, *adj.* unleaded.

Bleistift, -e, *n.m.* pencil.

blenden, *vb.* blind, dazzle.

blended, *adj.* great splendid.

Blick, -e, *n.m.* look, glance.

blicken, *vb.* look, glance.

blind, *adj.* blind.

Blinddarm, -̈e, *n.m.* appendix.

Blinddarmentzündung, -en, *n.f.* appendicitis.

Blindheit, -en, *n.f.* blindness.

blinken, *vb.* blink.

Blinklicht, -er, *n.nt.* blinker.

blinzeln, *vb.* blink; wink.

Blitz, -e, *n.m.* lightning.

blitzen, *vb.* flash, emit lightning.

blitzsauber, *adj.* immaculate.

Block, -s, *n.m.* bloc; block; (paper) pad.

Blocka'de, -n, *n.f.* blockade.

blockfrei, *adj.* non-aligned.

blockie'ren, *vb.* block; (account) freeze.

blöd(e), *adj.* stupid, dumb.

Blödsinn, *n.m.* idiocy, nonsense.

blödsinnig, *adj.* idiotic.

blond, *adj.* blond.

bloß, 1. *adj.* bare. **2.** *adv.* only, merely.

Blöße, -n, *n.f.* nakedness; *(fig.)* weak spot.

Bloßstellung, -en, *n.f.* exposure.

Bluejeans, *n.pl.* blue jeans.

Bluff, -s, *n.m.* bluff.

bluffen, *vb.* bluff.

blühen, *vb.* bloom; flourish.

blühend, *adj.* prosperous.

Blume, -n, *n.f.* flower.

Blumengeschäft, -e, *n.nt.* flower shop.

Blumenhändler, -, *n.m.* florist.

Blumenhändlerin, -nen, *n.f.* florist.

Blumenkohl, -e, *n.m.* cauliflower.

Blumenstrauß, -e, *n.m.* bouquet.

blumig, *adj.* flowery.

Bluse, -n, *n.f.* blouse.

Blut, *n.nt.* blood.

blutarm, *adj.* anemic; *(fig.)* penniless.

Blutarmut, *n.f.* anemia.

Blutdruck, -e, *n.m.* blood pressure.

Blüte, -n, *n.f.* bloom, blossom; *(fig.)* prime.

bluten, *vb.* bleed.

blütenreich, *adj.* florid.

Bluterguß, -̈sse, *n.m.* hemorrhage.

Bluterkrankheit, *n.f.* hemophilia.

Bluthund, -e, *n.m.* bloodhound.

blutig, *adj.* bloody.

Blutspender, -, *n.m.* blood donor.

Blutspenderin, -nen, *n.f.* blood donor.

blutlos, *adj.* bloodless.

blutunterlaufen, *adj.* bloodshot.

Blutvergießen, *n.nt.* bloodshed.

Blutvergiftung, -en, *n.f.* blood poisoning.

Bö, -en, *n.f.* squall.

Bock, -e, *n.m.* buck.

bockig, *adj.* obstinate.

Bockwurst, -e, *n.f.* sausage.

Boden, -, *n.m.* ground, soil, bottom, floor; attic; **(Grund und B.)** real estate.

bodenlos, *adj.* bottomless; outrageous.

Bodensatz, *n.m.* dregs.

Bogen, -, *n.m.* arch; bow; (paper) sheet.

Bogenschießen, *n.nt.* archery.

Bogenschütze, -n, -n, *n.m.* archer.

Böhme, -n, -n, *n.m.* Bohemian.

Böhmen, *n.nt.* Bohemia.

böhmisch, *adj.* Bohemian.

Bohne, -n, *n.f.* bean; **(grüne B.)** string bean.

bohren, *vb.* bore, drill.

Bohrer, -, *n.m.* drill.

Bolivien, *n.nt.* Bolivia.

Bollwerk, -e, *n.nt.* bulwark.

bombardie'ren, *vb.* bombard.

Bombe, -n, *n.f.* bomb, bombshell.

bomben, *vb.* bomb.

Bombenflugzeug, -e, *n.nt.* bomber.

bombensicher, *adj.* bombproof.

Boot, -e, *n.nt.* boat.

Bord, -e, *n.nt.* shelf; board; **(an B.)** aboard; **(an B. gehen)** board.

Bordell', -e, *n.nt.* brothel.

Bordstein, -e, *n.m.* curb, curbstone.

borgen, *vb.* borrow.

borniert', *adj.* stupid.

Börse, -n, *n.f.* purse; stock exchange.

Borste, -n, *n.f.* bristle.

Borte, -n, *n.f.* trimming, braid.

Bös, -, *n.nt.* evil.

bösartig, *adj.* malicious; (*med.*) malignant.

Böschung, -en, *n.f.* bank, embankment.

böse, *adj.* bad, evil; angry, mad.

Bösewicht, -e, *n.m.* scoundrel.

boshaft, *adj.* malicious.

Bosheit, -en, *n.f.* malice.

böswillig, *adj.* malevolent.

Bota'nik, *n.f.* botany.

bota'nisch, *adj.* botanical.

Bote, -n, -n, *n.m.* messenger.

Botin, -nen, *n.f.* messenger.

Botschaft, -en, *n.f.* message; embassy.

Botschafter, -, *n.m.* ambassador.

Botschafterin, -nen, *n.f.* ambassador.

Bouillon', -s, *n.f.* consommé.

boxen, *vb.* box, spar.

Boxkampf, -e, *n.m.* boxing match.

Boykott, -e, *n.m.* boycott.

boykottie'ren, *vb.* boycott.

Brand, -e, *n.m.* conflagration; blight.

branden, *vb.* surge.

brandmarken, *vb.* brand.

Brandstifter, -, *n.m.* arsonist.

Brandstiftung, -en, *n.f.* arson.

Brandung, -en, *n.f.* surf, breakers.

Branntwein, -e, *n.m.* brandy.

Brasi'lien, *n.nt.* Brazil.

braten*, *vb.* roast, fry.

Braten, -, *n.m.* roast.

Bratpfanne, -n, *n.f.* frying pan, griddle.

Bratrost, -e, *n.m.* oven rack; broiler.

Bratsche, -n, *n.f.* viola.

Bräu, *n.nt.* brew.

Brauch, -e, *n.m.* custom, usage.

brauchbar, *adj.* useful.

brauchen, *vb.* need, require; use.

brauen, *vb.* brew.

Brauer, -, *n.m.* brewer.

Brauerei, -en, *n.f.* brewery.

braun, *adj.* brown.

bräunen, *vb.* brown; tan.

brausen, *vb.* roar.

Braut, -e, *n.f.* bride.

Brautführer, -, *n.m.* usher (at a wedding).

Bräutigam, -e, *n.m.* bridegroom.

Brautjungfer, -n, *n.f.* bridesmaid.

brav, *adj.* upright; (of children) good.

Bravour', *n.f.* bravado.

brechen*, *vb.* break; *(med.)* fracture.

Brechmittel, -, *n.nt.* emetic.

Brei, -e, *n.m.* pap; porridge; *(fig.)* pulp.

breit, *adj.* broad, wide.

Breite, -n, *n.f.* breadth; width; latitude.

Bremse, -n, *n.f.* brake; horsefly.

bremsen, *vb.* brake, put on the brake.

brennbar, *adj.* combustible.

brennen*, *vb.* burn, scorch.

brennend, *adj.* burning; fervid.

Brenner, -, *n.m.* burner.

Brennholz, *n.nt.* firewood.

Brennpunkt, -e, *n.m.* focus.

Brennstoff, -e, *n.m.* fuel.

brenzlich, *adj.* risky, precarious.

Brett, -er, *n.nt.* board, plank.

Bretterbude, -n, *n.f.* shack.

Brezel, -n, *n.f.* pretzel.

Brief, -e, *n.m.* letter.

Briefkasten, -, *n.m.* mailbox.

Briefmarke, -n, *n.f.* stamp.

Briefpapier, *n.nt.* stationery.

Brieftasche, -n, *n.f.* wallet, billfold.

Briefträger, -, *n.m.* mail carrier.

Briefträgerin, -nen, *n.f.* mail carrier.

Briefumschlag, -̈e, *n.m.* envelope.

Briefwechsel, *n.m.* correspondence.

Briga'de, -n, *n.f.* brigade.

Brille, -n, *n.f.* spectacles, glasses.

bringen*, *vb.* bring; take.

Brise, -n, *n.f.* breeze.

Britan'nien, *n.nt.* Britain.

Brite, -n, -n, *n.m.* Briton.

Britin, -nen, *n.f.* Briton.

britisch, *adj.* British.

Brocken, -, *n.m.* crumb.

Brombeere, -n, *n.f.* blackberry.

bronchial', *adj.* bronchial.

Bronchi'tis, *n.f.* bronchitis.

Bronze, -n, *n.f.* brooch.

Broschü're, -n, *n.f.* pamphlet, booklet.

Brot, -e, *n.nt.* bread; **(beleg'tes B.)** sandwich.

Brötchen, -, *n.nt.* roll, bun.

Bruch, -̈e, *n.m.* break, breach, fracture; hernia; *(fig.)* violation.

brüchig, *adj.* brittle.

Bruchrechnung, *n.f.* fractions.

Bruchstück, -e, *n.nt.* fragment.

Bruchteil, -e, *n.m.* fraction.

Brücke, -n, *n.f.* bridge.

Bruder, -̈, *n.m.* brother.

brüderlich, *adj.* brotherly, fraternal.

Brüderschaft, -en, *n.f.* fraternity; intimate friendship.

Brühe, -n, *n.f.* broth.

brühen, *vb.* scald.

brüllen, *vb.* yell, bellow, howl.

brummen, *vb.* hum, buzz; grumble.

brünett', *adj.* dark-haired.

Brunnen, -, *n.m.* well, fountain.

brünstig, *adj.* fervent.

brüsk, *adj.* brusque.

Brust, -̈e, *n.f.* breast, chest.

brüsten, *vb.* **(sich b.)** boast.

Brut, -en, *n.f.* brood.

brutal', *adj.* brutal.

Brutalität', -en, *n.f.* brutality.

brüten, *vb.* brood.

brutto, *adj.* gross.

Bube, -n, -n, *n.m.* boy; (cards) jack.

Buch, -̈er, *n.nt.* book.

Buchbinderei, -ei'en, *n.f.* bookbindery.

Buche, -n, *n.f.* beech.

buchen, *vb.* book, reserve (plane seat, hotel).

Bücherei, -en, *n.f.* library.

Bücherregal, -e, *n.nt.* bookcase.

Bücherschrank, -̈e, *n.m.* bookcase.

Buchführung, -en, *n.f.* accounting, bookkeeping.

Buchhalter, -, *n.m.* accountant, bookkeeper.

Buchhalterin, -nen, *n.f.* accountant, bookkeeper.

Buchhändler, -, *n.m.* bookseller.

Buchhändlerin, -nen, *n.f.* bookseller.

Buchhandlung, -en, *n.f.* bookstore.

Büchse, -n, *n.f.* can.

Büchsenöffner, -, *n.m.* can opener.

Buchstabe(n), -, (or **-n, -n),** *n.m.* letter (of the alphabet).

buchstabie'ren, *vb.* spell; **(falsch b.)** misspell.

buchstäblich, *adj.* literal.

Bucht, -en, *n.f.* bay.

Buchweizen, *n.m.* buckwheat.

Buckel, -, *n.m.* hump, protuberance; hunchback.

buckelig, *adj.* hunchbacked.

bücken, *vb.* **(sich b.)** bend down, stoop.

Bude, -n, *n.f.* booth, stall, stand.

Büfett', -s, *n.nt.* buffet.

Büffel, -, *n.m.* buffalo.

Bug, -e, *n.m.* bow.

Bügeleisen, -, *n.nt.* flatiron.

bügeln, *vb.* iron, press.

Bühne, -n, *n.f.* stage.

Bühnenausstattung, -en, *n.f.* scenery.

Bulldogge, -n, *n.f.* bulldog.

Bulle, -n, -n, *n.m.* bull.

Bummel, -, *n.m.* spree, stroll.

bummeln, *vb.* stroll.

Bund, ⁻e, *n.nt.* league, federation.

Bund, -e, *n.m.* bunch, bundle.

Bündel, -, *n.nt.* bundle.

Bundes, *cpds.* federal.

Bundesbahn, *n.f.* German Federal Railway.

Bundeskanzler, *n.m.* chancellor of Germany.

Bundesrat, *n.m.* upper house of German parliament.

bundesstaatlich, *adj.* federal.

Bundestag, *n.m.* lower house of German parliament.

Bündnis, -se, *n.nt.* alliance.

bunt, *adj.* colorful; varicolored, motley.

Bürde, -n, *n.f.* burden.

Bürge, -n, -n, *n.m.* sponsor, guarantor.

Bürger, -, *n.m.* citizen.

Bürgerin, -nen, *n.f.* citizen.

bürgerlich, *adj.* civil; bourgeois.

Bürgermeister, -, *n.m.* mayor.

Bürgermeisterin, -nen, *n.f.* mayor.

Bürgerrechte, *n.pl.* civil rights.

Bürgerschaft, *n.f.* citizenry.

Bürgersteig, -e, *n.m.* sidewalk.

Burgfriede(n), -n, *n.m.* truce.

Bürgschaft, -en, *n.f.* guaranty, bond, bail.

Burgun'der, -, *n.m.* burgundy (wine).

Büro', -s, *n.nt.* office, bureau.

Bursche, -n, -n, *n.m.* chap, fellow.

Bürste, -n, *n.f.* brush.

bürsten, *vb.* brush.

Bus, -se, *n.m.* bus.

Busch, -e, *n.m.* bush, shrub.

Büschel, -, *n.nt.* bunch.

buschig, *adj.* bushy.

Busen, -, *n.m.* bosom.

Buße, -n, *n.f.* atonement, penitence; fine, penalty.

büßen, *vb.* do penance, atone for.

Büste, -n, *n.f.* bust.

Büstenhalter, -, *n.m.* brassiere.

Butter, *n.f.* butter.

Butterblume, -n, *n.f.* buttercup.

Butterbrot, -e, *n.nt.* slice of bread and butter.

Buttermilch, *n.f.* buttermilk.

buttern, *vb.* churn.

C

Café', -s, *n.nt.* café.

CD-Spieler, *n.m.* compact disk player.

Cellist', -en, -en, *n.m.* cellist.

Cellis'tin, -nen, *n.f.* cellist.

Cello, -s, *n.nt.* cello.

Chance, -n, *n.f.* opportunity, odds.

chao'tisch, *adj.* chaotic.

Charak'ter, -e're, *n.m.* character.

charakterisie'ren, *vb.* characterize.

charakteris'tisch, *adj.* characteristic.

Charis'ma, *n.nt.* charisma.

Charme, *n.m.* charm.

Charterflug, ⁻e, *n.m.* charter flight.

Chauffeur', -e, *n.m.* chauffeur.

Chaussee', -e'en, *n.f.* highway.

Chef, -s, *n.m.* chef; boss.

Chefin, -nen, *n.f.* boss.
Chemie', *n.f.* chemistry.
Chemika'lien, *n.pl.* chemicals.
Chemiker, -, *n.m.* chemist.
Chemikerin, -nen, *n.f.* chemist.
chemisch, *adj.* chemical.
Chemotherapie', *n.f.* chemotherapy.
Chiffre, -n, *n.f.* cipher.
China, *n.nt.* China.
Chine'se, -n, -n, *n.m.* Chinese.
Chinesin, -nen, *n.f.* Chinese.
chine'sisch, *adj.* Chinese.
Chinin', *n.nt.* quinine.
Chiroprak'tiker, -, *n.m.* chiropractor.
Chiroprak'tikerin, -nen, *n.f.* chiropractor.
Chirurg', -en, -en, *n.f.* surgeon.
Chirur'gin, -nen, *n.f.* surgeon.
Chirurgie', *n.f.* surgery.
Chlor, -s, *n.nt.* chlorine.
Chloroform', *n.nt.* chloroform.
Cholera, *n.f.* cholera.
chole'risch, *adj.* choleric.
Chor, -s, ̈e, *n.m.* choir; chorus.
Chorgang, ̈e, *n.m.* aisle.
Chorsänger, -, *n.m.* chorister.

Christ, -en, -en, *n.m.* Christian.
Christenheit, *n.f.* Christendom.
Christentum, *n.nt.* Christianity.
christlich, *adj.* Christian.
Christus, *n.m.* Christ.
Chrom, *n.nt.* chrome, chromium.
Chronik, -en, *n.f.* chronicle.
chronisch, *adj.* chronic.
Chronologie', -i'en, *n.f.* chronology.
chronolo'gisch, *adj.* chronological.
Chrysanthe'me, -en, *n.f.* chrysanthemum.
Clown, -s, *n.m.* clown.
Cocktail, -s, *n.m.* cocktail.
College, -s, *n.nt.* college.
Compu'ter, -, *n.m.* computer.
Comu'terspiel, -e, *n.nt.* computer game.
Couch, -es, *n.f.* couch.
Coupon, -s, *n.m.* coupon.
Cousin', -s, *n.m.* (male) cousin.
Cousi'ne, -en, *n.f.* (female) cousin.
Cowboy, -s, *n.m.* cowboy.
Crème, -s, *n.f.* cream.

D

da, 1. *conj.* because, since, as. **2.** *adv.* there; here; then.
dabei', *adv.* near it; present; in so doing, at the same time.
Dach, ̈er, *n.nt.* roof.
Dachrinne, -n, *n.f.* eaves.
Dachstube, -n, *n.f.* garret.
Dachtraufe, -n, *n.f.* gutter.
dadurch', *adv.* thereby.
dafür', *adv.* for that; instead.
dage'gen, *adv.* against it; on the other hand.
daher', *adv.* therefore, hence.
dahin', *adv.* (to) there.
dahin'ter, *adv.* behind it.
damals, *adv.* then, at that time.
Dame, -n, *n.f.* lady; checkers.
Damebrett, -er, *n.nt.* checkerboard.
Damenhut, ̈e, *n.m.* lady's hat.
Damenunterwäsche, *n.f.* lingerie.
Damespiel, *n.nt.* checkers.

damit', 1. *conj.* in order that. **2.** *adv.* with it, with them, at that.
Damm, ̈e, *n.m.* dam, causeway, levee.
dämmern, *vb.* dawn.
Dämmerung, -en, *n.f.* twilight.
Dämon, -o'nen, *n.m.* demon.
Dampf, ̈e, *n.m.* steam, vapor fume.
Dampfboot, -e, *n.nt.* steamboat.
dampfen, *vb.* steam.
dämpfen, *vb.* muffle; (cooking) steam.
Dampfer, -, *n.m.* steamship.
Däne, -n, -n, *n.m.* Dane.
Dänemark, *n.nt.* Denmark.
dänisch, *adj.* Danish.
dank, *prep.* owing to.
Dank, *n.m.* thanks.
dankbar, *adj.* thankful, grateful.
Dankbarkeit, -en, *n.f.* gratitude.

danken, *vb.* thank.
dann, *adv.* then, after that.
darauf', *adv.* on it, on them; after that, thereupon.
dar·bieten*, *vb.* present.
Darbietung, -en, *n.f.* presentation; entertainment.
dar·legen, *vb.* state.
Darlegung, -en, *n.f.* exposé, exposition.
Darlehen, -, *n.nt.* loan.
Darm, -e, *n.m.* intestine.
dar·stellen, *vb.* represent, constitute; present; portray.
Darstellung, -en, *n.f.* presentation; representation; depiction; **(graphische D.)** diagram.
Dasein, *n.nt.* existence.
daß, *conj.* that.
Datenverarbeitung, -en, *n.f.* data processing.
datie'ren, *vb.* date.
Dattel, -n, *n.f.* date.
Datum, -ten, *n.nt.* date.
Dauer, *n.f.* duration, length.
dauerhaft, *adj.* durable, lasting.
Dauerhaftigkeit, *n.f.* durability.
dauern, *vb.* last, continue; take (a while).
dauernd, *adj.* lasting, continual.
Dauerwelle, -n, *n.f.* permanent wave.
Daumen, -, *n.m.* thumb.
Daune, -n, *n.f.* down.
dazu', *adv.* in addition.
dazwi'schen·kommen*, *vb.* intervene.
dazwi'schen·treten*, *vb.* intercede.
Dazwi'schentreten, *n.nt.* intervention.
DDR (Deutsche Demokratische Republik) East Germany (German Democratic Republic).
Deba'kel, -, *n.nt.* debacle.
Debat'te, -n, *n.f.* debate.
Debet, -s, *n.nt.* debit.
Debüt', *-s,* *n.nt.* debut.
Debütan'tin, -nen, *n.f.* debutante.
Deck, -s, *n.nt.* deck.
Decke, -n, *n.f.* cover; blanket; ceiling.
Deckel, -n, *n.m.* lid.

decken, *vb.* cover; **(sich d.)** coincide, jibe.
Deckung, -en, *n.f.* cover(ing); collateral.
defekt', *adj.* defective.
Defekt', -e, *n.m.* defect.
Defensi've, -n, *n.f.* defensive.
Definition', -en, *n.f.* definition.
definitiv', *adj.* definite; definitive.
Defizit, -e, *n.nt.* deficit.
Deflation', -en, *n.f.* deflation.
Degen, -, *n.m.* sword; epée.
Degeneration', *n.f.* degeneration.
degeneriert', *adj.* degenerate.
dehnen, *vb.* stretch, expand; drawl.
Dehnung, -en, *n.f.* stretch(ing), expansion.
Deich, -e, *n.m.* dike.
Dekan', -e, *n.m.* dean.
Deklamation', -en, *n.f.* declamation.
deklamie'ren, *vb.* declaim.
deklarie'ren, *vb.* declare.
Deklination', -en, *n.f.* declension.
deklinie'ren, *vb.* decline.
Dekorateur', -e, *n.m.* decorator; window dresser.
Dekorateu'rin, -nen, *n.f.* decorator, window dresser.
dekorativ', *adj.* decorative, ornamental.
dekorie'ren, *vb.* decorate.
Dekret', -e, *n.nt.* decree.
Delegation', -en, *n.f.* delegation.
delegie'ren, *vb.* delegate.
Delegiert', -, *n.m.&f.* delegate.
delikat', *adj.* delicate, dainty.
Delikates'se, -n, *n.f.* delicacy.
Deli'rium, -rien, *n.nt.* delirium.
Demago'ge, -n, -n, *n.m.* demagogue.
demgemäß', *adv.* accordingly.
demnächst', *adv.* shortly, soon.
demobilisie'ren, *vb.* demobilize.
Demobilisie'rung, -en, *n.f.* demobilization.
Demokrat', -en, -en, *n.m.* democrat.
Demokratie', -n, *n.f.* democracy.
demokra'tisch, *adj.* democratic.
demolie'ren, *vb.* wreck.

demonstrativ', *adj.* demonstrative.

demonstrie'ren, *vb.* demonstrate.

demoralisie'ren, *vb.* demoralize.

Demut, *n.f.* humility.

demütig, *adj.* humble.

demütigen, *vb.* humiliate.

Demütigung, -en, *n.f.* humiliation.

demzufolge, *adv.* accordingly; consequently.

denkbar, *adj.* imaginable.

denken*, *vb.* think, reason.

Denker, -, *n.m.* thinker.

Denkmal, -̈er, *n.nt.* monument, memorial.

Denkungsart, *n.f.* mode of thinking, mentality.

denkwürdig, *adj.* memorable.

denn, 1. *conj.* for. 2. *adv.* do tell me; I wonder.

dennoch, *adv.* still, yet, nevertheless.

denunzie'ren, *vb.* denounce, inform.

Deportation', -en, *n.f.* deportation.

deportie'ren, *vb.* deport.

Depot', -s, *n.nt.* depot.

Depression', -en, *n.f.* depression.

deprimie'ren, *vb.* depress.

der, das, die, 1. *art.&adj.* the, that. 2. *pron.* he, she, it; they; that one. 3. *rel. pron.* who, which, that.

derart, 1. *adj.* such, of such a kind. 2. *adv.* in such a way.

derb, *adj.* coarse; stout; earthy.

dermaßen, *adv.* to such a degree, in such a manner.

Deserteur', -e, *n.m.* deserter.

Desertion', -en, *n.f.* desertion.

deshalb, *adv.* therefore, hence.

Desi'gner, -, *n.m.* designer.

Desi'gnerin, -nen, *n.f.* designer.

desinfizie'ren, *vb.* disinfect.

desodorisie'ren, *vb.* deodorize.

Despot', -en, -en, *n.m.* despot.

despo'tisch, *adj.* despotic.

Destillation', -en, *n.f.* distillation.

destillie'ren, *vb.* distill.

desto, *adv.* (d. besser) so much the better; (je mehr, d. besser) the more the better.

deswegen, *adv.* therefore, that's why.

Detail', -s, *n.nt.* detail.

Detektiv', -e, *n.m.* detective.

deuten, *vb.* interpret; point.

deutlich, *adj.* clear, distinct.

deutsch, *adj.* German.

Deutsch-, *n.m.&f.* German.

Deutschland, -, *n.nt.* Germany.

Deutung, -en, *n.f.* interpretation.

Dezem'ber, -, *n.m.* December.

dezentralisie'ren, *vb.* decentralize.

Dezi'bel, -n, *n.f.* decibel.

Dezimal'-, *cpds.* decimal.

dezimie'ren, *vb.* decimate.

Diagno'se, -n, *n.f.* diagnosis.

diagnostizie'ren, *vb.* diagnose.

diagonal', *adj.* diagonal.

Diagramm', -e, *n.nt.* graph.

Dialekt', -e, *n.m.* dialect.

Dialog', -e, *n.m.* dialogue.

Diamant', -en, *n.m.* diamond.

diametral', *adj.* diametrical.

Diät', -en, *n.f.* diet.

diät'gemäß, *adj.* dietary.

dicht, *adj.* dense, thick; tight.

Dichte, -n, *n.f.* density.

Dichter, -, *n.m.* poet.

Dichterin, -nen, *n.f.* poet.

dichterisch, *adj.* poetic.

Dichtheit, *n.f.* thickness.

Dichtung, -en, *n.f.* poetry; *(tech.)* packing, gasket.

dick, *adj.* thick, fat, stout.

Dickdarm, *n.m.* colon.

Dicke, -n, *n.f.* thickness.

dicken, *vb.* thicken.

Dickicht, -e, *n.nt.* thicket, brush.

dicklich, *adj.* chubby.

Dieb, -e, *n.m.* thief, robber.

Diebin, -nen, *n.f.* thief, robber.

Diebstahl, -̈e, *n.m.* theft, larceny.

Diele, -n, *n.f.* hall, hallway.

dienen, *vb.* serve.

Diener, -, *n.m.* valet, butler.

Dienerin, -nen, *n.f.* maid, servant.

Dienerschaft, -en, *n.f.* servant.

Dienst, -e, *n.m.* service.

Dienstag, -e, *n.m.* Tuesday.

dienstbeflissen, *adj.* assiduous; officious.

Dienstmädchen, -, *n.nt.* maid.

Dienstpflicht, *n.f.* compulsory military service, draft.
Dienstvorschrift, -en, *n.f.* regulation.
Dieselmotor, -en, *n.m.* diesel engine.
dieser, -es, -e, *pron.&adj.* this.
differential', *adj.* differential.
differenzie'ren, *vb.* differentiate.
Diktat', -e, *n.nt.* dictation.
Dikta'tor, -o'ren, *n.m.* dictator.
diktato'risch, *adj.* dictatorial.
Diktatur', -en, *n.f.* dictatorship.
diktie'ren, *vb.* dictate.
Dilem'ma, -s, *n.nt.* dilemma, predicament.
Dilettant', -en, -en, *n.m.* dilettante.
Dill, *n.m.* dill.
Ding, -e, *n.nt.* thing.
dingen*, *vb.* hire.
Diphtherie', *n.f.* diphtheria.
Diplom', -e, *n.nt.* diploma.
Diplomat', -en, -en, *n.m.* diplomat.
Diploma'tin, -nen, *n.f.* diplomat.
Diplomatie', *n.f.* diplomacy.
diploma'tisch, *adj.* diplomatic.
direkt', *adj.* direct; downright.
Direkti've, -n, *n.f.* directive.
Direk'tor, -o'ren, *n.m.* director, manager.
Direkto'rin, -nen, *n.f.* director, manager.
Direkto'rium, -ien, *n.nt.* directorate, directory.
Dirigent', -en, -en, *n.m.* conductor.
Dirigen'tin, -nen, *n.f.* conductor.
dirigie'ren, *vb.* conduct.
Diskont', -e, *n.m.* discount.
Diskont'satz, -̈e, *n.m.* interest rate.
Diskothek', -en, *n.f.* discotheque.
diskret', *adj.* discreet.
Diskretion', *n.f.* discretion.
diskriminie'ren, *vb.* discriminate.
Diskriminie'rung, -en, *n.f.* discrimination.
Diskussion', -en, *n.f.* discussion.
diskutie'ren, *vb.* discuss.

disqualifizie'ren, *vb.* disqualify.
Dissertation', -en, *n.f.* dissertation.
Disziplin', *n.f.* discipline.
disziplinie'ren, *vb.* discipline.
Diva, -s, *n.f.* diva.
divers', *adj.* miscellaneous.
Division', -en, *n.f.* division.
D-Mark, -, *n.f.* (= deutsche Mark) mark, German unit of currency.
doch, 1. *conj.* yet. **2.** *adv.* yet; indeed; oh yes.
Docht, -e, *n.m.* wick.
Dock, -s, *n.nt.* dock.
docken, *vb.* dock.
Dogma, -men, *n.nt.* dogma.
dogma'tisch, *adj.* dogmatic.
Doktor, -o'ren, *n.m.* doctor.
Doktorat', -e, *n.nt.* doctorate.
doktrinär', *adj.* doctrinaire.
Dokument', -e, *n.nt.* document.
dokumenta'risch, *adj.* documentary.
dokumentie'ren, *vb.* document, authenticate.
Dolch, -e, *n.m.* dagger.
Dollar, -s, *n.m.* dollar.
dolmetschen, *vb.* interpret.
Dolmetscher, -, *n.m.* interpreter.
Dolmetscherin, -nen, *n.f.* interpreter.
Dom, -e, *n.m.* cathedral, dome.
Domi'nion, -s, *n.nt.* dominion.
Donau, *n.f.* Danube.
Donner, -, *n.m.* thunder.
donnern, *vb.* thunder.
Donnerstag, -e, *n.m.* Thursday.
Donnerwetter, *n.nt.* (**zum D.**) confound it!; (what) in thunder.
Doppel-, *cpds.* double, dual.
Doppelgänger, -, *n.m.* double.
doppelkohlensaur, *adj.* (**d. es Natron**) bicarbonate of soda.
Doppelpunkt, -e, *n.m.* colon.
doppelt, *adj.* double.
Dorf, -̈er, *n.nt.* village.
Dorn, -en, *n.m.* thorn.
dörren, *vb.* dry, parch.
dort, *adv.* there.
Dose, -n, *n.f.* (small) box, can.
dösen, *vb.* doze.
Dosie'rung, -en, *n.f.* dosage.
Dosis, -sen, *n.f.* dose.

Drache, -n, -n, *n.m.* dragon.
Draht, ̈-e, *n.m.* wire.
Drahtaufnahmegerät, -e, *n.nt.* wire recorder.
drahtlos, *adj.* wireless.
drall, *adj.* buxom.
Drama, -men, *n.nt.* drama.
Drama'tiker, -, *n.m.* dramatist.
drama'tisch, *adj.* dramatic.
dramatisie'ren, *vb.* dramatize.
Drang, -e, *n.m.* urge.
drängeln, *vb.* crowd.
drängen, *vb.* urge, press.
Drangsal, -e, *n.f.* distress.
drapie'ren, *vb.* drape.
drastisch, *adj.* drastic.
draußen, *adv.* outside.
Dreck, *n.m.* dirt, mud.
dreckig, *adj.* filthy.
Drehbuch, ̈-er, *n.nt.* scenario (film).
drehen, *vb.* turn; make (a movie).
Drehpunkt, -e, *n.m.* pivot, fulcrum.
Drehung, -en, *n.f.* turning.
drei, *num.* three.
Dreieck, -e, *n.nt.* triangle.
dreifach, *adj.* triple.
dreifältig, *adj.* threefold.
dreimal, *adv.* thrice, three times.
Dreirad, ̈-er, *n.nt.* tricycle.
dreißig, *num.* thirty.
dreißigst-, *adj.* thirtieth.
Dreißigstel, -, *n.nt.* thirtieth part; **(ein d.)** one-thirtieth.
dreist, *adj.* bold; fresh, nervy.
dreizehn, *num.* thirteen.
dreschen*, *vb.* thresh, thrash.
Drill, *n.m.* drill.
Drillbohrer, -, *n.m.* drill.
dringen*, *vb.* force one's way, penetrate; insist.
dringend, *adj.* urgent.
dringlich, *adj.* pressing.
Dringlichkeit, *n.f.* urgency.
drinnen, *adv.* inside.
dritt-, *adj.* third.
Drittel, -, *n.nt.* third part; **(ein d.)** one-third.
drittens, *adv.* in the third place, thirdly.
Dritte Welt, *n.f.* Third World.
drittletzt, *adj.* third from last.

Droge, -n, *n.f.* drug.
Drogerie', -i'en, *n.f.* drug store.
Drogist, -en, *n.m.* druggist.
Drogis'tin, -nen, *n.f.* druggist.
drohen, *vb.* threaten.
dröhnen, *vb.* sound, boom, roar.
Drohung, -en, *n.f.* threat.
drollig, *adj.* droll, funny.
Droschke, -n, *n.f.* hack, cab.
Drossel, -n, *n.f.* thrush.
drosseln, *vb.* throttle, cut down.
drüben, *adv.* over there.
Druck, -e, *n.m.* print(ing), impression.
Druck, ̈-e, *n.m.* pressure.
drucken, *vb.* print.
Drucken, *n.nt.* printing.
drücken, *vb.* press, squeeze; oppress; **(sich d.)** get out of work, shirk.
drückend, *adj.* pressing, oppressive.
Druckerpresse, -n, *n.f.* printing-press.
drunter, *adv.* underneath.
Drüse, -n, *n.f.* gland.
Dschungel, -, *n.m. or nt. (-n f.)* jungle.
du, *pron.* you (familiar); thou.
ducken, *vb.* **(sich d.)** duck.
Duell', -e, *n.nt.* duel.
Duett', -e, *n.nt.* duet.
Duft, ̈-e, *n.m.* fragrance.
duftig, *adj.* fragrant.
dulden, *vb.* tolerate.
duldsam, *adj.* tolerant.
Duldsamkeit, *n.f.* tolerance.
dumm(-), *adj.* stupid, dumb.
Dummheit, -en, *n.f.* stupidity.
Dummkopf, ̈-e, *n.m.* dullard, idiot.
dumpf, *adj.* dull, musty.
Düne, -n, *n.f.* dune.
Dung, *n.m.* dung.
düngen, *vb.* fertilize.
Dünger, *n.m.* fertilizer, manure.
dunkel, *adj.* dark; obscure.
Dunkel, *n.nt.* dark(ness).
Dünkel, *n.m.* pretension.
dünken, *vb.* seem; **(mich dünkt)** methinks.
dünn, *adj.* thin.
Dunst, ̈-e, *n.m.* haze, vapor.
dunsten, *vb.* steam, fume.
dünsten, *vb.* steam, stew.

dunstig, *adj.* hazy.
Duplikat', **-e,** *n.nt.* duplicate.
Dur, *n.nt.* major; **(A-Dur)** A-major.
durch, *prep.* through; by means of.
durchaus', *adv.* entirely, by all means.
durchblät'tern, *vb.* leaf through.
Durchblick, **-e,** *n.m.* view (through something); grasp.
durch·blicken, *vb.* look through; be visible.
durchbli'cken, *vb.* see through, discern.
durchboh'ren, *vb.* pierce.
Durchbruch, **-̈e,** *n.m.* breakthrough.
durchdacht', *adj.* thought out.
durch·drehen, *vb.* panic.
durch·dringen*, *vb.* force one's way through, penetrate.
durchdrin'gen*, *vb.* permeate, impregnate.
durcheinan'der, *adv.* through one another; all mixed up.
Durcheinan'der, *n.nt.* confusion, turmoil, mess.
Durchfahrt, **-en,** *n.f.* passage, transit.
Durchfall, *n.m.* diarrhea.
durch·fallen*, *vb.* fail (a test).
durchführbar, *adj.* practicable.
durch·führen, *vb.* carry out.
Durchgang, **-̈e,** *n.m.* passage through; passageway; **(D. ges- perrt!)** closed to traffic.
durch·gehen*, *vb.* go through; bolt, run away.
durchgehend, *adj.* nonstop.
durch·helfen*, *vb.* help through; **(sich d.)** get along somehow.
durch·kreuzen, *vb.* cross out.
durchkreu'zen, *vb.* cross, intersect; thwart.
durch·leuchten, *vb.* shine through.
durchleuch'ten, *vb.* illuminate, irradiate, X-ray.
durchlö'chern, *vb.* perforate, puncture.
Durchlö'cherung, **-en,** *n.f.* perforation.
Durchmesser, **-,** *n.m.* diameter.
durchnäs'sen, *vb.* drench, soak.

Durchreise, **-n,** *n.f.* journey through; **(auf der D.)** passing through.
durch·schauen, *vb.* look through.
durchschau'en, *vb.* see through, understand.
durch·schneiden*, *vb.* cut in two.
durchschnei'den*, *vb.* cut, bisect, intersect.
Durchschnitt, **-e,** *n.m.* average.
durchschnittlich, *adj.* average.
durch·sehen*, *vb.* see through.
durchse'hen*, *vb.* look over, scrutinize; revise.
durch·setzen, *vb.* put through, get accepted.
durchset'zen, *vb.* intersperse, permeate.
Durchsicht, *n.f.* view; perusal.
durchsichtig, *adj.* transparent.
durch·sickern, *vb.* leak through, seep through.
durch·stechen*, *vb.* stick through.
durchste'chen*, *vb.* puncture, pierce.
durchsu'chen, *vb.* search.
Durchsu'chung, **-en,** *n.f.* search.
durch·wählen, *vb.* dial direct.
durchwüh'len, *vb.* ransack.
dürfen*, *vb.* be permitted, may.
dürftig, *adj.* meager.
dürr, *adj.* dry, barren; skinny.
Dürre, **-n,** *n.f.* drought, barrenness.
Durst, *n.m.* thirst.
dürsten, *vb.* thirst.
durstig, *adj.* thirsty.
Dusche, **-n,** *n.f.* shower.
Düse, **-n,** *n.f.* nozzle, jet.
Dusel, *n.m.* good luck.
duselig, *adj.* fizzy; stupid.
Düsenflugzeug, **-e,** *n.nt.* jet plane.
Düsenkampfflugzeug, *n.nt.* jet fighter plane.
düster, *adj.* gloomy.
Düsterheit, *n.f.* gloom.
Dutzend, **-e,** *n.nt.* dozen.
duzen, *vb.* call a person *du.*
Dyna'mik, *n.f.* dynamics.
dyna'misch, *adj.* dynamic.
Dynamit', *n.nt.* dynamite.

Dyna'mo, -s, *n.m.* dynamo.
Dynastie', -i'en, *n.f.* dynasty.
Dyslexie', *n.f.* dyslexia.

D-Zug, ⁼e, *n.m.* (= Durchgangs-zug) train with corridors in the cars; express train.

E

Ebbe, *n.f.* low tide.
ebben, *vb.* ebb.
eben, *adj.* even, level.
eben, *adv.* just; exactly.
Ebene, -n, *n.f.* plain, level ground; plane.
ebenfalls, *adv.* likewise.
ebenso, *adv.* likewise; **(e. groß)** just as big.
ebnen, *vb.* level, make smooth.
Echo, -s, *n.nt.* echo.
echt, *adj.* genuine, real.
Echtheit, -en, *n.f.* authenticity, genuineness.
Ecke, -n, *n.f.* corner.
eckig, *adj.* angular.
edel, *adj.* noble.
Edelstein, -e, *n.m.* jewel.
Efeu, *n.m.* ivy.
EG (Europäische Gemein-schaft), *n.f.* European Commu-nity.
egal', *adj.* equal; **(es ist mir e.)** I don't care, it makes no difference to me.
Egois'mus, *n.m.* egoism.
Egoist', -en, -en, *n.m.* egotist.
Egotis'mus, *n.m.* egotism.
ehe, *conj.* before.
Ehe, -n, *n.f.* marriage, matri-mony.
Ehebrecher, -, *n.m.* adulterer.
Ehebrecherin, -nen, *n.f.* adulter-ess.
Ehebruch, ⁼e, *n.m.* adultery.
ehedem, *adv.* formerly.
Ehefrau, -en, *n.f.* wife.
Ehegatte, -n, -n, *n.m.* spouse; husband.
Ehegattin, -nen, *n.f.* wife.
Eheleute, *n.pl.* married people.
ehelich, *adj.* marital; legitimate.
ehelos, *adj.* celibate.
Ehelosigkeit, *n.f.* celibacy.
ehemalig, *adj.* former.
ehemals, *adv.* formerly.
Ehemann, ⁼er, *n.m.* husband.

Ehepaar, -e, *n.nt.* married couple.
eher, *adv.* sooner, earlier; rather.
ehern, *adj.* brazen, brass.
Ehescheidung, -en, *n.f.* divorce.
Ehestand, *n.m.* matrimony.
ehrbar, *adj.* honorable.
Ehre, -n, *n.f.* honor.
ehren, *vb.* honor.
ehrenamtlich, *adj.* honorary, un-paid.
Ehrengast, ⁼e, *n.m.* guest of honor.
Ehrenplatz, ⁼e, *n.m.* place of honor.
ehrenvoll, *adj.* honorable.
ehrenwert, *adj.* worthy.
Ehrenwort, *n.nt.* word of honor.
ehrerbietig, *adj.* respectful.
Ehrerbietung, -en, *n.f.* rever-ence, obeisance.
Ehrfurcht, *n.f.* awe, respect, rev-erence.
Ehrgeiz, *n.m.* ambition.
ehrgeizig, *adj.* ambitious.
ehrlich, *adj.* honest, sincere.
Ehrlichkeit, -en, *n.f.* honesty.
ehrlos, *adj.* dishonorable.
Ehrlosigkeit, *n.f.* dishonor.
ehrsam, *adj.* honest, respectable.
Ehrsamkeit, *n.f.* respectability.
Ehrung, -en, *n.f.* tribute.
ehrwürdig, *adj.* reverend, vener-able.
Ei, -er, *n.nt.* egg.
Eiche, -n, *n.f.* oak.
Eichhörnchen, -, *n.nt.* squirrel.
Eid, -e, *n.m.* oath.
eidesstattlich, *adj.* under oath; **(eidesstattliche Erklä'rung)** affida-vit.
Eidgenosse, -n, -n, *n.m.* confed-erate.
Eidgenossenschaft, -en, *n.f.* confederation; **(Schweizerische E.)** Swiss Confederation.
eidgenössisch, *adj.* federal; Swiss.

Eifer, *n.m.* zeal, eagerness.
Eifersucht, *n.f.* jealousy.
eifersüchtig, *adj.* jealous.
eifrig, *adj.* zealous, eager, ardent.
Eigelb, -e, *n.nt.* yolk.
eigen, *adj.* own; typical of.
Eigenart, -en, *n.f.* peculiarity, inherent nature.
eigenartig, *adj.* peculiar.
Eigenheit, -en, *n.f.* peculiarity.
eigenmächtig, *adj.* arbitrary.
Eigenname(n), -, - *n.m.* proper name.
Eigennutz, *n.m.* selfishness.
eigennützig, *adj.* selfish.
Eigenschaft, -en, *n.f.* quality.
Eigenschaftswort, -̈er, *n.nt.* adjective.
Eigensinn, *n.m.* obstinacy, willfulness.
eigensinnig, *adj.* obstinate, willful.
eigentlich, 1. *adj.* actual. **2.** *adv.* as a matter of fact.
Eigentum, *n.nt.* property.
Eigentümer, -, *n.m.* owner.
Eigentümerin, -nen, *n.f.* owner.
Eigentumswohnung, -en, *n.f.* condominium.
eigenwillig, *adj.* willful; individual.
eignen, *vb.* **(sich e.)** be suited.
Eilbote, -n, -n, *n.m.* special delivery messenger; **(per E.n)** by special delivery.
Eilbrief, -e, *n.m.* special delivery letter.
Eile, *n.f.* haste, hurry.
eilen, *vb.* hurry.
eilig, *adj.* hasty, urgent.
Eilpost, *n.f.* special delivery.
Eimer, -, *n.m.* pail.
ein, -, -e, *art. & adj.* a, an; (stressed) one.
einan·der, *pron.* one another, each other.
ein·äschern, *vb.* cremate.
Einäscherung, -en, *n.f.* cremation.
ein·atmen, *vb.* inhale.
Einbahn-, *cpds.* one-way.
Einband, -̈e, *n.m.* binding.
ein·bauen, *vb.* install.
ein·behalten*, *vb.* withhold.

ein·berufen*, *vb.* summon, convoke.
ein·bilden, (sich e.) imagine.
Einbildung, -en, *n.f.* imagination; conceit.
ein·bringen*, *vb.* bind.
Einblick, -e, *n.m.* insight.
ein·bringen*, *vb.* yield.
Einbrecher, -, *n.m.* burglar.
Einbruch, -̈e, *n.m.* burglary.
Einbuchtung, -en, *n.f.* dent; bay.
ein·bürgern, *vb.* naturalize.
Einbuße, *n.f.* forfeiture.
ein·büßen, *vb.* forfeit.
ein·dämmen, *vb.* dam.
eindeutig, *adj.* clear, unequivocal.
ein·drängen, vb. (sich e.) encroach upon.
ein·dringen*, *vb.* penetrate, intrude, invade.
Eindringling, -e, *n.m.* intruder.
Eindruck, -̈e, *n.m.* impression.
eindrucksvoll, *adj.* impressive.
ein·engen, *vb.* hem in.
einer, -es, -e, *pron.* one, a person; one thing.
einerlei, *adj.* of one kind; **(es ist mir e.)** it's all the same to me.
einerseits, *adv.* on the one hand.
einfach, *adj.* simple, plain.
Einfachheit, *n.f.* simplicity.
Einfahrt, -en, *n.f.* gateway, entrance.
Einfall, -e, *n.m.* collapse; bright idea.
ein·fallen*, *vb.* fall in; invade; occur to.
einfältig, *adj.* simple.
Einfamilienhaus, -̈er, *n.nt.* one family home.
ein·fassen, *vb.* edge, trim.
ein·finden*, vb. (sich e.) present oneself, show up.
ein·flößen, *vb.* administer, instill.
Einfluß, -̈sse, *n.m.* influence.
einflußreich, *adj.* influential.
ein·fordern, *vb.* demand, reclaim.
einförmig, *adj.* uniform.
ein·fügen, *vb.* insert; **(sich e.)** adapt oneself.
Einfuhr, *n.f.* import, importation.
ein·führen, *vb.* import, induct.
Einführung, -en, *n.f.* induction; introduction.

Eingabe, -n, *n.f.* petition; (computer) input.

Eingang, ⁼e, *n.m.* entrance.

ein·geben*, *vb.* give; inspire.

eingebildet, *adj.* conceited.

eingeboren, *adj.* native, indigenous.

Eingeborene, *n.m.&f.* native.

Eingebung, -en, *n.f.* inspiration.

eingedenk, *adj.* mindful.

eingefleischt, *adj.* inveterate.

ein·gehen*, *vb.* enter; shrink; cease, perish.

eingehend, *adj.* detailed, thorough.

Eingemacht-, *n.nt.* preserves.

eingenommen, *adj.* partial, prejudiced.

Eingesessen-, *n.m.&f.* inhabitant.

Eingeständnis, -se, *n.nt.* confession, admission.

ein·gestehen*, *vb.* confess, admit.

Eingeweide, *n.pl.* intestines.

ein·gewöhnen, *vb.* acclimate.

ein·graben*, *vb.* bury.

ein·greifen*, *vb.* intervene.

Eingriff, -e, *n.m.* intervention.

ein·halten*, *vb.* check, stop; observe, keep.

ein·händigen, *vb.* hand in.

einheimisch, *adj.* native.

Einheimisch-, *n.m.&f.* native.

Einheit, -en, *n.f.* unit.

einheitlich, *adj.* uniform.

einher', *adv.* along.

ein·holen, *vb.* gather; overtake.

ein·hüllen, *vb.* wrap up, enfold.

einig, *adj.* united, agreed.

einige, *pron.&adj.* some, several.

einigen, *vb.* unite; (**sich e.**) agree.

einigermaßen, *adv.* to some extent, somewhat.

Einigkeit, *n.f.* unity.

ein·impfen, *vb.* inoculate.

ein·kassieren, *vb.* collect.

Einkauf, ⁼e, *n.m.* purchase.

ein·kaufen, *vb.* purchase.

Einkaufsbummel, *n.m.* shopping spree.

ein·kehren, *vb.* put up (at an inn).

ein·kerkern, *vb.* incarcerate.

ein·klammern, *vb.* bracket; put in parentheses.

Einklang, ⁼e, *n.m.* harmony.

ein·kleiden, *vb.* clothe.

ein·klemmen, *vb.* wedge in.

Einkommen, -, *n.nt.* income.

Einkommensteuer, -n, *n.f.* income tax.

ein·kreisen, *vb.* encircle.

Einkünfte, *n.pl.* revenue.

ein·laden*, *vb.* invite.

Einladung, -en, *n.f.* invitation.

Einlage, -n, *n.f.* enclosure, filling; deposit.

Einlaß, ⁼sse, *n.m.* admission, entrance.

ein·laufen*, *vb.* enter; shrink.

ein·legen, *vb.* insert; deposit; pickle.

ein·leiten, *vb.* introduce.

einleitend, *adj.* introductory.

Einleitung, -en, *n.f.* introduction.

ein·leuchten, *vb.* make sense.

einleuchtend, *adj.* plausible.

ein·lösen, *vb.* redeem; cash.

Einlösung, -en, *n.f.* redemption.

ein·machen, *vb.* preserve, can.

einmal, *adv.* once; (**auf e.**) all of a sudden; (**noch e.**) once again; (**nicht e.**) not even.

einmalig, *adj.* occurring only once, single, unique.

Einmarsch, ⁼e, *n.m.* marching into, entry.

ein·mauern, *vb.* wall in.

ein·mengen, *vb.* mix in; (**sich e.**) interfere.

ein·mischen, *vb.* mix in; (**sich e.**) intervene, meddle.

Einmischung, -en, *n.f.* intervention.

Einnahme, -n, *n.f.* receipt; capture.

ein·nehmen*, *vb.* take; captivate.

Einöde, *n.f.* desolate place, solitude.

ein·ordnen, *vb.* arrange, file.

ein·packen, *vb.* pack up, wrap up.

ein·pflanzen, *vb.* plant.

ein·prägen, *vb.* impress.

ein·rahmen, *vb.* frame.

ein·räumen, *vb.* concede; put away.

ein·rechnen, *vb.* include, allow for.

Einrede, -n, *n.f.* objection.

ein·reden, *vb.* talk into, persuade.

ein•reihen, vb. arrange.

ein•reißen*, vb. tear down.

ein•richten, vb. furnish, arrange, establish.

Einrichtung, -en, n.f. arrangement, institution.

ein•rücken, vb. move in; indent.

eins, num. one.

einsam, adj. lone(ly), lonesome.

Einsamkeit, n.f. loneliness, solitude.

ein•sammeln, vb. gather in.

Einsatz, ¨e, n.m. inset; stake (in betting); (mil.) sortie; mission.

ein•schalten, vb. switch on, shift into, tune in.

ein•schärfen, vb. inculcate.

ein•schätzen, vb. assess, estimate.

ein•schiffen, vb. (sich e.) embark.

ein•schlafen*, vb. go to sleep.

Einschlag, ¨e, n.m. impact; envelope.

ein•schlagen*, vb. drive in; strike, break; take.

einschlägig, adj. pertinent, relevant.

ein•schließen*, vb. lock up, in; enclose, include, involve.

einschließlich, adj. inclusive.

ein•schmeicheln, vb. (sich e.) insinuate oneself.

ein•schnappen, vb. snap shut; get annoyed.

Einschnitt, -e, n.m. cut, notch, segment.

ein•schränken, vb. limit, restrict.

Einschränkung, -en, n.f. restriction.

Einschreibebrief, -e, n.m. registered letter.

ein•schreiben*, vb. inscribe; (sich e.) register.

ein•schüchtern, vb. intimidate.

Einschüchterung, -en, n.f. intimidation.

ein•segnen, vb. consecrate, confirm.

ein•sehen*, vb. look into, realize.

ein•seifen, vb. soap, lather.

einseitig, adj. one-sided.

ein•setzen, vb. set in; appoint; install.

Einsicht, -en, n.f. insight; inspection.

Einsiedler, -, n.m. hermit.

ein•spannen, vb. stretch; harness, enlist.

ein•sperren, vb. lock up, imprison.

ein•spritzen, vb. inject.

Einspritzung, -en, n.f. injection.

Einspruch, ¨e, n.m. protest; (E. erhe′ben′) to protest.

einst, adv. once, one day.

ein•stecken, vb. put in one's pocket.

ein•stehen*, vb. (e. für) stand up for, take the place of.

ein•steigen*, vb. get in; (e.!) allaboard!

ein•stellen, vb. put in, tune in, engage; stop, suspend.

Einstellung, -en, n.f. attitude; adjustment; suspension.

ein•stimmen, vb. chime in, join in, agree.

einstimmig, adj. unanimous.

Einstimmigkeit, n.f. unanimity.

ein•studieren, vb. practice, rehearse.

Einsturz, ¨e, n.m. collapse.

einstweilen, adv. in the meantime.

ein•tauchen, vb. dip.

ein•tauschen, vb. exchange, swap.

ein•teilen, vb. divide, arrange, classify.

Einteilung, -en, n.f. classification.

eintönig, adj. monotonous.

Eintracht, n.f. harmony, concord.

ein•tragen*, vb. register, enter, record; bring in.

einträglich, adj. profitable.

Eintragung, -en, n.f. entry.

ein•treffen*, vb. arrive, happen.

ein•treten*, vb. enter.

Eintritt, -e, n.m. entry; beginning; admission.

Eintrittskarte, -n, n.f. ticket of admission.

ein•üben, vb. practice.

ein•verleiben, vb. incorporate, annex.

Einvernehmen, -, n.nt. accord.

Einverständnis, -se, n.nt. agreement.

Einwand, -e, n.m. objection.
Einwanderer, -, n.m. immigrant.
ein•wandern, vb. immigrate.
Einwanderung, -en, n.f. immigration.
einwandfrei, adj. sound, unobjectionable; perfect.
ein•wechseln, vb. change, cash.
ein•weichen, vb. soak.
ein•weihen, vb. consecrate, initiate.
Einweihung, -en, n.f. consecration, inauguration.
ein•wenden*, vb. wrap up.
ein•werfen*, vb. throw in; object, interject.
ein•wickeln, vb. wrap up.
ein•willigen, vb. consent.
Einwilligung, -en, n.f. consent, approval.
Einwirkung, -en, n.f. influence.
Einwohner, -, n.m. inhabitant, resident.
Einwohnerin, -nen, n.f. inhabitant, resident.
Einwurf, -e, n.m. slot; objection.
ein•zahlen, vb. pay in, deposit.
Einzahlung, -en, n.f. deposit.
Einzäunung, -en, n.f. enclosure.
ein•zeichnen, vb. inscribe.
Einzelheit, -en, n.f. detail.
einzeln, adj. single, individual.
ein•ziehen*, vb. (tr.) pull in, furl, seize, draft; (intr.) move in, march in.
einzig, adj. only, sole, single.
einzigartig, adj. unique.
Einzug, -e, n.m. entry.
ein•zwängen, vb. force in, squeeze in.
Eis, n.nt. ice; ice cream.
Eisberg, -e, n.m. iceberg.
Eisdiele, -n, n.f. ice-cream parlor.
Eisen, n.nt. iron.
Eisenbahn, -en, n.f. railroad.
Eisenbahnwagen, -, n.m. railroad coach.
Eisenwaren, n.pl. hardware.
eisern, adj. iron.
eisig, adj. icy.
eiskalt, adj. ice cold.
Eiskunstlauf, n.m. figure skating.
Eisregen, n.m. sleet.
Eisschrank, -e, n.m. refrigerator.
eitel, adj. vain.

Eitelkeit, -en, n.f. vanity.
Eiter, n.m. pus.
Eiterbeule, -n, n.f. abscess.
Eitergeschwulst, -e, n.f. abscess.
Eiweiß, -e, n.nt. white of egg.
Ekel, n.m. disgust.
ekelerregend, adj. nauseating.
ekelhaft, adj. disgusting.
ekeln, vb. arouse disgust; (sich vor) be disgusted by.
EKG (Elektrokardiogramm', -e), n.nt. electrocardiogram.
Eksta'se, -n, n.f. ecstasy.
eksta'tisch, adj. ecstatic.
Ekzem', -e, n.nt. eczema.
elas'tisch, adj. elastic.
Elefant', -en, -en, n.m. elephant.
elegant', adj. elegant, chic, smart.
Eleganz', n.f. elegance.
elektrifizie'ren, vb. electrify.
Elek'triker, -, n.m. electrician.
elek'trisch, adj. electric.
Elektrizität', n.f. electricity.
Elek'tron, -o'nen, n.nt. electron.
Elektro'nenrechner, -, n.m. computer.
Elektro'nenwissenschaft, n.f. electronics.
Element', -e, n.nt. element.
elementar', adj. elemental, elementary.
Elend, n.nt. misery.
elend, adj. miserable, wretched; sick.
elf, num. eleven.
Elfenbein, n.nt. ivory.
elft-, adj. eleventh.
Elftel, -, n.nt. eleventh part; (ein e.) one-eleventh.
Eli'te, n.f. elite.
Elixier', -e, n.nt. elixir.
Ellbogen, -, n.m. elbow.
Elle, -, n.f. ell, yard.
Elsaß, n.f. Alsace.
elterlich, adj. parental.
Eltern, n.pl. parents.
Emai'lle, n.f. enamel.
emanzipie'ren, vb. emancipate.
Embar'go, -s, n.nt. embargo.
Emblem', -e, n.nt. emblem.
Embryo, -s, n.m. embryo.
Empfang, -e, n.m. reception.
empfan'gen*, vb. receive; conceive (child).

Empfäng'er, -, *n.m.* receiver, recipient, addressee.

empfäng'lich, *adj.* susceptible.

Empfäng'nisverhütung, *n.f.* birth control, contraception.

Empfangs'bestätigung, -, *n.f.* receipt.

empfeh'len*, *vb.* recommend, commend.

empfeh'lenswert, *adj.* (re)commendable.

Empfeh'lung, -en, *n.f.* recommendation.

empfin'den*, *vb.* feel, sense.

empfind'lich, *adj.* sensitive.

empfind'sam, *adj.* sentimental; sensitive.

Empfin'dung, -en, *n.f.* feeling, sensation.

empfin'dungslos, *adj.* insensitive.

empor', *adv.* upward, aloft.

empö'ren, *vb.* make indignant; (**sich e.**) be furious; rebel.

empor'•ragen, *vb.* rise up, tower.

empor'•schwingen*, *vb.* (**sich e.**) soar upward.

Empö'rung, -en, *n.f.* indignation; rebellion.

emsig, *adj.* busy, industrious.

Emulsion', -en, *n.f.* emulsion.

Ende, -n, *n.nt.* end.

enden, *vb.* end.

endgültig, *adj.* definitive, conclusive, final.

endigen, *vb.* end.

endlich, 1. *adj.* final; finite. **2.'** *adv.* at last.

endlos, *adj.* endless.

Endstation, -en, *n.f.* terminus.

Energie', -n, *n.f.* energy.

energie'los, *adj.* languid.

ener'gisch, *adj.* energetic.

eng, *adj.* narrow, tight.

engagie'ren, *vb.* engage, hire.

Enge, -n, *n.f.* narrowness; narrow place; (**in die E. treiben***) drive into a corner.

Engel, -, *n.m.* angel.

England, *n.nt.* England.

Engländer, -, *n.m.* Englishman.

Engländerin, -nen, *n.f.* Englishwoman.

englisch, *adj.* English.

engstirnig, *adj.* narrow-minded.

Enkel, -, *n.m.* grandson.

Enkelin, -nen, *n.f.* granddaughter.

Enkelkind, -er, *n.nt.* grandchild.

enorm', *adj.* enormous.

Ensem'ble, -s, *n.nt.* ensemble.

entar'ten, *vb.* degenerate.

entbeh'ren, *vb.* go without.

entbehr'lich, *adj.* dispensable.

Entbeh'rung, -en, *n.f.* privation.

entbin'den*, *vb.* set free; deliver.

Entbin'dung, -en, *n.f.* delivery.

entblö'ßen, *vb.* denude, uncover, bare.

entde'cken, *vb.* discover.

Entde'ckung, -en, *n.f.* discovery.

Ente, -n, *n.f.* duck.

enteh'ren, *vb.* dishonor.

enteig'nen, *vb.* dispossess.

enter'ben, *vb.* disinherit.

entfa'chen, *vb.* kindle.

entfal'len*, *vb.* be cancelled; slip from (memory).

entfal'ten, *vb.* unfold.

entfer'nen, *vb.* remove.

Entfer'nung, -en, *n.f.* removal; distance.

entfes'seln, *vb.* unchain, release.

entflam'men, *vb.* inflame.

entflie'hen*, *vb.* flee, escape.

entfrem'den, *vb.* estrange, alienate.

entfüh'ren*, *vb.* carry off, abduct, kidnap.

Entfüh'rung, -en, *n.f.* abduction.

entge'gen, *adv.&prep.* opposite, contrary to; towards.

entge'gengesetzt, *adj.* opposite.

entge'gen•kommen*, *vb.* come towards; be obliging.

entge'gen•setzen, *vb.* oppose.

entge'gnen, *vb.* reply, retort.

entge'hen*, *vb.* elude.

Entgelt', *n.nt.* remuneration.

entglei'sen*, *vb.* jump the track; make a slip.

Entglei'sung, -en, *n.f.* derailment; blunder.

enthal'ten*, *vb.* hold, contain; (**sich e.**) refrain.

enthalt'sam, *adj.* abstemious.

Enthalt'samkeit, -en, *n.f.* abstinence.

Enthal'tung, *n.f.* forbearance.

enthe'ben*, *vb.* oust.

Enthe'bung, -en, *n.f.* ouster.
enthül'len, *vb.* unveil, disclose.
Enthül'lung, -en, *n.f.* disclosure, exposé.
Enthusiast', -en, -en, *n.m.* enthusiast.
entklei'den, *vb.* undress, divest.
entkom'men*, *vb.* escape.
entkräf'ten, *vb.* debilitate.
entla'den*, *vb.* unload.
entlang', *adv. &prep.* along.
entlas'sen*, *vb.* dismiss, release.
Entlas'sung, -en, *n.f.* dismissal, release.
entlau'fen*, *vb.* run away.
entle'digen, *vb.* free from, exempt.
entle'gen, *adj.* remote.
entmilitarisie'ren, *vb.* demilitarize.
entmu'tigen, *vb.* discourage.
Entmu'tigung, -en, *n.f.* discouragement.
entneh'men*, *vb.* take from, infer from.
entner'ven, *vb.* enervate.
entrah'men, *vb.* skim.
enträt'seln, *vb.* decipher.
entrei'ßen*, *vb.* snatch from.
entrich'ten, *vb.* pay, settle.
entrin'nen*, *vb.* run away from.
entrüs'ten, *vb.* make indignant; **(sich e.)** become indignant.
entrüs'tet, *adj.* indignant.
Entrüs'tung, -en, *n.f.* indignation.
entsa'gen, *vb.* renounce, abjure.
entschä'digen, *vb.* compensate, indemnify.
Entschä'digung, -en, *n.f.* compensation, indemnification.
entschei'den*, *vb.* decide.
entschei'dend, *adj.* decisive.
Entschei'dung, -en, *n.f.* decision.
entschie'den, *adj.* decided, definite.
entschlie'ßen*, *vb.* **(sich e.)** decide.
entschlo'ssen, *adj.* determined.
Entschlos'senheit, *n.f.* determination.
entschlüp'fen, *vb.* slip away from.
Enschluß', -sse, *n.m.* decision.

entschul'digen, *vb.* excuse; **(sich e.)** apologize.
Entschul'digung, -en, *n.f.* excuse, apology.
entset'zen, *vb.* dismiss; horrify; **(sich e.)** be horrified.
Entset'zen, *n.nt.* horror.
entsetz'lich, *adj.* horrible.
entsin'nen*, *vb.* **(sich e.)** recollect.
Entsor'gung, *n.f.* safe disposal of waste.
entspan'nen, *vb.* relax.
Entspan'nung, *n.f.* détente; relaxation.
entspre'chen*, *vb.* correspond.
entspre'chend, *adj.* corresponding (to), respective.
entste'hen*, *vb.* arise, originate.
entstel'len, *vb.* disfigure, deform, distort, mutilate, garble.
enttäu'schen, *vb.* disappoint.
Enttäu'schung, -en, *n.f.* disappointment.
entthro'nen, *vb.* dethrone.
entwaff'nen, *vb.* disarm.
entwäs'sern, *vb.* drain.
entweder, *conj.* **(e. . . . oder)** either . . . or.
entwei'chen*, *vb.* escape.
entwen'den*, *vb.* steal.
entwer'fen*, *vb.* sketch, draft, plan.
entwer'ten, *vb.* depreciate; cancel.
entwi'ckeln, *vb.* develop.
Entwick'ler, -, *n.m.* developer.
Entwicklung, -en, *n.f.* development.
Entwick'lungshilfe, *n.f.* foreign aid.
Entwick'lungsland, -ᵉʳ, *n.nt.* developing nation.
entwir'ren, *vb.* disentangle.
entwi'schen, *vb.* slip away from.
entwöh'nen, *vb.* wean; cure (from drugs).
entwür'digen, *vb.* dishonor.
Entwurf', -ᵉ, *n.m.* sketch, design, draft, plan.
entzie'hen*, *vb.* remove, extract.
entzü'cken, *vb.* delight.
Entzü'cken, -, *n.nt.* delight.
entzü'ckend, *adj.* delightful, charming.

Entzü'ckung, **-en**, *n.f.* rapture.
entzünd'bar, *adj.* inflammable.
entzün'den, *vb.* inflame.
entzün'det, *adj.* infected.
Entzün'dung, **-en**, *n.f.* inflammation, infection.
entzwei', *adv.* in two, apart.
Enzy'klika, **-ken**, *n.f.* encyclical.
Enzyklopädie', **-i'en**, *n.f.* encyclopaedia.
Epidemie', **-i'en**, *n.f.* epidemic.
epide'misch, *adj.* epidemic.
Epilepsie', *n.f.* epilepsy.
Epilog', **-e**, *n.m.* epilogue.
Episo'de, **-n**, *n.f.* episode.
Epo'che, **-n**, *n.f.* epoch.
Epos (pl. **Epopen**), *n.nt.* epic poem.
er, *pron.* he, it.
erach'ten, *vb.* consider.
erbar'men, *vb.* have pity; (**sich e.**) pity.
Erbar'men, *n.nt.* pity.
erbärm'lich, *adj.* pitiful.
erbar'mungslos, *adj.* pitiless.
erbau'en, *vb.* construct; edify.
erbau'lich, *adj.* edifying.
Erbau'ung, *n.f.* edification.
Erbe, **-n**, **-n**, *n.m.* heir.
Erbe, *n.nt.* inheritance, heritage.
erben, *vb.* inherit.
Erbfolge, *n.f.* succession.
erbie'ten*, *vb.* (**sich e.**) offer, volunteer.
Erbin, **-nen**, *n.f.* heiress.
erbit'ten, *vb.* ask for.
erbit'tern, *vb.* embitter.
erblas'sen, *vb.* turn pale.
erblei'chen*, *vb.* turn pale.
erblich, *adj.* hereditary.
Erblichkeit, *n.f.* heredity.
erblicken, *vb.* catch sight of.
erbo'sen, *vb.* make angry; (**sich e.**) get angry.
erbre'chen*, *vb.* break open; (**sich e.**) vomit.
Erbschaft, **-en**, *n.f.* inheritance.
Erbse, **-n**, *n.f.* pea.
Erbstück, **-e**, *n.nt.* heirloom.
Erdbeben, **-**, *n.nt.* earthquake.
Erdbeere, **-n**, *n.f.* strawberry.
Erdboden, *n.m.* ground, soil.
Erde, *n.f.* earth.
erden, *vb.* ground.
erden'ken*, *vb.* think up.

erdenk'lich, *adj.* imaginable.
Erdgeschoß, *n.nt.* ground floor.
Erdhügel, **-**, *n.m.* mound.
erdich'ten, *vb.* invent, imagine.
erdich'tet, *adj.* fictional.
Erdich'tung, *n.f.* fiction.
erdig, *adj.* earthy.
Erdkreis, **-e**, *n.m.* sphere.
Erdkugel, **-n**, *n.f.* globe.
Erdkunde, *n.f.* geography.
Erdnuß, **-sse**, *n.f.* peanut.
Erdöl, **-e**, *n.nt.* petroleum.
erdrei'sten, *vb.* (**sich e.**) be so bold.
erdros'seln, *vb.* strangle.
erdrü'cken, *vb.* crush (to death), stifle.
Erdteil, **-e**, *n.m.* continent.
erdul'den, *vb.* endure.
ereig'nen, *vb.* (**sich e.**) happen.
Ereig'nis, **-se**, *n.nt.* event.
ereig'nisreich, *adj.* eventful.
erfah'ren*, *vb.* come to know, learn, experience.
erfah'ren, *adj.* experienced, adept.
Erfah'rung, **-en**, *n.f.* experience.
erfas'sen, *vb.* grasp, realize; apprehend.
erfin'den*, *vb.* invent; contrive.
Erfin'der, **-**, *n.m.* inventor.
Erfin'derin, **-nen**, *n.f.* inventor.
erfin'derisch, *adj.* inventive; ingenious.
Erfin'dung, **-en**, *n.f.* invention.
Erfolg', **-e**, *n.m.* success.
erfolg'los, *adj.* unsuccessful.
erfolg'reich, *adj.* successful; (**e. sein***) to succeed.
erfor'derlich, *adj.* required.
erfor'dern, *vb.* require.
Erfor'dernis, **-se**, *n.nt.* requirement, requisite.
erfor'schen, *vb.* explore.
Erfor'schung, **-en**, *n.f.* exploration.
erfreu'en, *vb.* delight; gratify; (**sich e.**) enjoy.
erfreu'lich, *adj.* enjoyable, pleasing; welcome.
erfrie'ren*, *vb.* freeze.
erfri'schen, *vb.* refresh, invigorate.
Erfri'schung, **-en**, *n.f.* refreshment.

erfül'len, *vb.* fill; fulfill.
Erfül'lung, -en, *n.f.* fulfillment.
ergän'zen, *vb.* supplement; amend.
Ergän'zung, -en, *n.f.* supplement, complement.
erge'ben*, *vb.* yield; result in; **(sich e.)** result, follow; surrender.
erge'ben, *adj.* devoted.
Ergeb'nis, -se, *n.nt.* result, outcome.
ergie'big, *adj.* productive.
ergöt'zen, *vb.* delight.
ergötz'lich, *adj.* delectable.
ergrei'fen*, *vb.* grasp, seize.
Ergrif'fenheit, *n.f.* emotion.
Erguß', -sse, *n.m.* effusion.
erha'ben, *adj.* elevated; lofty, sublime.
Erha'benheit, *n.f.* grandeur.
erhal'ten*, *vb.* maintain, preserve; get, obtain.
Erhal'tung, *n.f.* maintenance, preservation; acquisition.
erhär'ten, *vb.* harden.
erha'schen, *vb.* snatch.
erhe'ben*, *vb.* raise.
erheb'lich, *adj.* considerable.
erhei'tern, *vb.* brighten, cheer.
erhel'len, *vb.* illuminate.
erhit'zen, *vb.* heat.
erhö'hen, *vb.* raise, heighten; ennoble.
Erhö'hung, -en, *n.f.* elevation, rise; enhancement; increase.
erho'len, *vb.* **(sich e.)** get better, recuperate.
Erho'lung, *n.f.* recuperation, recreation.
erhö'ren, *vb.* hear.
erin'nern, *vb.* remind; **(sich e.)** remember, recollect.
Erin'nerung, -en, *n.f.* remembrance, memory.
erkäl'ten, *vb.* **(sich e.)** catch cold.
Erkäl'tung, -en, *n.f.* cold.
erken'nen*, *vb.* recognize.
erkennt'lich, *adj.* recognizable; thankful.
Erkennt'nis, -se, *n.f.* realization, knowledge.
erklä'ren, *vb.* explain, declare.
erklä'rend, *adj.* explanatory.
Erklä'rung, -en, *n.f.* explanation; declaration.

erklet'tern, *vb.* climb up, scale.
erklin'gen*, *vb.* (re)sound.
erkran'ken, *vb.* be taken ill.
erkun'digen, *vb.* **(sich e.)** inquire.
Erkun'digung, -en, *n.f.* inquiry.
erlan'gen, *vb.* obtain, attain.
Erlaß', -sse, *n.m.* decree.
erlas'sen*, *vb.* decree; forgive.
erlau'ben, *vb.* allow, permit.
Erlaub'nis, -se, *n.f.* permission, permit.
erläu'tern, *vb.* illustrate; elucidate.
Erläu'terung, -en, *n.f.* illustration; elucidation.
Erleb'nis, -se, *n.nt.* event, experience.
erle'digen, *vb.* take care of, settle.
erle'digt, *adj.* settled; exhausted.
erleich'tern, *vb.* lighten, facilitate; relieve.
Erleich'terung, -en, *n.f.* ease, relief.
erlei'den*, *vb.* suffer.
erle'sen, *adj.* chosen, choice, select.
erleuch'ten, *vb.* illuminate.
erlie'gen*, *vb.* succumb.
Erlös', *n.m.* proceeds.
erlö'schen*, *vb.* go out, be extinguished; become extinct.
erlö'sen, *vb.* deliver, redeem.
Erlö'ser, *n.m.* redeemer.
Erlö'sung, -en, *n.f.* deliverance, redemption.
ermäch'tigen, *vb.* empower, enable.
Ermäch'tigung, -en, *n.f.* authorization.
ermah'nen, *vb.* admonish.
erman'geln, *vb.* lack.
ermä'ßigen, *vb.* reduce.
Ermä'ßigung, -en, *n.f.* reduction.
ermat'ten, *vb.* tire.
ermes'sen*, *vb.* calculate; comprehend.
ermit'teln, *vb.* ascertain.
Ermitt'lung, -en, *n.f.* detection; investigation.
ermög'lichen, *vb.* make possible, enable.
ermor'den, *vb.* murder.
Ermor'dung, -en, *n.f.* murder, assassination.

ermü'den, *vb.* tire; (sich e.) get tired.

ermun'tern, *vb.* rouse; cheer up.

ermu'tigen, *vb.* encourage.

Ermu'tigung, -en, *n.f.* encouragement.

ernäh'ren, *vb.* nourish, nurture.

Ernäh'rung, *n.f.* nourishment, nutrition.

ernen'nen*, *vb.* appoint, nominate.

Ernen'nung, -en, *n.f.* appointment, nomination.

erneu'ern, *vb.* renew.

Erneu'erung, -en, *n.f.* renewal.

ernie'drigen, *vb.* debase, degrade.

Ernie'drigung, -en, *n.f.* degradation.

ernst, *adj.* earnest; severe, serious.

Ernst, *n.m.* earnestness; gravity, seriousness.

Ernte, -n, *n.f.* harvest, crop.

ernten, *vb.* harvest, reap.

Ero'berer, -, *n.m.* conqueror.

ero'bern, *vb.* conquer.

Ero'berung, -en, *n.f.* conquest.

eröff'nen, *vb.* open.

Eröff'nung, -en, *n.f.* opening.

erör'tern, *vb.* discuss, debate.

Erör'terung, -en, *n.f.* discussion, debate.

Ero'tik, *n.f.* eroticism.

ero'tisch, *adj.* erotic.

erpicht', *adj.* intent.

erpres'sen, *vb.* blackmail.

Erpres'sung, -en, *n.f.* blackmail, extortion.

erqui'cken, *vb.* refresh.

erra'ten*, *vb.* guess.

erre'gen, *vb.* arouse, excite.

Erre'gung, -en, *n.f.* excitement; emotion.

errei'chen, *vb.* reach; achieve.

errich'ten, *vb.* erect, establish.

Errich'tung, -en, *n.f.* erection.

errin'gen*, *vb.* achieve; gain.

Errun'genschaft, -en, *n.f.* achievement, attainment.

Ersatz', *n.m.* compensation; substitute; *cpds.* spare.

erschaf'fen*, *vb.* create.

Erschaf'fung, -en, *n.f.* creation.

erschei'nen*, *vb.* appear.

Erschei'nung, -en, *n.f.* appearance; apparition; phenomenon.

erschie'ßen*, *vb.* shoot (dead).

erschla'gen*, *vb.* slay.

erschlie'ßen*, *vb.* open, unfold.

erschöp'fen, *vb.* exhaust.

erschöpft', *adj.* weary, exhausted.

Erschöp'fung, *n.f.* exhaustion.

erschre'cken, *vb.* scare, frighten, startle.

erschre'cken*, *vb.* become scared, become frightened, be startled.

erschüt'tern, *vb.* shake, shock.

Erschüt'terung, -en, *n.f.* shock; vibration.

erschwe'ren, *vb.* make more difficult, aggravate.

erschwing'lich, *adj.* within one's means.

erse'hen*, *vb.* see, learn.

erset'zen, *vb.* make good, replace; supersede.

ersicht'lich, *adj.* evident.

ersin'nen*, *vb.* devise.

erspa'ren, *vb.* save.

erst, 1. *adj.* first. 2. *adv.* not until, only.

erstar'ren, *vb.* get numb, stiffen; congeal.

erstat'ten, *vb.* refund, recompense.

erstau'nen, *vb.* astonish, amaze.

Erstau'nen, *n.nt.* amazement, astonishment.

erstaun'lich, *adj.* amazing.

erste'hen*, *vb.* arise; get, obtain.

erstei'gen*, *vb.* climb.

erstens, *adv.* in the first place, firstly.

erster-, *adj.* former.

ersti'cken, *vb.* stifle, suffocate, smother.

Ersti'ckung, -en, *n.f.* suffocation, asphyxiation, choking.

erstklassig, *adj.* first-class, first-rate.

erstre'ben, *vb.* aspire to.

erstre'cken, vb. (sich e.) extend, range.

ersu'chen, *vb.* request.

ertap'pen, *vb.* catch, surprise.

ertei'len, *vb.* give, administer.

Ertrag', -e, *n.m.* yield, return.

ertrag'bar, *adj.* bearable.

extra'gen*, *vb.* bear, endure.

erträg'lich, *adj.* passable, tolerable.

erträn'ken, *vb.* (tr.) drown.

ertrin'ken*, *vb.* (intr.) drown.

erü'brigen, *vb.* (sich e.) not be necessary.

erwa'chen, *vb.* wake.

erwach'sen*, *vb.* arise, grow, grow up.

erwach'sen, *adj.* grown, grown-up, adult.

Erwach'sen-, *n.m.&f.* adult.

erwä'gen, *vb.* deliberate, ponder.

Erwä'gung, -en, *n.f.* consideration.

erwäh'nen, *vb.* mention.

Erwäh'nung, -en, *n.f.* mention.

erwar'ten, *vb.* expect, await.

Erwar'tung, -en, *n.f.* expectation, anticipation.

erwe'cken, *vb.* awaken.

erwei'chen, *vb.* soften, mollify; (sich e. lassen*) relent.

erwei'sen*, *vb.* prove; render.

erwei'tern, *vb.* widen, extend.

erwer'ben*, *vb.* acquire.

Erwer'bung, -en, *n.f.* acquisition.

erwi'dern, *vb.* reply; return, reciprocate.

Erwi'derung, -en, *n.f.* reply; return.

erwir'ken, *vb.* bring about.

erwi'schen, *vb.* catch, get hold of.

erwünscht', *adj.* desired.

erwür'gen, *vb.* strangle.

erzäh'len, *vb.* tell, narrate, relate.

Erzäh'lung, -en, *n.f.* story, narrative, tale.

Erzbischof, ⁼e, *n.m.* archbishop.

Erzdiözese, -n, *n.f.* archdiocese.

erzeu'gen, *vb.* create, produce; *(elec.)* generate.

Erzeug'nis, -se, *n.nt.* product.

Erzherzog, ⁼e, *n.m.* archduke.

erzie'hen*, *vb.* educate.

Erzie'her, -, *n.m.* educator.

Erzie'herin, -nen, *n.f.* governess, educator, teacher.

erzie'herisch, *adj.* education; breeding.

Erzie'hung, *n.f.* upbringing; education.

Erziehungsanstalt, *n.f.* reform school.

erzür'nen, *vb.* (sich e.) become angry.

erzwin'gen*, *vb.* force.

es, *pron.* it.

Esche, -n, *n.f.* ash (tree).

Esel, -, *n.m.* donkey, ass, jackass.

Eskalation, *n.f.* escalation.

eskalie'ren, *vb.* escalate.

eßbar, *adj.* edible.

essen*, *vb.* eat.

Essen, *n.nt.* food.

Essenz', -en, *n.f.* essence; flavoring.

Essig, *n.m.* vinegar.

Eßlöffel, -, *n.m.* tablespoon.

Eßstäbchen, -, *n.nt.* chopstick.

Eßzimmer, -, *n.nt.* dining room.

Estland, *n.nt.* Estonia.

Eta'ge, -n, *n.f.* floor, story.

Etat', -s, *n.m.* budget.

ethnisch, *adj.* ethnic.

Etikett', -e, *n.nt.* tag, label, sticker.

Etiket'te, *n.f.* etiquette.

etliche, *pron.* several.

etwa, *adv.* about, approximately, more or less, maybe.

etwaig, *adj.* eventual.

etwas, 1. *pron.* something. 2. *adv.* somewhat.

Eule, -n, *n.f.* owl.

Euro'pa, *n.nt.* Europe.

Europä'er, -, *n.m.* European.

Europä'erin, -nen, *n.f.* European.

europä'isch, *adj.* European.

Europä'ische Gemeinschaft, *n.f.* European Community.

evakuie'ren, *vb.* evacuate.

evange'lisch, *adj.* evangelical, Protestant.

Evangelist', -en, -en, *n.m.* evangelist.

Evange'lium, *n.nt.* gospel.

Eventualität', -en, *n.f.* contingency.

eventuell', *adj.* possible, potential.

ewig, 1. *adj.* eternal, everlasting. 2. *adv.* forever.

Ewigkeit, -en, *n.f.* eternity.

Exa'men, -, *n.nt.* examination.
Exemplar', -e, *n.nt.* specimen, copy.
exerzie'ren, *vb.* drill.
Existenz', -en, *n.f.* existence.
existie'ren, *vb.* exist.
exo'tisch, *adj.* exotic.
Experiment', -e, *n.nt.* experiment.
experimentie'ren, *vb.* experiment.
Exper'te, -n, *n.m.* expert.
explodie'ren, *vb.* explode, detonate.

Explosion', -en, *n.f.* explosion.
explosiv', *adj.* explosive.
Export', -e, *n.m.* export.
exportie'ren, *vb.* export.
Expreß', -sse, *n.m.* express train.
extra, *adj.* extra; on purpose.
Extravaganz', -en, *n.f.* extravagance.
extrem', *adj.* extreme.
Exzellenz', -en, *n.f.* Excellency.
exzen'trisch, *adj.* eccentric.
Exzentrizität', -en, *n.f.* eccentricity.

F

Fabel, -n, *n.f.* fable.
fabelhaft, *adj.* fabulous, wonderful.
Fabrik', -en, *n.f.* factory, plant.
Fabrikant', -en, -en, *n.m.* manufacturer.
Fabrikat', -e, *n.nt.* manufactured article; **(deutsches F.)** made in Germany.
Fach, ̈-er, *n.nt.* compartment; profession; (academic) subject.
Fächer, -, *n.m.* fan.
fächern, *vb.* fan.
Fachhochschule, -n, *n.f.* technical university.
fachmännisch, *adj.* professional.
Fachwort, ̈-er, *n.nt.* technical term.
Fackel, -, *n.f.* torch.
fade, *adj.* flavorless, insipid.
Faden, ̈-, *n.m.* thread, filament.
fadenscheinig, *adj.* threadbare.
fähig, *adj.* able, capable, competent.
Fähigkeit, -en, *n.f.* ability, capability, competence.
fahnden, *vb.* search.
Fahne, -n, *n.f.* flag.
Fahnenflucht, *n.f.* desertion.
Fahnenflüchtig, -n.m. deserter.
Fähnrich, -e, *n.m.* ensign.
Fahrbahn, -en, *n.f.* lane.
Fähre, -n, *n.f.* ferry.
fahren*, *vb.* drive, ride, go.
Fahrer, -, *n.m.* driver.
Fahrerin, -nen, *n.f.* driver.
Fahrgeld, -er, *n.nt.* fare.

Fahrgemeinschaft, *n.f.* car pool.
Fahrkarte, -n, *n.f.* ticket.
Fahrkartenautomat, -en, *n.m.* ticket machine.
Fahrkartenschalter, -, *n.m.* ticket office.
fahrlässig, *adj.* negligent.
Fahrplan, ̈-e, *n.m.* timetable, schedule.
fahrplanmäßig, *adj.* scheduled.
Fahrpreis, -e, *n.m.* fare.
Fahrrad, ̈-er, *n.nt.* bicycle.
Fahrrinne, -n, *n.f.* lane.
Fahrschein, -e, *n.m.* ticket.
Fahrstuhl, ̈-e, *n.m.* elevator.
Fahrt, -en, *n.f.* fare; trip.
Fährte, -n, *n.f.* track, trail.
Fahrzeug, -e, *n.nt.* vehicle, conveyance.
Faktor, -o'ren, *n.m.* factor.
Fakultät', -en, *n.f.* faculty.
fakultativ', *adj.* optional.
Fall, ̈-e, *n.m.* fall; case.
Falle, -n, *n.f.* trap; pitfall.
fallen*, *vb.* fall, drop; **(f. lassen*)** drop.
fällen, *vb.* fell.
fällig, *adj.* due; **(f. werden*)** become due, mature.
Fälligkeit, *n.f.* maturity.
falls, *conj.* in case, if.
falsch, *adj.* false, wrong; fake; deceitful.
fälschen, *vb.* forge, counterfeit.
Fälscher, -, *n.m.* forger.
Falschheit, -en, *n.f.* falseness, deceit.

Fälschung, -en, *n.f.* forgery.
Falte, -n, *n.f.* fold, crease, pleat; wrinkle.
falten, *vb.* fold, pleat, crease.
familiär', *adj.* familiar; intimate.
Fami'lie, -n, *n.f.* family.
Fami'liennamen(n), -, *n.m.* surname.
famos', *adj.* splendid.
Fana'tiker, -, *n.m.* fanatic.
fana'tisch, *adj.* fanatic, rabid.
Fanatis'mus, *n.m.* fanaticism.
Fanfa're, -n, *n.f.* fanfare.
Fang, ̈-e, *n.m.* catch.
fangen*, *vb.* catch, capture.
Fänger, -, *n.m.* catcher.
Farbe, -n, *n.f.* color; paint; dye; (cards) suit.
färben, *vb.* color, dye.
farbenreich, *adj.* colorful.
Färber, -, *n.m.* dyer.
farbig, *adj.* colored.
farblos, *adj.* colorless, drab.
Farbstoff, -e, *n.m.* dye (stuff).
Farbton, ̈-e, *n.m.* shade.
Farbtönung, -en, *n.f.* tint.
Färbung, -en, *n.f.* coloring, hue.
Farce, -n, *n.f.* farce.
Farmer, -, *n.m.* farmer.
Fasching, *n.m.* carnival, Mardi Gras.
Faschis'mus, *n.m.* fascism.
Faschist', -en, -en, *n.m.* fascist.
faschis'tisch, *adj.* fascist.
faseln, *vb.* talk nonsense.
Faser, -n, *n.f.* fiber.
Faß, ̈-sser, *n.nt.* barrel, keg, vat, cask.
Fassa'de, -n, *n.f.* façade.
fassen, *vb.* grasp; seize; **(sich f.)** compose oneself; **(fasse dich kurz!)** make it short.
Fasson', -s, *n.f.* shape.
Fassung, -en, *n.f.* version; gem setting; *(fig.)* composure; **(aus der F. bringen*)** rattle.
fassungslos, *adj.* bewildered, staggered.
Fassungsvermögen, -, *n.nt.* capacity; comprehension.
fast, *adv.* almost, nearly.
fasten, *vb.* fast.
Fastenzeit, -, *n.f.* Lent.
faszinie'ren, *vb.* fascinate.
fauchen, *vb.* puff; (of cats) spit.

faul, *adj.* lazy; rotten.
faulenzen, *vb.* loaf.
Faulenzer, -, *n.m.* loafer.
Faulenzerin, -nen, *n.f.* loafer.
Fäulnis, *n.f.* decay, putrefaction.
Faultier, -e, *n.nt.* sloth.
Faust, ̈-e, *n.f.* fist.
faxen, *vb.* fax.
Februar, -e, *n.m.* February.
fechten*, *vb.* fence.
Feder, -n, *n.f.* feather, plume; pen.
federleicht, *adj.* feathery.
federn, *vb.* feather; have good springs.
Fee, Fe'en, *n.f.* fairy.
Fegefeuer, *n.nt.* purgatory.
Fehde, -n, *n.f.* feud.
fehlbar, *adj.* fallible.
fehlen, *vb.* lack; be absent or missing.
Fehler, -, *n.m.* mistake, error; flaw, imperfection, defect; blunder.
fehlerfrei, *adj.* flawless.
fehlerhaft, *adj.* faulty, imperfect, defective.
fehlerlos, *adj.* faultless.
fehl-gebären*, *vb.* abort, have a miscarriage.
Fehlgeburt, -en, *n.f.* miscarriage, abortion.
fehl-gehen*, *vb.* err, go astray.
Fehlschlag, ̈-e, *n.m.* failure; setback.
Fehltritt, -e, *n.m.* slip.
Feier, -n, *n.f.* celebration.
Feierabend, *n.m.* end of work.
feierlich, *adj.* ceremonious; solemn.
Feierlichkeit, -en, *n.f.* ceremony, solemnity.
feiern, *vb.* celebrate.
Feiertag, -e, *n.m.* holiday.
feige, *adj.* cowardly.
Feige, -n, *n.f.* fig.
Feigheit, -en, *n.f.* cowardice.
Feigling, -e, *n.m.* coward.
Feile, -n, *n.f.* file.
feilen, *vb.* file.
feilschen, *vb.* bargain, haggle.
fein, *adj.* fine, delicate; elegant; subtle.
Feind, -e, *n.m.* foe, enemy.
Feindin, -nen, *n.f.* enemy.

feindlich, *adj.* hostile.

Feindschaft, -en, *n.f.* enmity; feud.

Feindseligkeit, -en, *n.f.* hostility.

Feingefühl, *n.nt.* sensitivity.

Feinheit, -en, *n.f.* purity; delicacy; elegance; subtlety.

Feinschmecker, -, *n.m.* gourmet.

feinsinnig, *adj.* ingenious.

feist, *adj.* fat, plump.

Feld, -er, *n.nt.* field.

Feldbett, -en, *n.nt.* cot.

Feldherr, -n, -en, *n.m.* commander.

Feldstecher, -, *n.m.* binoculars.

Feldzug, =e, *n.m.* campaign.

Fell, -e, *n.nt.* skin, pelt, hide.

Fels(en), -, *n.m.* rock, boulder.

Felsblock, =e, *n.m.* boulder.

felsig, *adj.* rocky, craggy.

Fenster, -, *n.nt.* window.

Fensterladen, =, *n.m.* shutter.

Fensterscheibe, -n, *n.f.* windowpane.

Ferien, *n.pl.* vacation.

Ferienort, -e, *n.m.* resort.

fern, *adj.* far, distant, remote.

Fernanruf, -e, *n.m.* long-distance call.

ferner, *adv.* moreover, furthermore.

Ferngespräch, -e, *n.nt.* long-distance call.

Fernglas, =er, *n.nt.* binocular(s).

Fernrohr, -e, *n.nt.* telescope.

Fernsehen, *n.nt.* television.

Fernsprecher, -, *n.m.* telephone.

Ferse, -n, *n.f.* heel.

fertig, *adj.* finished, complete, ready, done; **(f. sein*)** be through; **(f. bringen*)** complete, accomplish.

Fertigkeit, -en, *n.f.* dexterity, knack.

fesch, *adj.* chic.

Fessel, -n, *n.f.* fetter, irons, handcuffs; ankle.

Fesselgelenk, -e, *n.nt.* ankle.

fesseln, *vb.* chain; *(fig.)* captivate, fascinate.

fest, *adj.* firm, solid; fixed, steady; tight.

Fest, -e, *n.nt.* feast, celebration.

Feste, -n, *n.f.* fort, stronghold.

Festessen, -, *n.nt.* banquet, feast.

fest·fahren*, *vb.* run aground; *(fig.)* come to an impasse.

fest·halten*, *vb.* hold fast to, adhere to; detain.

festigen, *vb.* solidify, consolidate.

Festigkeit, *n.f.* firmness, solidity.

fest·klammern, *vb.* clamp; **(sich f.)** hold fast.

Festland, *n.nt.* mainland.

fest·legen, *vb.* fix, lay down.

festlich, *adj.* festive.

Festlichkeit, -en, *n.f.* festivity.

fest·machen, *vb.* fasten, make fast.

Festmahl, -e, *n.nt.* feast.

Festnahme, -n, *n.f.* arrest.

fest·nehmen*, *vb.* arrest.

fest·setzen, *vb.* fix, establish; determine.

Festspiel, -e, *n.nt.* festival.

fest·stehen*, *vb.* be stable; be certain.

feststehend, *adj.* stationary.

fest·stellen, *vb.* determine, ascertain; state.

Festtag, -e, *n.m.* holiday.

Festung, -en, *n.f.* fortress.

Fete, -n, *n.f.* party.

fett, *adj.* fat, greasy.

Fett, -e, *n.nt.* fat, grease.

fetten, *vb.* grease.

fettig, *adj.* fatty, greasy, oily.

fettleibig, *adj.* obese.

Fetzen, -, *n.m.* rag; scrap.

feucht, *adj.* moist, damp, humid.

Feuchtigkeit, *n.f.* moisture, dampness, humidity.

feuchtkalt, *adj.* clammy.

Feuer, -, *n.nt.* fire, *(fig.)* verve.

Feueralarm, -e, *n.m.* fire alarm.

feuergefährlich, *adj.* inflammable.

Feuerleiter, -n, *n.f.* fire escape.

Feuermelder, -, *n.m.* fire alarm (box).

feuern, *vb.* fire.

Feuersbrunst, *n.f.* conflagration.

Feuerspritze, -n, *n.f.* fire engine.

Feuerstein, -e, *n.m.* flint.

Feuerwaffe, -n, *n.f.* firearm.

Feuerwechsel, -, *n.m.* skirmish.

Feuerwehrmann, =er, *n.m.* fireman.

Feuerwerk, -e, *n.nt.* fireworks.

Feuerzeug, -e, *n.nt.* cigarette lighter.
feurig, *adj.* fiery.
Fichte, -n, *n.f.* pine, fir.
fidel', *adj.* jolly.
Fieber, *n.nt.* fever.
fieberhaft, *adj.* feverish.
fiebern, *vb.* be feverish.
Fieberwahnsinn, -e, *n.m.* delirium.
Fiedel, -n, *n.f.* fiddle.
Figur', -en, *n.f.* figure.
figür'lich, *adj.* figurative.
Fiktion', -en, *n.f.* figment; fiction.
Filet', -s, *n.nt.* fillet.
Filia'le, -n, *n.f.* branch.
Film, -e, *n.m.* film, movie, motion-picture.
filmen, *vb.* film.
Filmschauspieler, -, *n.m.* movie actor.
Filmschauspielerin, -nen, *n.f.* movie actress.
Filter, -, *n.m.* filter.
filtrie'ren, *vb.* filter.
Filz, -e, *n.m.* felt.
Fina'le, -s, *n.nt.* finale.
Finan'zen, *n.pl.* finances.
finanziell', *adj.* financial.
finanzie'ren, *vb.* finance.
Finanz'mann, -er, *n.m.* financier.
Finanz'wirtschaft, -en, *n.f.* finance.
finden*, *vb.* find, locate.
Finderlohn, *n.m.* reward (for returning lost articles).
findig, *adj.* ingenious, resourceful.
Findigkeit, *n.f.* ingenuity.
Findling, -e, *n.m.* foundling.
Finger, -, *n.m.* finger.
Fingerabdruck, -e, *n.m.* fingerprint.
Fingernagel, -, *n.m.* fingernail.
fingie'ren, *vb.* feign, simulate.
fingiert', *adj.* fictitious.
finster, *adj.* dark; saturnine.
Finsternis, -se, *n.f.* darkness; eclipse.
Firma *(pl.* **Firmen)***, n.f.* firm, company.
Firnis, -se, *n.m.* varnish.
firnissen, *vb.* varnish.
Fisch, -e, *n.m.* fish.
fischen, *vb.* fish.
Fischer, -, *n.m.* fisherman.

Fischgeschäft, -e, *n.nt.* fish-store.
Fixie'rung, -en, *n.f.* fixation.
flach, *adj.* flat, shallow.
Fläche, -n, *n.f.* plane, area.
Flachheit, -en, *n.f.* flatness.
Flachs, *n.m.* flax.
flackern, *vb.* flare, flicker.
Flagge, -n, *n.f.* flag.
Flak, -(s), *n.f.* (= Fliegerabwehrkanone) antiaircraft (fire, troops).
Flak-, *cpds.* antiaircraft.
Flame, -n, -n, *n.m.* Fleming.
Flamme, -n, *n.f.* flame, blaze.
flammend, *adj.* flaming; *(fig.)* enthusiastic.
Flanell', -e, *n.m.* flannel.
Flanke, -n, *n.f.* flank.
flankie'ren, *vb.* flank.
Flasche, -n, *n.f.* bottle, flask.
Flaschenöffner, -, *n.m.* bottle opener.
flattern, *vb.* flutter, flap.
flau, *adj.* slack, dull.
Flaum, *n.m.* down, fuzz.
flaumig, *adj.* downy, fuzzy, fluffy.
Flechte, -n, *n.f.* braid.
flechten*, *vb.* weave, plait, bind.
Fleck, -e, *n.m.* spot, stain, blotch.
Fledermaus, -e, *n.f.* bat.
Flegel, -, *n.m.* rowdy, boor.
flehen, *vb.* implore, beseech.
flehentlich, *adj.* beseeching.
Fleisch, *n.nt.* flesh, meat.
Fleischerei, *n.f.* butcher's shop.
fleischig, *adj.* fleshy.
fleischlich, *adj.* carnal.
Fleiß, *n.m.* diligence, hard work.
fleißig, *adj.* industrious, hard working.
flicken, *vb.* patch.
Flicken, -, *n.m.* patch.
Flickwerk, *n.nt.* patchwork.
Flieder, *n.m.* lilac.
Fliege, -n, *n.f.* fly.
fliegen*, *vb.* fly.
Flieger, -, *n.m.* flier, aviator.
fliehen*, *vb.* flee.
Fliese, -n, *n.f.* tile, flagstone.
fließen*, *vb.* flow.
fließend, *adj.* fluent.
flimmern, *vb.* flicker.
flink, *adj.* nimble, spry.
Flirt, -s, *n.m.* flirt, flirtation.
flirten, *vb.* flirt.

Flitterwochen, n.pl. honeymoon.
Flocke, -n, n.f. flake.
Floh, ̈-e, n.m. flea.
Floß, ̈-e, n.m. float, raft.
Flosse, -n, n.f. fin.
Flöte, -n, n.f. whistle; flute.
flott, adj. afloat; smart, dashing.
Flotte, -n, n.f. fleet, navy.
Fluch, -e, n.m. curse.
fluchen, vb. swear, curse.
Flucht, -en, n.f. escape, flight, getaway; **(in die F. schlagen*)** rout.
flüchten, vb. flee.
flüchtig, adj. fleeting, cursory; superficial.
Flüchtling, -en, n.m. refugee, fugitive.
Flug, ̈-e, n.m. flight.
Flugblatt, ̈-er, n.nt. leaflet.
Flügel, -, n.m. wing.
Flughafen, ̈-, n.m. airport.
Flugpersonal, n.nt. flight attendants.
Flugzeug, -e, n.nt. airplane.
Flunder, -n, n.nf. flounder.
flunkern, vb. fib.
fluoreszie'rend, adj. fluorescent.
Fluß, ̈-sse, n.m. river; flux.
flüssig, adj. liquid, fluid; **(f. machen)** liquefy.
Flüssigkeit, -en, n.f. fluid, liquid.
flüstern, vb. whisper.
Flut, -en, n.f. flood, high tide.
fluten, vb. flood.
Föhn, n.m. foehn wind.
Folge, -n, n.f. consequence, outgrowth; succession; **(zur F. haben*)** result in.
folgen, vb. follow; succeed.
folgend, adj. subsequent.
folgenreich, adj. consequential.
folgenschwer, adj. momentous.
folgerichtig, adj. consistent.
folgern, vb. infer, deduce.
Folgerung, -en, n.f. inference, deduction.
folglich, adv. consequently.
Folter, -n, n.f. torture.
Fön, n.m. hair-dryer.
Fond, -s, n.m. fund.
Fondant', -s, n.m. bonbon.
Förderer, -, n.m. sponsor.
förderlich, adj. helpful, conducive.
fordern, vb. demand.

fördern, vb. promote; further; *(mining)* mine, haul.
Forderung, -en, n.f. demand, claim.
Förderung, -en, n.f. furtherance, advancement.
Forel'le, -n, n.f. trout.
Form, -en, n.f. form, shape; mold; **(in F. sein*)** be fit, be in fine shape.
Formalität', -en, n.f. formality.
Format', -e, n.nt. format; *(fig.)* stature.
Formation', -en, n.f. formation.
Formel, -n, n.f. formula.
formell', adj. formal.
formen, vb. form, shape, mold.
Förmlichkeit, -en, n.f. formality.
formlos, adj. formless.
Formular', -e, n.nt. form, blank.
formulie'ren, vb. formulate.
forschen, vb. explore, search.
Forscher, -, n.m. investigator, researcher.
Forscherin, -nen, n.f. investigator, researcher.
Forschung, -en, n.f. research.
fort, adv. away, gone; forward.
Fortbildung, -en, n.f. further education, training.
Fortdauer, n.f. continuity.
fortdauernd, adj. continuous.
fort•fahren*, vb. drive away; proceed, continue.
fort•gehen*, vb. leave; continue.
fortgeschritten, adj. advanced.
fort•pflanzen, vb. propagate.
fort•schreiten*, vb. progress.
Fortschritt, -e, n.m. progress, advance.
fortschrittlich, adj. progressive.
fort•setzen, vb. continue.
Fortsetzung, -en, n.f. continuation.
fortwährend, adj. continuous.
Foto, -s, n.nt. photograph.
Fotograf', -en, n.m. photographer.
Fotogra'fin, -nen, n.f. photographer.
Fotokopie', -n, n.f. photocopy.
Foyer', -s, n.nt. foyer.
Fracht, -en, n.f. freight, cargo.
Frachtbrief, -e, n.m. bill of lading.
Frachter, -, n.m. freighter.

Frachtschiff, -e, *n.nt.* freighter.
Frachtspesen, *n.pl.* freight charges.
Frage, -n, *n.f.* question.
Fragebogen, -, *n.m.* questionnaire.
fragen, *vb.* ask, inquire.
fragend, *adj.* interrogative.
Fragezeichen, -, *n.nt.* question mark.
fraglich, *adj.* questionable.
fragmenta'risch, *adj.* fragmentary.
fragwürdig, *adj.* questionable.
Fraktur', *n.f.* (*med.*) fracture; German type (*print.*).
Frankreich, *n.nt.* France.
Franse, -n, *n.f.* fringe.
Franzo'se, -n, -n, *n.m.* Frenchman.
Franzö'sin, -nen, *n.f.* Frenchwoman.
franzö'sisch, *adj.* French.
frappant', *adj.* striking.
fraternisie'ren, *vb.* fraternize.
Fratze, -n, *n.f.* grimace; face, mug.
Frau, -en, *n.f.* woman, wife; Mrs.
Frauenarzt, -̈e, *n.m.* gynecologist.
Frauenärztin, -nen, *n.f.* gynecologist.
Frauenrechtler, -, *n.m.* feminist.
Frauenrechtlerin, -nen, *n.f.* feminist.
Fräulein, -, *n.nt.* Miss.
fraulich, *adj.* womanly.
frech, *adj.* impudent; saucy.
Frechheit, -en, *n.f.* impertinence; effrontery.
frei, *adj.* free; frank; vacant.
Frei-, *n.nt.* outdoors.
Freibad, -̈er, *n.nt.* open-air swimming pool.
Freier, -, *n.m.* suitor.
freigebig, *adj.* generous.
Freigebigkeit, *n.f.* liberality, generosity.
freigestellt, *adj.* optional.
frei•halten*, *vb.* keep free; treat.
Freiheit, -en, *n.f.* liberty, freedom.
Freiherr, -n, -en, *n.m.* baron.
frei•lassen*, *vb.* free; leave blank.
freilich, *adv.* to be sure.

Freimarke, -n, *n.f.* stamp.
Freimaurer, -, *n.m.* Mason.
freimütig, *adj.* candid, heart-to-heart.
freisinnig, *adj.* liberal.
frei•sprechen*, *vb.* acquit, absolve.
Freispruch, -̈e, *n.m.* acquittal.
Freitag, -e, *n.m.* Friday.
freiwillig, *adj.* voluntary; (sich f. melden) volunteer; enlist.
Freiwillig-, *n.m.&f.* volunteer.
Freizeit, *n.f.* leisure time.
fremd, *adj.* strange; foreign, alien.
Fremd-, *n.m.&f.* stranger.
Fremdenführer, -, *n.m.* guide.
Fremdenführerin, -nen, *n.f.* guide.
Fremdenverkehr, *n.m.* tourism.
Fremdenverkehrsbüro, *n.nt.* tourist office.
Fremdenzimmer, -, *n.nt.* guest room, room to let.
frequentie'ren, *vb.* habituate.
Frequenz', -en, *n.f.* frequency.
Fresko, -ken, *n.nt.* fresco.
fressen*, *vb.* (of animals) eat; stuff oneself.
Freude, -n, *n.f.* joy, pleasure.
Freudenfeuer, -, *n.nt.* bonfire.
freudig, *adj.* joyful, joyous.
freudlos, *adj.* cheerless.
freuen, *vb.* make glad; (sich f.) be glad, rejoice.
Freund, -e, *n.m.* friend.
Freundin, -nen, *n.f.* friend (female).
freundlich, *adj.* friendly, kind.
freundlicherweise, *adv.* kindly.
Freundlichkeit, -en, *n.f.* kindness, friendliness.
freundlos, *adj.* friendless.
Freundschaft, -en, *n.f.* friendship.
freundschaftlich, *adj.* amicable.
Frevel, -, *n.m.* outrage.
frevelhaft, *adj.* sacrilegious; flagrant.
Friede(n), *n.m.* peace.
Friedensvertrag, -̈e, *n.m.* peace treaty.
friedfertig, *adj.* peaceable.
Friedhof, -̈e, *n.m.* cemetery, graveyard.
friedlich, *adj.* peaceable, peaceful.

frieren*, *vb.* freeze.

Frikassee', **-s**, *n.nt.* fricassee.

frisch, *adj.* fresh, crisp.

Frische, *n.f.* freshness.

Friseur', **-e**, *n.m.* barber, hairdresser.

Friseu'se, **-n**, *n.f.* hairdresser (female).

frisie'ren, *vb.* dress the hair; *(fig.)* tamper with.

Frist, **-en**, *n.f.* limited period; respite; deadline.

Frisur', **-en**, *n.f.* coiffure, hairdo.

frivol', *adj.* frivolous.

froh, *adj.* glad.

fröhlich, *adj.* gay, cheerful, happy, merry.

Fröhlichkeit, *n.f.* cheerfulness, merriment.

frohlo'cken, *vb.* rejoice.

fromm (**-, -**), *adj.* pious, religious, devout.

Frömmelei', **-en**, *n.f.* bigotry.

Frömmigkeit, *n.f.* piety.

Frömmler, **-**, *n.m.* bigot.

frönen, *vb.* indulge.

Front, **-en**, *n.f.* front.

Frosch, **⸚e**, *n.m.* frog.

Frost, *n.m.* frost, chill.

frösteln, *vb.* feel chilly.

frostig, *adj.* frosty.

Frucht, **⸚e**, *n.f.* fruit.

fruchtbar, *adj.* fruitful, fertile; prolific.

Fruchtbarkeit, *n.f.* fertility.

fruchtlos, *adj.* fruitless.

früh, *adj.* early.

früher, *adj.* earlier; former.

Frühjahr, **-e**, *n.nt.* spring.

Frühling, **-e**, *n.m.* spring.

frühreif, *adj.* precocious.

Frühstück, **-e**, *n.nt.* breakfast.

frühzeitig, *adj.* early.

Fuchs, **⸚e**, *n.m.* fox.

fügen, *vb.* join; (**sich f.**) comply, submit.

fügsam, *adj.* docile.

fühlbar, *adj.* tangible.

fühlen, *vb.* feel, sense.

führen, *vb.* lead, guide, direct.

Führer, **-**, *n.m.* leader, guide.

Führerin, **-nen**, *n.f.* leader, guide.

Führerschein, **-e**, *n.m.* driver's license.

Fülle, *n.f.* fullness, wealth; (**in Hülle und F.**) galore.

füllen, *vb.* fill.

Füllfederhalter, **-**, *n.m.* fountain pen.

Füllung, **-en**, *n.f.* filling.

Fund, **-e**, *n.m.* find, discovery.

Fundament', **-e**, *n.nt.* foundation.

fundie'ren, *vb.* base.

fünf, *num.* five.

fünf -, *adj.* fifth.

Fünftel, **-**, *n.nt.* fifth part; (**ein f.**) one-fifth.

fünfzig, *num.* fifty.

fünfzigst-, *adj.* fiftieth.

Fünfzigstel, **-**, *n.nt.* fiftieth part; (**ein f.**) one-fiftieth.

Funke(n), **-**, *n.m.* spark.

funkeln, *vb.* sparkle.

funkelnagelneu, *adj.* brand-new.

funken, *vb.* radio.

Funktion', **-en**, *n.f.* function.

Funktionär', **-e**, *n.m.* functionary, official.

Funktionärin, **-nen**, *n.f.* functionary, official.

funktionie'ren, *vb.* function.

für, *prep.* for.

Furche, **-n**, *n.f.* furrow.

Furcht, *n.f.* fright, fear, dread.

furchtbar, *adj.* terrible.

fürchten, *vb.* fear; (**sich f. vor**) be afraid of.

furchtlos, *adj.* fearless.

Furchtlosigkeit, *n.f.* fearlessness.

furchtsam, *adj.* fearful.

Fürsorge, *n.f.* care; welfare.

Fürst, **-en**, **-en**, *n.m.* prince, ruler.

Fürstin, **-nen**, *n.f.* princess.

fürstlich, *adj.* princely.

Furt, **-en**, *n.f.* ford.

Furun'kel, **-**, *n.m.* boil.

Fürwort, **⸚er**, *n.nt.* pronoun.

Fusion', **-en**, *n.f.* fusion, merger.

Fuß, **⸚e**, *n.m.* foot.

Fußball, **⸚e**, *n.m.* football.

Fußboden, **⸚**, *n.m.* floor; flooring.

Fußgänger, **-**, *n.m.* pedestrian.

Fußgängerzone, **-n**, *n.f.* pedestrian zone.

Fußnote, **-n**, *n.f.* footnote.

Fußpfleger, **-**, *n.m.* chiropodist.

Futter, -, *n.nt.* feed, fodder; lining.

füttern, *vb.* feed; (clothing) line.
Futurologie', *n.f.* futurology.

G

Gabardine, *n.m.* gabardine.
Gabe, -n, *n.f.* gift, donation; faculty.
Gabel, -n, *n.f.* fork.
gaffen, *vb.* gape.
gähnen, *vb.* yawn.
galant', *adj.* gallant.
Galanterie', -en, *n.f.* gallantry.
Gala-Uniform, *n.f.* full dress.
Galerie', -'i'en, *n.f.* gallery.
Galgen, -, *n.m.* gallows.
Galle, -n, *n.f.* gall, bile.
Gallenblase, -n, *n.f.* gall bladder.
gallertartig, *adj.* gelatinous.
gallig, *adj.* bilious.
Galopp', -s, *n.m.* gallop; (leichter G.) canter.
galoppie'ren, *vb.* galvanize.
galvanisie'ren, *vb.* galvanize.
Gang, ⸚e, *n.m.* walk; corridor, aisle; course; (auto) gear.
Gangrän', -e, *n.f.* gangrene.
Gangster, -, *n.m.* gangster.
Gans, ⸚e, *n.f.* goose.
Gänsemarsch, *n.m.* single file.
ganz, 1. *adj.* whole, entire. 2. *adv.* quite, rather; (g. gut) pretty good; (g. und gar) completely.
Ganz-, *n.nt.* whole (thing).
Ganzheit, *n.f.* entirety.
gänzlich, *adj.* complete.
Ganztagsbeschäftigung, *n.f.* full-time job.
gar, 1. *adj.* cooked, done. 2. *adv.* (g. nicht) not at all; (g. nichts) nothing at all.
Gara'ge, -n, *n.f.* garage.
Garantie', -'i'en, *n.f.* guarantee.
garantie'ren, *vb.* guarantee, warrant.
Garbe, -n, *n.f.* sheaf.
Gardero'be, -n, *n.f.* clothes; cloakroom.
gären, *vb.* ferment.
Garn, -e, *n.nt.* yarn; thread.
Garne'le, -n, *n.f.* shrimp.
garnie'ren, *vb.* garnish.
Garnison', -en, *n.f.* garrison.
Garnitur', -en, *n.f.* set.

garstig, *adj.* nasty.
Garten, ⸚, *n.m.* garden, yard.
Gartenbau, *n.m.* horticulture.
Gärtner, -, *n.m.* gardener.
Gärtnerin, -nen, *n.f.* gardener.
Gas, -e, *n.nt.* gas.
Gashebel, -, *n.m.* accelerator.
gasig, *adj.* gassy.
Gasse, -n, *n.f.* narrow street, alley.
Gast, ⸚e, *n.m.* guest.
Gastarbeiter, -, *n.m.* foreign worker.
gastfrei, *adj.* hospitable.
Gastfreiheit, *n.f.* hospitality.
gastfreundlich, *adj.* hospitable.
Gastfreundschaft, *n.f.* hospitality.
Gastgeber, -, *n.m.* host.
Gastgeberin, -nen, *n.f.* hostess.
Gasthaus, ⸚er, *n.nt.* inn; restaurant.
gastrono'misch, *adj.* gastronomical.
Gaststube, -n, *n.f.* taproom; restaurant.
Gatte, -n, -n, *n.m.* husband.
Gattin, -nen, *n.f.* wife.
Gattung, -en, *n.f.* species, genus.
Gau, -e, *n.m.* district, province.
Gaul, ⸚e, *n.m.* nag.
Gaumen, -, *n.m.* palate.
Gaze, -n, *n.f.* gauze.
Geäch'tet, -, *n.m.* outlaw.
Gebäck', *n.nt.* pastry.
Gebär'de, -n, *n.f.* gesticulation; gesture.
geba'ren, *vb.* (sich g.) behave.
gebä'ren*, *vb.* bear.
Gebäu'de, -, *n.nt.* building.
ge'ben*, *vb.* give; deal (cards); (es gibt) there is, there are.
Geber, -, *n.m.* giver.
Gebet', -e, *n.nt.* prayer.
Gebiet', -e, *n.nt.* territory, region, field.
gebie'ten*, *vb.* command.
Gebie'ter, -, *n.m.* master.
Gebil'de, -, *n.nt.* form, structure.

gebil′det, *adj.* educated, civilized, cultured.
Gebir′ge, -, *n.nt.* mountainous area, mountains; mountain range.
gebir′gig, *adj.* mountainous.
Gebiß′, -sse, *n.nt.* teeth; denture; (horse) bit.
Geblüt′, *n.nt.* descent, family.
gebo′ren, *adj.* born.
Gebor′genheit, *n.f.* safety.
Gebot′, -e, *n.nt.* command(ment).
Gebräu′, -e, *n.nt.* brew, concoction.
Gebrauch′, ⸚e, *n.m.* use; usage, custom.
gebrau′chen, *vb.* use.
gebräuch′lich, *adj.* customary.
Gebrauchs′anweisung, -en, *n.f.* directions (for use).
gebraucht′, *adj.* second-hand, used.
Gebre′chen, -, *n.nt.* infirmity.
gebrech′lich, *adj.* decrepit.
Gebrü′der, *n.pl.* brothers.
Gebrüll′, *n.nt.* roar, howl.
gebückt′, *adj.* stooped.
Gebühr′, -en, *n.f.* charge, fee; **(nach G.)** duly; **(über alle G.)** excessively.
gebüh′ren, *vb.* be due; **(sich g.)** be proper.
gebüh′rend, *adj.* duly.
gebühr′lich, *adj.* proper.
Geburt′, -en, *n.f.* birth; childbirth; **(von G. an)** congenital.
Geburtenkontrolle, *n.f.* birth control.
gebür′tig, *adj.* native.
Geburts′datum, -ten, *n.nt.* date of birth.
Geburts′helfer, -, *n.m.* obstetrician.
Geburts′ort, -e, *n.m.* birthplace.
Geburts′schein, -e, *n.m.* birth certificate.
Geburts′tag, -e, *n.m.* birthday.
Gebüsch′, -e, *n.nt.* bushes, shrubbery.
Geck, -en, -en, *n.m.* dandy.
Gedächt′nis, -sse, *n.nt.* memory.
Gedächt′nisfeier, -n, *n.f.* commemoration.
Gedan′ke(n), -, *n.m.* thought, idea.

gedan′kenlos, *adj.* thoughtless, unthinking.
gedan′kenvoll, *adj.* thoughtful.
Gedeck′, -e, *n.nt.* cover, table setting.
gedei′hen*, *vb.* thrive.
geden′ken*, *vb.* remember; commemorate.
Gedicht′, -e, *n.nt.* poem.
gedie′gen, *adj.* solid.
Gedrän′ge, *n.nt.* crush, crowd.
gedrängt′, *adj.* concise.
Geduld′, *n.f.* patience.
gedul′den, *vb.* **(sich g.)** have patience, forbear.
gedul′dig, *adj.* patient.
geehrt′, *adj.* honored.
geeig′net, *adj.* qualified; suitable.
Gefahr′, -en, *n.f.* danger, jeopardy.
gefähr′den, *vb.* endanger, jeopardize.
gefähr′lich, *adj.* dangerous.
gefahr′los, *adj.* without danger.
Gefähr′te, -n, -n, *n.m.* companion.
gefal′len*, *vb.* please; **(es gefällt mir)** I like it.
Gefal′len, -, *n.m.* favor.
gefäl′lig, *adj.* obliging, pleasing.
Gefan′gen-, *n.m.&f.* prisoner, captive.
Gefan′gennahme, -n, *n.f.* capture.
Gefan′genschaft, -en, *n.f.* captivity.
Gefäng′nis, -se, *n.nt.* prison, jail.
Gefäng′niswärter, -, *n.m.* jailer.
Gefäß′, -e, *n.nt.* container.
gefaßt′, *adj.* composed.
Gefecht′, -e, *n.nt.* battle, engagement.
gefeit′, *adj.* fortified against.
Gefie′der, *n.nt.* plumage.
gefleckt′, *adj.* dappled.
gefliss′entlich, *adj.* intentional; studied.
Geflü′gel, *n.nt.* poultry.
Geflüs′ter, *n.nt.* whispering.
Gefol′ge, *n.nt.* retinue.
gefrä′ßig, *adj.* gluttonous.
Gefrei′te, -n, -n, *n.m.* corporal.
gefrie′ren*, *vb.* freeze.
Gefrier′fach, ⸚er, *n.nt.* freezer (in refrigerator).

Gefro′ren -, *n.nt.* ice (cream).
gefü′gig, *adj.* compliant.
Gefühl′, -e, *n.nt.* feeling, sensation; emotion, sentiment.
gefühl′los, *adj.* insensible, callous.
gefühls′mäßig, *adj.* emotional.
gefühl′voll, *adj.* sentimental.
gegen, *prep.* against; toward; about.
Gegenangriff, -e, *n.m.* counterattack.
Gegend, -en, *n.f.* region.
Gegengewicht, -e, *n.nt.* counterbalance.
Gegengift, -e, *n.nt.* antidote, antitoxin.
Gegenmaßnahme, -n, *n.f.* countermeasure.
Gegensatz, ̈e, *n.m.* contrast, opposite.
gegenseitig, *adj.* mutual.
Gegenstand, ̈e, *n.m.* object.
Gegenteil, *n.nt.* reverse, opposite.
gegenü′ber, *prep.&adv.* opposite.
gegenü′ber-stellen, *vb.* confront.
Gegenwart, *n.f.* present, presence.
gegenwärtig, *adj.* present.
Gegenwirkung, -en, *n.f.* counteraction.
Gegner, -, *n.m.* adversary, opponent.
Gehalt′, -e, *n.m.* content, substance.
Gehalt′, ̈er, *n.nt.* salary, pay.
gehar′nischt, *adj.* armed; *(fig.)* vehement.
gehäs′sig, *adj.* malicious.
Gehäu′se, -, *n.nt.* casing.
geheim′, *adj.* secret, cryptic.
Geheim′dienst, -e, *n.m.* secret service.
geheim-′halten*, *vb.* keep secret.
Geheim′nis, -se, *n.nt.* secret, mystery.
geheim′nisvoll, *adj.* secretive, mysterious.
Geheiß′, *n.nt.* command, behest.
gehemmt′, *adj.* inhibited, self-conscious.
gehen*, *vb.* go, walk; **(wie geht es Ihnen?)** how are you?

gehen·lassen*, *vb.* **(sich g.)** let oneself go.
Gehil′fe, -n, -n, *n.m.* helper, assistant.
Gehil′fin, -nen, *n.f.* assistant.
Gehirn′, -e, *n.nt.* brain.
Gehirn′erschütterung, -en, *n.f.* concussion.
Gehöft′, -e, *n.nt.* farmstead.
Gehölz′, -e, *n.nt.* woods.
Gehör′, -e, *n.nt.* hearing.
gehor′chen, *vb.* obey.
gehö′ren, *vb.* belong to.
gehö′rig, *adj.* belonging to; thorough, sound; appropriate.
gehor′sam, *adj.* obedient.
Gehor′sam, *n.m.* obedience, allegiance.
Geige, -n, *n.f.* violin.
geil, *adj.* horny, *(fam.)* awesome.
Geisel, -n, *n.f.* hostage.
Geiser, -, *n.m.* geyser.
Geißel, -n, *n.f.* whip, scourge.
geißeln, *vb.* flagellate, scourge.
Geist, -er, *n.m.* mind, spirit; ghost; **(Heiliger G.)** Holy Spirit, Ghost.
geistesabwesend, *adj.* absent-minded.
Geistesgegenwart, *n.f.* presence of mind.
geistesgestört, *adj.* deranged.
Geisteswissenschaften, *n.pl.* arts.
geistig, *adj.* mental, spiritual.
geistlich, *adj.* ecclesiastic(al).
Geistlich -, *n.m.&f.* minister, clergy.
Geistlichkeit, *n.f.* clergy.
geistlos, *adj.* inane, vacuous.
geistreich, *adj.* bright, witty.
geisttötend, *adj.* tedious.
Geiz, -er, *n.m.* avarice; meanness.
Geizhals, ̈e, *n.m.* miser.
Geizkragen, -, *n.m.* miser.
geizig, *adj.* avaricious, miserly.
Geklap′per, *n.nt.* clatter.
Gekrit′zel, *n.nt.* scribbling.
gekün′stelt, *adj.* contrived.
Geläch′ter, *n.nt.* laughter.
Gela′ge, -, *n.nt.* banquet.
gelähmt′, *adj.* crippled.
Gelän′de, -, *n.nt.* terrain.
Gelän′der, -, *n.nt.* railing, banister.

gelan'gen, *vb.* reach, get to.
gelas'sen, *adj.* placid, composed.
Gelati'ne, -n, *n.f.* gelatine.
geläu'fig, *adj.* familiar, fluent.
Geläu'figkeit, *n.f.* fluency.
gelaunt', *adj.* (**gut g.**) in good humor.
gelb, *adj.* yellow.
gelbbraun, *adj.* tan.
Geld, -er, *n.nt.* money.
Geldbeutel, -, *n.m.* purse.
geldlich, *adj.* monetary.
Geldschein, -, *n.m.* bill.
Geldschrank, -̈e, *n.m.* safe.
Geldstrafe, -n, *n.f.* fine; (**zu einer G. verurteilen**) fine.
Geldwechsler, -, *n.m.* money-changer.
Gelee', -s, *n.nt.* jelly.
gele'gen, *adj.* situated; opportune.
Gele'genheit, -en, *n.f.* occasion, chance.
Gele'genheitskauf, *n.m.* bargain.
gele'gentlich, *adj.* occasional.
Gelehr'samkeit, *n.f.* erudition, scholarship.
gelehrt', *adj.* learned, erudite.
Gelehr'-t-, - *n.m.&f.* scholar.
Gelei'se, -, *n.nt.* track.
Geleit', -e, *n.nt.* accompaniment; (**freies G.**) safe conduct.
gelei'ten, *vb.* escort.
Geleit'zug, -̈e, *n.m.* convoy.
Gelenk', -e, *n.nt.* joint.
gelen'kig, *adj.* supple.
geliebt', *adj.* beloved.
Gelieb'-t-, - *n.m.&f.* beloved, lover.
gelind', *adj.* mild, light.
gelin'gen*, *vb.* succeed.
gellen, *vb.* shriek.
gellend, *adj.* shrill.
gelo'ben, *vb.* vow, pledge.
gelten*, *vb.* be valid, apply, hold; be intended for; be considered; (**das gilt nicht**) that's not fair.
Geltung, *n.f.* standing, value.
Gelüb'de, -, *n.nt.* vow.
Gelüst', -e, *n.nt.* lust.
gemach', *adv.* slowly, gently.
Gemach', -̈er, *n.nt.* chamber.
gemäch'lich, *adj.* leisurely, slow and easy.

Gemahl', -e, *n.m.* husband; consort.
Gemah'lin, -nen, *n.f.* wife.
gemäß', *prep.* according to.
gemä'ßigt, *adj.* moderate.
gemein, 1. *adj.* mean, vile, vicious. 2. *adv.* in common.
Gemein'de, -n, *n.f.* community; municipality; congregation.
gemein'gültig, *adj.* generally accepted.
Gemein'platz, -̈e, *n.m.* platitude.
gemein'sam, *adj.* common, joint.
Gemein'schaft, -, *n.f.* community, fellowship.
Gemur'mel, -, *n.nt.* murmur.
Gemü'se, -, *n.nt.* vegetable.
Gemüt', -er, *n.nt.* mind, spirit, temper, heart.
gemüt'lich, *adj.* comfortable, homey, genial.
Gemüts'art, -en, *n.f.* temperament.
Gemüts'ruhe, *n.f.* placidity.
genau', *adj.* accurate, exact; fussy.
Genau'igkeit, -en, *n.f.* accuracy.
geneh'migen, *vb.* grant, approve.
Geneh'migung, -en, *n.f.* permission, license.
geneigt', *adj.* inclined.
General', -̈e, *n.m.* general.
Genera'tor, -o'ren, *n.m.* generator.
gene'sen*, *vb.* recover.
Gene'sung, *n.f.* convalescence, recovery.
genial', *adj.* ingenious, having genius.
Geniali'tät, *n.f.* ingenuity, genius.
Genie', -s, *n.nt.* genius.
genie'ren, *vb.* embarrass.
genie'ßen*, *vb.* enjoy, relish.
Geni'tiv, -e, *n.m.* genitive.
Genos'se, -n, *n.m.* companion; *(derogatory)* character.
Genos'senschaft, -en, *n.f.* association, co-operative society.
genug', *adj.* enough.
genü'gen, *vb.* be enough, suffice.
genü'gend, *adj.* satisfactory, sufficient.
genüg'sam, *adj.* modest.
Genüg'samkeit, *n.f.* frugality.
Genug'tuung, -en, *n.f.* satisfaction.

Genuß', **-sse**, *n.m.* enjoyment; relish.

Geograph', **-en**, **-en**, *n.m.* geographer.

Geographie', *n.f.* geography.

geogra'phisch, *adj.* geographical.

Geometrie', *n.f.* geometry.

geome'trisch, *adj.* geometric.

geord'net, *adj.* orderly.

Gepäck', *n.nt.* luggage, baggage.

Gepäck'träger, **-**, *n.m.* porter.

Gepäck'schein, **-e**, *n.m.* baggage check.

Geplau'der, *n.nt.* chat, small talk.

Geprä'ge, *n.nt.* stamp; character.

gera'de, 1. *adj.* straight, even. 2. *adv.* just; (**g. aus**) straight ahead.

gera'de·stehen*, *vb.* stand straight; answer for.

geradezu', *adv.* downright.

Gerad'heit, *n.f.* erectness; directness.

Gerät', **-e**, *n.nt.* tool, appliance, utensil.

Geratewohl', *n.nt.* (**aufs G.**) at random, haphazardly.

geraum', *adj.* considerable.

geräu'mig, *adj.* spacious.

Geräusch', **-e**, *n.nt.* noise.

geräusch'los, *adj.* noiseless.

gerben, *vb.* tan (leather).

gerecht', *adj.* just, fair.

Gerech'tigkeit, *n.f.* justice.

Gere'de, *n.nt.* chatter; (**ins G. bringen**) make someone the talk of the town.

gereift', *adj.* mellow.

gereizt', *adj.* irritated, edgy.

Gereizt'heit, *n.f.* irritability.

gereu'en, *vb.* repent, regret.

Gericht', **-e**, *n.nt.* court, bar, tribunal; (food) course; (**Jüngstes G.**) doomsday, judgment day.

gericht'lich, *adj.* legal, judicial, forensic.

Gerichts'barkeit, *n.f.* jurisdiction.

Gerichts'gebäude, **-**, *n.nt.* courthouse.

Gerichts'saal, **-säle**, *n.m.* courtroom.

Gerichts'verhandlung, **-en**, *n.f.* court proceedings, trial.

gerie'ben, *adj.* cunning, sly.

gering', *adj.* slight, slim.

gering'·achten, *vb.* look down upon.

gering'fügig, *adj.* negligible, petty.

gering'·schätzen, *vb.* hold in low esteem.

gering'schätzig, *adj.* disparaging, derogatory.

gerin'nen*, *vb.* curdle, clot, coagulate.

Gerip'pe, **-**, *n.nt.* skeleton.

geris'sen, *adj.* shrewd.

Germa'ne, **-n**, **-n**, *n.m.* Teuton.

germa'nisch, *adj.* Germanic.

gern, *adv.* gladly, readily; (**g. haben***) like, be fond of; (**g. tun***) like to do.

Gerste, **-n**, *n.f.* barley.

Gerstenkorn', **-̈er**, *n.nt.* barleycorn; sty.

Geruch', **-̈e**, *n.m.* smell, odor, scent.

Gerücht', **-e**, *n.nt.* rumor.

geru'hen, *vb.* (**g. zu**) deign.

Gerüst', **-e**, *n.nt.* scaffold, scaffolding.

gesamt', *adj.* total.

Gesamt'heit, *n.f.* entirety.

Gesandt'-, *n.m.&f.* ambassador, envoy.

Gesandt'schaft, **-en**, *n.f.* legation.

Gesang', **-̈e**, *n.m.* song, chant.

Gesang'buch, **-̈er**, *n.nt.* hymnal.

Geschäft', **-e**, *n.nt.* business, deal; shop, store.

geschäf'tig, *adj.* busy.

Geschäf'tigkeit, *n.f.* bustle.

Geschäfts'mann, **-̈er**, *or* **-leute**, *n.m.* businessman.

geschäfts'mäßig, *adj.* businesslike.

Geschäfts'viertel, **-**, *n.nt.* downtown, business section.

Geschäfts'zeiten, *n.pl.* hours of business.

gesche'hen*, *vb.* occur, happen.

Gesche'nis, **-se**, *n.nt.* happening, occurrence.

gescheit', *adj.* bright, clever.

Geschenk', **-e**, *n.nt.* present.

Geschich'te, **-n**, *n.f.* story; history.

Geschick', *n.nt.* skill.

Geschick'lichkeit, -en, *n.f.* dexterity, facility.

geschickt', *adj.* skillful, clever, deft.

Geschirr', -e, *n.nt.* dishes; harness.

Geschlecht', -er, *n.nt.* genus, sex; gender; lineage, family.

geschlecht'lich, *adj.* sexual.

Geschmack', -̈e, *n.m.* taste, flavor.

geschmack'los, *adj.* tasteless; in bad taste.

geschmei'dig, *adj.* lithe.

Geschöpf', -e, *n.nt.* creature.

Geschoß', -sse, *n.nt.* missile, projectile.

Geschrei', *n.nt.* clamor.

Geschütz', -e, *n.nt.* gun.

Geschwa'der, -, *n.nt.* squadron.

Geschwätz', *n.nt.* idle talk, babble.

geschwät'zig, *adj.* talkative, gossipy.

geschwind', *adj.* swift.

Geschwin'digkeit, -en, *n.f.* speed, velocity.

Geschwin'digkeitsgrenze, -n, *n.f.* speed limit.

Geschwo'rene-, *n.m.&f.* juror; *(pl.)* jury.

Geschwulst', -e, *n.nt.* swelling, growth.

Geschwür', -e, *n.nt.* abscess, ulcer.

geseg'net, *adj.* blessed.

Gesel'le, -n, -n, *n.m.* journeyman; fellow.

gesel'len, *vb.* **(sich g.)** join.

gesel'lig, *adj.* sociable, gregarious.

Gesell'schaft, -en, *n.f.* society; company; party.

Gesell'schafter, -, *n.m.* companion.

Gesell'schafterin, -nen, *n.f.* companion.

gesell'schaftlich, *adj.* social.

Gesell'schaftskleidung, -en, *n.f.* evening dress, dress clothes.

Gesell'schaftsreise, -n, *n.f.* group tour.

Gesetz', -e, *n.nt.* law, act.

Gesetz'antrag, -̈e, *n.m.* bill.

gesetz'gebend, *adj.* legislative.

Gesetz'geber, -, *n.m.* legislator.

Gesetz'geberin, -nen, *n.f.* legislator.

Gesetz'gebung, *n.f.* legislation.

gesetz'lich, *adj.* lawful, legal.

gesetz'los, *adj.* lawless.

gesetz'mäßig, *adj.* legal.

Gesetz'mäßigkeit, *n.f.* legality.

gesetz'widrig, *adj.* illegal, unlawful.

Gesicht', -er, *n.nt.* face.

Gesichts'ausdruck, -̈e, *n.m.* facial expression, mien.

Gesichts'farbe, *n.f.* complexion.

Gesichts'kreis, *n.m.* horizon.

Gesichts'massage, -n, *n.f.* facial.

Gesichts'punkt, -e, *n.m.* point of view, aspect.

Gesichts'zug, -̈e, *n.m.* feature.

Gesin'del, *n.nt.* rabble.

gesinnt', *adj.* **(g. sein*)** be of a mind, be disposed.

Gesin'nung, -en, *n.f.* attitude, way of thinking, views.

gesit'tet, *adj.* well-mannered, civilized.

gespannt', *adj.* tense; eager to know, curious.

Gespenst', -er, *n.nt.* ghost.

Gespie'le, -n, -n, *n.m.* playmate.

Gespräch', -e, *n.nt.* talk, conversation.

gesprä'chig, *adj.* talkative.

Gestalt', -en, *n.f.* figure, form, shape.

gestal'ten, *vb.* form, shape, fashion.

Gestal'tung, -en, *n.f.* formation, fashioning.

Gestam'mel, *n.nt.* stammering.

gestän'dig, *adj.* **(g. sein*)** make a confession.

Gestånd'nis, -se, *n.nt.* confession, avowal.

Gestank', *n.m.* stench.

gestat'ten, *vb.* permit.

Geste, -n, *n.f.* gesture.

geste'hen, *vb.* confess, avow.

Gestein', *n.nt.* rock.

Gestell', -e, *n.nt.* stand, rack, frame.

gestern, *adv.* yesterday.

gestikulie'ren, *vb.* gesticulate.

Gestirn', -e, *n.nt.* star; constellation.

Gestirns'bahn, -en, n.f. orbit.
Gestrüpp', n.nt. scrub, brush.
Gesuch', -e, n.nt. application, petition, request.
gesucht', adj. far-fetched, contrived.
gesund', adj. healthy, sound, wholesome.
gesun'den, vb. recover.
Gesund'heit, n.f. health, fitness; **(geistige G.)** sanity.
Gesund'heitsamt, n.nt. Department of Public Health.
Gesund'heitsattest, -e, n.nt. certificate of health.
gesund'heitsschädlich, adj. unhealthy.
Gesund'heitswesen, n.nt. sanitation.
Gesun'dung, n.f. recovery.
Getö'se, n.nt. uproar.
Geträn'k, -e, n.nt. drink, beverage; **(alkoholfreies G.)** soft drink.
getrau'en, vb. **(sich G.)** dare.
Getrei'de, -, n.nt. grain, cereal.
getrennt', adj. separate.
getreu', adj. faithful.
Getrie'be, -n, n.nt. gear.
getrost', adv. confidently.
Getu'e, n.nt. fuss.
geübt', adj. experienced.
Gewächs', -e, n.nt. growth.
gewagt', adj. daring, hazardous.
Gewähr', n.f. guarantee.
gewäh'ren, vb. grant.
gewähr'leisten, vb. warrant, guarantee.
Gewahr'sam, n.m. custody.
Gewalt', -en, n.f. force, power.
Gewalt'herrschaft, n.f. despotism.
gewal'tig, adj. powerful, tremendous.
gewalt'sam, adj. forcible, violent.
gewalt'tätig, adj. violent.
Gewalt'tätigkeit, -en, n.f. violence.
Gewand', ⁻er, n.nt. garb, garment.
gewandt', adj. facile, versatile.
Gewandt'heit, -en, n.f. deftness.
gewär'tig, adv. **(g. sein*)** be prepared.
Gewäs'ser, n.nt. waters.
Gewe'be, -, n.nt. tissue, texture.

Gewehr', -e, n.nt. rifle, gun.
Gewer'be, -, n.nt. trade, business.
Gewerk'schaft, -en, n.f. labor union.
Gewicht' -e, n.nt. weight.
gewiegt', adj. crafty.
gewillt', adj. willing.
Gewinn', -e, n.m. gain, profit.
gewinn'bringend, adj. lucrative.
gewin'nen*, vb. win, gain.
Gewin'ner, -, -nen, n.f. winner.
gewinn'süchtig, adj. mercenary, greedy.
Gewirr', n.nt. tangle, confusion.
gewiß', adj. certain.
Gewis'sen, -, n.nt. conscience.
gewis'senhaft, adj. conscientious.
gewis'senlos, adj. unprincipled.
Gewis'sensbiß, -sse, n.m. remorse, qualms.
gewisserma'ßen, adv. so to speak, as it were.
Gewiß'heit, -en, n.f. certainty.
Gewit'ter, -, n.nt. thunderstorm.
gewitz'igt, adj. clever.
gewo'gen, adj. **(g. sein*)** be disposed towards.
gewöh'nen, vb. accustom; **(sich g. an)** become accustomed to.
Gewohn'heit, -en, n.f. habit, custom, practice.
gewohn'heitsmäßig, adj. customary, habitual.
gewöhn'lich, adj. ordinary, usual, regular; common, vulgar.
gewohnt', adj. accustomed.
Gewöl'be, -, n.nt. vaulting, vault.
Gewühl', n.nt. shuffle, melee.
gewun'den, adj. coiled; sinuous.
Gewürz', -e, n.nt. spice, condiment, seasoning.
Gewürz'kraut ⁻er, n.nt. herb.
Gezei'ten, n.pl. tide.
gezie'men, vb. be proper, befit.
Gicht, -en, n.f. gout, arthritis.
Giebel, -, n.m. gable.
Gier, n.f. greed(iness).
gierig, adj. greedy.
gießen*, vb. pour; cast (metal).
Gift, -e, n.nt. poison.
giftig, adj. poisonous.
Giftmüll, n.m. toxic waste.
Gilde, -n, n.f. guild.

Gin, -s, *n.m.* gin.
Gipfel, -, *n.m.* peak.
Gipfelkonferenz, *n.f.* summit.
gipfeln, *vb.* culminate.
Gips, -e, *n.m.* gypsum, plaster.
Giraf'fe, -n, *n.f.* giraffe.
Girant', -en, -en, *n.m.* endorser.
Girat', -en, -en, *n.m.* endorsee.
girie'ren, *vb.* endorse (a check, note, etc.), put into circulation.
Giro, -s, *n.nt.* endorsement, circulation (of endorsed notes, etc.).
Girokonto, -s, *n.nt.* checking account.
Gischt, -e, *n.m.* spray, foam.
Gitar're, -n, *n.f.* guitar.
Gitter, -, *n.nt.* grating; gate.
Gitterwerk, -e, *n.nt.* grating.
glaciert', *adj.* glacé.
Glanz, *n.m.* shine, sheen, gloss; brilliance, splendor.
glänzen, *vb.* shine.
glänzend, *adj.* shiny, brilliant.
Glas, ̈-er, *n.nt.* glass.
Glaser, -, *n.m.* glazier.
gläsern, *adj.* made of glass.
glasie'ren, *vb.* glaze.
glasig, *adj.* glassy.
Glasscheibe, -n, *n.f.* pane.
Glasur, -en, *n.f.* glaze.
Glasware, -n, *n.f.* glassware.
glatt, *adj.* smooth, slippery; outright.
glätten, *vb.* smooth.
Glatzkopf, ̈-e, *n.m.* bald head.
Glaube(n), -, *n.m.* belief, faith.
glauben, *vb.* believe.
Glaubensbekenntnis, -se, *n.nt.* confession of faith; creed.
glaubhaft, *adj.* believable.
gläubig, *adj.* believing, devout.
Gläubig-, *n.m.&f.* believer; creditor.
glaublich, *adj.* credible.
glaubwürdig, *adj.* credible.
Glaubwürdigkeit, *n.f.* credibility.
gleich, 1. *adj.* equal, same, even. 2. *adv.* right away.
gleichaltig, *adj.* of the same age.
gleichartig, *adj.* similar, homogeneous.
gleichberechtigt, *adj.* having equal rights.
Gleichberechtigung, -en, *n.f.* equality of rights.

gleichen*, *vb.* be like, equal, resemble.
gleichfalls, *adv.* likewise.
gleichförmig, *adj.* uniform.
gleichgesinnt, *adj.* like-minded.
gleichgestellt, *adj.* coordinate.
Gleichgewicht, *n.nt.* equilibrium.
gleichgültig, *adj.* indifferent.
Gleichgültigkeit, *n.f.* indifference.
Gleichheit, *n.f.* equality.
gleich·machen, *vb.* equalize.
Gleichmaß, *n.nt.* proportion, symmetry.
gleichmäßig, *adj.* even, regular.
Gleichmut, *n.m.* equanimity.
gleichmütig, *adj.* even-tempered.
Gleichnis, -se, *n.nt.* simile, parable.
gleichsam, *adv.* as it were.
gleichseitig, *adj.* equilateral.
gleich·setzen, *vb.* equate.
Gleichstrom, ̈-e, *n.m.* direct current.
gleich·tun*, *vb.* do like, match up to.
Gleichung, -en, *n.f.* equation.
gleichwertig, *adj.* equivalent.
gleich·wie, *adv.&conj.* just as.
gleich·wohl, *adv.* nevertheless.
gleichzeitig, *adj.* simultaneous.
Gleis, -e, *n.nt.* track.
gleiten*, *vb.* glide, slide, slip.
Gletscher, -, *n.m.* glacier.
Gletscherspalte, -n, *n.f.* crevasse.
Glied, -er, *n.nt.* limb; link.
gliedern, *vb.* segment, classify.
Gliederung, -en, *n.f.* arrangement, structure.
Gliedmaßen, *n.pl.* limbs, extremities.
glimmen*, *vb.* glow, glimmer.
glitschig, *adj.* slippery.
glitzern, *vb.* glitter.
Globus, -ben (-busse), *n.m.* globe.
Glocke, -n, *n.f.* bell.
Glockenschlag, ̈-e, *n.m.* stroke of the clock.
Glockenspiel, -e, *n.nt.* chimes, carillon.
Glockenturm, ̈-, *n.m.* belfry, bell-tower.
Glorie, -n, *n.f.* glory.

Glorienschein, -e, n.m. halo.

glorreich, adj. glorious.

glotzen, vb. stare.

Glück, n.nt. happiness, luck.

gluckern, vb. gurgle.

glücklich, adj. happy.

glücklicherweise, adj. fortunately.

glückse'lig, adj. blissful.

Glückse'ligkeit, -en, n.f. bliss.

glucksen, vb. gurgle.

Glücksfall, ⁼e, n.m. stroke of luck.

Glücksspiel, -e, n.nt. gamble; gambling.

Glücksspieler, -, n.m. gambler.

Glücksspielerin, -nen, n.f. gambler.

Glückwunsch, ⁼e, n.m. congratulation.

Glühbirne, -n, n.f. electric light bulb.

glühen, vb. glow.

glühend, adj. glowing, incandescent; ardent.

Glut, -en, n.f. heat, live coals; ardor, passion.

Glyzerin', n.nt. glycerine.

G.m.b.H., abbr. (= Gesell'schaft mit beschränk'ter Haftung) incorporated, inc.

Gnade, n.f. grace, mercy.

gnadenreich, adj. merciful.

gnädig, adj. gracious, merciful; (g.e Frau) madam.

Gold, n.nt. gold.

Goldbarren, -, n.m. bullion.

golden, adj. golden.

Goldfisch, -e, n.m. goldfish.

goldig, adj. darling, cute.

Goldschmied, -e, n.m. goldsmith.

Golf, -e, n.m. gulf, bay.

Golf, n.nt. golf.

Golfplatz, ⁼e, n.m. golf course.

Gondel, -n, n.f. gondola.

gönnen, vb. grant, not begrudge; (sich g.) allow oneself; (das gönne ich ihm!) that serves him right!

Gör, -en, n.nt. brat, kid.

Goril'la, -s, n.m. gorilla.

Gosse, -n, n.f. gutter, drain.

Gotik, n.f. Gothic architecture.

gotisch, adj. Gothic.

Gott, ⁼er, n.m. god, deity.

gottähnlich, adj. godlike.

Götterdämmerung, n.f. twilight of the gods.

Gottesacker, ⁼, n.m. cemetery.

Gottesdienst, -e, n.m. (church) service.

Gottesgabe, -, n.f. godsend.

Gotteshaus, ⁼er, n.nt. church.

Gotteslästerung, -en, n.f. blasphemy.

Gottheit, -en, n.f. deity, divinity.

Göttin, -nen, n.f. goddess.

göttlich, adj. godly, divine.

gottlob', interj. praise God.

gottlos, adj. godless.

Götze, -n, -n, n.m. idol, false god.

Götzenbild, -er, n.nt. idol.

Götzendienst, -e, n.m. idolatry.

Gouvernan'te, -n, n.f. governess.

Gouverneur', -e, n.m. governor.

Gouverneu'rin, -nen, n.f. governor.

Gouverneurs'amt, ⁼er, n.nt. governorship.

Grab, ⁼er, n.nt. grave.

graben*, vb. dig.

Graben, ⁼, n.m. trench, ditch.

Grablegung, -en, n.f. burial.

Grabmal, ⁼er, n.nt. tomb(stone).

Grabschrift, -e, n.f. epitaph.

Grabstein, -e, n.m. gravestone.

Grad, -e, n.m. degree.

Graf, -en, -en, n.m. count.

Gräfin, -nen, n.f. countess.

Grafschaft, -en, n.f. county.

Gram, n.m. grief, care.

grämen, vb. (sich g.) grieve, fret.

Gramm, -, n.nt. gram.

Gramma'tik, -en, n.f. grammar.

Gramma'tiker, -, n.m. grammarian.

Gramma'tikerin, -nen, n.f. grammarian.

gramma'tisch, adj. grammatical.

Grammophon', -e, n.nt. phonograph.

Granat', -e, n.m. garnet.

Grana'te, -n, n.f. grenade.

Granit', -e, n.m. granite.

granulie'ren, vb. granulate.

Graphiker, -, n.m. illustrator, commercial artist.

Graphikerin, -nen, n.f. illustrator, commercial artist.

graphisch, *adj.* graphic.
Gras, ̈-er, *n.nt.* grass.
grasartig, *adj.* grasslike, grassy.
grasen, *vb.* graze.
grasig, *adj.* grassy.
gräßlich, *adj.* hideous.
Grat, -e, *n.m.* ridge.
Gräte, -n, *n.f.* bone (of a fish).
gratis, *adj.* gratis.
Gratisprobe, -n, *n.f.* free sample.
gratulie'ren, *vb.* congratulate.
grau, *adj.* gray.
Grauen, *n.nt.* horror.
grauenhaft, *adj.* ghastly.
grausam, *adj.* cruel.
grausig, *adj.* lurid.
Graveur', -e, *n.m.* engraver.
Graveu'rin, -nen, *n.f.* engraver.
gravie'ren, *vb.* engrave.
gravitie'ren, *vb.* gravitate.
Grazie, -n, *n.f.* grace, charm.
graziös', *adj.* graceful.
greifbar, *adj.* tangible.
greifen*, *vb.* seize, grasp.
Greis, -e, *n.m.* old man.
Greisenalter, -, *n.nt.* old age.
Greisin, -nen, *n.f.* old woman.
grell, *adj.* garish, gaudy, shrill.
Grenze, -n, *n.f.* limit, border, boundary.
grenzen, *vb.* **(g. an)** border on.
grenzenlos, *adj.* boundless.
Greuel, -, *n.m.* horror, outrage.
greulich, *adj.* horrible.
Grieche, -n, *n.m.* Greek.
Griechenland, *n.nt.* Greece.
Griechin, -nen, *n.f.* Greek.
griechisch, *adj.* Greek.
Griesgram, -e, *n.m.* grouch.
griesgrämig, *adj.* sullen.
Grieß, -e, *n.m.* semolina, coarse meal; gravel.
Griff, -e, *n.m.* grasp, grip, handle.
Grill, -s, *n.m.* grill; grillroom.
Grille, -n, *n.f.* cricket; whim.
grillen, *vb.* broil.
grillenhaft, *adj.* whimsical.
Grimas'se, -n, *n.f.* grimace.
Grimm, *n.m.* anger.
grimmig, *adj.* angry.
grinsen, *vb.* grin.
Grinsen, *n.nt.* grin.
Grippe, -n, *n.f.* grippe, influenza.
grob(-), *adj.* coarse, rough, crude.

Grobian, -e, *n.m.* boor, ruffian.
Grog, -s, *n.m.* grog.
Groll, *n.m.* anger, grudge.
grollen, *vb.* be angry, bear a grudge.
Gros, -se, *n.nt.* gross.
Groschen, -, *n.m.* ten pfennig piece; 1/100 of an Austrian schilling.
groß(-), *adj.* big, tall, great.
großartig, *adj.* grand, magnificent.
Großbritan'ien, *n.nt.* Great Britain.
Größe, -n, *n.f.* size, height, greatness.
Großeltern, *n.pl.* grandparents.
großenteils, *adv.* in large part, largely.
Größenwahnsinn, *n.m.* megalomania.
Großhandel, *n.m.* wholesale trade.
großherzig, *adj.* magnanimous.
großjährig, *adj.* of age.
Großmacht, ̈-e, *n.f.* major power.
Großmut, *n.m.* magnanimity, generosity.
großmütig, *adj.* magnanimous, generous.
Großmutter, ̈-, *n.f.* grandmother.
Großrechenanlage, -n, *n.f.* (computer) mainframe.
großsprecherisch, *adj.* boastful.
Großstaat, -en, *n.m.* major power.
Großstadt, ̈-e, *n.f.* large city, metropolis.
Großstädter, -e, *n.m.* big city person.
Großstädterin, -nen, *n.f.* big city person.
größtenteils, *adv.* for the most part, mostly.
groß-tun*, *vb.* act big, boast.
Großvater, ̈-, *n.m.* grandfather.
groß-ziehen*, *vb.* bring up, raise.
großzügig, *adj.* on a grand scale, generous, broadminded.
grotesk', *adj.* grotesque.
Grotte, -n, *n.f.* grotto.
Grube, -n, *n.f.* pit; mine.
grübeln, *vb.* brood.

Grubenarbeiter, -, *n.m.* miner.
Gruft, ⁓e, *n.f.* crypt, vault.
grün, *adj.* green.
Grund, ⁓e, *n.m.* ground, bottom, basis, reason; **(G. und Boden)** land, real estate.
Grundbegriff, -e, *n.m.* basic concept.
Grundbesitz, -e, *n.m.* landed property.
Grundbesitzer, -, *n.m.* landholder.
Grundbesitzerin, -nen, *n.f.* landholder.
gründen, *vb.* found.
Grundgesetz, -e, *n.nt.* basic law; constitution.
Grundlage, -n, *n.f.* basis.
grundlegend, *adj.* fundamental.
gründlich, *adj.* thorough.
Grundlinie, -n, *n.f.* base.
grundlos, *adj.* bottomless; unfounded.
Grundriß, -sse, *n.m.* outline, sketch.
Grundsatz, ⁓e, *n.m.* principle.
grundsätzlich, *adj.* fundamental, on principle.
Grundschule, -n, *n.f.* elementary school.
Grundstoff, -e, *n.m.* basic material.
Grundstück, -e, *n.nt.* lot.
Gründung, -en, *n.f.* founding, establishment.
grunzen, *vb.* grunt.
Gruppe, -n, *n.f.* group.
gruppie'ren, *vb.* group.
gruselig, *adj.* uncanny, creepy.
Gruß, ⁓e, *n.m.* greeting; salute.
grüßen, *vb.* greet; salute.
gucken, *vb.* look.
gültig, *adj.* valid.
Gültigkeit, *n.f.* validity.
Gummi, -s, *n.m.* rubber; eraser.
Gummi, -s, *n.nt.* gum.
gummiartig, *adj.* gummy.
Gummiband, ⁓er, *n.nt.* rubber band.

Gummischuhe, *n.pl.* overshoes, galoshes, rubbers.
Gunst, ⁓e, *n.f.* favor.
günstig, *adj.* favorable.
Günstling, -e, *n.m.* favorite.
gurgeln, *vb.* gargle.
Gurgel, -n, *n.f.* throat, gullet.
Gurke, -n, *n.f.* cucumber; **(saure G.)** pickle.
Gurt, -e, *n.m.* girth, harness.
Gürtel, -, *n.m.* belt, girdle.
gürten, *vb.* gird.
Guru, -s, *n.m.* guru.
Guß, ⁓sse, *n.m.* downpour; frosting; casting.
Gußstein, -e, *n.m.* sink, drain.
gut, 1. *adj.* good. **2.** *adv.* well.
Gut, ⁓er, *n.nt.* property; landed estate; *(pl.)* goods.
Gutachten, -, *n.nt.* (expert) opinion, (legal) advice.
gutaussehend, *adj.* good-looking.
Gutdünken, *n.nt.* opinion, discretion.
Güte, *n.f.* kindness; quality, purity.
gutgläubig, *adj.* credulous.
Guthaben, -, *n.nt.* credit; assets.
gut•heißen*, *vb.* approve.
gutherzig, *adj.* good-hearted.
gütig, *adj.* kind, friendly, gracious.
gütlich, *adj.* kind, friendly.
gut•machen, *vb.* make good; **(wieder g.)** make amends for.
gutmütig, *adj.* good-natured.
gut•schreiben*, *vb.* credit.
Gutschrift, -en, *n.f.* credit.
Gymna'sium, -ien, *n.nt.* secondary school preparing for university.
Gymnas'tik, *n.f.* gymnastics.
gymnas'tisch, *adj.* gymnastic.
Gynäkologe, -n, *n.m.* gynaecologist.
Gynäkologin, -nen, *n.f.* gynaecologist.

H

ha, *abbr.* (= Hektar') hectare.
Haar, -e, *n.nt.* hair.

haarig, *adj.* hairy.
Haarklammer, -n, *n.f.* bobby pin.

Haarnadel, -n, *n.f.* hairpin.
haarscharf, *adj.* very sharp.
Haarschneiden, -, *n.nt.* haircut.
Haarschnitt, -e, *n.m.* (style of) haircut.
Haarspray, *n.m.* hairspray.
haarsträubend, *adj.* hair-raising.
Habe, -n, *n.f.* property; **(Hab und Gut)** goods and chattels, all one's property.
haben*, *vb.* have.
Haben, *n.nt.* credit; **(Soll und H.)** debit and credit.
Habgier, *n.f.* greed.
habgierig, *adj.* greedy.
Habseligkeiten, *n.pl.* belongings.
Habsucht, *n.f.* greed.
habsüchtig, *adj.* greedy.
Hacke, -n, *n.f.* hoe, pick; heel.
hacken, *vb.* chip.
Hader, *n.m.* quarrel, strife.
hadern, *vb.* quarrel.
Hafen, -, *n.m.* harbor, port.
Hafenstadt, -̈e, *n.f.* seaport.
Hafer, *n.m.* oats.
Hafergrütze, *n.f.* oatmeal.
Haft, *n.f.* arrest, detention.
haftbar, *adj.* liable.
Haftbefehl, -e, *n.m.* warrant.
haften, *vb.* stick, adhere; be responsible.
Haftpflicht, -en, *n.f.* liability.
Hagel, *n.m.* hail.
Hagelwetter, -, *n.nt.* hailstorm.
hager, *adj.* gaunt.
Hahn, -̈e, *n.m.* rooster; faucet.
Hähnchen, -, *n.nt.* chicken.
Haifisch, -e, *n.m.* shark.
Hain, -e, *n.m.* grove.
Haken, -, *n.m.* hook.
halb, *adj.* half.
halber, *prep.* because of, for the sake of.
halbie'ren, *vb.* halve.
Halbinsel, -n, *n.f.* peninsula.
halbjährlich, *adj.* semiannual.
Halbkreis, -e, *n.m.* semicircle.
Halbkugel, -n, *n.f.* hemisphere.
Halbmesser, -, *n.m.* radius.
Halbschuhe, *n.pl.* shoes.
halbtags, *adv.* part-time, half-day.
halbwegs, *adv.* halfway.
Hälfte, -n, *n.f.* half.
Halfter, -, *n.f.* halter.

Halle, -n, *n.f.* hall.
hallen, *vb.* sound, echo.
Hallenbad, -̈er, *n.nt.* indoor swimming pool.
Halm, -e, *n.m.* blade, stalk.
hallo, *interj.* hello.
Hals, -̈e, *n.m.* neck.
Halsband, -̈er, *n.nt.* necklace.
halsbrecherisch, *adj.* breakneck.
Halskette, -n, *n.f.* necklace.
Halsschmerzen, *n.pl.* sore throat.
halsstarrig, *adj.* obstinate.
Halstuch, -̈er, *n.nt.* kerchief.
Halsweh, *n.nt.* sore throat.
halt, *interj.* halt.
halt, *adv.* after all; I think.
Halt, -e, *n.m.* halt; hold, support.
haltbar, *adj.* tenable; durable; not perishable.
halten*, *vb.* hold, keep, stop; **(h. für)** consider as.
Halter, -, *n.m.* holder.
Haltestelle, -n, *n.f.* stop.
halt-machen, *vb.* halt, stop.
Haltung, -en, *n.f.* attitude, posture.
Hammelbraten, -, *n.m.* roast mutton.
Hammelfleisch, *n.nt.* mutton.
Hammelkeule, -n, *n.f.* leg of mutton.
Hammer, -̈, *n.m.* hammer.
hämmern, *vb.* hammer.
Hämorrhoi'de, -n, *n.f.* hemorrhoid.
hamstern, *vb.* hoard.
Hand, -̈e, *n.f.* hand.
Handarbeit, -en, *n.f.* manual labor; needlework.
Handbremse, -n, *n.f.* hand brake.
Handbuch, -̈er, *n.nt.* handbook, manual.
Händedruck, *n.m.* handshake.
Handel, *n.m.* trade, commerce.
handeln, *vb.* act, trade, deal; **(es handelt sich um ...)** it is a question of . . .
Handelsabkommen, *n.nt.* trade agreement.
Handelsgeist, *n.m.* commercialism.
Handelsmarine, *n.f.* merchant marine.
Handelsreisend-, *n.m.&f.* traveling salesperson.

handfest, adj. sturdy.
Handfläche, -n, n.f. palm.
Handgelenk, -e, n.nt. wrist.
handhaben, vb. handle, manage.
Handikap, -s, n.nt. handicap.
Handlanger, -, n.m. handy man.
Händler, -, n.m. dealer, trader.
Händlerin, -nen, n.f. dealer, trader.
handlich, adj. handy.
Handlung, -en, n.f. action; plot.
Handschelle, -n, n.f. handcuff.
Handschrift, -en, n.f. handwriting.
Handschuh, -e, n.m. glove.
Handtasche, -n, n.f. pocketbook.
Handtuch, -̈er, n.nt. towel.
Handvoll, n.f. handful.
Handwerk, n.nt. handicraft, handiwork.
Handwerker, -, n.m. craftsman, artisan.
Handwerkerin, -nen, n.f. craftswoman, artisan.
Hang, -̈e, n.m. slope; inclination.
Hängebrücke, -n, n.f. suspension bridge.
Hängematte, -n, n.f. hammock.
hängen*, vb. (intr.) hang, be suspended; **(an jemandem h.)** be attached to someone; (tr.) hang, suspend.
Hans, n.m. Hans; **(H. Dampf in allen Gassen)** jack-of-all-trades.
hänseln, vb. tease.
hantie'ren, vb. handle, manipulate.
hapern, vb. get stuck, be wrong.
Happen, -, n.m. morsel.
Harfe, -n, n.f. harp.
Harke, -n, n.f. rake.
harken, vb. rake.
Harm, n.m. grief.
harmlos, adj. harmless.
Harmonie, -i'en, n.f. harmony.
Harmo'nika, -s, n.f. harmonica.
harmo'nisch, adj. harmonious.
harmonisie'ren, vb. harmonize.
Harn, n.m. urine.
Harnblase, -n, n.f. (urinary) bladder.
harnen, vb. urinate.
Harnisch, -e, n.m. harness; armor.
Harpu'ne, -n, n.f. harpoon.

hart (-̈), adj. hard, severe.
Härte, -n, n.f. hardness, severity.
härten, vb. harden, temper.
hartgekocht, adj. hard-boiled.
hartherzig, adj. hard-hearted.
hartnäckig, adj. stubborn.
Harz, -e, n.nt. resin, rosin.
Hasch, n.nt. marijuana.
haschen, vb. catch, snatch.
Hase, -n, n.m. hare.
Haselnuß, -̈sse, n.f. hazelnut.
Hasenbraten, -, n.m. roast hare.
Haspe, -n, n.f. hasp, hinge.
Haß, n.m. hatred.
hassen, vb. hate.
häßlich, adj. ugly.
Häßlichkeit, n.f. ugliness.
Hast, n.f. haste, hurry.
hasten, vb. hasten, hurry.
hastig, adj. hasty.
Haube, -n, n.f. hood.
Hauch, -e, n.m. breath.
hauchdünn, adj. extremely thin.
hauen*, vb. hew, chop, strike, spank; **(sich h.)** fight.
Haufen, -, n.m. pile, heap; crowd.
häufen, vb. heap.
häufig, adj. frequent.
Häufigkeit, -en, n.f. frequency.
Häufung, -en, n.f. accumulation.
Haupt, -̈er, n.nt. head.
Hauptamt, -̈er, n.nt. main office.
Hauptbahnhof, -̈e, n.m. main railroad station.
Häuptling, -e, n.m. chieftain.
Hauptmann, -leute, n.m. captain.
Hauptquartier, -e, n.nt. headquarters.
Hauptsache, -n, n.f. main, essential thing; principal matter.
hauptsächlich, adj. main, principal.
Hauptstadt, -̈e, n.f. capital.
Hauptwort, -̈er, n.nt. noun, substantive.
Haus, -̈er, n.nt. house.
Hausangestellt-, n.m.&f. servant.
Hausarbeit, -en, n.f. housework.
Hausaufgabe, -n, n.f. homework.
hausbacken, adj. homemade; plain.
hausen, vb. dwell, reside.
Häuserblock, -s, n.m. block.

Hausfrau, -en, *n.f.* housewife.
Haushalt, -e, *n.m.* household.
haus·halten*, *vb.* economize.
Haushälterin, -nen, *n.f.* housekeeper.
Haushaltung, *n.f.* housekeeping.
hausie′ren, *vb.* peddle.
Hausie′rer, -, *n.m.* peddler.
häuslich, *adj.* domestic.
Hausmeister, -, *n.m.* janitor.
Hausrat, *n.m.* household goods.
Hausschuh, -e, *n.m.* slipper.
Haut, ⁼e, *n.f.* skin, hide.
hautstraffend, *adj.* astringent.
Hebamme, -n, *n.f.* midwife.
Hebel, -, *n.m.* lever.
heben*, *vb.* raise, lift.
Hebrä′er, -, *n.m.* Hebrew.
Hebrä′erin, -nen, *n.f.* Hebrew.
hebrä′isch, *adj.* Hebrew.
hecheln, *vb.* heckle.
Hecht, -e, *n.m.* pike (fish).
Heck, -e, *n.nt.* stern, rear, tail.
Hecke, -n, *n.f.* hedge.
Heer, -e, *n.nt.* army.
Heft, -e, *n.nt.* notebook; handle, hilt.
heften, *vb.* fasten, pin, stitch, tack.
Hefter, -, *n.m.* folder.
heftig, *adj.* vehement.
Heftigkeit, *n.f.* vehemence.
Heftklammer, -n, *n.f.* staple.
Heftzwecke, -n, *n.f.* thumbtack.
hegen, *vb.* nurture.
Heide, -n, -n, *n.m.* heathen.
Heide, -n, *n.f.* heath.
Heidelbeere, -n, *n.f.* huckleberry.
heidnisch, *adj.* heathen.
heikel, *adj.* ticklish, tricky, delicate.
Heil, *n.nt.* welfare, safety, salvation.
heil, *adj.* whole; well, healed, unhurt.
Heiland, *n.m.* Savior.
Heilbad, ⁼er, *n.nt.* spa.
heilbar, *adj.* curable.
Heilbutt, -e, *n.m.* halibut.
heilen, *vb.* heal, cure.
heilig, *adj.* holy, sacred.
Heilig, -, n.m.&f. saint.
Heiligabend, *n.m.* Christmas Eve.
heiligen, *vb.* hallow, sanctify.
Heiligenschein, -e, *n.m.* halo.

Heiligkeit, *n.f.* holiness, sanctity.
Heiligtum, ⁼er, *n.nt.* sanctuary.
Heiligung, -en, *n.f.* sanctification, consecration.
Heilmittel, -, *n.nt.* remedy, cure.
Heilung, -en, *n.f.* healing, cure.
Heim, -e, *n.nt.* home.
heim, *adv.* home.
Heimat, *n.f.* home (town, country).
Heimatland, ⁼er, *n.nt.* homeland.
heimatlich, *adj.* native.
heimatlos, *adj.* homeless.
Heimchen, -, *n.nt.* cricket.
heimisch, *adj.* domestic, homelike.
heimlich, *adj.* secret.
heim·suchen, *vb.* scourge.
Heimsuchung, -en, *n.f.* scourge.
heimtückisch, *adj.* malicious, treacherous.
heimwärts, *adv.* homeward.
Heimweh, *n.nt.* homesickness.
Heirat, -en, *n.f.* marriage.
heiraten, *vb.* marry.
Heiratsantrag, ⁼e, *n.m.* proposal.
heiser, *adj.* hoarse.
heiß, *adj.* hot.
heissen*, *vb.* be called, be named; mean; call, order.
heiter, *adj.* cheerful; clear.
heizen, *vb.* heat, have the heat on.
Heizkörper, -, *n.m.* radiator.
Heizvorrichtung, -en, *n.f.* heater.
Hektar, -e, *n.m.* hectare.
hektisch, *adj.* hectic.
Hektogramm′, -e, *n.nt.* hectogram.
Held, -en, -en, *n.m.* hero.
heldenhaft, *adj.* heroic.
Heldenmut, *n.m.* heroism.
Heldin, -nen, *n.f.* heroine.
helfen*, *vb.* help, aid, assist.
Helfer, -, *n.m.* helper.
Helferin, -nen, *n.f.* helper.
Helfershelfer, -, *n.m.* confederate, accomplice.
hell, *adj.* bright, light.
Helligkeit, *n.f.* brightness.
Helm, -e, *n.m.* helmet.
Hemd, -en, *n.nt.* shirt.
hemmen, *vb.* stop, hinder.
Hemmnis, -se, *n.nt.* hindrance, obstacle.

Hemmschuh, -e, *n.m.* brake.
Hemmung, -en, *n.f.* restraint, inhibition.
hemmungslos, *adj.* uninhibited, unrestrained.
Henkel, -, *n.m.* handle.
Henker, -, *n.m.* executioner.
Henna, *n.f.* henna.
Henne, -n, *n.f.* hen.
her, *adv.* towards here; ago.
herab', *adv.* downwards.
herab'·hängen, *vb.* droop.
herab'·lassen*, *vb.* let down; **(sich h.)** condescend.
herab'lassend, *adj.* condescending.
Herab'lassung, -en, *n.f.* condescension.
herab'·setzen, *vb.* set down, lower, reduce, disparage.
Herab'setzung, -en, *n.f.* reduction, disparagement.
heran', *adv.* up to, toward.
heran'·gehen*, *vb.* walk up to, approach.
heran'·nahen, *vb.* approach, draw near.
heran'·wachsen*, *vb.* grow up.
herauf', *adv.* upwards.
heraus', *adv.* out.
heraus'·bringen*, *vb.* bring out, publish.
Heraus'forderer, -, *n.m.* challenger.
heraus'·fordern, *vb.* challenge.
heraus'fordernd, *adj.* defiant.
Heraus'forderung, -en, *n.f.* challenge, defiance.
heraus'·geben*, *vb.* edit, publish.
Heraus'geber, -, *n.m.* editor, publisher.
Heraus'geberin, -nen, *n.f.* editor, publisher.
heraus'·kommen*, *vb.* come out, be published.
heraus'·lassen*, *vb.* let out.
heraus'·putzen, *vb.* dress up.
heraus'·stellen, *vb.* put out; **(sich h.)** turn out to be.
heraus'·ziehen*, *vb.* extract.
herb, *adj.* tart, bitter.
herbei', *adv.* toward here.
herbei'·schaffen, *vb.* procure.
Herberge, -n, *n.f.* hostel.

herbergen, *vb.* shelter, lodge.
Herbheit, -en, *n.f.* tartness.
Herbst, -e, *n.m.* fall, autumn.
herbstlich, *adj.* autumnal.
Herd, -e, *n.m.* kitchen stove; hearth.
Herde, -n, *n.f.* herd.
herein', *adv.* in; **(h.!)** come in!
Hergang, ⁻e, *n.m.* course of events.
hergebracht, *adj.* customary.
hergelaufen, *adj.* of uncertain origin.
Hering, -e, *n.m.* herring.
Herkommen, -, *n.nt.* tradition; origin.
herkömmlich, *adj.* traditional.
Herkunft, ⁻e, *n.f.* origin, extraction.
her·leiten, *vb.* derive.
herme'tisch, *adj.* hermetic.
hernach', *adv.* afterwards.
hernie'der, *adv.* downwards, from above.
Herr, -n, -en, *n.m.* Mr., gentleman, lord, master.
Herrenbekleidung, *n.f.* menswear.
Herrenfriseur, -e, *n.m.* men's barber.
Herrenvolk, ⁻er, *nt.* master race.
her·richten, *vb.* set up, arrange.
Herrin, -nen, *n.f.* mistress.
herrisch, *adj.* imperious.
herrlich, *adj.* wonderful, splendid.
Herrlichkeit, *n.f.* glory, magnificence.
Herrschaft, *n.f.* rule, reign; estate.
Herrschaften, *n.pl.* master and mistress of the house; people of high rank; **(meine H.)** ladies and gentlemen.
herrschen, *vb.* rule, reign.
herrschend, *adj.* ruling, prevailing.
Herrscher, -, *n.m.* ruler.
Herrscherin, -nen, *n.f.* ruler.
herrschsüchtig, *adj.* imperious, tyrannical.
her·sagen, *vb.* recite.
her·stellen, *vb.* make, manufacture.
Herstellung, -n, *n.f.* manufacture.

Hertz, *n.nt.* hertz.

herü'ber, *adv.* over (towards here).

herum', *adv.* around, about.

herum'·kriegen, *vb.* talk over, win over.

herum'·lungern, *vb.* loaf around.

herum'·nörgeln, *vb.* nag.

herum'·pfuschen, *vb.* tamper.

herum'·schnüffeln, *vb.* pry, snoop.

herum'·stehen*, *vb.* stand around, loiter.

herun'ter, *adv.* down.

herun'tergekommen, *adj.* run-down, down at the heels.

herun'ter·lassen*, *vb.* lower.

herun'ter·machen, *vb.* dress down, tear apart, pan.

hervor', *adv.* forth, forward.

hervor'·brechen*, *vb.* erupt.

hervor'·bringen*, *vb.* bring forth, produce.

hervor'·heben*, *vb.* emphasize.

hervor'·quellen*, *vb.* gush; ooze.

hervor'ragend, *adj.* prominent, outstanding, superb.

hervor'·rufen*, *vb.* evoke; provoke.

hervor'·schießen*, *vb.* spurt.

hervor'·stehen*, *vb.* protrude.

Herz(en), -, *n.nt.* heart.

her·zeigen, *vb.* show.

herzen, *vb.* hug, cuddle.

herzhaft, *adj.* hearty.

herzig, *adj.* lovable, darling.

Herzinfarkt, -e, *n.m.* heart attack.

herzlich, *adj.* cordial, affectionate.

Herzlichkeit, *n.f.* cordiality.

herzlos, *adj.* heartless.

Herzog, -e, *n.m.* duke.

Herzogin, -nen, *n.f.* duchess.

Herzogtum, -̈er, *n.nt.* dukedom, duchy.

heterosexuell', *adj.* heterosexual.

Hetze, -n, *n.f.* rush; agitation, inflammatory talk; hassle.

hetzen, *vb.* rush; hound, agitate, rabble-rouse.

Hetzerei', -en, *n.f.* rush; demagoguery.

hetzerisch, *adj.* inflammatory, demagogic.

Hetzredner, -, *n.m.* rabble rouser, demagogue.

Heu, *n.nt.* hay.

Heuchelei', -en, *n.f.* hypocrisy.

heucheln, *vb.* fake, feign; play the hypocrite.

Heuchler, -, *n.m.* hypocrite.

Heuchlerin, -nen, *n.f.* hypocrite.

heuchlerisch, *adj.* hypocritical.

heuer, *adv.* this year.

Heugabel, -n, *n.f.* pitchfork.

Heuhaufen, -, *n.m.* haystack.

heulen, *vb.* howl; cry.

heurig, *adj.* of this year.

Heuschnupfen, -, *n.m.* hay fever.

heute, *adv.* today; (**h. abend**) tonight.

heutig, *adj.* today's.

heutzutage, *adv.* nowadays.

Heuwiese, -n, *n.f.* hayfield.

Hexe, -n, *n.f.* witch.

hexen, *vb.* perform witchcraft; be a magician.

Hexenschuß, *n.m.* lumbago.

Hieb, -e, *n.m.* blow, stroke.

hienie'den, *adv.* here below.

hier, *adv.* here.

hierar'chisch, *adj.* hierarchical.

hierbei, *adv.* hereby.

hierher, *adv.* hither.

hiermit, *adv.* hereby, herewith.

Hifi, *n.nt.* high fidelity.

Hilfe, -n, *n.f.* help, aid.

hilfeflehend, *adj.* imploring.

Hilfeleistung, -en, *n.f.* assistance, aid.

hilflos, *adj.* helpless, defenseless.

Hilflosigkeit, *n.f.* helplessness.

hilfreich, *adj.* helpful.

hilfsbedürftig, *adj.* needy.

hilfsbereit, *adj.* cooperative.

Hilfsmittel, -, *n.nt.* aid.

Hilfsquelle, -n, *n.f.* resource.

Himbeere, -n, *n.f.* raspberry.

Himmel, -, *n.m.* heaven, sky.

Himmelfahrt, -en, *n.f.* ascension to heaven; (**H. Christi**) Ascension (Day) (40 days after Easter); (**Mari'ä H.**) Assumption (of the Blessed Virgin) (August 15).

himmelhochjauchzend, *adj.* jubilant.

himmelschreiend, *adj.* scandalous.

Himmelsrichtung, -en, *n.f.* point of the compass, direction.

himmlisch, *adj.* heavenly.

hin, *adv.* to there; gone; **(h. und her)** back and forth; **(h. und wieder)** now and then.

hinab', *prep.* down.

hinaus', *adv.* out.

hinaus'·zögern, *vb.* procrastinate.

Hinblick, *n.m.* aspect. **(in H. auf . . .)** with regard to . . .

hinderlich, *adj.* hindering, inconvenient.

hindern, *vb.* hinder, deter.

Hindernis, -se, *n.nt.* hindrance, obstacle.

hin·deuten, *vb.* point to.

hinein', *adv.* in.

hin·fallen*, *vb.* fall down.

Hingabe, *n.f.* fervency.

hin·geben*, *vb.* give away; up; **(sich h.)** devote oneself; surrender.

Hingebung, *n.f.* devotion.

hingestreckt, *adj.* prostrate.

hin·halten*, *vb.* (*fig.*) delay.

hinken, *vb.* limp.

hin·legen, *vb.* lay down; **(sich h.)** lie down.

hin·purzeln, *vb.* tumble.

hin·reißen*, *vb.* **(sich h. lassen)** let oneself be carried away.

hinreißend, *adj.* captivating, ravishing.

hin·richten, *vb.* execute.

Hinrichtung, -en, *n.f.* execution.

Hinsicht, *n.f.* respect, regard.

hinsichtlich, *prep.* in regard to, regarding, concerning.

hinten, *adv.* behind.

hintenherum', *adv.* from behind; (*fig.*) roundabout, through the back door.

hinter, *prep.* behind, beyond.

hinter-, *adj.* hind, back.

Hintergedanke(n), -, *n.m.* ulterior motive.

hinterge'hen*, *vb.* doublecross.

Hintergrund, ⁼e, *n.m.* background.

Hinterhalt, -e, *n.m.* ambush.

hinterher', *adv.* afterward(s).

Hinterland, *n.nt.* hinterland.

hinterle'gen, *vb.* deposit.

Hinterlist, *n.f.* insidiousness, underhanded act.

hinterlistig, *adj.* insidious, designing, underhanded.

Hintern, *n.m.* (*fam.*) bottom, behind.

Hintertreffen, *n.nt.* **(ins H. geraten)** fall behind.

Hintertür, -en, *n.f.* back door; (*fig.*) loophole.

hinterzie'hen*, *vb.* (*fig.*) defraud.

hinü'ber, *adv.* over, across.

hinun'ter, *adv.* down.

Hinweis, -e, *n.m.* reference; indication.

hin·weisen*, *vb.* point, refer, allude.

hinzu'·fügen, *vb.* add.

Hirn, -e, *n.nt.* brain.

Hirsch, -e, *n.m.* stag.

Hirschleder, -, *n.nt.* deerskin.

Hirt, -en, -en (*Biblical* **Hirte, -n, -n**), *n.m.* shepherd.

hissen, *vb.* hoist.

Histo'riker, -, *n.m.* historian.

Historikerin, -nen, *n.f.* historian.

histo'risch, *adj.* historic(al).

Hitze, *n.m.* heat.

hitzig, *adj.* heated, fiery, heady.

hitzköpfig, *adj.* hot-headed.

Hitzschlag, ⁼e, *n.m.* heatstroke.

Hobel, -, *n.m.* plane.

hobeln, *vb.* plane.

hoch (hoh-, höher, höchst), 1. *adj.* high, tall. **2.** *adv.* up.

Hochebene, -n, *n.f.* plateau.

hochachtungsvoll, *adv.* yours sincerely.

Hochdeutsch, *n.nt.* standard High German.

hocherfreut, *adj.* elated.

hochgradig, *adj.* intense, extreme.

Hochmut, *n.m.* haughtiness, pride.

hochmütig, *adj.* haughty, arrogant.

Hochsaison, *n.f.* peak season.

hoch·schätzen, *vb.* treasure.

Hochschule, -n, *n.f.* university.

Hochsommer, -, *n.m.* midsummer.

höchst, *adv.* highly, extremely.

Hochstapler, -, *n.m.* swindler, impersonator.
höchstenfalls, *adv.* at best, at the outside.
höchstens, *adv.* at best, at the outside.
Höchstgrenze, -n, *n.f.* top limit.
hochtrabend, *adj.* pompous, grandiloquent.
Hochverrat, *n.m.* high treason.
Hochzeit, -en, *n.f.* wedding.
Hochzeitsreise, -n, *n.f.* honeymoon.
hoch•ziehen*, *vb.* hoist.
hocken, *vb.* squat.
Hocker, -, *n.m.* stool.
Höcker, -, *n.m.* bump, hump.
Hockey, *n.nt.* hockey.
Hof, ⁼e, *n.m.* court, courtyard; (**den H. machen**) court.
hoffen, *vb.* hope.
hoffentlich, *adv.* I hope.
Hoffnung, -en, *n.f.* hope.
hoffnungslos, *adj.* hopeless.
hoffnungsvoll, *adj.* hopeful.
höfisch, *adj.* courtly.
höflich, *adj.* polite, courteous, respectful, civil.
Höflichkeit, -en, *n.f.* courtesy.
Höhe, -n, *n.f.* height, altitude, elevation.
Hoheit, -en, *n.f.* Highness.
Höhepunkt, -e, *n.m.* high point, highlight, climax, culmination.
höher, *adj.* higher.
hohl, *adj.* hollow.
Höhle, -n, *n.f.* cave, den.
Hohlraum, ⁼e, *n.m.* hollow space, vacuum.
Hohn, *n.m.* mockery, derision.
höhnisch, *adj.* derisive, mocking.
hohnlächeln, *vb.* sneer, deride.
hold, *adj.* gracious, lovely.
holdselig, *adj.* gracious.
holen, *vb.* (go and) get, fetch.
Holland, *n.nt.* Holland.
Holländer, -, *n.m.* Dutchman.
Holländerin, -nen, *n.f.* Dutchwoman.
holländisch, *adj.* Dutch.
Hölle, *n.f.* inferno, hell.
höllisch, *adj.* infernal, hellish.
Hologramm', -e, *n.nt.* hologram.
Holographie', *n.f.* holography.
holprig, *adj.* bumpy.

Holz, ⁼er, *n.nt.* wood, lumber, timber.
hölzern, *adj.* wooden.
Holzklotz, ⁼e, *n.m.* block (of wood); log.
Holzkohle, -n, *n.f.* charcoal.
Holzschnitt, -e, *n.m.* woodcut.
homosexuell', *adj.* homosexual.
Honig, *n.m.* honey.
Honorar', -e, *n.nt.* honorarium.
honorie'ren, *vb.* honor; remunerate.
Hopfen, -, *n.m.* hop(s).
hopsen, *vb.* hop, skip.
hops•gehen*, *vb.* go down the drain, go west.
hörbar, *adj.* audible.
horchen, *vb.* listen to; eavesdrop.
Horde, -n, *n.f.* horde.
hören, *vb.* hear.
Hörensagen, *n.nt.* hearsay.
Hörer, -, *n.m.* (telephone) receiver; (student) auditor.
hörig, *adj.* submissive; subservient.
Horizont', -e, *n.m.* horizon.
horizontal', *adj.* horizontal.
Hormon', -e, *n.nt.* hormone.
Horn, ⁼er, *n.nt.* horn.
hörnen, *adj.* horny.
Hornhaut, ⁼e, *n.f.* callous skin; cornea.
hornig, *adj.* horny.
Hornis'se, -n, *n.f.* hornet.
Horoskop', -e, *n.nt.* horoscope.
Hörsaal, -säle, *n.m.* lecture hall.
Hort, -e, *n.m.* hoard; refuge, retreat.
Hörweite, *n.f.* earshot.
Hose, -n, *n.f.* trousers, pants.
Hosenband, ⁼er, *n.nt.* garter.
Hostie, *n.f.* host.
Hotel', -s, *n.nt.* hotel.
Hotel'boy, -s, *n.m.* bellboy.
Hovercraft, *n.nt.* hovercraft.
hübsch, *adj.* pretty, handsome.
Hubschrauber, -, *n.m.* helicopter.
Huf, -e, *n.m.* hoof.
Hüfte, -n, *n.f.* hip.
Hügel, -, *n.m.* hill.
Huhn, ⁼er, *n.nt.* chicken, fowl.
Hühnerauge, -n, *n.nt.* corn (on the foot).
huldigen, *vb.* do homage to.
Hülle, -n, *n.f.* covering, casing; (**in**

H. und Fülle) abundantly, in profusion.

hüllen, vb. clothe, wrap, envelop.

Hülse, -n, n.f. hull, husk; case.

human', adj. humane.

Humanis'mus, n.m. humanism.

Humanist', -en, -en, n.m. humanist.

humanitär', adj. humanitarian.

Humanität', n.f. humanity.

Hummel, -n, n.f. bumblebee.

Hummer, -, n.m. lobster.

Humor', n.m. humor, wit.

Humorist', -en, -en, n.m. humorist.

humor'voll, adj. humorous.

humpeln, vb. hobble.

Hund, -e, n.m. dog, hound.

hundert, num. a hundred.

Hundert, -e, n.nt. hundred.

Hundertjahr'feier, -n, n.f. centenary, centennial.

hundertjährig, adj. centennial.

hundertst -, adj. hundredth.

Hundertstel, -, n.nt. hundredth part; **(ein h.)** one one-hundredth.

Hundezwinger, -, n.m. kennel.

Hündin, -nen, n.f. bitch.

hünenhaft, adj. gigantic.

Hunger, n.m. hunger.

hungern, vb. starve.

Hungersnot, ⸚e, n.f. famine.

Hungertod, n.m. starvation.

hungrig, adj. hungry.

Hupe, -n, n.f. auto horn.

hupen, vb. blow the horn.

hüpfen, vb. hop.

Hürde, -n, n.f. hurdle.

Hure, -n, n.f. whore.

husten, vb. cough.

Husten, n.m. cough.

Hut, ⸚e, n.m. hat.

Hut, n.f. care, protection; **(auf der H. sein*)** be on the alert.

hüten, vb. tend; **(sich h.)** beware, be careful not to do.

Hütte, -n, n.f. hut; shed, hovel; *(tech.)* foundry.

Hyazin'the, -n, n.f. hyacinth.

Hydrant', -en, -en, n.m. hydrant.

Hygie'ne, n.f. hygiene.

hygie'nisch, adj. hygienic, sanitary.

Hymne, -n, n.f. hymn, anthem.

Hypno'se, -n, n.f. hypnosis.

hypno'tisch, adj. hypnotic.

hypnotisie'ren, vb. hypnotize.

Hypothek', -en, n.f. mortgage.

Hypothe'se, -n, n.f. hypothesis.

hypothe'tisch, adj. hypothetical.

Hysterie', n.f. hysteria, hysterics.

hyste'risch, adj. hysterical.

I

ich, pron. I.

Ich, n.nt. ego.

ideal', adj. ideal.

Ideal', -e, n.nt. ideal.

idealisie'ren, vb. idealize.

Idealis'mus, n.m. idealism.

Idee', -e'en, n.f. idea, notion; **(fixe I.)** obsession.

identifizier'bar, adj. identifiable.

identifizie'ren, vb. identify.

iden'tisch, adj. identical.

Identität', -en, n.f. identity.

Idiot', -en, -en, n.m. idiot.

idio'tisch, adj. idiotic.

Idyll', -e, n.nt. idyl.

idyl'lisch, adj. idyllic.

ignorie'ren, vb. ignore.

illuminie'ren, vb. illuminate.

illuso'risch, adj. illusive, illusory.

Illustration', -en, n.f. illustration.

illustrie'ren, vb. illustrate.

imaginär', adj. imaginary.

Imam, -e, n.m. imam.

Imbiß, -sse, n.m. snack.

Imbißstube, -n, n.f. snack bar.

Imita'tor, -o'ren, n.m. impersonator.

imitie'ren, vb. imitate.

immatrikulie'ren, vb. **(sich i.)** register in a university.

immer, adv. always.

immergrün, adj. evergreen.

immerhin', adv. after all, anyway.

Immobi'lien, n.pl. real estate.

immun', adj. immune.

Immun'schwäche, n.f. immunodeficiency.

Immunität', -en, n.f. immunity.

Imperfekt, -e, *n.nt.* imperfect tense.

Imperialis'mus, *n.m.* imperialism.

imperialis'tisch, *adj.* imperialist.

impfen, *vb.* vaccinate.

Impfstoff, -e, *n.m.* vaccine.

Impfung, -en, *n.f.* vaccination.

implizi'te, *adv.* by implication.

implizie'ren, *vb.* imply, implicate.

imponie'ren, *vb.* impress.

Import, -e, *n.m.* import.

importie'ren, *vb.* import.

imposant', *adj.* imposing.

impotent', *adj.* impotent.

Impotenz', *n.f.* impotence.

imprägnie'ren, *vb.* waterproof.

Impresa'rio, -s, *n.m.* impresario.

improvisie'ren, *vb.* improvise.

Impuls, -e, *n.m.* impulse.

impulsiv', *adj.* impulsive.

Impulsivität', *n.f.* spontaneity.

imstan'de, *adj.* able, capable.

in, *prep.* in, into.

Inbegriff, -e, *n.m.* essence, embodiment.

inbegriffen, *adj.* included; implicit.

Inbrunst, *n.f.* ardor, fervor.

inbrünstig, *adj.* zealous, ardent.

Inder, -, *n.m.* Indian.

Inderin, -nen, *n.f.* Indian.

Index, -e *or* **-dizes,** *n.m.* index.

India'ner, -, *n.m.* (American) Indian, Native American.

India'nerin, -nen, *n.f.* *American) Indian, Native American.

india'nisch, *adj.* (American) Indian, Native American.

Indien, *n.nt.* India.

Indikativ, -e, *n.m.* indicative.

Indika'tor, -o'ren, *n.m.* indicator.

indirekt, *adj.* indirect.

indisch, *adj.* Indian.

indiskret, *adj.* indiscreet.

Individualität', -en, *n.f.* individuality.

individuell', *adj.* individual.

Indivi'duum, -duen, *n.nt.* individual.

Indone'sien, *n.nt.* Indonesia.

Induktion', -en, *n.f.* induction.

induktiv', *adj.* inductive.

Industrie', -i'en, *n.f.* industry.

industriell', *adj.* industrial.

Industriell'e, -n, -n, *n.m.&f.* industrialist.

induzie'ren, *vb.* induce.

infam', *adj.* infamous; beastly.

Infanterie', -n, *n.f.* infantry.

Infanterist, -en, -en, *n.m.* infantryman.

Infinitiv, -e, *n.m.* infinitive.

infiltrie'ren, *vb.* infiltrate.

infizie'ren, *vb.* infect.

Inflation', -en, *n.f.* inflation.

infolgedes'sen, *adv.* consequently.

informie'ren, *vb.* inform.

Ingenieur', -e, *n.m.* engineer.

Ingenieu'rin, -nen, *n.f.* engineer.

Ingwer, -, *n.m.* ginger.

Inhaber, -, *n.m.* proprietor; (of an apartment) occupant.

Inhaberin, -nen, *n.f.* proprietor; (of an apartment) occupant.

Inhalt, *n.m.* content, volume, capacity.

Inhaltsangabe, -n, *n.f.* table of contents.

inhaltsschwer, *adj.* momentous, weighty.

Inhaltsverzeichnis, -se, *n.nt.* table of contents, index.

Initiati've, -n, *n.f.* initiative.

inkog'nito, *adv.* incognito.

Inland, -e, *n.nt.* homeland; (im Inund Ausland) at home and abroad.

inländisch, *adj.* domestic.

inmit'ten, *prep.* amid, in the midst of.

innen, *adv.* inside.

Innen-, *cpds.* interior, inner; domestic.

Innenpolitik, *n.f.* domestic policy.

Innenseite, -n, *n.f.* inside.

inner-, *adj.* inner, interior, internal.

Inner-, *n.nt.* interior, inside; soul.

innerhalb, *prep.* within.

innerlich, *adj.* inward, intrinsic.

innerst-, *adj.* innermost.

innig, *adj.* intimate; fervent.

Innigkeit, *n.f.* fervor.

Innung, -en, *n.f.* guild.

Input, -s, *n.m.* input.

Insasse, -n, -n, *n.m.* occupant; inmate.

Insassin, -nen, *n.f.* occupant; inmate.

insbeson'dere, *adv.* especially.

Inschrift, -en, *n.f.* inscription.

Insekt', -en, *n.nt.* insect.

Insek'tenpulver, -, *n.nt.* insecticide.

Insel, -n, *n.f.* island.

Inserat', -e, *n.nt.* advertisement.

Inserent', -en, -en, *n.m.* advertiser.

insgeheim', *adv.* secretly.

insgesamt', *adv.* altogether.

Insig'nien, *n.pl.* insignia.

inso'fern, inso'weit, *adv.* to that extent, to this extent.

insofern, insoweit, *conj.* insofar as, to the extent that.

Inspek'tor, -o'ren, *n.m.* inspector.

Inspekto'rin, -nen, *n.f.* inspector.

inspizie'ren, *vb.* inspect.

Installation', -en, *n.f.* installation.

instand·'halten*, *vb.* keep up, keep in good repair.

Instand'haltung, *n.f.* maintenance.

inständig, *adj.* earnest.

instand·'setzen, *vb.* repair, recondition; enable.

Instanz', -en, *n.f.* instance.

Instan'zenweg, -e, *n.m.* stages of appeal, channels.

Instinkt', -e, *n.m.* instinct.

instinktiv', *adj.* instinctive.

Institut', -e, *n.nt.* institute, institution.

Instrument', -e, *n.nt.* instrument.

Insulin', *n.nt.* insulin.

inszenie'ren, *vb.* stage.

Inszenie'rung, -en, *n.f.* scenario.

intakt', *adj.* intact.

integrie'ren, *vb.* integrate.

Intellekt', -e, *n.m.* intellect.

intellektuell', *adj.* intellectual.

Intellektuell'-, *n.m. & f.* intellectual, highbrow; egghead.

intelligent', *adj.* intelligent.

Intelligenz', *n.f.* intelligence.

intensiv', *adj.* intense, intensive.

interessant', *adj.* interesting.

Interes'se, -n, *n.nt.* interest, concern.

interessie'ren, *vb.* interest.

Interjektion', -en, *n.f.* interjection.

Internat', -e, *n.nt.* boarding school.

international', *adj.* international.

internie'ren, *vb.* intern.

Internist', -en, -en, *n.m.* specialist for internal medicine.

interpretie'ren, *vb.* interpret.

interpunktie'ren, *vb.* punctuate.

Interpunktion', *n.f.* punctuation.

Interview', -s, *n.nt.* interview.

interview'en, *vb.* interview.

intim', *adj.* intimate.

Intoleranz', *n.f.* intolerance.

intransitiv', *adj.* intransitive.

intravenös', *adj.* intravenous.

Intri'ge, -n, *n.f.* intrigue.

intrigie'ren, *vb.* plot, scheme.

Intuition', -en, *n.f.* intuition.

intuitiv', *adj.* intuitive.

Invali'de, -n, -n, *n.m.* invalid.

Invasion', -en, *n.f.* invasion.

Inventar', -e, *n.nt.* inventory.

investie'ren, *vb.* invest.

inwendig, *adj.* inward, inner.

inzwi'schen, *adv.* in the meantime.

Irak', *n.nt.* Iraq.

Iran', *n.nt.* Iran.

irdisch, *adj.* earthly.

Ire, -n, -n, *n.m.* Irishman.

irgendein, -, -e, *adj.* any (at all), any old.

irgendeiner, -e, *pron.* anyone, anybody.

irgendetwas, *pron.* something or other, anything at all.

irgendjemand, *pron.* somebody or other.

irgendwann', *adv.* somewhere.

irgendwelcher, -es, -e, *adj.* any.

irgendwie', *adv.* somehow.

irgendwo', *adv.* somewhere, anywhere.

irgendwohin', *adv.* (to) somewhere, anywhere.

Irin, -nen, *n.f.* Irishwoman.

irisch, *adj.* Irish.

Irland, *n.nt.* Ireland.
Irländer, -, *n.m.* Irishman.
Irländerin, -nen, *n.f.* Irishwoman.
Ironie', *n.f.* irony.
iro'nisch, *adj.* ironical.
irre, *adj.* astray, wrong; wandering, lost; insane.
irre·führen, *vb.* mislead.
irreführend, *adj.* misleading.
irren, *vb.* err, go astray; **(sich i.)** err, be mistaken.
irrig, *adj.* mistaken.
irritie'ren, *vb.* irritate, annoy.
Irrsinn, *n.m.* nonsense, lunacy.
irrsinnig, *adj.* lunatic.

Irrtum, ‑er, *n.m.* error.
irrtümlich, *adj.* erroneous.
Isolationist', -en, -en, *n.m.* isolationist.
Isola'tor, -o'ren, *n.m.* insulator.
isolie'ren, *vb.* isolate; insulate.
Isolie'rung, -en, *n.f.* isolation; insulation.
Israel, *n.nt.* Israel.
Israe'li, -s, *n.m.* Israeli.
israe'lisch, *adj.* Israeli.
Israelit', -en, -en, *n.m.* Israelite.
Ita'lien, *n.nt.* Italy.
Italie'ner -, *n.m.* Italian.
Italie'nerin, -nen, *n.f.* Italian.
italie'nisch, *adj.* Italian.

J

ja, 1. *interj.* yes. **2.** *adv.* as is well known, to be sure.
Jacht, -en, *n.f.* yacht.
Jacke, -n, *n.f.* jacket.
Jade, *n.m.* jade.
Jagd, -en, *n.f.* hunt; chase; pursuit.
jagen, *vb.* hunt; chase.
Jäger, -, *n.m.* hunter.
jäh, *adj.* sudden.
Jahr, -e, *n.nt.* year.
jahraus, jahrein, *adv.* year in, year out.
Jahrbuch, ‑er, *n.nt.* yearbook, almanac, annual; *(pl.)* annals.
Jahrestag, -e, *n.m.* anniversary.
Jahreszeit, -en, *n.f.* season.
Jahrgang, ‑e, *n.m.* (school) class; (wine) vintage.
Jahrhun'dert, -e, *n.nt.* century.
jährlich, *adj.* yearly, annual.
Jahrmarkt, ‑e, *n.m.* fair.
Jahrzehnt', -e, *n.nt.* decade.
Jähzorn, *n.m.* quick temper.
jähzornig, *adj.* quick-tempered.
Jammer, *n.m.* misery.
jämmerlich, *adj.* miserable; dismal.
Januar, -e, *n.m.* January.
Japan, *n.nt.* Japan.
Japa'ner, -, *n.m.* Japanese.
Japanerin, -nen, *n.f.* Japanese.
japa'nisch, *adj.* Japanese.
Jargon', -s, *n.m.* jargon, slang.
jäten, *vb.* weed.

jauchzen, *vb.* jubilate, cheer.
jawohl', *interj.* yes, sir.
Jazz, *n.m.* jazz.
je, *adv.* ever; apiece, each; **(j. nach)** in each case according to; **(j. nachdem')** according to whether, as the case may be; **(je mehr, je desto, umso besser)** the more the better.
Jeans, *n.pl.* jeans.
Jeansstoff, -e, *n.m.* denim.
jeder, -es, -e, *pron. & adj.* each, every.
jedoch', *conj.* yet; nevertheless.
jemals, *adv.* ever.
jemand, *pron.* someone, somebody; anyone, anybody.
jener, -es, -e, *pron & adj.* that, yonder; the former.
jenseits, *adv. & prep.* beyond, on the other side.
Jenseits, *n.nt.* beyond, life after death.
Jeru'salem, *n.nt.* Jerusalem.
Jesuit', -en, -en, *n.m.* Jesuit.
jetzig, *adj.* present.
jetzt, *adv.* now.
jeweilig, *adj.* in question, under consideration.
Joch, -e, *n.nt.* yoke.
Jockei, -s, *n.m.* jockey.
Jod, *n.nt.* iodine.
jodeln, *vb.* yodel.
**Joghurt', ** *n.m. or nt.* yogurt.
johlen, *vb.* howl.

Joker, -, *n.m.* joker.
jonglie'ren, *vb.* juggle.
Jota, -s, *n.nt.* iota.
Journalist', -en, -en, *n.m.* journalist.
Journalis'tin, -nen, *n.f.* journalist.
Jubel, *n.m.* jubilation, rejoicing.
jubeln, *vb.* shout with joy, rejoice.
Jubilä'um, -en, *n.nt.* jubilee.
jucken, *vb.* itch.
Jude, -n, -n, *n.m.* Jew.
Judentum, *n.nt.* Judaism, Jewry.
Judenverfolgung, -en, *n.f.* pogrom.
Jüdin, -nen, *n.f.* Jew.
jüdisch, *adj.* Jewish.
Jugend, *n.f.* youth.
Jugendherberge, -n, *n.f.* youth hostel.
jugendlich, *adj.* youthful; adolescent, juvenile.
Jugendverbrecher, -, *n.m.* juvenile delinquent.
Jugendzeit, -en, *n.f.* youth, adolescence.
Jugosla'we, -n, -n, *n.m.* Yugoslav.

Jugoslä'win, -nen, *n.f.* Yugoslav.
Jugosla'wien, *n.nt.* Yugoslavia.
jugosla'wisch, *adj.* Yugoslavian.
Juli, *n.m.* July.
jung (-), *adj.* young.
Jung-, *n.nt.* young (of an animal).
Junge, -n, -n, *n.m.* boy.
jungenhaft, *adj.* boyish.
Jünger, -, *n.m.* disciple.
Jungfer, -n, *n.f.* (alte J.) old maid, spinster.
Jungfrau, -en, *n.f.* virgin.
Junggeselle, -n, -n, *n.m.* bachelor.
Jüngling, -e, *n.m.* young man.
Juni, *n.m.* June.
Junker, -, *n.m.* aristocratic landowner (especially in Prussia).
Jurist', -en, -en, *n.m.* jurist, lawyer; law student.
Juris'tin, -nen, *n.f.* jurist, lawyer; law student.
juris'tisch, *adj.* juridical, legal.
Justiz', *n.f.* justice.
Juwel', -e, *n.nt.* jewel.
Juwelier', -e, *n.m.* jeweler.
Juwelie'rin, -nen, *n.f.* jeweler.
Jux, *n.m.* fun.

K

Kabarett', -e, *n.nt.* cabaret.
Kabel, -, *n.nt.* cable; cablegram.
Kabeljau, -e, *n.m.* cod.
kabeln, *vb.* cable.
Kabi'ne, -n, *n.f.* cabin, stateroom.
Kabinett', -e, *n.nt.* cabinet.
Kabriolett', -s, *n.nt.* convertible.
Kachel, -n, *n.f.* tile.
Kada'ver, -, *n.m.* carcass.
Kadett', -en, -en, *n.m.* cadet.
Käfer, -, *n.m.* beetle, bug.
Kaffee, *n.m.* coffee.
Kaffein', *n.nt.* caffeine.
Käfig, -e, *n.m.* cage.
kahl, *adj.* bald; bare.
Kahn, -̈e, *n.m.* boat, barge.
Kaiser, -, *n.m.* emperor.
Kajü'te, -n, *n.f.* cabin (on a boat).
Kaka'o, -s, *n.m.* cocoa.
Kalb, -̈er, *n.nt.* calf.
Kalbfleisch, *n.nt.* veal.
Kalbleder, -, *n.nt.* calfskin.
Kalen'der, -, *n.m.* calendar.

Kali, *n.nt.* potash, potassium.
Kali'ber, -, *n.nt.* caliber.
Kalium, *n.nt.* potassium.
Kalk, -e, *n.m.* lime, chalk, calcium.
Kalkstein, *n.m.* limestone.
Kalorie', -i'en, *n.f.* calorie.
kalt(-), *adj.* cold.
kaltblütig, *adj.* cold-blooded.
Kälte, -n, *n.f.* cold(ness).
Kalva'rienberg, *n.m.* Calvary.
Kalzium, *n.nt.* calcium.
Kame'e, -n, *n.f.* cameo.
Kamel', -e, *n.nt.* camel.
Kamera, -s, *n.f.* camera.
Kamerad', -en, -en, *n.m.* companion, friend; comrade.
Kamera'din, -nen, *n.f.* companion, friend.
Kamerad'schaft, -en, *n.f.* comradeship, camaraderie; friendship.
Kamil'le, -n, *n.f.* camomile.

Kamin', **-e**, n.m. fireplace, hearth; fireside.

Kamm, **e**, n.m. comb; (mountain) crest.

kämmen, vb. comb.

Kammer, **-n**, n.f. room; chamber.

Kammermusik, n.f. chamber music.

Kampag'ne, **-n**, n.f. campaign.

Kampf, **e**, n.m. fight, fighting, combat.

kämpfen, vb. fight.

Kampfer, **-n**, n.f. camphor.

Kämpfer, **-**, n.m. fighter, combatant; champion.

kampfunfähig, adj. disabled.

Kanada, n.nt. Canada.

Kana'dier, **-**, n.m. Canadian.

Kana'dierin, **-nen**, n.f. Canadian.

kana'disch, adj. Canadian.

Kanal', **e**, n.m. canal, channel; duct.

Kanalisation', n.f. canalization; sewer.

kanalisie'ren, vb. canalize; drain by sewer.

Kana'rienvogel, **-**, n.m. canary.

Kanda're, **-n**, n.f. curb (of a horse); (an die K. nehmen) take a person in hand.

Kandidat', **-en**, **-en**, n.m. candidate, nominee.

Kandida'tin, **-nen**, n.f. candidate, nominee.

Kandidatur', **-en**, n.f. candidacy, nomination.

kandiert', adj. candied.

Känguruh', **-s**, n.nt. kangaroo.

Kanin'chen, **-**, n.nt. rabbit, bunny.

Kanne, **-n**, n.f. can, jug, pitcher.

Kanniba'le, **-n**, **-n**, n.m. cannibal.

Kanon', **-s**, n.m. canon.

Kanona'de, **-n**, n.f. cannonade.

Kano'ne, **-n**, n.f. cannon.

Kano'nenboot, **-e**, n.nt. gunboat.

Kanonier', **-e**, n.m. cannoneer.

kano'nisch, adj. canonical.

kanonisie'ren, vb. canonize.

Kanta'te, **-n**, n.f. cantata.

Kante, **-n**, n.f. edge, border.

Kanti'ne, **-n**, n.f. canteen.

Kanu', **-s**, n.nt. canoe.

Kanzel, **-n**, n.f. pulpit.

Kanzlei', **-en**, n.f. chancellery.

Kanzler, **-**, n.m. chancellor.

Kap, **-s**, n.nt. cape.

Kapaun', **-e**, n.m. capon.

Kapel'le, **-n**, n.f. chapel; orchestra, band.

Kapell'meister, **-**, n.m. conductor, bandmaster.

kapern, vb. capture.

kapie'ren, vb. understand.

kapital', adj. capital.

Kapital', **-ien**, n.nt. capital (funds).

kapitalisie'ren, vb. capitalize.

Kapitalis'mus, n.m. capitalism.

kapitalis'tisch, adj. capitalistic.

Kapitän', **-e**, n.m. captain.

Kapi'tel, **-**, n.nt. chapter.

kapitulie'ren, vb. capitulate.

Kappe, **-n**, n.f. cap, hood.

Kapsel, **-n**, n.f. capsule.

kaputt', adj. broken, busted; (k. machen) bust, wreck.

Kapu'ze, **-n**, n.f. hood.

Karabi'ner, **-**, n.m. carbine.

Karaf'fe, **-n**, n.f. decanter, carafe.

Karamel', n.nt. caramel.

Kara'te, n.nt. karate.

Karawa'ne, **-n**, n.f. caravan.

Karbid', n.nt. carbide.

Karbun'kel, **-**, n.m. carbuncle.

Kardinal', **e**, n.m. cardinal.

Karfrei'tag, n.m. Good Friday.

Karies, n.f. caries.

Karikatur', **-en**, n.f. caricature; cartoon.

karikie'ren, vb. caricature.

karmin'rot(-), adj. crimson.

Karneval', n.nt. carnival.

Karo, n.nt. (cards) diamond(s).

Karpfen, **-**, n.m. carp.

Karre, **-n**, n.f. cart.

Karree', **-s**, n.nt. square.

Karren, **-**, n.m. cart.

Karrie're, **-n**, n.f. career; (K. machen) be successful, get far in one's profession.

Karte, **-n**, n.f. card; chart, map.

Kartei', **-en**, n.f. card index, file.

Kartell', **-e**, n.nt. cartel.

Kartenspiel, **-e**, n.nt. card game; deck of cards.

Kartof'fel, **-n**, n.f. potato.

Karton', **-s**, n.m. carton.

Karussell', **-s**, *n.nt.* merry-go-round.

Karwoche, *n.f.* Holy Week.

Kaschmir, **-e**, *n.m.* cashmere.

Käse, *n.m.* cheese.

Kaser'ne, **-n**, *n.f.* barracks.

Kasi'no, **-s**, *n.nt.* casino.

Kasse, **-n**, *n.f.* cash box; cash register; box-office; **(bei K. sein*)** be flush; **(an der K. bezahlen)** pay the cashier.

Kassenzettel, **-**, *n.m.* sales slip.

Kasset'te, **-n**, *n.f.* cassette.

kassie'ren, *vb.* collect (money due); dismiss.

Kassie'rer, **-**, *n.m.* teller, cashier.

Kassie'rerin, **-nen**, *n.f.* teller, cashier.

Kaste, **-n**, *n.f.* caste.

kastei'en, **-e**, *n.m.* chastise, mortify.

Kasten, **̈-**, *n.m.* box, case.

Katalog', **-e**, *n.m.* catalogue.

Katapult', **-e**, *n.m.* catapult.

Katarrh', **-e**, *n.m.* catarrh.

Katas'ter, **-**, *n.nt.* register.

katastrophal', *adj.* disastrous, ruinous.

Katastro'phe, **-n**, *n.f.* disaster.

Katechis'mus, **-men**, *n.m.* catechism.

Kategorie', **-i'en**, *n.f.* category.

katego'risch, *adj.* categorical.

Kater, **-**, *n.m.* tomcat; hangover.

Kathedra'le, **-n**, *n.f.* cathedral.

Katho'de, **-n**, *n.f.* cathode.

Katholik', **-en**, **-en**, *n.m.* Catholic.

katho'lisch, *adj.* Catholic.

Katholizis'mus, **-men**, *n.m.* Catholicism.

Kattun', **-e**, *n.m.* gingham, calico.

Kätzchen, **-**, *n.nt.* kitten.

Katze, **-n**, *n.f.* cat.

katzenartig, *adj.* feline.

Katzenjammer, *n.m.* hangover.

kauen, *vb.* chew.

kauern, *vb.* crouch, cower.

Kauf, **̈-e**, *n.m.* purchase.

kaufen, *vb.* purchase, buy.

Käufer, **-**, *n.m.* buyer.

Käuferin, **-nen**, *n.f.* buyer.

Kauffrau, **-en**, *n.f.* businesswoman.

Kaufkontrakt, **-e**, *n.m.* bill of sale.

Kaufmann, **-leute**, *n.m.* businessman, merchant.

kaufmännisch, *adj.* commercial.

Kaugummi, **-s**, *n.nt.* chewing gum.

kaum, *adv.* scarcely, hardly, barely.

Kausalität', **-en**, *n.f.* causation.

Kaution', **-en**, *n.f.* surety; security; bail.

Kavalier', **-e**, *n.m.* cavalier.

Kavallerie', **-n**, *n.f.* cavalry.

Kaviar, **-e**, *n.m.* caviar.

keck, *adj.* saucy.

Kegel, **-**, *n.m.* cone.

kegelförmig, *adj.* conic.

kegeln, *vb.* bowl.

Kehle, **-n**, *n.f.* throat.

Kehlkopfentzündung, **-en**, *n.f.* laryngitis.

kehren, *vb.* turn; brush, sweep.

Kehricht, *n.m.* sweepings; garbage.

Kehrseite, **-n**, *n.f.* reverse side; other side of the picture.

kehrt•machen, *vb.* turn around, about-face.

Kehrtwendung, *n.f.* about face.

keifen, *vb.* nag, scold.

Keil, **-e**, *n.m.* wedge.

Keilerei, **-en**, *n.f.* fracas, brawl.

Keim, **-e**, *n.m.* germ, bud.

keimen, *vb.* germinate.

keimfrei, *adj.* germ free, sterile.

keimtötend, *adj.* germicidal.

kein, **-**, **-e**, *adj.* not a, not any, no.

keiner, **-es**, **-e**, *pron.* no one, not any, none.

keinerlei, *adj.* not of any sort.

keineswegs, *adv.* by no means.

Keks, **-e**, *n.m.* biscuit, cookie.

Kelch, **-e**, *n.m.* cup, goblet, chalice; calyx.

Kelchglas, **̈-er**, *n.nt.* goblet.

Kelle, **-n**, *n.f.* ladle, scoop.

Keller, **-**, *n.m.* cellar.

Kellner, **-**, *n.m.* waiter.

Kellnerin, **-nen**, *n.f.* waitress.

kennen*, *vb.* know, be acquainted with.

kennen•lernen, *vb.* meet, become acquainted with.

Kenner, **-**, *n.m.* connoisseur.

Kennerin, **-nen**, *n.f.* connoisseur, expert.

Kennkarte, -n, *n.f.* identity card.
kenntlich, *adj.* recognizable.
Kenntnis, -se, *n.f.* knowledge, notice.
Kennzeichen, -, *n.nt.* sign, distinguishing mark, feature.
kennzeichnen, *vb.* mark, stamp, distinguish, characterize.
kentern, *vb.* capsize.
Kera'mik, -en, *n.f.* ceramics.
kera'misch, *adj.* ceramic.
Kerbe, -n, *n.f.* notch.
kerben, *vb.* notch.
Kerker, -, *n.m.* jail, prison.
Kerl, -e, *n.m.* fellow, guy.
Kern, -e, *n.m.* kernel, pit, core; nucleus; gist.
Kernenergie, *n.f.* nuclear energy.
Kerngehäuse, -, *n.nt.* core.
Kernhaus, -̈er, *n.nt.* core.
Kernkraftwerk, -e, *n.nt.* nuclear power plant.
Kernphysik, *n.f.* nuclear physics.
Kernspaltung, -en, *n.f.* nuclear fission.
Kerosin', *n.nt.* kerosene.
Kerze, -n, *n.f.* candle.
Kessel, -, *n.m.* kettle, boiler.
Kette, -n, *n.f.* chain.
ketten, *vb.* chain, link.
Kettenreaktion, -en, *n.f.* chain reaction.
Ketzer, -, *n.m.* heretic.
Ketzerei', *n.f.* heresy.
keuchen, *vb.* gasp.
Keuchhusten, *n.m.* whooping-cough.
Keule, -n, *n.f.* club, cudgel; (meat) leg, joint.
keusch, *adj.* chaste.
Keuschheit, *n.f.* chastity.
kichern, *vb.* giggle.
Kiefer, -, *n.m.* jaw.
Kiefer, -n, *n.f.* pine.
Kiel, -e, *n.m.* keel.
Kielwasser, *n.nt.* wake.
Kieme, -n, *n.f.* gill.
Kiepe, -n, *n.f.* basket (carried on the back).
Kies, -e, *n.m.* gravel.
Kilo, -s, *n.nt.* kilogram.
Kilohertz, *n.nt.* kilohertz.
Kilome'ter, *n.m. or nt.* kilometer.
Kilowatt', -, *n.nt.* kilowatt.
Kind, -er, *n.nt.* child.

Kinderarzt, -̈e, *n.m.* pediatrician.
Kinderärztin, -nen, *n.f.* pediatrician.
Kinderbett, -en, *n.nt.* crib.
Kindergarten, -̈, *n.m.* kindergarten.
Kinderlähmung, -en, *n.f.* infantile paralysis, polio.
kinderlos, *adj.* childless.
Kinderraub, -en, *n.m.* kidnapping.
Kinderräuber, -, *n.m.* kidnapper.
Kindersportwagen, -, *n.m.* stroller.
Kinderwagen, -, *n.m.* baby carriage.
Kinderzimmer, -, *n.nt.* nursery.
Kindheit, -en, *n.f.* childhood.
kindisch, *adj.* childish.
kindlich, *adj.* childlike.
Kinn, -e, *n.nt.* chin.
Kino, -s, *n.nt.* movie theater.
Kiosk', -e, *n.m.* kiosk, newsstand.
kippen, *vb.* tip, tilt.
Kirche, -n, *n.f.* church.
Kirchenlied, -er, *n.nt.* hymn.
Kirchenschiff, -e, *n.nt.* nave.
Kirchenstuhl, -̈e, *n.m.* pew.
Kirchhof, -̈e, *n.m.* churchyard.
kirchlich, *adj.* ecclesiastical.
Kirchspiel, -e, *n.nt.* parish.
Kirchturm, -̈e, *n.m.* steeple.
Kirsche, -n, *n.f.* cherry.
Kissen, -, *n.nt.* cushion, pillow.
Kissenbezug, -̈e, *n.m.* pillowcase.
Kiste, -n, *n.f.* crate, chest.
Kitsch, *n.m.* trash.
Kittel, -, *n.m.* smock.
kitzeln, *vb.* tickle.
kitzlig, *adj.* ticklish.
klaffen, *vb.* gape, yawn.
Klage, -n, *n.f.* complaint; suit.
Kläger, -, *n.m.* plaintiff.
Klägerin, -nen, *n.f.* plaintiff.
kläglich, *adj.* miserable.
Klammer, -n, *n.f.* clamp, clasp; parenthesis.
Klamot'ten, *n.pl.* duds, rags, stuff.
Klampe, -n, *n.f.* cleat.
Klang, -̈e, *n.m.* sound, ring(ing).
Klappbett, -en, *n.nt.* folding bed.
Klappe, -n, *n.f.* flap, lid, valve.
klappen, *vb.* (*tr.*) flap, fold; (*intr.*) come out right.
klappern, *vb.* clatter, chatter, rattle.

Klaps, -e, *n.m.* slap.

klar, *adj.* clear.

klären, *vb.* clear.

Klarheit, -en, *n.f.* clarity.

Klarinet'te, -n, *n.f.* clarinet.

klar·legen, *vb.* clarify.

klar·stellen, *vb.* clarify.

Klasse, -e, *n.f.* class.

Klassenkamerad, -en, -en, *n.m.* classmate.

Klassenkameradin, -nen, *n.f.* classmate.

Klassenzimmer, -, *n.nt.* classroom.

klassifizie'ren, *vb.* classify.

Klassifizie'rung, -en, *n.f.* classification.

klassisch, *adj.* classic(al).

Klatsch, -e, *n.m.* gossip.

klatschen, *vb.* clap; gossip.

Klaue, -n, *n.f.* claw.

klauen, *vb.* snitch.

Klausel, -n, *n.f.* clause, proviso.

Klavier', -e, *n.nt.* piano.

Klebemittel, -, *n.nt.* glue, adhesive.

kleben, *vb.* paste; stick.

Klebgummi, *n.m.* mucilage.

klebrig, *adj.* sticky.

Klebstoff, -e, *n.m.* paste.

kleckern, *vb.* spill, make a spot.

Klecks, -e, *n.m.* spot, stain.

Klee, *n.m.* clover.

Kleid, -er *n.nt.* dress; *(pl.)* clothes.

kleiden, *vb.* clothe, dress.

Kleiderbügel, -, *n.m.* hanger.

Kleiderhändler, -, *n.m.* clothier.

Kleiderschrank, ⁼e, *n.m.* clothes closet, wardrobe.

kleidsam, *adj.* becoming.

Kleidung, -en, *n.f.* clothing.

Kleidungsstück, -e, *n.nt.* garment.

klein, *adj.* little, small.

Kleingeld, -er, *n.nt.* change.

Kleinheit, -en, *n.f.* smallness.

Kleinigkeit, -en, *n.f.* trifle.

kleinlaut, *adj.* meek, subdued.

kleinlich, *adj.* petty.

Kleinod, -ien, *n.nt.* jewel, gem.

Kleister, -, *n.m.* paste.

Klemme, -n, *n.f.* clamp; dilemma, jam, tight spot.

klemmen, *vb.* pinch, jam.

Klempner, -, *n.m.* plumber.

Klepper, -, *n.m.* hack.

klerikal', *adj.* clerical.

Kleriker, -, *n.m.* clergyman.

Klerus, *n.m.* clergy.

klettern, *vb.* climb.

klicken, *vb.* click (computer).

Klient', -en, -en, *n.m.* client.

Klien'tin, -nen, *n.f.* client.

Klima, -a'te, *n.nt.* climate.

Klimaanlage, -n, *n.f.* air conditioning (system).

klima'tisch, *adj.* climatic.

klimatisie'ren, *vb.* air-condition.

klimmen*, *vb.* climb.

Klinge, -n, *n.f.* blade.

Klingel, -n, *n.f.* (small) bell; buzzer.

klingeln, *vb.* ring.

klingen*, *vb.* ring, sound.

Klinik, -en, *n.f.* clinic, hospital.

klinisch, *adj.* clinical.

Klippe, -n, *n.f.* cliff, crag.

Klistier', -e, *n.nt.* enema.

Klo, -s, *n.nt.* (short for **Klosett'**) bathroom, toilet.

Kloa'ke, -n, *n.f.* sewer, drain.

klobig, *adj.* clumsy.

klopfen, *vb.* knock, beat.

Klops, -e, *n.m.* meatball.

Klosett', -e, *n.nt.* water closet.

Kloß, ⁼e, *n.m.* clump; dumpling.

Kloster, ⁼, *n.nt.* monastery, nunnery.

Klosterbruder, ⁼, *n.m.* friar.

Klostergang, ⁼e, *n.m.* cloister(s).

Klotz, ⁼e, *n.m.* block.

Klub, -s, *n.m.* club (social).

Kluft, ⁼e, *n.f.* gap, cleft, fissure.

klug(⁻), *adj.* clever, smart.

Klugheit, -en, *n.f.* cleverness.

Klumpen, -, *n.m.* lump.

klumpig, *adj.* lumpy.

knabbern, *vb.* nibble.

Knabe, -n, -n, *n.m.* lad, youth.

knacken, *vb.* click.

Knall, -e, *n.m.* bang, crack, pop.

knallen, *vb.* bang, pop.

knapp, *adj.* scarce, scant, tight, terse.

Knappheit, -en, *n.f.* scarcity, shortage, terseness.

knarren, *vb.* creak, rattle.

Knäuel, -, *n.m. or nt.* clew, ball; throng, crowd.

knauserig, *adj.* stingy.
Knebel, -, *n.m.* cudgel; gag.
knebeln, *vb.* bind, gag.
Knecht, -e, *n.m.* servant, farm hand.
Knechtschaft, -en, *n.f.* bondage, servitude.
kneifen*, *vb.* pinch.
Kneifzange, -n, *n.f.* pliers.
Kneipe, -n, *n.f.* tavern, pub, joint.
kneten, *vb.* knead.
Knick, -e, *n.m.* bend, crack.
knicken, *vb.* bend, fold, crack.
Knicks, -e, *n.m.* curtsy.
Knie, -i'e, *n.nt.* knee.
kni'en, *vb.* kneel.
Kniff, -e, *n.m.* pinch; trick.
knifflig, *adj.* tricky.
knipsen, *vb.* snap, punch (ticket), take a snapshot, snap one's fingers.
knirschen, *vb.* grate, crunch; gnash (teeth).
knistern, *vb.* crackle.
knittern, *vb.* wrinkle.
Knöchel, -, *n.m.* knuckle.
Knochen, -, *n.m.* bone.
knochenlos, *adj.* boneless.
knochig, *adj.* bony.
Knödel, -, *n.m.* dumpling.
Knopf, -̈e, *n.m.* button.
Knopfloch, -̈er, *n.nt.* buttonhole.
Knorpel, -, *n.m.* cartilage.
Knorren, -, *n.m.* knot, gnarl.
knorrig, *adj.* knotty, gnarled.
Knospe, -n, *n.f.* bud.
knospen, *vb.* bud.
Knoten, -, *n.m.* knot.
knoten, *vb.* knot.
Knotenpunkt, -e, *n.m.* junction.
knüpfen, *vb.* tie, knot.
Knüppel, -, *n.m.* cudgel, club.
knurren, *vb.* growl.
knusp(e)rig, *adj.* crisp, crusty.
Kobalt, *n.m.* cobalt.
Koch, -̈e, *n.m.* cook.
Kochbuch, -̈er, *n.nt.* cookbook.
kochen, *vb.* cook, boil.
Köchin, -nen, *n.f.* cook.
Kode, -s, *n.m.* code.
Kodein', *n.nt.* codein.
ködern, *vb.* decoy.
Kodex, -dizes, *n.m.* code.
kodifizie'ren, *vb.* codify.
Koffein', -e, *n.nt.* caffeine.

koffein'frei, *adj.* decaffeinated.
Koffer, -, *n.m.* suitcase, trunk.
Kofferkuli, -s, *n.m.* baggage cart (airport).
Kofferraum, *n.m.* trunk (auto).
Kognak, -s, *n.m.* brandy, cognac.
Kohl, -e, *n.m.* cabbage.
Kohle, -n, *n.f.* coal.
kohlen, *vb.* char.
Kohlenoxyd', *n.nt.* carbon monoxide.
Kohlenstoff, -e, *n.m.* carbon.
Koje, -n, *n.f.* bunk.
Kokain', *n.nt.* cocaine.
kokett', *adj.* coquettish.
Koket'te, -n, *n.f.* coquette.
kokettie'ren, *vb.* flirt.
Kokon', -s, *n.m.* cocoon.
Koks, -e, *n.m.* coke.
Kolben, -, *n.m.* butt; piston.
Kolle'ge, -n, -n, *n.m.* colleague.
Kolle'gin, -nen, *n.f.* colleague.
kollektiv', *adj.* collective.
Koller, *n.m.* rage, frenzy.
kölnisch Wasser, *n.nt.* eau-de-cologne.
kolonial', *adj.* colonial.
Kolonial'waren, *n.pl.* groceries.
Kolonial'warenhändler, -, *n.m.* grocer.
Kolonie', -i'en, *n.f.* colony.
Kolonisation', *n.f.* colonization.
kolonisie'ren, *vb.* colonize.
Kolon'ne, -n, *n.f.* column.
Kolorit', -e, *n.nt.* color(ing).
kolossal', *adj.* colossal.
Koma, *n.nt.* coma.
Kombi, -s, *n.m.* station wagon.
Kombination', -en, *n.f.* combination.
kombinie'ren, *vb.* combine.
Komet', -en, -en, *n.m.* comet.
Komiker, -, *n.m.* comedian.
Komikerin, -nen, *n.f.* comedienne.
komisch, *adj.* funny.
Komitee', -s, *n.nt.* committee.
Komma, -s, *(or -ta), n.nt.* comma.
Kommandant', -en, -en, *n.m.* commander, commanding officer.
Kommandantur', -en, *n.f.* commander's office.
kommen*, *vb.* come.

Kommentar', -e, *n.m.* commentary.

Kommenta'tor, -o'ren, *n.m.* commentator.

kommentie'ren, *vb.* comment on.

Kommissar', -e, *n.m.* commissary, commissioner.

Kommissa'rin, -nen, *n.f.* commissary, commissioner.

Kommission', -en, *n.f.* commission.

Kommo'de, -n, *n.f.* bureau.

kommunal', *adj.* communal, municipal.

Kommunikant', -en, -en, *n.m.* communicant.

Kommunion', -en, *n.f.* communion.

Kommuniqué', -s, *n.nt.* communiqué.

Kommunis'mus, *n.m.* communism.

Kommunist', -en, -en, *n.m.* communist.

Kommunis'tin, -nen, *n.f.* communist.

kommunis'tisch, *adj.* communistic.

kommunizie'ren, *vb.* commune; communicate.

Komödiant', -en, -en, *n.m.* comedian.

Komödian'tin, -nen, *n.f.* comedienne.

Komö'die, -n, *n.f.* comedy.

Kompagnon', -s, *n.m.* (business) partner.

kompakt', *adj.* compact.

Komparative, -e, *n.m.* comparative (degree).

Kompaß', -sse, *n.m.* compass.

kompensie'rend, *adj.* compensatory.

kompetent', *adj.* competent, authoritative.

Kompetenz', -en, *n.f.* competence, authority, jurisdiction.

komplex', *adj.* complex.

Komplex', -e, *n.m.* complex.

Komplikation', -en, *n.f.* complication.

Kompliment', -e, *n.nt.* compliment.

Kompli'ze, -n, -n, *n.m.* accomplice.

Kompli'zin, -nen, *n.f.* accomplice.

komplizie'ren, *vb.* complicate.

kompliziert', *adj.* complicated.

Komplott', -e, *n.nt.* plot.

komponie'ren, *vb.* compose.

Komponist', -en, -en, *n.m.* composer.

Komponis'tin, -nen, *n.f.* composer.

Komposition', -en, *n.f.* composition.

Kompott', -e, *n.nt.* compote.

Kompres'se, -n, *n.f.* compress.

Kompression', -en, *n.f.* compression.

Kompres'sor, -o'ren, *n.m.* compressor.

Kompromiß', -sse, *n.m.* compromise.

kompromittie'ren, *vb.* compromise.

Kompu'ter, -, *n.m.* computer.

Kondensation', -en, *n.f.* condensation.

Kondensa'tor, -o'ren, *n.m.* condenser.

kondensie'ren, *vb.* condense.

Kondi'tor, -o'ren, *n.m.* confectioner, pastry baker.

Konditorei', -ei'en, *n.f.* café and pastry shop.

Kondom', -e, *n.m.* condom.

Konfekt', -e, *n.nt.* candy.

Konfektion', *n.f.* ready-made clothing.

Konferenz', -en, *n.f.* conference.

Konfirmation', -en, *n.f.* confirmation.

konfiszie'ren, *vb.* confiscate.

Konfitü're, -n, *n.f.* jam.

Konflikt', -e, *n.m.* conflict.

konform', *adj.* in conformity.

konfrontie'ren, *vb.* confront.

konfus', *adj.* confused.

Kongreß', -sse, *n.m.* congress.

König, -e, *n.m.* king.

Königin, -nen, *n.f.* queen.

königlich, *adj.* royal.

Königreich, -e, *n.nt.* kingdom.

Königtum, *n.nt.* kingship, royalty.

Konjugation', -en, *n.f.* conjugation.

konjugie'ren, *vb.* conjugate.

Konjunktion', -en, *n.f.* conjunction.

Konjunktiv, -e, *n.m.* subjunctive.

konkav', *adj.* concave.

konkret', *adj.* concrete.

Konkurrent', -en, -en, *n.m.* competitor.

Konkurren'tin, -nen, *n.f.* competitor.

Konkurrenz', -en, *n.f.* competition.

konkurrie'ren, *vb.* compete.

Konkurs', -e, *n.m.* bankruptcy.

können*, *vb.* can, be able to.

konsequent', *adj.* consistent.

Konservatis'mus, *n.m.* conservatism.

konservativ', *adj.* conservative.

Konservato'rium, -en, *n.nt.* conservatory.

Konser'venfabrik, -en, *n.f.* cannery.

konservie'ren, *vb.* preserve.

Konservie'rung, -en, *n.f.* conservation.

Konsistenz', -en, *n.f.* consistency.

konsolidie'ren, *vb.* consolidate.

Konsonant', -en, -en, *n.m.* consonant.

konstant', *adj.* constant.

Konstellation', -en, *n.f.* constellation.

konstituie'ren, *vb.* constitute.

Konstitution', -en, *f.* constitution.

konstitutionell', *adj.* constitutional.

konstruie'ren, *vb.* construct.

Konstrukteur', -e, *n.m.* constructor, designer.

Konstruktion', -en, *n.f.* construction.

Konsul, -n, *n.m.* consul.

konsula'risch, *adj.* consular.

Konsulat', -e, *n.nt.* consulate.

Konsum', -s, *n.m.* consumption; (short for **Konsum'laden**, -̈, *n.m.*) cooperative store, co-op.

Konsument', -en, -en, *n.m.* consumer.

Konsum'verein, -e, *n.m.* cooperative (society).

Kontakt', -e, *n.m.* contact.

Kontinent, -e, *n.m.* continent.

kontinental', *adj.* continental.

Konto, -s *or* -ten *or* -ti, *n.nt.* account.

Kontobuch, -̈er, *n.nt.* bankbook, account book.

Kontor', -e, *n.nt.* office.

Kontorist', -en, *n.m.* clerk.

Kontoris'tin, -nen, *n.f.* clerk.

Kontrast', -e, *n.m.* contrast.

Kontroll'abschnitt, -e, *n.m.* stub.

Kontrol'le, -n, *n.f.* control, check.

kontrollier'bar, *adj.* controllable.

kontrollie'ren, *vb.* control, check.

Kontroll'marke, -n, *n.f.* check.

Kontur', -en, *n.f.* contour, outline.

Konvaleszenz', *n.f.* convalescence.

Konvention', -en, *n.f.* convention.

konventionell', *adj.* conventional.

konvergie'ren, *vb.* converge.

konvertie'ren, *vb.* convert.

konvex', *adj.* convex.

Konvulsion', -en, *n.f.* convulsion.

konvulsiv', *adj.* convulsive.

Konzentration', -en, *n.f.* concentration.

Konzentrations'lager, -, *n.nt.* concentration camp.

konzentrie'ren, *vb.* concentrate.

konzen'trisch, *adj.* concentric.

Konzept', -e, *n.nt.* plan, draft; (aus dem K. bringen*) confuse.

Konzern', -e, *n.m.* (business) trust, pool.

Konzert', -e, *n.nt.* concert.

Konzert'saal, -säle, *n.m.* concert hall.

Konzession', -en, *n.f.* concession.

koordinie'ren, *vb.* coordinate.

Kopf, -̈e, *n.m.* head.

Kopfhaut, -̈e, *n.f.* scalp.

Kopfhörer, -, *n.m.* earphone.

Kopfkissen, -, *n.nt.* pillow.

Kopfsalat, -e, *n.m.* lettuce.

Kopfschmerzen, *n.pl.* headache.
Kopfsprung, **ë,** *n.m.* dive.
Kopftuch, **ër,** *n.nt.* kerchief.
Kopie', **-i'en,** *n.f.* copy.
kopie'ren, *vb.* copy, duplicate.
Kopier'maschine, -n, *n.f.* photo-copier; copying machine.
koppeln, *vb.* couple.
Koral'le, -n, *n.f.* coral.
Korb, **ë,** *n.m.* basket.
Korbball, **ë,** *n.m.* basketball.
Korbwiege, -n, *n.f.* bassinet.
Korduanleder, -, *n.nt.* cordovan.
Kore'a, *n.nt.* Korea.
Korin'the, -n, *n.f.* currant.
Kork, -e, *n.m.* cork (material).
Korken, -, *n.m.* cork (stopper).
Korkenzieher, -, *n.m.* corkscrew.
Korn, -, *n.m.* grain whiskey.
Korn, -e, *n.m.* (type of) grain.
Korn, **ër,** *n.nt.* (individual) grain.
Körnchen, -, *n.nt.* granule.
Kornett', -e, *n.nt.* cornet.
körnig, *adj.* granular.
Kornkammer, -n, *n.f.* granary.
Kornspeicher, -, *n.m.* granary.
Körper, -, *n.m.* body.
Körperbau, *n.m.* physique.
Körperbehinderung, -en, *n.f.* physical disability.
Körperchen, -, *n.nt.* corpuscle.
Körperkraft, *n.f.* physical strength.
körperlich, *adj.* physical, corporeal.
Körperpflege, *n.f.* hygiene.
Körperschaft, -en, *n.f.* corporation.
Korps, -, *n.nt.* corps.
korpulent', *adj.* corpulent.
korrekt', *adj.* correct.
Korrekt'heit, -en, *n.f.* correctness.
korrektiv', *adj.* corrective.
Korresponden't, -en, -en, *n.m.* correspondent.
Korresponden'tin, -nen, *n.f.* correspondent.
Korrespondenz', -en, *n.f.* correspondence.
korrespondie'ren, *vb.* correspond.
Korridor, -e, *n.m.* corridor.
korrigie'ren, *vb.* correct.
korrumpie'ren, *vb.* corrupt.

korrupt', *adj.* corrupt.
Korruption', -en, *n.f.* corruption.
Korsett', -s, *n.nt.* corset.
kosen, *vb.* fondle, caress.
Kosename(n), -, *n.m.* pet name.
Kosme'tik, *n.f.* cosmetics.
kosme'tisch, *adj.* cosmetic.
kosmisch, *adj.* cosmic.
kosmopoli'tisch, *adj.* cosmopolitan.
Kosmos, *n.m.* cosmos.
Kost, *n.f.* food, fare, board.
kostbar, *adj.* costly, precious.
kosten, *vb.* cost; taste.
Kosten, *n.pl.* cost, charges, expenses.
Kostenanschlag, **ë,** *n.m.* estimate.
kostenfrei, *adj.* free of charge.
kostenlos, *adj.* free, without cost.
Kostgänger, -, *n.m.* boarder.
köstlich, *adj.* delicious.
kostspielig, *adj.* expensive.
Kostspieligkeit, -en, *n.f.* costliness.
Kostüm', -e, *n.nt.* costume; matching coat and skirt.
Kot, *n.m.* dirt, mud, filth.
Kotelett', -s, *n.nt.* cutlet, chop.
Köter, -, *n.m.* cur.
kotzen, *vb.* vomit.
Krabbe, -n, *n.f.* shrimp, crab.
Krach, -e, *or* -s, *n.m.* bang, crash, racket; row, fight.
krachen, *vb.* crash.
Kraft, -, *n.f.* strength, force, power.
kraft, *prep.* by virtue of.
Kraftbrühe, -, *n.f.* bouillon.
Kraftfahrer, -, *n.m.* motorist.
Kraftfahrerin, -nen, *n.f.* motorist.
Kraftfahrzeug, -e, *n.nt.* motor vehicle.
kräftig, *adj.* strong.
kraftlos, *adj.* powerless.
kraftstrotzend, *adj.* vigorous.
kraftvoll, *adj.* powerful.
Kraftwagen, -, *n.m.* automobile.
Kragen, -, *n.m.* collar.
Krähe, -n, *n.f.* crow.
Kralle, -n, *n.f.* claw.
Kram, **ë,** *n.m.* stuff, junk; business, affairs; retail trade, goods.
kramen, *vb.* rummage.

Krämer, -, *n.m.* small tradesman.

Krampf, -̈e, *n.m.* cramp, spasm.

krampfhaft, *adj.* spasmodic.

Kran, -̈e, *n.m.* crane, derrick.

Kranich, -e, *n.m.* crane.

krank(-), *adj.* sick.

kranken, *vb.* suffer from, ail.

kränken, *vb.* offend.

Krankenauto, -s, *n.nt.* ambulance.

Krankenhaus, -̈er, *n.nt.* hospital.

Krankenkasse, *n.f.* health insurance.

Krankenpfleger, -, *n.m.* male nurse.

Krankenschwester, -n, *n.f.* nurse.

Krankenwagen -, *n.m.* ambulance.

krankhaft, *adj.* morbid.

Krankheit, -en, *n.f.* sickness, disease.

kränklich, *adj.* sickly.

Kränkung, -en, *n.f.* offense.

Kranz, -̈e, *n.m.* wreath.

kraß, *adj.* crass, gross.

Kraßheit, -en, *n.f.* grossness.

kratzen, *vb.* scrape, scratch.

kraulen, *vb.* crawl.

kraus, *adj.* curly, crisp.

Krause, -n, *n.f.* frill.

kräuseln, *vb.* curl, ruffle.

Kraut, -̈er, *n.nt.* herb, plant.

Krawat'te, -n, *n.f.* necktie.

Krebs, -e, *n.m.* crayfish; *(med.)* cancer.

krebserregend, *adj.* carcinogenic.

kreden'zen, *vb.* serve, offer.

Kredit', -e, *n.m.* credit.

Kredit'karte, -n, *n.f.* credit card.

Kreide, -n, *n.f.* chalk.

kreidig, *adj.* chalky.

Kreis, -e, *n.m.* circle; district.

Kreisbahn, -en, *n.f.* orbit.

kreischen, *vb.* shriek.

Kreisel, -, *n.m.* top.

kreiseln, *vb.* spin like a top, gyrate.

kreisen, *vb.* circle, revolve.

kreisförmig, *adj.* circular.

Kreislauf, -̈e, *n.m.* circulation, circuit.

Kremato'rium, -ien, *n.nt.* crematorium.

Krempe, -n, *n.f.* brim.

Krepp, *n.m.* crepe.

Kretonn'e, -s, *n.m.* cretonne.

Kreuz, -e, *n.nt.* cross; back; *(music)* sharp.

kreuzen, *vb.* cross; cruise, tack.

Kreuzer, -, *n.m.* cruiser.

Kreuzgang, -̈e, *n.m.* cloister.

kreuzigen, *vb.* crucify.

Kreuzigung, -en, *n.f.* crucifixion.

kreuz und quer, *adv.* criss-cross.

Kreuzung, -en, *n.f.* cross(breed); crossing, intersection.

Kreuzverhör, -e, *n.nt.* cross-examination.

Kreuzzug, -̈e, *n.m.* crusade.

Kreuzzügler, -, *n.m.* crusader.

kribbelig, *adj.* jittery.

kriechen*, *vb.* crawl, creep; grovel.

Krieg, -e, *n.m.* war.

kriegen, *vb.* get.

Krieger, -, *n.m.* warrior.

kriegerisch, *adj.* warlike.

Kriegsdienst, -e, *n.m.* military service.

Kriegsdienstverweigerer, -, *n.m.* conscientious objector.

Kriegsgefangen-, *n.m.* prisoner of war.

Kriegsgericht, -e, *n.nt.* court-martial.

Kriegslist, -en, *n.f.* stratagem.

Kriegslust, -̈e, *n.f.* belligerence.

kriegslustig, *adj.* bellicose.

Kriegsmacht, -̈e, *n.f.* military forces.

Kriegsschiff, -e, *n.nt.* warship.

Kriegsverbrechen, -, *n.nt.* war crime.

kriegsversehrt, *adj.* disabled (by war).

Kriegszug, -̈e, *n.m.* military expedition.

Kriegszustand, -̈e, *n.m.* state of war.

kriminal', *adj.* criminal.

Kriminal'film, -e, *n.m.* thriller.

Krippe, -n, *n.f.* crib.

Krise, -n, *n.f.* crisis.

Kristall', -e, *n.nt.* crystal.

Kristall', -e, *n.m.* crystal, crystalline.

kristal'len, *adj.* crystal, crystalline.

kristallisie'ren, *vb.* crystallize.

Kritik', **-en**, *n.f.* criticism, critique, review.

Kritiker, **-**, *n.m.* critic.

Kritikerin, **-nen**, *n.f.* critic.

kritisch, *adj.* critical.

kritisie'ren, *vb.* criticize.

kritzeln, *vb.* scribble.

Krocket·spiel, **-e**, *n.nt.* croquet.

Krokodil', **-e**, *n.nt.* crocodile.

Krone, **-n**, *n.f.* crown.

krönen, *vb.* crown.

Kronleuchter, **-**, *n.m.* chandelier.

Kronprinz, **-en**, **-en**, *n.m.* crown prince.

Krönung, **-en**, *n.f.* coronation.

Kropf, **̈-e**, *n.m.* crop; goiter.

Krücke, **-n**, *n.f.* crutch.

Krug, **̈-e**, *n.m.* pitcher.

Krümel, **-**, *n.m.* crumb.

krümeln, *vb.* crumble.

krumm (**̈-**, **-**), *adj.* crooked.

krümmen, *vb.* bend; **(sich k.)** warp, buckle, double up (with pain or laughter).

Krümmung, **-en**, *n.f.* bend, curve; curvature.

Krüppel, **-**, *n.m.* cripple.

Kruste, **-n**, *n.f.* crust.

Kruzifix, **-e**, *n.nt.* crucifix.

Kübel, **-**, *n.m.* bucket.

Kubik'-, *cpds.* cubic.

kubisch, *adj.* cubic.

Küche, **-n**, *n.f.* kitchen.

Kuchen, **-**, *n.m.* cake.

Küchenchef, **-s**, *n.m.* chef.

Küchenzettel, **-**, *n.m.* menu, bill of fare.

Kugel, **-n**, *n.f.* sphere, ball, bullet.

kugelförmig, *adj.* spherical; globular.

Kuh, **̈-e**, *n.f.* cow.

kühl, *adj.* cool.

Kühle, *n.f.* coolness.

kühlen, *vb.* cool.

Kühler, **-**, *n.m.* auto radiator.

Kühlschrank, **̈-e**, *n.m.* refrigerator.

kühn, *adj.* bold.

Kühnheit, **-en**, *n.f.* boldness.

Küken, **-**, *n.nt.* chick.

kulina'risch, *adj.* culinary.

Kult, **-e**, *n.m.* cult.

kultivie'ren, *vb.* cultivate.

kultiviert', *adj.* cultured.

Kultivie'rung, *n.f.* cultivation.

Kultur', **-en**, *n.f.* culture.

kulturell', *adj.* cultural.

Kümmel, *n.m.* caraway.

Kummer, **-**, *n.m.* sorrow, grief.

kümmerlich, *adj.* miserable.

kümmern, *vb.* grieve, trouble, concern; **(sich k. um)** care about, look out for.

kummervoll, *adj.* sorrowful.

kund, *adj.* known.

Kunde, **-n**, **-n**, *n.m.* customer, client.

Kundin, **-nen**, *n.f.* customer, client.

Kunde, **-n**, *n.f.* knowledge, information.

kund·geben*, *vb.* make known.

Kundgebung, **-en**, *n.f.* demonstration.

kundig, *adj.* well informed, knowing.

kündigen, *vb.* give notice; cancel.

Kündigung, **-en**, *n.f.* cancellation.

Kundschaft, **-en**, *n.f.* clientele.

künftig, *adj.* future.

Kunst, **̈-e**, *n.f.* art.

künsteln, *vb.* contrive.

kunstfertig, *adj.* skillful.

Künstler, **-**, *n.m.* artist.

Künstlerin, **-nen**, *n.f.* artist.

künstlerisch, *adj.* artistic.

Künstlertum, *n.nt.* artistry.

künstlich, *adj.* artificial.

kunstlos, *adj.* artless.

Kunstseide, **-n**, *n.f.* rayon.

Kunststoff, **-e**, *n.m.* plastic.

Kunststück, **-e**, *n.nt.* feat, stunt.

kunstvoll, *adj.* artistic.

Kunstwerk, **-e**, *n.nt.* work of art.

Kunstwissenschaft, *n.f.* fine arts.

Kupfer, *n.nt.* copper.

kuppeln, *vb.* couple, join; pander.

Kuppelung, **-en**, *n.f.* clutch.

Kur, **-en**, *n.f.* cure.

Kurbel, **-n**, *n.f.* crank.

Kürbis, **-se**, *n.m.* pumpkin, gourd.

Kurier', **-e**, *n.m.* courier.

kurie'ren, *vb.* cure.

kurios', *adj.* odd, strange.

Kuriosität', **-en**, *n.f.* curio.

Kurio'sum, **-sa**, *n.nt.* freak.

Kurort, -e, *n.m.* resort.
Kurs, -e, *n.m.* course; rate of exchange.
Kursbuch, ̈-er, *n.nt.* timetable.
kursie'ren, *vb.* circulate.
kursiv', *adj.* italic.
Kursus, Kurse, *n.m.* course.
Kurve, -n, *n.f.* curve.
kurz(̈-), *adj.* short; **(k. und bündig)** short and to the point.
Kürze, -n, *n.f.* shortness, brevity.
kürzen, *vb.* shorten.
kürzlich, *adj.* recently.

Kurzschluß, *n.m.* short circuit.
kurzsichtig, *adj.* near-sighted.
kurzum', *adv.* in short.
Kürzung, -en, *n.f.* shortening, cut.
Kurzwaren, *n.pl.* notions.
Kusi'ne, -n, *n.f.* cousin.
Kuß, ̈-sse, *n.m.* kiss.
küssen, *vb.* kiss.
Küste, -n, *n.f.* coast, shore.
Küster, -, *n.m.* sexton.
Kutsche, -n, *n.f.* coach.
Kuvert', -s, *n.nt.* envelope.

L

Labe, -n, *n.f.* refreshment, comfort.
laben, *vb.* refresh, comfort.
Laborato'rium, -rien, *n.nt.* laboratory.
Labsal, -e, *n.nt.* refreshment, comfort.
Labyrinth', -e, *n.nt.* labyrinth.
Lache, -n, *n.f.* puddle.
lächeln, *vb.* smile.
Lächeln, -, *n.nt.* smile.
lachen, *vb.* laugh.
Lachen, -, *n.nt.* laugh(ing).
lächerlich, *adj.* ridiculous.
Lachs, -, *n.m.* salmon.
Lack, -e, *n.m.* lacquer.
Lackleder, -, *n.nt.* patent leather.
Lade, -n, *n.f.* box, chest, drawer.
laden*, *vb.* load, charge; summon.
Laden, ̈-, *n.m.* shop; shutter.
Ladendieb, -e, *n.m.* shop-lifter.
Ladendiebin, -nen, *n.f.* shop-lifter.
Ladenkasse, -n, *n.f.* till.
Ladentisch, -e, *n.m.* counter.
Ladung, -en, *n.f.* load, cargo, shipment; charge.
Lage, -n, *n.f.* location, situation, condition.
Lager, -, *n.nt.* camp, lair, bed; deposit, depot, supply; bearing.
Lagerhaus, ̈-er, *n.nt.* storehouse.
lagern, *vb.* lay down, store, deposit; **(sich l.)** camp; be deposited.
Lagerung, -en, *n.f.* storage, bearing; stratification, grain.
Lagu'ne, -n, *n.f.* lagoon.
lahm, *adj.* lame.

lähmen, *vb.* lame, cripple, paralyze.
Lähmung, -en, *n.f.* paralysis.
Laib, -e, *n.m.* loaf.
Laie, -n, -n, *n.m.* layman.
Laienstand, *n.m.* laity.
Laken, -, *n.nt.* sheet.
Lamm, ̈-er, *n.nt.* lamb.
Lampe, -n, *n.f.* lamp.
lancie'ren, *vb.* launch.
Land, ̈-er, *n.nt.* land, country.
Landbau, *n.m.* agriculture.
Landebahn, -en, *n.f.* flight strip, runway.
landen, *vb.* land.
Landesverrat, *n.m.* high treason.
Landkarte, -n, *n.f.* map.
landläufig, *adj.* usual, ordinary.
ländlich, *adj.* rural.
Landschaft, -en, *n.f.* landscape, countryside.
Landser, -, *n.m.* common soldier, GI.
Landsmann, -leute, *n.m.* compatriot.
Landsmännin, -en, *n.f.* compatriot.
Landstraße, -n, *n.f.* highway.
Landstrich, -e, *n.m.* region.
Landung, -en, *n.f.* landing.
Landwirt, -e, *n.m.* farmer.
Landwirtin, -nen, *n.f.* farmer.
Landwirtschaft, *n.f.* agriculture.
landwirtschaftlich, *adj.* agricultural.
lang (̈-), *adj.* long, tall.
lange, *adv.* for a long time.
Länge, -n, *n.f.* length; longitude.

langen, *vb.* hand; suffice.
Langeweile, *n.f.* boredom.
langlebig, *adj.* long-lived.
länglich, *adj.* oblong.
Langmut, *n.m.* patience.
langmütig, *adj.* long-suffering.
längs, *adv. & prep.* along.
langsam, *adj.* slow.
Langsamkeit, *n.f.* slowness.
längst, *adv.* long since.
langweilen, *vb.* bore.
langweilig, *adj.* boring.
langwierig, *adj.* lengthy.
Lanze, -n, *n.f.* lance.
Lappa'lie, -n, *n.f.* trifle.
Lappen, -, *n.m.* rag; lobe.
Lärm, *n.m.* noise.
Larve, -n, *n.f.* mask; larva.
Laserstrahl, -en, *n.m.* laser beam.
lassen*, *vb.* let, permit; cause to, have (someone do something, something done); leave; leave off, stop.
lässig, *adj.* indolent, careless.
Last, -en, *n.f.* burden, encumbrance; load, weight, cargo.
Lastauto, -s, *n.nt.* truck.
lasten, *vb.* weigh heavily, be a burden.
Laster, -, *n.nt.* vice.
lasterhaft, *adj.* vicious, wicked.
lästern, *vb.* slander, blaspheme.
lästig, *adj.* troublesome, disagreeable.
Lastkraftwagen, -, *n.m.* (motor) truck.
Lastwagen, -n, *n.m.* (motor) truck.
Latein', *n.nt.* Latin.
latei'nisch, *adj.* Latin.
Later'ne, -n, *n.f.* lantern.
Latri'ne, -n, *n.f.* latrine.
latschen, *vb.* shuffle, slouch.
Latz, -e, *n.m.* bib, flap.
lau, *adj.* tepid, lukewarm.
Laub, *n.nt.* foliage.
Lauer, *n.f.* ambush.
lauern, *vb.* lurk, lie in wait for.
Lauf, -e, *n.m.* course, race, run; (gun) barrel.
Laufbahn, -en, *n.f.* career; runway, race track.
laufen*, *vb.* run, walk.
laufend, *adj.* running, current.

Läufer, -, *n.m.* runner; stair carpet; (chess) bishop.
Läuferin, -nen, *n.f.* runner.
Lauge, -n, *n.f.* lye.
Laune, -n, *n.f.* whim, caprice, fancy; mood, humor.
launenhaft, *adj.* capricious.
launig, *adj.* humorous.
launisch, *adj.* moody.
Laus, -e, *n.f.* louse.
lauschen, *vb.* listen.
lausig, *adj.* lousy.
laut, *adj.* loud, aloud.
laut, *prep.* according to.
Laut, -e, *n.m.* sound.
Laute, -n, *n.f.* lute.
lauten, *vb.* read, say.
läuten, *vb.* ring, peal, sound.
lauter, *adj.* pure, sheer, nothing but.
Lauterkeit, -en, *n.f.* purity.
läutern, *vb.* purify.
lautlos, *adj.* soundless, silent.
Lautsprecher, -, *n.m.* loudspeaker.
lauwarm, *adj.* lukewarm; halfhearted.
Lava, *n.f.* lava.
Laven'del, *n.m.* lavender.
lax, *adj.* lax.
Laxheit, -en, *n.f.* laxity.
leben, *vb.* live, be alive.
Leben, -, *n.nt.* life.
lebend, *adj.* living.
leben'dig, *adj.* living, alive; lively.
Leben'digkeit, *n.f.* liveliness, vivacity.
lebenserfahren, *adj.* experienced, sophisticated.
Lebensgefahr, -en, *n.f.* danger (to life).
lebensgefährlich, *adj.* highly dangerous.
Lebenskraft, *n.f.* vitality.
lebenslänglich, *adj.* lifelong, for life.
Lebensmittel, *n.pl.* provisions, groceries.
Lebensmittelgeschäft, -e, *n.nt.* grocery store.
Lebensstandard, *n.m.* standard of living.
Lebensstil, *n.m.* life style.
Lebensunterhalt, *n.m.* livelihood.

Leber, -n, *n.f.* liver.
Lebewesen, -, *n.nt.* living being, organism.
lebewohl', *interj.* farewell, adieu.
lebhaft, *adj.* lively.
leblos, *adj.* lifeless.
Lebzeiten, *n.pl.* lifetime.
lechzen, *vb.* thirst, languish.
leck, *adj.* leaky, having a leak.
Leck, -e, *n.nt.* leak.
lecken, *vb.* leak; lick.
lecker, *adj.* tasty, appetizing.
Leder, -, *n.nt.* leather.
ledern, *adj.* leather(y).
ledig, *adj.* unmarried, single; vacant; exempt.
lediglich, *adv.* merely.
leer, *adj.* empty, vacant, blank.
Leere, -, *n.f.* emptiness.
leeren, *vb.* empty.
Leerlauf, *n.m.* neutral (gear).
legal', *adj.* legal.
legalisie'ren, *vb.* legalize.
Legat', -e, *n.nt.* bequest.
legen, *vb.* lay, place, put; (**sich l.**) lie down, subside.
legendär', *adj.* legendary.
Legen'de, -n, *n.f.* legend.
Legie'rung, -en, *n.f.* alloy.
Legion', -en, *n.f.* legion.
legitim', *adj.* legitimate.
legitimie'ren, *vb.* legitimize; (**sich l.**) prove one's identity.
Lehm, *n.m.* loam, clay.
Lehne, -n, *n.f.* back, arm (of a chair), support.
lehnen, *vb.* lean.
Lehnstuhl, -̈e, *n.m.* armchair.
Lehrbuch, -̈er, *n.nt.* textbook.
Lehre, -n, *n.f.* doctrine, teaching, lesson; apprenticeship.
lehren, *vb.* teach.
Lehrer, -, *n.m.* teacher.
Lehrerin, -nen, *n.f.* teacher.
Lehrgang, -̈e, *n.m.* course of instruction.
Lehrplan, -̈e, *n.m.* curriculum.
lehrreich, *adj.* instructive.
Lehrsatz, -̈e, *n.m.* proposition.
Lehrstunde, -n, *n.f.* lesson.
Leib, -er, *n.m.* body; abdomen; womb.
leibhaft(ig), *adj.* incarnate, personified.
leiblich, *adj.* bodily.

Leiche, -n, *n.f.* corpse.
leicht, *adj.* light; easy.
Leichtathletik, *n.f.* track and field.
Leichter, -, *n.m.* barge.
leichtfertig, *adj.* frivolous.
Leichtfertigkeit, *n.f.* frivolity.
leichtgläubig, *adj.* gullible, credulous.
Leichtigkeit, -en, *n.f.* ease.
Leichtsinn, *n.m.* frivolity.
leichtsinnig, *adj.* frivolous, reckless.
leid, *adj.* (**es tut* mir l.**) I'm sorry.
Leid, *n.nt.* suffering, sorrow, harm.
leiden*, *vb.* suffer; stand, endure; (**gern l. mögen***) like.
Leiden, -, *n.nt.* suffering; illness.
Leidenschaft, -en, *n.f.* passion.
leidenschaftlich, *adj.* passionate.
leidenschaftslos, *adj.* dispassionate.
leider, *adv.* unfortunately.
leidig, *adj.* unpleasant.
leidlich, *adj.* tolerable.
Leier, -n, *n.f.* lyre.
leihen*, *vb.* lend; borrow.
leihweise, *adv.* on loan.
Leim, *n.m.* glue.
leimen, *vb.* glue.
Leine, -n, *n.f.* line, leash.
leinen, *adj.* linen.
Leinen, -, *n.nt.* linen.
Leinsamen, *n.m.* linseed.
Leinwand, *n.f.* canvas; (movie) screen.
leise, *adj.* soft, quiet, gentle.
leisten, *vb.* perform, accomplish; (**sich l.**) afford.
Leisten, -, *n.m.* last.
Leistung, -en, *n.f.* performance, accomplishment, achievement, output.
leistungsfähig, *adj.* efficient.
Leitartikel, -, *n.m.* editorial.
leiten, *vb.* lead, direct, conduct, manage.
Leiter, -, *n.m.* leader, director, manager.
Leiter, -n, *n.f.* ladder.
Leiterin, -nen, *n.f.* leader, director, manager.
Leitfaden, -̈, *n.m.* key, guide.

Leitsatz, -̈e, *n.m.* guiding principle.
Leitung, -en, *n.f.* guidance, direction, management; wire, line, duct, tube; conduction.
Leitungswasser, -, *n.nt.* tap water.
Leitungsrohr, -e, *n.nt.* conduit.
Lektion', -en, *n.f.* lesson.
Lektor, -o'ren, *n.m.* university instructor.
Lekto'rin, -nen, *n.f.* university instructor.
Lektü're, -n, *n.f.* reading.
Lende, -n, *n.f.* loin.
Lendenstück, -e, *n.nt.* sirloin.
lenkbar, *adj.* steerable, dirigible, manageable.
lenken, *vb.* direct, steer, guide.
Lenkung, -en, *n.f.* guidance, steering, control.
Lenz, -e, *n.m.* spring.
Leopard', -en, -en, *n.m.* leopard.
Lerche, -n, *n.f.* lark.
lernen, *vb.* learn.
Lesart, -e, *n.f.* reading, version.
lesbar, *adj.* legible; worth reading.
lesbisch, *adj.* lesbian.
Lese, -n, *n.f.* vintage.
Lesebuch, -̈er, *n.nt.* reader.
lesen*, *vb.* read; lecture; gather.
Leser, -, *n.m.* reader.
leserlich, *adj.* legible.
Lethargie', *n.f.* lethargy.
lethar'gisch, *adj.* lethargic.
Lettland, *n.nt.* Latvia.
letzt-, *adj.* last.
letzter-, *adj.* latter.
leuchten, *vb.* give forth light, shine.
Leuchter, -, *n.m.* candlestick.
Leuchtschirm, -e, *n.m.* fluorescent screen, television screen.
Leuchtsignal, -e, *n.nt.* flare.
Leuchtturm, -̈e, *n.m.* lighthouse.
leugnen, *vb.* deny.
Leukoplast', -, *n.nt.* adhesive tape, band-aid.
Leumund, -e, *n.m.* reputation.
Leute, *n.pl.* people.
Leutnant, -s *or* **-e,** *n.m.* lieutenant.
leutselig, *adj.* affable.
Lexikon, -ka, *n.nt.* dictionary.
Liaison', -s, *n.f.* liaison.
liberal', *adj.* liberal.

Liberalis'mus, *n.m.* liberalism.
Libret'to, -s, *n.nt.* libretto.
Licht, -er, *n.nt.* light.
Lichtbild, -er, *n.nt.* photograph.
Lichtschimmer, -, *n.m.* glint.
Lichtspiel, -e, *n.nt.* moving picture.
Lid, -er, *n.nt.* eyelid.
lieb, *adj.* dear.
liebäugeln, *vb.* make eyes at.
Liebchen, -, *n.nt.* dearest, darling.
Liebe, -n, *n.f.* love.
Liebelei', -en, *n.f.* flirtation.
liebeln, *vb.* flirt, make love.
lieben, *vb.* love.
liebenswert, *adj.* lovable.
liebenswürdig, *adj.* amiable, kind.
lieber, *adv.* rather.
Liebesaffäre, -n, *n.f.* love affair.
liebevoll, *adj.* loving, affectionate.
lieb-haben*, *vb.* love.
Liebhaber, -, *n.m.* lover.
Liebhaberei', -en, *n.f.* hobby.
liebkosen, *vb.* fondle, caress.
Liebkosung, -en, *n.f.* caress.
lieblich, *adj.* lovely.
Liebling, -e, *n.m.* darling.
Lieblings-, *cpds.* favorite.
lieblos, *adj.* loveless.
Liebreiz, -e, *n.m.* charm.
Liebschaft, -en, *n.f.* love affair.
Liebst-, *n.m.* & *f.* dearest, sweetheart.
Lied, -er, *n.nt.* song.
liederlich, *adj.* slovenly; dissolute.
Lieferant', -en, -en, *n.m.* supplier.
liefern, *vb.* supply, deliver.
Lieferung, -en, *n.f.* delivery.
Lieferwagen, -, *n.m.* delivery van.
liegen*, *vb.* lie, be located.
Lift, -e, *n.m.* elevator.
Likör', -e, *n.m.* liqueur.
lila, *adj.* lilac, purple.
Lilie, -n, *n.f.* lily.
Limona'de, -n, *n.f.* lemonade.
Limo'ne, -n, *n.f.* lime.
Limousi'ne, -n, *n.f.* limousine, sedan.
lind, *adj.* mild, gentle.
lindern, *vb.* alleviate, ease, soothe.
Lineal', -e, *n.nt.* ruler.
linear', *adj.* linear.
Linguist', -en, -en, *n.m.* linguist.

Linguis'tin, -nen, *n.f.* linguist.
linguis'tisch, *adj.* linguistic.
Linie, -n, *n.f.* line.
link-, *adj.* left.
Link-, *n.f.* left.
linkisch, *adj.* awkward, clumsy.
links, *adv.* to the left.
Linse, -n, *n.f.* lens; lentil.
Lippe, -n, *n.f.* lip.
Lippenstift, -e, *n.m.* lipstick.
liquidie'ren, *vb.* liquidate.
lispeln, *vb.* lisp, whisper.
List, -e, *n.f.* cunning, trick, ruse.
Liste, -n, *n.f.* list.
listig, *adj.* cunning, crafty.
Litanei', -en, *n.f.* litany.
Litauen, *n.nt.* Lithuania.
Liter, -, *n.m. or nt.* liter.
litera'risch, *adj.* literary.
Literatur', -en, *n.f.* literature.
Lithographie', -i'en, *n.f.* lithograph(y).
Liturgie', -i'en, *n.f.* liturgy.
litur'gisch, *adj.* liturgical.
Livree', -e'en, *n.f.* livery.
Lizenz', -en, *n.f.* license.
Lob, -e, *n.nt.* praise.
loben, *vb.* praise.
lobenswert, *adj.* praiseworthy.
löblich, *adj.* praiseworthy.
lobpreisen, *vb.* praise, extol.
Lobrede, -n, *n.f.* eulogy.
Loch, -er, *n.nt.* hole.
lochen, *vb.* put a hole in, punch.
Locke, -n, *n.f.* lock, curl.
locken, *vb.* curl; lure.
locker, *adj.* loose.
lockern, *vb.* loosen.
lockig, *adj.* curly.
lodern, *vb.* blaze.
Löffel, -, *n.m.* spoon.
Logbuch, -er, *n.nt.* log.
Loge, -n, *n.f.* loge, box; (fraternal) lodge.
Logik, *n.f.* logic.
logisch, *adj.* logical.
Lohn, -e, *n.m.* reward; wages.
lohnen, *vb.* reward, pay, be of value; **(sich l.)** be worth the trouble.
Lohnerhöhung, (-en) *n.f.* raise.
lokal', *adj.* local.
Lokal', -e, *n.nt.* night club, bar, place of amusement; premises.

Lokomoti've, -n, *n.f.* locomotive.
Lokus, -se, *n.m.* toilet.
los, *adj.* loose; wrong; **(was ist l.?)** what's the matter?
Los, -e, *n.nt.* lot.
lösbar, *adj.* soluble.
los•binden*, *vb.* untie.
Löschblatt, -er, *n.nt.* blotter.
löschen, *vb.* extinguish, quench; unload.
lose, *adj.* loose, slack, lax, dissolute.
Lösegeld, -er, *n.nt.* ransom.
lösen, *vb.* undo, solve, dissolve; buy (a ticket).
los•fahren*, *vb.* start out.
los•gehen*, *vb.* start out, go off, begin.
los•kommen*, *vb.* get loose.
los•lassen*, *vb.* get loose, let go.
los•lösen, *vb.* disconnect.
los•machen, *vb.* unfasten, free.
Lösung, -en, *n.f.* solution.
Lösungsmittel, -, *n.nt.* solvent.
los•werden*, *vb.* get rid of.
Lot, -e, *n.nt.* lead, plumbline.
löten, *vb.* solder.
lotrecht, *adj.* perpendicular.
Lotse, -n, -n, *n.m.* pilot.
lotsen, *vb.* pilot.
Lotterie, -i'en, *n.f.* lottery.
Löwe, -n, -n, *n.m.* lion.
Lücke, -n, *n.f.* gap.
lückenhaft, *adj.* with gaps, incomplete.
lückenlos, *adj.* without gaps, complete.
Luder, -, *n.nt.* scoundrel, slut; carrion.
Luft, -e, *n.f.* air.
Luftabwehr, *n.f.* anti-aircraft, air defense.
Luftangriff, -e, *n.m.* air raid.
Luftballon, -s, *n.m.* balloon.
Luftblase, -n, *n.f.* bubble.
Luftbrücke, -n, *n.f.* air lift.
luftdicht, *adj.* airtight.
Luftdruck, -e, *n.m.* air pressure.
lüften, *vb.* air, ventilate.
Luftfahrt, *n.f.* aviation.
Luftflotte, -n, *n.f.* air fleet.
luftig, *adj.* airy.
luftkrank, -, *adj.* air-sick.

Luftlinie, -n, *n.f.* air line.
Luftpirat, -en, -en, *n.m.* hijacker.
Luftpost, *n.f.* airmail.
Luftsack, ̈-e, *n.m.* airbag (automobile).
Luftschiff, -e, *n.nt.* airship, dirigible.
Luftsprung, ̈-e, *n.m.* caper.
Luftstützpunkt, -e, *n.m.* air base.
Lüftung, *n.f.* ventilation.
Luftverpestung, *n.f.* air pollution.
Luftverschmutzung, *n.f.* air pollution.
Luftwaffe, -n, *n.f.* air force.
Luftzug, ̈-e, *n.m.* draft.
Lüge, -n, *n.f.* lie.
lugen, *vb.* peep.
lügen*, ̈-e, *vb.* lie.
Lügner, -, *n.m.* liar.
Lügnerin, -nen, *n.f.* liar.
Lümmel, -, *n.m.* lout.
Lump, -en, -en, *n.m.* bum.

Lumpen, -, *n.m.* rag.
Lunge, -n, *n.f.* lung.
Lungenentzündung, -en, *n.f.* pneumonia.
Lust, ̈-e, *n.f.* pleasure, desire; (L. haben*) feel like (doing something).
lüstern, *adj.* lecherous.
lustig, *adj.* merry, gay.
Lüstling, -e, *n.m.* libertine.
lustlos, *adj.* listless.
Lustspiel, -e, *n.nt.* comedy.
Lutheraner, -, *n.m.* Lutheran.
lutherisch, *adj.* Lutheran.
lutschen, *vb.* suck.
luxuriös, *adj.* luxurious.
Luxus, *n.m.* luxury.
Luxus-, *cpds.* de luxe.
Lymphe, -n, *n.f.* lymph.
lynchen, *vb.* lynch.
Lyrik, *n.f.* lyric poetry.
lyrisch, *adj.* lyric.
Lyzeum, -e'en, *n.nt.* girls' high school.

M

Maat, -e, *n.m.* mate.
machbar, *adj.* feasible.
machen, *vb.* make, do.
Macht, ̈-e, *n.f.* power.
Machterweiterung, -en, *n.f.* aggrandizement.
mächtig, *adj.* powerful.
machtlos, *adj.* powerless.
Mädchen, -, *n.nt.* girl.
mädchenhaft, *adj.* girlish.
Mädel, -, *n.nt.* girl.
Mafia, *n.f.* mafia.
Magazin', -e, *n.nt.* magazine, storeroom, store.
Magd, ̈-e, *n.f.* hired girl.
Magen, - or ̈-, *n.m.* stomach.
Magenbeschwerden, *n.pl.* indigestion.
Magengeschwür, -e, *n.nt.* stomach ulcer.
Magenschmerzen, *n.pl.* stomach ache.
Magenverstimmung, -en, *n.f.* stomach upset.
mager, *adj.* lean.
Magermilch, *n.f.* skim milk.
Magie', *n.f.* magic.

magisch, *adj.* magic.
Magnat', -en, -en, *n.m.* magnate, tycoon.
Magne'sium, *n.nt.* magnesium.
Magnet', -e, *or* **-en, -en,** *n.m.* magnet.
magne'tisch, *adj.* magnetic.
Magnetophon', -e, *n.nt.* tape recorder.
Mahago'ni, *n.nt.* mahogany.
mähen, *vb.* mow.
Mahl, -e, *or* **̈-er,** *n.nt.* meal, repast.
mahlen, *vb.* grind.
Mahlzeit, -en, *n.f.* meal.
mahnen, *vb.* remind, urge, warn, dun.
Mahnung, -en, *n.f.* admonition, warning.
Mähre, -n, *n.f.* mare.
Mai, *n.m.* May.
Mais, *n.m.* corn, maize.
Maiskolben, -, *n.m.* corncob.
Majestät', -en, *n.f.* majesty.
majestä'tisch, *adj.* majestic.
Major', -e, *n.m.* major.
Majorität', -en, *n.f.* majority.
Majus'kel, -n, *n.f.* capital letter.

Makel, -, *n.m.* stain, blemish, flaw.
makellos, *adj.* spotless, flawless, immaculate.
Makkaro'ni, *n.pl.* macaroni.
Makler, -, *n.m.* broker.
Maklerin, -nen, *n.f.* broker.
Makre'le, -n, *n.f.* mackerel.
Makro'ne, -n, *n.f.* macaroon.
¹Mal, -e, *n.nt.* mark, sign, spot, mole.
²Mal, -e, *n.nt.* time; **(das erste M.)** the first time; **(2 mal 2)** 2 times 2.
mal, *adv.* (= einmal) once, just; **(nicht m.)** not even.
Mala'ria, *n.f.* malaria.
malen, *vb.* paint.
Maler, -, *n.m.* painter.
Malerei', -en, *n.f.* painting.
Malerin, -nen, *n.f.* painter.
malerisch, *adj.* picturesque.
Malz, *n.nt.* malt.
man, *pron.* one, a person.
Manager, -, *n.m.* manager.
Managerin, -nen, *n.f.* manager.
mancher, -es, -e, *pron. & adj.* many, many a.
mancherlei, *adj.* various.
manchmal, *adv.* sometimes.
Mandat', -e, *n.nt.* mandate.
Mandel, -n, *n.f.* almond; tonsil.
Mandoli'ne, -n, *n.f.* mandolin.
Mangel, ⁻, *n.m.* lack, dearth, defect.
Mangel, -n, *n.f.* mangle.
mangelhaft, *adj.* faulty.
mangeln, *vb.* be lacking, deficient; **(es mangelt mir an . . . .)** I lack . . . .
mangels, *prep.* for lack of.
Manie', -i'en, *n.f.* mania.
Manier', -en, *n.f.* manner.
manier'lich, *adj.* mannerly, polite.
manikü'ren, *vb.* manicure.
manipulie'ren, *vb.* manipulate.
Manko, -s, *n.nt.* defect, deficiency.
Mann, ⁻er, *n.m.* man, husband.
Männchen, -, *n.nt.* male (animal).
Mannesalter, -, *n.nt.* manhood.
mannhaft, *adj.* manly.
mannigfach, *adj.* manifold.
mannigfaltig, *adj.* manifold.
Mannigfaltigkeit, -en, *n.f.* diversity.
männlich, *adj.* male, masculine.

Männlichkeit, *n.f.* manliness.
Mannschaft, -en, *n.f.* crew, team, squad; *(pl.)* enlisted men.
Manö'ver, -, *n.nt.* maneuver.
manö'vrie'ren, *vb.* maneuver.
Manschet'te, -n, *n.f.* cuff.
Mantel, ⁻, *n.m.* overcoat.
Manufaktur', -en, *n.f.* manufacture, factory.
Manuskript', -e, *n.nt.* manuscript.
Mappe, -n, *n.f.* portfolio, briefcase, folder.
Märchen, -, *n.nt.* fairy tale.
märchenhaft, *adj.* fabulous.
Märchenland, ⁻er, *n.nt.* fairyland.
Margari'ne, *n.f.* margarine.
Marihua'na, *n.nt.* marijuana.
Mari'ne, -n, *n.f.* navy.
marinie'ren, *vb.* marinate.
Marionet'te, -n, *n.f.* marionette, puppet.
Mark, -, *n.f.* mark (unit of money); **(Deutsche M.)** German mark.
Mark, -en, *n.f.* border(land).
Marke, -n, *n.f.* mark; brand, sort; postage stamp, check, ticket.
markie'ren, *vb.* mark.
Marki'se, -n, *n.f.* awning.
Markstein, -e, *n.m.* boundary stone, landmark.
Markt, ⁻e, *n.m.* market.
Marktplatz, ⁻e, *n.m.* market place.
Marmela'de, -n, *n.f.* jam.
Marmor, -e, *n.m.* marble.
Maro'ne, -n, *n.f.* chestnut.
Marot'te, -n, *n.f.* whim, fad.
Marsch, ⁻e, *n.m.* march.
Marsch, -en, *n.f.* marsh.
Marschall, ⁻e, *n.m.* marshal.
marschie'ren, *vb.* march.
Marter, -n, *n.f.* torture.
martern, *vb.* torture.
Märtyrer, -, *n.m.* martyr.
Märtyrerin, -nen, *n.f.* martyr.
Märtyrertum, *n.nt.* martyrdom.
März, *n.m.* March.
Marzipan', -e, *n.m. or nt.* marzipan, almond paste.
Masche, -n, *n.f.* stitch, mesh.
Maschi'ne, -n, *n.f.* machine.

Maschi'nenbau, *n.m.* mechanical engineering.

Maschi'nengewehr, -e, *n.nt.* machine gun.

Maschinist', -en, -en, *n.m.* machinist.

Masern, *n.pl.* measles.

Maske, -n, *n.f.* mask.

Maskera'de, -n, *n.f.* masquerade.

maskie'ren, *vb.* mask.

Maskot'te, -n, *n.f.* mascot.

maskulin', *adj.* masculine.

Maß, -e, *n.nt.* measure(ment), dimension, extent, rate, proportion.

Massa'ge, -n, *n.f.* massage.

Masse, -n, *n.f.* mass.

massenhaft, *adj.* in large quantity.

Massenmedien, *n.pl.* mass media.

Massenversammlung, -en, *n.f.* mass meeting.

massenweise, *adv.* in large numbers.

Masseur', -e, *n.m.* masseur.

Masseu'se, -n, *n.f.* masseuse.

maßgebend, *adj.* authoritative, standard.

maßgeblich, *adj.* authoritative, standard.

massie'ren, *vb.* massage.

massig, *adj.* bulky, solid.

mäßig, *adj.* moderate.

mäßigen, *vb.* moderate.

Mäßigkeit, *n.f.* temperance.

Mäßigung, *n.f.* moderation.

massiv', *adj.* massive.

maßlos, *adj.* immoderate, excessive.

Maßnahme, -n, *n.f.* measure, step.

Maßregel, -n, *n.f.* measure, step.

maßregelnd, *adj.* disciplinary.

Maßstab, -̈e, *n.m.* scale, rate, gauge, standard.

maßvoll, *adj.* moderate.

Mast, -e *or* **-en,** *n.m.* mast.

mästen, *vb.* fatten.

Material', -ien, *n.nt.* material.

Materialis'mus, *n.m.* materialism.

Mate'rie, -n, *n.f.* matter, stuff.

materiell', *adj.* material.

Mathematik', *n.f.* mathematics.

Mathema'tiker, -, *n.m.* mathematician.

Mathema'tikerin, -nen, *n.f.* mathematician.

mathema'tisch, *adj.* mathematical.

Matrat'ze, -n, *n.f.* mattress.

Mätres'se, -n, *n.f.* mistress.

Matro'se, -n, -n, *n.m.* sailor.

matschig, *adj.* muddy, slushy; pulpy.

matt, *adj.* dull, tired.

Matte, -n, *n.f.* mat.

Mattigkeit, *n.f.* lassitude.

Mätzchen, -, *n.nt.* antic, foolish trick.

Mauer, -n, *n.f.* (outside) wall.

Maul, -̈er, *n.nt.* mouth, snout.

Maulkorb, -̈e, *n.m.* muzzle.

Maultier, -e, *n.nt.* mule.

Maulwurf, -̈e, *n.m.* mole.

Maure, -n, -n, *n.m.* Moor.

Maurer, -, *n.m.* mason, bricklayer.

Maus, -̈e, *n.f.* mouse.

Mausole'um, -le'en, *n.nt.* mausoleum.

maximal', *adj.* maximum.

Maximum, -ma, *n.nt.* maximum.

Mayonnai'se, -n, *n.f.* mayonnaise.

m. E., *abbr.* (= meines Erach'tens) in my opinion.

Mecha'nik, *n.f.* mechanics, mechanism.

Mecha'niker, -, *n.m.* mechanic.

Mecha'nikerin, -nen, *n.f.* mechanic.

mecha'nisch, *adj.* mechanical.

mechanisie'ren, *vb.* mechanize.

Mechanis'mus, -men, *n.m.* mechanism.

Medai'lle, -n, *n.f.* medal.

Medikament', -e, *n.nt.* drug, medicine.

Medium, -ien, *n.nt.* medium.

Medizin', -en, *n.f.* medicine.

Medizi'ner, -, *n.m.* medical man, medical student.

Medizi'nerin, -nen, *n.f.* medical student.

medizi'nisch, *adj.* medical.

Meer, -e, *n.nt.* sea.

Meerbusen, -, *n.m.* bay.

Meerenge, -n, *n.f.* strait.

Meeresboden, *n.m.* seabed.

Meeresbucht, -en, *n.f.* bay.

Meerrettich, -e, *n.m.* horseradish.

Meerschweinchen, -, *n.nt.* guinea pig.

Megahertz, *n.nt.* megahertz.

Mehl, *n.nt.* flour, meal.

mehr, *adj.* more.

mehren, *vb.* increase.

mehrere, *adj.* several.

mehrfach, *adj.* multiple.

Mehrheit, -en, *n.f.* majority.

mehrmalig, *adj.* repeated.

mehrmals, *adv.* repeatedly.

Mehrwertsteuer, -n, *n.f.* value-added tax.

Mehrzahl, -en, *n.f.* majority; plural.

meiden*, *vb.* avoid.

Meile, -n, *n.f.* mile.

Meilenstein, -e, *n.m.* milestone.

mein, -, -e, *adj.* my.

Meineid, *n.m.* perjury.

meinen, *vb.* mean, think.

meiner, -es, -e, *pron.* mine.

meinetwegen, *adv.* for my sake; for all I care.

Meinung, -en, *n.f.* opinion.

Meinungsumfrage, -n, *n.f.* poll.

Meißel, -, *n.m.* chisel.

meist, 1. *adj.* most (of). **2.** *adv.* mostly, usually.

meistens, *adv.* mostly, usually.

Meister, -, *n.m.* master; champion.

meisterhaft, *adj.* masterly.

Meisterin -nen, *n.f.* master; champion.

Meisterschaft, -en, *n.f.* championship.

Meisterstück, -e, *n.nt.* masterpiece.

Melancholie', *n.f.* melancholy.

melancho'lisch, *adj.* melancholy.

Melas'se, *n.f.* molasses.

melden, *vb.* announce, notify, report.

Meldung, -en, *n.f.* announcement, notification, report.

melken, *vb.* milk.

Melodie', -i'en, *n.f.* melody, tune.

melo'disch, *adj.* melodious.

Melo'ne, -n, *n.f.* melon; derby.

Membra'ne, -n, *n.f.* membrane.

Memoi'ren, *n.pl.* memoirs.

Memoran'dum, -den, *n.nt.* memorandum.

Menagerie', -i'en, *n.f.* menagerie.

Menge, -n, *n.f.* quantity; crowd, multitude; **(eine M.)** a lot.

Mensa, -sen, *n.f.* cafeteria.

Mensch, -en, -en, *n.m.* human being, person; man.

Menschenfeind, -e, *n.m.* misanthrope.

Menschenfreund, -e, *n.m.* humanitarian.

Menschenliebe, *n.f.* philanthropy.

Meschenmenge, -n, *n.f.* mob.

Menschenrechte, *n.pl.* human rights.

Menschenverstand, *n.m.* **(gesunder M.)** common sense.

Menschheit, *n.f.* mankind, humanity.

menschlich, *adj.* human; humane.

Menschlichkeit, *n.f.* humanity.

Menstruation', *n.f.* menstruation.

Mentalität', *n.f.* mentality.

Menthol', *n.nt.* menthol.

Menü, -s, *n.nt.* menu.

merken, *vb.* realize, notice; **(sich m.)** keep in mind; **(sich nichts m. lassen*)** not give oneself away.

Merkmal, -e, *n.nt.* mark, characteristic.

merkwürdig, *adj.* peculiar, odd, queer.

Messe, -n, *n.f.* fair; *(eccles.)* mass.

messen*, *vb.* measure; gauge; **(sich m.)** match.

Messer, -, *n.nt.* knife.

Messi'as, *n.m.* Messiah.

Messing, *n.nt.* brass.

Metall', -e, *n.nt.* metal.

metal'len, *adj.* metallic.

Metall'waren, *n.pl.* hardware.

Meteor', -e, *n.m. or nt.* meteor.

Meteorologie', *n.f.* meteorology.

Meter, -, *n.m. or nt.* meter.

Metho'de, -n, *n.f.* method.

metrisch, *adj.* metric.

Metzger, -, *n.m.* butcher.

Metzgerei', **-en**, *n.f.* butcher shop.

Meuterei', **-en**, *n.f.* mutiny.

meutern, *vb.* mutiny.

Mexika'ner, **-**, *n.m.* Mexican.

Mexika'nerin, **-nen**, *n.f.* Mexican.

mexika'nisch, *adj.* Mexican.

Mexiko, *n.nt.* Mexico.

Mieder, **-**, *n.nt.* bodice.

Miene, **-n**, *n.f.* mien.

Mienenspiel, **-e**, *n.nt.* pantomine.

Miete, **-n**, *n.f.* rent, rental.

mieten, *vb.* rent, lease, hire.

Mieter, **-**, *n.m.* tenant.

Mieterin, **-nen**, *n.f.* tenant.

Mietvertrag, **ꞏe**, *n.m.* lease.

Mietwagen, **-**, *n.m.* rented car.

Mietwohnung, **-en**, *n.f.* flat, apartment.

Migrä'ne, *n.f.* migraine.

Mikro'be, **-n**, *n.f.* microbe.

Mikrofilm, **-e**, *n.m.* microfilm.

Mikrophon', **-e**, *n.nt.* microphone.

Mikroskop', **-e**, *n.nt.* microscope.

Milbe, **-n**, *n.f.* mite.

Milch, *n.f.* milk.

Milchhändler, **-**, *n.m.* dairyman.

milchig, *adj.* milky.

Milchmann, **ꞏer**, *n.m.* milkman.

Milchwirtschaft, **-en**, *n.f.* dairy.

mild, *adj.* mild, gentle, lenient.

Milde, *n.f.* mildness, leniency, clemency.

mildern, *vb.* mitigate, alleviate, soften; **(mildernde Umstände)** extenuating circumstances.

Milderung, **-en**, *n.f.* alleviation.

Militär', **-s**, *n.nt.* military.

Militär'dienstpflicht, **-en**, *n.f.* conscription.

militä'risch, *adj.* military.

Militaris'mus, *n.m.* militarism.

militaris'tisch, *adj.* militaristic.

Miliz', **-en**, *n.f.* militia.

Millime'ter, **-**, *n.nt.* millimeter.

Million', **-en**, *n.f.* million.

Millionär', **-e**, *n.m.* millionaire.

Millionä'rin, **-nen**, *n.f.* millionairess.

Milz, **-en**, *n.f.* spleen.

Minderheit, **-en**, *n.f.* minority.

minderjährig, *adj.* minor, not of age.

Minderjährigkeit, *n.f.* minority.

mindern, *vb.* reduce.

minderwertig, *adj.* inferior.

Minderwertigkeitskomplex, *n.m.* inferiority complex.

mindestens, *adv.* at least.

Mine, **-n**, *n.f.* mine.

Mineral', **-e** *or* **-ien**, *n.nt.* mineral.

minera'lisch, *adj.* mineral.

Miniatur', **-en**, *n.f.* miniature.

minimal, *adj.* minimum, minute.

Minimum, **-ma**, *n.nt.* minimum.

Mini'ster, **-**, *n.m.* (cabinet) minister.

Mini'sterin, **-nen**, *n.f.* (cabinet) minister.

Miniſte'rium, **-rien**, *n.nt.* ministry, department.

Mini'sterpräsident, **-en**, **-en**, *n.m.* prime minister.

Mini'sterpräsidentin, **-nen**, *n.f.* prime minister.

minus, *adv.* minus.

Minu'te, **-n**, *n.f.* minute.

Minz'e, **-n**, *n.f.* mint.

mischen, *vb.* mix, mingle, blend.

Mischmasch, **-e**, *n.m.* hodgepodge.

Mischung, **-en**, *n.f.* mixture, blend.

mißachten, *vb.* disregard; slight.

Mißachtung, **-en**, *n.f.* disdain.

Mißbildung, **-en**, *n.f.* abnormality, deformity.

mißbilligen, *vb.* disapprove.

Mißbrauch, **ꞏe**, *n.m.* abuse, misuse.

mißbrau'chen, *vb.* abuse.

mißdeu'ten, *vb.* misconstrue.

missen, *vb.* do without.

Mißerfolg, **-e**, *n.m.* failure.

Missetat, **-en**, *n.f.* misdeed, crime.

Missetäter, **-**, *n.m.* offender.

mißfal'len*, *vb.* displease.

Mißfallen, *n.nt.* displeasure.

Mißgeburt, **-en**, *n.f.* freak.

Mißgeschick, **-e**, *n.nt.* adversity, misfortune.

mißglü'cken, *vb.* fail.

mißglückt', *adj.* unsuccessful, abortive.

mißgön'nen, *vb.* begrudge.

mißhan'deln, *vb.* mistreat, maltreat.

Mission', -en, *n.f.* mission.

Missionar', -e, *n.m.* missionary.

Missiona'rin, -nen, *n.f.* missionary.

Mißklang, ⸚e, *n.m.* discord.

mißlin'gen*, *vb.* miscarry, fail.

mißra'ten, *adj.* ill-bred, low.

mißtrau'en, *vb.* distrust.

Mißtrauen, *n.nt.* distrust.

mißtrauisch, *adj.* suspicious, distrustful.

mißvergnügt, *adj.* cranky.

Mißverhältnis, -se, *n.nt.* disproportion.

Mißverständnis, -se, *n.nt.* misunderstanding.

mißverstehen*, *vb.* misunderstand.

Mist, *n.m.* manure, muck.

mistig, *adj.* misty.

mit, *prep.* with.

Mitarbeit, *n.f.* cooperation, collaboration.

mit·arbeiten, *vb.* collaborate.

Mitarbeiter, -, *n.m.* collaborator; colleague; (**anonymer M.**) ghost writer.

Mitarbeiterin, -nen, *n.f.* collaborator; colleague.

Mitbewerber, -, *n.m.* competitor.

mit·bringen*, *vb.* bring along; bring a present.

Mitbürger, -, *n.m.* fellow citizen.

Mitbürgerin, -nen, *n.f.* fellow citizen.

miteinan'der, *adv.* together, jointly.

mitein'begriffen, *adj.* included; implied.

mitempfunden, *adj.* sympathizing; vicarious.

mit·fühlen, *vb.* sympathize.

mitfühlend, *adj.* sympathetic.

Mitgefühl, *n.nt.* sympathy.

mitgenommen, *adj.* the worse for wear.

Mitgift, -en, *n.f.* dowry.

Mitglied, -er, *n.nt.* member, fellow.

Mitgliedschaft, *n.f.* membership.

Mithelfer, -, *n.m.* accessory.

Mithelferin, -nen, *n.f.* accessory.

Mitleid, *n.nt.* pity, compassion; mercy.

mitleidig, *adj.* compassionate.

mit·machen, *vb.* string along, join, conform.

Mitmacher, -, *n.m.* conformer.

Mitmensch, -en, -en, *n.m.* fellow-man.

Mitschuld, *n.f.* complicity.

mitschuldig, *adj.* being an accessory.

Mitschüler, -, *n.m.* classmate.

Mitschülerin, -nen, *n.f.* classmate.

Mitspieler, -, *n.m.* player.

Mitspielerin, -nen, *n.f.* player.

Mittag, *n.m.* midday, noon.

Mittagessen, -, *n.nt.* noon meal, lunch, dinner.

Mittäter, -, *n.m.* accomplice.

Mitte, -n, *n.f.* middle, midst, center.

mitteilbar, *adj.* communicable.

mit·teilen, *vb.* inform, communicate.

Mitteilung, -en, *n.f.* information, communication.

Mittel, -, *n.nt.* means, measure, expedient; medium.

mittel, *adj.* mean.

Mittelalter, *n.nt.* Middle Ages.

mittelalterlich, *adj.* medieval.

mittellos, *adj.* penniless, destitute.

mittelmäßig, *adj.* mediocre.

Mittelmeer, *n.nt.* Mediterranean Sea.

Mittelpunkt, -e, *n.m.* center, focus.

mittels, *prep.* by means of.

Mittelstand, *n.m.* middle class.

Mitternacht, *n.f.* midnight.

mittler-, *adj.* medium, middle.

Mittler-Osten, *n.m.* Middle East.

mittschiffs, *adv.* amidships.

Mittwoch, -e, *n.m.* Wednesday.

mit·wirken, *vb.* cooperate, assist, contribute.

mitwirkend, *adj.* contributory.

Möbel, -, *n.nt.* piece of furniture; (*pl.*) furniture.

Möbelwagen, -, *n.m.* moving van.

mobil', *adj.* mobile; (*fig.*) hale and hearty.

mobilisie'ren, *vb.* mobilize.

mobilisiert', *adj.* mobile.

möblie'ren, *vb.* furnish.

Mode, -n, *n.f.* mode, fashion.
Modell', -e, *n.nt.* model.
modellie'ren, *vb.* model.
Modenschau *n.f.* fashion show.
modern, *vb.* rot.
modern', *adj.* modern, fashionable.
modernisie'ren, *vb.* modernize.
Modeschöpfer, -, *n.m.* designer.
modifizie'ren, *vb.* modify.
modisch, *adj.* modish, fashionable.
Mofa, -s, *n.nt.* moped.
mögen*, *vb.* like; may.
möglich, *adj.* possible; potential.
möglicherweise, *adv.* possibly.
Möglichkeit, -en, *n.f.* possibility; potential; facility.
Mohammeda'ner, -, *n.m.* Moslem.
Mohammeda'nerin, -nen, *n.f.* Moslem.
Mohr, -en, -en, *n.m.* Moor.
Mohrrübe, -n, *n.f.* carrot.
Mole, -n, *n.f.* mole, jetty, breakwater.
Molkerei', -en, *n.f.* dairy.
Moll, *n.nt.* minor.
mollig, *adj.* plump; snug.
Moment, -e, *n.m.* moment, instant.
Moment', -e, *n.nt.* factor, impulse, motive.
momentan', *adj.* momentary.
Monarch', -en, -en, *n.m.* monarch.
Monarchie', -i'en, *n.f.* monarchy.
Monat, -e, *n.m.* month.
monatlich, *adj.* monthly.
Monatsschrift, -en, *n.f.* monthly.
Mönch, -e, *n.m.* monk.
Mond, -e, *n.m.* moon.
Mondschein, *n.m.* moonlight.
Mondsichel, -n, *n.f.* crescent moon.
Monolog', -e, *n.m.* monologue.
Monopol', -e, *n.m.* monopoly.
monopolisie'ren, *vb.* monopolize.
monoton', *adj.* monotonous.
Monotonie', *n.f.* monotony.

monströs', *adj.* monstrous, freak.
Montag, -e, *n.m.* Monday.
Montan'union, *n.f.* European Coal and Steel Community.
montie'ren, *vb.* assemble, mount.
monumental', *adj.* monumental.
Moor, -e, *n.nt.* moor.
Moos, -e, *n.nt.* moss.
Mop, -s, *n.m.* mop.
**Moral', ** *n.f.* morals; morality; morale.
mora'lisch, *adj.* moral, ethical.
Moralist', -en, -en, *n.m.* moralist.
Morast', -e, *n.m.* morass, bog.
Mord, -e, *n.m.* murder, assassination.
morden, *vb.* murder.
**Mörder, -, ** *n.m.* murderer.
Mörderin, -nen, *n.f.* murderess.
Mords-, *cpds.* mortal; heck of a . . . .
morgen, *adv.* tomorrow.
**Morgen, -, ** *n.m.* morning; acre.
Morgendämmerung, -en, *n.f.* dawn.
Morgenrock, ⁻e, *n.m.* dressing gown.
morgens, *adv.* in the morning.
Morphium, *n.nt.* morphine.
morsch, *adj.* rotten.
Mörser, -, *n.m.* mortar.
Mörtel, -, *n.m.* mortar.
Mosaik', -e, *n.nt.* mosaic.
Moschee', -n, *n.f.* mosque.
Moskau, *n.nt.* Moscow.
Most, -e, *n.m.* grape juice, new wine; **(Apfelmost)** cider.
Mostrich, *n.m.* mustard.
Motiv', -e, *n.nt.* motif.
motivie'ren, *vb.* motivate.
Motivie'rung, -en, *n.f.* motivation.
Motor('), -o'ren, *n.m.* motor, engine.
motorisie'ren, *vb.* motorize, mechanize.
Motor(')rad, ⁻er, *n.nt.* motorcycle.
Motte, -n, *n.f.* moth.
Motto, -s, *n.nt.* motto.
Mücke, -n, *n.f.* mosquito.

mucksen, *vb.* stir.
müde, *adj.* tired, sleepy; weary.
Müdigkeit, *n.f.* fatigue.
Muff, -e, *n.m.* muff.
muffig, *adj.* musty.
Mühe, -n, *n.f.* trouble, inconvenience; effort; **(machen Sie sich keine M.)** don't bother.
mühelos, *adj.* effortless.
mühen, *vb.* **(sich m.)** try, take the trouble.
Mühle, -n, *n.f.* mill.
Muhme, -n, *n.f.* aunt.
Mühsal, -e, *n.f.* trouble, hardship.
mühsam, *adj.* difficult, tedious, inconvenient.
mühselig, *adj.* laborious.
Mull, *n.m.* gauze.
Müll, *n.m.* garbage.
Mullah, -s, *n.m.* mullah.
Müller, -, *n.m.* miller.
Müllerin, -nen, *n.f.* miller.
multinational′, *adj.* multinational.
Multiplikation′, -en, *n.f.* multiplication.
multiplizie′ren, *vb.* multiply.
Mumie, -n, *n.f.* mummy.
München, *n.nt.* Munich.
Mund, -̈er, *n.m.* mouth.
Mundart, -en, *n.f.* dialect.
Mündel, -, *n.nt.* ward.
münden, *vb.* run, flow into, end.
mündlich, *adj.* oral, verbal.
Mündung, -en, *n.f.* (river) mouth; (gun) muzzle.
Munition′, -en, *n.f.* ammunition, munition.
munkeln, *vb.* rumor.
Münster, *n.nt.* cathedral.
munter, *adj.* awake; sprightly, lusty.
Münze, -n, *n.f.* coin; mint.
mürbe, *adj.* mellow; (meat) tender; (cake) crisp; (fig.) weary.
murmeln, *vb.* murmur, mutter.
murren, *vb.* grumble.
mürrisch, *adj.* disgruntled, petulant, glum.
Mürrischkeit, *n.f.* glumness.
Muschel, -n, *n.f.* shell; mussel, clam.
Muse, -n, *n.f.* muse.
Muse′um, -e′en, *n.nt.* museum.
Musik′, *n.f.* music.

musika′lisch, *adj.* musical.
Musikant′, -en, -en, *n.m.* musician.
Musiker, -, *n.m.* musician.
Musikerin, -nen, *n.f.* musician.
Musik′kapelle, -n, *n.f.* band, orchestra.
Musik′pavillon, -s, *n.m.* bandstand.
Muskat′, -n, *n.m.* nutmeg.
Muskel, -n, *n.m.* muscle.
Muskelkraft, -̈e, *n.f.* muscular strength, brawn.
muskulös′, *adj.* muscular.
Muße, *n.f.* leisure.
Musselin′, -e, *n.m.* muslin.
müssen*, *vb.* must, have to.
müßig, *adj.* idle.
Müßigkeit, *n.f.* idleness.
Muster, -, *n.nt.* model; sample; pattern, design.
Musterbeispiel, -e, *n.nt.* paragon, perfect example.
mustergültig, *adj.* exemplary, model.
musterhaft, *adj.* exemplary.
mustern, *vb.* examine; (mil.) muster.
Musterung, -en, *n.f.* examination; (mil.) muster; (pattern) figuring.
Mut, *n.m.* courage, fortitude.
Mutation′, -en, *n.f.* mutation.
mutig, *adj.* courageous.
Mutigkeit, *n.f.* pluck.
mutmaßen, *vb.* conjecture.
mutmaßlich, *adj.* presumable.
Mutmaßung, -en, *n.f.* conjecture.
Mutter, -̈, *n.f.* mother.
Mutterleib, *n.m.* womb.
mütterlich, *adj.* maternal.
Mutterschaft, *n.f.* maternity.
mutterseelenallein′, *adj.* all alone.
Muttersprache, -n, *n.f.* native language.
mutwillig, *adj.* deliberate, wilful.
Mütze, -n, *n.f.* cap, bonnet.
Myrte, -n, *n.f.* myrtle.
mysteriös′, *adj.* mysterious.
Mystik, *n.f.* mysticism.
mystisch, *adj.* mystic.
Mythe, -n, *n.f.* myth.
Mythologie′, *n.f.* mythology.

N

na, *interj.* well; (**n. also**) there you are; (**n. und ob**) I should say so.

Nabe, -n, *n.f.* hub.

nach, *prep.* towards; to; after; according to; (**n. und n.**) by and by, gradually.

nach·affen, *vb.* ape, imitate.

nach·ahmen, *vb.* imitate, simulate.

Nachahmung, -en, *n.f.* imitation.

Nachbar, (-n,) -n, *n.m.* neighbor.

Nachbarin, -nen, *n.f.* neighbor.

Nachbarschaft, -en, *n.f.* neighborhood.

nachdem', *conj.* after.

nach·denken*, *vb.* think, meditate, reflect.

nachdenklich, *adj.* contemplative, pensive.

Nachdruck, *n.m.* emphasis.

nachdrücklich, *adj.* emphatic.

nach·eifern, *vb.* emulate.

Nachfolger, -, *n.m.* successor.

Nachfolgerin, -nen, *n.f.* successor.

Nachforschung, -en, *n.f.* investigation; research.

Nachfrage, -n, *n.f.* inquiry; (**Angebot und N.**) supply and demand.

nach·fühlen, *vb.* understand, appreciate.

nach·füllen, *vb.* refill.

nach·geben*, *vb.* give in, yield.

nach·gehen*, *vb.* follow; seek; (clock) be slow.

nachgiebig, *adj.* compliant.

nachhaltig, *adj.* lasting.

nach·helfen*, *vb.* assist, boost.

nachher, *adv.* afterward(s).

Nachhilfe, *n.f.* assistance.

Nachhilfelehrer, -, *n.m.* tutor.

Nachhilfelehrerin, -nen, *n.f.* tutor.

nach·holen, *vb.* make up for.

Nachkomme, -n, -n, *n.m.* descendant.

Nachlaß, -sse, *n.m.* estate.

nach·lassen*, *vb.* abate, subside.

nachlässig, *adj.* negligent, careless, derelict.

Nachlässigkeit, -en, *n.f.* negligence, carelessness.

nach·machen, *vb.* imitate.

Nachmittag, -e, *n.m.* afternoon.

Nachmittagsvorstellung, -en, *n.f.* matinée.

Nachnahme, -n, *n.f.* (**per N.**) C.O.D.

nach·prüfen, *vb.* check up, verify.

Nachricht, -en, *n.f.* information, message, notice; (*pl.*) news.

Nachrichtensendung, -en, *n.f.* newscast.

nach·schlagen*, *vb.* look up, refer to.

Nachschrift, -en, *n.f.* postscript.

nach·sehen*, *vb.* look after; look up; examine, check; (*fig.*) excuse, indulge.

Nachsehen, *n.nt.* (**das N. haben***) be the loser.

nach·senden*, *vb.* forward, send on.

Nachsicht, -en, *n.f.* indulgence, forbearance.

nachsichtig, *adj.* lenient, indulgent.

Nachspiel, -e, *n.nt.* postlude.

nach·spüren, *vb.* track down.

nächst-, *adj.* next nearest.

nach·stehen*, *vb.* be inferior.

nach·stellen*, *vb.* pursue; (clock) put back.

Nächstenliebe, *n.f.* charity.

nächstens, *adv.* soon.

Nacht, ⸚e, *n.f.* night.

Nachteil, -e, *n.m.* disadvantage, drawback.

nachteilig, *adj.* disadvantageous, adverse.

Nachthemd, -en, *n.nt.* nightgown.

Nachtigall, -en, *n.f.* nightingale.

Nachtisch, -e, *n.m.* dessert.

nächtlich, *adj.* nocturnal.

Nachtlokal, -e, *n.nt.* night club.

Nachtrag, ⸚e, *n.m.* supplement.

nach·tragen*, *vb.* carry behind; (*fig.*) resent, bear a grudge.

nachträglich, *adj.* belated.

Nachtwache, -n, *n.f.* vigil.

Nachweis, -e, *n.m.* proof, certificate.

nachweisbar, *adj.* demonstrable.

nach•weisen*, *vb.* demonstrate, prove.

Nachwelt, *n.f.* posterity.

Nachwirkung, -en, *n.f.* aftereffect.

nach•zählen, *vb.* count over again, count up.

nach•zeichnen, *vb.* trace.

nackt, *adj.* naked, nude; bare.

Nacktheit, *n.f.* nakedness, bareness.

Nadel, -n, *n.f.* needle, pin.

Nagel, ⸚, *n.m.* nail.

nagen, *vb.* gnaw.

Nagetier, -e, *n.nt.* rodent.

nah(e) (näher, nächst-), *adj.* near.

Nähe, *n.f.* vicinity, proximity.

nähen, *vb.* sew.

Näherin, -nen, *n.f.* seamstress.

nähern, *vb.* (**sich n.**) approach.

nähren, *vb.* nourish; nurture.

nahrhaft, *adj.* nutritious, nourishing.

Nahrung, -en, *n.f.* nourishment, food.

Nahrungsmittel, *n.pl.* foodstuffs.

Naht, ⸚e, *n.f.* seam.

naiv', *adj.* naïve.

Name(n), -, *n.m.* name.

namentlich, *adv.* by name, namely; considerable.

namhaft, *adj.* renowned.

nämlich, *adv.* that is to say, namely.

nanu', *interj.* well, what do you know?

Naphtha, *n.nt.* naphtha.

Narbe, -n, *n.f.* scar.

Narko'se, -n, *n.f.* anesthetic.

narko'tisch, *adj.* narcotic, anesthetic.

Narr, -en, -en, *n.m.* fool; (**zum N. halten***) fool, make a fool of.

narrensicher, *adj.* foolproof.

närrisch, *adj.* foolish, daffy.

Narzis'se, -n, *n.f.* narcissus; (**gelbe N.**) daffodil.

nasal', *adj.* nasal.

naschen, *vb.* nibble (secretly) on sweets.

Nase, -n, *n.f.* nose.

näselnd, *adj.* nasal.

Nasenbluten, *n.nt.* nosebleed.

Nasenloch, ⸚er, *n.nt.* nostril.

Nasenschleim, *n.m.* mucus.

naseweis, *adj.* fresh, know-it-all.

naß(⸚), *adj.* wet.

Nässe, *n.f.* wetness, moisture.

nässen, *vb.* wet.

Nation', -en, *n.f.* nation.

national', *adj.* national.

Nationalis'mus, *n.m.* nationalism.

Nationalität', -en, *n.f.* nationality.

National'ökonomie, *n.f.* political economics.

Natrium, *n.nt.* sodium.

Natron, *n.nt.* sodium.

Natur', -en, *n.f.* nature.

Natura'lien, *n.pl.* food produce.

naturalisie'ren, *vb.* naturalize.

Naturalist', -en, -en, *n.m.* naturalist.

Natur'forscher, -, *n.m.* naturalist.

Natur'forscherin, -nen, *n.f.* naturalist.

Natur'kunde, *n.f.* nature study.

natür'lich, 1. *adj.* natural. **2.** *adv.* of course.

Natür'lichkeit, *n.f.* naturalness.

Natur'wissenschaftler, *n.m.* scientist.

Natur'wissenschaftlerin, -nen, *n.f.* scientist.

nautisch, *adj.* nautical.

Navigation', *n.f.* navigation.

Nebel, -, *n.m.* fog, mist.

Nebelfleck, -e, *n.m.* nebula.

nebelhaft, *adj.* nebulous.

neb(e)lig, *adj.* foggy.

neben, *prep.* beside.

Nebenanschluß, ⸚sse, *n.m.* (telephone) extension.

nebenbei', *adv.* besides; by the way, incidentally.

Nebenbuhler, -, *n.m.* rival.

nebeneinan'der, *adv.* beside one another, abreast.

Nebengebäude, -, *n.nt.* annex.

Nebenprodukt, -e, *n.nt.* by-product.

Nebensache, -n, *n.f.* incidental matter.

nebensächlich, *adj.* incidental, irrelevant.
Nebenweg, -e, *n.m.* byway.
nebst, *prep.* with, including.
necken, *vb.* tease, kid.
neckisch, *adj.* playful, cute.
Neffe, -n, -n, *n.m.* nephew.
negativ, *adj.* negative.
Negativ, -e, *n.nt.* negative.
Neger, -, *n.m.* Negro.
Negligé, -s, *n.nt.* negligée.
nehmen*, *vb.* take.
Neid, *n.m.* envy.
neidisch, *adj.* envious.
neigen, *vb.* *(tr.)* incline, bow, bend; *(intr.)* lean, slant; *(fig.)* tend.
Neigung, -en, *n.f.* inclination; slant; tendency, trend; affection.
nein, *interj.* no.
Nelke, -n, *n.f.* carnation.
nennen*, *vb.* name, call.
nennenswert, *adj.* considerable, worth mentioning.
Nenner, -, *n.m.* denominator.
Nennwert, -e, *n.m.* denomination; face value.
Neon, *n.nt.* neon.
Nerv, -en, *n.m.* nerve.
Nervenarzt, ⸚e, *n.m.* neurologist.
Nervenärztin, -nen, *n.f.* neurologist.
Nervenkitzel, -, *n.m.* thrill.
nervös', *adj.* nervous, jittery; high-strung.
Nervosität', *n.f.* nervousness.
Nerz, -e, *n.m.* mink.
Nessel, -n, *n.f.* nettle.
Nest, -er, *n.nt.* nest.
nett, *adj.* nice, enjoyable.
netto, *adj.* net.
Netz, -e, *n.nt.* net, web; network.
Netzhaut, ⸚e, *n.f.* retina.
neu, *adj.* new; **(aufs neue, von neuem)** anew.
Neubelebung, -en, *n.f.* revival.
Neuerung, -en, *n.f.* innovation.
Neugierde, -n, *n.f.* curiosity.
neugierig, *adj.* curious, inquisitive.
Neuheit, -en, *n.f.* novelty.
Neuigkeit, -en, *n.f.* news; novelty.
Neujahr, *n.nt.* New Year; **(Fröhliches N.)** Happy New Year.

neulich, *adv.* the other day, recently.
Neuling, -e, *n.m.* novice.
neun, *num.* nine.
neunt-, *adj.* ninth.
Neuntel, -, *n.nt.* ninth part; **(ein n.)** one-ninth.
neunzig, *num.* ninety.
neunzigst-, *adj.* ninetieth.
Neunzigstel, -, *n.nt.* ninetieth part; **(ein n.)** one-ninetieth.
Neuralgie, -, *n.f.* neuralgia.
neuro'tisch, *adj.* neurotic.
neutral', *adj.* neutral.
Neutralität', *n.f.* neutrality.
Neutron, -o'nen, *n.nt.* neutron.
Neutro'nenbombe, -n, *n.f.* neutron bomb.
nicht, *adv.* not; **(n. wahr)** isn't that so, don't you, aren't we, won't they, etc.
Nichtachtung, *n.f.* disregard, disrespect.
Nichtanerkennung, -en, *n.f.* nonrecognition; repudiation.
Nichtbeachtung, *n.f.* disregard.
Nichte, -n, *n.f.* niece.
nichtig, *adj.* null, void.
nichts, *pron.* nothing.
Nichts, *n.nt.* nothingness, nonentity.
nichtsdestoweniger, *adv.* notwithstanding, nevertheless.
Nichtswisser, -, *n.m.* ignoramus.
nichtswürdig, *adj.* worthless, condemnable.
Nickel, *n.nt.* nickel.
nicken, *vb.* nod.
nie, *adv.* never.
nieder, *adv.* down.
Niedergang, *n.m.* decline.
niedergedrückt, *adj.* depressed.
niedergeschlagen, *adj.* dejected.
Niederkunft, *n.f.* childbirth.
Niederlage, -n, *n.f.* defeat; branch office.
Niederlande, *n.pl.* Netherlands.
Niederländer, -, *n.m.* Netherlander, Dutchman.
Niederländerin, -nen, *n.f.* Dutchwoman.
niederländisch, *adj.* Netherlandic, Dutch.
nieder•lassen*, *vb.* **(sich n.)** settle.

Niederlassung, -en, *n.f.* settlement.

nieder-metzeln, *vb.* massacre.

Niederschlag, ⸚e, *n.m.* precipitation; sediment.

Niedertracht, *n.f.* meanness, infamy.

niederträchtig, *adj.* mean, vile, infamous.

niedlich, *adj.* pretty, cute.

niedrig, *adj.* low; base, menial.

niemals, *adv.* never.

niemand, *pron.* no one, nobody.

Niere, -n, *n.f.* kidney.

nieseln, *vb.* drizzle.

niesen, *vb.* sneeze.

Niete, -n, *n.f.* rivet; (lottery) blank; failure, washout.

Nihilis'mus, *n.m.* nihilism.

Nikotin', *n.nt.* nicotine.

nimmer, *adv.* never.

nimmermehr, *adv.* never again.

nirgends, nirgendwo, *adv.* nowhere.

Nische, -n, *n.f.* recess, niche.

nisten, *vb.* nestle.

Niveau', -s, *n.nt.* level.

nobel, *adj.* noble; liberal.

noch, *adv.* still, yet; **(n. einmal)** once more; **(n. ein)** another, an additional; **(weder . . . n.)** neither . . . nor.

nochmalig, *adj.* additional, repeated.

nochmal(s), *adv.* once more.

Noma'de, -n, -n, *n.m.* nomad.

nominal', *adj.* nominal.

Nonne, -n, *n.f.* nun.

Nonnenkloster, ⸚e, *n.nt.* convent.

Nord, Norden, *n.m.* north.

nördlich, *adj.* northern; to the north.

Nordos'ten, *n.m.* northeast.

nordöst'lich, *adj.* northeastern; to the northeast.

Nordpol, *n.m.* North Pole.

Nordwes'ten, *n.m.* northwest.

nordwest'lich, *adj.* northwestern; to the northwest.

nörgeln, *vb.* gripe.

Norm, -en, *n.f.* norm, standard.

normal', *adj.* normal.

Norwegen, *n.nt.* Norway.

Norweger, -, *n.m.* Norwegian.

Norwegerin, -nen, *n.f.* Norwegian.

norwegisch, *adj.* Norwegian.

Not, ⸚e, *n.f.* need, necessity; hardship; distress.

Notar', -e, *n.m.* notary.

Notausgang, ⸚e, *n.m.* emergency exit.

Notbehelf, *n.m.* makeshift, stopgap.

Notdurft, *n.f.* want; need.

notdürftig, *adj.* scanty, bare.

Note, -n, *n.f.* note; grade.

Notfall, ⸚e, *n.m.* emergency.

notgedrungen, *adv.* perforce.

notie'ren, *vb.* note, make a note.

Notie'rung, -en, *n.f.* quotation.

nötig, *adj.* necessary.

nötigen, *vb.* urge.

Notiz', -en, *n.f.* note.

Notiz'block, ⸚e, *n.m.* notepaper pad.

Notiz'buch, ⸚er, *n.nt.* notebook.

notleidend, *adj.* needy.

notwendig, *adj.* necessary.

Notwendigkeit, -en, *n.f.* necessity.

Novel'le, -n, *n.f.* short story; novella.

Novem'ber, *n.m.* November.

Nu, *n.m.* jiffy.

nüchtern, *adj.* sober; **(auf nüchternen Magen)** on an empty stomach.

Nüchternheit, *n.f.* sobriety; unimaginativeness.

Nudeln, *n.pl.* noodles.

nuklear', *adj.* nuclear.

Null, -en, *n.f.* cipher; zero.

numerie'ren, *vb.* number.

Num'mer, -, -n, *n.f.* number.

nun, *adv.* now; **(von n. an)** henceforth.

nur, *adv.* only

Nuß, ⸚sse, *n.f.* nut.

Nußschale, -n, *n.f.* nutshell.

Nüster, -n, *n.f.* nostril.

Nutzbarkeit, *n.f.* utility.

Nutzen, *n.m.* benefit.

nützen, *vb.* *(tr.)* use, utilize; *(intr.)* be of use, help, benefit.

nützlich, *adj.* useful, beneficial.

nutzlos, *adj.* useless, futile.
Nutzlosigkeit, *n.f.* futility.

Nylon, *n.nt.* nylon.
Nymphe, -n, *n.f.* nymph.

O

Oa'se, -n, *n.f.* oasis.
ob, *conj.* whether; **(als o.)** as if.
Obdach, *n.nt.* shelter.
obdachlos, *adj.* homeless.
oben, *adv.* above; upstairs.
ober-, *adj.* upper.
Ober, -, *n.m.* (= Oberkellner) headwaiter, waiter; **(Herr O.!)** waiter!
Oberbefehlshaber, -, *n.m.* commander-in-chief.
Oberfläche, -n, *n.f.* surface.
oberflächlich, *adj.* superficial.
Oberhaupt, -, *n.nt.* chief.
Oberherrschaft, *n.f.* sovereignty.
Oberschicht, *n.f.* upper stratum; upper classes.
oberst-, *adj.* supreme, paramount.
Oberst, -en, -en, *n.m.* colonel.
Oberstleut'nant, -s, *n.m.* lieutenant colonel.
obgleich', *conj.* although.
Obhut, *n.f.* keeping, charge.
obig, *adj.* above, aforesaid.
Objekt' -e, *n.nt.* object.
objektiv', *adj.* objective.
Objektiv', -e, *n.nt.* objective; lens.
Objektivität', *n.f.* objectivity, detachment.
Obliegenheit, -en, *n.f.* duty, obligation.
Obligation', -en, *n.f.* bond; obligation.
obligato'risch, *adj.* obligatory.
Obrigkeit, -en, *n.f.* authorities, government.
obschon', *conj.* although.
ob•siegen, *vb.* be victorious over.
Obst, *n.nt.* fruit.
Obstgarten, -, *n.m.* orchard.
obszön', *adj.* obscene.
Obus, -se, *n.m.* (= Oberleitungsomnibus) trolley bus.
ob•walten, *vb.* prevail, exist.
obwohl', *conj.* although.

Ochse, -n, -n *or* **Ochs, -en, -en,** *n.m.* ox.
öde, *adj.* bleak, desolate.
Öde, -n, *n.f.* bleakness, waste place.
oder, *conj.* or.
Ofen, -, *n.m.* stove, oven, furnace.
offen, *adj.* open, frank.
offenbar, *adj.* evident.
offenba'ren, *vb.* reveal.
Offenba'rung, -en, *n.f.* revelation.
Offenba'rungsschrift, -en, *n.f.* scripture.
Offenheit, *n.f.* frankness.
offenkundig, *adj.* manifest.
offensichtlich, *adj.* obvious.
Offensi've, -n, *n.f.* offense, offensive.
öffentlich, *adj.* public.
Öffentlichkeit, *n.f.* public.
offiziell', *adj.* official.
Offizier', -e, *n.m.* officer.
öffnen, *vb.* open.
Öffnung, -en, *n.f.* opening, aperture.
Öffnungszeiten, *n. pl.* opening hours.
oft (-), *adv.* often.
öfters, *adv.* quite often.
oftmals, *adv.* often (times).
ohne, *prep.* without.
ohneglei'chen, *adv.* unequalled.
ohnehin, *adv.* in any case.
Ohnmacht, *n.f.* faint, unconsciousness; **(in O. fallen*)** faint.
ohnmächtig, *adj.* in a faint, powerless.
Ohr, -en, *n.nt.* ear.
Öhr, -e, *n.nt.* eye (of a needle, etc.).
Ohrenschmerzen, *n.pl.* earache.
Ohrfeige, -n, *n.f.* slap.
Ohrring, -e, *n.m.* earring.
okay, *pred. adv.* okay.
okkult', *adj.* occult.

Ökologie, *n.f.* ecology.
ökologisch, *adj.* ecological.
Ökonom', **-en**, **-en**, *n.m.* farmer, manager.
Ökonomie', **-i'en**, *n.f.* economy; agriculture.
öko'nomisch, *adj.* economical.
Okta've, **-n**, *n.f.* octave.
Okto'ber, *n.m.* October.
ökume'nisch, *adj.* ecumenical.
Okzident', *n.m.* occident.
Öl, **-e**, *n.nt.* oil.
ölen, *vb.* oil.
ölig, *adj.* oily.
Oli've, **-n**, *n.f.* olive.
Ölung, **-en**, *n.f.* oiling; anointment; (letzt Ö.) extreme unction.
Oma, **-s**, *n.f.* granny, grandma.
Ombudsmann, **ẹ̈r**, *n.m.* ombudsman.
Omelett', **-e**, *n.nt.* omelet.
Omnibus, **-se**, *n.m.* (omni)bus.
ondulie'ren, *vb.* wave (hair).
Onkel, **-**, *n.m.* uncle.
Opa, **-s**, *n.m.* grandpa.
Opal', **-e**, *n.m.* opal.
Oper, **-n**, *n.f.* opera.
Operation', **-en**, *n.f.* operation.
operativ', *adj.* operative.
Operet'te, **-n**, *n.f.* operetta.
operie'ren, *vb.* operate.
Opernglas, **ẹ̈r**, *n.nt.* opera glasses.
Opfer, **-**, *n.nt.* offering, sacrifice; victim, casualty.
opfern, *adv.* sacrifice.
Opium, *n.nt.* opium.
opponie'ren, *vb.* oppose.
Opposition', **-en**, *n.f.* opposition.
Optik, *n.f.* optics.
Optiker, **-**, *n.m.* optician.
Optikerin, **-nen**, *n.f.* optician.
Optimis'mus, *n.m.* optimism.
optimis'tisch, *adj.* optimistic.
optisch, *adj.* optic.
Oran'ge, **-n**, *n.f.* orange.
Orches'ter, **-**, *n.nt.* orchestra.
Orchide'e, **-n**, *n.f.* orchid.
Orden, **-**, *n.m.* order, medal, decoration.
ordentlich, *adj.* orderly, decent, regular.
ordinär, *adj.* vulgar.

ordnen, *vb.* put in order, sort, arrange.
Ordnung, **-en**, *n.f.* order.
Organ', **-e**, *n.nt.* organ.
Organisation', **-en**, *n.f.* organization.
orga'nisch, *adj.* organic.
organisie'ren, *vb.* organize; scrounge.
Organis'mus, **-men**, *n.m.* organism.
Organist', **-en**, **-en**, *n.m.* organist.
Organis'tin, **-nen**, *n.f.* organist.
Orgel, **-n**, *n.f.* organ.
Orgie, **-n**, *n.f.* orgy.
Orient', *n.m.* Orient.
orienta'lisch, *adj.* oriental.
orientie'ren, *vb.* orient(ate).
Orientie'rung, **-en**, *n.f.* orientation.
Original', **-e**, *n.nt.* original.
Originalität', **-en**, *n.f.* originality.
originell', *adj.* original.
Ort, **-e**, *n.m.* place, locality, town.
Orter, **-**, *n.m.* navigator.
orthodox', *adj.* orthodox.
örtlich, *adj.* local.
ortsansässig, *adj.* resident, indigenous.
Ortschaft, **-en**, *n.f.* town, village.
Ortsgespräch, **-e**, *n.nt.* local call.
Ost, **Osten**, *n.m.* east.
Ostblockstaaten, *n.m.pl.* Eastern European nations.
Ostern, *n.nt.* Easter.
Österreich, *n.nt.* Austria.
Österreicher, **-**, *n.m.* Austrian.
Österreicherin, **-nen**, *n.f.* Austrian.
österreichisch, *adj.* Austrian.
östlich, *adj.* eastern, easterly.
Ostsee, *n.f.* Baltic Sea.
ostwärts, *adv.* eastward.
Otter, **-**, *n.m.* otter.
Otter, **-n**, *n.f.* adder.
Ouvertü're, **-n**, *n.f.* overture.
oval', *adj.* oval.
Ozean, **-e**, *n.m.* ocean.
Ozeandampfer, **-**, *n.m.* ocean liner.
Ozon', **-e**, *n.nt.* ozone.

Paar, -e, *n.nt.* pair, couple; **(ein paar)** a few.

paaren, *vb.* mate.

Pacht, -en, *n.f.* lease, tenure.

Pachtbrief, -e, *n.m.* lease (document).

pachten, *vb.* lease (from).

Pächter, -, *n.m.* tenant.

Pächterin, -nen, *n.f.,* tenant.

Pachtzins, *n.m.* rent (money).

Pack, -̈e, *n.nt.* pack; rabble.

Päckchen, -, *n.nt.* parcel.

packen, *vb.* pack, seize, thrill.

Packen, -, *n.m.* pack.

Packung, -en, *n.f.* packing, wrapper, pack(age).

Pädago'ge, -n, -n, *n.m.* pedagogue.

Pädago'gik, *n.f.* pedagogy.

Pädago'gin, -nen, *n.f.* pedagogue.

Paddel, -, *n.nt.* paddle.

paff, *interj.* bang.

Page, -n, -n, *n.m.* page.

Pakt, -e, *n.m.* pact.

Palast', -̈e, *n.m.* palace.

Palet'te, -n, *n.f.* palette.

Palme, -n, *n.f.* palm.

Pampelmu'se, -n, *n.f.* grapefruit.

Panik, *n.f.* panic.

Panne, -n, *n.f.* breakdown; flat tire.

Panora'ma, -men, *n.nt.* panorama.

Panther, -, *n.m.* panther.

Pantof'fel, -n, *n.f.* slipper.

Pantomi'me, -n, *n.f.* pantomime.

Panzer, -, *n.m.* armor; tank.

Panzer-, *cpds.* armored.

Papagei', -en, -en, *n.m.* parrot.

Papier', -e, *n.nt.* paper.

Papier'bogen, -̈, *n.m.* sheet of paper.

Papier'korb, -̈e, *n.m.* wastebasket.

Papier'krieg, -e, *n.m.* red tape, paperwork.

Papier'waren, *n.pl.* stationery.

Papp, -e, *n.m.* pap, paste.

Pappe, -n, *n.f.* cardboard.

Papst, -̈e, *n.m.* pope.

päpstlich, *adj.* papal.

Papsttum, *n.nt.* papacy.

Para'de, -n, *n.f.* parade.

Paradies', *n.nt.* paradise.

paradox', *adj.* paradoxical.

Paradox', -e, *n.nt.* paradox.

Paraffin', -e, *n.nt.* paraffin.

Paragraph', -en, -en, *n.m.* paragraph.

parallel', *adj.* parallel.

Paralle'le, -n, *n.f.* parallel.

Paraly'se, -n, *n.f.* paralysis.

Parenthe'se, -n, *n.f.* parenthesis.

Parfüm', -e, *n.nt.* perfume.

pari, *adv.* at par.

Pari, *n.nt.* par.

Paris', *n.nt.* Paris.

Pari'ser, -, *n.m.* Parisian.

Pari'serin, -nen, *n.f.* Parisian.

Park, -e *or* **-s,** *n.m.* park.

parken, *vb.* park.

Parkuhr, -en, *n.f.* parking meter.

Parkverbot, -e, *n.nt.* no parking.

Parlament', -e, *n.nt.* parliament.

parlamenta'risch, *adj.* parliamentary.

Parodie', -i'en, *n.f.* parody.

Paro'le, -n, *n.f.* password.

Partei', -en, *n.f.* party.

Partei'genosse, -n, -n, *n.m.* party comrade.

partei'isch, *adj.* partisan, biased.

partei'lich, *adj.* partisan, biased.

partei'los, *adj.* impartial.

Parter're, -s, *n.nt.* ground floor; orchestra (seats in theater).

Partie', -i'en, *n.f.* match.

Partisan', (-en,) -en, *n.m.* partisan; guerilla.

Partitur', -en, *n.f.* score.

Partizip', -ien, *n.nt.* participle.

Partner, -, *n.m.* partner, associate.

Partnerin, -nen, *n.f.* partner, associate.

Parzel'le, -n, *n.f.* lot, plot.

Paß, -̈sse, *n.m.* pass; passport.

passa'bel, *adj.* passable.

Passagier', -e, *n.m.* passenger.

Passant', -en, -en, *n.m.* passerby.

passen, *vb.* suit, fit; **(p. zu)** match.

passend, *adj.* fitting, suitable, proper.
passie'ren, *vb.* happen; pass.
Passion', *n.f.* passion.
passiv, *adj.* passive.
Passiv', *n.nt.* passive.
Pasta, -sten, *n.f.* paste.
Paste, -n, *n.f.* paste.
Paste'te, -n, *n.f.* meat pie.
pasteurisie'ren, *vb.* pasteurize.
Pastil'le, -n, *n.f.* lozenge.
Pastor, -o'ren, *n.m.* minister.
Pate, -n, *n.m.* godfather.
Pate, -n, *n.f.* godmother.
Patenkind, -er, *n.nt.* godchild.
Patenonkel, -, *n.m.* godfather.
Patent', -e, *n.nt.* patent.
Patentante, -n, *n.f.* godmother.
Pathos, *n.nt.* pathos.
Patient', -en, -en, *n.m.* patient.
Patien'tin, -nen, *n.f.* patient.
Patin, -nen, *n.f.* godmother.
patrio'tisch, *adj.* patriotic.
Patriot', -en, -en, *n.m.* patriot.
Patriotis'mus, *n.m.* patriotism.
Patro'ne, -n, *n.f.* cartridge; pattern.
Patrouil'le, -n, *n.f.* patrol.
Pauschal'preis, -e, *n.m.* total price.
Pause, -n, *n.f.* pause, intermission, recess.
Pavillon, -s, *n.m.* pavillion.
Pazifis'mus, *n.m.* pacifism.
Pazifist', -en, -en, *n.m.* pacifist.
Pech, *n.nt.* pitch, bad luck.
Pedal', -e, *n.nt.* pedal.
Pedant', -en, -en, *n.m.* pedant.
Pein, *n.f.* pain, agony.
peinigen, *vb.* torment.
peinlich, *adj.* embarrassing; meticulous.
Peitsche, -n, *n.f.* whip.
peitschen, *vb.* whip.
Pelz, -e, *n.m.* fur.
Pelzhändler, -, *n.m.* furrier.
Pendel, -, *n.m. or nt.* pendulum.
pendeln, *vb.* swing, oscillate.
Pendler, -, *n.m.* commuter.
Penis, -se, *n.m.* penis.
Penizillin', *n.nt.* penicillin.
Pension', -en, *n.f.* pension; board, boarding house.
pensionie'ren, *vb.* pension; (**sich p. lassen***) retire.

per, *prep.* per, by, with.
perfekt', *adj.* perfect.
Perfekt', -e, *n.nt.* perfect (tense).
Pergament', -e, *n.nt.* parchment.
Perio'de, -n, *n.f.* period, term.
perio'disch, *adj.* periodic.
Peripherie', -i'en, *n.f.* periphery.
Perle, -n, *n.f.* pearl.
Perlmutter, *n.f.* mother-of-pearl.
Persia'ner, *n.m.* Persian lamb.
Persien, *n.nt.* Persia.
Person', -en, *n.f.* person.
Personal', *n.nt.* personnel, staff.
Persona'lien, *n.pl.* personal data.
Perso'nenzug, -e, *n.m.* passenger train.
persön'lich, *adj.* personal.
Persön'lichkeit, -en, *n.f.* personage; personality.
Perspekti've, -n, *n.f.* perspective.
pervers', *adj.* perverse.
Pessimis'mus, *n.m.* pessimism.
pessimis'tisch, *adj.* pessimistic.
Pest, *n.f.* plague, pestilence.
Petersi'lie, -n, *n.f.* parsley.
Petro'leum, *n.nt.* petroleum.
Petschaft, -en, *n.nt.* seal.
Pfad, -e, *n.m.* path.
Pfadfinder, -, *n.m.* boy scout.
Pfahl, -e, *n.m.* pole, pile, post, stake.
Pfand, -er, *n.m.* pawn, pledge, security; deposit.
Pfandbrief, -e, *n.m.* bond, mortgage bond.
pfänden, *vb.* seize, attach, impound.
Pfandhaus, -er, *n.nt.* pawnshop.
Pfanne, -n, *n.f.* pan.
Pfannkuchen, -, *n.m.* pancake.
Pfarrer, -, *n.m.* minister, priest.
Pfau, -en, *n.m.* peacock.
Pfeffer, *n.m.* pepper.
Pfefferkuchen, -, *n.m.* gingerbread.
Pfeffermin'ze, *n.f.* peppermint.
Pfeife, -n, *n.f.* pipe, whistle.
pfeifen*, *vb.* whistle.
Pfeil, -e, *n.m.* arrow.
Pfeiler, -, *n.m.* pillar, pier.
Pfennig, -e, *n.m.* penny.
Pferd, -e, *n.nt.* horse.
Pferdestärke, -n, *n.f.* horsepower.
Pfiff, -e, *n.m.* whistle; trick.

pfiffig, *adj.* tricky, sly.
Pfingsten, *n.m.* Pentecost, Whitsuntide.
Pfirsich, -e, *n.m.* peach.
Pflanze, -n, *n.f.* plant.
pflanzen, *vb.* plant.
Pflaster, -, *n.nt.* plaster; pavement.
pflastern, *vb.* plaster, pave.
Pflaume, -n, *n.f.* plum.
Pflege, -n, *n.f.* care, nursing, cultivation.
Pflegeeltern, *n.pl.* foster parents.
pflegen, *vb.* take care of, nurse, cultivate; be accustomed.
Pflicht, -en, *n.f.* duty.
pflichtgemäß, *adj.* dutiful.
Pflock, -e, *n.m.* peg.
pflücken, *vb.* pick, gather.
Pflug, -e, *n.m.* plow.
pflügen, *vb.* plow.
Pforte, -n, *n.f.* gate, door, entrance.
Pförtner, -, *n.m.* janitor, doorman.
Pfosten, -, *n.m.* post, jamb.
Pfote, -n, *n.f.* paw.
Pfropf, -e, Pfropfen, -, *n.m.* stopper, plug.
pfropfen, *vb.* graft.
Pfund, -e, *n.nt.* pound.
pfuschen, *vb.* botch, bungle.
Pfütze, -n, *n.f.* puddle.
Phänomen', -e, *n.nt.* phenomenon.
Phantasie', -i'en, *n.f.* fantasy.
phantas'tisch, *adj.* fantastic.
Phase, -n, *n.f.* phase.
Philosoph', -en, -en, *n.m.* philosopher.
Philosophie', -i'en, *n.f.* philosophy.
Philo'sophin, -nen, *n.f.* philosopher.
philoso'phisch, *adj.* philosophical.
phlegma'tisch, *adj.* phlegmatic.
phone'tisch, *adj.* phonetic.
Phosphor, *n.m.* phosphorus.
Photoapparat, -e, *n.m.* camera.
photoelek'trisch, *adj.* photoelectric.
Photograph', -en, -en, *n.m.* photographer.

Photographie', -i'en, *n.f.* photograph(y).
Photogra'phin, -nen, *n.f.* photographer.
Photokopie', -i'en, *n.f.* photocopy.
photokopie'ren, *vb.* photocopy.
Photokopier'maschine, -n, *n.f.* photocopier.
Physik', *n.f.* physics.
Physiker, -, -en, *n.m.* physicist.
Physikerin, -nen, *n.f.* physicist.
Physiologie', *n.f.* physiology.
physisch, *adj.* physical.
Pianist', -en, -en, *n.m.* pianist.
Pianis'tin, -nen, *n.f.* pianist.
Pickel, -, *n.m.* pimple; ice axe.
picken, *vb.* peck.
Picknick, -s, *n.nt.* picnic.
piepsen, *vb.* peep.
Pier, -s, *n.m.* pier.
Pietät', *n.f.* piety.
Pigment', -e, *n.nt.* pigment.
pikant', *adj.* piquant.
Pilger, -, *n.m.* pilgrim.
Pilgerin, -nen, *n.f.* pilgrim.
Pille, -n, *n.f.* pill.
Pilot', -en, -en, *n.m.* pilot.
Pilo'tin, -nen, *n.f.* pilot.
Pilz, -e, *n.m.* mushroom.
Pinsel, -, *n.m.* brush.
Pinzet'te, -n, *n.f.* tweezers.
Pionier', -e, *n.m.* pioneer; *(mil.)* engineer.
Pisto'le, -n, *n.f.* pistol.
Pisto'lenhalter, -, *n.m.* holster.
Pizza, -s, *n.f.* pizza.
Plackerei', -en, *n.f.* drudgery.
plädie'ren, *vb.* plead.
Plädoyer', -s, *n.nt.* plea.
Plage, -n, *n.f.* trouble, affliction.
plagen, *vb.* plague, annoy, afflict.
Plagiat', -, *n.nt.* plagiarism.
Plakat', -e, *n.nt.* placard, poster.
Plan, -e, *n.m.* plan.
planen, *vb.* plan.
Planet', -en, -en, *n.m.* planet.
Planke, -n, *n.f.* plank.
planlos, *adj.* aimless.
planmäßig, *adj.* according to plan; scheduled.
planschen, *vb.* splash.
Planta'ge, -n, *n.f.* plantation.
Plappermaul, -er, *n.nt.* chatterbox.

plappern, vb. babble.
Plasma, -men, n.nt. plasma.
Plastik, -en, n.f. sculpture.
plastisch, adj. plastic.
Plateau, -s, n.nt. plateau.
Platin, n.nt. platinum.
platt, adj. flat.
Plättbrett, -er, n.nt. ironing board.
Platte, -n, n.f. plate, slab, sheet, tray; (photographic) slide; (phonograph) record.
Plätteisen, -, n.nt. (flat) iron.
plätten, vb. iron.
Plattenspieler, -, n.m. record player.
Plattform, -en, n.f. platform.
Plattfuß, ̈-e, n.m. flat foot.
plattieren, vb. plate.
Platz, ̈-e, n.m. place, seat, square.
platzen, vb. burst.
Plauderei', -en, n.f. chat.
plaudern, vb. chat.
pleite, adj. broke.
Plombe, -n, n.f. (tooth) filling.
plötzlich, adj. sudden.
plump, adj. clumsy, tactless.
Plunder, n.m. old clothes, rubbish.
plündern, vb. plunder, pillage.
Plünderung, -en, n.f. pillage.
Plural, -e, n.m. plural.
plus, adv. plus.
Plüsch, -e, n.m. plush.
Plutokrat', -en, -en, n.m. plutocrat.
pneuma'tisch, adj. pneumatic.
Pöbel, n.m. mob, rabble.
pöbelhaft, adj. vulgar.
pochen, vb. knock, throb.
Pocke, -n, n.f. pock; (pl.) smallpox.
Podium, -ien, n.nt. rostrum.
Poesie', i'en, n.f. poetry.
Poet', -en, -en, n.m. poet.
poe'tisch, adj. poetic.
Poin'te, -n, n.f. point (of a joke), punch line.
Pokal', -e, n.m. goblet, cup.
Pol, -e, n.m. pole.
polar', adj. polar.
Polar'stern, n.m. North Star.
Pole, -n, -n, n.m. Pole.
Polen, n.nt. Poland.

Poli'ce, -n, n.f. (insurance) policy.
polie'ren, vb. polish.
Politik', n.f. politics, policy.
Poli'tiker, -, n.m. politician.
Poli'tikerin, -nen, n.f. politician.
poli'tisch, adj. politic(al).
Politur', -en, n.f. polish.
Polizei', -en, n.f. police.
polizei'lich, adj. by the police.
Polizei'präsident, -en, -en, n.m. chief of police.
Polizei'präsidium, -ien, n.nt. police headquarters.
Polizei'revier, -e, n.nt. police station.
Polizei'richter, -, n.m. police state.
Polizei'staat, -en, n.m. police state.
Polizei'stunde, -n, n.f. curfew.
Polizei'wache, -n, n.f. police station.
Polizist', -en, -en, n.m. policeman.
Polizis'tin, -nen, n.f. police officer.
polnisch, adj. Polish.
Polonä'se, -n, n.f. polonaise.
Polster, -, n.nt. pad, cushion.
polstern, vb. pad, upholster.
Polsterung, -en, n.f. padding, upholstery.
poltern, vb. rattle, bluster.
Polygamie', n.f. polygamy.
Poly'pen, n.pl. adenoids.
Polytech'nikum, -ken, n.nt. technical college.
Pomeran'ze, -n, n.f. orange.
Pommes frites, n.pl. French fries.
Pony, -s, n.nt. pony; (pl.) bangs.
populär', adj. popular.
popularisie'ren, vb. popularize.
Popularität', n.f. popularity.
Pore, -n, n.f. pore.
porös', adj. porous.
Portal', -e, n.nt. portal.
Portefeuille', -s, n.nt. portfolio.
Portemonnaie', -s, n.nt. purse.
Portier', -s, n.m. doorman, concierge.
Portion', -en, n.f. portion, helping.
Porto, n.nt. postage.

Porträt', -s, *n.nt.* portrait.
Portugal, *n.nt.* Portugal.
Portugie'se, -n, -n, *n.m.* Portuguese.
Portugie'sin, -nen, *n.f.* Portuguese.
portugie'sisch, *adj.* Portuguese.
Porzellan', -en, *n.nt.* porcelain, china.
Posau'ne, -n, *n.f.* trumpet.
Pose, -n, *n.f.* pose.
posie'ren, *vb.* strike a pose.
Position', -en, *n.f.* position.
positiv, *adj.* positive.
Posse, -n, *n.f.* prank, antic; farce.
Post, *n.f.* mail; post office.
Postamt, -̈er, *n.nt.* post office.
Postanweisung, -en, *n.f.* money order.
Postbote, -n, -n, *n.m.* mail carrier.
Postbotin, -nen, *n.f.* mail carrier.
Posten, -, *n.m.* post, station; item.
Postfach, -̈er, *n.nt.* post office box.
Postkarte, -n, *n.f.* postcard.
postlagernd, *adv.* general delivery.
Postleitzahl, -en, *n.f.* zip code.
Poststempel, -, *n.m.* postmark.
Pracht, *n.f.* splendor.
prächtig, *adj.* splendid.
prachtvoll, *adv.* gorgeous.
Prädikat', -e, *n.nt.* predicate.
Präfix, -e, *n.nt.* prefix.
prägen, *vb.* stamp, coin, impress.
Prägung, -en, *n.f.* coinage.
prähistorisch, *adj.* prehistoric.
prahlen, *vb.* boast.
praktisch, *adj.* practical.
Prali'ne, -n, *n.f.* chocolate candy.
prallen, *vb.* bounce, be reflected.
Prämie, -n, *n.f.* premium, prize.
präpa'rie'ren, *vb.* prepare.
Präposition', -en, *n.f.* preposition.
Präsens, *n.nt.* present.
präsentie'ren, *vb.* present.
Präservativ', -e, *n.nt.* condom.
Präsident', -en, -en, *n.m.* president.
Präsiden'tin, -nen, *n.f.* president.
prasseln, *vb.* patter, crackle.

Praxis, *n.f.* practice; doctor's office.
Präzedenz'fall, -̈e, *n.m.* precedent.
Präzision', *n.f.* precision.
predigen, *vb.* preach.
Prediger, -, *n.m.* preacher.
Predigt, -en, *n.f.* sermon.
Preis, -e, *n.m.* price, cost; prize, praise.
Preiselbeere, -n, *n.f.* cranberry.
preisen*, *vb.* praise.
Preisgabe, -n, *n.f.* surrender, abandonment.
preis•geben*, *vb.* surrender, abandon.
prellen, *vb.* toss; cheat.
Premie're, -n, *n.f.* première.
Premier'minister, -, *n.m.* prime minister.
Premier'ministerin, -nen, *n.f.* prime minister.
Presse, *n.f.* press.
pressen, *vb.* press.
Prestige, -, *n.nt.* prestige.
Preuße, -n, -n, *n.m.* Prussian.
Preußen, *n.nt.* Prussia.
preußisch, *adj.* Prussian.
Priester, -, *n.m.* priest.
prima, *adj.* first class, swell.
primär', *adj.* primary.
Primel, -n, *n.f.* primrose.
primitiv', *adj.* primitive.
Prinz, -en, -en, *n.m.* prince.
Prinzes'sin, -nen, *n.f.* princess.
Prinzip', -ien, *n.nt.* principle.
Priorität', -en, *n.f.* priority.
Prise, -n, *n.f.* pinch.
Prisma, -men, *n.nt.* prism.
privat', *adj.* private.
Privileg', -ien, *n.nt.* privilege.
pro, *prep.* per.
Probe, -n, *n.f.* experiment, test; rehearsal; sample.
proben, *vb.* rehearse.
probeweise, *adj.* tentative.
Probezeit, -en, *n.f.* probation.
probie'ren, *vb.* try (out).
Problem', -e, *n.nt.* problem.
Produkt', -e, *n.nt.* product.
Produktion', *n.f.* production.
produktiv', *adj.* productive.
Produzent', -en, -en, *n.m.* producer.
produzie'ren, *vb.* produce.

profan', *adj.* profane.
Profes'sor, **-o'ren**, *n.m.* professor.
Professo'rin, **-nen**, *n.f.* professor.
Profil', **-e**, *n.nt.* profile.
Profit', **-e**, *n.m.* profit.
profitie'ren, *vb.* profit.
Progno'se, **-n**, *n.f.* prognosis.
Programm', **-e**, *n.nt.* program.
Projekt', **-e**, *n.nt.* project.
Projektion', **-en**, *n.f.* projection.
Projek'tor, **-o'ren**, *n.m.* projector.
projizie'ren, *vb.* project.
Proklamation', **-en**, *n.f.* proclamation.
Prokurist', **-en**, **-en**, *n.m.* manager.
Prokuris'tin, **-nen**, *n.f.* manager.
Proletariat', *n.nt.* proletariat.
Proleta'rier, **-**, *n.m.* proletarian.
proleta'risch, *adj.* proletarian.
Prolog', **-e**, *n.m.* prologue.
prominent', *adj.* prominent.
Prono'men, **-mina**, *n.nt.* pronoun.
Propagan'da, *n.f.* propaganda, publicity.
Propel'ler, **-**, *n.m.* propeller.
Prophet', **-en**, **-en**, *n.m.* prophet.
prophe'tisch, *adj.* prophetic.
prophezei'en, *vb.* prophesy.
Prophezei'ung, **-en**, *n.f.* prophecy.
Proportion', **-en**, *n.f.* proportion.
proppenvoll, *adj.* chock full.
Prosa, *n.f.* prose.
prosa'isch, *adj.* prosaic.
Prospekt', **-e**, *n.m.* prospectus.
Prostituiert'-, *n.f.* prostitute.
Protein', *n.nt.* protein.
Protest', **-e**, *n.m.* protest.
Protestant', **-en**, **-en**, *n.m.* Protestant.
protestie'ren, *vb.* protest.
Protokoll', **-e**, *n.nt.* minutes, record.
protzen, *vb.* show off.
protzig, *adj.* gaudy.
Proviant', *n.m.* food, supplies.
Provinz', **-en**, *n.f.* province.
provinziell', *adj.* provincial.
Provision', **-en**, *n.f.* commission.

proviso'risch, *adj.* temporary.
Provokation', **-en**, *n.f.* provocation.
provozie'ren, *vb.* provoke.
Prozent', **-e**, *n.nt.* per cent.
Prozent'satz, **-e**, *n.m.* percentage.
Prozeß', **-sse**, *n.m.* process; trial, lawsuit.
Prozession', **-en**, *n.f.* procession.
prüde, *adj.* prudish.
prüfen, *vb.* test, examine, verify.
Prüfung, **-en**, *n.f.* test, examination, scrutiny.
Prügel, **-**, *n.m.* cudgel; *(pl.)* beating.
Prügelei', **-en**, *n.f.* brawl.
prügeln, *vb.* beat, thrash.
Prunk, *n.m.* pomp, show.
prunkvoll, *adj.* pompous, showy.
PS, *abbr.* (= Pferdestärke) horsepower.
Psalm, **-en**, *n.m.* psalm.
Pseudonym', **-e**, *n.nt.* pseudonym.
psychede'lisch, *adj.* psychedelic.
Psychia'ter, **-**, *n.m.* psychiatrist.
Psychia'terin, **-nen**, *n.f.* psychiatrist.
Psychiatrie', *n.f.* psychiatry.
Psychoanaly'se, **-n**, *n.f.* psychoanalysis.
Psycholo'ge, **-n**, **-n**, *n.m.* psychologist.
Psychologie', *n.f.* psychology.
Psycholo'gin, **-nen**, *n.f.* psychologist.
psycholo'gisch, *adj.* psychological.
Psycho'se, **-n**, *n.f.* psychosis.
Pubertät', *n.f.* puberty.
Publikation', **-en**, *n.f.* publication.
Publikum, *n.nt.* public, audience.
publizie'ren, *vb.* publish.
Pudding, **-e**, *n.m.* pudding.
Pudel, **-**, *n.m.* poodle.
Puder, **-**, *n.m.* powder.
Puderdose, **-n**, *n.f.* compact.
pudern, *vb.* powder.
Puderquaste, **-n**, *n.f.* powder puff.
Puffer, **-**, *n.m.* buffer.
Pulli, **-s**, *n.m.* sweater.
Pullo'ver, **-**, *n.m.* sweater.
Puls, **-e**, *n.m.* pulse.

Pulsader, -n, *n.f.* artery.
Pulsar, -s *n.m.* pulsar.
pulsie'ren, *vb.* pulsate, throb.
Pult, -e, *n.nt.* desk, lectern.
Pulver, -, *n.nt.* powder.
Pumpe, -n, *n.f.* pump.
pumpen, *vb.* pump; borrow, lend.
Pumps, *n.pl.* pumps.
Punkt, -e, *n.m.* point, dot, period.
Punktgleichheit, *n.f.* tie.
pünktlich, *adj.* punctual.
Punktzahl, -en, *n.f.* score.
Punsch, *n.m.* punch.
Pupil'le, -n, *n.f.* pupil.
Puppe, -n, *n.f.* doll; chrysalis.

pur, *adj.* pure; (alcohol) straight.
Püree', -s, *n.nt.* purée.
Purpur, *n.m.* purple.
purpurn, *adj.* purple.
Puter, -, *n.m.* turkey.
Putsch, -e, *n.m.* attempt to overthrow the government.
Putz, *n.m.* finery.
putzen, *vb.* clean, polish.
Putzfrau, -en, *n.f.* cleaning woman.
putzig, *adj.* funny, droll, quaint.
Putzwaren, *n.pl.* millinery.
Puzzle, -s, *n.nt.* puzzle.
Pyja'ma, -s, *n.m.* pajamas.
Pyrami'de, -n, *n.f.* pyramid.

Q

quadraphon', *adj.* quadraphonic.
Quadrat', -e, *n.nt.* square.
Quadrat'-, *cpds.* square.
quadra'tisch, *adj.* square.
quaken, *vb.* quack, croak.
Qual, -en, *n.f.* torment, agony, ordeal.
quälen, *vb.* torment, torture.
Qualifikation', -en, *n.f.* qualification.
qualifizie'ren, *vb.* qualify.
Qualität', -en, *n.f.* quality.
qualmen, *vb.* smoke.
qualvoll, *adj.* agonizing.
Quantität', -en, *n.f.* quantity.
Quaranta'ne, -n, *n.f.* quarantine.
Quark, *n.m.* curds.
Quarkkäse, -, *n.m.* cottage cheese.
Quartal', -e, *n.nt.* quarter of a year.
Quartett', -e, *n.nt.* quartet.
Quartier', -e, *n.nt.* lodging, billet.

Quarz, -e, *n.m.* quartz.
Quasar, -e, *n.m.* quasar.
Quaste, -n, *n.f.* tuft.
Quatsch, *n.m.* nonsense, bunk, baloney.
Quecksilber, *n.nt.* mercury.
Quelle, -n, *n.f.* spring, source, well, fountain.
quellen*, *vb.* well, gush, flow.
quer, *adj.* cross(wise), diagonal.
Querschnitt, -, *n.m.* cross section.
Querstraße, -n, *n.f.* cross street.
Querverweis, -e, *n.m.* cross reference.
quetschen, *vb.* squeeze, bruise.
Quetschung, -en, *n.f.* contusion.
quietschen, *vb.* squeak.
Quintett', -e, *n.nt.* quintet.
quitt, *adj.* quits, even, square.
quittie'ren, *vb.* receipt.
Quittung, -en, *n.f.* receipt.
Quote, -n, *n.f.* quota.

R

Rabatt', -e, *n.m.* discount.
Rabau'ke, -n, -n, *n.m.* tough.
Rabbi'ner, -, *n.m.* rabbi.
Rabe, -n, -n, *n.m.* raven.
Rache, *n.f.* revenge.
rächen, *vb.* revenge, avenge.
Rachen, -, *n.m.* throat, jaws.
Rad, -er, *n.nt.* wheel.
Radar, *n.nt.* radar.

Radau', *n.m.* noise, racket.
radeln, *vb.* (bi)cycle.
rad-fahren*, *vb.* (bi)cycle.
Radfahrer, -, *n.m.* (bi)cyclist.
Radfahrerin, -nen, *n.f.* bicyclist.
radie'ren, *vb.* erase; etch.
Radier'gummi, -s, *n.m.* (rubber) eraser.
Radie'rung, -en, *n.f.* etching.

Radies'chen, -, *n.nt.* radish.
radikal', *adj.* radical.
Radio, -s, *n.nt.* radio.
radioaktiv', *adj.* radioactive.
radioaktiv'-Niederschlag, *n.m.* fallout.
Radioapparat, -e, *n.m.* radio set.
Radioempfänger, -, *n.m.* radio receiver.
Radiosender, -, *n.m.* radio transmitter, broadcasting station.
Radiosendung, -en, *n.f.* radio broadcast.
Radium, *n.nt.* radium.
Radius, -ien, *n.m.* radius.
Radspur, -en, *n.f.* rut.
Radweg, -e, *n.m.* bike path.
raffinie'ren, *vb.* refine.
raffiniert', *adj.* tricky, shrewd; sophisticated.
ragen, *vb.* extend, loom.
Rahm, *n.m.* cream.
rahmen, *vb.* frame.
Rahmen, -, *n.m.* frame.
Rake'te, -n, *n.f.* rocket.
Rake'tenwaffe, -n, *n.f.* missile.
rammen, *vb.* ram.
Rampe, -n, *n.f.* ramp.
Rand, -er, *n.m.* edge, brim, margin.
Rang, -e, *n.m.* rank.
rangie'ren, *vb.* switch, shunt.
Rangordnung, -en, *n.f.* hierarchy.
ranzig, *adj.* rancid.
Rapier', -e, *n.nt.* foil.
rasch, *adj.* quick.
rascheln, *vb.* rustle.
rasen, *vb.* rage.
Rasen, *n.m.* lawn, turf.
rasend, *adj.* frenzied.
Raserei', -en, *n.f.* frenzy.
Rasierapparat, -e, *n.m.* safety razor.
rasie'ren, *vb.* shave.
Rasier'klinge, -n, *n.f.* razor blade.
Rasier'messer, -, *n.nt.* (straight) razor.
Rasse, -n, *n.f.* race; breed.
rasseln, *vb.* rattle.
Rast, -en, *n.f.* rest.
rasten, *vb.* rest.
rastlos, *adj.* restless.
Rasur', -en, *n.f.* erasure; shave.

Rat, -e, *n.m.* advice; councilor.
Rate, -n, *n.f.* payment, installment.
raten*, *vb.* guess, advise.
Ratenzahlung, *n.f.* payment by installments.
ratifizie'ren, *vb.* ratify.
Ration', -en, *n.f.* ration.
rationell', *adj.* rational, reasonable.
rationie'ren, *vb.* ration.
ratlos, *adj.* helpless, perplexed, at one's wit's end.
Ratlosigkeit, *n.f.* perplexity.
ratsam, *adj.* advisable.
Ratsamkeit, *n.f.* advisability.
Rätsel, -, *n.nt.* riddle, puzzle; enigma, mystery.
rätselhaft, *adj.* puzzling, mysterious.
Ratte, -n, *n.f.* rat.
rattern, *vb.* rattle.
Raub, *n.m.* robbery, plunder.
rauben, *vb.* rob.
Räuber, -, *n.m.* robber.
Rauch, *n.m.* smoke.
rauchen, *vb.* smoke.
Raucher, -, *n.m.* smoker.
räuchern, *vb.* smoke (fish, meat).
raufen, *vb.* pull, tear; **(sich r.)** fight, brawl.
Rauferei', -en, *n.f.* brawl.
rauh, *adj.* rough; harsh; rugged.
Rauheit, -en, *n.f.* roughness.
Raum, -e, *n.m.* room, space.
räumen, *vb.* vacate.
Raumfahrt, *n.f.* space travel.
Rauminhalt, *n.m.* volume, capacity, contents.
räumlich, *adj.* spatial.
Raumtransporter, *n.m.* space shuttle.
Räumung, *n.f.* (*comm.*) clearance; (*mil.*) evacuation.
raunen, *vb.* whisper.
Rausch, -e, *n.m.* intoxication.
rauschen, *vb.* roar, rustle.
Rauschgift, -e, *n.nt.* narcotic, dope.
Razzia, -ien, *n.f.* raid.
reagie'ren, *vb.* react, respond.
Reaktion', -en, *n.f.* reaction, response.
Reaktionär', -e, *n.m.* reactionary.

reaktionär', *adj.* reactionary.
reaktivie'ren, *vb.* recommission.
Reak'tor, -o'ren, *n.m.* reactor.
realisie'ren, *vb.* realize, put into effect.
Realisie'rung, -en, *n.f.* realization.
Realis'mus, *n.m.* realism.
Realist', -en, -en, *n.f.* realist.
Realität', -en, *n.f.* reality.
Rebe, -n, *n.f.* vine; grape.
Rebstock, ⁼e, *n.m.* vine.
Rechen, -, *n.m.* rake.
Rechenaufgabe, -n, *n.f.* arithmetic problem.
Rechenmaschine, -n, *n.f.* calculating machine.
Rechenschaft, *n.f.* account, responsibility; (**R. ablegen**) account for.
Rechenschieber, -, *n.m.* slide rule.
rechnen, *vb.* count, do sums, figure.
Rechnen, *n.nt.* arithmetic.
Rechnung, -en, *n.f.* figuring, computation; bill; (**R. tragen***) take into account.
Rechnungsbuch, ⁼er, *n.nt.* account book.
recht, *adj.* right; (**r. haben***) be right.
Recht, -e, *n.nt.* right; (system of) law.
Rechteck, -e, *n.nt.* rectangle.
rechteckig, *adj.* rectangular, oblong.
rechtfertigen, *vb.* justify; vindicate.
Rechtfertigung, -en, *n.f.* justification.
rechtlich, *adj.* legal, judicial.
rechtmäßig, *adj.* lawful.
rechts, *adv.* (to the) right.
Rechtsanwalt, ⁼e, *n.m.* lawyer.
Rectsanwältin, -nen, *n.f.* lawyer.
rechtschaffen, *adj.* honest, righteous.
Rechtschaffenheit, *n.f.* honesty, righteousness.
Rechtschreibung, *n.f.* orthography, spelling.
Rechtsgelehrt-, *n.m.* jurist.
Rechtsprechung, *n.f.* jurisdiction.

Rechtsspruch, ⁼e, *n.m.* judgment, sentence.
Rechtsstreit, -e, *n.m.* litigation.
Rechtswissenschaft, *n.f.* jurisprudence.
recken, *vb.* stretch.
Redakteur', -e, *n.m.* editor.
Redaktion', -en, *n.f.* editorial office; editor.
Rede, -n, *n.f.* speech, talk; (**eine R. halten***) give a speech; (**keine R. sein* von**) be no question of; (**jemanden zur R. stellen**) confront a person with, take to task.
redegewandt, *adj.* eloquent.
Redekunst, *n.f.* rhetoric, oratory.
reden, *vb.* talk, speak; (**vernünftig r. mit**) reason with.
Redensart, -en, *n.f.* way of speaking; saying, idiom.
Redeteil, -e, *n.m.* part of speech.
Redewendung, -en, *n.f.* phrase, figure of speech.
redlich, *adj.* honest, upright.
Redner, -, *n.m.* speaker, orator.
Rednerin, -nen, *n.f.* speaker, orator.
redselig, *adj.* loquacious.
Reduktion', -en, *n.f.* reduction.
reduzie'ren, *vb.* reduce.
reell', *adj.* honest, sound.
reflektie'ren, *vb.* reflect.
Reflex', -e, *n.m.* reflex.
Reflexion', -en, *n.f.* reflection.
Reform', -en, *n.f.* reform.
reformie'ren, *vb.* reform.
Refrain', -s, *n.m.* refrain.
Regal', -e, *n.nt.* shelf.
rege, *adj.* alert; active.
Regel, -n, *n.f.* rule.
regelmäßig, *adj.* regular.
Regelmäßigkeit, *n.f.* regularity.
regeln, *vb.* regulate.
regelrecht, *adj.* regular, downright.
Regelung, -en, *n.f.* regulation.
regen, *vb.* (**sich r.**) stir, move.
Regen, -, *n.m.* rain.
Regenbogen, -, *n.m.* rainbow.
Regenguß, ⁼sse, *n.m.* downpour.
Regenmantel, -, *n.m.* raincoat.
Regenschirm, -e, *n.m.* umbrella.
Regie', *n.f.* direction.
regie'ren, *vb.* govern.

Regie'rung, -en, *n.f.* government.

Regi'me, -s, *n.nt.* regime.

Regiment', -er, *n.nt.* regiment.

Region', -en, *n.f.* region.

Regisseur', -e, *n.m.* director.

Regis'ter, -, *n.nt.* register, index.

Registrie'rung, -en, *n.f.* registration.

regnen, *vb.* rain.

regnerisch, *adj.* rainy.

regsam, *adj.* alert, quick.

regulie'ren, *vb.* regulate.

Reh, -e, *n.nt.* deer, roe.

rehabilitie'ren, *vb.* rehabilitate.

Rehleder, -, *n.nt.* deerskin.

Reibe, -n, *n.f.* grater.

reiben*, *vb.* rub; grate; chafe.

Reibung, -en, *n.f.* friction.

reich, *adj.* rich.

Reich, -e, *n.nt.* kingdom, empire, realm.

reichen, *vb. (tr.)* pass, hand, reach; *(intr.)* extend.

reichlich, *adj.* plentiful, ample, abundant.

Reichtum, -er, *n.m.* wealth, affluence.

Reichweite, *n.m.* reach, range.

reif, *adj.* ripe, mature.

Reife, *n.f.* maturity.

reifen, *vb.* ripen, mature.

Reifen, -, *n.m.* hoop; (auto, etc.) tire.

Reifenpanne, -n, *n.f.* puncture, blowout.

reiflich, *adj.* carefully considerate.

Reigen, -, *n.m.* (dance) round; (music) song.

Reihe, -n, *n.f.* row; series, succession.

reihen, *vb.* (sich r.) rank.

Reihenfolge, -n, *n.f.* sequence, succession.

Reim, -, *n.m.* rhyme.

rein, *adj.* clean, pure.

Reinfall, -e, *n.m.* flop.

rein·fallen*, *vb.* be taken in.

Reinheit, *n.f.* purity.

reinigen, *vb.* clean, cleanse.

Reinigung, -en, *n.f.* cleaning, cleansing; (chemische R.) dry-cleaner, dry-cleaning.

rein·legen, *vb.* trick, take in.

Reis, *n.m.* rice.

Reise, -n, *n.f.* trip, journey.

Reiseandenken, -, *n.nt.* souvenir.

Reisebüro, -s, *n.nt.* travel agency.

Reiseführer, -, *n.m.* guidebook.

reisen, *vb.* travel.

Reisend-, *n.m.&f.* traveler.

Reiseroute, -n, *n.f.* itinerary.

Reisescheck, -s, *n.m.* traveler's check.

reißen*, *vb.* rip, tear; (sich r. um) scramble for.

reißend, *adj.* rapid, racing.

Reißer, -, *n.m.* thriller, bestseller.

reiten*, *vb.* ride, horseback.

Reiter, -, *n.m.* rider.

Reiterin, -nen, *n.f.* rider.

Reiz, -e, *n.m.* charm, appeal; irritation.

reizbar, *adj.* sensitive, irritable.

reizen, *vb.* excite, tempt; irritate.

reizend, *adj.* adorable, lovely.

Reizfaktor, -en, *n.m.* irritant.

Reizmittel, -, *n.nt.* stimulant.

Reizung, -en, *n.f.* irritation.

rekeln, *vb.* (sich r.) stretch, sprawl.

Reklame, -n, *n.f.* advertisement, advertising, publicity.

reklamie'ren, *vb.* reclaim; complain.

Rekord', -e, *n.m.* record.

Rekrut', -en, -en, *n.m.* draftee, recruit.

Rektor, -o'ren, *n.m.* headmaster; (university) president, chancellor.

relativ', *adj.* relative.

Religion', -en, *n.f.* religion.

religiös', *adj.* religious.

Rendezvous, -, *n.nt.* rendezvous, tryst.

Rennen, -, *n.nt.* race.

rennen*, *vb.* run, dash; race.

Renntier, -e, *n.nt.* reindeer.

renovie'ren, *vb.* renovate.

renta'bel, *adj.* profitable.

Rente, -n, *n.f.* pension, income.

rentie'ren, *vb.* (sich r.) be profitable.

Reparation', -en, *n.f.* reparation.

Reparatur', -en, *n.f.* repair.

reparie'ren, *vb.* repair.

repatriie'ren, *vb.* repatriate.

Repertoire', -s, *n.nt.* repertoire.

Repor'ter, -, *n.m.* reporter.

Repor'terin, -nen, *n.f.* reporter.

Repräsentant', -en, -en, *n.m.* representative.
Repräsentation', -en, *n.f.* representation.
reproduzie'ren, *vb.* reproduce.
Reptil', -e *or* -ien, *n.nt.* reptile.
Republik', -en, *n.f.* republic.
republika'nisch, *adj.* republican.
requirie'ren, *vb.* requisition.
Requisition', -en, *n.f.* requisition.
Reservation', -en, *n.f.* reservation.
Reser've, -n, *n.f.* reserve.
reservie'ren, *vb.* reserve.
Reservoir', -s, *n.nt.* reservoir.
Residenz', -en, *n.f.* residence.
Resignation', -en, *n.f.* resignation.
resignie'ren, *vb.* resign.
resolut', *adj.* determined.
resonant', *adj.* resonant.
Resonanz', -en, *n.f.* resonance.
Respekt', *n.m.* respect, regard.
Rest, -e, *n.m.* rest, remnant.
Restaurant', -s, *n.nt.* restaurant.
restaurie'ren, *vb.* restore.
Restbestand, -̈e, *n.m.* residue.
restlos, *adj.* without remainder, entire.
Resultat', -e, *n.nt.* result.
Resümee', -s, *n.nt.* résumé.
retten, *vb.* rescue, save, salvage.
Retter, -, *n.m.* savior.
Rettung, -en, *n.f.* rescue; salvation.
Rettungsboot, -e, *n.nt.* lifeboat.
rettungslos, *adj.* irretrievable, hopeless.
Rettungsring, -e, *n.m.* life preserver.
Rettungswagen, -, *n.m.* ambulance.
Reue, *n.f.* repentance.
reuevoll, *adj.* repentant.
reuig, *adj.* penitent.
Revan'che, -n, *n.f.* revenge; return match.
Revers', -, *n.m.* lapel.
revidie'ren, *vb.* revise.
Revier', -e, *n.nt.* district.
Revision', -en, *n.f.* revision.
Revol'te, -n, *n.f.* revolt.
revoltie'ren, *vb.* revolt.
Revolution', -en, *n.f.* revolution.

revolutionär', *adj.* revolutionary.
Revol'ver, -, *n.m.* revolver, gun.
Rezept', -e, *n.nt.* receipt, recipe; prescription.
Rhabar'ber, *n.m.* rhubarb.
Rhapsodie', -i'en, *n.f.* rhapsody.
Rhein, *n.m.* Rhine.
rheto'risch, *adj.* rhetorical.
Rheuma, *n.nt.* rheumatism.
Rheumatis'mus, *n.m.* rheumatism.
rhythmisch, *adj.* rhythmical.
Rhythmus, -men, *n.m.* rhythm.
richten, *vb.* set right; (**r. auf**) turn to; (**sich r. an**) turn to; (**sich r. nach**) go by, be guided by, depend on; *(jur.)* judge.
Richter, -, *n.m.* judge.
Richterin, -nen, *n.f.* judge.
richterlich, *adj.* judicial, judiciary.
Richterstand, *n.m.* judiciary.
richtig, *adj.* true, correct.
Richtigkeit, *n.f.* correctness.
Richtung, -en, *n.f.* direction; tendency.
riechen*, *vb.* smell.
Riecher, -, *n.m.* (*fig.*) hunch.
Riegel, -, *n.m.* bolt.
Riemen, -, *n.m.* strap; oar.
Riese, -n, -n, *n.m.* giant.
riesenhaft, *adj.* gigantic.
riesig, *adj.* tremendous, vast.
rigoros', *adj.* rigorous.
Rind, -er, *n.nt.* ox, cow, cattle.
Rinde, -n, *n.f.* bark.
Rindfleisch, *n.nt.* beef.
Rindsleder, -, *n.nt.* cowhide.
Ring, -e, *n.m.* ring.
ringeln, *vb.* curl.
ringen*, *vb.* struggle, wrestle.
Ringkampf, -̈e, *n.m.* wrestling match.
Rinne, -n, *n.f.* rut, groove.
rinnen*, *vb.* run, flow.
Rinnstein, -e, *n.m.* curb, gutter.
Rippe, -n, *n.f.* rib.
Rippenfellentzündung, -en, *n.f.* pleurisy.
Risiko, -s *or* -ken, *n.nt.* risk, hazard, gamble.
riskie'ren, *vb.* risk, gamble.
Riß, -sse, *n.m.* tear, crack.
Ritt, -e, *n.m.* ride.
Ritter, -, *n.m.* knight.

ritterlich, *adj.* chivalrous.
rittlings, *adv.* astride.
Rituele, -e, *n.nt.* ritual.
rituell', *adj.* ritual.
Ritus, -en, *n.m.* rite.
Ritze, -n, *n.f.* crack.
Riva'le, -n, -n, *n.m.* rival.
Riva'lin, -nen, *n.f.* rival.
rivalisie'ren, *vb.* rival.
Rivalität', -en, *n.f.* rivalry.
Rizinusöl, -n, *n.nt.* castor oil.
Robbe, -n, *n.f.* seal.
Roboter, -, *n.m.* robot.
robust', *adj.* robust.
röcheln, *vb.* breathe heavily.
Rock, -̈e, *n.m.* (men) jacket; (women) skirt; (music) rock.
Rockmusik, *n.f.* rock music.
rodeln, *vb.* go sledding.
Rodelschlitten, -, *n.m.* sled.
Rogen, -, *n.m.* roe.
Roggen, *n.m.* rye.
roh, *adj.* raw, crude; (*fig.*) brutal.
Roheit, -en, *n.f.* crudeness, brutality.
Rohling, -e, *n.m.* rowdy.
Rohr, -e, *n.nt.* pipe; (gun) barrel; (bamboo, sugar) cane.
Röhre, -n, *n.f.* pipe, tube.
Rohrflöte, -n, *n.f.* reed pipe.
Rolle, -n, *n.f.* roll, coil; spool; role, part.
rollen, *vb.* roll.
Roller, -, *n.m.* scooter.
Rolltreppe, -n, *n.f.* escalator.
Rom, *n.nt.* Rome.
Roman', -e, *n.m.* novel.
roma'nisch, *adj.* Romance.
Roman'schriftsteller, -, *n.m.* novelist.
Roman'schriftstellerin, -nen, *n.f.* novelist.
Roman'tik, *n.m.* romanticism, Romantic Movement.
roman'tisch, *adj.* romantic.
Roman'ze, -n, *n.f.* romance.
Römer, -, *n.m.* Roman.
Römerin, -nen, *n.f.* Roman.
römisch, *adj.* Roman.
röntgen, *vb.* x-ray.
Röntgenaufnahme, -n, *n.f.* x-ray.
Röntgenstrahlen, *n.pl.* x-rays.
rosa, *adj.* pink.
Rose, -n, *n.f.* rose.

Rosenkranz, -̈e, *n.m.* rosary.
rosig, *adj.* rosy.
Rosi'ne, -n, *n.f.* raisin.
Roß, -sse, *n.nt.* horse, steed.
Rost, *n.m.* rust; (oven) grate.
rosten, *vb.* rust.
rösten, *vb.* roast; toast.
rostig, *adj.* rusty.
rot (-̈), *adj.* red.
rotbraun, *adj.* red-brown, maroon.
Röteln, *n.pl.* German measles.
rotie'ren, *vb.* rotate.
Rotwein, -e, *n.m.* red wine, claret.
Roué', -s, *n.m.* roué, rake.
Rouge, *n.nt.* rouge.
Roula'de, -n, *n.f.* meat roll.
Route, -n, *n.f.* route.
Routi'ne, -n, *n.f.* routine.
routiniert', *adj.* experienced.
Rowdy, -s, *n.m.* hoodlum.
Rübe, -n, *n.f.* (gelbe R.) carrot; (rote R.) beet; (weisse R.) turnip.
Rubin', -e, *n.m.* ruby.
Rubrik', -en, *n.f.* category, heading.
ruchbar, *adj.* notorious.
ruchlos, *adj.* infamous, profligate.
Ruck, -e, *n.m.* jerk, wrench.
Rückantwort, -en, *n.f.* reply.
ruckartig, *adj.* jerky.
rückbezüglich, *adj.* reflexive.
Rückblick, *n.m.* retrospect.
rücken, *vb.* move, move over.
Rücken, -, *n.m.* back.
rückerstatten, *vb.* refund.
Rückfahrkarte, -n, *n.f.* return ticket.
Rückfahrt, -en, *n.f.* return trip.
Rückfall, -̈e, *n.m.* relapse.
Rückgabe, *n.f.* return, restitution.
Rückgang, -̈e, *n.m.* retrogression, decline.
rückgängig, *adj.* declining; (r. machen) cancel, revoke.
Rückgrat, -e, *n.nt.* spine, backbone.
Rückhalt, *n.m.* support, reserve.
rückhaltlos, *adj.* unreserved, frank.
Rückhand, -̈, *n.f.* backhand.
Rückkaufswert, -e, *n.m.* equity (mortgage, etc.).
Rückkehr, *n.f.* return; reversion.

Rückkopplung, -en, *n.f.* feedback.
Rückmarsch, ⁼e, *n.m.* retreat.
Rucksack, ⁼e, *n.m.* knapsack.
Rückschlag, ⁼e, *n.m.* reverse, upset.
Rückschluß, ⁼sse, *n.m.* conclusion.
Rückseite, -n, *n.f.* reverse, rear.
Rücksicht, -en, *n.f.* consideration.
Rücksichtnahme, *n.f.* consideration.
rücksichtslos, *adj.* inconsiderate; reckless, ruthless.
Rücksichtslosigkeit, -en, *n.f.* lack of consideration, ill-mannered behavior; ruthlessness.
rücksichtsvoll, *adj.* thoughtful, considerate.
Rückstand, ⁼e, *n.m.* arrears; (**in R. geraten**) fall behind, lag.
rückständig, *adj.* in arrears; backward, antiquated.
Rücktritt, -e, *n.m.* resignation.
rückwärts, *adv.* backward(s).
Rückwärtsgang, ⁼e, *n.m.* reverse (gear).
ruckweise, *adv.* by fits and starts.
Rückzug, ⁼e, *n.m.* retreat.
Rudel, -, *n.nt.* pack.
Ruder, -, *n.nt.* oar.
Ruderboot, -e, *n.nt.* rowboat.
rudern, *vb.* row.
Ruf, -e, *n.m.* call; reputation, standing.
rufen*, *vb.* call, shout.
Rufnummer, -n, *n.f.* (telephone) number.
Rüge, -n, *n.f.* reprimand.
rügen, *vb.* reprimand.
Ruhe, *n.f.* rest; calmness, tranquility; silence.
ruhelos, *adj.* restless.
ruhen, *vb.* rest, repose.
Ruhestand, *n.m.* retirement.
Ruhestätte, -n, *n.f.* resting place.
ruhig, *adj.* calm, composed; quiet; (**das kannst du r. machen**) go ahead and do it.
Ruhm, *n.m.* fame, glory.
rühmen, *vb.* praise, extol.

rühmenswert, *adj.* praiseworthy.
rühmlich, *adj.* laudable.
ruhmlos, *adj.* inglorious.
ruhmreich, *adj.* glorious.
Ruhr, *n.f.* dysentery.
Rührei, -er, *n.nt.* scrambled eggs.
rühren, *vb.* move, stir; (**sich r.**) stir.
rührend, *adj.* touching, pathetic.
rührig, *adj.* lively, bustling.
Rührung, *n.f.* emotion, compassion.
Rui'ne, -n, *n.f.* ruin.
ruinie'ren, *vb.* ruin.
Rum, *n.m.* rum.
Rummel, *n.m.* hubbub, racket.
Rummelplatz, *n.m.* amusement park, fair.
rumpeln, *vb.* rumble.
Rumpf, ⁼e, *n.m.* torso, fuselage, hull.
rund, *adj.* round, circular.
Runde, -n, *n.f.* round; (sports) lap.
Rundfunk, *n.m.* radio.
Rundfunksendung, -en, *n.f.* broadcast.
Rundfunksprecher, -, *n.m.* broadcaster.
Rundfunkübertragung, -en, *n.f.* broadcast.
rundlich, *adj.* plump.
Rundreise, -n, *n.f.* tour.
Rundschreiben, -, *n.nt.* circular.
Runzel, -n, *n.f.* wrinkle.
runzeln, *vb.* wrinkle; (**die Stirn r.**) frown.
rupfen, *vb.* pluck.
Rüsche, -n, *n.f.* ruffle.
Ruß, *n.m.* soot, grime.
Russe, -n, *n.m.* Russian.
Rüssel, -n, *n.m.* trunk.
Russin, -nen, *n.f.* Russian.
russisch, *adj.* Russian.
Rußland, *n.nt.* Russia.
rüsten, *vb.* prepare; (*mil.*) arm.
rüstig, *adj.* vigorous, spry.
Rüstung, -en, *n.f.* armament; armor.
rutschen, *vb.* slide, skid.
rütteln, *vb.* shake, jolt.

Saal, Säle, *n.m.* large room, hall.
Saat, -en, *n.f.* seed, sowing.
Sabbat, -en, *n.m.* Sabbath.
Säbel, -, *n.m.* saber.
Sabota'ge, *n.f.* sabotage.
Saboteur', -e, *n.m.* saboteur.
sabotie'ren, *vb.* sabotage.
Sacharin', *n.nt.* saccharine.
Sache, -n, *n.f.* thing, matter; cause.
Sachkundig-, *n.m.* expert.
sachlich, *adj.* objective, relevant, matter-of-fact; (art) functional.
Sachlichkeit, *n.f.* objectivity, detachment.
sacht, *adj.* soft.
sachte, *adv.* cautiously, gingerly.
Sachverständig-, *n.m.&f.* expert.
Sack, -̈e, *n.m.* sack, bag.
Sadis'mus, *n.m.* sadism.
Sadist', -en, -en, *n.m.* sadist.
sadis'tisch, *adj.* sadistic.
säen, *vb.* sow.
Saft, -̈e, *n.m.* juice, sap.
saftig, *adj.* juicy, succulent.
Sage, -n, *n.f.* myth.
Säge, -n, *n.f.* saw.
sagen, *vb.* say, tell.
sägen, *vb.* saw.
sagenhaft, *adj.* mythical, fabulous.
Sago, *n.nt.* tapioca.
Sahne, *n.f.* cream.
Sahneneis, *n.nt.* ice cream.
Saison', -s, *n.f.* season.
Saite, -n, *n.f.* string, chord.
Sakrament', -e, *n.nt.* sacrament.
Sakrileg', -e, *n.nt.* sacrilege.
Sakristei, -en, *n.f.* sacristy, vestry.
Salat', -e, *n.m.* salad.
Salat'soße, -n, *n.f.* salad dressing.
Salbe, -n, *n.f.* salve, ointment.
salben, *vb.* anoint.
Saldo, -den, *n.m.* balance, remainder.
Salm, -e, *n.m.* salmon.
Salon', -s, *n.m.* salon.
salopp', *adj.* nonchalant.
salutie'ren, *vb.* salute.
Salve, -n, *n.f.* salvo.

Salz, -e, *n.nt.* salt.
salzen, *vb.* salt.
salzig, *adj.* salty.
Salzwasser, -, *n.nt.* brine.
Samen, -, *n.m.* seed.
sammeln, *vb.* collect, gather; (sich s.) (mil.) rally.
Sammler, -, *n.m.* collector.
Sammlerin, -nen, *n.f.* collector.
Sammlung, -en, *n.f.* collection.
Samstag, -e, *n.m.* Saturday.
Samt, *n.m.* velvet.
samt, *adv.&prep.* together with.
sämtlich, *adj.* entire.
Sanato'rium, -rien, *n.nt.* sanatorium.
Sand, -e, *n.m.* sand.
Sanda'le, -n, *n.f.* sandal.
sandig, *adj.* sandy.
Sandtorte, -n, *n.f.* pound cake.
sanft, *adj.* gentle, meek.
Sanftmut, *n.m.* gentleness.
sanftmütig, *adj.* gentle, meek.
Sänger, -, *n.m.* singer.
Sängerin, -nen, *n.f.* singer.
sang- und klanglos, *adv.* quietly.
Sankt, *adj.* Saint.
Saphir', -e, *n.m.* sapphire.
Sardel'le, -n, *n.f.* anchovy.
Sardi'ne, -n, *n.f.* sardine.
Sarg, -̈e, *n.m.* coffin.
Sarkas'mus, *n.m.* sarcasm.
sarkas'tisch, *adj.* sarcastic.
Satan, *n.m.* Satan.
sata'nisch, *adj.* diabolical.
Satellit', -en, -en, *n.m.* satellite.
Satin', *-s, n.m.* satin.
Sati're, -n, *n.f.* satire.
sati'risch, *adj.* satirical.
satt, *adj.* satiated; (ich bin s.) I have had enough to eat; (ich habe es s.) I am sick of it; (sich s. essen*, sehen*) have one's fill.
Sattel, -, *n.m.* saddle.
satteln, *vb.* saddle.
sättigen, *vb.* satiate, saturate.
Sättigung, *n.f.* satiation, saturation.
sattsam, *adv.* sufficiently.
Satz, -̈e, *n.m.* (gram.) sentence, clause; (music) movement; (dishes, tennis) set.

Satzlehre, *n.f.* syntax.
Satzung, -en, *n.f.* statute, by-law.
Satzzeichen,-, *n.nt.* punctuation mark.
Sau, ̈e, *n.f.* sow.
sauber, *adj.* clean, neat.
Sauberkeit, *n.f.* cleanliness, neatness.
säuberlich, *adj.* clean, careful.
säubern, *vb.* cleanse, purge.
Säuberungsaktion, -en, *n.f.* purge.
sauer, *adj.* sour, acid.
Säuerlichkeit, -en, *n.f.* acidity.
Sauerstoff, *n.m.* oxygen.
saufen*, *vb.* drink heavily, guzzle.
Säufer, -, *n.m.* drunkard.
saugen*, *vb.* suck.
Saugen, *n.nt.* suction.
Sauger, -, *n.m.* nipple (baby's bottle).
Säugetier, -e, *n.nt.* mammal.
Säugling, -e, *n.m.* infant, baby.
Säule, -n, *n.f.* pillar, column.
Saum, ̈e, *n.m.* seam, hem.
säumen, *vb.* hem; delay.
säumig, *adj.* tardy, delinquent.
Säure, -n, *n.f.* acid.
säuseln, *vb.* rustle.
sausen, *vb.* (wind) whistle; run, dash.
S-Bahn, *n.f.* city and suburban train.
schaben, *vb.* scrape.
Schabernack, -e, *n.m.* hoax.
schäbig, *adj.* shabby.
Schach, *n.nt.* chess; **(in S. halten*)** keep at bay.
Schachbrett, -er, *n.nt.* chessboard.
Schachfigur, -en, *n.f.* chessman.
schachmatt', *adj.* checkmate; *(fig.)* exhausted.
Schachspiel, -e, *n.nt.* chess.
Schacht, -e, *n.m.* shaft.
Schachtel, -n, *n.f.* box.
schade, *adv.* too bad.
Schädel, -, *n.m.* skull.
schaden, *vb.* harm; be harmful.
Schaden, -, *n.m.* harm, damage.
Schadenersatz, *n.m.* indemnity, compensation, damages.
schadenfroh, *adj.* gloating; **(s. sein*)** gloat.
schadhaft, *adj.* defective.

schädigen, *vb.* wrong, damage.
schädlich, *adj.* harmful, injurious.
Schädling, -e, *n.m.* pest, destructive insect.
Schädlingsbekämpfungsmittel, *n.nt.* pesticide.
Schaf, -e, *n.nt.* sheep.
Schäfer, -, *n.m.* shepherd.
schaffen*, *vb.* make, create.
schaffen, *vb.* get done, achieve; **(sich zu s. machen mit)** to busy oneself with, tangle.
Schaffner, -, *n.m.* conductor.
Schaffnerin, -nen, *n.f.* conductor.
Schafott', -e, *n.nt.* scaffold.
Schafskopf, ̈e, *n.m.* idiot.
Schaft, -e, *n.m.* shaft.
Schakal', -e, *n.m.* jackal.
Schal, -s, *n.m.* shawl, scarf.
schal, *adj.* stale.
Schale, -n, *n.f.* skin, rind; shell; dish, bowl.
schälen, *vb.* pare, peel.
Schalk, -e, *n.m.* roguе.
schalkhaft, *adj.* roguish.
Schall, ̈e, *n.m.* sound, ring.
Schalldämpfer, -, *n.m.* (auto) muffler; (gun) silencer.
schallen*, *vb.* ring, resound.
Schallgrenze, -n, *n.f.* sound barrier.
Schallplatte, -n, *n.f.* phonograph record.
Schalotte, -n, *n.f.* scallion.
Schaltanlage, -n, *n.f.* switchboard.
Schaltbrett, -er, *n.nt.* switchboard; control panel.
schalten, *vb.* shift; command; **(s. und walten)** do as one pleases.
Schalter, -, *n.m.* (elec.) switch; (ticket, etc.) window.
Schaltjahr, -e, *n.nt.* leap year.
Schaltung, -en, *n.f.* (elec.) connection; (auto) shift.
Scham, *n.f.* shame; chastity.
schämen, *vb.* shame; **(sich s.)** be ashamed.
Schamgefühl, -e, *n.nt.* sense of modesty.
schamhaft, *adj.* modest, chaste.
schamlos, *adj.* shameless, infamous.

Schamlosigkeit, *n.f.* shamelessness.

Schampun', -s, *n.nt.* shampoo.

schandbar, *adj.* shameful, disgraceful.

Schande, *n.f.* shame, dishonor.

schänden, *vb.* dishonor, ravish.

Schandfleck, -e, *n.m.* blemish, stigma.

schändlich, *adj.* infamous.

Schandtat, -en, *n.f.* crime.

Schändung, -en, *n.f.* desecration; rape.

Schankstube, -n, *n.f.* barroom.

Schanze, -n, *n.f.* entrenchment; **(sein Leben in die S. schlagen*)** risk one's life.

Schar, -en, *n.f.* flock, group, host.

scharf (-), *adj.* sharp, acute, keen.

Scharfblick, *n.m.* quick eye; acuteness.

Schärfe, -n, *n.f.* sharpness, acuteness.

schärfen, *vb.* sharpen.

Scharfrichter, -, *n.m.* executioner.

Scharfsinn, *n.m.* acumen, discernment.

scharfsinnig, *adj.* acute, shrewd.

Scharlach, *n.m.* scarlet fever.

scharlachrot, *adj.* scarlet.

Scharnier', -e, *n.nt.* hinge.

Schärpe, -n, *n.f.* sash.

Scharte, -n, *n.f.* crack.

Schatten, -, *n.m.* shade; shadow.

Schattenbild, -er, *n.nt.* silhouette.

Schattengestalt, -en, *n.f.* phantom, phantasm.

Schattenseite, -n, *n.f.* shady side; *(fig.)* disadvantage, drawback.

schattie'ren, *vb.* shade.

schattig, *adj.* shady.

Schatz, -e, *n.m.* treasure.

schätzen, *vb.* treasure, prize; estimate, gauge; esteem.

schätzenswert, *adj.* estimable.

Schatzmeister, -, *n.m.* treasurer.

Schätzung, -en, *n.f.* estimate.

schätzungsweise, *adv.* approximately.

Schau, *n.f.* show, exhibition; **(zur S. tragen*)** display.

Schauder, -, *n.m.* shudder, shiver.

schauderhaft, *adj.* horrible, ghastly.

schaudern, *vb.* shudder.

schauen, *vb.* see, look.

Schauer, -, *n.m.* shower; (fever) chill.

schauerlich, *adj.* gruesome.

Schaufel, -n, *n.f.* shovel; dustpan.

Schaufenster, -, *n.nt.* store window, display window.

Schaukel, -n, *n.f.* swing.

schaukeln, *vb.* swing, rock.

Schaukelstuhl, -e, *n.m.* rocking chair.

Schaum, *n.m.* froth, foam; lather.

schäumen, *vb.* froth, foam; lather.

Schaumgummi, *n.m.* foam rubber.

Schaumwein, -e, *n.m.* champagne.

Schauplatz, -e, *n.m.* scene, theater, locale.

schaurig, *adj.* horrible.

Schauspiel, -e, *n.nt.* drama; spectacle.

Schauspieler, -, *n.m.* actor.

Schauspielerin, -nen, *n.f.* actress.

Schaustellung, *n.f.* exhibition; ostentation.

Scheck, -s, *n.m.* check.

scheel, *adj.* **(s. an'sehen*)** look askance at.

Scheffel, -, *n.m.* bushel.

Scheibe, -n, *n.f.* disk; slice; pane.

Scheibenwischer, -, *n.m.* windshield wiper.

Scheich, -e, *n.m.* sheikh.

Scheide, -n, *n.f.* sheath; (water) divide; vagina.

scheiden*, *vb.* leave, part; **(sich s. lassen*)** get divorced.

Scheidewand, -e, *n.f.* partition.

Scheideweg, -e, *n.m.* crossroads.

Scheidung, -en, *n.f.* divorce.

Schein, *n.m.* shine, light, shimmer; brilliance.

scheinbar, *adj.* apparent; imaginary.

scheinen*, *vb.* shine, seem.

scheinheilig, *adj.* hypocritical.

Scheinwerfer, -, *n.m.* spotlight; headlight.

Scheinwerferlicht, *n.nt.* floodlight.

Scheitel, -, *n.m.* part (in the hair).

scheitern, *vb.* fail.

Schelle, -n, *n.f.* bell.

schellen, *vb.* ring.

Schelm, -e, *n.m.* rogue.

schelmisch, *adj.* roguish, mischievous.

Schelte, *n.f.* scolding.

schelten*, *vb.* scold.

Schema, -s, *n.nt.* scheme.

Schenke, -n, *n.f.* tavern, bar.

Schenkel, -, *n.m.* thigh.

schenken, *vb.* give (as a present).

Schenkstube, -n, *n.f.* taproom, bar.

Schenkung, -en, *n.f.* donation.

Schere, -n, *n.f.* scissors, shears.

scheren*, *vb.* shear.

Schererei, -en, *n.f.* bother.

Scherz, -e, *n.m.* joke, jest.

scherzen, *vb.* joke, jest, kid.

scherzhaft, *adj.* jocular.

scheu, *adj.* shy.

Scheu, *n.f.* timidity.

scheuchen, *vb.* scare, shoo.

scheuen, *vb.* shy, shun.

Scheuer, -n, *n.f.* barn, shed.

scheuern, *vb.* scour.

Scheuklappe, -n, *n.f.* blinder.

Scheune, -n, *n.f.* barn, shed.

Scheusal, -e, *n.nt.* monster, fright.

scheußlich, *adj.* horrible.

Schi, -er, *n.m.* ski.

Schicht, -en, *n.f.* layer, stratum, class.

schick, *adj.* chic, stylish.

Schick, *n.m.* skill; stylishness.

schicken, *vb.* send; **(sich s.)** be proper.

Schickeri'a, *n.f. (slang)* jet-set.

schicklich, *adj.* proper.

Schicksal, -e, *n.nt.* fate.

schicksalsschwer, *adj.* fateful.

Schickung, *n.f.* providence.

Schiebedach, *n.nt.* sun-roof.

schieben*, *vb.* push, shove; engage in illegal transactions.

Schieber, -, *n.m.* profiteer.

Schiebung, -en, *n.f.* racketeering.

Schiedsrichter, -, *n.m.* umpire, referee.

schief, *adj.* crooked, askew.

Schiefer, *n.m.* slate.

schielen, *vb.* be cross-eyed, look cross-eyed.

Schienbein, -e, *n.nt.* shin.

Schiene, -n, *n.f.* rail; *(med.)* splint.

schier, 1. *adj.* sheer, pure. **2.** *adv.* almost.

Schierling, *n.m.* hemlock.

schießen*, *vb.* shoot.

Schießgewehr, -e, *n.nt.* gun.

Schiff, -e, *n.nt.* ship; nave (of a church).

Schiffahrt, *n.f.* navigation.

schiffbar, *adj.* navigable.

Schiffbau, *n.m.* ship building.

Schiffbruch, -̈e, *n.m.* shipwreck.

Schiffer, -, *n.m.* mariner.

Schiffsrumpf, -̈e, *n.m.* hull.

schi·laufen*, *vb.* ski.

Schild, -e, *n.m.* shield.

Schild, -er, *n.nt.* sign.

Schilddrüse, -n, *n.f.* thyroid gland.

schildern, *vb.* portray.

Schilderung, -en, *n.f.* portrayal.

Schildkröte, -n, *n.f.* turtle, tortoise.

Schilf, *n.nt.* reed.

Schilift, -s, *n.m.* ski lift.

schillern, *vb.* be iridescent.

Schilling, -e, *n.m.* shilling.

Schimmel, -, *n.m.* mold, mildew; white horse.

schimmelig, *adj.* moldy.

Schimmer, -, *n.m.* glimmer, gleam.

Schimpan'se, -n, -n, *n.m.* chimpanzee.

Schimpf, -e, *n.m.* insult, abuse, disgrace.

schimpfen, *vb.* insult, abuse, complain, gripe.

Schimpfwort, -e, *n.nt.* term of abuse.

schinden*, *vb.* flay; *(fig.)* torment; **(sich s.)** work hard, slave.

Schinken, -, *n.m.* ham.

Schirm, -e, *n.m.* screen; umbrella, parasol; shelter.

schirmen, *vb.* protect.

Schirmherr, -n, -en, *n.m.* patron.

Schlacht, -en, *n.f.* battle.

schlachten, *vb.* slaughter.

Schlächter, -, *n.m.* butcher.

Schlachtfeld, -er, n.nt. battle-field.

Schlachtschiff, -e, n.nt. battle-ship.

Schlacke, -n, n.f. slag, clinker, cinder.

Schlaf, n.m. sleep.

Schlafanzug, ̈-e, n.m. pajamas.

Schläfe, -n, n.f. temple.

schlafen*, vb. sleep, be asleep.

Schlafenszeit, -en, n.f. bedtime.

schlaff, adj. limp.

Schlaffheit, n.f. limpness, laxity.

Schlaflosigkeit, n.f. insomnia.

Schlafmittel, -, n.nt. sleeping pill.

schläfrig, adj. sleepy.

Schlafrock, ̈-e, n.m. dressing gown.

Schlafwagen, -, n.m. sleeping car.

Schlafzimmer, -, n.nt. bedroom.

Schlag, ̈-e, n.m. blow, stroke, shock.

Schlagader, -n, n.f. artery.

Schlaganfall, ̈-e, n.m. stroke; apoplexy.

Schlagbaum, ̈-e, n.m. wooden bar, (railroad customs) barrier.

schlagen*, vb. hit, strike, beat; fell (trees); coin (money).

Schlager, -, n.m. hit (song, play, book).

Schläger, -, n.m. hitter; bat, club.

Schlägerei, -en, n.f. brawl.

Schlagholz, ̈-er, n.nt. bat, club.

Schlagobers, n.nt. whipped cream.

Schlagsahne, n.f. whipped cream.

Schlagseite, n.f. list.

Schlagwort, -e, n.nt. slogan.

Schlagzeile, -n, n.f. headline.

Schlamm, n.m. muck, mud.

schlampig, adj. frowsy.

Schlange, -n, n.f. snake, serpent.

schlängeln, vb. (sich s.) wind, wriggle.

schlank, adj. slender, slim.

schlapp, adj. slack, flabby.

Schlappe, -n, n.f. rebuff, setback, defeat.

schlau, adj. sly, clever, astute.

Schlauch, ̈-e, n.m. hose, tube.

Schlaufe, -n, n.f. loop.

schlecht, adj. bad.

schlechterdings, adv. absolutely.

schlechthin, adv. quite, simply.

Schlegel, -, n.m. mallet, sledge hammer, drumstick.

schleichen*, vb. sneak, slink, crawl.

Schleier, -, n.m. veil.

schleierhaft, adj. veil-like; inexplicable, mysterious.

Schleife, -n, n.f. bow.

schleifen, vb. drag.

schleifen*, vb. grind, polish, sharpen.

Schleifmittel, -, n.nt. abrasive.

Schleifstein, -e, n.m. grindstone.

Schleim, n.m. slime; mucus.

Schleimhaut, ̈-e, n.f. mucous membrane.

schleimig, adj. slimy; mucous.

schlendern, vb. saunter, stroll.

schlenkern, vb. shamble, dangle, swing.

Schleppe, -n, n.f. train.

schleppen, vb. drag, lug, haul, tow.

Schlepper, -, n.m. tugboat, tractor.

Schleuder, -n, n.f. slingshot, catapult, centrifuge.

schleudern, vb. hurl, fling; skid.

schleunig, adj. speedy.

Schleuse, -n, n.f. sluice, lock.

Schlich, -e, n.m. trick.

schlicht, adj. plain, simple.

schlichten, vb. smooth; arbitrate.

Schlichter, -, n.m. arbitrator.

Schlichtung, -en, n.f. arbitration.

schließen*, vb. shut; close; conclude.

Schließfach, ̈-er, n.nt. baggage locker.

schließlich, 1. adj. final. **2.** adv. at last.

Schliff, -e, n.m. cut, polish(ing), grind(ing); good manners, style; (letzter S.) final touch.

schlimm, adj. bad, serious.

Schlinge, -n, n.f. sling, noose.

schlingen*, vb. twist, wind; gulp.

schlingern, vb. roll; (fig.) stagger.

Schlips, -e, n.m. necktie.

Schlitten, -, n.m. sled, sleigh.

Schlittschuh, -e, n.m. skate.

schlittschuh·laufen*, *vb.* skate.
Schlitz, -e, *n.m.* slit, slot, slash.
schlitzen, *vb.* slit, slash.
Schloß, -sser, *n.nt.* lock; castle.
Schlot, -e, *n.m.* chimney, flue.
schlottern, *vb.* hang loosely, flop, shake.
Schlucht, -en, *n.f.* gorge, gulch.
schluchzen, *vb.* sob.
Schluck, -e, *n.m.* swallow.
Schluckauf, *n.m.* hiccup(s).
Schlückchen, -, *n.nt.* nip.
schlucken, *vb.* swallow.
Schlummer, *n.m.* slumber.
schlummern, *vb.* slumber.
Schlund, -̈e, *n.m.* throat, gullet; chasm.
schlüpfen, *vb.* slip.
Schlüpfer, -, *n.m.* panties.
schlüpfrig, *adj.* slippery.
schlürfen, *vb.* sip.
Schluß, -̈sse, *n.m.* end, close, conclusion.
Schlüssel, -, *n.m.* key.
Schlußfolgerung, -e, *n.f.* deduction, conclusion.
Schmach, *n.f.* disgrace, insult.
schmachten, *vb.* languish.
schmächtig, *adj.* slim, slight.
schmachvoll, *adj.* ignominious.
schmackhaft, *adj.* tasty.
schmähen, *vb.* abuse, revile.
schmal (-, -̈), *adj.* narrow.
schmälern, *vb.* curtail, detract from.
Schmalz, *n.nt.* lard.
schmarotzen, *vb.* sponge (on).
Schmarot′zer, -, *n.m.* hanger-on; parasite.
schmatzen, *vb.* smack one's lips.
Schmaus, -̈e, *n.m.* feast.
schmausen, *vb.* feast.
schmecken, *vb.* taste.
Schmeichelei′, -en, *n.f.* flattery.
schmeichelhaft, *adj.* flattering.
schmeicheln, *vb.* flatter.
schmeißen*, *vb.* throw, hurl, chuck, hit.
schmelzen*, *vb.* melt.
Schmerz, -en, *n.m.* ache, pain.
schmerzen, *vb.* ache, pain, hurt.
Schmerzgeld, *n.nt.* punitive damages.
schmerzhaft, *adj.* painful.
schmerzlos, *adj.* painless.

Schmetterling, -e, *n.m.* butterfly.
schmettern, *vb.* dash, smash; bray, blare.
Schmied, -e, *n.m.* blacksmith.
Schmiede, -n, *n.f.* forge.
schmieden, *vb.* forge.
schmiegen, *vb.* bend, press close, nestle, cling.
schmiegsam, *adj.* pliant, flexible.
Schmiere, -n, *n.f.* grease.
schmieren, *vb.* grease, smear, scribble; **(wie geschmiert′)** like clockwork.
schmierig, *adj.* greasy, dirty, sordid.
Schmiermittel, -, *n.nt.* lubricant.
Schminke, -n, *n.f.* rouge, make-up, grease paint.
schminken, *vb.* put on make-up.
Schmiß, -̈sse, *n.m.* stroke, cut; dueling scar; verve.
schmökern, *vb.* browse.
schmollen, *vb.* pout, sulk.
schmoren, *vb.* stew.
schmuck, *adj.* smart, trim.
Schmuck, *n.m.* ornament, jewelry.
schmücken, *vb.* decorate.
Schmucknadel, -n, *n.f.* clip.
Schmuggel, -, *n.m.* smuggling.
schmuggeln, *vb.* smuggle.
Schmuggelware, -n, *n.f.* contraband.
Schmuggler, -, *n.m.* smuggler.
schmunzeln, *vb.* smirk, grin.
schmusen, *vb.* cuddle, neck.
Schmutz, *n.m.* dirt, filth.
schmutzig, *adj.* dirty.
Schnabel, -̈, *n.m.* beak.
Schnake, -n, *n.f.* gnat.
Schnalle, -n, *n.f.* buckle, clasp.
schnallen, *vb.* buckle.
schnalzen, *vb.* click (one's tongue), snap (one's fingers), crack (a whip).
schnappen, *vb.* snap, snatch, grab, catch, gasp (for breath).
Schnappschuß, -̈sse, *n.m.* snapshot.
Schnaps, -̈, *n.m.* hard liquor, whisky, brandy.
schnarchen, *vb.* snore.
schnarren, *vb.* buzz, whir, rattle, burr.

schnattern, vb. cackle.
schnauben, vb. pant, snort.
schnaufen, vb. breathe hard.
Schnauze, -n, n.f. snout.
Schnecke, -n, n.f. snail.
Schnee, n.m. snow.
Schneepflug, -̈e, n.m. snowplow.
Schneesturm, -̈e, n.m. blizzard.
Schneid, n.m. bravado.
Schneide, -n, n.f. edge.
schneiden*, vb. cut.
schneidend, adj. cutting, scathing.
Schneider, -, n.m. tailor.
Schneiderin, -nen, n.f. dressmaker.
schneidig, adj. dashing.
schneien, vb. snow.
schnell, adj. quick.
schnellen, vb. flip, jerk.
Schnelligkeit, -en, n.f. swiftness.
Schnellzug, -̈e, n.m. express train.
schneuzen, vb. (sich s.) blow one's nose.
schnippisch, adj. saucy.
Schnitt, -e, n.m. cut, slice, incision.
Schnittbohne, -n, n.f. string bean.
Schnitte, -n, n.f. slice, sandwich.
Schnittlauch, n.m. chive(s).
Schnittmuster, -, n.nt. pattern.
Schnittpunkt, -e, n.m. intersection.
Schnittstelle, -n, f. (computer) interface.
Schnittwaren, n.pl. dry goods.
Schnittwunde, -n, n.f. cut.
Schnitzel, -, n.nt. chip; cutlet.
schnitzen, vb. carve, whittle.
Schnitzwerk, -e, n.nt. carving.
schnodd(e)rig, adj. insolent.
schnöde, adj. scornful, base.
Schnorchel, -, n.m. snorkel.
schnüffeln, vb. sniffle, snoop.
Schnuller, -, n.m. pacifier.
Schnupfen, -, n.m. cold (in the head).
Schnupftuch, -̈er, n.nt. handkerchief.
Schnuppe, -n, n.f. shooting star; **(das ist mir S.)** I don't care a hoot.
Schnur, -̈e, n.f. cord, string.
schnüren, vb. lace.

Schnurrbart, -̈e, n.m. mustache.
Schnürsenkel, -, n.m. shoelace.
Schock, -s, n.m. shock.
schockie'ren, vb. shock.
schofel(ig), adj. shabby, mean.
Schokola'de, -n, n.f. chocolate.
Scholle, -n, n.f. clod, soil.
schon, adv. already; even.
schön, adj. beautiful, nice.
schonen, vb. treat carefully, spare.
Schönheit, -en, n.f. beauty.
Schönheitssalon, -s, n.m. beauty parlor.
Schonung, -en, n.f. careful treatment, consideration.
schonungslos, adj. merciless.
Schopf, -̈e, n.m. forelock, crown.
schöpfen, vb. draw (water, breath); take from.
Schöpfer, n.m. creator.
schöpferisch, adj. creative.
Schöpfkelle, -n, n.f. scoop.
Schöpflöffel, -, n.m. ladle, dipper.
Schöpfung, n.f. creation.
Schoppen, -, n.m. glass of beer or wine; pint.
Schorf, n.m. scab.
Schornstein, -e, n.m. chimney, smokestack.
Schoß, -̈e, n.m. lap.
Schößling, -e, n.m. shoot.
Schote, -n, n.f. pod.
Schotte, -n, -n, n.m. Scotsman.
Schottin, -nen, n.f. Scotswoman.
schottisch, adj. Scotch.
Schottland, n.nt. Scotland.
schräg, adj. oblique.
Schrägschrift, -, n.f. italics.
Schramme, -n, n.f. scratch.
Schrank, -̈e, n.m. wardrobe, locker, cupboard, cabinet.
Schranke, -n, n.f. barrier.
Schrapnell', -s, n.nt. shrapnel.
Schraube, -n, n.f. screw.
schrauben, vb. screw.
Schraubenschlüssel, -, n.m. wrench.
Schraubenzieher, -, n.m. screwdriver.
Schreck, -e, n.m. fright, scare.
schrecken*, vb. frighten.
Schrecken, -, n.m. terror, fear.

schreckhaft, *adj.* easily frightened.

schrecklich, *adj.* awful, terrible.

Schrei, -e, *n.m.* cry, scream, shout.

schreiben*, *vb.* write.

Schreiben, -, *n.nt.* letter.

Schreiber, -, *n.m.* clerk, scribe.

Schreibheft, -e, *n.nt.* notebook.

Schreibkraft, ⁼e, *n.f.* typist; clerk.

Schreibmaschine, -n, *n.f.* typewriter.

Schreibtisch, -e, *n.m.* desk.

Schreibung, -en, *n.f.* spelling.

Schreibwaren, *n.pl.* stationery.

schreien*, *vb.* cry, scream, shout.

schreiend, *adj.* flagrant.

Schrein, -e, *n.m.* shrine, casket, cabinet.

schreiten*, *vb.* stride, step.

Schrift, -en, *n.f.* writing, script; (Heilige S.) scripture(s).

Schriftführer, -, *n.m.* secretary (of an organization).

schriftlich, *adj.* written, in writing.

Schriftsatz, ⁼e, *n.m.* type.

Schriftsteller, -, *n.m.* writer, author.

Schriftstellerin, -nen, *n.f.* writer, author.

schrill, *adj.* shrill.

Schritt, -e, *n.m.* step, pace; crotch (of trousers).

schroff, *adj.* steep, abrupt, curt.

Schrotmehl, *n.nt.* coarse meal, grits.

schrubbe(r)n, *vb.* scrub.

Schrulle, -n, *n.f.* whim.

schrumpfen, *vb.* shrink.

Schub, ⁼e, *n.m.* shove, thrust; batch.

Schublade, -n, *n.f.* drawer.

Schubschiff, -e, *n.nt.* tugboat.

schüchtern, *adj.* shy, bashful.

Schüchternheit, -en, *nf.* bashfulness, shyness.

Schuft, -e, *n.m.* cad, scoundrel.

schuften, *vb.* work hard, drudge.

schuftig, *adj.* mean, shabby.

Schuh, -e, *n.m.* shoe.

Schuhmacher, -, *n.m.* shoemaker.

Schuhmacherin, -nen, *n.f.* shoemaker.

Schuhputzer, -, *n.m.* bootblack.

Schuhwerk, -e, *n.nt.* footwear.

Schularbeiten, *n.pl.* homework.

Schulbeispiel, -e, *n.nt.* typical example.

Schuld, -en, *n.f.* fault, guilt, blame, debt.

schulden, *vb.* owe.

schuldhaft, *adj.* culpable.

schuldig, *adj.* guilty; due, owing.

Schuldigkeit, *n.f.* duty.

Schuldigsprechung, -en, *n.f.* conviction.

Schuldirektor, -en, *n.m.* headmaster, principal.

Schuldirektorin, -nen, *n.f.* headmistress, principal.

schuldlos, *adj.* guiltless.

Schuldner, -, *n.m.* debtor.

Schuldnerin, -nen, *n.f.* debtor.

Schule, -n, *n.f.* school.

schulen, *vb.* train, indoctrinate.

Schüler, -, *n.m.* (boy) pupil.

Schülerin, -nen, *n.f.* (girl) pupil.

Schulgeld, -er, *n.nt.* tuition.

Schulter, -n, *n.f.* shoulder.

schultern, *vb.* shoulder.

schummeln, *vb.* cheat.

Schund, -, *n.m.* trash.

Schupo, -s, *n.m.* (= Schutzpolizist) cop.

Schuppe, -n, *n.f.* scale; (*pl.*) dandruff.

Schuppen, -, *n.m.* shed, hangar.

schüren, *vb.* poke, stir up, foment.

Schurke, -n, -n, *n.m.* villain, scoundrel.

Schürze, -n, *n.f.* apron.

Schuß, ⁼sse, *n.m.* shot.

Schüssel, -n, *n.f.* dish, bowl.

schustern, *vb.* repair shoes.

Schuster, -, *n.m.* shoemaker.

Schutt, -, *n.m.* rubbish.

schütteln, *vb.* shake.

schütten, *vb.* shed, pour.

Schutz, -, *n.m.* protection.

Schütze, -n, -n, *n.m.* rifleman, marksman, shot.

schützen, *vb.* protect.

Schutzengel, -, *n.m.* guardian angel.

Schützengraben, -̈, n.m. trench, dugout.
Schutzhaft, n.f. protective custody.
Schutzheilig-, n.m.&f. patron saint.
Schutzherr, -n, -en, n.m. patron.
schutzlos, adj. unprotected, defenseless.
Schutzmann, -̈er, n.m. patrolman.
Schutzmarke, -n, n.f. trade mark.
schwach (-̈), adj. weak.
Schwäche, -n, n.f. weakness.
schwächen, vb. weaken.
Schwachheit, -en, n.f. frailty.
schwächlich, adj. feeble.
Schwächling, -e, n.m. weakling.
Schwachsinn, n.m. feeble-mindedness.
schwachsinnig, adj. feeble-minded.
Schwager, -̈r, n.m. brother-in-law.
Schwägerin, -nen, n.f. sister-in-law.
Schwalbe, -n, n.f. swallow.
Schwall, -e, n.m. flood.
Schwamm, -̈e, n.m. sponge.
Schwan, -̈e, n.m. swan.
schwanger, adj. pregnant.
Schwangerschaft, -en, n.f. pregnancy.
Schwangerschaftsverhütung, n.f. contraception.
schwanken, vb. totter, sway, vacillate, waver.
Schwankung, -en, n.f. fluctuation.
Schwanz, -̈e, n.m. tail.
schwänzen, vb. cut (a class).
Schwarm, -̈e, n.m. swarm.
schwärmen, vb. swarm; (s. für) be crazy about.
Schwärmer, -, n.m. enthusiast.
schwarz(-̈), adj. black; illegal.
Schwarz-, n. m. & f. Black (person).
Schwarzbrot, -e, n.nt. black bread.
schwärzen, vb. blacken.
Schwarzmarkt, -̈e, n.m. black market.

Schwarzseher, -, n.m. alarmist, pessimist.
schwatzen, schwätzen, vb. chatter, gab.
Schwebe, n.f. suspense, suspension; (in der S.) undecided.
schweben, vb. hover, be suspended, be pending.
Schwebezustand, -̈e, n.m. abeyance.
Schwede, -n, -n, n.m. Swede.
Schweden, n.nt. Sweden.
Schwedin, -nen, n.f. Swede.
schwedisch, adj. Swedish.
Schwefel, n.m. sulphur.
Schweif, -e, n.m. tail, train.
schweifen, vb. roam, range.
schweigen*, vb. keep quiet, be silent.
Schweigen, n.nt. silence.
schweigsam, adj. silent.
Schwein, -e, n.nt. swine, hog, pig; good luck.
Schweinebraten, -, n.m. roast of pork.
Schweinefleisch, n.nt. pork.
Schweinerei', -en, n.f. awful mess, dirty business.
Schweinestall, -̈e, n.m. pigsty.
Schweinsleder, n.nt. pigskin.
Schweiß, n.m. sweat.
Schweiz, n.f. Switzerland.
Schweizer, -, n.m. Swiss.
Schweizerin, -nen, n.f. Swiss.
schweizerisch, adj. Swiss.
schwelen, vb. smolder.
schwelgen, vb. revel.
Schwelgerei', -en, n.f. revelry.
Schwelle, -n, n.f. sill, threshold; (railroad) tie.
schwellen*, vb. swell.
schwenken, vb. wave, flourish, brandish.
schwer, adj. heavy; difficult.
Schwere, n.f. heaviness.
schwerfällig, adj. clumsy, ponderous, stolid.
Schwergewicht, n.nt. heavyweight.
schwerhörig, adj. hard of hearing.
Schwerkraft, n.f. gravity.
schwerlich, adj. with difficulty, hardly.
Schwermut, n.f. melancholy.

schwermütig, *adj.* moody, melancholy.

Schwerpunkt, *n.m.* center of gravity; emphasis.

Schwert, -er, *n.nt.* sword; centerboard.

schwerwiegend, *adj.* grave.

Schwester, -n, *n.f.* sister; nurse.

Schwiegereltern, *n.pl.* parents-in-law.

Schwiegermutter, ̈, *n.f.* mother-in-law.

Schwiegersohn, ̈e, *n.m.* son-in-law.

Schwiegertochter, ̈, *n.f.* daughter-in-law.

Schwiegervater, ̈, *n.m.* father-in-law.

Schwiele, -n, *n.f.* callous, weal.

schwielig, *adj.* callous.

schwierig, *adj.* difficult.

Schwierigkeit, -en, *n.f.* difficulty, trouble.

Schwimmbad, ̈er, *n.nt.* swimming pool.

schwimmen*, *vb.* swim.

Schwimmweste, -n, *n.f.* lifejacket.

Schwindel, -, *n.m.* dizziness; swindle, hoax; bunk.

Schwindelgefühl, *n.nt.* vertigo.

schwindeln, *vb.* swindle, cheat, fraud.

schwinden*, *vb.* disappear.

Schwindler, -, *n.m.* swindler, cheat, fraud.

schwindlig, *adj.* dizzy.

Schwindsucht, *n.f.* consumption.

schwindsüchtig, *adj.* consumptive.

schwingen*, *vb.* swing, brandish, oscillate.

Schwingung, -en, *n.f.* oscillation.

Schwips, *n.m.* **(einen S. haben*)** be tipsy.

schwirren, *vb.* whir.

schwitzen, *vb.* sweat.

schwören*, *vb.* swear.

schwul, *adj.* homosexual.

schwül, *adj.* sultry, muggy.

Schwulst, ̈e, *n.m.* bombast.

Schwund, *n.m.* disappearance, loss.

Schwung, ̈e, *n.m.* swing, verve, animation, motion.

Schwungkraft, *n.f.* drive.

schwunglos, *adj.* lackadaisical.

schwungvoll, *adj.* spirited.

Schwur, ̈e, *n.m.* oath.

sechs, *num.* six.

sechst-, *adj.* sixth.

Sechstel, -, *n.nt.* sixth part; **(ein s.)** one-sixth.

sechzig, *num.* sixty.

sechzigst-, *adj.* sixtieth.

Sechzigstel, -, *n.nt.* sixtieth part; **(ein s.)** one-sixtieth.

See, Se'en, *n.m.* lake.

See, Se'en, *n.f.* sea.

See-, *cpds.* naval, marine.

Seegang, *n.m.* (rough, calm) sea.

Seehund, -e, *n.m.* seal.

seekrank, *adj.* seasick.

Seekrankheit, *n.f.* seasickness.

Seele, -n, *n.f.* soul, spirit, mind.

Seeleute, *n.pl.* seamen.

seelisch, *adj.* spiritual.

Seelsorge, *n.f.* ministry.

Seemann, -leute, *n.m.* mariner.

Seemeile, -n, *n.f.* nautical mile.

Seeräuber, -, *n.m.* pirate.

Seereise, -n, *n.f.* cruise.

Seetang, *n.m.* seaweed.

seetüchtig, *adj.* seaworthy.

Seezunge, -n, *n.f.* sole.

Segel, -, *n.nt.* sail.

Segelboot, -e, *n.nt.* sailboat.

Segelflug, *n.m.* gliding.

Segelflugzeug, -e, *n.nt.* glider, sailplane.

segeln, *vb.* sail.

Segeltuch, *n.nt.* canvas, duck.

Segen, -, *n.m.* blessing.

Segment, -e, *n.nt.* segment.

segnen, *vb.* bless.

Segnung, -en, *n.f.* blessing, benediction.

sehen*, *vb.* see.

sehenswert, *adj.* worth seeing.

Sehenswürdigkeit, -en, *n.f.* sight(s).

Seher, -, *n.m.* seer, prophet.

Sehkraft, ̈e, *n.f.* (power of) sight, vision.

Sehne, -n, *n.f.* tendon, ligament, sinew.

sehnen, *vb.* **(sich s.)** long, yearn.

Sehnsucht, *n.f.* longing.

sehnsüchtig, *adj.* longing.
sehnsuchtsvoll, *adj.* longing.
sehr, *adv.* very, much, a lot.
Sehweite, -n, *n.f.* range of sight.
seicht, *adj.* shallow, insipid.
Seide, -n, *n.f.* silk.
Seidel, -, *n.nt.* beer mug.
seiden, *adj.* silk.
Seidenpapier, *n.nt.* tissue paper.
seidig, *adj.* silky.
Seife, -n, *n.f.* soap.
Seifenschaum, *n.m.* suds.
seihen, *vb.* strain.
Seil, -e, *n.nt.* rope, cable.
Seilbahn, -en, *n.f.* cableway.
sein*, *vb.* be.
sein, -, -e, *adj.* his, its.
Sein, *n.nt.* being.
seiner, -es, -e, *pron.* his, its.
seinerseits, *adv.* for his part.
seinerzeit, *adv.* at the time.
seinesgleichen, *pron.* equal to
him, such as he.
seinetwegen, *adv.* for his sake;
for all he cares.
seinetwillen, *adv.* (um s.) for his
sake, because of him.
seit, 1. *prep.* since, for. **2.** *conj.*
since.
seitab', *adv.* aside.
seitdem, 1. *conj.* since. **2.** *adv.*
since then.
Seite, -n, *n.f.* side; page.
seitenlang, *adj.* going on for
pages.
seitens, *prep.* on behalf of.
Seitensprung, -̈e, *n.m.* escapade.
Seitenstraße, -n, *n.f.* side street.
Seitenzahl, -en, *n.f.* number of
pages.
seither, *adv.* since then.
seitlich, *adj.* lateral.
seitwärts, *adv.* sideways.
Sekretär', -e, *n.m.* secretary.
Sekretä'rin, -nen, *n.f.* secretary.
Sekt, -e, *n.m.* champagne.
Sekte, -n, *n.f.* sect, denomination.
Sekundant', -en, -en, *n.m.* second (at a duel).
sekundär', *adj.* secondary.
Sekun'de, -n, *n.f.* second.
selb-, *adj.* same.
selber, *adv.* (my-, your-, him-,
etc.) self; (our-, your-, them-)
selves.

selbst, *adv.* even; (my-, your-,
him-, etc.) self; (our-, your-,
them-) selves.
Selbstachtung, *n.f.* self-respect.
selbständig, *adj.* independent.
Selbständigkeit, *n.f.* independence.
Selbstbeherrschung, *n.f.* self-
control.
Selbstbestimmung, *n.f.* self-de-
termination.
selbstbewußt, *adj.* self-conscious.
Selbstbiographie, -n, autobiography.
selbstgefällig, *adj.* self-satisfied,
smug.
selbstgefertigt, *adj.* homemade.
selbstgerecht, *adj.* self-righ-
teous.
Selbstgespräch, -e, *n.nt.* monologue.
selbstlos, *adj.* unselfish.
Selbstmord, -e, *n.m.* suicide.
selbstredend, *adj.* self-evident.
selbstsicher, *adj.* self-confident.
Selbstsucht, *n.f.* selfishness.
selbstsüchtig, *adj.* selfish.
selbsttätig, *adj.* automatic.
selbstverständlich, *adj.* obvious.
Selbstverwaltung, *n.f.* home
rule.
selbstzufrieden, *adj.* complacent.
Selbstzufriedenheit, *n.f.* complacency.
selig, *adj.* blessed; blissfully
happy; deceased, late.
Seligkeit, -en, *n.f.* salvation,
bliss.
selig·sprechen*, *vb.* beatify.
Sellerie, *n.m.* celery.
selten, 1. *adj.* rare, scarce. **2.** *adv.*
seldom.
Seltenheit, -en, *n.f.* rarity.
Selters, Selter(s)wasser, *n.nt.*
soda water.
seltsam, *adj.* strange, queer, curious.
Seman'tik, *n.f.* semantics.
seman'tisch, *adj.* semantic.
Semes'ter, -, *n.nt.* semester, term.
Semiko'lon, -s, *n.nt.* semicolon.
Seminar', -e, *n.nt.* seminar(y).
Semit', -en, -en, *n.m.* Semite.

semi'tisch, *adj.* Semitic.
Semmel, -n, *n.f.* roll.
Senat', -e, *n.m.* senate.
Sena'tor, -o'ren, *n.m.* senator.
Senato'rin, -nen, *n.f.* senator.
senden*, *vb.* send, ship.
senden, *vb.* broadcast.
Sender, -, *n.m.* sender, transmitter, broadcasting station.
Sendung, -en, *n.f.* shipment; broadcast, transmission.
Senf, *n.m.* mustard.
sengen, *vb.* scorch, singe.
Senior, -o'ren, *n.m.* senior citizen.
senken, *vb.* sink, lower, reduce.
senkrecht, *adj.* perpendicular.
Senkung, -en, *n.f.* depression, reduction.
Sensation', -en, *n.f.* sensation, thrill.
sensationell', *adj.* sensational.
Sense, -n, *n.f.* scythe.
sensi'bel, *adj.* sensitive.
sentimental', *adj.* sentimental.
Septem'ber, -, *n.m.* September.
Serbe, -n, -n, *n.m.* Serbian.
Serbien, *n.nt.* Serbia.
Serbin, -nen, *n.f.* Serbian.
serbisch, *adj.* Serbian.
Serie, -n, *n.f.* series.
Serum, -ra, *n.nt.* serum.
Servi'ce, -, *n.nt.* service, set.
servie'ren, *vb.* serve.
Servier'platte, -n, *n.f.* platter.
Serviet'te, -n, *n.f.* napkin.
Sessel, -, *n.m.* easy-chair.
seßhaft, *adj.* settled, established.
setzen, *vb.* set, put, place; **(sich s.)** sit down.
Seuche, -n, *n.f.* plague, epidemic.
seufzen, *vb.* sigh.
Seufzer, -, *n.m.* sigh.
sexuell', *adj.* sexual.
Siam, *n.nt.* Siam.
Siame'se, -n, -n, *n.m.* Siamese.
siame'sisch, *adj.* Siamese.
Sibi'rien, *n.nt.* Siberia.
sich, *pron.* (him-, her-, it-, your-)self, (them-, your-)selves; each other, one another.
Sichel, -n, *n.f.* sickle; crescent.
sicher, *adj.* sure, certain, safe, secure.

Sicherheit, -en, *n.f.* safety, security, certainty.
Sicherheitsnadel, -n, *n.f.* safety-pin.
sicherlich, *adv.* surely.
sichern, *vb.* secure, safeguard.
Sicherung, -en, *n.f.* fuse.
Sicht, *n.f.* sight.
sichtbar, *adj.* visible.
sichten, *vb.* sift; sight.
sickern, *vb.* seep.
sie, *pron.* she; they.
Sie, *pron.* you (normal polite).
Sieb, -e, *n.nt.* sieve, strainer.
sieben, *vb.* sift, strain.
sieben, *num.* seven.
sieb(en)t-, *adj.* seventh.
Sieb(en)tel,-, *n.nt.* seventh part; **(ein s.)** one-seventh.
siebzig, *num.* seventy.
siebzigst-, *adj.* seventieth.
Siebzigstel, -, *n.nt.* seventieth part; **(ein s.)** one-seventieth.
siedeln, *vb.* settle.
sieden*, *vb.* boil.
Siedler, -, *n.m.* settler.
Siedlerin, -nen, *n.f.* settler.
Siedlung, -en, *n.f.* settlement.
Sieg, -e, *n.m.* victory.
Siegel, -, *n.nt.* seal.
siegeln, *vb.* seal.
siegen, *vb.* win, be victorious.
Sieger, -, *n.m.* winner, victor.
sieghaft, *adj.* triumphant.
siegreich, *adj.* victorious.
Signal', -e, *n.nt.* signal.
Signal'horn, -̈er, *n.nt.* bugle.
Silbe, -n, *n.f.* syllable.
Silber, *n.nt.* silver.
silbern, *adj.* silver.
Silberwaren, *n.f.* silverware.
silbisch, *adj.* syllabic.
silbrig, *adj.* silvery.
Silves'ter, *n.nt.* New Year's Eve.
Sims, -e, *n.m.* cornice; ledge, sill, mantelpiece.
singen*, *vb.* sing.
Singular, -e, *n.m.* singular.
sinken*, *vb.* sink, decline, fall.
Sinn, -e, *n.m.* sense, mind, meaning, taste.
Sinnbild, -er, *n.nt.* symbol.
sinnen*, *vb.* think, meditate, plot.
sinnig, *adj.* thoughtful, appropriate.

sinnlich, *adj.* sensual.
sinnlos, *adj.* senseless.
Sintflut, *n.f.* flood, deluge.
Sippe, -n, *n.f.* kin; clan, tribe.
Sire'ne, -n, *n.f.* siren.
Sirup, -e, *n.m.* molasses; syrup.
Sitte, -n, *n.f.* custom; (*pl.*) mores, manners, morals.
Sittenlehre, -n, *n.f.* ethics.
sittenlos, *adj.* immoral.
sittig, *adj.* chaste, well-bred.
sittlich, *adj.* moral.
Situation', -en, *n.f.* situation.
Sitz, -e, *n.m.* seat; residence.
sitzen*, *vb.* sit, be seated; fit; be in jail.
sitzen·bleiben*, *vb.* remain seated; get stuck (with); not be promoted.
sitzen·lassen*, *vb.* jilt.
Sitzplatz, -̈e, *n.m.* seat.
Sitzung, -en, *n.f.* session.
Sizilia'ner, -, *n.m.* Sicilian.
Sizilia'nerin, -nen, *n.f.* Sicilian.
sizilia'nisch, *adj.* Sicilian.
Sizi'lien, *n.nt.* Sicily.
Skala, -len, *n.f.* scale.
Skandal', -e, *n.m.* scandal.
Skandina'vien, *n.nt.* Scandinavia.
Skandina'vier, -, *n.m.* Scandinavian.
Skandina'vierin, -nen, *n.f.* Scandinavian.
skandina'visch, *adj.* Scandinavian.
Skelett, -e, *n.nt.* skeleton.
Skepsis, *n.f.* skepticism.
Skeptiker, -, *n.m.* skeptic.
skeptisch, *adj.* skeptic(al).
Ski, -er, *n.m.* ski.
ski·laufen*, *vb.* ski.
Skilehrer, -, *n.m.* ski instructor.
Skilehrerin, -nen, *n.f.* ski instructor.
Skilift, -s, *n.m.* ski lift.
Skizze, -n, *n.f.* sketch.
skizzie'ren, *vb.* sketch.
Sklave, -n, -n, *n.m.* slave.
Sklaverei', -, *n.f.* slavery.
Sklavin, -nen, *n.f.* slave.
Skrupel, -, *n.m.* scruple.
skrupellos, *adj.* unscrupulous.
Slang, *n.m.* slang.
Slawe, -n, -n, *n.m.* Slav.

slawisch, *adj.* Slavic.
Slowa'ke, -n, -n, *n.m.* Slovak.
Slowakei', *n.f.* Slovakia.
Slowa'kin, -nen, *n.f.* Slovak.
slowa'kisch, *adj.* Slovakian.
Smaragd', -e, *n.m.* emerald.
Smoking, -s, *n.m.* dinner jacket, tuxedo.
Snob, -s, *n.m.* snob.
so, *adv.* so, thus; **(s. groß wie)** as big as.
Socke, -n, *n.f.* sock.
Sockenhalter, -, *n.m.* garter.
Soda, *n.nt.* soda.
Sodbrennen, *n.nt.* heartburn.
soe'ben, *adv.* just now.
Sofa, -s, *n.nt.* sofa.
sofort', *adv.* immediately.
sofor'tig, *adj.* instantaneous.
Software, -, *n.f.* software.
Sog, -e, *n.m.* suction; undertow.
sogar', *adv.* yet, even.
sogenannt, *adj.* so-called.
Sohle, -n, *n.f.* sole.
Sohn, -̈e, *n.m.* son.
solch(er, -es, -e), *adj.* such.
solcherlei, *adj.* of such a kind.
solchermaßen, *adv.* in such a way.
Sold, -e, *n.m.* pay.
Soldat', -en, -en, *n.m.* soldier.
solid', *adj.* solid.
Solidarität', *n.f.* solidarity.
Solist', -en, -en, *n.m.* soloist.
Solis'tin, -nen, *n.f.* soloist.
Soll, *n.nt.* debit; quota.
sollen*, *vb.* be supposed to, be said to; shall; **(er sollte gehen*)** he should, ought to go; **(er hätte gehen* sollen)** he should, ought to have gone.
Solo, -s, *n.nt.* solo.
Sommer, -, *n.m.* summer.
Sommersprosse, -n, *n.f.* freckle.
Sommerzeit, -en, *n.f.* summer time; daylight-saving time.
Sona'te, -n, *n.f.* sonata.
Sonde, -n, *n.f.* probe.
sonder, *prep.* without.
Sonder-, *cpds.* special.
Sonderangebot, -e, *n.nt.* bargain, special sale.
sonderbar, *adj.* strange, queer.
sonderbarerwei'se, *adv.* strange to say.

sonderglei'chen, *adv.* without equal, unparalleled.
sonderlich, *adj.* peculiar.
sondern, *vb.* separate.
sondern, *conj.* but (on the contrary).
sondie'ren, *vb.* sound, probe.
Sonett', *-e, n.nt.* sonnet.
Sonnabend, -e, *n.m.* Saturday.
Sonne, -n, *n.f.* sun.
sonnen, *vb.* (sich s.) sun oneself, bask.
Sonnenbrand, -̈e, *n.m.* sunburn.
Sonnenbräune, *n.f.* sun tan.
sonnenklar, *adj.* clear as daylight.
Sonnenschein, *n.m.* sunshine.
Sonnenstich, -e, *n.m.* sun stroke.
sonnenverbrannt, *adj.* sunburned.
sonnig, *adj.* sunny.
Sonntag, -e, *n.m.* Sunday.
sonst, *adv.* otherwise, else; formerly.
sonstig, *adj.* other; former.
sonstwie, *adv.* in some other way.
sonstwo, *adv.* somewhere else.
sonstwoher, *adv.* from some other place.
sonstwohin, *adv.* to some other place.
Sopran', -e, *n.m.* soprano.
Sorbett, -e, *n.nt.* sherbet.
Sorge, -n, *n.f.* sorrow; worry, anxiety, apprehension; care.
sorgen, *vb.* (s. für) care for, provide; (sich s.) worry, concern oneself.
sorgenfrei, *adj.* carefree.
sorgenvoll, *adj.* worried, care-worn.
Sorgfalt, *n.f.* care.
sorgfältig, *adj.* careful, meticulous.
sorglos, *adj.* carefree.
sorgsam, *adj.* careful, painstaking.
Sorte, -n, *n.f.* sort, kind.
sortie'ren, *vb.* sort, assort, classify.
Soße, -n, *n.f.* sauce, gravy.
souverän', *adj.* sovereign.
Souveränität', *n.f.* sovereignty.
soviel, *adv.* so much, as much.
sowie, *conj.* as well as; as soon as.
sowieso', *adv.* in any case.

Sowjet, -s, *n.m.* Soviet.
sowje'tisch, *adj.* Soviet.
Sowjetunion, *n.f.* Soviet Union.
sowohl, *adv.* as well; (s. A als B, s. A wie B) both A and B.
sozial', *adj.* social.
sozialisie'ren, *vb.* socialize, nationalize.
Sozialis'mus, *n.m.* socialism.
Sozialist', -en, -en, *n.m.* socialist.
Sozialis'tin, -nen, *n.f.* socialist.
sozialis'tisch, *adj.* socialistic.
Soziologie', *n.f.* sociology.
sozusagen, *adv.* as it were, so to speak.
Spaghet'ti, *n.pl.* spaghetti.
Spalt, -e, *n.m.* crack, chink.
spaltbar, *adj.* fissionable.
Spalte, -n, *n.f.* crevice, gap; (newspaper) column.
spalten, *vb.* split.
Spaltung, -en, *n.f.* cleavage; fission.
Spange, -n, *n.f.* clasp, buckle.
Spanien, *n.nt.* Spain.
Spanier, -, *n.m.* Spaniard.
Spanierin, -nen, *n.f.* Spaniard.
spanisch, *adj.* Spanish.
Spann, -e, *n.m.* arch, instep.
Spanne, -n, *n.f.* span.
spannen, *vb.* stretch; tighten.
spannend, *adj.* exciting, gripping.
Spannkraft, *n.f.* elasticity; (fig.) energy.
Spannung, -en, *n.f.* tension; (fig.) close attention, suspense.
sparen, *vb.* save.
Spargel, -, *n.m.* asparagus.
Sparkasse, -n, *n.f.* savings bank.
spärlich, *adj.* sparse, meager.
Sparren, -, *n.m.* spar, rafter.
sparsam, *adj.* thrifty, economical.
Sparsamkeit, *n.f.* thrift.
Spaß, -̈e, *n.m.* joke, fun.
spaßeshalber, *adv.* for the fun of it.
spaßig, *adj.* funny.
Spaßmacher, -, *n.m.* jester.
spät, *adj.* late.
Spaten, -, *n.m.* spade.
spätestens, *adv.* at the latest.
Spatz, -en, *n.m.* sparrow.
spazie'ren-gehen*, *vb.* go for a walk, stroll.

Spazier'fahrt, -en, *n.f.* drive.
Spazier'gang, ̈-, *n.m.* walk.
Specht, -e, *n.m.* woodpecker.
Speck, *n.m.* fat; bacon.
spedie'ren, *vb.* dispatch.
Spediteur', -e, *n.m.* shipping agent.
Speer, -e, *n.m.* spear; javelin.
Speiche, -n, *n.f.* spoke.
Speichel, *n.m.* saliva.
Speicher, -, *n.m.* loft, storage place.
speien*, *vb.* spit.
Speise, -n, *n.f.* food, nourishment.
Speisekammer, -n, *n.f.* pantry.
Speisekarte, -n, *n.f.* bill of fare, menu.
speisen, *vb. (tr.)* feed; *(intr.)* eat.
Speiseröhre, -n, *n.f.* esophagus.
Speisewagen, -, *n.m.* diner, dining-car.
Speisezettel, -, *n.m.* menu.
Speisung, -en, *n.f.* feeding.
Spekta'kel, -, *n.m.* noise, racket.
spekulie'ren, *vb.* speculate.
spenda'bel, *adj.* free and easy with money; **(s. sein*)** splurge.
Spende, -n, *n.f.* donation.
spenden, *vb.* give; donate.
Sperling, -e, *n.m.* sparrow.
Sperre, -n, *n.f.* barrier, blockade; gate.
sperren, *vb.* block, obstruct, blockade; (money) freeze.
Sperrfeuer, -, *n.nt.* barrage.
Sperrstunde, -n, *n.f.* curfew.
Spesen, *n.pl.* charges, expenses, **(auf S.)** on an expense account.
spezialisie'ren, *vb.* specialize.
Spezialist', -en, -en, *n.m.* specialist.
Spezialis'tin, -en, *n.f.* specialist.
Spezialität', -en, *n.f.* specialty.
speziell', *adj.* special, specific.
spezi'fisch, *adj.* specific.
spezifizie'ren, *vb.* specify.
Sphäre, -n, *n.f.* sphere.
Sphinx, -en, *n.f.* sphinx.
spicken, *vb.* lard, interlard.
Spiegel, -, *n.m.* mirror.
spiegeln, *vb.* mirror, reflect.
Spiegelung, -en, *n.f.* reflection.
Spiel, -e, *n.nt.* play, game; gambling; pack (of cards).

Spielbank, -en, *n.f.* gambling casino.
spielen, *vb.* play, act; **(um Geld s.)** gamble.
Spieler, -, *n.m.* player.
Spielerin, -nen, *n.f.* player.
spielerisch, *adj.* playful.
Spielgefährte, -n, -n, *n.m.* playmate.
Spielgefährtin, -nen, *n.f.* playmate.
Spielplatz, ̈-e, *n.m.* playground.
Spielraum, ̈-, *n.m.* room for action, range; elbow room; margin.
Spielverderber, -, *n.m.* spoilsport.
Spielwaren, *n.pl.* toys.
Spielzeug, -e, *n.nt.* toy.
Spieß, -e, *n.m.* spear; top sergeant.
Spinat', *n.m.* spinach.
Spindel, -n, *n.f.* spindle.
Spinett', -e, *n.nt.* spinet, harpsichord.
Spinne, -n, *n.f.* spider.
spinnen*, *vb.* spin; be crazy.
Spinngewebe, -, *n.nt.* cobweb.
Spion', -e, *n.m.* spy.
Spionag'e, *n.f.* espionage.
spionie'ren, *vb.* spy.
Spira'le, -n, *n.f.* spiral.
spiral'förmig, *adj.* spiral.
Spiritis'mus, *n.m.* spiritism.
Spiritualis'mus, *n.m.* spiritualism.
Spirituo'sen, *n.pl.* liquor, spirits.
spitz, *adj.* pointed, acute.
Spitzbart, ̈-e, *n.m.* goatee.
Spitze, -n, *n.f.* point, tip, top; lace.
spitzenartig, *adj.* lacy.
spitzfindig, *adj.* shrewd; subtle.
Spitzhacke, -n, *n.f.* pick.
Spitzname(n), -, *n.m.* nickname.
spleißen*, *vb.* splice.
Splitter, -, *n.m.* splinter, chip.
splittern, *vb.* splinter, shatter.
spontan', *adj.* spontaneous.
spora'disch, *adj.* sporadic.
Sporn, Sporen, *n.m.* spur.
Sport, -e, *n.m.* sport.
Sportler, -, *n.m.* sportsman; athlete.
Sportlerin, -nen, *n.f.* athlete.

sportlich, *adj.* athletic; sportsmanlike.

Sportplatz, ̈e, *n.m.* athletic field, stadium.

Spott, *n.m.* mockery, ridicule.

spottbillig, *adj.* dirt cheap.

spotten, *vb.* mock, scoff.

Spötter, -, *n.m.* scoffer.

spöttisch, *adj.* derisive.

Sprache, -n, *n.f.* speech; language.

spracheigen, *adj.* idiomatic.

Sprachfehler, -, *n.m.* speech impediment.

Sprachführer, -, *n.m.* phrase book.

sprachgewandt, *adj.* fluent.

sprachlos, *adj.* speechless.

Sprachschatz, *n.m.* vocabulary.

Sprachwissenschaft, -en, *n.f.* linguistics, philology.

sprechen*, *vb.* speak, talk.

Sprecher, -, *n.m.* speaker, spokesman.

Sprecherin, -nen, *n.f.* speaker, spokesperson.

Sprechstunde, -n, *n.f.* office hour.

spreizen, *vb.* spread apart.

sprengen, *vb.* explode, break; sprinkle.

Sprengstoff, -e, *n.m.* explosive.

Sprichwort, ̈er, *n.nt.* proverb, adage.

sprichwörtlich, *adj.* proverbial.

sprießen*, *vb.* sprout.

Springbrunnen, -, *n.m.* fountain.

springen*, *vb.* jump; crack.

Springer, -, *n.m.* (chess) knight.

Springquell, -e, *n.m.* fountain.

sprinten, *vb.* sprint.

Spritze, -n, *n.f.* spray; injection; hypodermic.

spritzen, *vb.* spray, squirt, splash, inject.

spröde, *adj.* brittle; chapped; reserved, prim.

Sproß, -sse, *n.m.* sprout.

Sprößling, -e, *n.m.* shoot; offspring.

Sprotte, -n, *n.f.* sprat.

Spruch, ̈e, *n.m.* saying.

Sprudel, -, *n.m.* bubbling water; soda water.

sprudeln, *vb.* bubble.

Sprudeln, *n.nt.* effervescence.

sprühen, *vb.* spark, sparkle.

Sprühregen, *n.m.* drizzle.

Sprung, ̈e, *n.m.* jump; fissure, crack.

Sprungbrett, -er, *n.nt.* diving board; (*fig.*) stepping stone.

sprunghaft, *adj.* jumpy; erratic.

Sprungschanze, -n, *n.f.* ski-jump.

Spucke, *n.f.* spit, saliva.

spucken, *vb.* spit.

Spuk, -e, *n.m.* spook, ghost.

Spule, -n, *n.f.* spool, reel; (*elec.*) coil; bobbin.

spulen, *vb.* reel, wind.

spülen, *vb.* rinse, wash; (toilet) flush.

Spülstein, -e, *n.m.* sink.

Spund, -e, *n.m.* spigot, tap.

Spur, -en, *n.f.* trace, track.

spuren, *vb.* follow the prescribed pattern.

spüren, *vb.* feel; trace.

spurlos, *adj.* without a trace.

Spurweite, -n, *n.f.* width of track, gauge.

sputen, *vb.* (**sich s.**) hurry up.

Staat, -en, *n.m.* state, government.

Staatenbund, ̈e, *n.m.* federation.

staatlich, *adj.* national, governmental.

Staatsangehörig-, *n.m.&f.* national citizen.

Staatsangehörigkeit, -en, *n.f.* citizenship, nationality.

Stattsanwalt, ̈e, *n.m.* district attorney.

Staatsanwältin, -nen, *n.f.* district attorney.

staatsfeindlich, *adj.* subversive.

Staatskunst, *n.f.* statesmanship.

Staatsmann, ̈er, *n.m.* statesman.

Staatssekretär, -e, *n.m.* undersecretary of a ministry.

Staatsstreich, -e, *n.m.* coup d'état.

Stab, ̈e, *n.m.* staff, rod.

stabil', *adj.* stable.

stabilisie'ren, *vb.* stabilize.

Stabilität', *n.f.* stability.

Stachel, -n, *n.m.* sting, thorn, spike.

Stachelbeere, -n, *n.f.* gooseberry.

Stachelschwein, -e, *n.nt.* porcupine.

Stadion, -dien, *n.nt.* stadium.

Stadium, -dien, *n.nt.* stage.

Stadt, ̈e, *n.f.* town, city.

stadtbekannt, *adj.* known all over town, notorious.

städtisch, *adj.* municipal; urban.

Stadtplan, ̈e, *n.m.* city map.

Stadtteil, -e, *n.m.* borough.

Staffel, -n, *n.f.* rung, step; (*mil.*) echelon, squadron.

staffeln, *vb.* graduate, stagger.

Stagflation', *n.f.* stagflation.

stagnie'ren, *vb.* stagnate.

stagnie'rend, *adj.* stagnant.

Stahl, -e, *n.m.* steel.

Stahlhelm, -e, *n.m.* steel helmet.

Stahlwaren, *n.pl.* cutlery; hardware.

Stall, ̈e, *n.m.* stall, stable, barn.

Stamm, ̈e, *n.m.* (tree) trunk; (word) stem; tribe, clan.

Stammbaum, ̈e, *n.m.* family tree; pedigree.

stammeln, *vb.* stammer.

stammen, *vb.* stem, originate, be descended.

Stammgast, ̈e, *n.m.* habitué.

stämmig, *adj.* sturdy, burly.

stampfen, *vb.* stamp, trample.

Stand, ̈e, *n.m.* stand(ing), position; level; status; class, estate.

Standard, -s, *n.m.* standard.

standardisie'ren, *vb.* standardize.

Ständchen, -, *n.nt.* serenade.

Ständer, -, *n.m.* rack, stand.

Standesamt, ̈er, *n.nt.* marriage bureau; registrar.

standesbewußt, *adj.* class-conscious.

standesgemäß, *adj.* according to one's rank.

standhaft, *adj.* steadfast.

Standhaftigkeit, *n.f.* constancy.

stand·halten, *vb.* hold one's ground, withstand.

Standpunkt, -e, *n.m.* standpoint, point of view.

Stange, -n, *n.f.* rod, bar, pole; carton (of cigarettes).

Stapel, -, *n.m.* pile; stock; (ship) slip; (**vom S. lassen***) launch.

stapeln, *vb.* pile up.

stapfen, *vb.* stamp, plod.

Star, -e, *n.m.* (eye) cataract; (bird) starling; (film) star.

stark (-), *adj.* strong.

Stärke, -n, *n.f.* strength; starch.

stärken, *vb.* strengthen; starch.

Stärkungsmittel, -, *n.nt.* tonic.

starr, *adj.* rigid.

starren, *vb.* stare.

Starrheit, *n.f.* rigidity.

starrköpfig, *adj.* stubborn, headstrong.

Starrsinn, *n.m.* obstinacy.

Start, -s, *n.m.* start.

Startbahn, -en, *n.f.* runway.

starten, *vb.* start.

Startklappe, -n, *n.f.* choke (auto).

Station', -en, *n.f.* station.

stationär', *adj.* stationary.

Stations'vorsteher, -, *n.m.* station master.

statisch, *adj.* static.

Statist', -en, -en, *n.m.* (theater) extra; (*fig.*) dummy.

Statis'tik, *n.f.* statistics.

Stativ', -e, *n.nt.* (photo) tripod.

statt, *prep.* instead of.

Stätte, -n, *n.f.* place.

statt·finden*, *vb.* take place.

stattlich, *adj.* imposing.

Statue, -n, *n.f.* statue.

Staub, -, *n.m.* dust.

staubig, *adj.* dusty.

Staubsauger, -, *n.m.* vacuum cleaner.

Staudamm, ̈e, *n.m.* dam.

stauen, *vb.* dam up; (**sich s.**) be dammed up, get jammed up.

staunen, *vb.* be astonished, wonder.

Stausee, -n, *n.m.* reservoir.

Stauung, -en, *n.f.* congestion.

stechen*, *vb.* prick, sting; pierce, stab.

Stechschritt, *n.m.* goose step.

Steckdose, -n, *n.f.* (*elec.*) outlet, socket.

stecken(*), *vb. intr.* be located, be hidden; (**wo steckt er denn?**) where *is* he, anyhow?; (**s. bleiben***) get stuck.

stecken, vb. tr. put, stick, pin, hide.

Steckenpferd, -e, n.nt. hobbyhorse; hobby.

Stecknadel, -n, n.f. pin.

Steckrübe, -n, n.f. turnip.

Steg, -e, n.m. path; footbridge.

stehen*, vb. stand, be located; be becoming; (**sich gut s.**) be on good terms; (**es steht dahin'**) it has yet to be shown.

stehen•bleiben*, vb. stop.

stehen•lassen*, vb. leave standing; leave behind, forget.

stehlen*, vb. steal.

Stehplatz, -̈e, n.m. standing room.

steif, adj. stiff, rigid.

Steifheit, -en, n.f. stiffness, rigidity.

Steig, -e, n.m. path.

steigen*, vb. climb, rise.

steigern, vb. increase, boost; (**sich s.**) increase, (fig.) work oneself up.

Steigung, -en, n.f. rise, slope, ascent.

steil, adj. steep.

Stein, -e, n.m. stone, rock.

Steingut, n.nt. earthenware, crockery.

steinigen, vb. stone.

Stelldichein, n.nt. rendezvous.

Stelle, -n, n.f. place, spot, point.

stellen, vb. place, put, set.

Stellenangebot, -e, n.nt. position offered.

Stellenvermittlung, -en, n.f. employment agency.

stellenweise, adv. in parts; in places.

Stellung, -en, n.f. position, place, stand; job; (**S. nehmen**) comment.

Stellungnahme, -n, n.f. comment, attitude.

stellvertretend, adj. assistant, deputy.

Stellvertreter, -, n.m. representative, deputy, alternate.

Stellvertreterin, -nen, n.f. representative, deputy, alternate.

stemmen, vb. stem; (**sich s. gegen**) oppose, resist.

Stempel, -, n.m. stamp.

stempeln, vb. stamp; (**s. gehen**) be on the dole.

Stenographie', -i'en, n.f. shorthand.

stenographie'ren, vb. take shorthand, write shorthand.

Stenotypis'tin, -nen, n.f. stenographer.

Steppdecke, -n, n.f. quilt comforter.

Steppe, -n, n.f. steppe.

steppen, vb. stitch.

sterben*, vb. die.

sterblich, adj. mortal.

stereophon', adj. stereophonic, stereo.

steril', adj. sterile.

sterilisie'ren, vb. sterilize.

Sterilität', n.f. sterility.

Sterling, n.nt. pound sterling.

Stern, -e, n.m. star.

Sternbild, -er, n.nt. constellation.

Sternchen, -, n.nt. asterisk.

Sternkunde, -, n.f. astronomy.

Sternwarte, -n, n.f. observatory.

stet(ig), adj. steady.

stets, adv. always.

Steuer, -, n.nt. rudder, helm.

Steuer, -n, n.f. tax.

Steuererklärung, -en, n.f. tax return.

steurfrei, adj. tax-free; duty-free.

steuern, vb. steer, pilot, navigate.

Steuerruder, -, n.nt. rudder.

Steuerzahler, -, n.m. taxpayer.

Steward, -s, n.m. steward.

Stewardeß, -ssen, n.f. stewardess.

Stich, -e, n.m. stab; bite, sting; stitch.

stichhaltig, adj. valid, sound.

Stichwort, -̈er, n.nt. cue.

sticken, vb. embroider.

Stickerei', -en, n.f. embroidery.

Stickstoff, n.m. nitrogen.

stieben*, vb. fly (about), scatter.

Stief-, cpds. step-; (**Stiefvater**) stepfather; etc.

Stiefel, -, n.m. boot.

Stiel, -e, n.m. handle; stalk, stem.

stier, adj. glassy (look).

Stier, -e, n.m. steer.

stieren, vb. stare.

Stift, -e, n.m. peg, pin, tack; crayon, pencil.

Stift, -e(r), *n.nt.* charitable institution.
stiften, *vb.* donate; found; endow.
Stiftung, -en, *n.f.* foundation; donation.
Stil, -e, *n.m.* style.
stilgerecht, *adj.* in good style, in good taste.
still, *adj.* still, quiet.
Stille, *n.f.* stillness, silence.
Stilleben, -, *n.nt.* still-life.
stillen, *vb.* still, quench; nurse (a baby).
stillos, *adj.* in bad taste.
stillschweigend, *adj.* silent; tacit, implicit.
Stillstand, *n.m.* halt.
Stimmabgabe, -n, *n.f.* vote; voting.
Stimmband, ⁼er, *n.nt.* vocal cord.
Stimme, -n, *n.f.* voice; vote.
stimmen, *vb.* tune; vote; be correct.
Stimmengleichheit, *n.f.* tie vote.
Stimmenprüfung, -en, *n.f.* recounting of votes.
Stimmrecht, -e, *n.nt.* suffrage, franchise.
Stimmung, -en, *n.f.* mood; morale.
stimmungsvoll, *adj.* festive, moving; intimate.
Stimmzettel, -, *n.m.* ballot.
stinken*, *vb.* stink.
Stinktier, -e, *n.nt.* skunk.
Stint, -e, *n.m.* smelt.
Stipendium, -dien, *n.nt.* scholarship, grant.
Stirn, -en, *n.f.* forehead, brow.
Stirnhöhle, -n, *n.f.* sinus.
Stock, ⁼e, *n.m.* stick, cane.
stockdunkel, *adj.* pitch-dark.
stocken, *vb.* stop, come to a halt; falter.
Stockung, -en, *n.f.* stop, standstill; deadlock.
Stockwerk, -e, *n.nt.* floor, story.
Stoff, -e, *n.m.* matter, substance; material; cloth.
stofflich, *adj.* material.
stöhnen, *vb.* groan.
Stoiker, -, *n.m.* stoic.
stoisch, *adj.* stoical.
Stola, -len, *n.f.* stole.
stolpern, *vb.* stumble, trip.

stolz, *adj.* proud.
Stolz, *n.m.* pride.
stolzie'ren, *vb.* strut.
stopfen, *vb.* stuff; (socks, etc.) darn.
stoppen, *vb.* stop.
Stöpsel, -, *n.m.* stopper; (elec.) plug.
Stör, -e, *n.m.* sturgeon.
Storch, ⁼e, *n.m.* stork.
stören, *vb.* disturb, bother.
Störenfried, -e, *n.m.* intruder, troublemaker.
Störung, -en, *n.f.* disturbance; (radio) interference, static.
Stoß, ⁼e, *n.m.* blow, hit, thrust.
stoßen*, *vb.* push, kick, hit, thrust.
Stoßstange, -n, *n.f.* bumper.
stottern, *vb.* stutter.
Strafanstalt, -en, *n.f.* penal intitution.
strafbar, *adj.* liable to punishment.
Strafe, -n, *n.f.* punishment; fine; sentence.
strafen, *vb.* punish.
straff, *adj.* taut, tight.
straffen, *vb.* tighten.
Strafgebühr, -en, *n.f.* fine.
Strafgericht, -e, *n.nt.* criminal court.
Strafkammer, -n, *n.f.* criminal court.
Sträfling, -e, *n.m.* convict.
Strafmandat, -e, *n.nt.* traffic ticket.
Strafporto, *n.nt.* postage due.
Strahl, -en, *n.m.* ray, beam; (water) spout.
strahlen, *vb.* beam, gleam, radiate.
Strahlen, *n.nt.* radiance.
strahlend, *adj.* radiant.
Strahlflugzeug, -e, *n.nt.* jet plane.
Strahlung, -en, *n.f.* radiation.
Strähne, -n, *n.f.* strand; streak.
stramm, *adj.* tight, tight; (fig.) strapping.
strampeln, *vb.* kick.
Strand, -e, *n.m.* beach, shore.
stranden, *vb.* strand.
Strandgut, *n.nt.* jetsam.

Strang, ⁻e, *n.m.* rope; (über die Stränge schlagen*) run riot.

Strapa'ze, -n, *n.f.* exertion, drudgery.

strapazier'fähig, *adj.* durable.

Straße, -n, *n.f.* street, road.

Straßenbahn, -en, *n.f.* streetcar, trolley.

Strategie', *n.f.* strategy.

strate'gisch, *adj.* strategic.

Stratosphä're, *n.f.* stratosphere.

sträuben, *vb.* (sich s.) bristle; (*fig.*) struggle against, resist.

Strauch, ⁻er, *n.m.* shrub.

straucheln, *vb.* falter, stumble.

Strauß, ⁻e, *n.m.* bouquet; ostrich.

streben, *vb.* strive, endeavor, aspire.

Streben, *n.nt.* pursuit.

Strebepfeiler, -, *n.m.* flying buttress.

Streber, -, *n.m.* (school) grind; (society) social climber.

strebsam, *adj.* zealous.

Strecke, -n, *n.f.* stretch, distance.

strecken, *vb.* stretch; (die Waffen s.) lay down one's arms.

Streich, -e, *n.m.* stroke, blow; prank.

streicheln, *vb.* stroke, caress.

streichen*, *vb.* scratch; paint.

Streichholz, ⁻er, *n.nt.* match.

Streichorchester, -, *n.nt.* string orchestra.

Streichung, -en, *n.f.* deletion.

Streife, -n, *n.f.* patrol.

streifen, *vb.* touch lightly.

Streifen, -, *n.m.* strip.

Streik, -s, *n.m.* strike.

Streikposten, -, *n.m.* picket.

Streit, -e, *n.m.* quarrel, dispute.

streiten*, *vb.* fight; (sich s.) quarrel.

Streitfrage, -n, *n.f.* controversy.

Streitpunkt, -e, *n.m.* point at issue.

streitsüchtig, *adj.* pugnacious.

streng, *adj.* strict, stern, severe.

strenggläubig, *adj.* orthodox.

streuen, *vb.* strew, scatter, sprinkle.

Strich, -e, *n.m.* stroke, line; (nach S. und Faden) thoroughly; (gegen den S.) against the grain.

Strick, -e, *n.m.* rope.

stricken, *vb.* knit.

strittig, *adj.* controversial.

Stroh, *n.nt.* straw.

Strolch, -e, *n.m.* vagabond.

Strom, ⁻e, *n.m.* stream; (*elec.*) current.

strömen, *vb.* stream, flow.

Stromkreis, -e, *n.m.* circuit.

stromlinienförmig, *adj.* streamlined.

Stromspannung, -en, *n.f.* voltage.

Strömung, -en, *n.f.* current; trend, drift.

Strudel, -, *n.m.* whirlpool.

Struktur', -en, *n.f.* structure.

Strumpf, ⁻e, *n.m.* stocking.

Strumpfband, ⁻er, *n.nt.* garter.

Strumpfbandgürtel, *n.m.* girdle.

Strumpfhose, -n, *n.f.* panty hose.

Strumpfwaren, *n.pl.* hosiery.

struppig, *adj.* shaggy.

Stube, -n, *n.f.* room.

Stuck, -, *n.m.* stucco.

Stück, -e, *n.nt.* piece; (theater) play.

stückeln, *vb.* patch, piece together.

stücken, *vb.* piece.

Student', -en, -en, *n.m.* student.

Studen'tin, -nen, *n.f.* student.

Studie, -n, *n.f.* study.

Studiengeld, -er, *n.nt.* tuition.

studie'ren, *vb.* study (at a university), be a student.

Studium, -dien, *n.nt.* study.

Stufe, -n, *n.f.* step.

stufenweise, *adj.* gradual, step by step.

Stuhl, ⁻e, *n.m.* chair.

stumm, *adj.* mute, silent.

Stummel, -, *n.m.* stub, butt.

Stümper, -, *n.m.* beginner, amateur.

stumpf, *adj.* blunt; stupid; (angle) obtuse.

Stumpf, ⁻e, *n.m.* stump.

Stunde, -n, *n.f.* hour; (school) class.

Stundenplan, ⁻e, *n.m.* schedule.

stündlich, *adj.* hourly.

stupsen, *vb.* joggle.

stur, *adj.* stubborn; obtuse.

Sturm, ⁻e, *n.m.* storm.

stürmen, *vb.* storm.

stürmisch, *adj.* stormy.
Sturz, ⁻e, *n.m.* fall; overthrow.
stürzen, *vb.* plunge, hurl, overthrow; rush, crash.
Stute, -n, *n.f.* mare.
Stütze, -n, *n.f.* support, prop, help.
stutzen, *vb.* trim.
stützen, *vb.* support.
Stützpunkt, -e, *n.m.* base.
Subjekt', -e, *n.nt.* subject.
subjektiv, *adj.* subjective.
sublimie'ren, *vb.* sublimate.
Substantiv, -e, *n.nt.* noun.
Substanz', -en, *n.f.* substance.
subtil', *adj.* subtle.
subtrahie'ren, *vb.* subtract.
Subvention', -en, *n.f.* subvention, subsidy.
Suche, *n.f.* search.
suchen, *vb.* search, seek, look for.
Sucht, *n.f.* addiction.
süchtig, *adj.* addicted.
Süd, Süden, *n.m.* south.
südlich, *adj.* southern; to the south.
Südos'ten, *n.m.* southeast.
südöst'lich, *adj.* southeast.
Südpol, *n.m.* South Pole.
Südwe'sten, *n.m.* southwest.
südwest'lich, *adj.* southwest.
suggerie'ren, *vb.* suggest.
Sühne, -n, *n.f.* atonement, expiation.
sühnen, *vb.* atone for, expiate.
Sülze, *n.f.* jellied meat.
summa'risch, *adj.* summary.
Summe, -n, *n.f.* sum.
summen, *vb.* hum, buzz.
Sumpf, ⁻e, *n.m.* swamp, mire.
Sünde, -n, *n.f.* sin.

Sündenbock, *n.m* scapegoat.
Sündenvergebung, *n.f.* absolution.
Sünder, -, *n.m.* sinner.
Sünderin, -nen, *n.f.* sinner.
Sündflut, *n.f.* the Flood; cataclysm.
sündhaft, *adj.* sinful.
sündigen, *vb.* sin.
super, *adj.* super.
Superstar, -s, *n.m.* superstar.
Suppe, -n, *n.f.* soup.
surren, *vb.* buzz.
suspendie'ren, *vb.* suspend.
süß, *adj.* sweet.
Süße, *n.f.* sweetness.
Süßigkeiten, *n.pl.* sweets.
Sylve'ster, *n.nt.* New Year's Eve.
Symbol', -e, *n.nt.* symbol.
symbo'lisch, *adj.* symbolic.
Sympathie', -i'en, *n.f.* sympathy.
sympa'tisch, *adj.* likable, congenial; *(med.)* sympathetic.
Symphonie', -i'en, *n.f.* symphony.
sympho'nisch, *adj.* symphonic.
Symptom', -e, *n.nt.* symptom.
symptoma'tisch, *adj.* symptomatic.
Synago'ge, -n, *n.f.* synagogue.
synchronisie'ren, *vb.* synchronize.
Syndrom', -e, *n.nt.* syndrome.
Synonym', -e, *n.nt.* synonym.
Synthe'se, -n, *n.f.* synthesis.
synthe'tisch, *adj.* synthetic.
Syphilis, *n.f.* syphilis.
System', -e, *n.nt.* system.
systema'tisch, *adj.* systematic.
Szene, -n, *n.f.* scene.

T

Tabak, *n.m.* tobacco.
Tabel'le, *n.f.* chart.
Tablett', -e, *n.nt.* tray.
Tablet'te, -n, *n.f.* tablet.
Tadel, -, *n.m.* reproof, reprimand; (school) demerit.
tadeln, *vb.* reprove, find fault with.
tadelnswert, *adj.* reprehensible.

Tafel, -n, *n.f.* tablet; table; chart; blackboard; bar (of chocolate).
täfeln, *vb.* panel.
Tag, ⁻e, *n.m.* day; **(guten T.)** how do you do.
Tagebuch, ⁻er, *n.nt.* diary.
Tagesanbruch, ⁻e, *n.m.* daybreak.
Tageslicht, *n.nt.* daylight.
Tageszeitung, -en, *n.f.* daily newspaper.

täglich, *adj.* daily.
Tagung, -en, *n.f.* convention, meeting.
Taille, -n, *n.f.* waist.
Takt, *n.m.* tact; rhythm.
taktisch, *adj.* tactical.
Tal, ̈-er, *n.nt.* valley.
Talent', -e, *n.nt.* talent.
talentiert', *adj.* talented.
tändeln, *vb.* dally.
Tango, -s, *n.m.* tango.
Tank, -s, *n.m.* tank.
Tankstelle, -n, *n.f.* filling station.
Tanne, -n, *n.f.* fir, spruce.
Tante, -n, *n.f.* aunt.
Tantie'me, -n, *n.f.* bonus.
Tanz, ̈-e, *n.m.* dance.
tänzeln, *vb.* flounce, caper.
tanzen, *vb.* dance.
Tänzer, -, *n.m.* dancer.
Tänzerin, -nen, *n.f.* dancer.
Tanzsaal, -säle, *n.m.* dance hall, ballroom.
Tape'te, -n, *n.f.* wallpaper.
Tapezie'rer, -, *n.m.* upholsterer.
tapfer, *adj.* brave, valiant.
Tapisserie, -i'en, *n.f.* tapestry.
tappen, *vb.* grope.
tapsig, *adj.* gawky.
tarnen, *vb.* screen, camouflage.
Tarnung, -en, *n.f.* screen, camouflage.
Tasche, -n, *n.f.* pocket; handbag.
Taschenausgabe, -n, *n.f.* paperback.
Taschendieb, -e, *n.m.* pickpocket.
Taschenformat, *n.nt.* pocketsize.
Tachengeld, -er, *n.nt.* allowance, pocket money.
Taschenlampe, -n, *n.f.* flashlight.
Taschenrechner, -, *n.m.* calculator.
Taschentuch, ̈-er, *n.nt.* handkerchief.
Tasse, -n, *n.f.* cup.
Tastatur', -en, *n.f.* keyboard.
Taste, -n, *n.f.* key.
tasten, *vb.* feel; grope.
Tastentelefon, -e, *n.nt.* touch tone phone.
Tastsinn, *n.m.* sense of touch.
Tat, -en, *n.f.* act, deed; **(in der T.)** indeed.

Tatbestand, *n.m.* facts, findings.
Täter, -, *n.m.* culprit.
Täterin, -nen, *n.f.* culprit.
tätig, *adj.* active.
Tätigkeit, -en, *n.f.* activity.
Tatkraft, ̈-e, *n.f.* energy.
tatkräftig, *adj.* energetic.
tätlich, *adj.* violent.
Tätlichkeit, -en, *n.f.* violence.
Tatsache, -n, *n.f.* fact.
tatsächlich, *adj.* actual, real.
Tatze, -n, *n.f.* paw, claw.
Tau, *n.m.* dew.
Tau, -e, *n.nt.* rope.
taub, *adj.* deaf.
Taube, -n, *n.f.* pigeon, dove.
tauchen, *vb.* dive, plunge, dip.
Taucher, -, *n.m.* diver.
Taucherin, -nen, *n.f.* diver.
tauen, *vb.* melt, thaw.
Taufe, -n, *n.f.* baptism, christening.
taufen, *vb.* baptize, christen.
Taufkapelle, -n, *n.f.* baptistry.
taugen, *vb.* be worth; be of use.
Taugenichts, *n.m.* good-for-nothing.
tauglich, *adj.* useful, qualified.
taumeln, *vb.* stagger.
taumelnd, *adj.* groggy.
Tausch, *n.m.* exchange, trade.
tauschen, *vb.* exchange.
täuschen, *vb.* deceive, delude, fool.
täuschend, *adj.* deceptive.
Tauschhandel, *n.m.* barter.
Täuschung, -en, *n.f.* deception, delusion, fallacy.
tausend, *num.* a thousand.
Tausend, -e, *n.nt.* thousand.
tausendst-, *adj.* thousandth.
Tausendstel, -, *n.nt.* thousandth part; **(ein t.)** one one-thousandth.
Taxe, -n, *n.f.* tax; taxi.
taxie'ren, *vb.* appraise, estimate.
Technik, *n.f.* technique; technology.
technisch, *adj.* technical.
Tee, -s, *n.m.* tea.
Teekanne, -n, *n.f.* tea-pot.
Teelöffel, -, *n.m.* teaspoon.
Teer, -, *n.m.* tar.
Teich, -e, *n.m.* pond, pool.
Teig, -e, *n.m.* dough, batter.

Teil, -e, *n.m.* part, portion, section.

teilbar, *adj.* divisible.

teilen, *vb.* divide, share.

teil·haben*, *vb.* share.

Teilhaber, -, *n.m.* partner.

Teilhaberin, -nen, *n.f.* partner.

Teilnahme, *n.f.* participation; sympathy.

teilnahmslos, *adj.* lethargic.

teil·nehmen*, *vb.* participate, partake.

Teilnehmer, -, *n.m.* participant, partner.

Teilnehmerin, -nen, *n.f.* participant, partner.

teils, *adv.* partly.

Teilung, -en, *n.f.* partition, division.

teilweise, *adv.* partly.

Teint, -s, *n.m.* complexion.

Telefon', -e, *n.nt.* telephone.

Telegramm', -e, *n.nt.* telegram.

Telegraph', -en, -en, *n.m.* telegraph.

telegraphie'ren, *vb.* telegraph.

Telephon', -e, *n.nt.* telephone.

Telephon'buch, ⸚er, *n.nt.* telephone directory.

telephonie'ren, *vb.* telephone.

Telephonist', -en, *n.m.* operator.

Telephonis'tin, -nen, *n.f.* operator.

Telephon'zelle, -n, *n.f.* telephone booth.

Teller, -, *n.m.* plate.

Temperament', *n.nt.* temperament, disposition; vivacity.

temperament'voll, *adj.* temperamental; vivacious.

Temperatur', -en, *n.f.* temperature.

Tempo, -s, *n.nt.* speed; tempo.

Tendenz', -en, *n.f.* tendency, trend.

Tender, -, *n.m.* tender.

Tennis, *n.nt.* tennis.

Tennisschläger, -, *n.m.* tennis racket.

Tennisschuh, -e, *n.m.* sneaker.

Tenor', -e, *n.m.* tenor.

Teppich, -e, *n.m.* rug, carpet.

Termin', -e, *n.m.* deadline; appointment.

Terpentin', *n.nt.* turpentine.

Terras'se, -n, *n.f.* terrace.

Terror, *n.m.* terror.

Terroranschlag, ⸚e, *n.m.* terrorist attack.

Terroris'mus, *n.m.* terrorism.

Testament', -e, *n.nt.* testament, will.

testamenta'risch, *adj.* testamentary, noted in the will.

teuer, *adj.* expensive, dear.

Teuerung, *n.f.* rising cost of living.

Teufel, -, *n.m.* devil.

teuflisch, *adj.* diabolic.

Text, -e, *n.m.* text.

Texti'lien, *n.pl.* textiles.

Textil'ware, -n, *n.f.* textile.

Thea'ter, -, *n.nt.* theater; spectacle.

Thea'terkasse, -n, *n.f.* box office.

Thea'terstück, -e, *n.nt.* play.

Thea'terwissenschaft, -en, *n.f.* dramaturgy.

theatra'lisch, *adj.* theatrical.

Thema, -men, *n.nt.* theme, subject, topic.

Theolo'ge, -n, -n, *n.m.* theologian.

theore'tisch, *adj.* theoretical.

Theorie', -i'en, *n.f.* theory.

Therapie', *n.f.* therapy.

Thermome'ter, -, *n.nt.* thermometer.

These, -n, *n.f.* thesis.

Thron, -e, *n.m.* throne.

Thunfisch, -e, *n.m.* tuna.

tief, *adj.* deep, low; profound.

Tiefe, -n, *n.f.* depth.

Tiefebene, -n, *n.f.* plain, lowland.

tiefgründig, *adj.* profound.

Tiefkühler, -, *n.m.* freezer.

Tiefkühltruhe, -n, *n.f.* deep freeze.

tiefsinnig, *adj.* profound; pensive.

tieftraurig, *adj.* heartbroken.

Tier, -e, *n.nt.* animal.

Tierarzt, ⸚e, *n.m.* veterinarian.

Tierärztin, -nen, *n.f.* veterinarian.

tierisch, *adj.* animal, bestial.

Tiger, -, *n.m.* tiger.

tilgen, *vb.* obliterate; delete; pay off, amortize.

Tilgung, -en, *n.f.* liquidation, amortization.

Tinte, -n, *n.f.* ink.

Tintenfisch, -e, *n.m.* octopus.

Tip, -s, *n.m.* hint, suggestion.

tippen, *vb.* type.

Tisch, -e, *n.m.* table.

Tischdecke, -n, *n.f.* tablecloth.

Tischler, -, *n.m.* carpenter.

Tischtuch, -̈er, *n.nt.* tablecloth.

Titel, -, *n.m.* title.

Toast, -, *n.m.* toast.

toben, *vb.* rave, rage.

Tochter, -̈, *n.f.* daughter.

Tod, - *n.m.* death.

Todesfall, -̈e, *n.m.* (case of) death.

Todesstrafe, -n, *n.f.* capital punishment.

tödlich, *adj.* deadly, mortal; lethal.

Toilette, -n, *n.f.* toilet.

Toilettenartikel, *n.pl.* toilet articles.

tolerant, *adj.* tolerant.

Toleranz', - *n.f.* tolerance.

toll, *adj.* mad, crazy.

tollkühn, *adj.* foolhardy.

Tollwut, *n.f.* rabies.

tölpelhaft, *adj.* clumsy.

Tomate, -n, *n.f.* tomato.

Ton, -̈e, *n.m.* tone, sound; clay.

tonangebend, *adj.* setting the style.

Tonart, -en, *n.f.* key.

Tonband, -̈er, *n.nt.* magnetic tape.

Tonbandaufnahme, -n, *n.f.* tape recording.

Tonbandgerät, -e, *n.nt.* tape recorder.

tönen, *vb.* sound, resound, ring.

Tonfall, -̈e, *n.m.* intonation, inflection.

Tonfilm, -e, *n.m.* sound movie.

Tonhöhe, -n, *n.f.* pitch.

Tonleiter, -n, *n.f.* scale.

Tonne, -n, *n.f.* ton; barrel.

Tonstufe, -n, *n.f.* (music) pitch.

Tonwaren, *n.pl.* earthenware.

Topf, -̈e, *n.m.* pot.

Töpferware, -n, *n.f.* pottery.

Tor, -en, -en, *n.m.* fool.

Tor, -e, *n.nt.* gate, gateway; (sport) goal.

Torbogen, -̈, *n.m.* archway.

Torheit, -en, *n.f.* folly.

töricht, *adj.* foolish.

torkeln, *vb.* lurch, stagger.

Tornister, -, *n.m.* knapsack, pack.

torpedieren, *vb.* torpedo.

Torpedo, -s, *n.m.* torpedo.

Törtchen, -, *n.nt.* tart.

Torte, -n, *n.f.* tart, layer cake.

Tortur', -en, *n.f.* torture.

Torwart, -e, *n.m.* goalie.

tosen, *vb.* rage, roar.

tot, *adj.* dead.

total', *adj.* total.

totalitär', *adj.* totalitarian.

töten, *vb.* kill.

Totenwache, -n, *n.f.* wake.

Toto, *n.m.* lottery.

Totschlag, -̈e, *n.m.* (case of) manslaughter.

Tour, -en, *n.f.* tour, excursion, trip.

Touris'mus, *n.m.* tourism.

Tourist', -en, -en, *n.m.* tourist.

Touris'tin, -nen, *n.f.* tourist.

Trab, *n.m.* trot.

traben, *vb.* trot.

Tracht, -en, *n.f.* costume.

trachten, *vb.* seek, endeavor.

Tradition', -en, *n.f.* tradition.

traditionell', *adj.* traditional.

Tragbahre, -n, *n.f.* stretcher.

tragbar, *adj.* portable; bearable.

träge, *adj.* indolent, sluggish.

tragen*, *vb.* carry, bear; wear.

Träger, -, *n.m.* carrier; girder; (lingerie) straps.

Tragik, *n.f.* tragic art; calamity.

tragisch, *adj.* tragic.

Tragö'die, -n, *n.f.* tragedy.

Tragweite, -n, *n.f.* range; significance, consequence.

Trainer, -, *n.m.* coach.

Trainerin, -nen, *n.f.* coach.

trainie'ren, *vb.* train, work out; coach.

Trambahn, -en, *n.f.* trolley.

trampeln, *vb.* trample.

Tranchier'messer, -, *n.nt.* carving-knife.

Träne, -n, *n.f.* tear.

tränen, *vb.* water (eye).

Trank, -̈e, *n.m.* potion.

tränken, vb. water (animals).
Transaktion', -en, n.f. transaction.
Transforma'tor, -o'ren, n.m. transformer, converter.
Transfusion', -en, n.f. transfusion.
transpirie'ren, vb. perspire.
transponie'ren, vb. transpose.
Transport', -e, n.m. transport.
transportie'ren, vb. transport.
transsexual', adj. transsexual.
Transvestit', -en, -en, n.m. transvestite.
Trapez', -e, n.nt. trapeze.
Traube, -n, n.f. grape.
trauen, vb. (intr.) trust; (tr.) marry, join in marriage.
Trauer, n.f. grief; mourning.
trauern, vb. grieve, mourn.
trauervoll, adj. mournful.
Traufe, -n, n.f. gutter; (vom Regen in die T.) out of the frying pan into the fire.
Traum, ⁼e, n.m. dream; (böser T.) nightmare.
träumen, vb. dream; (vor sich hin⁓t.) daydream.
Träumer, -, n.m. dreamer.
Träumerei', -en, n.f. daydream, reverie.
Träumerin, -nen, n.f. dreamer.
träumerisch, adj. fanciful, far-away.
traumhaft, adj. dreamlike; dreamy.
traurig, adj. sad.
Trauring, -e, n.m. wedding ring.
Travelerscheck, -s, n.m. traveler's check.
Trecker, -, n.m. tractor.
Treff, n.nt. clubs (cards).
treffen*, vb. hit; meet; (sich t.) meet.
treffend, adj. pertinent.
Treffer, -, n.m. hit.
trefflich, adj. excellent.
treiben*, vb. (tr.) drive; be engaged in; (intr.) drift, float.
Treibstoff, n.m. fuel.
Trend, -s, n.m. trend.
trennen, vb. separate, divide; hyphenate; (sich t.) part.
Trennung, -en, n.f. separation, division.

treppab', adv. down the stairs.
treppauf', adv. up the stairs.
Treppe, -n, n.f. staircase, stairs.
Tresor', -e, n.m. vault.
treten*, vb. step, tread.
treu, adj. true, faithful, loyal.
Treue, n.f. faith, loyalty; allegiance.
Treueid, -e, n.m. oath of allegiance.
Treuhänder, -, n.m. trustee.
treuherzig, adj. trusting, guileless.
treulich, adv. faithfully.
treulos, adj. disloyal.
Treulosigkeit, -e, n.f. disloyalty.
Tribü'ne, -n, n.f. grandstand.
Trichter, -, n.m. funnel.
Trick, -s, n.m. trick.
Trickfilm, -e, n.m. animated cartoon.
Tricktrack, n.nt. backgammon.
Trieb, -e, n.m. sprout, shoot; urge.
triebhaft, adj. instinctive, unrestrained.
Triebfeder, -n, n.f. mainspring.
Triebwagen, -, n.m. railcar.
triefen*, vb. drip.
triftig, adj. weighty.
Trikot', -s, n.nt. knitted cloth.
trimmen, vb. trim.
trinkbar, adj. drinkable.
trinken*, vb. drink.
Trinker, -, n.m. drunkard.
Trinkerin, -nen, n.f. drinker.
Trinkgeld, -er, n.nt. tip.
Trinkspruch, ⁼e, n.m. toast.
Tripper, -, n.m. gonorrhea.
Tritt, -e, n.m. step; kick.
Trittleiter, -n, n.f. stepladder.
Triumph', -e, n.m. triumph.
triumphie'ren, vb. triumph.
trivial', adj. trivial.
trocken, adj. dry.
Trockenhaube, -n, n.f. hair drier.
trocken-legen, vb. (land) drain; (baby) change the diapers.
trocknen, vb. dry.
trödeln, vb. dawdle.
Trog, ⁼e, n.m. trough.
trollen, vb. (sich t.) toddle off.
Trommel, -n, n.f. drum.
Trommelfell, -e, n.nt. eardrum.
Trompe'te, -n, n.f. trumpet.
Tropen, n.pl. tropics.

Tropfen, -, *n.m.* drop.
tropfen, *vb.* drip.
Tropfer, -, *n.m.* dropper.
Trophä'e, -n, *n.f.* trophy.
tropisch, *adj.* tropical.
Trost, *n.m.* consolation, solace, comfort.
trösten, *vb.* console, comfort.
trostlos, *adj.* desolate, dreary.
trostreich, *adj.* comforting.
Trott, *n.m.* trot.
Trottel, -, *n.m.* idiot, dope.
Trotz, *n.m.* defiance, spite.
trotz, *prep.* in spite of, despite, notwithstanding.
trotzdem, 1. *conj.* although, despite the fact that. 2. *adv.* nevertheless.
trotzen, *vb.* defy.
trotzig, *adj.* defiant.
trübe, *adj.* dim; muddy; cloudy.
Trubel, *n.m.* bustle, confusion.
trüben, *vb.* dim.
Trübsal, *n.f.* misery, sorrow.
trübselig, *adj.* sad, gloomy.
Trübsinn, *n.m.* dejection, gloom.
trübsinnig, *adj.* gloomy.
Trüffel, -n, *n.f.* truffle.
Trug, *n.m.* deceit; delusion.
trügen*, *vb.* (tr.) deceive; (intr.) be deceptive.
trügerisch, *adj.* deceptive; illusory; treacherous.
Trugschluß, -sse, *n.m.* fallacy.
Truhe, -n, *n.f.* chest.
Trümmer, *n.pl.* ruins, debris.
Trunk, ⸚e, *n.m.* drink; draught.
Trunkenbold, -e, *n.m.* drunkard.
Trunkenheit, *n.f.* drunkenness.
Trupp, -s, *n.m.* troop, squad.
Truppe, -n, *n.f.* troops.
Truppeneinheit, -en, *n.f.* unit, outfit.
Trust, -s, *n.m.* trust.
Truthahn, ⸚e, *n.m.* turkey.
Tscheche, -n, -n, *n.m.* Czech.
Tschechei', *n.f.* Czechoslovakia.
Tschechin, -nen, *n.f.* Czech.
tschechisch, *adj.* Czech.
Tschechoslowa'ke, -n, -n, *n.m.* Czechoslovakian.
Tschechoslowa'kin, -nen, *n.f.* Czechoslovakian.

Tschechoslowakei', *n.f.* Czechoslovakia.
tschechoslowa'kisch, *adj.* Czechoslovakian.
T-shirt, -s, *n.nt.* T-shirt.
Tube, -n, *n.f.* tube.
Tuberkulo'se, *n.f.* tuberculosis.
Tuch, ⸚er, *n.nt.* cloth.
tüchtig, *adj.* able, efficient.
Tüchtigkeit, *n.f.* ability, efficiency.
Tücke, -n, *n.f.* malice, perfidy.
tückisch, *adj.* malicious, treacherous.
Tugend, -en, *n.f.* virtue.
tugendhaft, *adj.* virtuous.
tugendsam, *adj.* virtuous.
Tüll, *n.m.* tulle.
Tülle, -n, *n.f.* spout.
Tulpe, -n, *n.f.* tulip.
tummeln, *vb.* move about; romp.
Tummelplatz, ⸚e, *n.m.* playground.
Tumor, -o'ren, *n.m.* tumor.
Tümpel, -, *n.m.* pool.
Tumult, -e, *n.m.* tumult, uproar; hubbub.
tun*, *vb.* do.
Tünche, -n, *n.f.* whitewash; (fig.) veneer.
Tunichtgut, -e, *n.m.* ne'er-do-well.
Tunke, -n, *n.f.* sauce, gravy.
tunken, *vb.* dunk.
Tunnel, -, *n.m.* tunnel.
tupfen, *vb.* dab.
Tür, -en, *n.f.* door; (mit der T. ins Haus fallen*) blurt out.
Turbi'nenjäger, -, *n.m.* turbo-jet plane.
Turbi'nenpropellertriebwerk, -e, *n.nt.* turbo-prop.
Türeingang, ⸚e, *n.m.* doorway.
Türke, -n, -n, *n.m.* Turk.
Türkei', *n.f.* Turkey.
Türkin, -nen, *n.f.* Turk.
Türkis, -e, *n.m.* turquoise.
türkisch, *adj.* Turkish.
Turm, ⸚e, *n.m.* tower, spire, steeple; (chess) castle, rook; (spitzer T.) spire.
türmen, *vb.* (tr.) pile up; (intr.) beat it; (sich t.) rise high.

turnen, *vb.* do gymnastics.
Turner, -, *n.m.* gymnast.
Turnerin, -nen, *n.f.* gymnast.
Turnhalle, -n, *n.f.* gym(nasium).
Turnhose, -n, *n.f.* gym shorts.
Turnier', -e, *n.nt.* tournament.
Turnschuh, -e, *n.m.* sneaker.
tuscheln, *vb.* whisper.
Tuschkasten, -, *n.m.* paint box.
Tüte, -n, *n.f.* (paper) bag, sack.
Tütelchen, -, *n.nt.* dot.

TÜV, *n.m.* car inspection.
Typ, -en, *n.m.* type.
Type, -n, *n.f.* (printing) type.
Typhus, *n.m.* typhus, typhoid fever.
typisch, *adj.* typical.
Typographie', *n.f.* typography.
Tyrann', -en, -en, *n.m.* tyrant.
Tyrannei', -en, *n.f.* tyranny.
tyrannisie'ren, *vb.* tyrannize, oppress.

U

U-Bahn, -en, *n.f.* (= Untergrundbahn) subway.
übel, *adj.* bad; nasty; nauseated.
Übel, *n.nt.* evil; nuisance.
Übelkeit, *n.f.* nausea.
übel-nehmen, *vb.* hold against, resent.
Übeltat, -en, *n.f.* offence.
Übeltäter, -, *n.m.* offender.
üben, *vb.* practice.
über, *prep.* over, about, above, across, beyond.
überall, *adv.* everywhere.
überar'beiten, *vb.* work over; (sich ü.) overwork.
überaus, *adv.* exceedingly.
überbelichten, *vb.* overexpose.
überbie'ten*, *vb.* outbid; surpass.
Überbleibsel, -, *n.nt.* rest, leftover.
Überblick, -e, *n.m.* survey; general view.
überbli'cken, *vb.* survey.
überbrin'gen*, *vb.* deliver.
Überbrin'ger, -, *n.m.* bearer.
Überbrin'gerin, -nen, *n.f.* bearer.
überbrü'cken, *vb.* bridge.
überdau'ern, *vb.* outlive, outlast.
überdies, *adv.* furthermore.
Überdruß, *n.m.* boredom; (bis zum Ü.) ad nauseam.
überdrüssig, *adj.* tired of, sick of.
übereilt, *adj.* rash, hasty.
übereinan'der, *adv.* one on top of the other.
überein'kommen*, *vb.* agree.
Überein'kommen, -, *n.nt.* agreement.

Überein'kunft, ⁼e, *n.f.* agreement.
überein'-stimmen, *vb.* agree.
Überein'stimmung, -en, *n.f.* agreement, accord.
überfah'ren*, *vb.* drive over, run over.
Überfahrt, -en, *n.f.* passage, crossing.
Überfall, ⁼e, *n.m.* raid; hold-up.
überfallen*, *vb.* attack suddenly, hold up.
überfällig, *adj.* overdue.
überflie'gen*, *vb.* fly over; (fig.) scan.
über-fließen*, *vb.* overflow.
überflü'geln, *vb.* surpass.
Überfluß, -üsse, *n.m.* abundance.
überflüssig, *adj.* superfluous.
überflu'ten, *vb.* overflow.
überfüh'ren, *vb.* transfer, transport; convict.
Überfüh'rung, -en, *n.f.* transport, transfer; (railroad) overpass.
überfüllt, *adj.* overcrowded, jammed.
Übergabe, *n.f.* delivery; surrender.
Übergang, ⁼e, *n.m.* passage; transition.
überge'ben*, *vb.* hand over, deliver; (sich ü.) vomit.
über-gehen*, *vb.* go over to.
überge'hen*, *vb.* pass over, skip.
Übergewicht, *n.nt.* overweight, preponderance; (das Ü. bekommen*) get the upper hand.
über-greifen*, *vb.* spread; encroach.

Übergriff, -e, *n.m.* encroachment.

über-haben*, *vb.* be sick of, be fed up with.

überhand'nehmen*, *vb.* spread, become dominant.

überhäu'fen, *vb.* overwhelm.

überhaupt', *adv.* in general; altogether, at all.

überheb'lich, *adj.* overbearing.

überho'len, *vb.* overhaul; drive past, pass.

überholt', *adj.* out-of-date.

überhö'ren, *vb.* purposely not hear, ignore.

überla'den, *adj.* ornate.

überlas'sen*, *vb.* give to, yield, leave to.

über-laufen*, *vb.* defect, desert; boil over, run over.

überlau'fen, *adj.* overrun.

Überläu'fer, -, *n.m.* deserter.

überle'ben, *vb.* outlive, survive.

Überle'ben, *n.nt.* survival.

überle'gen, *vb.* reflect on, think over.

überle'gen, *adj.* superior.

überlegt', *adj.* deliberate.

Überle'gung, -en, *n.f.* deliberation, consideration.

überlie'fern, *vb.* hand over.

Überlie'ferung, -en, *n.f.* tradition.

überlis'ten, *vb.* outwit.

Übermacht, *n.f.* superiority.

überman'nen, *vb.* overpower.

Übermaß, *n.nt.* excess.

übermäßig, *adj.* excessive.

Übermensch, -en, -en, *n.m.* superman.

übermit'teln, *vb.* transmit, convey.

übermorgen, *adv.* the day after tomorrow.

Übermü'dung, *n.f.* overfatigue, exhaustion.

Übermut, *n.m.* high spirits; arrogance.

übernächst, *adj.* next but one.

übernach'ten, *vb.* spend the night, stay overnight.

übernatürlich, *adj.* supernatural.

überneh'men*, *vb.* take over.

überparteilich, *adj.* nonpartisan.

überprü'fen, *vb.* examine, check.

Überprü'fung, -en, *n.f.* checking, check-up.

überque'ren, *vb.* cross.

überra'gen, *vb.* surpass.

überra'gend, *adj.* superior.

überra'schen, *vb.* surprise.

Überra'schung, -en, *n.f.* surprise.

überre'den, *vb.* persuade.

Überre'dung, -en, *n.f.* persuasion.

überreich, *adj.* abundant, profuse.

überrei'chen, *vb.* hand over, present.

Überrest, -e, *n.m.* remains, relics.

überrum'peln, *vb.* take by surprise.

Überschallgeschwindigkeit, -en, *n.f.* supersonic speed.

überschat'ten, *vb.* overshadow.

überschät'zen, *vb.* overestimate.

überschau'en, *vb.* survey, get the whole view of.

Überschlag, -̈e, *n.m.* estimate.

überschla'gen*, *vb.* pass over, skip; (sich ü.) turn over.

Überschrift, -en, *n.f.* title, heading, headline.

Überschuhe, *n.pl.* galoshes.

Überschuß, -̈sse, *n.m.* surplus.

überschüt'ten, *vb.* overwhelm.

überschwem'men, *vb.* inundate.

Überschwem'mung, -en, *n.f.* flood.

Übersee, *n.f.* oversea(s).

Überseedampfer, -, *n.m.* transoceanic liner.

überseh'bar, *adj.* capable of being taken in at a glance; foreseeable.

überse'hen*, *vb.* view; overlook, not notice, ignore.

Überse'hen, -, *n.nt.* oversight.

übersen'den*, *vb.* send, transmit; consign, remit.

überset'zen, *vb.* translate.

Überset'zer, -, *n.m.* translator.

Überset'zerin, -nen, *n.f.* translator.

Überset'zung, -en, *n.f.* translation.

Übersicht, -en, *n.f.* overview; summary, outline.

übersichtlich, adj. clear; easily understandable.
überspannt', adj. eccentric.
überspringen*, vb. skip.
übersprudelnd, adj. exuberant.
überste'hen*, vb. endure, survive.
überstei'gen*, vb. surpass.
überstim'men, vb. outvote, overrule.
Überstunde, -n, n.f. hour of overtime work; (pl.) overtime.
überstür'zen, vb. precipitate.
überstürzt', adj. headlong, precipitate.
übertrag'bar, adj. transferable.
übertra'gen*, vb. transfer, transmit; translate; (im Radio ü.) broadcast; (im Fernseh ü.) televise.
Übertra'gung, -en, n.f. transfer; translation; broadcast.
übertref'fen*, vb. surpass, excel.
übertrei'ben*, vb. exaggerate.
Übertrei'bung, -en, n.f. exaggeration.
über'treten*, vb. pass; overflow; (pol.) go over; (eccl.) convert.
übertre'ten*, vb. trespass, violate, infringe.
Übertre'tung, -en, n.f. violation, infringement.
übertrie'ben, adj. exaggerated, extravagant.
übervor'teilen, vb. get the better of (someone).
überwa'chen, vb. watch over, keep under surveillance, control.
Überwa'chung, -en, n.f. surveillance, control.
überwäl'tigen, vb. overpower, overwhelm.
überwei'sen*, vb. transfer; remit.
Überwei'sung, -en, n.f. remittance.
überwer'fen*, vb. (sich ü.) have a falling-out with.
überwie'gen*, vb. outweigh; predominate.
überwie'gend, adj. preponderant.
überwin'den*, vb. conquer, overcome.
Überwin'dung, -en, n.f. conquest; effort, reluctance.
überwin'tern, vb. hibernate.

Überzahl, n.f. numerical superiority.
überzäh'lig, adj. surplus.
überzeu'gen, vb. convince.
überzeu'gend, adj. convincing.
Überzeu'gung, -en, n.f. conviction.
Überzeu'gungskraft, n.f. forcefulness.
Überzieher, -, n.m. overcoat.
üblich, adj. customary, usual.
U-Boot, -e, n.nt. (= Unterseeboot) submarine.
übrig, adj. remaining, left over. **(es bleibt mir nichts anderes übrig)** I have no other choice.
übrigens, adv. incidentally, by the way.
übrig•haben*, vb. have left over; **(nichts ü. für)** have no use for.
Übung, -en, n.f. practice; exercise.
Übungsbeispiel, -e, n.nt. paradigm.
UdSSR, abbr. (= Union' der Soziali'stischen Sowjetrepubliken) Union of Soviet Socialist Republics.
Ufer, -, n.nt. shore, bank.
Ufereinfassung, -en, n.f. embankment.
uferlos, adj. limitless.
Uhr, -en, n.f. watch, clock; **(wieviel Uhr ist es?)** what time is it?; **(sieben U.)** seven o'clock.
Uhrmacher, -, n.m. watchmaker.
Uhu, -s, n.m. owl.
Ulk, -e, n.m. fun.
ulkig, adj. funny.
Ultra-, cpds. ultra.
um, prep. around; at (clock time); **(um . . . zu)** in order to; **(u. so mehr)** the more, all the more so.
um•adressieren, vb. readdress.
um•arbeiten, vb. rework, revise.
umar'men, vb. embrace.
Umar'mung, -en, n.f. embrace.
um•bauen, vb. remodel.
um•biegen*, vb. turn, turn around.
um•bringen*, vb. kill.
um•drehen, vb. turn around, rotate, revolve.

Umdre'hung, -en, *n.f.* turn, revolution, rotation.

um·erzie'hen*, *vb.* reeducate.

umfah'ren*, *vb.* circumnavigate, circle.

um·fal'len*, *vb.* fall over.

Umfang, =e, *n.m.* circumference; extent; volume.

umfang'reich, *adj.* extensive; comprehensive; voluminous.

umfas'sen, enclose, surround; comprise.

umfas'send, *adj.* comprehensive.

um·for'men, *vb.* remodel, transform, convert.

Umfrage, -n, *n.f.* inquiry, poll.

Umgang, *n.m.* intercourse, association.

Umgangssprache, *n.f.* colloquial speech, vernacular.

umge'ben*, *vb.* surround.

Umge'bung, -en, *n.f.* surroundings, environment; vicinity.

um·ge'hen*, *vb.* go around, circulate; (u. mit) deal with, handle; (mit dem Gedanken u.) contemplate, plan.

umge'hen*, *vb.* evade, circumvent.

Umge'hen, -, *n.nt.* evasion.

Umge'hung, -en, *n.f.* circumvention; (mil.) flanking movement.

Umge'hungsstraße, -n, *n.f.* bypass.

umgekehrt, 1. *adj.* reverse, inverse. 2. *adv.* the other way round.

um·gestal'ten, *vb.* transform, alter, modify.

umgren'zen, *vb.* enclose; circumscribe.

um·gucken, *vb.* (sich u.) look around.

um·haben*, *vb.* have on.

Umhang, =e, *n.m.* wrap.

umher', *adv.* around, about.

umher'·gehen*, *vb.* walk around.

umher'·wandern, *vb.* wander.

Umkehr, *n.f.* return; reversal.

um·kehren, *vb.* turn (back, round, inside out, upside down).

Umkehrung, -en, *n.f.* reversal, reversing.

um·kippen, *vb.* turn over, tip over.

um·kleiden*, *vb.* (sich u.) change one's clothes.

Umkleideraum, =e, *n.m.* dressing-room.

um·kommen*, *vb.* perish.

Umkreis, -e, *n.m.* circumference; range, radius.

umkrei'sen, *vb.* circle around, rotate around.

Umlauf, *n.m.* circulation.

um·laufen*, *vb.* circulate.

um·legen, *vb.* put on; change the position, shift; change the date.

um·leiten, *vb.* divert.

Umleitung, -en, *n.f.* detour.

um·lernen, *vb.* learn anew, readjust one's views.

umliegend, *adj.* surrounding.

umrah'men, *vb.* frame.

umran'den, *vb.* edge.

um·rechnen, *vb.* convert.

umrei'ßen*, *vb.* outline.

umrin'gen, *vb.* surround.

Umriß, -sse, *n.m.* contour, outline.

um·rühren, *vb.* stir.

Umsatz, =e, *n.m.* turnover, sales.

Umsatzsteuer, -n, *n.f.* sales tax.

um·schalten, *vb.* switch.

Umschau, *n.f.* (U. halten*) look around.

umschichtig, *adv.* in turns.

Umschlag, =e, *n.m.* envelope; (book) cover; turnover; compress.

umschlie'ßen*, *vb.* encircle, encompass.

umschlin'gen*, *vb.* embrace.

um·schreiben*, *vb.* rewrite.

umschrei'ben*, *vb.* circumscribe, paraphrase.

Umschrei'bung, -en, *n.f.* paraphrase.

Umschrift, -en, *n.f.* transcription.

Umschwung, =e, *n.m.* change, about-face.

um·sehen*, *vb.* (sich u.) look around.

um·setzen, *vb.* transpose; (goods) sell.

Umsicht, *n.f.* circumspection.

umsichtig, *adj.* circumspect, prudent.

umso, *adv.* **(u. besser)** so much the better; **(je mehr, u. besser)** the more the better.

umsonst, *adv.* in vain; gratis, free of charge.

Umstand, "e, *n.m.* circumstance, condition; *(pl.)* formalities, fuss; **(in anderen Umständen)** pregnant.

umständlich, *adj.* complicated, fussy.

Umstandskleid, -er, *n.nt.* maternity dress.

Umstandswort, "er, *n.nt.* adverb.

Umstehend-, *adj.m.&f.* bystander.

um•steigen*, *vb.* transfer, change.

Umsteiger, -, *n.m.* transfer (ticket).

um•stellen*, *vb.* change the position of; **(sich u. auf)** readjust, convert to; computerize.

umstel'len, *vb.* surround.

um•steuern, *vb.* reverse.

um•stimmen, *vb.* make someone change his mind.

um•stoßen*, *vb.* overturn, overthrow, upset.

Umsturz, "e, *n.m.* overthrow, revolution.

um•stürzen, *vb.* overturn.

Umtausch, -e, *n.m.* exchange; **(vom U. ausgeschlossen)** no exchange.

umtauschbar, *adj.* exchangeable.

um•tauschen, *vb.* exchange.

Umtrieb, -e, *n.m.* intrigue, machinations.

um•tun*, *vb.* **(sich nach etwas u.)** look for, apply for.

Umwälzung, -en, *n.f.* upheaval, revolution.

um•wandeln, *vb.* transform; change; convert.

um•wechseln, *vb.* change, convert.

Umweg, -e, *n.m.* detour.

Umwelt, *n.f.* environment.

Umweltschutz, *n.m.* environmental protection.

Umweltschtzer, -, *n.m.* environmentalist.

Umweltverschmutzung, *n.f.* pollution.

umwer'ben*, *vb.* woo, court.

Umwer'bung, *n.f.* courtship.

um•werfen*, *vb.* overthrow; upset.

um•ziehen*, *vb.* move; **(sich u.)** change one's clothes.

umzin'geln, *vb.* surround.

Umzug, "e, *n.m.* move; procession.

unabhängig, *adj.* independent.

Unabhängigkeit, *n.f.* independence.

unabkömmlich, *adj.* indispensable.

unabläs'sig, *adj.* incessant.

unabseh'bar, *adj.* unforeseeable.

unabwend'bar, *adj.* inevitable.

unachtsam, *adj.* inattentive; careless.

unähnlich, *adj.* dissimilar, unlike.

unangebracht, *adj.* out of place.

unangemessen, *adj.* unsuitable, improper.

unangenehm, *adj.* unpleasant, distasteful.

Unannehmlichkeit, -en, *n.f.* trouble.

unansehnlich, *adj.* plain, inconspicuous.

unanständig, *adj.* indecent, obscene.

unanwendbar, *adj.* inapplicable.

unappetitlich, *adj.* unappetizing; nasty.

Unart, -en, *n.f.* rudeness, bad manners.

unartig, *adj.* naughty.

unauffällig, *adj.* inconspicuous.

unaufhör'lich, *adj.* incessant.

unaufmerksam, *adj.* inattentive.

Unaufmerksamkeit, -en, *n.f.* inattentiveness; inadvertence.

unaufrichtig, *adj.* insincere.

Unaufrichtigkeit, -en, *n.f.* insincerity; lie.

unausbleib'lich, *adj.* inevitable.

unausgeglichen, *adj.* unbalanced, unstable.

unausgesetzt, *adj.* continual.

unaussteh'lich, *adj.* insufferable.

unbändig, *adj.* unruly; excessive.

unbarmherzig, *adj.* merciless.

unbeabsichtigt, *adj.* unintentional.

unbeachtet, *adj.* unnoticed; **(u. lassen*)** ignore.

unbedacht, *adj.* thoughtless.
unbedenklich, *adj.* harmless.
unbedeutend, *adj.* insignificant.
unbedingt', *adj.* absolute, unconditional.
unbefangen, *adj.* natural, naïve.
unbefleckt, *adj.* immaculate; **(unbefleckte Empfängnis)** Immaculate Conception.
unbefriedigend, *adj.* unsatisfactory.
unbefriedigt, *adj.* dissatisfied.
unbefugt, *adj.* unauthorized.
unbegabt, *adj.* untalented.
unbegreif'lich, *adj.* incomprehensible.
unbegrenzt, *adj.* limitless.
unbegründet, *adj.* unfounded.
Unbehagen, *n.nt.* discomfort.
unbehaglich, *adj.* uneasy.
unbeherrscht, *adj.* uncontrolled.
unbeholfen, *adj.* awkward, clumsy.
unbekannt, *adj.* unknown, unfamiliar.
unbekümmert, *adj.* unconcerned.
unbeliebt, *adj.* unpopular.
unbemerkbar, *adj.* imperceptible.
unbemerkt, *adj.* unnoticed.
unbenommen, *adj.* **(es bleibt* Ihnen u.)** you are at liberty to.
unbequem, *adj.* inconvenient; uncomfortable.
unbere'chenbar, *adj.* incalculable; unreliable, erratic.
unberechtigt, *adj.* unauthorized; unjustified.
unberufen!, *interj.* touch wood!
unbeschädigt, *adj.* undamaged.
unbescheiden, *adj.* immodest; selfish.
Unbescholtenheit, *n.f.* integrity.
unbeschreiblich, *adj.* indescribable.
unbeschrieben, *adj.* blank.
unbesehen, *adj.* unseen.
unbesieg'bar, *adj.* invincible.
unbesonnen, *adj.* thoughtless.
unbesorgt, *adj.* carefree, unconcerned.
unbeständig, *adj.* changeable.
unbestellbar, *adj.* undeliverable.
unbestimmt, *adj.* indefinite, vague.

unbestritten, *adj.* undisputed.
unbeträchtlich, *adj.* inconsiderable.
unbeugsam, *adj.* inflexible; obstinate.
unbewandert, *adj.* inexperienced.
unbewiesen, *adj.* not proved.
unbewohnbar, *adj.* uninhabitable.
unbewohnt, *adj.* uninhabited.
unbewußt, *adj.* unconscious; unknown.
unbezahl'bar, *adj.* priceless.
unbrauchbar, *adj.* useless.
und, *conj.* and.
Undank, *n.m.* ingratitude.
undankbar, *adj.* ungrateful.
undefinier'bar, *adj.* indefinable.
undenk'lich, *adj.* inconceivable; **(seit u. en Zeiten)** since time out of mind.
undeutlich, *adj.* unclear, indistinct.
undicht, *adj.* leaky.
Unding, *n.nt.* absurdity, nonsense.
unduldsam, *adj.* intolerant.
undurchführ'bar, *adj.* not feasible.
undurchsichtig, *adj.* opaque.
uneben, *adj.* uneven.
unecht, *adj.* not genuine, false, counterfeit; artificial.
unehelich, *adj.* illegitimate.
unehrenhaft, *adj.* dishonorable.
unehrerbietig, *adj.* disrespectful.
unehrlich, *adj.* dishonest; insincere.
uneingeschränkt, *adj.* unlimited.
uneinig, *adj.* **(u. sein*)** disagree.
Uneinigkeit, -en, *n.f.* disagreement, dissension.
unempfindlich, *adj.* insensitive.
unend'lich, *adj.* infinite; **(u. klein)** infinitesimal.
Unend'lichkeit, -en, *n.f.* infinity.
unentbehrlich, *adj.* indispensable.
unentgeltlich, *adj.* gratuitous.
unentschieden, *adj.* undecided; **(das Spiel ist u.)** the game is a draw.
unentschlossen, *adj.* undecided.
unentwegt, *adj.* constant.
unerfahren, *adj.* inexperienced.

Unerfahrenheit, -en, *n.f.* inexperience.
unerfreulich, *adj.* unpleasant.
unerheblich, *adj.* insignificant, irrelevant.
unerhört', *adj.* unheard of, outrageous.
unerkannt, *adj.* unrecognized.
unerkennbar, *adj.* unrecognizable.
unerklärlich, *adj.* inexplicable.
unerläßlich, *adj.* indispensable.
unerlaubt, *adj.* unlawful, illegal, illicit.
unermeß'lich, *adj.* immeasurable.
unermüdlich, *adj.* unpleasant.
unerquicklich, *adj.* unpleasant.
unersätt'lich, *adj.* insatiable.
unerschrocken, *adj.* intrepid.
unersetz'lich, *adj.* irreplaceable.
unersprieß'lich, *adj.* unpleasant.
unerträg'lich, *adj.* unbearable, insufferable.
unerwartet, *adj.* unexpected.
unerwünscht, *adj.* unwelcome.
unerzogen, *adj.* ill-bred, ill-mannered.
unfähig, *adj.* unable, incapable, incompetent.
unfair, *adj.* unfair.
Unfall, -̈e, *n.m.* accident.
unfaß'bar, *adj.* incomprehensible.
unfaß'lich, *adj.* incomprehensible.
unfehl'bar, *adj.* infallible.
Unfeinheit, -en, *n.f.* crudeness, crudity.
unförmig, *adj.* shapeless.
unfreiwillig, *adj.* involuntary.
unfreundlich, *adj.* unkind, unfriendly; rude.
unfruchtbar, *adj.* barren, sterile.
Unfug, *n.m.* mischief.
unfügsam, *adj.* unmanageable.
Ungar, -n, -n, *n.m.* Hungarian.
Ungarin, -nen, *n.f.* Hungarian.
ungarisch, *adj.* Hungarian.
Ungarn, *n.nt.* Hungary.
ungastlich, *adj.* inhospitable.
ungeachtet, *prep.* notwithstanding.
ungebildet, *adj.* uneducated.
ungebührlich, *adj.* improper.

ungebunden, *adj.* free.
Ungeduld, *n.f.* impatience.
ungeduldig, *adj.* impatient.
ungeeignet, *adj.* unqualified, unsuitable.
ungefähr, 1. *adj.* approximate. **2.** *adv.* approximately, about.
ungefährlich, *adj.* harmless.
ungefällig, *adj.* unobliging, impolite.
ungeheuchelt, *adj.* sincere.
ungeheuer, *adj.* tremendous, huge.
Ungeheuer, -, *n.nt.* monster.
ungeheu'erlich, *adj.* monstrous.
ungehobelt, *adj.* uncouth.
ungehörig, *adj.* improper, rude.
ungehorsam, *adj.* disobedient.
Ungehorsam, *n.m.* disobedience.
ungekünstelt, *adj.* unaffected, natural.
ungeläufig, *adj.* unfamiliar.
ungelegen, *adj.* inconvenient.
ungelenk, *adj.* clumsy.
ungelernt, *adj.* unskilled.
ungemein, *adv.* uncommonly.
ungemütlich, *adj.* uncomfortable.
ungeneigt, *adj.* disinclined.
ungeniert, *adj.* free and easy.
ungenießbar, *adj.* inedible; unbearable.
ungenügend, *adj.* insufficient; unsatisfactory.
ungerade, *adj.* uneven; (numbers) odd.
ungerecht, *adj.* unjust, unfair.
ungerechtfertigt, *adj.* unwarranted.
Ungerechtigkeit, -en, *n.f.* injustice.
ungern, *adv.* unwillingly; reluctantly.
ungesalzen, *adj.* unsalted.
ungeschehen, *adj.* **(u. machen)** to undo.
Ungeschicklichkeit, -en, *n.f.* clumsiness.
ungeschickt, *adj.* clumsy, awkward.
ungeschlacht, *adj.* uncouth.
ungesetzlich, *adj.* illegal.
ungesittet, *adj.* unmannerly.
ungestört, *adj.* undisturbed.

ungestraft, 1. *adj.* unpunished. **2.** *adv.* with impunity.

ungestüm, *adj.* impetuous.

ungesund, *adj.* unhealthy; unsound.

Ungetüm, -e, *n.nt.* monster.

ungewandt, *adj.* awkward.

ungewiß, *adj.* uncertain.

Ungewißheit, -en, *n.f.* uncertainty.

Ungewitter, -, *n.nt.* thunderstorm.

ungewöhnlich, *adj.* unusual, abnormal.

ungewohnt, *adj.* unaccustomed, unfamiliar.

ungewollt, *adj.* unintentional.

ungezählt, *adj.* innumerable.

ungezügelt, *adj.* unrestrained.

ungezwungen, *adj.* easygoing.

Ungläubig-, *n.m.&f.* infidel.

unglaublich, *adj.* incredible.

unglaubwürdig, *adj.* unreliable.

ungleich, *adj.* unequal, uneven, unlike.

ungleichartig, *adj.* dissimilar.

Ungleichheit, -en, *n.f.* unequality, dissimilarity.

Unglück, -e, *n.nt.* misfortune, calamity, disaster, accident.

unglücklich, *adj.* unhappy; unfortunate.

unglücklicherweise, *adv.* unfortunately.

unglückselig, *adj.* disastrous; utterly miserable.

Ungnade, *n.f.* disfavor.

ungnädig, *n.f.* ungracious.

ungültig, *adj.* invalid; null and void; **(für u. erklären)** annul, declare null and void.

ungünstig, *adj.* unfavorable.

unhalt'bar, *adj.* untenable.

unhandlich, *adj.* unwieldy.

Unheil, *n.nt.* harm, disaster.

unheil'bar, *adj.* incurable.

unheilbringend, *adj.* fatal, ominous.

unheilvoll, *adj.* ominous.

unheimlich, *adj.* scary, sinister.

unhöflich, *adj.* impolite, rude.

unhygienisch, *adj.* unsanitary.

Uniform', -en, *n.f.* uniform.

uninteressant, *adj.* uninteresting.

uninteressiert, *adj.* uninterested; disinterested.

unisex, *adj.* unisex.

universal', *adj.* universal.

Universität', -en, *n.f.* university.

Univer'sum, *n.n.t* universe.

unkenntlich, *adj.* unrecognizable.

unklar, *adj.* unclear, obscure.

unkleidsam, *adj.* unbecoming.

unkompliziert, *adj.* uncomplicated.

Unkosten, *n.pl.* expenses, overhead.

Unkraut, *n.nt.* weeds.

unlängst, *adv.* recently.

unlauter, *adj.* impure; unfair.

unleserlich, *adj.* illegible.

unlieb, *adj.* disagreeable.

unliebenswürdig, *adj.* unfriendly, impolite.

unlogisch, *adj.* illogical.

unlustig, *adj.* listless.

unmanierlich, *adj.* unmannered.

unmaßgeblich, *adj.* irrelevant; unauthoritative.

unmäßig, *adj.* immoderate.

Unmenge, -n, *n.f.* enormous quantity.

Unmensch, -en, -en, *n.m.* brute.

unmenschlich, *adj.* inhuman.

unmerklich, *adj.* imperceptible.

unmittelbar, *adj.* immediate.

unmodern, *adj.* old-fashioned, out of style.

unmöglich, *adj.* impossible.

unmoralisch, *adj.* immoral.

unmündig, *adj.* underage.

unnachahmlich, *adj.* inimitable.

unnah'bar, *adj.* inaccessible.

unnötig, *adj.* needless, unnecessary.

unnütz, *adj.* useless.

unordentlich, *adj.* disorderly, messy.

Unordnung, *n.f.* disorder.

unparteilisch, *adj.* impartial, neutral.

unpassend, *adj.* unsuitable; improper, off-color.

unpassier'bar, *adj.* impassable.

unpäßlich, *adj.* unwell, indisposed.

unpersönlich, *adj.* impersonal.

unpolitisch, *adj.* nonpolitical.

unpraktisch, *adj.* impractical.

unpünktlich, *adj.* not on time.

unrecht, *adj.* wrong; (**u. haben***) be wrong.

Unrecht, *n.nt.* wrong, harm, injustice.

unreell, *adj.* dishonest.

unregelmäßig, *adj.* irregular.

unreif, *adj.* immature.

unrein, *adj.* unclean; impure.

unrichtig, *adj.* incorrect.

Unruhe, **-n**, *n.f.* unrest, trouble, disturbance.

unruhig, *adj.* restless, troubled, uneasy.

unschädlich, *adj.* harmless.

unscheinbar, *adj.* insignificant.

unschicklich, *adj.* improper.

unschlüssig, *adj.* undecided.

Unschuld, *n.f.* innocence.

unschuldig, *adj.* innocent.

unselig, *adj.* unhappy, fatal.

unser, **-, -e**, *adj.* our.

uns(e)rer, **-es, -e**, *pron.* ours.

unsicher, *adj.* uncertain; unsafe.

Unsicherheit, **-en**, *n.f.* uncertainty, insecurity.

unsichtbar, *adj.* invisible.

Unsinn, *n.m.* nonsense.

unsinnig, *adj.* absurd, nonsensical.

Unsitte, **-n**, *n.f.* bad habit.

unsittlich, *adj.* immoral.

unsterblich, *adj.* immortal.

unstet, *adj.* unsteady.

Unstimmigkeit, **-en**, *n.f.* discrepancy, disagreement.

unsympatisch, *adj.* disagreeable.

untauglich, *adj.* unfit.

unteilbar, *adj.* indivisible.

unten, *adv.* below, down, downstairs.

unter, *prep.* under, beneath, below; among; (**u. uns**) just between you and me.

unter-, *adj.* under, lower.

Unterarm, **-e**, *n.m.* forearm.

unterbewußt, *adj.* subconscious.

Unterbewußtsein, *n.nt.* subconsciousness.

unterbie'ten*, *vb.* undercut; lower.

unterblei'ben*, *vb.* not get done.

unterbre'chen*, *vb.* interrupt.

Unterbre'chung, **-en**, *n.f.* interruption.

unterbrei'ten, *vb.* submit.

unter-bringen*, *vb.* lodge, accommodate.

unterdes'(sen), *adv.* meanwhile.

unterdrü'cken, *vb.* suppress, oppress, repress, stifle, subdue.

unterdrückt', *adj.* downtrodden.

Unterdrü'ckung, **-en**, *n.f.* suppression.

untereinan'der, *adv.* among them- (our-, your-) selves.

unterernährt, *adj.* undernourished.

Unterernährung, *n.f.* malnutrition.

Unterfüh'rung, **-en**, *n.f.* underpass.

Untergang, **̈-e**, *n.m.* downfall, decline.

unterge'ben, *adj.* subordinate.

Unterge'bene, *n.m.&f.* subordinate.

unter-gehen*, *vb.* perish; set (sun).

untergeordnet, *adj.* subordinate.

untergra'ben*, *vb.* undermine, subvert.

Untergrundbahn, **-en**, *n.f.* subway.

unterhalb, *prep.* below.

Unterhalt, *n.m.* maintenance, keep.

unterhal'ten*, *vb.* maintain, support; entertain; (**sich u.**) converse.

Unterhal'tung, **-en**, *n.f.* maintenance; entertainment, conversation.

Unterhand'lung, **-en**, *n.f.* negotiation.

Unterhaus, *n.nt.* lower house (of parliament, congress).

Unterhemd, **-en**, *n.nt.* undershirt.

Unterhose, **-n**, *n.f.* underpants.

unterjo'chen, *vb.* subjugate.

Unterkunft, **̈-e**, *n.f.* lodging.

Unterlage, **-n**, *n.f.* base, bed; evidence; bottom sheet.

unterlas'sen*, *vb.* omit, fail to do.

Unterlas'sung, **-en**, *n.f.* omission, default.

unterle'gen, *adj.* inferior.

Unterleib, **-er**, *n.m.* abdomen.

unterlie'gen*, *vb.* succumb to, be overcome by.

Untermieter, -, *n.m.* subtenant.

unterneh'men*, *vb.* undertake.

Unterneh'men, -, *n.nt.* enterprise.

unterneh'mend, *adj.* enterprising.

Unterneh'mer, -, *n.m.* entrepreneur, contractor.

Unterneh'merin, -nen, *n.f.* entrepreneur, contractor.

Unterneh'mung, -en, *n.f.* undertaking.

unterneh'mungslustig, *adj.* adventurous.

Unteroffizier, -e, *n.m.* non-commissioned officer, sergeant.

Unterpfand, *nt.* pledge, security.

Unterre'dung, -en, *n.f.* discussion, parley.

Unterricht, *n.m.* instruction.

unterrich'ten, *vb.* instruct.

Unterrich'tung, *n.f.* guidance.

Unterrock, -̈e, *n.m.* slip, petticoat.

untersa'gen, *vb.* prohibit.

Untersatz, -̈e, *n.m.* base; saucer.

unterschät'zen, *vb.* underestimate.

unterschei'den, *vb.* distinguish, differentiate; (sich u.) differ.

Unterschei'dung, -en, *n.f.* distinction.

Unterschied, -e, *n.m.* difference.

unterschiedslos, *adj.* indiscriminate.

unterschla'gen*, *vb.* embezzle, suppress.

unterschrei'ben*, *vb.* sign (one's name to).

Unterschrift, *n.f.* signature.

Unterseeboot, -e, *n.nt.* submarine.

untersetzt', *adj.* chunky, thickset.

Unterstand, -̈e, *n.m.* dugout.

unterste'hen*, *vb.* (sich u.) dare.

Unterstel'lung, -en, *n.f.* innuendo, insinuation.

unterstrei'chen*, *vb.* underline, underscore.

unterstüt'zen, *vb.* support, back.

Unterstüt'zung, -en, *n.f.* support, backing.

untersu'chen, *vb.* investigate, examine.

Untersu'chung, -en, *n.f.* investigation, examination.

Untertan, (-en), -en, *n.m.* subject.

Untertasse, -n, *n.f.* saucer.

unter-tauchen', *vb.* submerge.

Unterwäsche, *n.f.* underwear.

unterwegs', *adv.* on the way; bound for.

unterwei'sen*, *vb.* instruct.

Unterwei'sung, -en, *n.f.* instruction.

Unterwelt, *n.f.* underworld.

unterwer'fen*, *vb.* subjugate; subject to; (sich u.) submit (to).

Unterwer'fung, *n.f.* submission.

unterwor'fen, *adj.* subject (to).

unterwür'fig, *adj.* subservient.

unterzeich'nen, *vb.* sign.

unterzie'hen*, *vb.* (sich u.) undergo.

untief, *adj.* shallow.

untreu, *adj.* unfaithful, disloyal.

Untreue, *n.f.* unfaithfulness, disloyalty.

untröstlich, *adj.* disconsolate.

unüberlegt, *adj.* inconsiderate, thoughtless.

unüberwind'lich, *adj.* insuperable.

unumgäng'lich, *adj.* unavoidable.

unverän'derlich, *adj.* invariable.

unverant'wortlich, *adj.* irresponsible.

unverbes'serlich, *adj.* incorrigible.

unverbindlich, *adj.* without obligation.

unverblümt, *adj.* blunt.

unverdaulich, *adj.* indigestible.

unverein'bar, *adj.* incompatible.

unvergeßlich, *adj.* unforgettable.

unvergleich'lich, *adj.* incomparable.

unverheiratet, *adj.* unmarried.

unverhohlen, *adj.* frank, aboveboard.

unverkenn'bar, *adj.* unmistakable.

unvermeidlich, *adj.* inevitable.
unvermittelt, *adj.* abrupt.
unvermutet, *adj.* unexpected.
unverschämt, *adj.* shameless, impudent, nervy.
Unverschämtheit, -en, *n.f.* impertinence, gall.
unversehens, *adv.* unexpectedly.
unverständlich, *adj.* incomprehensible.
unverzüglich, *adj.* speedy, without delay.
unvollendet, *adj.* incomplete, unfinished.
unvollkommen, *adj.* incomplete, imperfect.
unvoreingenommen, *adj.* unbiased.
unvorher'gesehen, *adj.* unforeseen.
unvorsichtig, *adj.* careless.
unvorstell'bar, *adj.* unimaginable.
unwäg'bar, *adj.* imponderable.
unwahr(haftig), *adj.* untrue.
Unwahrheit, -en, *n.f.* untruth.
unwahrnehmbar, *adj.* imperceptible.
unwahrscheinlich, *adj.* improbable.
unweigerlich, *adj.* unhesitating; without fail.
unwesentlich, *adj.* immaterial, nonessential.
unwiderleg'bar, *adj.* irrefutable.
unwidersteh'lich, *adj.* irresistible.
unwillkürlich, *adj.* involuntary.
unwirksam, *adj.* ineffectual.
unwissend, *adj.* ignorant.
unwürdig, *adj.* unworthy.
Unzahl, *n.f.* tremendous number.
unzählig, *adj.* countless.
Unze, -n, *n.f.* ounce.
unzertrenn'lich, *adj.* inseparable.
Unzucht, *n.f.* lewdness.
unzüchtig, *adj.* lewd.

unzufrieden, *adj.* dissatisfied.
Unzufriedenheit, -en, *n.f.* dissatisfaction.
unzulänglich, *adj.* insufficient, inadequate.
unzurechnungsfähig, *adj.* insane.
unzureichend, *adj.* insufficient.
unzuverlässig, *adj.* unreliable.
Ur-, *cpds.* original; very old; tremendously.
uralt, *adj.* very old, ancient.
Uraufführung, -en, *n.f.* première.
Urenkel, -, *n.m.* great-grandson.
Urenkelin, -nen, *n.f.* great-granddaughter.
Urgroßeltern, *n.pl.* great-grandparents.
Urgroßmutter, ¨-, *n.f.* great-grandmother.
Urgroßvater, ¨-, *n.m.* great-grandfather.
Urheber, -, *n.m.* author, originator.
Urheberrecht, -e, *n.nt.* copyright.
Urin', -e, *n.nt.* urine.
urinie'ren, *vb.* urinate.
Urkunde, -n, *n.f.* document.
Urlaub, -e, *n.m.* leave, furlough.
Urlauber, -, *n.m.* vacationer.
Urlauberin, -nen, *n.f.* vacationer.
Urne, -n, *n.f.* urn; ballot box.
Urquell, -e, *n.m.* fountainhead.
Ursache, -n, *n.f.* cause; **(keine U.)** don't mention it.
Ursprung, ¨-e, *n.m.* origin.
ursprünglich, *adj.* original.
Urteil, -e, *n.nt.* judgment, sentence.
urteilen, *vb.* judge.
Urteilsspruch, ¨-e, *n.m.* verdict.
usurpie'ren, *vb.* usurp.
usw., *abbr.* (= und so weiter) etc., and so forth.
uto'pisch, *adj.* utopian.

V

Vagabund', -en, -en, *n.m.* tramp.
vage, *adj.* vague.
Vagi'na, (-nen), *n.f.* vagina.

Valu'ta, -ten, *n.f.* value; (foreign) currency.
Vanil'le, *n.f.* vanilla.

Variation', -en, *n.f.* variation.
Varieté', -s, *n.nt.* variety show, vaudeville.
varlie'ren, *vb.* vary.
Vase, -n, *n.f.* vase.
Vater, -̈, *n.m.* father.
Vaterland, *n.nt.* fatherland.
väterlich, *adj.* fatherly, paternal.
vaterlos, *adj.* fatherless.
Vaterschaft, -en, *n.f.* fatherhood, paternity.
Vaterun'ser, -, *n.nt.* Lord's Prayer.
Veilchen, -, *n.nt.* violet.
Vene, -n, *n.f.* vein.
vene'risch, *adj.* venereal.
Ventil', -e, *n.nt.* valve.
Ventilation', *n.f.* ventilation.
Ventila'tor, -o'ren, *n.m.* ventilator, fan.
ventilie'ren, *vb.* ventilate.
verab'reden, *vb.* agree upon; **(sich v.)** make an appointment, date.
Verab'redung, -en, *n.f.* appointment, engagement, date.
verab'scheuen, *vb.* abhor, detest.
verab'schieden, *vb.* dismiss; pass (a bill); **(sich v.)** take one's leave.
verach'ten, *vb.* scorn, despise.
verach'tenswert, *adj.* despicable.
veräch'tlich, *adj.* contemptuous.
Verach'tung, -en, *n.f.* contempt.
verallgemei'nern, *vb.* generalize.
Verallgemei'nerung, -en, *n.f.* generalization.
veral'tet, *adj.* obsolete.
Veran'da, -den, *n.f.* porch.
verän'derlich, *adj.* changeable.
verän'dern, *vb.* change.
Verän'derung, -en, *n.f.* change.
veran'kern, *vb.* anchor, moor.
veran'lassen*, *vb.* cause, motivate.
Veran'lassung, -en, *n.f.* cause, motivation.
veran'schaulichen, *vb.* illustrate.
veran'stalten, *vb.* arrange, put on.
Veran'staltung, -en, *n.f.* arrangement, performance.
verant'wortlich, *adj.* responsible.
Verant'wortlichkeit, -en, *n.f.* responsibility.

Verant'wortung, -en, *n.f.* responsibility; accounting, justification.
verant'wortungslos, *adj.* irresponsible.
verant'wortungsvoll, *adj.* carrying responsibility.
verar'beiten, *vb.* process.
verär'gern, *vb.* exasperate.
verar'men, *vb.* become poor.
Verb, -en, *n.nt.* verb.
verbal', *adj.* verbal.
Verband', -̈e, *n.m.* association; bandage, dressing.
verban'nen, *vb.* banish, exile.
Verban'nung, -en, *n.f.* banishment, exile.
verbau'en, *vb.* build badly; obstruct.
verber'gen*, *vb.* hide.
verbes'sern, *vb.* improve, correct.
Verbes'serung, -en, *n.f.* improvement, correction.
verbeu'gen, *vb.* **(sich v.)** bow.
Verbeu'gung, -en, *n.f.* bow.
verbeu'len, *vb.* dent, batter.
verbie'gen*, *vb.* bend (out of shape).
verbie'ten*, *vb.* forbid, prohibit, ban.
verbie'terisch, *adj.* prohibitive.
verbin'den*, *vb.* connect, join, combine; bandage.
verbind'lich, *adj.* binding, obligatory.
Verbin'dung, -en, *n.f.* connection, combination; (chemical) compound; (student) fraternity; **(in V. stehen* mit)** be in touch with; **(sich in V. setzen mit)** get in touch with.
verbis'sen, *adj.* suppressed; dogged.
verbit'ten*, *vb.* **(sich v.)** decline; not stand for.
verbit'tern, *vb.* embitter.
verblas'sen, *vb.* turn pale, fade.
Verbleib', *n.m.* whereabouts.
verblei'chen*, *vb.* grow pale, fade.
verblüf'fen, *vb.* dumbfound, flabbergast.
verbo'gen, *adj.* bent.
verbor'gen, *adj.* hidden.

Verbot', -e, *n.nt.* prohibition.

Verbrauch', *n.m.* consumption.

verbrau'chen, *vb.* consume, use up, wear out.

Verbrau'cher, -, *n.m.* consumer.

Verbrauchs'steuer, -n, *n.f.* excise tax.

Verbre'chen, -, *n.nt.* crime.

Verbre'cher, -, *n.m.* criminal.

Verbre'cherin, -nen, *n.f.* criminal.

verbre'cherisch, *adj.* criminal.

verbrei'ten, *vb.* disseminate, propagate, diffuse.

verbrenn'bar, *adj.* combustible.

verbren'nen*, *vb.* burn; cremate.

Verbren'nung, *n.f.* burning; cremation; combustion.

verbrin'gen*, *vb.* spend (time).

verbrüh'en, *vb.* scald.

verbun'den, *adj.* indebted, obliged.

verbün'den, *vb.* ally.

Verbün'det-, *n.m.&f.* ally, confederate.

verbür'gen, *vb.* guarantee.

Verdacht', *n.m.* suspicion.

verdäch'tig, *adj.* suspicious, suspected.

verdam'men, *vb.* damn, condemn.

verdam'menswert, *adj.* damnable.

Verdamm'nis, *n.f.* (eternal) damnation.

verdammt', *adj.* damned; damn it!

Verdam'mung, -en, *n.f.* damnation.

verdamp'fen, *vb.* evaporate.

verdau'en, *vb.* digest.

verdau'lich, *adj.* digestible.

Verdau'ung, *n.f.* digestion.

Verdau'ungsstörung, -en, *n.f.* indigestion.

Verdeck', -e, *n.nt.* deck covering; top (of an auto).

verden'ken*, *vb.* take amiss.

verder'ben*, *vb.* perish, spoil, ruin.

Verder'ben, *n.nt.* perdition, ruin, doom.

verderb'lich, *adj.* ruinous; perishable.

verderbt', *adj.* corrupt.

verdeut'lichen, *vb.* make clear.

verdich'ten, *vb.* thicken, solidify.

verdie'nen, *vb.* earn, deserve.

Verdienst', -e, *n.m.* earnings.

Verdienst', -e, *n.nt.* merit.

verdienst'lich, *adj.* meritorious.

verdient', *adj.* deserving, deserved.

verdol'metschen, *vb.* interpret, translate.

verdop'peln, *vb.* double.

Verdop'pelung, -en, *n.f.* doubling.

verdor'ren, *vb.* wither.

verdrän'gen, *vb.* push out, displace; suppress, inhibit.

Verdrän'gung, -en, *n.f.* displacement; repression, inhibition.

verdre'hen, *vb.* twist, distort, pervert.

verdrie'ßen*, *vb.* grieve, vex, annoy.

verdrieß'lich, *adj.* morose, sulky.

Verdruß', *n.m.* vexation, irritation.

verdun'keln, *vb.* darken.

Verdun'kelung, -en, *n.f.* blackout.

verdün'nen, *vb.* thin, dilute, rarefy.

verdut'zen, *vb.* bewilder.

vereh'ren, *vb.* adore, respect, revere.

Vereh'rer, -, *n.m.* admirer.

Vereh'rerin, -nen, *n.f.* admirer.

Vereh'rung, *n.f.* adoration, reverence.

verei'digen, *vb.* administer an oath to.

Verei'digung, -en, *n.f.* swearing-in.

Verein', -e, *n.m.* association.

verein'bar, *adj.* compatible.

verein'baren, *vb.* come to an agreement, reconcile.

Verein'barkeit, *n.f.* compatibility.

Verein'barung, -en, *n.f.* agreement.

verein'fachen, *vb.* simplify.

verein'heitlichen, *vb.* standardize, make uniform.

verei'nigen, *vb.* unite.

Verei'nigte Staaten von Ame'rika, *n.pl.* United States of America.

Verei'nigung, -en, *n.f.* union, alliance, association, merger.

Verein'te Natio'nen, *n.pl.* United Nations.

verein'zelt, *adj.* isolated, individual; scattered, stray.

verei'teln, *vb.* thwart, foil.

verer'ben, *vb.* bequeath.

vererb'lich, *adj.* hereditary.

Verer'bung, -en, *n.f.* heredity.

verfah'ren*, *vb.* act, proceed, deal; **(sich v.)** lose one's way.

Verfah'ren, -, *n.nt.* procedure, process.

Verfall', *n.m.* decay, decline, disrepair.

verfal'len*, *vb.* decay, decline, deteriorate; fall due, lapse.

verfäl'schen, *vb.* falsify, adulterate.

Verfäl'schung, -en, *n.f.* falsification, adulteration.

verfäng'lich, *adj.* captious, insidious.

verfas'sen, *vb.* compose, write.

Verfas'ser, -, *n.m.* author.

Verfas'serin, -nen, *n.f.* author.

Verfas'sung, -en, *n.f.* composition; state, condition; constitution.

verfas'sungsmäßig, *adj.* constitutional.

verfas'sungswidrig, *adj.* unconstitutional.

verfau'len, *vb.* rot.

verfault', *adj.* putrid.

verfecht'bar, *adj.* defensible.

verfeh'len, *vb.* miss.

verfei'nern, *vb.* refine.

Verfei'nerung, -en, *n.f.* refinement.

verfer'tigen, *vb.* manufacture.

verfil'men, *vb.* film, make a movie of.

verflie'ßen*, *vb.* flow away, lapse.

verflu'chen, *vb.* curse, damn.

verflucht', *adj.* cursed, damned; damn it!

verfol'gen, *vb.* pursue, haunt, persecute.

Verfol'gung, -en, *n.f.* pursuit, persecution.

Verfrach'ter, -, *n.m.* shipper.

verfrüht', *adj.* premature.

verfüg'bar, *adj.* available.

verfü'gen, *vb.* enact, order; **(v. über)** have at one's disposal.

Verfü'gung, -en, *n.f.* disposition, instruction, enactment; **(mir zur V. stehen*)** be at my disposal; **(mir zur V. stellen)** place at my disposal.

verfüh'ren, *vb.* lead astray, entice, pervert, seduce.

verfüh'rerisch, *adj.* seductive.

vergan'gen, *adj.* past, last.

Vergan'genheit, *n.f.* past.

vergäng'lich, *adj.* ephemeral, transitory.

Verga'ser, -, *n.m.* carburetor.

verge'ben*, *vb.* forgive; **(sich v.)** misdeal (at cards); **(sich etwas v.)** compromise oneself.

verge'bens, *adv.* in vain.

vergeb'lich, *adj.* vain, futile.

Verge'bung, *n.f.* forgiveness.

vergegenwär'tigen, *vb.* envisage, picture to oneself.

verge'hen*, *vb.* pass, elapse; **(sich v.)** err, sin, commit a crime.

Verge'hen, -, *n.nt.* misdemeanor.

vergel'ten*, *vb.* repay; retaliate.

Vergel'tung, -en, *n.f.* recompense; retaliation.

Vergel'tungsmaßnahme, -n, *n.f.* reprisal.

verges'sen*, *vb.* forget.

Verges'senheit, *n.f.* oblivion.

vergeß'lich, *adj.* forgetful.

vergeu'den, *vb.* squander.

vergewal'tigen, *vb.* use force on, rape.

Vergewal'tigung, -en, *n.f.* rape.

vergewis'sern, *vb.* confirm; reassure.

vergie'ßen*, *vb.* shed.

vergif'ten, *vb.* poison.

Vergiß'meinnicht, -e, *n.nt.* forget-me-not.

Vergleich', -e, *n.m.* comparison.

vergleich'bar, *adj.* comparable.

vergleich'en*, *vb.* compare.

vergnü'gen, *vb.* amuse.

Vergnü'gen, *n.nt.* fun; **(viel V.)** have a good time.

vergnügt', *adj.* in good spirits, gay.

Vergnü'gung, -en, *n.f.* pleasure, amusement, diversion.

vergöt'tern, *vb.* idolize.

vergrei'fen*, *vb.* **(sich v.)** do the wrong thing; **(sich an etwas v.)** attack, misappropriate.

vergrö'ßern, *vb.* enlarge, magnify.

Vergrö'ßerung, *vb.* enlarge, magnify.

Vergrö'ßerung, -en, *n.f.* enlargement.

Vergrö'ßerungsapparat, -e, *n.m.* enlarger.

Vergün'stigung, -en, *n.f.* favor; reduction.

vergü'ten, *vb.* pay back.

verhaf'ten, *vb.* arrest.

Verhaftung, -en, *n.f.* arrest.

verhal'ten*, *vb.* hold back; **(sich v.)** be, behave.

verhal'ten, *adj.* suppressed.

Verhal'ten, *n.nt.* behavior.

Verhält'nis, -se *n.nt.* relation(ship), proportion, ratio; love affair; *(pl.)* circumstances, conditions.

verhält'nismäßig, *adj.* relative, comparative.

verhan'deln, *vb.* negotiate.

Verhand'lung, -en, *n.f.* negotiation.

Verhand'lungsweise, *n.f.* procedure.

Verhäng'nis, -se *n.nt.* fate, destiny.

verhäng'nisvoll, *adj.* fatal, fateful.

verhar'ren, *vb.* remain, persist.

verhär'ten, *vb.* **(sich v.)** harden, stiffen.

verhaßt', *adj.* hateful, odious.

verhau'en*, *vb.* beat up; make a mess of.

verhed'dern, *vb.* **(sich v.)** get snarled, caught.

verhee'ren, *vb.* desolate.

verhee'rend, *adj.* disastrous.

verheim'lichen, *vb.* conceal.

verhei'raten, *vb.* marry off; **(sich v.)** get married.

verherr'lichen, *vb.* glorify.

verhin'dern, *vb.* prevent, hinder.

Verhin'derung, *n.f.* prevention, hindrance.

verhoh'len, *adj.* hidden, clandestine.

verhöh'nen, *vb.* mock, diride.

Verhör', -e, *n.nt.* interrogation, hearing.

verhö'ren, *vb.* interrogate.

verhun'gern, *vb.* starve to death.

verhü'ten, *vb.* prevent.

Verhü'tung, -en, *n.f.* prevention.

Verhü'tungsmittel, -, *n.nt.* contraceptive device.

verir'ren, *vb.* **(sich v.)** lose one's way, go astray.

Verkauf', -̈e, *n.m.* sale.

verkau'fen, *vb.* sell.

Verkäu'fer, -, *n.m.* clerk, salesman.

Verkäu'ferin, -nen, *n.f.* clerk, salesperson.

verkäuf'lich, *adj.* saleable.

Verkehr', *n.m.* trade, traffic; relations, intercourse.

verkeh'ren, *vb.* *(tr.)* change; *(intr.)* run, go; associate, consort, frequent.

Verkehrs'ampel, -n, *n.f.* traffic light.

Verkehrs'flugzeug, -e, *n.nt.* air liner.

Verkehrs'licht, -er, *n.nt.* traffic light.

Verkehrs'mittel, *n.nt.* means of transporation.

verkehrt', *adj.* reversed, wrong, backwards.

verken'nen*, *vb.* mistake, misunderstand.

verket'ten, *vb.* link.

verkla'gen, *vb.* sue, accuse.

Verklagt', -, *n.m.&f.* defendant.

verklärt', *adj.* transfigured, radiant.

verklei'den, *vb.* disguise; panel.

verklei'nern, *vb.* make smaller; belittle.

Verklei'nerung, -en, *n.f.* diminution; disparagement.

verknüp'fen, *vb.* connect, relate.

verkom'men*, *vb.* decay, come down in the world, die.

verkom'men, *adj.* squalid, dissolute.

verkör'pern, *vb.* embody.

verkör'pert, *adj.* incarnate.

Verkör'perung, -en, *n.f.* embodiment, epitome.

verkrü'ppelt, *adj.* crippled.

verküm'mern, *vb.* wither.

verkün'd(ig)en, *vb.* announce, proclaim.

Verkün'd(ig)ung, -en, *n.f.* announcement, Annunciation.

verkür'zen, *vb.* shorten.

verla'den*, *vb.* load, ship.

Verla'der, *n.m.* shipper.

Verlag', -e, *n.m.* publishing house.

verla'gern, *vb.* shift, displace.

verlan'gen, *vb.* demand, require, ask; **(v. nach)** desire, long for.

Verlan'gen, *n.nt.* demand, request, craving.

verlän'gern, *vb.* lengthen, prolong, extend, renew.

Verlän'gerung, -en, *n.f.* prolongation, extension, renewal.

verlang'samen, *vb.* slow down.

verlas'sen*, *vb.* leave, abandon, forsake; **(sich v. auf)** depend on, rely on.

verlas'sen, *adj.* abandoned, deserted, forlorn.

verläß'lich, *adj.* dependable.

Verlauf', *n.m.* course, lapse.

verlau'fen*, *vb.* pass, elapse; **(sich v.)** get lost.

verle'ben, *vb.* pass.

verlebt', *adj.* dissipated.

verle'gen, *vb.* move, shift; block; misplace; publish.

verle'gen, *adj.* embarrassed.

Verle'ger, -, *n.m.* publisher.

Verle'gerin, -nen, *n.f.* publisher.

Verle'gung, -en, *n.f.* transfer, removal.

verlei'hen*, *vb.* lend; confer, bestow.

Verlei'hung, -en, *n.f.* bestowal.

verlei'ten, *vb.* lead astray, inveigle.

verler'nen, *vb.* forget.

verletz'bar, *adj.* vulnerable.

verlet'zen, *vb.* hurt, offend; violate, infringe.

Verlet'zung, -en, *n.f.* injury; violation.

verleug'nen, *vb.* deny, disown.

verleum'den, *vb.* slander.

verleum'derisch, *adj.* libelous.

Verleum'dung, -en, *n.f.* libel, slander.

verlie'ben, vb. (sich v.) fall in love.

verliebt', *adj.* in love.

verlie'ren*, *vb.* lose.

verlo'ben, *vb.* affiance, betroth; **(sich v.)** get engaged.

verlobt', *adj.* engaged.

Verlobt'-, *n.m.* fiancé.

Verlobt'-, *n.f.* fiancée.

Verlo'bung, -en, *n.f.* engagement.

verlo'cken, *vb.* entice, lure.

verlö'schen*, *vb.* go out, be extinguished.

Verlust', -e, *n.m.* loss; *(pl.)* casualties.

verma'chen, *vb.* bequeath.

Vermächt'nis, -se, *n.nt.* bequest, legacy.

vermäh'len, *vb.* espouse.

Vermäh'lung, -en, *n.f.* espousal.

vermeh'ren, *vb.* augment, multiply, increase.

vermeid'bar, *adj.* avoidable.

vermei'den*, *vb.* avoid.

vermeint'lich, *adj.* supposed.

vermen'gen, *vb.* blend; mix up.

Vermerk', -e, *n.m.* note; entry.

vermer'ken, *vb.* note down.

vermes'sen*, *vb.* measure, survey; **(sich v.)** have the audacity.

Vermes'senheit, *n.f.* presumptuousness.

Vermes'sung, -en, *n.f.* survey.

vermie'ten, *vb.* rent (to someone).

vermin'dern, *vb.* diminish; **(sich v.)** decrease.

vermis'sen, *vb.* miss.

vermit'teln, *vb.* mediate, negotiate, arrange.

Vermitt'ler, *-, n.m.* mediator.

Vermitt'lerin, -nen, *n.f.* mediator.

Vermitt'lung, -en, *n.f.* mediation.

vermö'ge, *prep.* by virtue of.

vermö'gen*, *vb.* be able.

Vermö'gen, -, *n.nt.* fortune, wealth, estate; ability, power.

vermö'gend, *adj.* wealthy, well-to-do.

vermuten, *vb.* presume.

vermut'lich, *adj.* presumable.

Vermu'tung, -en, *n.f.* surmise.

vernach'lässigen, *vb.* neglect.

Vernach'lässigung, -en, *n.f.* neglect.

verneh'men*, *vb.* perceive, hear, learn; examine.

vernehm'lich, *adj.* perceptible.

Verneh'mung, -en, *n.f.* hearing.

vernei'gen *vb.* **(sich v.)** bow.

vernei'nen, *vb.* deny.

vernei'nend, *adj.* negative.

Vernei'nung, -en, *n.f.* denial.

vernich'ten, *vb.* annihilate, destroy.

vernich'tend, *adj.* devastating.

Vernich'tung, -en, *n.f.* annihilation, destruction.

Vernunft', *n.f.* reason.

vernunft'gemäß, *adj.* rational, according to reason.

vernünf'tig, *adj.* reasonable, sensible.

veröf'fentlichen, *vb.* publish.

Veröf'fentlichung, -en, *n.f.* publication.

verord'nen, *vb.* decree, order.

Verord'nung, -en, *n.f.* decree, ordinance, edict.

verpa'cken, *vb.* pack up, wrap up.

Verpa'ckung, *n.f.* packaging, wrapping.

verpas'sen, *vb.* miss.

verpes'ten, *vb.* infect.

verpfän'den, *vb.* pawn, pledge.

verpfle'gen, *vb.* care for; feed.

Verpfle'gung, -en, *n.f.* food, board.

verpflich'ten, *vb.* oblige; **(sich v.)** commit oneself.

Verpflich'tung, -en, *n.f.* obligation.

Verrat', *n.m.* treason, betrayal.

verra'ten*, *vb.* betray.

Verrä'ter, -, *n.m.* traitor.

Verrä'terin, -nen, *n.f.* traitor.

verrä'terisch, *adj.* treacherous.

verrech'nen, *vb.* reckon up; **(sich v.)** make a mistake in figuring, miscalculate.

verrei'sen, *vb.* go away on a trip.

verreist', *adj.* away on a trip.

verren'ken, *vb.* sprain.

verrich'ten, *vb.* do, perform, carry out.

verrin'gern, *vb.* decrease.

verros'ten, *vb.* rust.

verrucht', *adj.* infamous, wicked.

verrückt', *adj.* mad, crazy.

Verrückt'heit, -en, *n.f.* madness; folly.

Verruf', *n.m.* disrepute, notoriety.

verru'fen, *adj.* disreputable, notorious.

Vers, -e, *n.m.* verse.

versa'gen, *vb.* refuse; fail.

Versa'gen, *n.nt.* failure.

Versa'ger, -, *n.m.* failure, flop.

Versa'gerin, -nen, *n.f.* failure, flop.

versam'meln, *vb.* assemble.

Versamm'lung, -en, *n.f.* assembly, gathering, meeting.

Versand', *n.m.* dispatch.

versäu'men, *vb.* neglect, miss.

Versäum'nis, -se, *n.nt.* omission.

verschaf'fen, *vb.* procure.

verschämt', *adj.* bashful, coy.

verschan'zen, *vb.* entrench.

verschär'fen, *vb.* intensify.

verschei'den*, *vb.* expire.

verschen'ken, *vb.* give away.

verscher'zen, *vb.* throw away, lose frivolously.

verscheu'chen, *vb.* scare away.

verschi'cken, *vb.* send off.

verschie'ben*, *vb.* shift, displace; postpone.

Verschie'bung, -en, *n.f.* shift; postponement.

verschie'den, *adj.* different, distinct; various, assorted, separate.

verschie'denartig, *adj.* various; heterogeneous.

verschie'ßen*, *vb.* fire off; fade.

verschla'fen*, 1. *vb.* miss by sleeping too long; sleep off; **(sich v.)** oversleep. **2.** *adj.* sleepy.

Verschlag', -̈e, *n.m.* partition, compartment.

verschla'gen*, 1. *vb.* drive away; **(es verschlägt' mir den Atem)** it takes my breath away. **2.** *adj.* sly.

verschlech'tern, *vb.* make worse, impair; **(sich v.)** become worse, deteriorate.

Verschlech'terung, -en, *n.f.* deterioration.

verschlei'ern, *vb.* veil.

verschlep'pen, *vb.* delay; abduct.

verschleu'dern, vb. squander.

verschlie'ßen*, vb. close, lock.

verschlim'mern, vb. make worse, aggravate; **(sich v.)** become worse, deteriorate.

verschlin'gen*, vb. devour.

verschlis'sen, adj. worn out, frayed.

verschlos'sen, adj. closed, locked; reserved, taciturn.

verschlu'cken, vb. swallow; **(sich v.)** swallow the wrong way, choke.

Verschluß', -̈sse, n.m. closure; lock, plug, stopper; fastening, fastener; (camera) shutter.

verschmach'ten, vb. languish.

verschmel'zen*, vb. fuse, merge.

Verschmel'zung, -en, n.f. fusion.

verschneit', adj. covered with snow.

Verschnitt', n.m. adulteration; watered spirits.

verschnupft', adj. having a cold.

verschol'len, adj. missing, never heard of again.

verscho'nen, vb. spare.

verschö'nern, vb. beautify.

verschrei'ben*, vb. prescribe.

verschü'chtern, vb. intimidate.

verschul'det, adj. indebted.

verschüt'ten, vb. spill.

verschwei'gen*, vb. keep quiet about.

verschwen'den, vb. squander, waste, dissipate.

Verschwen'der, -, n.m. spendthrift.

Verschwen'derin, -nen, n.f. spendthrift.

verschwen'derisch, adj. wasteful, extravagant, prodigal.

Verschwen'dung, -en, n.f. extravagance, wastefulness.

verschwie'gen, adj. silent, discreet, reticent.

verschwin'den*, vb. disappear.

Verschwin'den, n.nt. disappearance.

verschwom'men, adj. blurred.

verschwö'ren*, vb. renounce; **(sich v.)** conspire.

Verschwö'rer, -, n.m. conspirator.

Verschwö'rerin, -nen, n.f. conspirator.

Verschwö'rung, -en, n.f. conspiracy.

verse'hen*, vb. provide; perform; **(sich v.)** make a mistake.

Verse'hen, -, n.nt. oversight, error; **(aus V.)** by mistake.

versen'den*, vb. send off.

versen'gen, vb. singe, scorch.

versen'ken, vb. sink.

verset'zen, vb. move, transfer; (school) promote; pawn, hock; reply.

versi'chern, vb. insure, assure; affirm, assert.

Versi'cherung, -en, n.f. insurance, assurance.

versie'geln, vb. seal.

versie'gen, vb. dry up.

versin'ken*, vb. sink.

versinn'bildlichen, vb. symbolize.

Version', -en, n.f. version.

versöh'nen, vb. reconcile.

versöh'nend, adj. conciliation.

versöhn'lich, adj. conciliatory.

Versöh'nung, -en, n.f. reconciliation.

versor'gen, vb. provide, supply.

Versor'gung, n.f. supply, maintenance.

verspä'ten, vb. **(sich v.)** be late.

verspä'tet, adj. late.

Verspä'tung, -en, n.f. lateness.

versper'ren, vb. bar, obstruct.

verspie'len, vb. gamble away; **(sich v.)** misplay.

verspielt', adj. playful.

verspot'ten, vb. mock, deride.

verspre'chen*, vb. promise; **(sich v.)** make a slip of the tongue.

Verspre'chen, -, n.nt. promise.

verstaat'lichen, vb. nationalize.

Verstand', n.m. mind, intellect, brains.

verstän'dig, adj. sensible, intelligent.

verstän'digen, vb. inform; **(sich v.)** make oneself understood, make an agreement.

Verstän'digung, -en, n.f. agreement, understanding.

verständ'lich, adj. understandable.

Verständ'nis, *n.nt.* understanding.

verständ'nisvoll, *adj.* understanding.

verstär'ken, *vb.* strengthen, reinforce, intensify, amplify.

Verstär'ker, -, *n.m.* amplifier.

Verstär'kung, -en, *n.f.* reinforcement.

verstau'ben, *vb.* get covered with dust.

verstäu'ben, *vb.* atomize.

verstau'chen, *vb.* sprain.

Versteck', -e, *n.nt.* hiding place; ambush; **(V. spielen)** play hide-and-go-seek.

verste'cken, *vb.* hide.

versteckt', *adj.* hidden; veiled, oblique, ulterior.

verste'hen*, *vb.* understand.

Verstei'gerung, -en, *n.f.* auction.

verstell'bar, *adj.* adjustable.

verstel'len, *vb.* adjust; change, disguise; **(sich v.)** pretend.

Verstel'lung, -en, *n.f.* adjustment; disguise, sham, hypocrisy.

versteu'ern, *vb.* pay tax on.

verstim'men, *vb.* annoy, upset.

verstimmt', *adj.* annoyed, cross; *(music)* out of tune.

verstockt', *adj.* obdurate; impenitent.

verstoh'len, *adj.* stealthy, surreptitious.

verstop'fen, *vb.* stop up, clog.

Verstop'fung, -en, *n.f.* obstruction, jam; *(med.)* constipation.

verstor'ben, *adj.* deceased.

verstört', *adj.* distracted, bewildered.

Verstoß, -̈e, *n.m.* violation, offence.

versto'ßen*, *vb.* expel, disown; **(v. gegen)** infringe on, offend.

verstrei'chen*, *vb.* elapse.

verstri'cken, *vb.* ensnare, enmesh.

verstüm'meln, *vb.* mutilate.

Verstüm'melung, -en, *n.f.* mutilation.

verstum'men, *vb.* become silent.

Versuch', -e, *n.m.* attempt; test, trial, experiment; effort.

versu'chen, *vb.* attempt, try, test; strive; entice, tempt.

versuchs'weise, *adv.* experimentally.

Versu'chung, -en, *n.f.* temptation.

versün'digen, *vb.* **(sich v.)** sin against.

versun'ken, *adj.* sunken; **(v. sein*)** be absorbed, be lost.

versü'ßen, *vb.* sweeten.

verta'gen, *vb.* adjourn.

Verta'gung, -en, *n.f.* adjournment.

vertau'schen, *vb.* exchange for; mistake for; substitute.

vertei'digen, *vb.* defend, advocate.

Vertei'diger, -, *n.m.* defender; *(jur.)* counsel for the defense.

Vertei'digerin, -nen, *n.f.* defender; (jur.) counsel for the defense.

Vertei'digung, -en, *n.f.* defense.

vertei'len, *vb.* distribute, disperse, divide.

Vertei'ler, -, *n.m.* distributor.

Vertei'lung, -en, *n.f.* distribution; dispersal, division.

vertie'fen, *vb.* deepen; **(sich v.)** deepen, become engrossed.

vertieft', *adj.* absorbed.

vertil'gen, *vb.* consume; exterminate.

Vertrag', -̈e, *n.m.* contract, treaty, pact.

vertra'gen*, *vb.* endure, tolerate, stand; **(sich v.)** agree, get along.

vertrag'lich, *adj.* contractual.

verträg'lich, *adj.* compatible, good-natured.

vertrau'en, *vb.* trust; confide in; rely on.

Vertrau'en, *n.nt.* trust, confidence, faith.

vertrau'ensvoll, *adj.* confident, reliant.

Vertrau'ensvotum, *n.nt.* vote of confidence.

vertrau'lich, *adj.* confidential.

Vertrau'lichkeit, -en, *n.f.* familiarity, intimacy; **(in aller V.)** in strict confidence.

vertraut', *adj.* acquainted, familiar; intimate.

Vertraut', -, *n.m.&f.* confidant(e).

Vertraut'heit, -en, *n.f.* familiarity; intimacy.

vertrei'ben*, *vb.* drive away, expel.

Vertrei'bung, -en, *n.f.* expulsion.

vertre'ten*, *vb.* represent; act as substitute; advocate.

Vertre'ter, -, *n.m.* representative, agent; deputy, substitute.

Vertre'terin, -nen, *n.f.* representative, agent; deputy, substitute.

Vertre'tung, -en, *n.f.* representation, agency; substitution.

Vertrieb', -e, *n.m.* sale, market.

Vertrie'ben-, *n.m.&f.* expellee, refugee.

Vertriebs'stelle, -n, *n.f.* distributor.

vertu'schen, *vb.* hush up.

verü'beln, *vb.* take amiss.

verü'ben, *vb.* commit.

verun'glücken, *vb.* meet with an accident; fail.

verun'reinigen, *vb.* pollute.

verun'stalten, *vb.* disfigure.

verun'zieren, *vb.* mar.

verur'sachen, *vb.* cause, bring about; result in.

verur'teilen, *vb.* condemn; *(jur.)* sentence.

Verur'teilung, *n.f.* condemnation; *(jur.)* sentence.

verviel'fachen, *vb.* multiply.

verviel'fältigen, *vb.* multiply; mimeograph; **(sich v.)** multiply.

vervoll'kommen, *vb.* perfect.

Vervoll'kommnung, *n.f.* perfection.

vervoll'ständigen, *vb.* complete.

verwach'sen*, *vb.* grow together; become deformed.

Verwach'sung, -en, *n.f.* deformity.

verwah'ren, *vb.* keep, hold in safe-keeping.

verwahr'losen, *vb.* neglect.

verwahr'lost, *adj.* neglected.

Verwah'rung, *n.f.* custody.

verwal'ten, *vb.* administer, manage.

Verwal'ter, -, *n.m.* administrator.

Verwal'terin, -nen, *n.f.* administrator.

Verwal'tung, -en, *n.f.* administration, management.

verwan'deln, *vb.* change, transform; **(sich v.)** metamorphose.

Verwand'lung, -en, *n.f.* change, transformation; metamorphosis.

verwandt', *adj.* related.

Verwandt'-, *n.m.&f.* relation, relative.

Verwandt'schaft, -en, *n.f.* relationship, affinity.

verwech'seln, *vb.* mistake for, confuse.

Verwechs'lung, -en, *n.f.* mistake, mix-up.

verwe'gen, *adj.* daring, bold.

verweh'ren, *vb.* prevent from; refuse.

verwei'gern, *vb.* refuse.

Verwei'gerung, -en, *n.f.* refusal.

verwei'len, *vb.* linger.

Verweis', -e, *n.m.* reprimand; **(einen V. erteilen)** reprimand.

verwei'sen*, *vb.* banish; **(v. auf)** refer to.

verwend'bar, *adj.* usable, applicable.

Verwend'barkeit, *n.f.* usability, applicability.

verwen'den(*), *vb.* use, supply; expend.

Verwen'dung, -en, *n.f.* use, application.

verwer'fen*, *vb.* reject.

verwe'sen, *vb.* putrify, decay.

verwi'ckeln, *vb.* entangle, involve, implicate.

verwi'ckelt, *adj.* involved, intricate, complicated.

Verwick'lung, -en, *n.f.* entanglement, implication; complication.

verwin'den*, *vb.* get over, overcome.

verwir'ken, *vb.* forfeit.

verwirk'lichen, *vb.* realize, materialize.

Verwirk'lichung, -en, *n.f.* realization.

verwir'ren, *vb.* confuse, bewilder, confound, puzzle, mystify.

Verwir'rung, -en, *n.f.* confusion, bewilderment, perplexity.

verwi'schen, *vb.* wipe out; smudge.

verwit'wet, *adj.* widowed.

verwor'fen, *adj.* depraved.
verwor'ren, *adj.* confused.
verwun'den, *vb.* wound.
verwun'dern, *vb.* astonish.
Verwun'dung, -en, *n.f.* wound, injury.
verwun'schen, *adj.* enchanted.
verwün'schen, *vb.* curse; bewitch.
verwüs'ten, *vb.* devastate.
verza'gen, *vb.* despair.
verzagt', *adj.* deponent.
verzäh'len, (sich v.) *vb.* miscount.
verzär'teln, *vb.* pamper.
verzau'bern, *vb.* bewitch.
verzeh'ren, *vb.* consume.
verzeich'nen, *vb.* register, list.
Verzeich'nis, -se, *n.nt.* list, index.
verzei'hen*, *vb.* pardon, forgive.
Verzei'hung, -en, *n.f.* pardon, forgiveness; **(ich bitte um V.)** I beg your pardon.
verzer'ren, *vb.* distort.
Verzicht', -e, *n.m.* renunciation; **(V. leisten)** renounce.
verzich'ten, *vb.* renounce, forego, waive.
verzie'hen*, *vb.* pull out of shape; **(child)** spoil; **(sich v.)** withdraw; vanish, disperse; **(wood)** warp.
verzie'ren, *vb.* embellish.
Verzie'rung, -en, *n.f.* ornament, embellishment.
verzin'sen, *vb.* pay interest; **(sich v.)** bear interest.
Verzin'sung, -en, *n.f.* interest return; payment of interest; interest rate.
verzo'gen, *adj.* moved away; **(child)** spoiled.
verzö'gern, *vb.* delay.
Verzö'gerung, -en, *n.f.* delay.
verzol'len, *vb.* pay duty on.
verzückt', *adj.* enraptured.
Verzug', -e, *n.m.* delay; default.
verzwei'feln, *vb.* despair.
verzwei'felt, *adj.* desperate.
Verzweif'lung, -en, *n.f.* desperation.
verzwickt', *adj.* complicated.
Vesper, -n, *n.f.* vespers.
Veterinär', -e, *n.m.* veterinarian.

Veterinärin', -nen, *n.f.* veterinarian.
Vetter, -n, *n.m.* cousin.
Viadukt', -e, *n.m.* viaduct.
Vibration', -en, *n.f.* vibration.
vibrie'ren, *vb.* vibrate.
Video, -s, *n.nt.* video.
Vieh, *n.nt.* cattle.
viehisch, *adj.* brutal.
Viehzucht, *n.f.* cattle breeding.
viel, *adj.* much; **(pl.)** many.
vielbedeutend, *adj.* significant.
vieldeutig, *adj.* ambiguous.
Vieleck, -e, *n.nt.* polygon.
vielerlei, *adj.* various, many.
vielfach, *adj.* manifold.
Vielfalt, *n.f.* variety.
vielfältig, *adj.* multiple.
Vielfältigkeit, *n.f.* multiplicity.
vielfarbig, *adj.* multicolored.
Vielfraß, -e, *n.m.* glutton.
Vielheit, -en, *n.f.* multiplicity.
vielleicht', *adv.* perhaps.
vielmals, *adv.* many times.
vielmehr, *adv.* rather.
vielsagend, *adj.* significant, highly suggestive.
vielseitig, *adj.* many-sided; versatile.
vielverheißend, *adj.* very promising.
vielversprechend, *adj.* very promising.
vier, *num.* four.
Viereck, -e, *n.nt.* square.
viereckig, *adj.* square.
vierfach, *adj.* fourfold.
Vierfüßler, -, *n.m.* quadruped.
vierschrötig, *adj.* thick-set.
viert-, *adj.* fourth.
vierteilen, *vb.* quarter.
Viertel, -, *n.nt.* fourth part, quarter; **(ein v.)** one-fourth.
vierzehn, *num.* fourteen.
vierzig, *num.* forty.
vierzigst-, *adj.* fortieth.
Vierzigstel, -, *n.nt.* fortieth part; **(ein v.)** one-fortieth.
violett', *adj.* violet.
Violi'ne, -n, *n.f.* violin.
Violinist', -en, -en, *n.m.* violinist.
Violini'stin, -nen, *n.f.* violinist.
Virtuo'se, -n, -n, *n.m.* virtuoso.
Visier', -e, *n.nt.* visor; **(gun)** sight.
visuell', *adj.* visual.

Visum, -sa, *n.nt.* visa.
Vitalität', *n.f.* vitality.
Vize-, *cpds.* vice-.
Vogel, -, *n.m.* bird.
vogelartig, *adj.* birdlike.
Vogelbauer, -, *n.nt.* bird cage.
Vogelscheuche, -n, *n.f.* scarecrow.
Vogt, -e, *n.m.* overseer.
Vokal', -e, *n.m.* vowel.
Volant', -s, *n.m.* flounce.
Volk, -er, *n.nt.* people, nation.
Völkerbund, *n.m.* League of Nations.
Völkerkunde, *n.f.* ethnology; (school) social studies.
Völkermord, *n.m.* genocide.
Völkerrecht, *n.nt.* international law.
Volksabstimmung, -en, *n.f.* plebiscite, referendum.
Volkscharakter, *n.m.* national character.
Volksentscheid, *n.m.* plebiscite, referendum.
Volksgenosse, -n, -n, *n.m.* fellow countryman.
Volkskunde, *n.f.* folklore.
Volkslied, -er, *n.nt.* folksong.
Volksmenge, *n.f.* crowd, mob.
Volksschule, -n, *n.f.* elementary school.
Volkstanz, -e, *n.m.* folk-dance.
volkstümlich, *adj.* popular.
Volkszählung, -en, *n.f.* census.
voll, *adj.* full.
Vollblut, *n.nt.* thoroughbred.
vollblütig, *adj.* full-blooded.
vollbrin'gen*, *vb.* accomplish, fulfill.
vollen'den, *vb.* finish, complete.
vollen'det, *adj.* accomplished.
vollends, *adv.* completely.
Völlerei, *n.f.* gluttony.
vollfüh'ren, *vb.* accomplish.
Vollgas, *n.nt.* full throttle.
völlig, *adj.* complete, entire.
volljährig, *adj.* of age.
vollkom'men, *adj.* perfect.
Vollkom'menheit, *n.f.* perfection.
Vollmacht, -e, *n.f.* authority, warrant, proxy, power of attorney.
vollständig, *adj.* complete.

voll·stopfen, *vb.* cram, stuff.
vollstre'cken, *vb.* execute, carry out.
Vollversammlung, *n.f.* (U.N.) General Assembly.
vollzählig, *adj.* complete.
vollzie'hen*, *vb.* execute, carry out; consummate; **(sich v.)** take place.
Volontär, -e, *n.m.* volunteer.
Volontär'arzt, -e, *n.m.* intern.
Volontär'ärztin, -nen, *n.f.* intern.
Volt, -, *n.nt.* volt.
Volu'men, -, *n.nt.* volume.
von, *prep.* before; in front of; ago.
vor, *prep.* before; in front of; ago.
Vorabend, -e, *n.m.* eve.
Vorahnung, -en, *n.f.* premonition, foreboding.
voran', *adv.* in front of, ahead; onward.
voran'·gehen*, *vb.* precede.
voran'·kommen, *vb.* get ahead.
Voranmeldung, -en, *n.f.* (telephone) person-to-person call.
Voranschlag, -e, *n.m.* estimate.
Vorarbeit, -en, *n.f.* preparatory work.
Vorarbeiter, -, *n.m.* foreman.
vorauf', *adv.* before, ahead.
voraus', *adv.* in advance, ahead; **(im v.)** in advance.
voraus'·bedingen*, *vb.* precede.
voraus'·bestellen, *vb.* order ahead, make reservations.
voraus'·gehen*, *vb.* precede.
voraus'gesetzt, *adv.* **(v. daß)** provided that.
voraus'·nehmen*, *vb.* state now, anticipate.
Voraus'sage, -n, *n.f.* prediction, forecast.
voraus'·sagen, *vb.* predict, forecast.
voraus'·setzen, *vb.* presume, presuppose.
Voraus'setzung, -en, *n.f.* supposition, assumption; prerequisite.
Voraus'sicht, *n.f.* foresight.
voraus'sichtlich, 1. *adj.* probable, prospective. **2.** *adv.* presumably.

voraus'•zahlen, vb. pay in advance, advance.

Vorbedacht, n.m. forethought.

Vorbedeutung, -en, n.f. omen.

Vorbedingung, -en, n.f. prerequisite.

Vorbehalt, n.m. reservation.

vor•behalten*, vb. reserve.

vorbei', adv. over, past.

vorbelastet, adj. having a questionable record; (jur.) having a criminal record.

vor•bereiten, vb. prepare.

vor•bestellen, vb. order in advance, make reservations.

vor•beugen, vb. prevent.

vorbeugend, adj. preventive.

Vorbild, -er, n.nt. model.

vorbildlich, adj. exemplary.

vor•bringen*, vb. state; propose.

vorder-, adj. front, anterior.

Vorderfront, -en, n.f. frontage; (fig.) forefront.

Vordergrund, n.m. foreground.

vorderhand, adv. for the time being; right now.

Vordermann, -er, n.m. person ahead of one.

Vorderseite, -n, n.f. front.

Vorderteil, -e, n.nt. front part.

vor•drängen, vb. (sich v.) elbow one's way forward.

vor•dringen*, vb. press forward, advance.

Vordruck, -e, n.m. form, blank.

voreilig, adj. rash, hasty.

voreingenommen, adj. prejudiced.

Voreingenommenheit, n.f. partiality.

vor•enthalten*, vb. withhold.

vorerst, adv. first of all.

Vorfahr, -en, -en, n.m. ancestor.

vor•fahren*, vb. drive up; (v. lassen*) let pass.

Vorfahrtsrecht, -e, n.nt. right of way.

Vorfall, -e, n.m. incident.

vor•fallen*, vb. occur.

vor•finden*, vb. find.

vor•führen, vb. show, demonstrate, produce.

Vorführung, -en, n.f. demonstration, show, production.

Vorgang, -e, n.m. occurrence, process, procedure.

Vorgänger, -, n.m. predecessor.

Vorgängerin, -nen, n.f. predecessor.

vor•geben*, vb. pretend, feign.

Vorgefühl, -e, n.nt. presentiment, hunch.

vor•gehen*, vb. advance; come first, precede.

Vorgehen, n.nt. procedure, policy.

Vorgericht, -e, n.nt. appetizer; first course.

Vorgeschichte, n.f. prehistory; history, background.

vorgeschrieben, adj. prescribed.

vorgesehen, adj. planned, scheduled.

Vorgesetzt-, n.m.&f. superior.

vorgestern, adv. the day before yesterday.

vorgetäuscht, adj. make-believe.

vor•greifen*, vb. anticipate.

vor•haben*, vb. plan, intention.

Vorhaben, n.nt. plan, intention.

Vorhalle, -n, n.f. lounge.

vor•halten*, vb. (fig.) reproach.

Vorhand, n.f. forehand.

vorhan'den, adj. existing, present, available.

Vorhang, -e, n.m. curtain, drapery.

vorher, adv. before, beforehand, previously.

vorher'gehend, adj. previous.

vor•herrschen, vb. prevail.

Vorherrschaft, n.f. predominance.

vorherrschend, adj. prevalent, predominant.

Vorher'sage, -n, n.f. prediction.

vorher'•sagen, vb. foretell.

vorher'•sehen*, vb. foresee.

Vorhut, n.f. vanguard.

vorig, adj. previous, last.

Vorjahr, -e, n.nt. preceding year.

Vorkämpfer, -, n.m. pioneer, champion.

Vorkenntnis, -se, n.f. preliminary knowledge; rudiments.

Vorkommen, n.nt. occurrence.

vor•kommen*, vb. occur.

Vorkommnis, -se, n.nt. occurrence.

Vorkriegs-, *cpds.* prewar.
vor·laden*, *vb.* summon.
Vorladung, -en, *n.f.* summons.
vor·lassen*, *vb.* let pass; admit.
Vorlassung, -en, *n.f.* admittance.
vorläufig, 1. *adj.* preliminary, tentative; temporary. 2. *adv.* for the time being.
vorlaut, *adj.* flippant, fresh.
vor·legen, *vb.* show, submit, produce.
vor·lesen*, *vb.* read out loud.
Vorlesung, -en, *n.f.* reading; lecture.
Vorlesungsverzeichnis, -se, *n.nt.* university catalogue.
vorletzt, *adj.* last but one.
Vorliebe, *n.f.* preference, fondness.
vorlieb·nehmen*, *vb.* be satisfied with.
vor·liegen*, *vb.* exist.
vorliegend, *adj.* present, at hand, in question.
vor·machen, *vb.* show how to do; (einem etwas v.) deceive, fool.
Vormachtstellung, -en, *n.f.* predominance.
vormalig, *adj.* former.
vormals, *adv.* heretofore.
Vormann, ̈-er, *n.m.* foreman.
Vormarsch, ̈-e, *n.m.* advance.
vor·merken, *vb.* make a note of; reserve.
Vormittag, -e, *n.m.* forenoon.
Vormund, -e, *n.m.* guardian.
vorn, *adv.* in front.
Vorname(n), -, *n.m.* first name.
vornehm, *adj.* noble, distinguished.
vor·nehmen*, *vb.* (sich v.) undertake, consider, take up, resolve.
vornehmlich, *adv.* chiefly.
Vorort, -e, *n.m.* suburb.
Vorortzug, ̈-, *n.m.* local (train).
Vorplatz, ̈-e, *n.m.* hall; court.
Vorrang, *n.m.* priority, precedence.
Vorrat, ̈-e, *n.m.* supply, provision, stock, stockpile.
vorrätig, *adj.* in stock.
Vorratskammer, -n, *n.f.* storeroom; pantry.
Vorrecht, -e, *n.nt.* privilege, prerogative.

Vorrede, -n, *n.f.* preface.
Vorrichtung, -en, *n.f.* arrangement; contrivance, device, fixture.
vor·rücken, *vb.* move forward, advance.
Vorsatz, ̈-e, *n.m.* purpose, intention; (jur.) premeditation.
vorsätzlich, *adj.* willful, intentional; (jur.) premeditated.
Vorschein, *n.m.* (zum V. kommen*) appear.
Vorschlag, ̈-e, *n.m.* proposal, proposition, suggestion.
vor·schlagen*, *vb.* propose, suggest.
vorschnell, *adj.* rash.
vor·schreiben*, *vb.* prescribe.
Vorschrift, -en, *n.f.* regulation.
vorschriftsmäßig, *adj.* as prescribed, regulation.
Vorschub, *n.m.* assistance.
Vorschule, -n, *n.f.* elementary school.
Vorschuß, ̈-sse, *n.m.* advance payment.
vor·schützen, *vb.* pretend, plead.
vor·sehen*, *vb.* earmark, plan, schedule; (sich v.) be careful.
Vorsehung, *n.f.* providence.
Vorsicht, *n.f.* caution.
vorsichtig, *adj.* careful, cautious.
vorsichtshalber, *adv.* as a precaution.
Vorsichtsmaßregel, -n, *n.f.* precaution.
Vorsilbe, -n, *n.f.* prefix.
Vorsitz, -e, *n.m.* chairmanship, presidency; (den V. führen) preside.
Vorsitzend-, *n.m.&f.* chairperson.
Vorsitzende(r), -n, *n.m.&f.* chairman; chairwoman.
Vorsorge, *n.f.* providence, foresight; (V. treffen*) take precautions.
vorsorglich, *adv.* as a precaution.
Vorspeise, -n, *n.f.* appetizer.
vor·spiegeln, *vb.* deceive, delude.
Vorspiel, -e, *n.nt.* prelude.
vor·springen*, *vb.* project.
Vorsprung, ̈-e, *n.m.* advantage; head start; (arch.) ledge.

Vorstadt, ⁻e, *n.f.* suburb, outskirts.

Vorstand, *n.m.* board; committee.

vorstellbar, *adj.* conceivable.

vor·stellen, *vb.* present, introduce; (clock) set ahead; (sich v.) imagine, picture.

Vorstellung, -en, *n.f.* presentation, introduction; imagination, idea, notion; (theater) performance, show.

Vorstellungsgespräch, -e, *n.nt.* interview.

Vorstoß, ⁻e, *n.m.* attack.

vor·stoßen*, *vb.* push forward.

vor·strecken, *vb.* stretch forward; (money) advance.

vor·täuschen, *vb.* make-believe, simulate.

Vorteil, -e, *n.m.* advantage.

vorteilhaft, *adj.* advantageous, profitable.

Vortrag, ⁻e, *n.m.* lecture, talk.

vor·tragen*, *vb.* lecture, recite, report.

Vortragende, *n.m.&f.* lecturer.

vortreff·lich, *adj.* excellent.

Vortritt, *n.m.* precedence.

vorü·ber, *adv.* past, gone.

vorü·ber·gehen*, *vb.* pass.

vorü·bergehend, *adj.* temporary.

Vorurteil, -e, *n.nt.* prejudice.

Vorväter, *n.pl.* forefathers.

Vorwahl, -en, *n.f.* primary election.

Vorwahlnummer, -n, *n.f.* area code (telephone).

Vorwand, ⁻e, *n.m.* pretense, pretext.

Vorwarnung, -en, *n.f.* forewarning.

vorwärts, *adv.* forward.

vorwärts·kommen*, *vb.* get ahead, make headway.

vorweg·nehmen*, *vb.* anticipate; forestall.

vor·werfen*, *vb.* reproach.

vorwiegend, *adv.* predominantly, mainly, chiefly.

Vorwort, -e, *n.nt.* preface.

Vorwurf, ⁻e, *n.m.* reproach.

vor·zeigen, *vb.* show, produce.

vorzeitig, *adj.* premature.

vor·ziehen*, *vb.* prefer.

Vorzimmer, -, *n.nt.* antechamber, anteroom.

Vorzug, ⁻e, *n.m.* preference; advantage.

vorzüg·lich, 1. *adj.* excellent, exquisite. 2. *adv.* especially.

Vorzüg·lichkeit, -en, *n.f.* excellence.

vorzugsweise, *adv.* preferably.

vulgär, *adj.* vulgar.

Vulkan', -e, *n.m.* volcano.

W

Waage, -n, *n.f.* scales.

waagerecht, *adj.* horizontal.

Waagschale, -n, *n.f.* scale.

Wabe, -n, *n.f.* honeycomb.

wach, *adj.* awake.

Wache, -n, *n.f.* watch, guard.

wachen, *vb.* be awake, stay awake; watch over.

wachhabend, *adj.* on duty.

Wachlokal, -e, *n.nt.* guardhouse, police station.

Wachposten, -, *n.m.* sentry.

Wachs, -e, *n.nt.* wax.

wachsam, *adj.* watchful, vigilant.

Wachsamkeit, *n.f.* vigilance.

wachsen*, *vb.* grow, increase.

wachsen, *vb.* wax.

Wachskerze, -n, *n.f.* candle.

Wachstum, *n.nt.* growth.

Wacht, *n.f.* guard, watch.

Wächter, -, *n.m.* watchman; keeper.

Wachtmeister, -, *n.m.* (police) sergeant.

wackelig, *adj.* shaky, wobbly.

wackeln, *vb.* shake, wobble.

wacker, *adj.* staunch, brave, stouthearted.

Wade, -n, *n.f.* calf (of the leg).

Waffe, -n, *n.f.* weapon, arm.

Waffel, -n, *n.f.* waffle.

Waffenfabrik, -en, *n.f.* arms factory.

Waffengattung, -en, *n.f.* arm; branch of the army.

waffenlos, *adj.* unarmed, defenseless.

Waffenstill'stand, ˵e, *n.m.* armistice, truce.

waffnen, *vb.* arm.

wagemutig, *adj.* venturesome.

wagen, *vb.* dare, risk, venture.

Wagen, -, *n.m.* carriage, coach, wagon, car.

wägen(*), *vb.* consider.

Wagenheber, -, *n.m.* auto jack.

Waggon', -s, *n.m.* railroad car.

Waggon'ladung, -en, *n.f.* carload.

waghalsig, *adj.* rash, risky.

Wagnis, -se, *n.nt.* venture.

Wahl, -en, *n.f.* choice, election, vote, ballot.

wählbar, *adj.* eligible; (nicht w.) ineligible.

wahlberechtigt, *adj.* eligible to vote.

Wahlbezirk, -e, *n.m.* constituency.

wählen, *vb.* choose; elect, vote; (telephone) dial.

Wähler, -, *n.m.* constituent, voter.

Wählerin -nen, *n.f.* constituent, voter.

wählerisch, *adj.* choosy, fastidious.

Wählerschaft, *n.f.* electorate.

Wahlgang, ˵e, *n.m.* ballot.

Wahlkampf, ˵e, *n.m.* election campaign.

Wahlliste, -n, *n.f.* ticket, slate.

Wahlrecht, -e, *n.nt.* franchise, suffrage; (W. erteilen) enfranchise; (W. entziehen*) disenfranchise.

Wählscheibe, -n, *n.f.* dial (on a telephone).

Wahlspruch, ˵e, *n.m.* slogan, motto.

Wahlstimme, -n, *n.f.* vote.

Wahn, *n.m.* delusion.

Wahnsinn, *n.m.* insanity.

wahnsinnig, *adj.* insane, delirious.

wahr, *adj.* true, truthful, real; (nicht w.?) isn't that so?

wahren, *vb.* keep, preserve.

währen, *vb.* continue, last.

während, 1. *prep.* during. 2. *conj.* while.

wahrhaftig, *adj.* true, sincere.

Wahrheit, ˵en, *n.f.* truth.

wahrnehmbar, *adj.* perceptible.

wahr·nehmen*, *vb.* perceive.

Wahrnehmung, -en, *n.f.* perception.

wahr·sagen, *vb.* prophesy, tell fortunes.

Wahrsager, -, *n.m.* fortune-teller.

Wahrsagerin, -nen, *n.f.* fortuneteller.

wahrschein'lich, *adj.* probable, likely.

Wahrschein'lichkeit, *n.f.* probability, likelihood.

Währung, -en, *n.f.* currency.

Wahrzeichen, -, *n.nt.* distinctive mark, landmark.

Waise, -n, *n.f.* orphan.

Waisenhaus, ˵er, *n.nt.* orphanage.

Wald, ˵er, *n.m.* wood, forest.

Walfisch, -e, *n.m.* whale.

Wall, ˵e, *n.m.* rampart.

wallen, *vb.* undulate; bubble.

Wallfahrer, -, *n.m.* pilgrim.

Wallfahrerin, -nen, *n.f.* pilgrim.

Wallfahrt, -en, *n.f.* pilgrimage.

Walnuß, ˵sse, *n.f.* walnut.

Walroß, ˵sse, *n.nt.* walrus.

walten, *vb.* rule.

Walze, -n, *n.f.* roll, roller.

walzen, *vb.* roll, roll out; waltz.

wälzen, *vb.* roll, revolve.

Walzer, -, *n.m.* waltz.

Wand, ˵e, *n.f.* wall.

Wandel, *n.m.* change.

wandelbar, *adj.* changeable.

Wandelhalle, -n, *n.f.* lobby.

wandeln, *vb.* go, wander; (sich w.) change.

wandern, *vb.* hike, wander, roam.

Wanderschaft, *n.f.* travels.

Wanderung, -en, *n.f.* hike, wandering; migration.

Wandgemälde, -, *n.nt.* mural.

Wandlung, -en, *n.f.* change, transformation.

Wandschrank, ˵e, *n.m.* (eingebauter W.) closet.

Wandtafel, -n, *n.f.* blackboard.

Wandteppich, -e, *n.m.* tapestry.

Wandverkleidung, -en, *n.f.* wall-covering.

Wange, -n, *n.f.* cheek.

wankelmütig, *adj.* fickle.

wanken, *vb.* stagger, sway.

wann, 1. *conj.* when. 2. *adv.* when.

Wanne, -n, *n.f.* tub.

Wanze, -n, *n.f.* bedbug.

Wappen, -, *n.nt.* coat of arms.

Ware, -n, *n.f.* article, commodity, merchandise, ware; *(pl.)* goods.

Warenhandel, *n.m.* trade, commerce.

Warenhaus, ̈er, *n.nt.* department store.

Warenrechnung, -en, *n.f.* invoice.

warm (-), *adj.* warm.

Wärme, *n.f.* warmth, heat.

wärmen, *vb.* warm.

Wärmflasche, -n, *n.f.* hot water bottle.

warnen, *vb.* warn, caution.

Warnung, -en, *n.f.* warning.

Warte, -n, *n.f.* watch-tower, lookout.

warten, *vb.* wait.

Wärter, -, *n.m.* keeper, guard.

Wärterin, -nen, *n.f.* keeper, guard.

Warteraum, ̈e, *n.m.* waiting room.

Wartezeit, -en, *n.f.* wait.

Wartezimmer, -, *n.nt.* waiting room.

warum', *adv. & conj.* why.

Warze, -n, *n.f.* wart.

was, *pron.* what.

Waschanstalt, -en, *n.f.* laundry.

waschbar, *adj.* washable.

Waschbecken, -, *n.nt.* washbasin.

Wäsche, *n.f.* laundry, linen.

waschecht, *adj.* colorfast; *(fig.)* dyed in the wool.

waschen*, *vb.* wash, launder.

Wäscherei', -en, *n.f.* laundry.

Wäscheschrank, ̈e, *n.m.* linen closet.

Waschfrau, -en, *n.f.* laundry.

Waschlappen, -, *n.m.* face cloth.

Waschleder, *n.nt.* chamois.

Waschmaschine, -n, *n.f.* washing machine.

Waschpulver, *n.nt.* soap powder.

Waschraum, ̈e, *n.m.* washroom.

Waschseife, -n, *n.f.* laundry soap.

Waschtisch, -e, *n.m.* washstand, washbowl.

Waschzettel, -, *n.m.* laundry list; (book) blurb; memo.

Wasser, -, *n.nt.* water.

wasserdicht, *adj.* watertight, waterproof.

Wasserfall, ̈e, *n.m.* waterfall.

Wasserflugzeug, -e, *n.nt.* hydroplane.

Wasserhahn, ̈e, *n.m.* faucet.

wässerig, *adj.* watery, aqueous.

Wasserleitung, -en, *n.f.* water main; aqueduct.

wässern, *vb.* water.

Wasserrinne, -n, *n.f.* gully, gutter.

Wasserstoff, *n.m.* hydrogen.

Wasserstoffbombe, -n, *n.f.* hydrogen bomb.

Wasserstoffsu'peroxyd, *n.nt.* hydrogen peroxide.

Wassersucht, *n.f.* dropsy.

Wasserverschmutzung, *n.f.* water pollution.

waten, *vb.* wade.

watscheln, *vb.* waddle.

Watte, *n.f.* cotton.

weben(*), *vb.* weave.

Webeschiffchen, -, *n.nt.* shuttle.

Webstuhl, ̈e, *n.m.* loom.

Wechsel, -, *n.m.* change, shift, rotation; *(comm.)* draft.

Wechselgeld, *n.nt.* change.

Wechseljahre, *n.pl.* menopause.

Wechselkurs, -e, *n.m.* rate of exchange.

wechseln, *vb.* change, exchange.

wechselnd, *adj.* intermittent.

Wechselstrom, ̈e, *n.m.* alternating current.

wecken, *vb.* wake, awaken.

Wecker, -, *n.m.* alarm clock.

wedeln, *vb.* wag.

weder, *adj.* (w. . . . . noch) neither . . . nor.

weg, *adv.* away; gone.

Weg, -e, *n.m.* way, path, route.

wegen, *prep.* because of.

weg•fahren*, *vb.* drive away, leave.

weg•fallen*, *vb.* be omitted; not take place.

weg•gehen*, *vb.* go away, leave.

weg•kommen*, *vb.* get away; get off.

weg•lassen*, *vb.* leave out.

weg·nehmen*, *vb.* take away.

weg·räumen, *vb.* remove.

weg·schicken, *vb.* send off.

weg·schnappen, *vb.* snatch.

Wegweiser, -, *n.m.* guidepost, signpost.

Wegzehrung, **-en**, *n.f.* provisions for a journey.

Weh, *n.nt.* woe, pain, ache.

Weh, *n.f.* while.

weh, *adj.* sore; (**w. tun***) hurt, be sore.

wehen, *vb.* (wind) blow; (flag) wave.

Wehen, *n.pl.* labor pains.

Wehklage, **-n**, *n.f.* lament, lamentation.

wehklagen, *vb.* wail, lament.

Wehmut, *n.f.* sadness.

wehmütig, *adj.* sad, melancholy.

Wehr, -e, *n.nt.* dam.

Wehr, **-en**, *n.f.* defense, resistance.

Wehrdienst, *n.m.* military service.

wehren, *vb.* (sich w.) defend oneself, fight.

wehrfähig, *adj.* fit to serve (in the army).

wehrlos, *adj.* defenseless.

Wehrmacht, *n.f.* armed forces; (specifically, German army to 1945).

Wehrpflicht, *n.f.* duty to serve in armed forces; (**allgemeine W.**) compulsory military service.

weh·tun*, *vb.* hurt, be sore.

Weib, **-er**, *n.nt.* woman.

Weibchen, -, *n.nt.* (*zool.*) female.

Weibersache, **-n**, *n.f.* women's affair.

weiblich, *adj.* female, feminine.

weich, *adj.* soft.

Weiche, **-n**, *n.f.* switch.

weichen*, *vb.* give way, yield.

weichen, *vb.* soften.

weichlich, *adj.* soft; effeminate.

Weide, **-n**, *n.f.* pasture; willow.

weiden, *vb.* graze; (sich w.) feast one's eyes, gloat.

weidlich, *adv.* thoroughly.

weigern, *vb.* (sich w.) refuse.

Weihe, **-n**, *n.f.* consecration.

weihen, *vb.* consecrate.

Weiher, -, *n.m.* pond.

weihevoll, *adj.* solemn.

Weihnachten, -, *n.nt.* Christmas.

Weihnachtslied, **-er**, *n.nt.* Christmas carol.

Weihnachtsmann, **-er**, *n.m.* Santa Claus.

Weihrauch, *n.m.* incense.

Weihung, **-en**, *n.f.* consecration.

weil, *conj.* because, since.

Weile, *n.f.* while.

weilen, *vb.* stay.

Weiler, -, *n.m.* hamlet.

Wein, **-e**, *n.m.* wine.

Weinbauer, -, *n.m.* wine grower.

Weinberg, **-e**, *n.m.* vineyard.

Weinbrand, -*e*, *n.m.* brandy.

weinen, *vb.* cry, weep.

Weingarten, -, *n.m.* vineyard.

Weinlese, *n.f.* vintage.

Weinrebe, **-n**, *n.f.* grapevine.

Weinstock, -*e*, *n.m.* grapevine.

Weinstube, **-n**, *n.f.* tap room.

Weintraube, **-n**, *n.f.* grape.

weise, *adj.* wise.

Weise, **-n**, *n.f.* manner, way, method.

weisen*, *vb.* show; (**von sich w.**) reject.

Weisheit, **-en**, *n.f.* wisdom.

weis·machen, *vb.* make someone believe, fool.

weiß, *adj.* white.

weissagen, *vb.* prophesy, tell fortunes.

Weissager, -, *n.m.* fortune teller.

Weissagerin, **-nen**, *n.f.* fortune teller.

Weißwaren, *n.pl.* linen goods.

Weisung, **-en**, *n.f.* order, direction.

weit, *adj.* far; wide, large.

weitab', *adv.* far away.

weitaus', *adv.* by far.

Weite, **-n**, *n.f.* width, largeness, expanse; size.

weiter, *adv.* farther, further; (**und so w.**) and so forth.

weiterhin, *adv.* furthermore.

weitgehend, *adj.* far-reaching.

weither', *adv.* from afar.

weitläufig, *adj.* lengthy, elaborate, complex.

weitreichend, *adj.* far-reaching.

weitsichtig, *adj.* far-sighted.

weittragend, *adj.* far-reaching.

weitverbreitet, *adj.* widespread.

weitverstreut, *adj.* far-flung.

Weizen, *n.m.* wheat.

welcher, -es, -e, *pron.&adj.* which, what.

welchergestalt, *adv.* in what manner.

welk, *adj.* wilted.

welken, *vb.* wilt.

Welle, -n, *n.f.* wave; (*tech.*) shaft.

wellen, *vb.* wave; (*tech.*) corrugate.

Wellenlänge, -n, *n.f.* wave length.

wellig, *adj.* wavy.

Welt, -en, *n.f.* world.

Weltall, *n.nt.* universe.

Weltanschauung, -en, *n.f.* philosophy of life.

Weltbürger, -, *n.m.* cosmopolite.

Weltbürgerin, -nen, *n.f.* cosmopolite.

weltgeschichtlich, *adj.* historical.

weltgewandt, *adj.* sophisticated.

weltklug (-), *adj.* worldly-wise.

Weltkrieg, -e, *n.m.* world war.

Weltkugel, -n, *n.f.* globe.

weltlich, *adj.* worldly, secular.

Weltmeister, -, *n.m.* world's champion.

Weltmeisterin, -nen, *n.f.* world's champion.

Weltmeisterschaft, -en, *n.f.* world's championship.

weltnah, *adj.* worldly, realistic.

Weltraum, *n.m.* outer space.

Weltreich, -e, *n.nt.* empire.

Weltschmerz, *n.m.* world-weariness.

Weltstadt, ̈-e, *n.f.* metropolis.

weltweit, *adj.* world-wide.

Wende, -n, *n.f.* turn, bend.

Wendekreis, -e, *n.m.* tropic; (W. des Krebses) tropic of Cancer; (W. des Steinbocks) tropic of Capricorn.

wenden*, *vb.* turn; (sich w. an) appeal to.

Wendepunkt, *n.m.* turning point.

wendig, *adj.* versatile, resourceful.

Wendung, -en, *n.f.* turn.

wenig, *adj.* few, little.

weniger, *adj.* fewer, less; minus.

Wenigkeit, -e, *n.f.* trifle; (meine W.) yours truly.

wenigstens, *adv.* at least.

wenn, *conj.* when, if.

wer, *pron.* who.

werben*, *vb.* recruit, enlist, advertise; woo.

Werbeplakat, -e, *n.nt.* poster.

Werber, -, *n.m.* suitor.

Werbung, -en, *n.f.* recruiting, advertising; courting.

Werdegang, ̈-e, *n.m.* development; career.

werden*, *vb.* become, get, grow.

werfen*, *vb.* throw, cast; (über den Haufen w.) upset.

Werft, -en, *n.f.* dockyard, shipyard.

Werk, -e, *n.nt.* work, labor, deed; factory, plant.

werken, *vb.* work, operate.

Werkstatt, ̈-e, *n.f.* plant, shop.

Werktag, -e, *n.m.* work day, weekday.

werktags, *adv.* weekdays.

Werkzeug, -e, *n.nt.* tool, instrument.

Wermut, *n.m.* vermouth.

Wert, -e, *n.m.* value, worth, merit.

wert, *adj.* worth, valued, esteemed.

Wertarbeit, -en, *n.f.* workmanship.

Wertbrief, -e, *n.m.* registered insured letter.

wertlos, *adj.* worthless, useless.

Wertlosigkeit, -en, *n.f.* worthlessness, uselessness.

Wertpapier, -e, *n.nt.* security, bond, stock.

Wertschätzung, -en, *n.f.* esteem, value.

Werturteil, -e, *n.nt.* value judgement.

Wertverminderung, -en, *n.f.* depreciation.

wertvoll, *adj.* valuable.

Wesen, -, *n.nt.* being, creature; nature, character; essence, substance.

Wesenheit, *n.f.* entity.

wesenlos, *adj.* unreal.

Wesenszug, ̈-e, *n.m.* characteristic.

wesentlich, *adj.* essential, material; substantial, vital.

weshalb, 1. *conj.* for which reason. **2.** *adv.* why.
Wespe, -n, *n.f.* wasp.
wessen, *pron.* whose.
West, Westen, *n.m.* west.
Weste, -n, *n.f.* vest, waistcoat.
westlich, *adj.* western; to the west.
westwärts, *adv.* westward.
Wettbewerb, -e, *n.m.* competition.
Wettbewerber, -, *n.m.* competitor, contestant.
Wettbewerberin, -nen, *n.f.* competitor, contestant.
Wette, -n, *n.f.* wager, bet.
wetteifern, *vb.* compete, rival.
wetten, *vb.* wager, bet.
Wetter, -, *n.nt.* weather.
Wetterfahne, -n, *n.f.* weather vane.
Wettermeldung, -en, *n.f.* weather report.
Wetterverhältnisse, *n.pl.* weather conditions.
Wettervorhersage, *n.f.* weather forecast.
Wettkampf, -̈e, *n.m.* match, contest; competition.
Wettlauf, -̈e, *n.m.* race (on foot).
Wettläufer, -, *n.m.* runner.
Wettläuferin, -nen, *n.f.* runner.
Wettrennen, -, *n.nt.* race.
Wettrüsten, -, *n.nt.* armament race.
Wettspiel, -e, *n.nt.* match, tournament.
Wettstreit, -e, *n.m.* contest, competition; match, race.
wetzen, *vb.* hone, sharpen.
Whisky, -s, *n.m.* whiskey.
wichsen, *vb.* polish; thrash.
Wicht, -e, *n.m.* little fellow.
wichtig, *adj.* important.
Wichtigkeit, *n.f.* importance.
Wichtigtuer, -, *n.m.* busybody, pompous fellow.
Wickel, -, *n.m.* wrapping, compress; curler.
wickeln, *vb.* wind, reel; wrap; curl.
wider, *prep.* against, contrary to.
widerfah'ren*, *vb.* happen to.
Widerhall, -e, *n.m.* reverberation.
wider•hallen, *vb.* resound, reverberate.

Widerhalt, *n.m.* support.
widerle'gen, *vb.* refute, disprove.
Widerle'gung, -en, *n.f.* refutation, disproof, rebuttal.
widerlich, *adj.* distasteful, repulsive.
widernatürlich, *adj.* perverse.
widerra'ten*, *vb.* dissuade.
widerrechtlich, *adj.* illegal.
Widerrede, -n, *n.f.* contradiction.
Widerruf, -e, *n.m.* revocation; cancellation.
widerru'fen*, *vb.* revoke, repeal; retract; cancel.
Widersacher, -, *n.m.* antagonist.
Widerschein, -e, *n.m.* reflection.
widerset'zen, *vb.* **(sich w.)** oppose.
Widersinn, *n.m.* absurdity.
widersinnig, *adj.* absurd, preposterous.
widerspenstig, *adj.* recalcitrant, contrary.
wider•spiegeln, *vb.* reflect.
widerspre'chen*, *vb.* contradict.
widerspre'chend, *adj.* contradictory.
Widerspruch, -̈e, *n.m.* contradiction, disagreement.
Widerstand, -̈e, *n.m.* resistance.
widerstandsfähig, *adj.* resistant, tough.
Widerstandskraft, -̈e, *n.f.* power of resistance, resilience.
widerstandslos, *adj.* without resistance.
widerste'hen*, *vb.* resist, withstand.
widerstre'ben, *vb.* resist, be repugnant.
Widerstre'ben, *n.nt.* reluctance.
widerstre'bend, *adj.* reluctant.
Widerstreit, -e, *n.m.* antagonism, conflict.
widerstrei'ten*, *vb.* resist, conflict with.
widerwärtig, *adj.* repugnant, repulsive.
Widerwille(n), *n.m.* distaste.
widerwillig, *adj.* unwilling, reluctant.
widmen, *vb.* dedicate, devote.
Widmung, -en, *n.f.* dedication.
widrig, *adj.* contrary.

widrigenfalls, *adv.* failing which, otherwise.

wie, 1. *conj.* how; as. **2.** *adv.* how.

wieder, *adv.* again; back, in return.

Wiederauf´bau, *n.m.* reconstruction.

wiederauf•bereiten, *vb.* recycle.

Wiederauf´erstehung, *n.f.* resurrection.

Wiederauf´rüstung, -en, *n.f.* rearmament.

Wiederauf´wertung, -en, *n.f.* revaluation.

Wiederbelebung, -en, *n.f.* revival.

wiederein´•setzen, *vb.* reinstate.

wiederein´•stellen, *vb.* reinstate.

wieder•erkennen*, *vb.* recognize.

Wiedererkennung, -en, *n.f.* recognition.

wieder•erlangen, *vb.* retrieve.

wieder•erstatten, *vb.* reimburse, refund.

wieder•finden*, *vb.* recover.

Wiedergabe, -n, *n.f.* return; rendition, reproduction.

wieder•geben*, *vb.* return, restore.

wiedergeboren, *adj.* born-again.

Wiedergeburt, *n.f.* rebirth.

wieder•gewinnen*, *vb.* recover, regain.

Wiedergewinnung, -en, *n.f.* recovery.

wiedergut´•machen, *vb.* redress, make amends for.

Wiedergut´machung, -en, *n.f.* restitution, redress.

wiederher´•stellen, *vb.* restore.

Wiederher´stellung, -en, *n.f.* restoration.

wiederho´len, *vb.* repeat; review.

Wiederho´lung, -en, *n.f.* repetition; review.

Wiederhören, *n.nt.* hearing again; **(auf W.)** good-bye (at the end of a telephone call).

Wiederinstand´setzung, -en, *n.f.* reconditioning.

Wiederkehr, *n.f.* return, recurrence.

wieder•kehren, *vb.* return.

Wiedersehen, *n.nt.* seeing again; **(auf W.)** good-bye.

Wiedervereinigung, *n.f.* reunification.

wieder•verheiraten, *vb.* **(sich w.)** remarry.

wieder•versöhnen, *vb.* reconcile.

Wiederversöhnung, -en, *n.f.* reconciliation.

Wiege, -n, *n.f.* cradle.

wiegen, *vb.* rock.

wiegen*, *vb.* weigh.

Wiegenlied, -er, *n.nt.* lullaby.

wiehern, *vb.* neigh.

Wiese, -n, *n.f.* meadow.

wieso´, *adv.* how so, why.

wild, *adj.* wild, ferocious, savage.

Wild, *n.nt.* game.

Wild-, *n.m.* savage.

Wildbret, *n.nt.* game.

Wildfang, -̈e, *n.m.* tomboy.

Wildheit, *n.f.* ferocity, fierceness.

Wildleder, -, *n.nt.* chamois, suede.

Wildnis, -se, *n.f.* wilderness.

Wille(n), *n.m.* will.

willenlos, *adj.* irresolute, passive, shifting.

Willenskraft, *n.f.* willpower.

willensstark (-), *adj.* strong-willed, resolute.

willfah´ren*, *vb.* comply with, gratify.

willfährig, *adj.* complaisant.

willig, *adj.* willing, ready.

Willkom´men, *n.nt.* welcome.

Willkür, *n.f.* arbitrariness, choice.

willkürlich, *adj.* arbitrary.

wimmeln, *vb.* swarm.

wimmern, *vb.* moan.

Wimper, -n, *n.f.* eyelash.

Wind, -e, *n.m.* wind.

Winde, -n, *n.f.* reel.

Windel, -n, *n.f.* diaper.

winden*, *vb.* wind, coil; **(sich w.)** squirm.

Windhund, -e, *n.m.* greyhound.

windig, *adj.* windy.

Windmühle, -n, *n.f.* windmill.

Windpocken, *n.pl.* chickenpox.

Windschutzscheibe, -n, *n.f.* windshield.

windstill, *adj.* calm.

Windstoß, -̈e, *n.m.* gust.

Windzug, *n.m.* draft.

Wink, -e, *n.m.* sign, wave; *(fig.)* hint, tip.

Winkel, -, *n.m.* angle, corner.

Winkelzug, ⁼e, *n.m.* dodge, subterfuge.

winken, *vb.* wave, beckon.

winseln, *vb.* whimper, wail.

Winter, -, *n.m.* winter.

Winterfrische, -, *n.f.* winter resort.

Wintergarten, -, *n.m.* conservatory.

winterlich, *adj.* wintry.

Winterschlaf, *n.m.* hibernation.

Winzer, -, *n.m.* wine-grower.

winzig, *adj.* tiny, minute.

Wippe, -n, *n.f.* seesaw.

wir, *pron.* we.

Wirbel, -, *n.m.* whirl, whirlpool; cowlick; vertebra.

wirbeln, *vb.* whirl.

Wirbelsäule, -n, *n.f.* vertebral column, spine.

Wirbelsturm, ⁼e, *n.m.* cyclone.

Wirbeltier, -e, *n.nt.* vertebrate.

wirken, *vb.* work, effect; **(w. auf)** effect.

wirklich, *adj.* real, actual.

Wirklichkeit, *n.f.* reality.

Wirlichkeitsflucht, *n.f.* escapism.

wirklichkeitsnah, *adj.* realistic.

wirksam, *adj.* effective.

Wirksamkeit, *n.f.* effectiveness, validity; **(in W. treten*)** take effect.

Wirkung, -en, *n.f.* effect.

Wirkungskraft, *n.f.* effect, efficacy.

wirkungslos, *adj.* ineffectual.

wirkungsvoll, *adj.* effective.

wirr, *adj.* confused.

Wirrnis, -se, *n.f.* tangle, confusion.

Wirrwarr, *n.nt.* confusion, maze.

Wirt, -e, *n.m.* host; landlord; proprietor.

Wirtin, -nen, *n.f.* hostess; landlady.

Wirtschaft, -en, *n.f.* inn, tavern; household; economy.

wirtschaften, *vb.* manage; keep house.

Wirtschafterin, -nen, *n.f.* housekeeper.

wirtschaftlich, *adj.* economic(al).

Wirtschaftlichkeit, *n.f.* economy.

Wirtschaftsabkommen, -, *n.nt.* trade agreement.

Wirtschaftsprüfer, -, *n.m.* certified public accountant.

Wirtschaftswissenschaft, *n.f.* economics.

Wirtschaftswunder, *n.nt.* economic miracle.

Wirtshaus, ⁼er, *n.nt.* inn.

Wisch, -e, *n.m.* scrap.

wischen, *vb.* wipe.

Wischlappen, -, *n.m.* cleaning rag.

wispern, *vb.* whisper.

Wißbegier, *n.f.* desire for knowledge; curiosity.

wissen*, *vb.* know.

Wissen, *n.nt.* learning, knowledge.

Wissenschaft, -en, *n.f.* learning, knowledge, science, scholarship.

wissenschaftlich, *adj.* scientific, scholarly.

wissenswert, *adj.* worth knowing.

wissentlich, *adv.* knowingly.

wittern, *vb.* smell; suspect.

Witterung, *n.f.* weather.

Witterungsverhältnisse, *n.pl.* weather conditions.

Witwe, -n, *n.f.* widow.

Witwer, -, *n.m.* widower.

Witz, -e, *n.m.* joke, pun, gag.

Witzbold, -e, *n.m.* joker, wise guy.

witzeln, *vb.* quip.

witzig, *adj.* witty, humorous.

witzlos, *adj.* pointless, fatuous.

wo, *adv.* where, in what place.

woan'ders, *adv.* elsewhere.

wobei', *adv.* whereby.

Woche, -n, *n.f.* week.

Wochenblatt, ⁼er, *n.nt.* weekly paper.

Wochenende, -n, *n.nt.* weekend.

Wochenschau, *n.f.* newsreel.

Wochentag, -e, *n.m.* weekday.

wöchentlich, *adj.* weekly.

wodurch', *adv.* through what; whereby.

wofern', *conj.* in so far as.

Woge, -n, *n.f.* wave, billow.

wogen, *vb.* wave, heave.

woher', *adv.* whence, from where.

wohl, *adv.* well; presumably, I suppose.

Wohl, *n.nt.* well-being, good health; (**zum W.**) here's to you.

wohlbedacht, *adj.* well-considered.

Wohlbehagen, *n.nt.* comfort.

Wohlergehen, *n.nt.* welfare.

wohlerzogen, *adj.* well brought up.

Wohlfahrt, *n.f.* welfare.

Wohlfahrtsstaat, -en, *n.m.* welfare state.

Wohlgefallen, *n.nt.* pleasure.

wohlgefällig, *adj.* pleasant, agreeable.

wohlgemerkt, *adv.* nota bene.

wohlgemut, *adj.* cheerful.

wohlgeneigt, *adj.* affectionate.

Wohlgeruch, -̈e, *n.m.* fragrance.

wohlhabend, *adj.* prosperous, well-to-do.

wohlig, *adj.* comfortable.

wohlklingend, *adj.* melodious.

wohlriechend, *adj.* fragrant.

wohlschmeckend, *adj.* tasty.

Wohlsein, *n.nt.* good health; (**zum W.**) your health.

Wohlstand, *n.m.* prosperity.

Wohltat, -en, *n.f.* benefit; pleasure.

Wohltäter, -, *n.m.* benefactor.

Wohltäterin, -nen, *n.f.* benefactress.

wohltätig, *adj.* charitable.

Wohltätigkeit, -en, *n.f.* charity.

wohltuend, *adj.* beneficial, pleasant, soothing.

wohlweislich, *adv.* wisely, prudently.

Wohlwollen, *n.nt.* benevolence, good will.

wohlwollend, *adj.* benevolent.

wohnen, *vb.* reside, live, dwell.

wohnhaft, *adj.* resident.

wohnlich, *adj.* comfortable, cozy.

Wohnort, -e, *n.m.* domicile, place of residence.

Wohnsitz, -e, *n.m.* residence.

Wohnung, -en, *n.f.* apartment, place of living.

Wohnwagen, -, *n.m.* trailer.

wölben, vb. (sich w.) arch over.

Wolf, -̈e, *n.m.* wolf.

Wolke, -n, *n.f.* cloud.

Wolkenbruch, -̈e, *n.m.* cloudburst.

Wolkenkratzer, -, *n.m.* skyscraper.

wolkenlos, *adj.* cloudless.

Wolle, *n.f.* wool.

wollen, *adj.* woolen.

wollen*, *vb.* want, be willing, intend.

wollig, *adj.* fluffy, fleecy.

Wollust, *n.f.* voluptuousness, lust.

wollüstig, *adj.* lascivious.

womög'lich, *adv.* if possible.

Wonne, -n, *n.f.* delight.

wonnig, *adj.* charming, delightful.

Wort, -e or **-̈er**, *n.nt.* word.

Wortart, -en, *n.f.* part of speech.

Wörterbuch, -̈er, *n.nt.* dictionary.

Wörterverzeichnis, -se, *n.nt.* vocabulary.

Wortführer, -, *n.m.* spokesman.

wortgetreu, *adj.* literal, verbatim.

wortkarg, *adj.* taciturn.

Wortlaut, -e, *n.m.* wording, text.

wörtlich, *adj.* literal.

wortlos, *adj.* speechless.

wortreich, *adj.* wordy, verbose.

Wortschatz, -̈e, *n.m.* vocabulary.

Wortspiel, -e, *n.nt.* pun.

Wortwechsel, -, *n.m.* altercation.

Wrack, -s, *n.nt.* wreck.

wringen*, *vb.* wring.

Wucher, *n.m.* usury.

wucherisch, *adj.* usurious.

Wuchs, *n.m.* growth, figure, height.

Wucht, *n.f.* weight; momentum.

wühlen, *vb.* burrow, rummage; *(fig.)* agitate.

wühlerisch, *adj.* inflammatory, subversive.

wulstig, *adj.* thick.

wund, *adj.* sore, wounded.

Wunde, -n, *n.f.* wound.

Wunder, -, *n.nt.* miracle, wonder.

wunderbar, *adj.* wonderful, miraculous.
Wunderdoktor, -en, *n.m.* quack.
Wunderkind, -er, *n.nt.* child prodigy.
wunderlich, *adj.* strange.
wundern, *vb.* surprise; **(sich w.)** be surprised.
wundersam, *adj.* wondrous.
wunderschön, *adj.* lovely, exquisite.
wundervoll, *adj.* wonderful.
Wundmal, -e, *n.nt.* scar; *(pl.)* stigmata.
Wundstarrkrampf, *n.m.* tetanus.
Wunsch, ⸚e, *n.m.* wish, desire.
wünschen, *vb.* wish, desire, want.
wünschenswert, *adj.* desirable.
Würde, *n.f.* dignity.
Würdenträger, -, *n.m.* dignitary.
würdig, *adj.* worthy, dignified.
würdigen, *vb.* honor, appreciate.
Wurf, ⸚e, *n.m.* throw; litter, brood.

Würfel, -, *n.m.* cube; *(pl.)* dice.
Würfelzucker, *n.m.* lump sugar.
Wurfpfeil, -e, *n.m.* dart.
würgen, *vb.* choke, retch; strangle.
Wurm, ⸚er, *n.m.* worm.
wurmen, *vb.* annoy, rankle.
wurmstichig, *adj.* wormy.
Wurst, ⸚e, *n.f.* sausage.
Würstchen, -, *n.nt.* **(heißes W.)** frankfurter.
Würze, -n, *n.f.* seasoning, flavor.
Wurzel, -n, *n.f.* root.
würzen, *vb.* season, spice.
würzig, *adj.* aromatic, spicy.
wüst, *adj.* waste, desolate; unkempt; wild; vulgar.
Wüste, -n, *n.f.* desert.
Wut, *n.f.* rage, fury.
Wutanfall, ⸚e, *n.m.* rage; tantrum.
wüten, *vb.* rage.
wütend, *adj.* furious.

X

X-beinig, *adj.* knock-kneed.
x-beliebig, *adj.* any old, any . . . at all; **(jeder x-beliebige)** every Tom, Dick, and Harry.

x-mal, *adv.* umpteen times.
X-Strahlen, *n.pl.* x-rays.
Xylophon', -e, *n.nt.* xylophone.

Y

Yacht, -en, *n.f.* yacht.

Z

Zacke, -n, *n.f.* jag; spike; (fork) prong; (dress) edging.
zacken, *vb.* indent, notch.
zackig, *adj.* jagged; notched; snappy.
zag, *adj.* faint-hearted.
zagen, *vb.* hesitate.
zaghaft, *adj.* timid.
zäh, *adj.* tough, tenacious.
zähflüssig, *adj.* viscous.
Zähigkeit, *n.f.* tenacity, perseverance.
Zahl, -en, *n.f.* number, figure.

zahlen, *vb.* pay; **(Bitte z.)** the check, please.
zählen, *vb.* count.
Zahlenangaben, *n.pl.* figures.
zahlenmäßig, *adj.* numerical.
Zähler, -, *n.m.* meter.
Zahlkarte, -n, *n.f.* money order.
zahllos, *adj.* countless.
zahlreich, *adj.* numerous.
Zahltag, -e, *n.m.* payday.
Zahlung, -en, *n.f.* payment.
zahlungsfähig, *adj.* solvent.
Zahlungsmittel, -, *n.nt.* tender, currency.

zahlungsunfähig, *adj.* insolvent.
Zahlwort, -̈er, *n.nt.* numeral.
zahm, *adj.* tame.
zähmen, *vb.* tame, domesticate.
Zahn, -̈e, *n.m.* tooth; (*tech.*) cog.
Zahnarzt, *n.m.* dentist.
Zahnärztin, -nen, *n.f.* dentist.
Zahnbürste, -n, *n.f.* toothbrush.
zahnen, *vb.* teethe.
Zahnfleisch, *n.nt.* gum.
Zahnheilkunde, *n.f.* dentistry.
Zahnpasta, -ten, *n.f.* toothpaste.
Zahnplombe, -n, *n.f.* filling.
Zahnputzmittel, -, *n.nt.* dentifrice.
Zahnradbahn, -en, *n.f.* cog railroad.
Zahnschmerzen, *n.pl.* toothache.
Zahnseide, *n.f.* dental floss.
Zahnstein, *n.m.* tartar.
Zahnstocher, -, *n.m.* toothpick.
Zahnweh, *n.nt.* toothache.
Zange, -n, *n.f.* pliers; forceps.
Zank, *n.m.* quarrel.
zanken, *vb.* (**sich z.**) quarrel, bicker.
zapfen, *vb.* tap.
Zapfen, -, *n.m.* peg, plug.
Zapfenstreich, *n.m.* (*mil.*) retreat.
zappelig, *adj.* fidgety.
zappeln, *vb.* flounder, fidget.
Zar, -en, -en, *n.m.* czar.
zart, *adj.* tender, dainty.
Zartheit, -en, *n.f.* tenderness, daintiness.
zärtlich, *adj.* tender, affectionate.
Zauber, -, *n.m.* enchantment, spell, charm, fascination.
Zauberei', *n.f.* sorcery, magic.
Zauberer, -, *n.m.* magician, wizard.
zauberhaft, *adj.* enchanting.
Zauberkraft, -̈e, *n.f.* magic power.
Zauberkunst, -̈e, *n.f.* magic.
Zauberspruch, -̈e, *n.m.* incantation, charm.
zaudern, *vb.* hesitate.
Zaum, -e, *n.m.* bridle.
zäumen, *vb.* bridle.
Zaun, -̈e, *n.m.* fence.
zausen, *vb.* tousle.
Zebra, -s, *n.nt.* zebra.

Zeche, -n, *n.f.* bill for drinks; mine, colliery.
zechen, *vb.* drink, carouse.
Zeder, -n, *n.f.* cedar.
Zeh, -en, *n.m.* toe.
Zehe, -n, *n.f.* toe.
Zehenspitze, -n, *n.f.* tip of the toe; (**auf Z.n gehen**) tiptoe.
zehn, *num.* ten.
zehnt-, *adj.* tenth.
Zehntel, -, *n.nt.* tenth part; (**ein z.**) one-tenth.
zehren, *vb.* (**z. an**) wear out, consume; (**z. von**) live on.
Zeichen, -, *n.nt.* sign, mark, token.
Zeichentrickfilm, -e, *n.m.* animated cartoon.
zeichnen, *vb.* draw; initial; (*comm.*) subscribe.
Zeichner, -, *n.m.* draftsman.
Zeichnerin, -nen, *n.f.* draftswoman.
Zeichnung, -en, *n.f.* drawing, (*comm.*) subscription.
Zeigefinger, -, *n.m.* forefinger.
zeigen, *vb.* show, indicate, point; demonstrate; exhibit.
Zeiger, -, *n.m.* (clock) hand.
Zeile, -n, *n.f.* line.
Zeit, -en, *n.f.* time.
Zeitalter, -, *n.nt.* age, era.
Zeitaufnahme, -n, *n.f.* time exposure.
Zeitdauer, *n.f.* period of time.
Zeitgeist, *n.m.* spirit of the times.
zeitgemäß, *adj.* timely.
Zeitgenosse, -n, -n, *n.m.* contemporary.
Zeitgenossin, -nen, *n.f.* contemporary.
zeitgenössisch, *adj.* contemporary.
zeitig, *adj.* early.
zeitlich, 1. *adj.* temporal. **2.** *adv.* in time.
zeitlos, *adj.* timeless, ageless.
Zeitmangel, *n.m.* lack of time.
Zeitpunkt, -e, *n.m.* time, moment.
zeitraubend, *adj.* time-consuming.
Zeitraum, -e, *n.m.* period.
Zeitschrift, -en, *n.f.* magazine, journal, periodical.

Zeitspanne, -n, *n.f.* period of time.
Zeitung, -en, *n.f.* newspaper.
Zeitungsanzeige, -n, *n.f.* ad, announcement.
Zeitungsausschnitt, -e, *n.m.* newspaper clipping.
Zeitungshändler, -, *n.m.* newsdealer.
Zeitungshändlerin, -nen, *n.f.* newsdealer.
Zeitungsjunge, -n, -n, *n.m.* paper-boy.
Zeitungsnotiz, -en, *n.f.* press item.
Zeitvertreib, *n.m.* pastime.
zeitweilig, *adj.* temporary.
Zeitwort, -er, *n.nt.* verb.
Zelle, -n, *n.f.* cell.
zellig, *adj.* cellular.
Zellophan, *n.nt.* cellophane.
Zellstoff, -e, *n.m.* cellulose.
Zelluloid, *n.nt.* celluloid.
Zellulo'se, *n.f.* cellulose.
Zelt, -e, *n.nt.* tent.
zelten, *vb.* live in a tent, camp.
Zelter, -, *n.m.* camper.
Zelterin, -nen, *n.f.* camper.
Zeltplatz, -e, *n.m.* campsite.
Zement, -, *n.m.* cement, concrete.
zensie'ren, *vb.* censor; (school) grade, mark.
Zensor, -'oren, *n.m.* censor.
Zensur', -en, *n.f.* censorship; (school) grade, mark.
Zensus, *n.m.* census.
Zentime'ter, -, *n.nt.* centimeter.
Zentner, -, *n.m.* 100 German pounds.
zentral', *adj.* central.
Zentral'heizung, *n.f.* central heating.
zentralisie'ren, *vb.* centralize.
Zentrum, -tren, *n.nt.* center.
zerbre'chen, *vb.* break to pieces, shatter.
zerbrech'lich, *adj.* fragile, frail.
zerbrö'ckeln, *vb.* crumble.
zerdrü'cken, *vb.* crush, shatter.
Zeremonie', -'i'en, *n.f.* ceremony.
zeremoniell', *adj.* ceremonial.
zerfah'ren, *adj.* absent-minded, scatter-brained.
Zerfall', *n.m.* ruin, decay.

zerfal'len*, *vb.* fall into ruin, disintegrate; (in Teile z.) be divided.
zerfet'zen, *vb.* tear into shreds.
zerflei'schen, *vb.* mangle.
zerfres'sen*, *vb.* erode, corrode.
zerge'hen*, *vb.* dissolve, melt.
zerglie'dern, *vb.* dismember, dissect.
zerklei'nern, *vb.* reduce to small pieces; crush; (wood) chop.
zerknau'tschen, *vb.* crumple.
zerknirscht', *adj.* contrite.
zerknül'len, *vb.* crumple.
zerlas'sen*, *vb.* dissolve, melt.
zerle'gen, *vb.* separate, cut up, carve.
zerlumpt', *adj.* ragged.
zermal'men, *vb.* crunch.
zermar'tern, *vb.* torture; (den Kopf z.) rack one's brain.
zermür'ben, *vb.* wear down.
Zermür'bung, -en, *n.f* attrition.
zerpflü'cken, *vb.* pick to pieces.
zerquet'schen, *vb.* squash.
Zerrbild, -er, *n.nt.* distorted picture, caricature.
zerrei'ßen*, *vb.* tear up, rend.
zerren, *vb.* tug, pull.
zerrin'nen*, *vb.* disappear, melt away.
zerrüt'ten, *vb.* ruin.
Zerrüt'tung, -en, *n.f.* ruin.
zerschla'gen*, *vb.* smash, shatter.
zerschmei'ßen*, *vb.* smash.
zerset'zen, *vb.* decompose.
zerset'zend, *adj.* subversive.
Zerset'zung, -en, *n.f.* decomposition; subversion.
zersprin'gen*, *vb.* burst.
zerstäu'ben, *vb.* pulverize; atomize; scatter.
zerstö'ren, *vb.* destroy, demolish.
zerstö'rend, *adj.* destructive.
Zerstö'rung, -en, *n.f.* destruction, demolition.
zerstreu'en, *vb.* scatter; divert, amuse.
zerstreut', *adj.* absent-minded.
Zerstreu'ung, -en, *n.f.* scattering; relaxation, amusement.
zertei'len, *vb.* cut up; separate, divide.
zertren'nen, *vb.* sever; (dress) cut up.

zertre'ten*, *vb.* trample.

zertrüm'mern, *vb.* wreck, demolish.

Zerwürf'nis, -se, *n.nt.* discord, quarrel.

zerzau'sen, *vb.* tousle, rumple.

Zettel, -, *n.m.* slip of paper, note, sticker, bill.

Zeug, -e, *n.nt.* stuff, material, cloth.

Zeuge, -n, -n, *n.m.* witness.

zeugen, *vb.* testify, give evidence; beget, create, produce.

Zeugenaussage, -n, *n.f.* testimony.

Zeugin, -nen, *n.f.* witness.

Zeugnis, -se, *n.nt.* testimony, evidence; reference (for a job); (school) report card.

Zicho'rie, -n, *n.f.* chickory.

Zickzack, -e, *n.m.* zigzag.

Ziege, -n, *n.f.* (she-)goat.

Ziegel, -, *n.m.* tile.

Ziegelstein, -e, *n.m.* brick.

Ziegenbock, -̈e, *n.m.* billy-goat.

Ziegenpeter, *n.m.* mumps.

ziehen*, *vb. (intr.)* move, go, draw, be drafty; *(tr.)* pull, drag, draw, tug; cultivate.

Ziehharmonika, -s, *n.f.* accordion.

Ziehung, -en, *n.f.* drawing.

Ziel, -e, *n.nt.* goal, target, end, objective.

zielbewußt, *adj.* with a clear goal, resolute.

zielen, *vb.* aim.

ziellos, *adj.* aimless, erratic.

Zielscheibe, -n, *n.f.* target.

ziemen, *vb.* be fitting for; **(sich z.)** be proper.

ziemlich, **1.** *adj.* suitable, fitting; pretty much of. **2.** *adv.* pretty, rather, quite.

Zier, *n.f.* ornament(ation).

Zierat, -e, *n.m.*, *or* -en, *n.f.* ornament, decoration.

Zierde, -n, *n.f.* ornament; honor.

zieren, *vb.* adorn, ornament.

zierlich, *adj.* dainty.

Ziffer, -n, *n.f.* figure, numeral.

Zifferblatt, -̈er, *n.nt.* dial, face (of a clock).

Zigaret'te, -n, *n.f.* cigarette.

Zigar're, -n, *n.f.* cigar.

Zigeu'ner, -, *n.m.* gypsy.

Zigeu'nerin, -nen, *n.f.* gypsy.

Zimbel, -n, *n.f.* cymbal.

Zimmer, -, *n.nt.* room.

Zimmerdecke, -n, *n.f.* ceiling.

Zimmermädchen, -, *n.nt.* chambermaid.

Zimmermann, -leute, *n.m.* carpenter.

zimperlich, *adj.* finicky, prim.

Zimt, -e, *n.m.* cinnamon.

Zinke, -n, *n.f.* prong.

Zinn, *n.nt.* tin, pewter.

Zins, -en, *n.m.* interest.

Zinseszins, -en, *n.m.* compound interest.

Zinssatz, -̈e, *n.m.* rate of interest.

Zipfel, -, *n.m.* tip.

Zirkel, -, *n.m.* compass (for making a circle).

zirkulie'ren, *vb.* circulate.

zirkulie'rend, *adj.* circulatory.

Zirkus, -se, *n.m.* circus.

zirpen, *vb.* chirp.

zischen, *vb.* hiss, sizzle; whiz.

ziselie'ren, *vb.* engrave, chase.

Zitadel'le, -n, *n.f.* citadel.

Zitat', -e, *n.nt.* quotation.

zitie'ren, *vb.* quote, cite.

Zitro'ne, -n, *n.f.* lemon.

zittern, *vb.* quiver, shiver, tremble.

zivil', *adj.* civil; reasonable.

Zivil', *n.nt.* civilians; civilian clothes.

Zivil'bevölkerung, -en, *n.f.* civilian population.

Zivilisa'tion, -en, *n.f.* civilization.

zivilisie'ren, *vb.* civilize.

Zivilist', -en, -en, *n.m.* civilian.

Zobel, *n.m.* sable.

zögern, *vb.* hesitate.

zögernd, *adj.* hesitant.

Zölibat', *n.m. or nt.* celibacy.

Zoll, -, *n.m.* inch.

Zoll, -̈e, *n.m.* tariff, duty, toll.

Zollamt, -̈er, *n.nt.* custom house.

Zollbeamt'-, *n.m.* customs officer.

Zollbeamtin, -nen, *n.f.* customs officer.

zollfrei, *adj.* duty free.

Zöllner, -, *n.m.* customs collector; (Bible) publican.

zollpflichtig, *adj.* subject to duty.

Zolltarif, -e, *n.m.* tariff.

Zollverein, -e, *n.m.* customs union.

Zollverschluß, *n.m.* customs seal; (unter Z.) under bond.

Zone, -, *n.f.* zone.

Zoo, -s, *n.m.* zoo.

Zoologie, *n.f.* zoology.

zoolo′gisch, *adj.* zoological.

Zorn, *n.m.* ire, wrath, anger.

zornig, *adj.* angry.

zottig, *adj.* shaggy.

zu, *adv.* too; closed.

zu, *prep.* to.

Zubehör, *n.nt.* accessories, appurtenances, trimmings.

zu•bereiten, *vb.* prepare.

Zubereitung, -en, *n.f.* preparation.

zu•bringen*, *vb.* bring to; pass, spend.

Zuch, -en, *n.f.* breed(ing), rearing, education, training, decency.

züchten, *vb.* breed, raise.

Züchter, -, *n.m.* breeder.

Züchterin, -nen, *n.f.* breeder.

Zuchthaus, ⸚er, *n.nt.* penitentiary.

züchtig, *adj.* chaste, demure.

züchtigen, *vb.* chasten, chastise.

zucken, *vb.* twitch, jerk, flash.

Zucker, *n.m.* sugar.

Zuckerbäcker, -, *n.m.* confectioner.

Zuckerguß, ⸚sse, *n.m.* icing.

Zuckerkrankheit, *n.f.* diabetes.

Zuckerwerk, *n.nt.* confectionery.

Zuckung, -en, *n.f.* twitch, convulsion.

zu•decken, *vb.* cover up.

zudem′, *adv.* in addition.

zudringlich, *adj.* intruding, obtrusive.

Zueignung, -en, *n.f.* dedication.

zueinan′der, *adv.* to one another.

zu•erkennen*, *vb.* award.

zuerst′, *adv.* first, at first.

Zufall, ⸚e, *n.m.* chance, coincidence.

zufällig, **1.** *adj.* chance, fortuitous. **2.** *adv.* by chance.

Zuflucht, *n.f.* refuge; recourse.

Zufluchtsort, -e, *n.m.* place of refuge.

Zufluß, ⸚sse, *n.m.* flowing in, influx.

zufol′ge, *prep.* as a result of; according to.

zufrie′den, *adj.* content, satisfied.

zufrie′den•stellen, *vb.* satisfy.

zu•frieren*, *vb.* freeze over, freeze up.

zu•fügen, *vb.* inflict.

Zufuhr, -en, *n.f.* bringing in, importation, supply.

zu•führen, *vb.* bring to, import, supply.

Zug, ⸚e, *n.m.* pull, drawing, draft; stroke; feature, trait; move; train; procession; trend; flight; (mil.) squad.

Zugabe, -n, *n.f.* bonus, premium, encore.

Zugang, ⸚e, *n.m.* access, approach.

zugänglich, *adj.* accessible, approachable.

zu•geben*, *vb.* give in addition; admit.

zugegebenerma′ßen, *adv.* admittedly.

zuge′gen, *adv.* present.

zugehörig, *adj.* belonging to, pertinent.

Zügel, -, *n.m.* rein; restraint.

zügellos, *adj.* unbridled, unrestrained.

zügeln, *vb.* bridle, curb, check.

zugestandenerma′ßen, *adv.* avowedly.

Zugeständnis, -se, *n.nt.* confession; concession.

zu•gestehen*, *vb.* confess, concede.

zugetan, *adj.* devoted to, fond of.

zugig, *adj.* drafty.

Zugkraft, *n.f.* pull, thrust.

zugleich′, *adv.* at the same time.

Zugluft, *n.f.* draft.

zu•greifen*, *vb.* lend a hand; help oneself.

zugrun′de, *adv.* at the bottom, as a basis; (z. gehen*) go to ruin, perish; (z. richten) ruin, destroy.

zugun′sten, *adv.&prep.* for the benefit of, in favor of.

zugu′te, *adv.* for the benefit of.

zu•haken, *vb.* hook.

zu•halten*, *vb.* keep shut.

zuhan'den, adv. at hand.
zu•hören, vb. listen to.
Zuhörer, -, n.m. listener, auditor; (pl.) audience.
Zuhörerin, -nen, n.f. listener.
Zuhörerraum, ̈-e, n.m. auditorium.
Zuhörerschaft, -en, n.f. audience.
zu•kleben, vb. paste together.
zu•knallen, vb. slam.
zu•knöpfen, vb. button up.
zu•knüpfen, vb. tie, knot, fasten.
zu•kommen*, vb. be one's due; be proper for.
Zukunft, n.f. future.
zukünftig, adj. future.
Zulage, -n, n.f. extra pay, pay raise.
zu•langen, vb. help oneself.
zulänglich, adj. adequate.
zu•lassen*, vb. leave closed; admit; permit.
zulässig, adj. permissible, admissible.
Zulauf, n.m. run; (Z. haben*) popular.
zu•laufen*, vb. run up to.
zu•legen, vb. add; (sich etwas z.) acquire.
zulei'de, adv. (z. tun*) hurt, harm.
zu•leiten, vb. lead to, direct to.
zuletzt', adv. at last, finally.
zulie'be, adv. for the sake of.
zu•machen, vb. shut.
zumal', 1. adv. especially; together. 2. conj. especially; because.
zu•mauern, vb. wall up.
zumeist', adv. for the most part.
zu•messen*, vb. allot.
zumin'dest, adv. at least.
zumu'te, adv. (z. sein*) feel, be in a mood.
zu•muten, vb. expect, demand.
Zumutung, -en, n.f. imposition.
zunächst', adv. first of all.
Zunahme, -n, n.f. increase.
Zuname(n), -, n.m. surname, last name.
zünden, vb. ignite; (fig.) inflame.
zündend, adj. inflammatory.
Zünder, -, n.m. fuse.
Zündholz, ̈-er, n.nt. match.
Zündkerze, -n, n.f. spark plug.

Zündschlüssel, -, n.m. ignition key.
Zündstoff, -e, n.m. fuel.
Zündung, n.f. ignition; detonation.
zu•nehmen*, vb. grow, increase; (moon) wax; put on weight.
zu•neigen, vb. incline.
Zuneigung, -en, n.f. inclination; affection.
Zunft, ̈-e, n.f. guild.
Zunge, -n, n.f. tongue.
zungenfertig, adj. glib.
zunich'te, adv. to nothing, ruined; (z. machen) ruin, frustrate.
zunut'ze, adv. (z. machen) profit by, utilize.
zuo'berst, adv. at the top.
zu•packen, vb. (fig.) get to work.
zupfen, vb. pull, (wool) pick.
zu•raten*, vb. advise in favor of.
zurechnungsfähig, adj. accountable.
zurecht', adv. right, in good order.
zurecht'•finden*, vb. (sich z.) find one's way.
zurecht'•machen, vb. prepare.
zu•reden, vb. urge, encourage.
zureichend, adj. sufficient.
zu•richten, vb. prepare; (übel z.) maul.
zürnen, vb. be angry.
Zurschau'stellung, -en, n.f. display.
zurück', adv. back, behind.
zurück'•behalten*, vb. keep back.
zurück'•bleiben*, vb. lag behind.
zurück'•bringen*, vb. return.
zurück'•drängen, vb. drive back.
zurück'•erstatten, vb. reimburse.
zurück'•fahren*, vb. drive back; recoil.
zurück'•fallen*, vb. fall back; relapse.
zurück'•führen, vb. lead back; trace back, attribute.
zurück'•geben*, vb. return.
zurück'geblieben, adj. backward.
Zurück'gebliebenheit, n.f. backwardness.

zurück'·gehen*, *vb.* go back; decline.

zurück'gesetzt, *adj.* (prices) reduced.

zurück'gezogen, *adj.* secluded.

Zurück'gezogenheit, *n.f.* seclusion.

zurück'·halten*, *vb.* retain; restrain; withhold.

zurück'haltend, *adj.* reticent.

Zurück'haltung, *n.f.* restraint.

zurück'·kehren, *vb.* return, revert.

zurück'·kommen*, *vb.* return.

zurück'·lassen*, *vb.* leave behind.

zurück'·legen, *vb.* lay aside; accomplish.

zurück'·lehnen, *vb.* (sich z.) lean back, recline.

zurück'·liegen*, *vb.* lie in the past.

zurück'·nehmen*, *vb.* take back; retract.

zurück'·prallen, *vb.* recoil, rebound.

zurück'·rufen*, *vb.* recall.

zurück'·schauen, *vb.* look back.

zurück'·schlagen*, *vb.* hit back, repulse.

zurück'·schrecken, *vb.* be startled; shrink (from).

zurück'·sehen*, *vb.* look back on; reflect.

zurück'·sehnen, *vb.* (sich z.) long to return.

zurück'·setzen, *vb.* put back; set aside; reduce.

zurück'·stehen*, *vb.* stand back; (*fig.*) be inferior.

zurück'·stellen, *vb.* set back; set aside; (*mil.*) defer.

zurück'·stoßen*, *vb.* repulse.

zurück'·strahlen, *vb.* reflect.

zurück'·treiben*, *vb.* repel.

zurück'·treten*, *vb.* resign.

zurück'·verfolgen, *vb.* trace.

zurück'·versetzen, *vb.* put back; (sich z.) go back to a time.

zurück'·weichen*, *vb.* retreat.

zurück'·weisen*, *vb.* send back; reject.

Zurück'weisung, **-en**, *n.f.* rebuff.

zurück'·zahlen, *vb.* refund, repay.

zurück'·ziehen*, *vb.* pull back, withdraw; (sich z.) withdraw, back out.

Zuruf', -e, *n.m.* call, shout; acclamation.

Zusage, -n, *n.f.* acceptance.

zu·sagen, *vb.* accept; (es sagt mir zu) it agrees with me.

zusam'men, *adv.* together.

Zusam'menarbeit, *n.f.* cooperation, collaboration.

zusam'men·arbeiten, *vb.* cooperate, collaborate.

Zusam'menbau, *n.m.* assemblage.

zusam'men·brauen, *vb.* concoct.

zusam'men·brechen*, *vb.* collapse.

Zusam'menbruch, **-̈e**, *n.m.* collapse.

zusam'men·drängen, *vb.* (sich z.) crowd together; huddle.

zusam'men·fahren*, *vb.* ride together; crash; be startled, wince.

zusam'men·fassen, *vb.* summarize, recapitulate.

zusam'menfassend, *adj.* comprehensive; summary.

Zusam'menfassung, **-en**, *n.f.* summary, condensation.

zusam'men·fügen, *vb.* join together.

zusam'men·gehören, *vb.* belong together.

zusam'men·geraten*, *vb.* collide.

zusam'mengesetzt, *adj.* composed; compound.

Zusam'menhang, **-̈e**, *n.m.* connection, relation; context; association.

zusam'men·hängen*, *vb.* hang together, be connected, cohere.

zusam'menhängend, *adj.* coherent.

zusam'men·häufen, *vb.* pile up.

zusam'men·kauern, *vb.* huddle.

zusam'men·kommen*, *vb.* get together, convene.

Zusam'menkunft, **-̈e**, *n.f.* meeting.

zusam'men·laufen*, *vb.* converge.

zusam'men·legen, *vb.* combine, pool, merge.

zusam'men·nehmen*, *vb.* (sich z.) pull oneself together.

zusam'men·passen, *vb.* go well together.

Zusam'menprall, -e, *n.m.* collision, impact.

zusam'men·pressen, *vb.* compress.

zusam'men·rechnen, *vb.* add up.

zusam'men·reißen*, *vb.* (sich z.) pull oneself together.

zusam'men·rotten, *vb.* (sich z.) band together.

zusam'men·rufen*, *vb.* summon, convene.

zusam'men·scharen, *vb.* scrape together; (sich z.) band together, cluster.

zusam'men·schließen*, *vb.* join together; (sich z.) close ranks.

Zusam'menschluß, -sse, *n.m.* federation, merger.

zusam'men·schrumpfen, *vb.* shrink, dwindle.

zusam'men·setzen, *vb.* combine, compound; (sich z.) consist, be composed.

Zusam'mensetzung, -en, *n.f.* combination, composition.

zusam'men·stehen*, *vb.* stand together, stick together.

zusam'men·stellen, *vb.* make up, compile.

Zusam'menstellung, -en, *n.f.* composition, arrangement.

Zusam'menstoß, -e, *n.m.* collision, clash.

zusam'men·stoßen*, *vb.* get together; collide, clash, crash.

zusam'men·strömen, *vb.* flow together, flock together.

zusam'men·stürzen, *vb.* collapse.

zusam'men·tragen*, *vb.* compile.

zusam'men·treffen*, *vb.* meet, encounter; coincide.

Zusam'mentreffen, -, *n.nt.* encounter; coincide.

zusam'men·treten*, *vb.* convene.

zusam'men·tun*, *vb.* put together; (sich z.) unite.

zusam'men·wirken, *vb.* act together, collaborate.

zusam'men·zählen, *vb.* sum up.

zusam'men·ziehen*, *vb.* draw together; (sich z.) contract, constrict.

Zusam'menziehung, -en, *n.f.* contraction.

Zusatz, -e, *n.m.* addition.

zusätzlich, *adj.* additional, supplementary.

zuschan'den·machen, *vb.* ruin.

zu·schauen, *vb.* look on, watch.

Zuschauer, -, *n.m.* spectator.

Zuschauerin, -nen, *n.f.* spectator.

zu·schicken, *vb.* send to, forward.

zu·schieben*, *vb.* shove towards; (die Schuld z.) put the blame on.

zu·schießen*, *vb.* contribute.

Zuschlag, -e, *n.m.* increase; additional charge.

zu·schlagen*, *vb.* strike; bang shut.

zu·schließen*, *vb.* lock.

zu·schneiden*, *vb.* cut out.

zu·schreiben*, *vb.* ascribe, attribute, impute.

Zuschrift, -en, *n.f.* communication.

Zuschuß, -sse, *n.m.* subsidy.

zu·sehen*, *vb.* look on, watch.

zusehends, *adv.* visibly.

zu·senden*, *vb.* send, forward.

zu·sichern, *vb.* assure, promise.

Zustand, -e, *n.m.* state, condition; situation.

zustan'de·bringen*, *vb.* bring about, achieve, accomplish.

zustan'de·kommen*, *vb.* come about, be accomplished.

zuständig, *adj.* competent, qualified.

Zuständigkeit, -en, *n.f.* competence; jurisdiction.

zustat'ten·kommen*, *vb.* be useful.

zu·stehen*, *vb.* be due to; become, suit; behoove.

zu·stellen, *vb.* deliver.

Zustellung, -en, *n.f.* delivery.

zu·stimmen, *vb.* agree, consent.

Zustimmung, -en, *n.f.* agreement, consent, approval.
zu•stopfen, *vb.* plug.
zu•stoßen*, *vb.* slam tight, meet with, befall.
Zustrom, *n.m.* influx.
Zutat, -en, *n.f.* ingredient.
zu•teilen, *vb.* allot, assign, allocate.
zu•trauen, *vb.* believe someone capable of doing.
Zutrauen, *n.nt.* confidence.
zutraulich, *adj.* trusting.
zu•treffen*, *vb.* prove right, apply.
zutreffend, *adj.* correct, applicable.
Zutritt, -e, *n.m.* admittance, admission.
Zutun, *n.nt.* assistance.
zuverlässig, *adj.* reliable, trustworthy.
Zuverlässigkeit, *n.f.* reliability.
Zuversicht, *n.f.* confidence, trust.
zuversichtlich, *adj.* confident, sure.
zuviel', *adv.* too much.
zuvor', *adv.* beforehand.
zuvor'derst, *adv.* up front.
zuvör'derst, *adv.* first of all.
zuvor'•kommen*, *vb.* anticipate, forestall.
zuvor'kommend, *adj.* obliging, polite.
Zuvor'kommenheit, *n.f.* civility.
Zuwachs, *n.m.* increase, rise, growth.
zu•wandern, *vb.* immigrate.
zuwe'ge•bringen*, *vb.* bring about, achieve.
zuwei'len, *adv.* at times.
zu•weisen*, *vb.* assign, apportion, allot.
Zuweisung, -en, *n.f.* assignment, allocation.
zu•wenden*, *vb.* turn towards; bestow upon.
Zuwendung, -en, *n.f.* donation.
zuwi'der, 1. *adv.* abhorrent, repugnant. **2.** *prep.* contrary to.
zuwi'der•handeln, *vb.* act contrary to, disobey.
zu•zahlen, *vb.* pay extra.
zu•ziehen*, *vb.* pull closed; (**sich etwas z.**) contract, incur.

Zuzug, *n.m.* move, influx.
zuzüglich, *adv.* plus.
Zwang, *n.m.* compulsion, coercion, duress; constraint.
zwanglos, *adj.* unrestrained, informal, casual.
Zwangsarbeit, *n.f.* forced labor; hard labor.
zwangsläufig, *adv.* necessarily.
zwangsräumen, *vb.* evict.
Zwangsverschleppt-, *n.m.&f.* displaced person.
zwangsweise, *adv.* forcibly.
Zwangswirtschaft, *n.f.* controlled economy.
zwanzig, *num.* twenty.
zwanzigst-, *adj.* twentieth.
Zwanzigstel, -, *n.nt.* twentieth part; (**ein z.**) one-twentieth.
zwar, *adv.* to be sure (means that a *but* is coming); (**und z.**) namely, to give further details.
Zweck, -e, *n.m.* purpose, end, aim.
zweckdienlich, *adj.* expedient.
Zwecke, -n, *n.f.* tack.
zweckmäßig, *adj.* expedient.
zwecks, *prep.* for the purpose of.
zwei, *num.* two.
zweideutig, *adj.* ambiguous.
Zweideutigkeit, -en, *n.f.* ambiguity.
zweierlei, *adj.* of two kinds.
zweifach, *adj.* twofold.
zweifältig, *adj.* twofold, double.
Zweifel, -, *n.m.* doubt.
zweifelhaft, *adj.* doubtful.
zweifellos, *adj.* doubtless.
zweifeln, *vb.* doubt.
Zweifler, -, *n.m.* doubter, sceptic.
Zweiflerin, -nen, *n.f.* doubter, sceptic.
Zweig, -e, *n.m.* branch, bough, twig.
Zweikampf, ̈-e, *n.m.* duel.
zweimal, *adv.* twice.
zweimalig, *adj.* repeated, done twice.
zweimonatlich, *adj.* bimonthly.
Zweirad, ̈-er, *n.nt.* bicycle.
zweiseitig, *adj.* two-sided, bilateral.
Zweisitzer, -, *n.m.* two-seater, roadster.
zweisprachig, *adj.* bilingual.

zweit-, *adj.* second.

zweitbest-, *adj.* second-best.

zweiteilig, *adj.* two-piece; bipartite.

zweitens, *adv.* in the second place, secondly.

zweitklassig, *adj.* second-class.

Zwerchfell, -e, *n.nt.* diaphragm.

Zwerg, -e, *n.m.* dwarf; midget.

zwergenhaft, *adj.* dwarfish, diminutive.

zwetschge, -n, *n.f.* plum.

zwicken, *vb.* pinch.

Zwickmühle, -n, *n.f.* dilemma, jam.

Zwieback, -e *or* **-e,** *n.m.* rusk.

Zwiebel, -n, *n.f.* onion.

zwiefach, *adj.* double.

Zwiegespräch, -e, *n.nt.* dialogue.

Zwielicht, *n.nt.* twilight.

zwielichtig, *adj.* shady.

Zwiespalt, -e, *n.m.* discrepancy; discord; schism.

zwiespältig, *adj.* discrepant, conflicting.

Zwilling, -e, *n.m.* twin.

zwingen*, *vb.* force, compel.

zwingend, *adj.* compelling.

Zwinger, -, *n.m.* cage; (dog) kennel.

zwinkern, *vb.* wink.

Zwirn, -e, *n.m.* thread; twine.

Zwirnfaden, -, *n.m.* thread.

zwischen, *prep.* between, among.

Zwischenakt, -e, *n.m.* entr'acte; interval.

Zwischenbemerkung, -en, *n.f.* incidental remark, interruption.

Zwischendeck, -e, *n.nt.* steerage.

Zwischending, -e, *n.nt.* something halfway between, mixture, cross.

zwischendurch', *adv.* in between; now and then.

Zwischenfall, -e, *n.m.* incident.

Zwischenhändler, -, *n.m.* jobber.

Zwischenhändlerin, -nen, *n.f.* jobber.

Zwischenlandung, -en, *n.f.* stopover.

Zwischenraum, -e, *n.m.* space in between.

Zwischenruf, -e, *n.m.* interjection, interruption.

Zwischenspiel, -e, *n.nt.* interlude, intermezzo.

Zwischenstock, -e, *n.m.* mezzanine.

Zwischenzeit, *n.f.* interval, interim.

Zwist, -e, *n.m.* quarrel, discord.

zwitschern, *vb.* twitter, chirp.

Zwitter, -, *n.m.* hybrid.

zwo, *num.* two (used especially on the telephone to avoid having *zwei* misunderstood as *drei*).

zwölf, *num.* twelve.

Zwölf'fingerdarm, -e, *n.m.* duodenum.

zwölft-, *adj.* twelfth.

Zwölftel, -, *n.nt.* twelfth part; (ein z.) one-twelfth.

zwot-, *adj.* second.

Zyklamat', -e, *n.nt.* cyclamate.

Zyklon', -e, *n.m.* cyclone.

Zyklotron', -e, *n.nt.* cyclotron.

Zyklus, -klen, *n.m.* cycle.

Zylin'der, -, *n.m.* cylinder; top hat.

Zyniker, -, *n.m.* cynic.

Zynikerin, -nen, *n.f.* cynic.

zynisch, *adj.* cynical.

Zypres'se, -n, *n.f.* cypress.

Zyste, -n, *n.f.* cyst.

a, *art.* ein, -, -e.

abandon, *vb.* verlas'sen*.

abandoned, *adj.* verlas'sen; *(depraved)* verwor'fen.

abandonment, *n.* Aufgeben *nt.*

abash, *vb.* beschä'men.

abate, *vb.* nach·las'sen*.

abatement, *n.* Vermin'derung, -en *f.*

abbess, *n.* Äbtis'sin, -nen *f.*

abbey, *n.* Abtei', -en *f.*, Kloster, ÷ *nt.*

abbot, *n.* Abt, ÷e *m.*

abbreviate, *vb.* ab·kürzen.

abbreviation, *n.* Abkürzung, -en *f.*

abdicate, *vb.* ab·danken.

abdication, *n.* Abdankung, -en *f.*

abdomen, *n.* Unterleib, -er *m.*

abdominal, *adj.* Leib- *(cpds.).*

abduct, *vb.* entfüh'ren.

abduction, *n.* Entfüh'rung, -en *f.*

abductor, *n.* Entfüh'rer, - *m.*

aberration, *n.* Abweichung, -en *f.*

abet, *vb.* an·treiben*, helfen*.

abetment, *n.* Beistand, -e *m.*

abettor, *n.* Helfershelfer, - *m.*

abeyance, *n.* Schwebezustand, ÷e *m.*

abhor, *vb.* verab'scheuen.

abhorrence, *n.* Abscheu, -e *m.*

abhorrent, *adj.* zuwi'der.

abide, *vb. (dwell)* wohnen; *(remain)* bleiben*; *(tolerate)* leiden*.

abiding, *adj.* dauernd.

ability, *n.* Fähigkeit, -en *f.*

abject, *adj.* elend, niedrig, unterwür'fig.

abjure, *vb.* ab·schwören*, entsa'gen.

ablative, *n.* Ablativ, -e *m.*

ablaze, *adj.* in Flammen.

able, *adj.* fähig, tüchtig; **(to be a.)** können*.

able-bodied, *adj.* kräftig.

ablution, *n.* Abwaschung, -en *f.*

ably, *adv.* fähig, tüchtig.

abnormal, *adj.* ungewöhnlich, abnorm'.

abnormality, *n.* Mißbildung, -en *f.*, Abnormität', -en *f.*

aboard, *adv.* an Bord.

abode, *n.* Wohnsitz, -e *m.*, Wohnung, -en *f.*

abolish, *vb.* ab·schaffen.

abolition, *n.* Aufhebung, -en *f.*

abominable, *adj.* abscheu'lich.

abominate, *vb.* verab'scheuen.

abomination, *n.* Abscheu, -e *m.*

aboriginal, *adj.* ursprüng'lich, Ur- *(cpds.).*

aborigine, *n.* Ureinwohner, - *m.*

abort, *vb.* fehl·gebären*, ab·treiben*.

abortion, *n.* Fehlgeburt, -en *f.*, Abtreibung, -en *f.*

abortive, *adj.* mißglückt'.

abound, *vb.* im Überfluß vorhanden sein.

about, **1.** *adv. (approximately)* etwa, ungefähr; *(around)* herum'; umher'; **(be a. to)** im Begriff sein*. **2.** *prep. (around)* um; *(concerning)* über.

about-face, *n.* Kehrtwendung *f.*

above, 1. *adj.* obig. **2.** *adv.* oben. **3.** *prep.* über.

aboveboard, *adj.* offen, unverhoh'len.

abrasion, *n.* Abschaben *nt.*, Abschleifen *nt.*

abrasive, 1. *n.* Schleifmittel, - *nt.* **2.** *adj.* abschaben, abschleifend.

abreast, *adv.* nebeneinan'der, Seite an Seite.

abridge, *vb.* ab·kürzen.

abridgment, *n.* Abkürzung, -en *f.*

abroad, *adv.* im Ausland.

abrupt, *adj.* schroff, abrupt'.

abruptness, *n.* Schroffheit, -en *f.*

abscess, *n.* Eitergeschwulst, -e *f.*

abscond, *vb.* durch·brennen*.

absence, *n.* Abwesenheit, -en *f.*

absent, *adj.* abwesend.

absentee, *n.* Abwesend- *m. & f.*

absent-minded, *adj.* zerstreut'.

absinthe, *n.* Absinth', -e *m.*

absolute, *adj.* absolut', unbedingt'.

absoluteness, *n.* Unbedingt'heit, -en *f.*

absolution, *n.* Absolution', -en *f.*

absolve, *vb.* frei·sprechen*, ent·la'sten.

absorb, *vb.* auf·saugen, absorbie'ren.

absorbed, *adj.* (*fig.*) vertieft'.

absorbent, 1. *n.* Absorbie'rungsmittel, -*nt.* **2.** *adj.* aufsaugend.

absorbing, *adj.* aufsaugend; (*interesting*) packend.

absorption, *n.* Absorption', -en *f.*

abstain, *vb.* sich enthal'ten*.

abstemious, *adj.* enthalt'sam.

abstinence, *n.* Enthalt'samkeit, -en *f.*

abstract, 1. *n.* (*book, article*) Auszug, -e *m.* **2.** *adj.* abstrakt'. **3.** *vb.* abstrahie'ren.

abstraction, *n.* Abstraktion', -en *f.*

abstruse, *adj.* abstrus'.

absurd, *adj.* unsinnig.

absurdity, *n.* Unsinnigkeit, -en *f.*

abundance, *n.* Überfluß, -sse *m.*

abundant, *adj.* Überreich.

abuse, 1. *n.* (*book, article*) Mißbrauch, -e *m.* **2.** *n.* Mißbrauch, -e *m.*

abusive, *adj.* mißbräuchlich, beschimp'fend.

abut, *vb.* an·grenzen.

abutment, *n.* Angrenzung, -en *f.*

abyss, *n.* Abgrund, -e *m.*

academic, *adj.* akade'misch.

academy, *n.* Akademie', -mi'en *f.*; Hochschule, -n *f.*

acanthus, *n.* Akan'thus, -se *m.*

accede, *vb.* ein·willigen.

accelerate, *vb.* beschleu'nigen.

acceleration, *n.* Beschleu'nigung, -en *f.*

accelerator, *n.* Gashebel, - *m.*

accent, 1. *n.* Akzent', -e *m.* **2.** *vb.* beto'nen.

accept, *vb.* an·nehmen*.

acceptability, *n.* Annehmbarkeit, -en *f.*

acceptable, *adj.* annehmbar.

acceptance, *n.* Annahme, -n *f.*

access, *n.* Zugang, -e *m.*

accessible, *adj.* zugänglich.

accessory, 1. *n.* (*person*) Mithelfer, - *m.*, Mithelferin, -nen *f.*; (*thing*) Zubehör *nt.* **2.** *adj.* zusätzlich.

accident, *n.* Unfall, -e *m*; (*chance*) Zufall, -e *m.*

accidental, *adj.* zufällig.

acclaim, 1. *n.* Beifall, -e *m.* **2.** *vb.* Beifall rufen*.

acclamation, *n.* Zuruf, -e *m*, Beifall, -e *m.*

acclimate, *vb.* akklamatisie'ren.

accommodate, *vb.* an·passen, (*lodge*) unter·bringen*.

accommodating, *adj.* entge'genkommend.

accommodation, *n.* Anpassung, -en *f.*, (*lodging*) Unterkunft, -e *f.*

accompaniment, *n.* Beglei'tung, -en *f.*

accompanist, *n.* Beglei'ter, - *m.*, Begle'terin, -nen *f.*

accompany, *vb.* beglei'ten.

accomplice, *n.* Mittäter, - *m.*, Mittäterin, -nen *f.*

accomplish, *vb.* leisten.

accomplished, *adj.* vollen'det.

accomplishment, *n.* Leistung, -en *f.*

accord, *n.* Einvernehmen, - *nt.*

accordance, *n.* Überein'stimmung, -en *f.*

accordingly, *adv.* demgemäß.

according to, *prep.* laut, gemäß'.

accordion, *n.* Ziehharmonika, -s *f.*

accost, *vb.* an·sprechen*.

account, *n.* (*comm.*) Konto, -ten *nt.*, (*narrative*) Bericht', -e *m.*

accountable, *adj.* verant'wortlich.

accountant, *n.* Buchhalter, - *m.*, Buchhalterin, -nen *f.*

accounting, *n.* Buchführung, -en *f.*

accredit, *vb.* akkreditie'ren, beglau'bigen.

accrual, *n.* Zuwachs *m.*

accrue, *vb.* an·wachsen*.

accumulate, *vb.* (sich) an·häufen.

accumulation, *n.* Anhäufung, -en *f.*

accumulator, *n.* Ansammler, - *m.*, Akkumula'tor, -to'ren *m.*

accuracy, *n.* Genau'igkeit, -en *f.*

accurate, *adj.* genau'.

accursed, *adj.* verflucht'.

accusation, *n.* Anklage, -n *f.*

accusative, 1. *n.* Akkusativ, -e *m.* **2.** *adj.* anklagend.

accuse, *vb.* an·klagen.

accused, n. Angeklagt- m. & f.

accuser, n. Ankläger, - m., Anklägerin, -nen f.

accustom, vb. gewöh'nen.

accustomed, adj. gewohnt', gewöhnt'; **(become a. to)** sich gewöh'nen an.

ace, n. As, -se nt.

acetate, n. Acetat', -e nt.

acetic, adj. ace'tisch.

acetylene, n. Acetylen' nt.

ache, 1. n. Schmerz, -en m. 2. vb. weh tun*, schmerzen.

achieve, vb. errei'chen.

achievement, n. Leistung, -en f.

acid, 1. n. Säure, -n f. 2. adj. sauer.

acidify, vb. in Säure verwandeln.

acidity, n. Säuerlichkeit, -en f.

acknowledge, vb. an•erkennen*, bestä'tigen.

acme, n. Höhepunkt, -e m.

acne, n. Akne, -n f.

acolyte, n. Altar'diener, - m.

acorn, n. Eichel, -n f.

acoustics, n. Aku'stik f.

acquaint, vb. bekannt'machen.

acquaintance, n. Bekannt'schaft, -en f.

acquainted, adj. bekannt', vertraut'.

acquiesce, vb. ein•willigen, ruhig hin•nehmen*.

acquiescence, n. Einwilligung, -en f.

acquire, vb. erwer'ben*.

acquisition, n. Erwer'bung, -en f.

acquisitive, adj. gewinn'süchtig.

acquit, vb. frei•sprechen*.

acquittal, n. Freispruch, -̈e m.

acre, n. Morgen, - m.

acreage, n. Flächeninhalt nach Morgen; Land.

acrimonious, adj. scharf, bitter.

acrimony, n. Bitterkeit, -en f.

acrobat, n. Akrobat', -en, -en m.

across, 1. prep. über. 2. adv. hinü'ber, herü'ber.

act, 1. n. (deed) Tat, -en f.; (drama) Akt, -e m.; (law) Gesetz', -e nt. 2. vb. handeln; (stage) spielen; (behave) sich beneh'men*.

acting, 1. n. (stage) Schauspielkunst, -̈e f. 2. adj. stellvertretend.

action, n. Handlung, -en f.

activate, vb. aktive'ren.

activation, n. Aktivie'rung, -en f.

active, adj. tätig, aktiv'.

activity, n. Tätigkeit, -en f.

actor, n. Schauspieler, - m.

actress, n. Schauspielerin, -nen f.

actual, adj. tatsächlich.

actuality, n. Wirklichkeit, -en f.

actually, adv. wirklich.

actuary, n. Gerichts'schreiber, - m.; Versi'cherungsmathema'tiker, - m.

acumen, n. Scharfsinn m.

acupuncture, n. Akupunktur', -en f.

acute, adj. scharf, scharfsinnig, akut'; (angle) spitz.

acuteness, n. Schärfe, -n f., Scharfsinnigkeit f.

adage, n. Sprichwort, -̈er nt.

adamant, adj. hartnäckig.

adapt, vb. an•passen, anpassen*.

adaptability, n. Anpassungsfähigkeit, -en f.

adaptable, adj. anpassungsfähig.

adaptation, n. Anwendung, -en f., Bear'beitung, -en f.

adapter, n. Bear'beiter, - m.; Adap'ter, m.

add, vb. hinzu'•fügen, addie'ren.

adder, n. Natter, -n f.

addict, n. (drug a.) Rauschgift'-süchtig- m. & f.; (alcohol a.) Alkoholsüchtig- m. & f.

addicted, adj. süchtig.

addition, n. Zusatz, -̈e m.

additional, adj. zusätzlich.

address, 1. n. (on letters, etc.) Adres'se, -n f.; (speech) Ansprache, -n f. 2. vb. (a letter) adressie'ren; (a person) an•sprechen*.

addressee, n. Empfäng'er, - m., Empfäng'erin, -nen f.

adenoid, n. Nasenwucherung f.; (pl.) Poly'pen pl.

adept, adj. erfah'ren, geschickt'.

adequacy, n. Angemessenheit, -en f.

adequate, adj. angemessen.

adhere, vb. haften, fest•halten*.

adherence, n. Festhalten nt.

adherent, n. Anhänger, - m.

adhesive, 1. n. Klebemittel, - nt. 2. adj. anhaftend; (a. tape) Leukoplast' nt. nt.

adieu, *interj.* lebewohl'!, ade'!

adjacent, *adj.* angrenzend.

adjective, *n.* Eigenschaftswort, ÷er *nt.*, Adjektiv, -e *nt.*

adjoin, *vb.* an-grenzen.

adjourn, *vb.* verta'gen.

adjournment, *n.* Verta'gung, -en *f.*

adjunct, 1. *n.* Zusatz, ÷e *m.* 2. *adj.* zusätzlich.

adjust, *vb.* passend machen, berich'tigen, aus-gleichen*.

adjuster, *n.* Ausgleicher, - *m.*

adjustment, *n.* Ausgleichung, -en *f.*

adjutant, *n.* Adjutant', -en, -en *m.*

administer, *vb.* verwal'ten; erteil'en.

administration, *n.* Verwal'tung, -en *f.*

administrative, *adj.* Verwal'tungs- (*cpds.*).

administrator, *n.* Verwal'ter, - *m.*

admirable, *adj.* bewun'dernswert.

admiral, *n.* Admiral', -e *m.*

admiralty, *n.* Admiralität', -en *f.*

admiration, *n.* Bewun'derung *f.*

admire, *vb.* bewun'dern.

admirer, *n.* Vereh'rer, - *m.* Vereh'rerin, -nen *f.*

admissible, *adj.* zulässig.

admission, *n.* (*entrance*) Eintritt, -e *m.*; (*confession*) Geständnis, -se *nt.*

admit, *vb.* (*permit*) zu-lassen*; (*concede*) zu-gestehen*.

admittance, *n.* Zutritt, -e *m.*

admittedly, *adv.* zugegebenerma'ßen; allerdings'.

admixture, *n.* Beimischung, -en *f.*

admonish, *vb.* ermah'nen.

admonition, *n.* Ermah'nung, -en *f.*

adolescence, *n.* das heran'wachsende Alter, Jugendzeit, -en *f.*

adolescent, 1. *n.* der heran'wachsende Junge, das heran'wachsende Mädchen. 2. *adj.* jugendlich.

adopt, *vb.* adoptie'ren, an-nehmen*.

adoption, *n.* Adoption', -en *f.*

adorable, *adj.* reizend, entzück'end.

adoration, *n.* Vereh'rung *f.*, Anbetung *f.*

adore, *vb.* vereh'ren, an-beten.

adorn, *vb.* schmücken, zieren.

adornment, *n.* Verzie'rung, -en *f.*

adrift, *adj.* treibend, Wind und Wellen preisgegeben.

adroit, *adj.* geschickt'.

adulation, *n.* Schmeichelei', -en *f.*

adult, 1. *n.* Erwach'sen- *m.&f.* 2. *adj.* erwach'sen.

adulterate, *vb.* verfäl'schen.

adultery, *n.* Ehebruch, ÷e *m.*

advance, 1. *n.* Fortschritt, -e *m.*; (*mil.*) Vormarsch, ÷e *m.*; (*pay*) Vorschuß, ÷sse; (**in a.**) im voraus'. 2. *vb.* Fortschritte machen; (*mil.*) vor-rücken; (*pay*) voraus'-zahlen; (*promote*) beför'dern.

advanced, *adj.* fortgeschritten, modern'.

advancement, *n.* Förderung, -en *f.*; Beför'derung, -en *f.*

advantage, *n.* Vorteil, -e *m.*

advantageous, *adj.* vorteilhaft.

advent, *n.* Ankunft, ÷e *f.*; (*eccl.*) Advent' *m.*

adventure, *n.* Abenteuer, - *nt.*

adventurer, *n.* Abenteurer, - *m.*

adventurous, *adj.* abenteuerlich; unterneh'mungslustig.

adverb, *n.* Abverb', -en *nt.*, Umstandswort, ÷er *nt.*

adverbial, *adj.* adverbial'.

adversary, *n.* Gegner, - *m.* Gegnerin, -nen *f.*

adverse, *adj.* ungünstig, nachteilig.

adversity, *n.* Mißgeschick, -e *nt.*

advertise, *vb.* an-zeigen, annoncie'ren, Rekla'me machen.

advertisement, *n.* Annon'ce, -n *f.*, Inserat', -e *nt.*, Rekla'me, -n *f.*

advertiser, *n.* Inserent', -en, -en *m.*, Anzeiger, - *m.*

advertising, *n.* Rekla'me, -n *f.*

advice, *n.* Rat *m.*

advisability, *n.* Ratsamkeit *f.*

advisable, *adj.* ratsam.

advise, *vb.* raten*, bera'ten*.

advisedly, *adv.* absichtlich.

adviser, *n.* Bera'ter, - *m.* Bera'terin, -nen *f.*

advocacy, *n.* Befür'wortung *f.*

advocate, 1. *n.* Anwalt, ÷e *m.*, Anwältin, -nen *f.* 2. *vb.* vertei'digen, befür'worten.

aerate, *vb.* mit Luft vermen'gen.

aerial, 1. *n.* Anten'ne, -n *f.* 2. *adj.* Luft- (*cpds.*).

aeronautics, *n.* Aeronau'tik *f.*

aesthetic, *adj.* ästhe'tisch.

aesthetics, *n.* Ästhe'tik *f.*

afar, *adv.* von ferne.

affability, *n.* Freundlichkeit *f.*

affable, *adj.* freundlich.

affair, *n.* Angelegenheit, -en *f.;* Affä're, -n *f.*

affect, 1. *n.* Affekt', -e *m.* 2. *vb.* wirken auf.

affectation, *n.* Affektiert'heit, -en *f.*

affected, *adj.* betrof'fen; (*unnatural*) affektiert'; affig.

affection, *n.* Zuneigung, -en *f.*, Liebe, -n *f.*

affectionately, *adv.* (*letter*) mit herzlichen Grüßen.

affidavit, *n.* eidesstattliche Erklä'rung, -en *f.*

affiliate, *vb.* an'gliedern.

affiliation, *n.* Angliederung, -en *f.*

affinity, *n.* Verwandt'schaft, -en *f.*

affirm, *vb.* (*declare*) erklä'ren; (*confirm*) bestä'tigen; (*say yes to*) beja'hen.

affirmation, *n.* Bestä'tigung, -en *f.;* Beja'hung, -en *f.*

affirmative, *adj.* beja'hend.

affix, 1. *n.* (*gram.*) Affix, -e *nt.* 2. *vb.* an'heften; (*add on*) bei'fügen.

afflict, *vb.* plagen.

affliction, *n.* Plage, -n *f.*, Leid *nt.*

affluence, *n.* Reichtum, ̈-er *m.*

affluent, *adj.* reich.

afford, *vb.* gewäh'ren; (*have the means to*) sich leisten.

affront, 1. *n.* Belei'digung, -en *f.* 2. *vb.* belei'digen.

afield, *adv.* (*far a.*) weit entfernt'.

afire, *adv.* in Flammen.

afraid, *adj.* bange; (*be a. of*) sich fürchten vor.

Africa, *n.* Afrika, *nt.*

African, 1. *n.* Afrika'ner, - *m.*, Afrika'nerin, -nen *f.* 2. *adj.* afrika'nisch.

aft, *adv.* achtern.

after, 1. *prep.* nach, hinter. 2. *conj.* nachdem'.

aftermath, *n.* Nachernte, -n *f.*

afternoon, *n.* Nachmittag, -e *m.*

afterward(s), *adv.* hinterher', nachher, anschließend.

again, *adv.* wieder, noch einmal.

against, *prep.* gegen.

age, 1. *n.* Alter, - *nt.;* (*era*) Zeitalter, - *nt.* 2. *vb.* altern.

aged, *adj.* bejahrt'.

ageless, *adj.* zeitlos.

age limit, *n.* Altersgrenze *f.*

agency, *n.* Vertre'tung, -en *f.*, Agentur', -en *f.*

agenda, *n.* Tagesordnung, -en *f.*

agent, *n.* Vertre'ter, - *m.*, Vertre'terin, -nen *f.*

aggrandizement, *n.* Machterweiterung, -en *f.*

aggravate, *vb.* verschlim'mern, erschwe'ren.

aggravation, *n.* Verschlim'merung, -en *f.*

aggregate, 1. *n.* Aggregat', -e *nt.* 2. *adj.* Gesamt- (*cpds.*).

aggregation, *n.* Anhäufung, -en *f.*

aggression, *n.* Angriff, -e *m.*, Aggression', -en *f.*

aggressive, *adj.* aggresiv'.

aggressiveness, *n.* Angriffslust *f.*

aggressor, *n.* Angreifer, - *m.*

aghast, *adj.* entsetzt'.

agile, *adj.* flink, behen'd(e).

agility, *n.* Behen'digkeit *f.*

agitate, *vb.* bewe'gen, beun'ruhigen.

agitation, *n.* Bewe'gung, -en *f.*, Beun'ruhigung, -en *f.*

agitator, *n.* Hetzredner, -.

agnostic, 1. *n.* Agno'stiker, - *m.* 2. *adj.* agno'stisch.

ago, *adv.* vor.

agony, *n.* Qual, -en *f.*

agree, *vb.* überein'stimmen.

agreeable, *adj.* angenehm.

agreement, *n.* Überein'stimmung, -en *f.*

agricultural, *adj.* landwirtschaftlich.

agriculture, *n.* Landwirtschaft *f.*

ahead, *adv.* voraus'; (*straight a.*) gera'de aus.

aid, n. Hilfe, -n f.; Hilfsmittel, nt. **2.** vb. helfen*.

aide, n. Adjutant', -en, -en m.

AIDS, n. Aids (no article).

ail, vb. kranken.

ailment, n. Krankheit, -en f.

aim, 1. n. (goal) Ziel, -e nt.; (purpose) Zweck, -e m. **2.** vb. zielen.

aimless, adj. ziellos.

air, 1. n. Luft, ⸗e f. **2.** vb. lüften.

airbag, n. (automobile) Luftsack, ⸗e m.

air base, n. Luftstützpunkt, -e m.

airborne, adj. in der Luft; (a. troops) Luftlandetruppen pl.

air-condition, vb. klimatisie'ren, mit Klima-Anlage verse'hen*.

air-conditioned, adj. klimatisiert', mit Klima-Anlage verse'hen.

air-conditioning, n. Klima-Anlage, -n f.

aircraft, n. Flugzeug, -e nt.

aircraft carrier, n. Flugzeugträger, -, m., Flugzeugmut'terschiff, -e nt.

air line, n. Luftlinie, -n f.

air liner, n. Verkehrs'flugzeug, -e nt.

airmail, n. Luftpost f.

airplane, n. Flugzeug, -e nt.

air pollution, n. Luftverpestung f., Luftverschmutzung f.

airport, n. Flughafen, ⸗ m.

air pressure, n. Luftdruck, -e m.

air raid, n. Luftangriff, -e m.

airsick, adj. luftkrank (-).

airtight, adj. luftdicht.

airy, adj. luftig.

aisle, n. Gang, ⸗e m.; (church) Chorgang, ⸗e m.

ajar, adj. angelehnt, halb offen.

akin, adj. verwandt'.

alarm, 1. n. Alarm', -e m. **2.** vb. alarmie'ren, beun'ruhigen.

albino, n. Albi'no, -s m.

album, n. Album, -ben nt.

albumen, n. Eiweißstoff, -e m., Albu'men nt.

alcohol, n. Alkohol, -e m.

alcoholic, 1. n. Alkoho'liker, - m. **2.** adj. alkoho'lisch.

alcove, n. Alko'ven, - m.

ale, n. englisches Bier, Ale nt.

alert, 1. n. Alarm', -e m., Vorwar-

nung, -en f. **2.** adj. aufmerksam. **3.** vb. alarmie'ren.

alfalfa, n. Alfal'fa nt.

algebra, n. Algebra f.

algebraic, adj. algebra'isch.

alias, adv. alias.

alibi, n. Alibi, -s nt.

alien, 1. n. Ausländer, - m., Ausländerin, -nen f. **2.** adj. fremd, ausländisch.

alienate, vb. entfrem'den.

alight, vb. sich nieder-lassen*; (dismount) ab'steigen*.

align, vb. aus'richten; (ally) zusam'men-tun*.

alike, adj. gleich.

alive, adj. leben'dig; (be a.) leben.

alkali, n. Alka'li nt.

alkaline, adj. alka'lisch.

all, adj. aller, -es, -e; (above a.) vor allem; (a. at once) auf einmal; (a. the same) gleich; (a. of you) Sie alle; (not at a.) gar nicht.

allay, vb. beru'higen, stillen.

allegation, n. Behaup'tung, -en f.

allege, vb. an'führen, behaup'ten.

allegiance, n. Treue f., Gehor'sam m.

allegory, n. Allegorie', -i'en f.; Sinnbild, -er nt.

allergy, n. Allergie', -i'en f.

alleviate, vb. erleich'tern, lindern.

alley, n. Gasse, -n f.; Durchgang, ⸗e m.; (blind a.) Sackgasse, -n f.

alliance, n. Bündnis, -se nt.; Allianz', -en f.

allied, adj. verbün'det; (related) verwandt'.

alligator, n. Alliga'tor, -to'ren m.

allocate, vb. zu'teilen.

allot, vb. zu'weisen*; zu'teilen.

allotment, n. Zuweisung, -en f.

allow, vb. erlau'ben, gestat'ten.

allowance, n. (money) Taschengeld, -er nt.; (permission) Erlaub'nis, -se f.; (make a.s for) Rücksicht nehmen-auf*.

alloy, 1. n. Legie'rung, -en f. **2.** vb. legie'ren.

all right, interj. gut, schön, in Ordnung.

allude, vb. hin-weisen*, an'spielen.

allure, 1. n. Charme m. **2.** vb. verlock'en.

allusion, n. Anspielung, -en f.

ally, 1. *n.* Verbün'det- *m.&f.*, Alli-iert'- *m. & f. 2.* *vb.* verbün'den.

almanac, *n.* Almanach, -e *m.*

almighty, *adj.* allmäch'tig.

almond, *n.* Mandel, -n *f.*

almost, *adv.* beinahe, fast.

alms, *n.* Almosen, - *nt.*

aloft, 1. *adv.* hochoben; empor'.

alone, 1. *adj.* allein'; **(leave a.)** in Ruhe lassen*.

along, 1. *adv.* entlang'; **(come a.)** mit-kommen*. **2.** *prep.* entlang', längs.

alongside, *prep.* neben.

aloof, 1. *adj.* gleichgültig. **2.** *adv.* abseits.

aloud, *adv.* laut.

alpaca, *n.* Alpa'ka, -s *nt.*

alphabet, *n.* Alphabet', -e *nt.*

alphabetical, *adj.* alphabe'tisch.

alphabetize, *vb.* alphabetisie'ren.

Alps, *n.pl.* Alpen *pl.*

already, *adv.* schon.

also, *adv.* auch.

altar, *n.* Altar', -e *m.*

alter, *vb.* ändern.

alteration, *n.* Änderung, -en *f.*

alternate, 1. *n.* Stellvertreter, - *m.*, Stellvertreterin, -nen *f.* **2.** *adj.* alternativ'. **3.** *vb.* ab-wechseln.

alternating current, *n.* Wechsel-strom, -e *m.*

alternative, 1. *n.* Alternati've, -n *f.* **2.** *adj.* alternativ'.

although, *conj.* obwohl', obgleich'.

altitude, *n.* Höhe, -n *f.*

alto, *n.* Altstimme, -n *f.*

altogether, *adv.* völlig, ganz und gar; alles in allem.

altruism, *n.* Altruis'mus *m.*

alum, *n.* Alaun', -e *f.*

aluminum, *n.* Alumi'nium *nt.*

always, *adv.* immer.

amalgamate, *vb.* amalgamie'ren.

amass, *vb.* an-sammeln.

amateur, *n.* Amateur', -e *m.*

amaze, *vb.* erstau'nen.

amazement, *n.* Erstau'nen *nt.*

amazing, *adj.* erstaun'lich.

ambassador, *n.* Botschafter, - *m.*, Botschafterin, -nen *f.*, Gesandt'- *m.&f.*

amber, *n.* Bernstein, -e *m.*

ambiguity, *n.* Zweideutigkeit, -en *f.*

ambiguous, *adj.* zweideutig.

ambition, *n.* Ehrgeiz *m.*, Ambition', -en *f.*

ambitious, *adj.* ehrgeizig.

ambulance, *n.* Krankenwagen, - *m.*, Krankenauto, -s *nt.*, Rettungswagen, - *m.*

ambush, 1. *n.* Hinterhalt *m.* **2.** *vb.* aus dem Hinterhalt überfallen*.

ameliorate, *vb.* verbes'sern.

amenable, *adj.* zugänglich.

amend, *vb.* verbes'sern, ergän'zen.

amendment, *n.* Gesetz'abän-derung, -en *f.*, Verfas'sungs-zusatz, -e *m.*

amenity, *n.* Annehmlichkeit, -en *f.*

America, *n.* Ame'rika *nt.*

American, 1. *n.* Amerika'ner, - *m.*, Amerika'nerin, -nen *f.* **2.** *adj.* amerika'nisch.

amethyst, *n.* Amethyst', -e *m.*

amiable, *adj.* liebenswürdig.

amicable, *adj.* freundschaftlich.

amid, *prep.* inmit'ten.

amidships, *adv.* mittschiffs.

amiss, *adj.* los, schief; **(take a.)** übel-nehmen*.

amity, *n.* Freundschaft, -en *f.*

ammonia, *n.* Ammoniak *nt.*; **(household a.)** Salmiak'geist *m.*

ammunition, *n.* Munition', -en *f.*

amnesia, *n.* Amnesie' *f.*

amnesty, *n.* Amnestie', -i'en *f.*

amniocentesis, *n.* Amniokente'se *f.*

amoeba, *n.* Amö'be, -n *f.*

among, *prep.* unter, zwischen, bei.

amorous, *adj.* verliebt'.

amortize, *vb.* tilgen, amortisie'ren.

amount, 1. *n.* (*sum*) Betrag', -e *m.*; **(large a.)** Menge, -n *f.* **2.** *vb.* **(a. to)** betra'gen*.

ampere, *n.* Ampere, - (*pron.* Ampär') *nt.*

amphibian, 1. *n.* Amphi'bie, -n *f.* **2.** *adj.* amphi'bisch.

amphibious, *adj.* amphi'bisch.

amphitheater, *n.* Amphi'theater, - *nt.*

ample, *adj.* reichlich.

amplify, vb. (enlarge) erwei'tern; (make louder) verstär'ken; (state more fully) ausführ'licher darstellen.

amputate, vb. amputie'ren.

amuse, vb. belus'tigen, amü-sie'ren.

amusement, n. Unterhal'tung, -en f.; Belus'tigung, -en f.

amusement park, n. Rummel-platz, *m*.

an, art. ein, -, -e.

anachronism, n. Anachronis'mus, -men *m*.

analogical, adj. analo'gisch.

analogous, adj. analog'.

analogy, n. Analogie', -i'en f.

analysis, n. Analy'se, -n f.

analyst, n. Analy'tiker, - *m*.

analytic, adj. analy'tisch.

analyze, vb. analysie'ren.

anarchy, n. Anarchie' -i'en f.

anatomy, n. Anatomie', -i'en f.

ancestor, n. Vorfahr, -en, -en, *m*., Vorfahrin, -nen f.

ancestral, adj. Stamm- (cpds.).

ancestry, n. Abstammung, -en f.

anchor, 1. n. Anker, - *m*. 2. vb. veran'kern.

anchovy, n. Sardel'le, -n f.

ancient, adj. alt, uralt.

and, conj. und.

anecdote, n. Anekdo'te, -n f.

anemia, n. Blutarmut f.

anemic, adj. blutarm.

anesthesia, n. Anästhesie' f.

anesthetic, 1. n. Narko'se -n f., Betäu'bungsmittel, - nt. 2. adj. betäu'bend, narko'tisch.

anew, adv. aufs neue, von neuem.

angel, n. Engel, - *m*.

anger, n. Zorn *m*., Ärger *m*.

angle, 1. n. (geom.) Winkel, - *m*.; (point of view) Gesichtspunkt, -e *m*. 2. vb. (fish) angeln.

angry, adj. böse, ärgerlich; (be a.) sich ärgern.

anguish, n. Qual, -en f.

angular, adj. eckig.

animal, 1. n. Tier, -e nt. 2. adj. tier-isch.

animate, vb. bele'ben.

animated, adj. lebhaft.

animated cartoon, n. Zeichen-trickfilm, -e *m*.

animation, n. Lebhaftigkeit, -en f.

animosity, n. Erbit'terung, -en f.

ankle, n. Fessel, -n f.; Fessel-gelenk, -e nt.

annals, n.pl. Anna'len pl.

annex, 1. n. Anhang, -̈e *m*.; (building) Nebengebäude, - nt. 2. vb. annektie'ren.

annexation, n. Annektie'rung, -en f.

annihilate, vb. vernich'ten.

anniversary, n. Jahrestag, -e *m*.

annotate, vb. mit Anmerkungen verse'hen*, annotie'ren.

announce, vb. an-kündigen, bekannt'-geben*.

announcement, n. Bekannt'ma-chung, -en f.

announcer, n. Ansager, - *m*. An-sagerin, -nen f.

annoy, vb. beläs'tigen, ärgern.

annoyance, n. Ärger *m*.; Beläs'-tigung, -en f.

annual, 1. n. Jahrbuch, -̈er nt. 2. adj. jährlich.

annuity, n. jährliche Rente, -n f.

annul, vb. annullie'ren.

anoint, vb. salben.

anomaly, n. Anomalie', -i'en f.

anonymous, adj. anonym'.

another, adj. (different) ein ander-; (additional) noch ein; (one a.) sich einan'der.

answer, 1. n. Antwort, -en f. 2. vb. antworten, beant'worten.

answerable, adj. beant'wortbar; verant'wortlich.

answering machine, n. Anruf-beantworter *m*.

ant, n. Ameise, -n f.

antagonism, n. Widerstreit, -e *m*.

antagonist, n. Widersacher, - *m*., Gegner, - *m*.

antagonistic, adj. wider-strei'tend.

antagonize, vb. vor den Kopf stoßen*.

antarctic, 1. n. Antark'tis, f. 2. adj. antark'tisch.

antecedent, 1. n. (gram.) Bezie'-hungswort, -̈er nt. 2. adj. vorher'-gehend.

antelope, n. Antilo'pe, -n f.

antenna, n. (radio) Anten'ne, -n f.; (insect) Fühler, - *m*.

anterior, *adj.* vorder-.

anteroom, *n.* Vorzimmer, - *nt.*

anthem, Hymne, -n *f.;* **(national a.)** National'hymne, -n *f.*

anthology, *n.* Anthologie', -i'en *f.*

anthracite, *n.* Anthrazit' *nt.*

anthropologist, *n.* Anthropolo'ge, -n, -n *m.*

anthropology, *n.* Anthropologie', -i'en *f.*

antiaircraft, *adj.* Flak (*cpds.*).

antibody, *n.* Antikörper, - *m.*

antic, *n.* Posse, -n *f.;* Mätzchen, - *nt.*

anticipate, *vb.* vorweg'nehmen*; erwar'ten.

anticipation, *n.* Erwar'tung, -en *f.*

anticlimax, *n.* enttäu'schende Wendung, -en *f.*

antidote, *n.* Gegengift, -e *nt.*

antinuclear, *adj.* antinuklear'.

antiquated, *adj.* veral'tet.

antique, *adj.* antik'.

antiques, *n.* Antiquitäten *pl.*

antiquity, *n.* Anti'ke *f.;* Altertum, ⁼er *nt.*

anti-Semitism, *n.* Antisemitis'mus *m.*

antiseptic, 1. *n.* antisep'tisches Mittel *nt.* **2.** *adj.* antisep'tisch.

antisocial, *adj.* antisozial'.

antitoxin, *n.* Gegengift, -e *nt.*

antlers, *n.pl.* Geweih', -e *nt.*

anvil, *n.* Amboß, -sse *m.*

anxiety, *n.* Angst, ⁼e *f.;* Besorg'nis, -se *f.*

anxious, *adj.* besorgt'; ängstlich.

any, *adj.* irgendein, -, -e; irgendwelcher, -es, -e; jeder, -es, -e; **(not a.)** kein, -, -e.

anybody, *pron.* jemand, irgendjemand; **(not . . . a.)** niemand.

anyhow, *adv.* sowieso'.

anyone, *pron.* jemand, irgendjemand; **(not . . . a.)** niemand.

anything, *pron.* etwas, irgendetwas; **(not . . . a.)** nichts.

anyway, *adv.* sowieso'.

anywhere, *adv* (*location*) irgendwo; (*direction*) irgendwohin'.

apart, *adv.* abseits, beisei'te; **(a. from)** abgesehen von; **(take a.)** auseinan'der-nehmen*.

apartheid, *n.* Apart'heid *f.*

apartment, *n.* Mietswohnung, -en *f.*

ape, 1. *n.* Affe, -n, -n *m.* **2.** *vb.* nach-affen.

aperture, *n.* Öffnung, -en *f.*

apex, *n.* Gipfel, - *m.*

aphorism, *n.* Aphoris'mus, -men *m.*

apiece, *adv.* **(ten dollars a.)** je zehn Dollar.

apologetic, *adj.* entschul'digend.

apologize, *vb.* sich entschul'digen.

apology, *n.* Entschul'digung, -en *f.*

apoplexy, *n.* Schlaganfall, ⁼e *m.*

apostle, *n.* Apos'tel, - *m.*

apostrophe, *n.* Apostroph *m.*

appall, *vb.* entset'zen.

apparatus, *n.* Apparat', -e *m.;* Ausrüstung, -en *f.*

apparel, *n.* Kleidung, -en *f.*

apparent, *adj.* (*visible*) sichtbar; (*clear*) klar; (*obvious*) offensichtlich; (*probable*) scheinbar.

apparition, *n.* Erschei'nung, -en *f.;* Gespenst', -er, -er *nt.*

appeal, 1. *n.* (*request*) Bitte, -n *f.;* (*charm*) Reiz, -e *m.;* (*law*) Beru'fung, -en *f.* **2.** *vb.* (*law*) Beru'fung ein-legen, appellie'ren; **(a. to, turn to)** sich wenden* an; **(a. to, please)** gefal'len*.

appear, *vb.* (*seem*) scheinen*; (*come into view*) erschei'nen*.

appearance, *n.* Erschei'nung, -en *f.,* Anschein, -e *m.*

appease, *vb.* beschwich'tigen.

appeasement, *n.* Beschwich'tigung, -en *f.*

appendage, *n.* Anhang, ⁼e *m.*

appendectomy, *n.* Blinddarmoperation -en *f.*

appendicitis, *n.* Blinddarmentzündung, -en *f.*

appendix, *n.* Anhang, ⁼e *m.;* (*med.*) Blinddarm, ⁼e *m.*

appetite, *n.* Appetit' *m.*

appetizer, *n.* Vorgericht, -e *nt.*

appetizing, *adj.* appetit'lich; lecker.

applaud, *vb.* applaudie'ren, Beifall klatschen.

applause, *n.* Beifall, ⁼e *m.*

apple, n. Apfel, ⁻ m.
applesauce, n. Apfelmus nt.
appliance, n. Gerät', -e nt.
applicable, adj. anwendbar.
applicant, n. Bewer'ber, - m., Bewer'berin, -nen f.
application, n. (request) Bewer'bung, -en f.; (use) Anwendung, -en f.
appliqué, adj. (a. work) Applikations'stickerei, -en f.
apply, vb. (make use of) an·wen'den*; (request) sich bewer'ben*.
appoint, vb. ernen'nen*.
appointment, n. (to a position) Ernen'nung, -en f.; (doctor's) Anmeldung, -en f.; (date) Verab'redung, -en f.
apportion, vb. proportional'vertei'len; zu·teilen.
appraisal, n. Abschätzung, -en f.
appraise, vb. ab·schätzen.
appreciable, adj. beträcht'lich.
appreciate, vb. schätzen; an·er·kennen*.
appreciation, n. Anerkennung, -en f.
apprehend, vb. (grasp) erfas'sen; (arrest) verhaf'ten; (fear) be·fürch'ten.
apprehension, n. (worry) Besorg'nis, -se f.; (arrest) Verhaf'tung, -en f.
apprehensive, adj. besorgt'.
apprentice, n. Lehrling, -e m.
apprise, vb. benach'richtigen.
approach, 1. n. (nearing) Annäherung, -en f.; (access) Zugang, ⁻e m.; (military) Anmarsch m. 2. vb. (come nearer) sich nähern; (turn to) sich wenden* an.
approachable, adj. zugänglich.
approbation, n. Geneh'migung, -en f.
appropriate, 1. adj. angemessen, passend. 2. vb. (seize) sich an·eignen; (vote funds) bewilligen.
appropriation, n. (seizure) Aneignung, -en f.; (approval) Bewil'ligung, -en f.
approval, n. Zustimmung, -en f., Einwilligung, -en f.
approve, vb. zu·stimmen, geneh'migen.

approximate, 1. vb. sich nähern. 2. adj. annähernd.
approximately, adv. ungefähr, etwa.
approximation, n. Annäherung, -en f.
apricot, n. Apriko'se, -n f.
April, n. April' m.
apron, n. Schürze, -n f.
apropos, 1. adj. treffend. 2. prep. hinsichtlich.
apt, adj. (fitting) passend; (likely) geneigt'; (able) fähig.
aptitude, n. Fähigkeit, -en f.
aquarium, n. Aqua'rium, -ien nt.
aquatic, adj. Wasser- (cpds.).
aqueduct, n. Wasserleitung, -en f.
Arab, 1. n. Araber, - m.; Araberin, -nen f. 2. adj. ara'bisch.
Arabian, adj. ara'bisch.
Arabic, adj. ara'bisch.
arable, adj. bestell'bar.
arbiter, n. Schlichter, - m.
arbitrary, adj. willkürlich.
arbitrate, vb. schlichten.
arbitration, n. Schlichtung, -en f.
arbitrator, n. Schlichter, - m.
arbor, n. Laube, -n f.
arc, n. Bogen, -(⁻) m.
arcade, n. Arka'de, -n f.
arch, n. Bogen, -(⁻) m.; (instep) Spann, -e m.
archaeology, n. Altertumskunde f., Archäologie' f.
archaic, adj. archa'isch, altertümlich.
archbishop, n. Erzbischof, ⁻e m.
archdiocese, n. Erzdiözese, -n f.
archduke, n. Erzherzog, ⁻e m.
archer, n. Bogenschütze, -n, -n m.
archery, n. Bogenschießen nt.
architect, n. Architekt', -en, -en m., Architek'tin, -nen f.
architectural, adj. architekto'nisch.
architecture, n. Architektur', -en f.
archives, n. Archiv', e nt.
archway, n. Torbogen, ⁻m.
arctic, 1. n. Arktis f. 2. adj. arktisch.
ardent, adj. eifrig, inbrünstig.
ardor, n. Eifer m., Inbrunst f.
arduous, adj. mühsam.

area, n. Fläche, -n f., Gebiet, -e nt.

area code, n. (phone) Vorwahlnummer, -n f.

arena, n. Are'na, -nen f.

Argentina, n. Argenti'nien nt.

argue, vb. argumentie'ren; (quarrel) sich streiten*.

argument, n. Argument', -e nt.

argumentative, adj. streitsüchtig.

aria, n. Arie, -n f.

arid, adj. dürr, trocken.

arise, vb. auf•stehen*, sich erhe'ben*; (come into being) entste'hen*.

aristocracy, n. Aristokratie', -i'en f.

aristocrat, n. Aristokrat', -en, -en m., Aristokra'tin, -nen f.

aristocratic, adj. aristokra'tisch.

arithmetic, n. Rechnen nt., Arithmetik' f.

ark, n. Arche, -n f.; (Noah's a.) Arche Noah.

arm, 1. n. Arm, -e m.; (weapon) Waffe, -n f. 2. v. bewaff'nen, rüsten.

armament, n. Bewaff'nung, -en f.; (weapons) Waffen pl.

armchair, n. Lehnstuhl, ⸚e m.

armful, n. Menge, -n f.

armhole, n. Armloch, ⸚er nt.

armistice, n. Waffenstill'stand m.

armor, Rüstung, -en f., Panzer, - m.

armored, adj. gepan'zert; Panzer- (cpds.)

armory, n. Exerzier'halle, -n f.; Waffenfabrik, -en f.

armpit, n. Achselhöhle, -n f.

arms, n.pl. Waffen pl.

army, n. Heer, -e nt., Armee', -me'en f.

aroma, n. Aro'ma, -s nt.

aromatic, adj. würzig.

around, 1. adv. herum'; (approximately) etwa, ungefähr. 2. prep. um.

arouse, vb. (excite) erre'gen; (waken) wecken.

arraign, vb. richterlich vor•führen.

arrange, vb. arrangie'ren, ab•sprechen*, ein•richten; (agree) verein'baren.

arrangement, n. Anordnung, -en f.

array, 1. n. Anordnung, -en f.; (fig.) Menge, -n f. 2. vb. ordnen.

arrears, n.pl. Schulden pl.; (in a.) in Rückstand.

arrest, 1. n. (law) Verhaf'tung, -en f. 2. vb. (law) verhaf'ten; (stop) an•halten*.

arrival, n. Ankunft, ⸚e f.

arrive, vb. an•kommen*.

arrogance, n. Anmaßung, -en f., Arroganz, -en f.

arrogant, adj. anmaßend, arrogant'.

arrow, n. Pfeil, -e m.

arsenal, n. Waffenlager, - nt.

arsenic, n. Arsen' nt.

arson, n. Brandstiftung, -en f.

art, n. Kunst, ⸚e f.

arterial, adj. Arte'rien- (cpds.); (a. highway) Hauptverkehrs'straße, -n f.

arteriosclerosis, n. Arte'rienverkalkung, -en f.

artful, adj. kunstvoll; (sly) schlau.

arthritis, n. Arthri'tis f.

artichoke, n. Artischock'e, -n f.

article, n. Arti'kel, - m.

articulate, 1. vb. (utter) artikulie'ren; (join) zusam'men•fügen. 2. adj. deutlich.

articulation, n. Artikulie'rung, -en f.

artifice, n. List, -en f.

artificial, adj. künstlich.

artificiality, n. Künstlichkeit, -en f.

artillery, n. Artillerie', -i'en f.

artisan, n. Handwerker, - m., Handwerkerin, -nen f.

artist, n. Künstler, - m., Künstlerin, -nen f.

artistic, adj. künstlerisch.

artistry, n. Künstlertum nt.

artless, adj. kunstlos.

as, conj.&adv. (when) wie, als; (because) da; (a. if) als ob; (with X a. Hamlet) mit X als Hamlet; (a. big a.) so groß wie; (just a. big a.) ebenso groß wie; (he a. well a. I) er sowohl wie ich.

asbestos, n. Asbest', -e m.

ascend, vb. (intr.) steigen*; (tr.) bestei'gen*.

ascent, n. Aufstieg, -e m.

ascertain, vb. fest·stellen.

ascetic, 1. n. Asket', -en, -en m. **2.** adj. aske'tisch.

ascribe, vb. zu·schreiben*.

ash, n. Asche, -n f.; (tree) Esche, -n f.

ashamed, adj. beschämt' (be a.) sich schämen.

ashen, adj. aschgrau.

ashes, n.pl. Asche f.

ashore, adv. an Land.

ashtray, n. Aschenbecher, - m., Aschbecher, - m.

Asia, n. Asien n.

Asian, 1. n. Asiat', -en, -en m., Asia'tin, -nen f. **2.** adj. asia'tisch.

aside, adv. beisei'te; (a. from) außer.

ask, vb. (question) fragen; (request) bitten*; (demand) verlangen.

asleep, adj. schlafend; (be a.) schlafen*.

asparagus, n. Spargel, - m.

aspect, n. Anblick, -e m.; (fig.) Gesichts'punkt, -e m.

aspersion, n. Verleum'dung, -en f.

asphalt, n. Asphalt', -e m.

asphyxiate, vb. ersticken.

aspirant, Anwärter, - m.

aspirate, 1. n. Hauchlaut, -e m. **2.** adj. aspiriert'. **3.** vb. aspirie'ren.

aspiration, n. Aspiration', -en f., Bestre'bung, -en f.

aspire, vb. streben.

aspirin, n. Aspirin' nt.

ass, n. Esel, - m.

assail, vb. an·greifen*.

assailable, adj. angreifbar.

assailant, n. Angreifer, - m., Angreiferin, -nen f.

assassin, n. Attentä'ter, - m., Attentä'terin, -nen f. Mörder, - m., Mörderin, -nen f.

assassinate, vb. ermor'den.

assassination, n. Ermor'dung, -en f., Attentat', -e nt.

assault, 1. n. Angriff, -e m.; (law) tätliche Belei'digung, -en f. **2.** vb. an·greifen*.

assay, 1. n. Probe, -n f. **2.** vb. prüfen.

assemblage, n. Versamm'lung, -en f.

assemble, vb. versam'meln; (tech.) montie'ren.

assembly, n. Versamm'lung, -en f.; (tech.) Monta'ge, -n f.

assent, 1. n. Zustimmung, -en f. **2.** vb. zu·stimmen.

assert, vb. behaup'ten.

assertion, n. Behaup'tung, -en f.

assertive, adj. bestimmt'.

assess, vb. ein·schätzen.

assessor, n. Steuerabschätzer, - m.

asset, n. Vorzug, -̈e m.; (comm.) Guthaben, -nt.

asseverate, vb. beteu'ern.

assiduous, adj. emsig.

assign, vb. zu·teilen, zu·weisen*; (homework) auf·geben*.

assignable, adj. bestimm'bar.

assignation, n. Anweisung, -en f.; (tryst) Stelldichein, - nt.

assignment, n. Anweisung, -en f.; (homework) Aufgabe, -n f.

assimilate, vb. an·gleichen*, assimilie'ren.

assimilation, n. Angleichung, -en f., Assimilie'rung, -en f.

assimilative, adj. angleichend.

assist, vb. unterstüt'zen, helfen*.

assistance, n. Unterstüt'zung, -en f., Hilfe, -n f.

assistant, 1. n. Gehil'fe, -n, -n m., Gehil'fin, -nen f. Assistent', -en, -en m., Assisten'tin, -nen f. **2.** adj. Hilfs- (cpds.) stellvertretend.

associate, 1. n. Partner, - m., Partnerin, -nen f. **2.** vb. verkeh'ren, assozie'ren.

association, n. Verbin'dung, -en f., Verei'nigung, -en f.

assonance, n. Assonanz', -en f.

assort, vb. sortie'ren.

assorted, adj. verschie'den.

assortment, n. Auswahl, -en f.

assuage, vb. beschwich'tigen.

assume, vb. an·nehmen*; (arrogate) sich an·maßen.

assuming, adj. anmaßend; (a. that) angenommen, daß.

assumption, n. Annahme, -n f.; (eccles.) Himmelfahrt f.

assurance, *n.* Versi'cherung, -en *f.,* Zusicherung, -en *f.*

assure, *vb.* versi'chern, zu-sichern.

assured, *adj.* sicher, zuversichtlich.

aster, *n.* Aster, -n *f.*

asterisk, *n.* Sternchen, - *nt.*

asthma, *n.* Asthma *nt.*

astigmatism, *n.* Astigmatis'mus, -men *nt.*

astonish, *vb.* erstau'nen; **(be astonished)** staunen.

astonishment, *n.* Erstau'nen, - *nt.*

astound, *vb.* erstau'nen.

astray, *adj.* irre; **(go a.)** sich verir'ren, auf Abwege gera'ten*.

astringent, *adj.* gefäß'spannend, hautstraffend, adstringie'rend.

astrology, *n.* Astrologie', -i'en *f.*

astronaut, *n.* Astronaut', -en *m.,* Astronau'tin, -nen *f.*

astronomy, *n.* Astronomie', -i'en *f.*

astute, *adj.* scharf (-), schlau.

asylum, *n.* *(refuge)* Asyl', -e *nt.;* *(institution)* Anstalt, -en *f.*

at, *prep.* an; **(at home)** zu Hause.

atheist, *n.* Atheist', -en, -en *m.,* Atheis'tin, -nen *f.*

athlete, *n.* Athlet', -en, -en *m.,* Sportler, - *m.,* Sportlerin, -nen *f.*

athletic, *adj.* athle'tisch, sportlich.

athletics, *n.* Sport, -e *m.*

Atlantic, 1. *n.* Atlan'tik *m.* 2. *adj.* atlan'tisch.

Atlantic Ocean, *n.* Atlan'tik *m.*

atlas, *n.* Atlas, -lan'ten *m.*

atmosphere, *n.* Atmosphä're, -n *f.*

atmospheric, *adj.* atmosphä'risch.

atoll, *n.* Atoll', -e *nt.*

atom, *n.* Atom', -e *nt.*

atomic, *adj.* atomar'; Atom'- *(cpds.)*.

atomize, *vb.* atomisie'ren.

atone, *vb.* büßen, sühnen.

atonement, *n.* Buße, -n *f.,* Sühne, -n *f.*

atrocious, *adj.* entsetz'lich, grausam.

atrocity, *n.* Grausamkeit, -en *f.*

atrophy, *n.* Atrophie', -i'en *f.*

attach, *vb.* an-heften, beifügen; *(attribute)* bei-messen*.

attaché, *n.* Attaché, -s *m.*

attachment, *n.* Beifügung, -en *f.;* *(device)* Vorrichtung, -en *f.,* Zubehör *nt.;* *(liking)* Zuneigung, -en *f.*

attack, 1. *n.* Angriff, -e *m.* 2. *vb.* an-greifen*.

attain, *vb.* errei'chen.

attainable, *adj.* erreich'bar.

attainment, *n.* Errun'genschaft, -en *f.*

attempt, 1. *n.* Versuch', -e *m.* 2. *vb.* versu'chen.

attend, *vb.* *(meeting)* bei-wohnen; *(lecture)* besu'chen, hören; *(patient)* behan'deln; *(person)* beglei'ten.

attendance, *n.* Anwesenheit, -en *f.,* Besuch', -e *m.*

attendant, 1. *n.* Beglei'ter, - *m.* 2. *adj.* beglei'tend, anwesend.

attention, *n.* Aufmerksamkeit, -en *f.;* **(a.!)** Achtung!; **(pay a.)** auf-passen.

attentive, *adj.* aufmerksam.

attenuate, *vb.* verdün'nen, vermin'dern; *(jur.)* mildern.

attest, *vb.* bezeu'gen.

attic, *n.* Dachboden, -̈ *m.,* Boden, -̈ *m.*

attire, 1. *n.* Kleidung, -en *f.* 2. *vb.* kleiden.

attitude, *n.* *n.* Haltung, -en *f.*

attorney, *n.* Anwalt, -̈e *m.,* Anwältin, -nen *f.*

attract, *vb.* an-ziehen*.

attraction, *n.* Anziehungskraft, -̈e *f.*

attractive, *adj.* anziehend.

attribute, 1. *n.* Eigenschaft, -en *f.* 2. *vb.* zu-schreiben*.

attribution, *n.* Beimessung, -en *f.*

auction, *n.* Verstei'gerung, -en *f.*

auctioneer, *n.* Verstei'gerer, - *m.,* Auktiona'tor, -to'ren *m.*

audacious, *adj.* kühn.

audacity, *n.* Kühnheit, -en *f.*

audible, *adj.* hörbar.

audience, *n.* Zuhörerschaft, -en *f.,* Publikum, -ka *nt.;* *(of a king)* Audienz', -en *f.*

audiovisual, *adj.* audiovisuell'.

audit, 1. n. Rechnungsprüfung, -en f. **2.** vb. prüfen.
audition, n. Vorführungsprobe, -n f.
auditor, n. Hörer, - m; (comm.) Rechnungsprüfer, - m.
auditorium, n. Zuhörerraum, ⸗e m., Auditorium, -rien nt.
augment, vb. vermeh'ren.
augur, 1. n. Augur', -en, -en m. **2.** vb. weissagen.
August, n. August' m.
aunt, n. Tante, -n f.
auspices, n.pl. Auspi'zien.
auspicious, adj. günstig.
austere, adj. streng.
austerity, n. Enthalt'samkeit, -en f.
Australia, n. Austra'lien nt.
Australian, 1. n. Austra'lier, - m., Austra'lierin, -nen f.
Austria, n. Österreich nt.
Austrian, 1. n. Österreicher, - m., Österreicherin, -nen f. **2.** adj. österreichisch.
authentic, adj. authen'tisch.
authenticate, vb. beglau'bigen.
authenticity, n. Echtheit, -en f.
author, n. Verfas'ser - m., Verfas'serin, -nen f.
authoritarian, adj. autoritär'.
authoritative, adj. maßgebend.
authority, n. Autorität', -en f.
authorization, n. Vollmacht, ⸗e f.
authorize, vb. bevoll'mächtigen.
auto, n. Auto, -s nt.
autobiography, n. Autobiographie', -i'en f.
autocracy, n. Autokratie', -i'en f.
autocrat, n. Autokrat', -en, -en m.
autograph, n. Autogramm', -e nt.
automatic, adj. automa'tisch.
automation, n. Automation' f.
automaton, n. Automat', -en, -en m.
automobile, n. Kraftwagen, - m.
automotive, adj. Auto (cpds.).
autonomous, adj. autonom'.
autonomy, n. Autonomie', -i'en f.

autopsy, n. Leichenöffnung, -en f.
autumn, n. Herbst, -e m.
auxiliary, adj. Hilfs- (cpds.).
avail, 1. n. Nutzen m. **2.** vb. nützen; (a. oneself of) benut'zen.
available, adj. vorhan'den.
avalanche, n. Lawi'ne, -n f.
avarice, n. Geiz, -e m.
avaricious, adj. geizig.
avenge, vb. rächen.
avenue, n. Allee', -e'en f.
average, 1. n. Durchschnitt, -e m. **2.** adj. durchschnittlich; Durchschnitts- (cpds.).
averse, adj. abgeneigt.
aversion, n. Abneigung, -en f.
aviation, n. Luftfahrt f.
aviator, n. Flieger, - m.
aviatrix, n. Fliegerin, -nen f.
avid, adj. begie'rig.
avocation, n. Nebenberuf, -e m.
avoid, vb. vermei'den*.
avoidable, adj. vermeid'lich.
avoidance, n. Vermei'dung, -en f.
avow, vb. geste'hen*.
avowal, n. Geständ'nis, -se nt.
await, vb. erwar'ten.
awake, adj. wach.
awaken, vb. (tr.) wecken, (intr.) erwach'en.
award, 1. n. Preis, -e m.; (jur.) Urteil, -e nt. **2.** vb. zu•erkennen*.
aware, adj. bewußt'.
away, adv. weg, fort.
awe, n. Ehrfurcht f.
awful, adj. schrecklich.
awhile, adv. eine Weile.
awkward, adj. (clumsy) ungeschickt; (embarrassing) peinlich.
awning, n. Marki'se, -n f.
awry, adj. schief.
axe, n. Axt, ⸗e f.
axiom, n. Axiom', -e nt.
axis, n. Achse, -n f.
axle, n. Achse, -n f.
ayatollah, n. Ajatol'lah, -s m.
azure, adj. azur'blau.

B

babble, 1. n. Geschwätz' nt. **2.** vb. schwatzen.

baboon, n. Pavian, -e m.
baby, n. Baby, -s nt.; Säugling, -e m.

bachelor, n. Junggeselle, -n, -n m.

back, 1. n. Rücken, - m.; Kreuz, -e nt.; (chair) Lehne, -n f. **2.** vb. rückwärts•fahren*; (support) unterstüt'zen. **3.** adj. hinter-. **4.** adv. zurück'.

backbone, n. Rückgrat, -e nt.

backfire, n. Fehlzündung, -en f.

background, n. Hintergrund, -̈e m.

backing, n. Unterstüt'zung, -en f.

backlash, n. Rückprall m.; Bewir'kung des Gegenteils f.

backpack, vb. mit Rucksack wandern.

backward, 1. adj. zurück'geblieben, rückständig. **2.** adv. rückwärts.

backwards, adv. rückwärts; (wrongly) verkehrt'.

bacon, n. Speck m.

bacterium, n. Bakte'rium, -rien nt.

bad, adj. (not good) schlecht; (serious) schlimm; (too b.) schade.

bag, n. Sack, -̈e m.; (paper) Tüte, -n f.; (luggage) Koffer, - m.; (woman's purse) Tasche, -n f.

baggage, n. Gepäck' nt.

baggage cart, n. (airport) Kofferkuli, -s m.

baggy, adj. bauschig.

bail, n. Kaution', -en f., Bürgschaft, -en f.

bail out, vb. (set free) Kaution' stellen für; (empty out water) schöpfen, aus•schöpfen; (make a parachute jump) ab•springen*.

bake, vb. backen*.

baking, n. Backen nt.

baking soda, n. Natriumbikarbonat' nt.

balance, 1. n. (equilibrium) Gleichgewicht nt.; (remainder) Rest, -e m; (trade) Bilanz', -en f. **2.** vb. balancie'ren; (make come out equal) aus•gleichen*.

balcony, n. Balkon', -s or -e m.

bald, adj. kahl; (b. head) Glatzkopf, -̈e m.; (b. spot) Glatze, -n f.

balk, vb. (hinder) verhin'dern; (b. at nothing) vor nichts zurück'•scheuen.

ball, n. (for throwing, game, dance) Ball, -̈e m.; (spherical object, bullet) Kugel, -n f.

ballerina, n. Balleri'na, -nen f.

ballet, n. (paper) Stimmzettel, - m.; (voting) Wahl, -en f.

ballpoint, n. Kugelschreiber m.

ballroom, n. Tanzsaal, -säle m.

balm, n. Balsam, -e m.

balmy, adj. sanft.

balsam, n. Balsam, -e m.

Baltic Sea, n. Ostsee f.

bamboo, n. Bambus, -se m.

ban, 1. n. Bann, -e m. **2.** vb. bannen, verbie'ten*.

banal, adj. banal'.

banana, n. Bana'ne, -n f.

band, n. Band, -̈er nt.; (gang) Bande, -n f.; (music) Musik'kapelle, -n f.

bandage, 1. n. Verband', -̈e m. **2.** vb. verbin'den*.

bandanna, n. Kopftuch, -̈er nt., Halstuch, -̈er nt.

bandit, n. Bandit', -en, -en m.

baneful, adj. giftig, verderb'lich.

bang, 1. n. Knall, -e m. **2.** vb. knallen.

banish, vb. verban'nen.

banishment, n. Verban'nung, -en f.

banister, n. Treppengeländer, - nt.

bank, n. Bank, -en f.; (river) Ufer, - nt.; (slope) Böschung, -en f.

bank account, n. Bankkonto nt.

bankbook, n. Kontobuch, -̈er nt.

banker, n. Bankier', -s m.

banking, n. Bankgeschäft, -e nt.

bank note, n. Banknote, -n, f.

bankrupt, adj. bankrott'.

bankruptcy, n. Konkurs', -e m.

banner, n. Banner, - nt.

banquet, n. Festessen, - nt.

banter, 1. n. Scherz, -e m. **2.** vb. scherzen.

baptism, n. Taufe, -n f.

baptismal, adj. Tauf- (cpds.).

Baptist, n. Baptist', -en, -en m.

baptistery, n. Taufkapelle, -n f., Taufstein, -e m.

baptize, vb. taufen.

bar, 1. n. Stange, -n f.; (for drinks) Bar, -s f.; (jur.) Gericht', -e nt. **2.** vb. aus•schließen*.

barb, n. Widerhaken, - m.

barbarian, 1. n. Barbar', -en, -en m. **2.** adj. barba'risch.

barbarism, n. Barbarei', -en f.

barbarous, adj. barba'risch.

barber, n. Herrenfriseur, -e m.

barbiturate, n. Barbitur'säurepräparat, -e nt.

bare, 1. adj. bloß, nackt. **2.** vb. entblö'ßen.

barefoot, adj. barfuß.

barely, adv. kaum.

bargain, 1. n. Gele'genheitskauf, ⸗e m. **2.** vb. feilschen, handeln.

barge, 1. n. Schleppkahn, ⸗e m., Leichter, - m. **2.** vb. stürmen.

baritone, n. Bariton, -e m.

barium, n. Barium f.

bark, 1. n. (tree) Rinde, -n f.; (boat) Barke, -n f.; (dog) Bellen nt. **2.** vb. bellen.

barley, n. Gerste, -n f., Graupen pl.

barn, n. (hay, grain) Scheune, -n f.; (animals) Stall, ⸗e m.

barnacle, n. Entenmuschel, -n f.

barnyard, n. Bauernhof, ⸗e m.

barometer, n. Barome'ter, - nt.

barometric, adj. barome'trisch.

baron, n. Baron', -e m.

baroness, n. Barones'se, -n f.

baroque, 1. n. Barock' nt. **2.** adj. barock'.

barracks, n. Kaser'ne, -n f.

barrage, n. Sperre, -n f.; (mil.) Sperrfeuer, -.

barrel, n. Faß, ⸗sser nt.

barren, adj. unfruchtbar, dürr.

barricade, 1. n. Barrika'de, -n f. **2.** vb. verbarrikadie'ren.

barrier, n. Schranke, -n f.

barroom, n. Schankstube, -n f.

bartender, n. Barmixer, - m.

barter, 1. n. Tauschhandel m. **2.** vb. tauschen.

base, 1. n. der unterste Teil, -e m.; (geom.) Grundlinie, -n f.; (mil.) Stützpunkt, -e m. **2.** vb. basie'ren. **3.** adj. niederträchtig.

baseball, n. Baseball, ⸗e m.

baseboard, n. Waschleiste, -n f.

basement, n. Keller, - m.

baseness, n. Niederträchtigkeit, -en f.

bashful, adj. schüchtern.

bashfulness, n. Schüchternheit, -en f.

basic, adj. grundlegend.

basin, n. Becken, - nt.

basis, n. Grundlage, -n f., Basis, -sen f.

basket, n. Korb, ⸗e m.

bass, n. (singer) Baß, ⸗sse m.; (fish) Barsch, -e m.

bassinet, n. Korbwiege, -n f.

bassoon, n. Fagott', -e nt.

bastard, n. uneheliches Kind nt., Bastard, -e m.

baste, vb. (thread) heften; (roast) begie'ßen*.

bat, n. Fledermaus, ⸗e f.; (sport) Schlagholz, ⸗er nt.

batch, n. Schub, ⸗e m.

bath, n. Bad, ⸗er nt.

bathe, vb. baden; (b.ing suit) Badeanzug, ⸗e m.

bather, n. Badend- m.&f.

bathrobe, n. Bademantel, ⸗ m.

bathroom, n. Badezimmer, - nt.

bathtub, n. Badewanne, -n f.

baton, n. Taktstock, ⸗e m.

battalion, n. Bataillon', -e nt.

batter, 1. n. (one who bats) Schläger, - m.; (cooking) Teig, -e m. **2.** vb. schlagen*.

battery, n. Batterie', -i'en f.

battle, 1. n. Schlacht, -en f. **2.** vb. kämpfen.

battlefield, n. Schlachtfeld, -er nt.

battleship, n. Schlachtschiff, -e nt.

bawl, vb. brüllen.

bay, 1. n. (geography) Bucht, -en f.; (plant) Lorbeer, -en m.; (at b.) in Schach. **2.** vb. bellen.

bayonet, n. Bajonett', -e nt.

bazaar, n. Bazar', -e m.

be, vb. sein*.

beach, n. Strand, -e m.

beachhead, n. Landekopf, ⸗e m.

beacon, n. Leuchtfeuer, - nt.

bead, n. Perle, -n f.; (drop) Tropfen, - m.

beading, n. Perlstickerei, -en f.

beak, n. Schnabel, ⸗ m.

beaker, n. Becher, - m.

beam, 1. n. (construction) Balken, - m.; (light) Strahl, -en m. **2.** vb. strahlen, glänzen.

beaming, adj. strahlend.

bean, n. Bohne, -n f.

bear, 1. n. (animal) Bär, -en, -en m. **2.** vb. (carry) tragen*; (endure) ertra'gen*; (give birth to) gebä'ren*.

bearable, adj. erträg'lich.

beard, n. Bart, ⁼e m.

bearer, n. Überbrin'ger, - m., Überbrin'gerin, -nen f.

bearing, n. (behavior) Haltung, -en f.; (affect) Bezug', ⁼e m.; (machinery) Lager, - nt.

beast, n. Vieh nt., Tier, -e nt., Bestie, - f.

beat, 1. n. Schlag, ⁼e m.; (music) Takt, -e m. **2.** vb. schlagen*.

beaten, adj. geschla'gen.

beatify, vb. selig-sprechen*.

beating, n. (punishment) Prügel pl., Schläge pl.; (defeat) Niederlage, -n f.

beatitudes, n.pl. (biblical) Seligpreisungen pl.

beau, n. Vereh'rer, - m.

beautiful, adj. schön.

beautify, vb. verschö'nern.

beauty, n. Schönheit, -en f.

beauty parlor, n. Schönheitssalon, -s m., Frisier'salon, -s m.

beaver, n. Biber, - m.

because, conj. weil; (b. of) wegen.

beckon, vb. winken.

become, vb. werden*.

becoming, adj. kleidsam.

bed, n. Bett, -en nt.; (garden) Beet, -e nt.

bedbug, n. Wanze, -n f.

bedding, n. Bettzeug nt.

bedroom, n. Schlafzimmer, - nt.

bedspread, n. Bettdecke, -n f.

bee, n. Biene, -n f.

beef, n. Rindfleisch nt.

beefsteak, n. Beefsteak, -s nt.

beehive, n. Bienenstock, ⁼e m.

beer, n. Bier, -e nt.

beet, n. Bete, -n f., Runkelrübe, -n f., rote Rübe, -n f.

beetle, n. Käfer, - m.

befall, vb. zu-stoßen*.

befit, vb. gezie'men.

befitting, adj. schicklich; (be b.) sich schicken.

before, 1. adv. (time) vorher; (place) voran'. **2.** prep. vor. **3.** conj. ehe, bevor'.

beforehand, adv. vorher.

befriend, vb. sich an-freunden mit.

befuddle, vb. verwir'ren.

beg, vb. betteln; (implore) bitten*.

beggar, n. Bettler, - m., Bettlerin, -nen f.

begin, vb. an-fangen*, begin'nen*.

beginner, n. Anfänger, - m. Anfängerin, -nen f.

beginning, n. Anfang, ⁼e m.

begrudge, vb. mißgön'nen.

beguile, vb. bestrick'en.

behalf, n. (on b. of) zugun'sten von, im Namen von.

behave, vb. sich beneh'men*.

behavior, n. Beneh'men, nt.

behead, vb. enthaup'ten.

behind, 1. adv. hinten, zurück'. **2.** prep. hinter.

behold, 1. vb. sehen*. **2.** interj. sieh(e) da.

beige, adj. beigefarben.

being, n. Sein nt., Wesen, - nt.

belated, adj. verspä'tet; nachträglich.

belch, vb. rülpsen.

belfry, n. Glockenturm, ⁼e m.

Belgian, 1. n. Belgier, - m., Belgierin, -nen f. **2.** adj. belgisch.

Belgium, n. Belgien nt.

belie, vb. Lügen strafen.

belief, n. Glaube(n), - m.

believable, adj. glaubhaft.

believe, vb. glauben.

believer, n. Gläubig- m.&f.

belittle, vb. bagatellisie'ren.

bell, n. (small) Klingel, -n f.; (large) Glocke, -n f.

bellboy, n. Hotel'boy, -s m.

belligerence, n. Kriegslust, ⁼e f.; Kriegszustand, ⁼e m.

belligerent, adj. kriegerisch, kriegsführend.

bellow, vb. brüllen.

bellows, n. Blasebalg, ⁼e m.

belly, n. Bauch, ⁼e m.

belong, vb. gehö'ren.

belongings, n.pl. Habseligkeiten pl.

beloved, adj. geliebt'.

below, 1. adv. unten. **2.** prep. unter.

belt, n. Gürtel, - m.

bench, n. Bank, ⁼e f.

bend, vb. biegen*.
beneath, 1. adv. unten. **2.** prep. unter.
benediction, n. Segen, - m.
benefactor, n. Wohltäter, - m.
benefactress, n. Wohltäterin, -nen f.
beneficent, adj. wohltätig.
beneficial, adj. wohltuend, nützlich.
beneficiary, n. Begün'stigt- m.&f.; Nutzniesser, - m.
benefit, 1. n. Wohltat, -en f.; (advantage) Nutzen - m., Vorteil, - m. **2.** vb. nützen; **(b. from)** Nutzen ziehen* aus.
benevolence, n. Wohlwollen nt.
benevolent, adj. wohlwollend.
benign, adj. gütig.
bent, adj. gebeugt'; (out of shape) verbo'gen.
benzine, n. Benzin' nt.
bequeath, vb. verma'chen.
bequest, n. Vermächt'nis, -se nt. Legat', -e nt.
berate, vb. aus•schelten*.
bereave, vb. berau'ben.
bereavement, n. Verlust durch Tod.
berry, n. Beere, -n f.
berth, n. Bettplatz, -̈e m.
beseech, vb. an•flehen.
beset, vb. bedrän'gen.
beside, prep. neben; **(b. oneself)** außer sich.
besides, 1. adv. außerdem. **2.** prep. außer.
besiege, vb. bela'gern.
best, 1. adj. best-. **2.** vb. übertref'fen*.
bestial, adj. bestia'lisch, tierisch.
bestow, vb. verlei'hen*.
bestowal, n. Verlei'hung, -en f.
bet, 1. n. Wette, -n f. **2.** vb. wetten.
betake oneself, vb. sich auf•machen.
betoken, vb. bezeich'nen.
betray, vb. verra'ten*.
betrayal, n. Verrat' m.
betroth, vb. verlo'ben; **(be b.ed)** sich verlo'ben.
betrothal, n. Verlo'bung, -en f.
better, 1. adj. besser. **2.** vb. verbes'sern.
between, prep. zwischen.

bevel, 1. n. schräger Anschnitt, -e m. **2.** vb. schräg ab•schneiden*.
beverage, n. Getränk', -e nt.
bewail, vb. bekla'gen.
beware, vb. sich hüten.
bewilder, vb. verwir'ren.
bewilderment, n. Verwir'rung, -en f.
bewitch, vb. bezau'bern; verzau'bern.
beyond, 1. adv. jenseits. **2.** prep. jenseits, über.
biannual, adj. halbjährlich.
bias, n. Vorurteil, -e nt.
bib, n. Lätzchen, - nt.
Bible, n. Bibel, -n f.
Biblical, adj. biblisch.
bibliography, n. Bibliographie', -i'en f.
bicarbonate, n. (of soda) doppelkohlensaures Natron nt.
biceps, n. Bizeps, -e m.
bicker, vb. sich zanken.
bicycle, n. Fahrrad, -̈er nt.
bicyclist, n. Radfahrer, - m., Radfahrerin, -nen f.
bid, 1. n. Angebot, -e nt. **2.** vb. bieten*.
bidder, n. Bieter, m., Bieterin, -nen f.
bide, vb. ab•warten.
biennial, adj. zweijährlich.
bier, n. Bahre, -n f.
bifocal, adj. bifokal'.
big, adj. groß (größer, größt-).
bigamist, n. Bigamist', -en, -en m.
bigamous, adj. biga'misch.
bigamy, n. Bigamie', -i'en f.
bigot, n. Frömmler, - m
bigoted, adj. bigott'.
bigotry, n. Frömmelei', -en f.
bilateral, adj. zweiseitig.
bile, n. Galle, -n f.
bilingual, adj. zweisprachig.
bilious, adj. gallig.
bill, n. (bird) Schnabel -̈ m.; (banknote) Geldschein, -e m.; (sum owed) Rechnung, -en f.; (legislative) Geset'zesvorlage, -n f.
billboard, n. Rekla'meschild, -er nt.
billet, 1. n. Quartier', -e nt. **2.** vb. ein•quartieren.
billfold, n. Brieftasche, -n f.

billiards, n. Billard nt.

billion, n. Billion', -en f.

bill of fare, n. Speisekarte, -n f.

bill of health, n. Gesund'heitsattest, -e nt.

bill of lading, n. Frachtbrief, -e m.

bill of sale, n. Kaufkontrakt, -e m.

billow, 1. n. Woge, -n f. 2. vb. wogen.

bimonthly, adj. zweimo'natlich.

bin, n. Kasten, -̈ m.

bind, vb. binden*; verbin'den*.

bindery, n. Buchbinderei', -en f.

binding, 1. n. (book) Einband, -̈e m.; (ski) Bindung, -en f. 2. adj. bindend.

binocular, n. Fernglas, -̈er nt.

biochemistry, n. Biochemie' f.

biodegradable, adj. orga'nisch abbaubar.

biofeedback, n. Biosignalrück'gabe, -n f.

biographer, n. Biograph', -en, -en m.

biographical, adj. biogra'phisch.

biography, n. Biographie', -i'en f.

biological, adj. biolo'gisch.

biology, n. Biologie', -i'en f.

bipartisan, adj. die Regierungs- und die Oppositionspartei vertretend.

bird, n. Vogel, -̈ m.

birth, n. Geburt', -en f.

birth control, n. Geburtenkontrolle f., Empfängnisverhütung f.

birthday, n. Geburts'tag, -e m.

birthmark, n. Muttermal, -e nt.

birthplace, n. Geburts'ort, -e m.

birth rate, n. Gebur'tenziffer, -n f.

birthright, n. Erstgeburtsrecht, -e nt.; angestammtes Recht nt.

biscuit, n. Biskuit', -e nt.; Keks, -e m.

bisect, vb. halbie'ren.

bishop, n. Bischof, -̈e, m.

bismuth, n. Wismut nt.

bison, n. Bison, -s m.

bit, n. (piece) Bißchen, - nt.; (a bit of) ein bißchen; (harness) Gebiß, -sse nt.; (computer) Bit, - nt.

bitch, n. Hündin, -nen f.

bite, 1. n. Bissen, - m. 2. vb. beißen*.

biting, adj. beißend.

bitter, adj. bitter.

bitterness, n. Bitterkeit, -en f.

biweekly, adj. zweiwöchentlich.

black, 1. adj. schwarz (-̈). 2. n. (person) Schwarz- m.&f.

blackberry, n. Brombeere, -n f.

blackbird, n. Amsel, -n f.

blackboard, n. Wandtafel, -n f.

blacken, vb. schwärzen.

blackmail, 1. n. Erpres'sung, -en f. 2. vb. erpres'sen.

black market, n. Schwarzmarkt, -̈e m.

blackout, n. Verdun'kelung, -en f.

blacksmith, n. Schmied, -e m.

bladder, n. Blase, -n f.

blade, n. (knife) Klinge, -n f.; (grass) Halm, -e m.

blame, 1. n. Schuld, -en f. 2. vb. beschul'digen.

blanch, vb. bleichen; bleich werden*.

bland, adj. mild.

blank, 1. n. (form) Formular', -e nt. 2. adj. unbeschrieben, leer.

blanket, n. Decke, -n f., Wolldecke, -n f.

blaspheme, vb. lästern.

blasphemer, n. Gotteslästerer, - m.

blasphemous, adj. gotteslästerlich.

blasphemy, n. Gotteslästerung, -en f., Blasphemie', -i'en f.

blast, 1. n. (of wind) Windstoß, -̈e m.; (explosion) Explosion', -en f. 2. vb. sprengen.

blatant, adj. laut, aufdring'lich.

blaze, 1. n. Flamme, -n f. 2. vb. lodern, leuchten.

bleach, vb. bleichen.

bleak, adj. öde.

bleed, vb. bluten.

blemish, n. Makel, - m.

blend, 1. n. Mischung, -en f. 2. vb. mischen.

bless, vb. segnen.

blessed, adj. gese'gnet, selig.

blessing, n. Segen, - m.

blight, 1. n. (bot.) Brand, -̈e m. 2. (fig.) verei'teln.

blind, 1. adj. blind. 2. vb. blenden.

blindfold, 1. n. Augenbinde -n f. 2. vb. die Augen verbin'den*.

blindness, n. Blindheit, -en f.
blink, vb. blinken, blinzeln.
blinker, n. Scheuklappe, -n f.; (signal) Blinklicht, -er nt.
bliss, n. Glückseligkeit, -en f.
blissful, adj. glückselig.
blister, n. Blase, -n f.
blithe, adj. fröhlich.
blizzard, n. Schneesturm, =e m.
bloat, vb. blähen.
bloated, adj. aufgedunsen.
bloc, n. Block, =e m.
block, 1. n. (wood) Holzblock, =e m.; (city) Häuserblock, =e m. **2.** vb. sperren.
blockade, n. Blocka'de, -n f.
blond, adj. blond.
blood, n. Blut nt.
blood donor, n. Blutspender, - m., Blutspenderin, -nen f.
bloodhound, n. Bluthund, -e m.
blood plasma, n. Plasma, -men nt.
blood poisoning, n. Blutvergiftung, -en f.
blood pressure, n. Blutdruck, =e m.
bloodshed, n. Blutvergießen, - nt.
bloodshot, adj. blutunterlaufen.
bloody, adj. blutig.
bloom, 1. n. Blüte, -n f. **2.** vb. blühen.
blossom, n. Blüte, -n f.
blot, 1. n. Fleck, -e m. **2.** vb. beflecken, (ink) löschen.
blotter, n. Löschpapier, -e nt.
blouse, n. Bluse, -n f.
blow, 1. n. Schlag, =e m., Stoß, =e, m. **2.** vb. blasen*.
blowout, n. Reifenpanne, -n f.
blubber, 1. n. Walfischspeck m. **2.** vb. heulen.
blue, adj. blau.
bluebird, n. Blaukehlchen, - nt.
blue jeans, n.pl. Bluejeans pl.
blueprint, n. Blaudruck, =e m.; (fig.) Plan, =e m.
bluff, 1. n. (cliff) Klippe, -n f., schroffer Felsen, - m.; (cards) Bluff, -s m. **2.** adj. schroff. **3.** vb. bluffen.
bluffer, n. Bluffer, - m.
bluing, n. Waschblau nt.
blunder, 1. n. Fehler, - m. **2.** vb. Fehler machen.
blunderer, n. Tölpel, - m.

blunt, adj. stumpf; (fig.) unverblümt.
blur, 1. n. Verschwom'menheit f. **2.** vb. (intr.) verschwim'men*; (tr.) trüben.
blurred, adj. verschwommen.
blush, 1. n. Errö'ten nt. **2.** vb. errö'ten.
bluster, vb. toben; (swagger) prahlen.
boar, n. Eber, - m.
board, 1. n. (plank) Brett, -er nt., Bord, -e nt.; (food) Verpfle'gung, -en f.; (committee) Ausschuß, =sse m.; (council) Behör'de, -n f.; (ship) Bord, -e m. **2.** vb. an Bord gehen*.
boarder, n. Kostgänger, - m.
boarding house, n. Pension', -en f.
boarding pass, n. Bordkarte, -n f.
boarding school, n. Internat', -e nt.
boast, 1. n. Angeberei', -en f. **2.** vb. prahlen, an'geben*.
boaster, n. Angeber, - m., Angeberin, -nen f.
boastful, adj. angeberisch.
boastfulness, n. Angeberei', -en f.
boat, n. Boot, -e nt., Schiff, -e nt.
bob, 1. n. (hair) Bubikopf m. **2.** vb. baumeln; (hair) kurz schneiden*.
bobby pin, n. Haarklammer, -n f.
bodice, n. Oberteil, -e nt.
bodily, adj. leiblich.
body, n. Körper, - m., Leib, -er m.
bodyguard, n. Leibwache, -n f.
bog, 1. n. Sumpf, =e m. **2.** vb. (b. down) stecken bleiben*.
Bohemian, 1. n. Böhme, -n, -n m. **2.** adj. böhmisch.
boil, 1. n. (med.) Furun'kel, - n f. **2.** vb. kochen.
boiler, n. Kessel, - m.
boisterous, adj. ungestüm.
bold, adj. kühn.
boldface, n. Fettdruck, -e m.
boldness, n. Kühnheit, -en f.
Bolivian, 1. n. Bolivia'ner, - m., Bolivia'nerin, -nen f. **2.** adj. bolivia'nisch.
bolster, 1. n. Polster, - nt. **2.** vb. (support) unterstüt'zen.
bolster up, vb. stärken.

bolt, 1. n. (lock) Riegel, - m.; (screw with nut) Schraube, -n f.; (lightning) Blitz, -e m. **2.** vb. (lock) verrie'geln; (dash, of persons) davon'stürzen, (of horses) durch'gehen*.

bomb, 1. n. Bombe, -n f. **2.** vb. bomben.

bombard, vb. bombardie'ren.

bombardier, n. Bombardier', -e m.

bombardment, n. Beschie'ßung, -en f.

bomber, n. Bombenflugzeug, -e nt.

bombproof, adj. bombensicher.

bombshell, n. Bombe, -n f.

bombsight, n. Bombenziel'vorrichtung, -en f.

bonbon, n. Fondant', -s m.

bond, n. Band, -e nt., Fessel, -n f.; (law) Bürgschaft, -en f.; (stock exchange) Obligation', -en f.

bondage, n. Knechtschaft, -en f.

bone, n. Knochen, - m.; (fish) Gräte, -n f.

bonfire, n. Freudenfeuer, - nt.

bonnet, n. Damenhut, -̈e m.

bonus, n. Extrazahlung, -en f.; Tantie'me, -n f.

bony, adj. knochig.

book, 1. n. Buch, -̈er nt. **2.** vb. buchen.

bookcase, n. Bücherschrank, -̈e m.

bookkeeper, n. Buchhalter, - m., Buchhalterin, -nen f.

bookkeeping, n. Buchführung, -en f.

booklet, n. Broschü're, -n f.

bookseller, n. Buchhändler, - m., Buchhändlerin, -nen f.

bookstore, n. Buchhandlung, -en f.

boom, n. Baum, -̈e m.; (econ.) Hochkonjunktur, -en f. **2.** vb. brummen, dröhnen.

boon, n. Geschenk', -e nt.; (fig.) Segen, - m.

boor, n. Grobian, -e m.

boorish, adj. grob (-).

boost, 1. n. (increase) Aufschwung, -̈e m.; (push) Antrieb, -e m. **2.** vb. (increase) steigern; (push) nachhelfen*.

boot, n. Stiefel, - m.

bootblack, n. Schuhputzer, - m.

booth, n. Bude, -n f.; (telephone) Fernsprechzelle, -n f.

border, 1. n. Grenze, -n f. **2.** vb. grenzen an.

borderline, n. Grenze, -n f.

bore, 1. n. (hole) Bohrloch, -̈er nt.; (cylinder) Bohrung, -en f.; (person) langweiliger Mensch, -en, -en m. **2.** vb. bohern; (annoy) langweilen.

boredom, n. Langeweile f.

boric, adj. Bor- (cpds.).

boring, adj. langweilig.

born, adj. gebo'ren.

born-again, adj. wiedergeboren.

borough, n. Stadtteil, -e m.

borrow, vb. borgen, leihen*.

bosom, n. Busen, - m.

boss, 1. n. Chef, -s m., Chefin, -nen f. **2.** adj. herrschsüchtig.

bossy, adj. herrschsüchtig.

botanical, adj. bota'nisch.

botany, n. Bota'nik f.

both, adj. & pron. beide.

bother, 1. n. Verdruß' m. **2.** vb. belās'tigen; (disturb) stören.

bothersome, adj. lästig.

bottle, n. Flasche, -n f.

bottle opener, n. Flaschenöffner, - m.

bottom, n. Grund, -̈e m.; Hintern m.

bottomless, adj. bodenlos.

boudoir, n. Boudoir', -s nt.

bough, n. Ast, -̈e m., Zweig, -e m.

bouillon, n. Kraftbrühe, -n f.

boulder, n. Felsblock, -̈e m.

boulevard, n. Boulevard', -s m.

bounce, vb. springen*.

bound, 1. n. (jump) Sprung, -̈e m. (b.s.) Grenzen pl. **2.** vb. (jump) springen*; (limit) begren'zen. **3.** adj. (tied) gebun'den; (duty b.) verpflich'tet; (b. for) unterwegs' nach.

boundary, n. Grenze, -n f.

bound for, adj. unterwegs' nach.

boundless, adj. grenzenlos.

bounty, n. Freigebigkeit, -en f.

bouquet, n. Blumenstrauß, -̈e m.

bourgeois, adj. bürgerlich.

bout, n. (boxing) Boxkampf, -̈e m.

bovine, adj. Rinder- (cpds.).

bow, 1. n. (for arrows, violin) Bogen, - m.; (greeting) Verbeu'gung, -en f.; (hair, dress) Schleife, -n f.; (of boats) Bug, -e m. **2.** vb. sich verbeu'gen.

bowels, n.pl. Eingeweide pl.

bowl, 1. n. Schüssel -n f., Schale, -n f. **2.** vb. kegeln.

bowlegged, adj. o-beinig.

bowler, n. Kegelspieler, - m., Kegelspielerin, -nen f.; (hat) Melo'ne, -n f.

bowling, n. Kegeln n.

box, 1. n. (small) Schachtel, -n f.; (large) Kasten, ∺ m.; (theater) Loge, -n f.; **(letter b.)** Briefkasten, ∺ m. **2.** (sport) boxen.

boxcar, n. Güterwagen, - m.

boxer, n. Boxer, - m.

boxing, n. Boxen nt.

box office, n. Thea'terkasse, -n f.

boy, n. Junge, -n, -n m., Bube, -n, -n m.

Boycott, 1. n. boykott', -e m. **2.** vb. boykottie'ren.

boyhood, n. Jugend, -en f.

boyish, adj. jungenhaft, jung.

bra, n. BH, -s m.

brace, 1. n. Klammer, -n f., Stütze, -n f. **2.** vb. absteifen.

bracelet, n. Armband, ∺er nt.

bracket, n. Klammer, -n f.; (typography) Klammer, -n f.; (group) Gruppe, -n f.

brag, vb. prahlen, an'geben*.

braggart, n. Angeber, - m.

braid, 1. n. Flechte, -n f. **2.** vb. flechten*.

brain, n. Gehirn', -e nt.

brake, 1. n. Bremse, -n f. **2.** vb. bremsen.

bran, n. Kleie, -n f.

branch, n. Ast, ∺e m., Zweig, -e m.; Filia'le, -n f.

brand, 1. n. (sort) Sorte, -n f.; (mark) Marke, -n f. **2.** vb. brandmarken.

brandish, vb. schwingen*.

brandy, n. Weinbrand, -e m., Kognak, -s m.

brash, adj. dreist.

brass, n. Messing nt.

brassiere, n. Büstenhalter, - m.

brat, n. Balg, ∺e m.

bravado, n. Bravour' f., Schneid m.

brave, adj. tapfer.

bravery, n. Tapferkeit, -en f.

brawl, n. Rauferei', -en f.

brawn, n. Muskelkraft, ∺e f.

bray, 1. n. Eselsgeschrei nt. **2.** vb. schreien*.

brazen, adj. ehern; (insolent) unverschämt.

Brazil, n. Brasi'lien nt.

Brazilian, 1. n. Brasilia'ner, - m., Brasilia'nerin, -nen f. **2.** adj. brasilia'nisch.

breach, n. Bruch, ∺e m.

bread, n. Brot, -e nt.

breadth, n. Breite, -n f.

break, 1. n. Bruch, ∺e m.; Pause, -n f. **2.** vb. brechen*.

breakable, adj. zerbrech'lich.

breakfast, n. Frühstück, -e nt.

breakneck, adj. halsbrecherisch.

breakwater, n. Mole, -n f.

breast, n. Brust, ∺e f.

breath, n. Atem, - m.

breathe, vb. atmen.

breathing, n. Atmen nt.

breathless, adj. atemlos.

breeches, n. Kniehose -n f.

breed, 1. n. Zucht, -en f. **2.** vb. (beget) erzeu'gen; (raise) züchten; (educate) erzie'hen*.

breeder, n. Züchter, - m., Züchterin, -nen f.

breeding, n. Erzie'hung, -en f.

breeze, n. Brise, -n f.

breezy, adj. luftig.

brevity, n. Kürze, -n f.

brew, 1. n. Gebräu, -e nt. **2.** vb. brauen.

brewer, n. Brauer, - m.

brewery, n. Brauerei', -en f.

briar, n. Dornbusch, ∺e m.; Bruyèreholz f.

bribe, vb. beste'chen*.

briber, n. Beste'cher, - m., Beste'cherin, -nen f.

bribery, n. Beste'chung, -en f.

brick, n. Backstein, -e m.; Ziegelstein, -e m.

bricklayer, n. Maurer, - m.

bridal, adj. Hochzeits- (cpds.).

bride, n. Braut, ∺e f.

bridegroom, n. Bräutigam, -e m.

bridesmaid, n. Brautjungfer, -n f.

bridge, 1. n. Brücke, -n f.; *(game)* Bridge nt. **2.** vb. überbrü'cken.
bridle, 1. n. Zaum, ‑e m.
brief, adj. kurz (‑).
brief case, n. Aktenmappe, -n f.
bright, adj. hell; *(smart)* gescheit'.
brighten, vb. erhel'len.
brightness, n. Klarheit, -en f.
brilliance, n. Glanz, -e m.
brilliant, adj. glänzend; *(smart)* hochbegabt.
brim, n. *(cup)* Rand, ‑er m.; *(hat)* Krempe, -n f.
brine, n. Salzwasser, - nt., Sole, -n f.
bring, vb. bringen*.
brink, n. Rand, ‑er m.
briny, adj. salzig.
brisk, adj. lebhaft.
brisket, n. *(meat)* Bruststück, -e nt.
briskness, n. Lebhaftigkeit, -en f.
bristle, 1. n. Borste, -n f. **2.** vb. sich sträuben.
Britain, n. Britan'nien nt.
British, adj. britisch.
Briton, n. Brite, -n, -n m., Britin, -nen f.
brittle, adj. brüchig, spröde.
broad, adj. breit, weit.
broadcast, 1. n. Rundfunksendung, -en f., Übertra'gung, -en f. **2.** vb. senden, im Radio übertra'gen*.
broadcaster, n. Rundfunksprecher, - m., Rundfunksprecherin, -nen f.
broadcloth, n. feiner Wäschestoff m.
broaden, vb. erwei'tern.
broadly, adv. allgemein'.
broadminded, adj. großzügig, tolerant'.
brocade, n. Brokat'-e m.
broil, vb. grillen.
broiler, n. Bratrost, -e m.
broke, adj. pleite.
broken, adj. gebro'chen; kaputt'.
broker, n. Makler, - m., Maklerin, -nen f.
brokerage, n. *(business)* Maklergeschäft, -e nt.; *(charge)* Maklergebühr, -en f.
bronchial, adj. bronchial'.

bronchitis, n. Bronchi'tis f.
bronze, n. Bronze, -n f.
brooch, n. Brosche, -n f.
brood, 1. n. Brut, -en f. **2.** vb. brüten.
brook, n. Bach, ‑e m.
broom, n. Besen, - m.
broomstick, n. Besenstiel, -e m.
broth, n. Brühe, -n f.
brothel, n. Bordell', - e nt.
brother, n. Bruder, ‑ m.
brotherhood, n. Brüderschaft, -en f.
brother-in-law, n. Schwager, ‑ m.
brotherly, adj. brüderlich.
brow, n. Stirn, -en f.
brown, adj. braun.
browse, vb. schmökern.
bruise, 1. n. Quetschung, -en f. **2.** vb. quetschen, stoßen*.
brunette, n. Brünet'te, -n f.
brunt, n. **(bear the b.)** die Hauptlast tragen*.
brush, 1. n. Bürste, -n f.; *(artist's)* Pinsel, - m. **2.** vb. bürsten.
brusque, adj. brüsk.
brutal, adj. brutal'.
brutality, n. Brutalität', -en f.
brutalize, vb. verro'hen.
brute, n. Unmensch, -en, -en m.
bubble, 1. n. Luftblase, -n f. **2.** vb. sprudeln.
buck, 1. n. Bock, ‑e m. **2.** vb. bocken; *(fig.)* sich gegen etwas auf-bäumen.
bucket, n. Eimer, - m.
buckle, 1. n. Schnalle, - f. **2.** vb. *(fasten)* schnallen; *(bend)* sich krümmen, sich biegen*.
buckwheat, n. Buchweizen m.
bud, 1. n. Knospe, -n f. **2.** vb. knospen.
budge, vb. sich rühren.
budget, n. Etat', -s m.
buffalo, n. Büffel, - m.
buffer, n. Puffer, - m.; **(b. state)** Pufferstaat, -en m.
buffet, 1. n. Büfett', -e, Buffet', -s nt. **2.** vb. schlagen*.
bug, n. Käfer, - m.
bugle, n. Signal'horn, ‑er nt.
build, vb. bauen.
builder, n. Baumeister, - m.
building, n. Gebäu'de, - nt.

bulb, n. Knolle, -n f.; (electric) Glühbirne, -n f.

bulge, 1. n. Ausbuchtung, -en f. **2.** vb. sich aus·buchten.

bulk, n. Umfang m., Hauptteil, -e m.

bulky, adj. umfangreich.

bull, n. Bulle, -n, -n m.

bulldog, n. Bulldogge, -n f.

bullet, n. Kugel, -n f.

bulletin, n. Bericht', -e m.

bully, 1. n. Kraftmeier, - m. **2.** vb. kraftmeiern.

bulwark, n. Bollwerk, -e nt.

bum, 1. n. (fam.) Lump, -en, -en m. **2.** vb. (fam.) pumpen.

bumblebee, n. Hummel, -n f.

bump, 1. n. Stoß, -"e m. **2.** vb. stoßen*.

bumper, n. Stoßstange, -n f.

bun, n. Brötchen, - nt.

bunch, n. Büschel, - nt.

bundle, n. Bündel, - nt.

bungle, vb. pfuschen.

bunion, n. Entzün'dung am großen Zeh.

bunny, n. Kanin'chen, - nt.

buoy, n. Boje, -n f.

buoyant, adj. schwimmend, tragfähig; (fig.) lebhaft.

burden, 1. n. Last, -en f. **2.** vb. belas'ten.

burdensome, adj. beschwer'lich.

bureau, n. Büro', -s nt.; (furniture) Kommo'de, -n f.

burglar, n. Einbrecher, - m., Einbrecherin, -nen f.

burglary, n. Einbruch, -"e m.

burial, n. Begräb'nis, -se nt.

burlap, n. grobe Leinwand f.

burly, adj. stämmig.

burn, 1. n. Verbren'nung, -en f. **2.** vb. (intr.) brennen*, (tr.) verbren'nen*.

burner, n. Brenner, - m.

burrow, 1. n. (of an animal) Bau, -e m. **2.** vb. sich ein·graben*.

burst, 1. n. Krach, -e m.; Explosion', -en f. **2.** vb. (intr.) platzen; (tr.) sprengen.

bury, vb. begra'ben*; eingraben*.

bus, n. Bus, -se m.

bush, n. Busch, -"e m.

bushel, n. Scheffel, - m.

bushy, adj. buschig.

business, n. Geschäft', -e nt.

businesslike, adj. geschäfts'mäßig.

businessman, n. Geschäfts'mann, -"er or -leute m.

businesswoman, n. Geschäfts'frau, -en f.

bust, 1. n. Büste, -n f. **2.** vb. (fam.) kaputt' machen.

bustle, n. Geschäf'tigkeit, -en f.

busy, adj. beschäf'tigt; geschäf'tig.

but, 1. prep. außer. **2.** conj. aber.

butcher, n. Fleischer, - m., Metzger, - m., Schlächter, - m., Schlachter, - m.

butler, n. Diener, - m.

butt, 1. n. (gun) Kolben, - m.; (aim) Ziel, -e nt. **2.** vb. mit dem Kopf stoßen*.

butter, n. Butter f.

butterfly, n. Schmetterling, -e m.

buttermilk, n. Buttermilch f.

buttocks, n.pl. Gesäß', -e nt.

button, n. Knopf, -"e m.

buttonhole, n. Knopfloch, -"er nt.

buttress, 1. n. Stütze, -n f.; (arch.) Strebepfeiler, - m. **2.** vb. stützen.

buxom, adj. drall.

buy, vb. kaufen.

buyer, n. Käufer, - m., Käuferin, -nen f.

buzz, vb. summen.

buzzard, n. Bussard, -e m.

buzzer, n. Klingel, -n f.

by, prep. von; (through) durch; (near) bei.

by-and-by, adv. später.

bygone, adj. vergan'gen.

by-pass, n. Umge'hungsstraße, -n f.

by-product, n. Nebenprodukt, -e nt.

bystander, n. Zuschauer, - m., Zuschauerin, -nen f.

byte, n. Byte, -s nt.

byway, n. Nebenweg, -e m.

C

cab, n. *(taxi)* Taxe, -n f., Taxi, -s nt.; *(locomotive)* Führerstand, -e m.

cabaret, n. Kabarett', -e nt.

cabbage, n. Kohl m.

cabin, n. Kabi'ne, -n f.

cabinet, n. Kabinett', -e nt.

cabinetmaker, n. Kunsttischler, - m.

cable, 1. n. Kabel, - nt. 2. vb. kabeln.

cablegram, n. Kabel, - nt.

cache, n. Versteck', -e nt.

cackle, vb. gackern.

cactus, n. Kaktus, -te'en m.

cad, n. Schuft, -e m.

cadaver, n. Leichnam, -e m.

cadet, n. Kadett', -en, -en m.

cadence, n. Tonfall, ⁻e m.; Kadenz', -en f.

cadmium, n. Kadmium nt.

café, n. Cafe', -s nt.; Konditorei', -en f.

cafeteria, n. Mensa, -sen f.

caffeine, n. Koffein', -e nt.

cage, n. Käfig, -e m.

cajole, vb. beschwat'zen.

cake, n. Kuchen, -- m.

calamity, n. Unglück, -e nt.

calcium, n. Kalzium nt.

calculable, adj. bere'chenbar.

calculate, vb. berech'nen.

calculating machine, n. Rechenmaschine, -n f.

calculation, n. Berech'nung, -en f.

calculator, n. Taschenrechner, - m.

calculus, n. Differential'rechnung, -en f.

caldron, n. Kessel, - m.

calendar, n. Kalen'der, - m.

calf, n. Kalb, ⁻er nt.

calfskin, n. Kalbleder, - nt.

caliber, n. Kali'ber, - nt.

calico, n. Kattun', -e m.

calipers, n.pl. Greifzirkel, - m.

calisthenics, n.pl. Leibesübungen pl.

call, 1. n. Ruf, -e m.; *(telephone)* Anruf, -e m. 2. vb. rufen*.

calling card, n. Visi'tenkarte, -n f.

callous, adj. schwielig; *(unfeeling)* gefühl'los.

callus, n. Schwiele, -n f.

calm, 1. adj. ruhig. 2. vb. beru'higen.

calmness, n. Ruhe f.

caloric, adj. kalo'risch.

calorie, n. Kalorie, -i'en f.

Calvary, n. Kalva'rienberg m.

calve, vb. kalben.

cambric, n. Batist', -e m.

camel, n. Kamel', -e nt.

cameo, n. Kame'e, -n f.

camera, n. Kamera, -s f.; Photoapparat, -e m.

camouflage, 1. n. Tarnung, -en f.; *(natural c.)* Mimikry f. Schutzfarbe, -n f. 2. vb. tarnen.

camp, 1. n. Lager, - nt. 2. vb. lagern.

campaign, 1. n. Feldzug, ⁻e m.; Kampag'ne, -n f. 2. vb. *(political)* Wahlreden halten*.

camper, n. Zelter, - m., Zelterin, -nen f.

camphor, n. Kampfer m.

camping, n. Zelten nt.

campsite, n. Zeltplatz, ⁻e m.

campus, n. Universitäts'gelände, - nt., College-Gelände, - nt.

can, 1. n. *(tin)* Büchse, -n f.; *(large)* Kanne, -n f. 2. vb. *(preserve)* ein•machen; *(be able)* können*.

Canada, n. Kanada nt.

Canadian, 1. n. Kana'dier, - m., Kana'dierin, -nen f. 2. adj. kana'disch.

canal, n. Kanal', ⁻e m.

canapé, n. Cocktailgebäck nt.

canary, n. Kana'rienvogel, ⁻ m.

cancel, vb. entwer'ten, rückgängig machen, auf•heben*.

cancellation, n. Aufhebung, -en f., Entwer'tung, -en f.

cancer, n. Krebs, -e m.

candelabrum, n. Armleuchter, - m.

candid, adj. offen, ehrlich.

candidacy, n. Kandidatur', -en f.

candidate, n. Kandidat', -en, -en m., Kandida'tin, -nen f.

candied, *adj.* kandiert'.

candle, *n.* Kerze, -n *f.*

candlestick, *n.* Leuchter, - *m.*

candor, *n.* Offenheit, -en *f.*

cane, *n.* Stock, ⸚e *m;* *(sugar)* Rohr, -e *nt.*

canine, *adj.* Hunde- *(cpds.).*

canister, *n.* Blechbüchse, -n *f.*

canker, *n.* Krebs, -e *m.*

canned, *adj.* eingemacht; Büchsen- *(cpds.).*

cannibal, *n.* Kanniba'le, -n, -n *m.*

canning, *n.* Einmachen *nt.*

cannon, *n.* Kano'ne, -n *f.*

cannot, *vb.* nicht können*.

canny, *adj.* schlau, umsichtig.

canoe, *n.* Kanu', -s *nt.*

canon, *n.* *(rule, song)* Kanon, -s *m.;* *(person)* Domherr, -n, -en *m.*

canonical, *adj.* kano'nisch.

canonize, *vb.* kanonisie'ren.

can opener, *n.* Büchsenöffner, - *m.*

canopy, *n.* Baldachin, -e *m.*

cant, *n.* Heuchelei', -en *f.*

cantaloupe, *n.* Melo'ne, -n *f.*

canteen, *n.* Kanti'ne, -n *f.*

canvas, *n.* *(material)* Segeltuch *nt.;* *(painter's)* Leinwand *f.*

canvass, **1.** *n.* Stimmenprüfung, -en *f.* **2.** *vb.* untersu'chen, prüfen.

canyon, *n.* Schlucht, -en *f.*

cap, *n.* Mütze, -n *f.*

capability, *n.* Fähigkeit, -en *f.*

capable, *adj.* fähig.

capacious, *adj.* geräu'mig.

capacity, *n.* *(content)* Inhalt *m.;* *(ability)* Fähigkeit, -en *f.;* *(quality)* Eigenschaft, -en *f.*

cape, *n.* *(clothing)* Umhang, ⸚e *m.;* *(geogr.)* Kap, -s *nt.*

caper, **1.** *n.* Luftsprung, ⸚e *m.* **2.** *vb.* Luftsprünge machen.

capital, **1.** *n.* *(money)* Kapital', -ien *nt.;* *(city)* Hauptstadt, ⸚e *f.* **2.** *adj.* kapital'.

capitalism, *n.* Kapitalis'mus *m.*

capitalist, *n.* Kapitalist', -en, -en *m.*

capitalistic, *adj.* kapitalistisch.

capitalization, *n.* Kapitalisie'rung, -en *f.*

capitalize, *vb.* kapitalisie'ren.

capitulate, *vb.* kapitulie'ren.

capon, *n.* Kapaun', -e *m.*

caprice, *n.* Laune, -n *f.*

capricious, *adj.* launenhaft.

capsize, *vb.* kentern.

capsule, *n.* Kapsel, -n *f.*

captain, *n.* Kapitän', -e *m.;* *(army)* Hauptmann, -leute *m.*

caption, *n.* Überschrift, -en *f.*

captious, *adj.* verfäng'lich.

captivate, *vb.* fesseln.

captive, **1.** *n.* Gefan'gener, - *m.&f.* **2.** *adj.* gefan'gen.

captivity, *n.* Gefan'genschaft, -en *f.*

captor, *n.* Fänger, - *m.*

capture, **1.** *n.* Gefan'gennahme, -n *f.* **2.** *vb.* *(person)* fangen*; *(city)* ero'bern.

car, *n.* Wagen, - *m.;* Auto, -s *nt.*

carafe, *n.* Karaf'fe, -n *f.*

caramel, *n.* Karamel' *nt.*

carat, *n.* Karat', -e *m.*

caravan, *n.* Karawa'ne, -n *f.*

caraway, *n.* Kümmel *m.*

carbide, *n.* Karbid' *nt.*

carbine, *n.* Karabi'ner, - *m.*

carbohydrate, *n.* Kohlehydrat, -e *nt.*

carbon, *n.* Kohlenstoff, -e *m.*

carbon dioxide, *n.* Kohlendioxyd *nt.*

carbon monoxide, *n.* Kohlenoxyd' *nt.*

carbon paper, *n.* Kohlepapier, -e *nt.*

carbuncle, *n.* Karbun'kel, - *m.;* *(gem)* Karfun'kel, - *m.*

carburetor, *n.* Verga'ser, - *m.*

carcass, *n.* Kada'ver, - *m.*

carcinogenic, *adj.* krebserregend.

card, *n.* Karte, -n *f.*

cardboard, *n.* Pappe, -n *f.*

cardiac, *adj.* Herz- *(cpds.).*

cardinal, **1.** *n.* Kardinal', -e *m.* **2.** *adj.* hauptsächlich.

care, **1.** *n.* *(worry)* Sorge, -n *f.;* *(prudence)* Vorsicht *f.;* *(accuracy)* Sorgfalt *f.;* **(take c. of)** sorgen für; **(c. for, like)** gern mögen*; **(c. about)** sich kümmern um.

careen, *vb.* wild fahren*.

career, *n.* Karrie're, -n *f.*

carefree, *adj.* sorglos.

careful, *adj.* *(prudent)* vorsichtig; *(accurate)* sorgfältig.

carefulness, n. (prudence) Vorsicht f.; (accuracy) Sorgfalt f.

careless, adj. (imprudent) unvorsichtig, leichtsinnig; (inaccurate) unsorgfältig, nachlässig.

carelessness, n. (imprudence) Unvorsichtigkeit, -en f.; (inaccuracy) Nachlässigkeit, -en f.

caress, 1. n. Liebkosung, -en f. 2. vb. liebkosen, streicheln.

caretaker, n. Verwal'ter, - m.

cargo, n. Ladung, -en f., Fracht, -en f.

caricature, 1. n. Karikatur', -en f. 2. vb. karikie'ren.

caries, n. Karies f.

carload, n. Waggon'ladung, -en f.

carnal, adj. fleischlich.

carnation, n. Nelke, -n f.

carnival, n. Karneval, -e m.

carnivorous, adj. fleischfressend.

carol, 1. n. Weihnachtslied, -er nt. 2. vb. singen*.

carouse, vb. zechen.

carousel, n. Karussell', -s nt.

carpenter, n. (construction) Zimmermann, -leute m; (finer work) Tischler, - m.

carpet, n. Teppich, -e m.

car pool, n. Fahrgemeinschaft, -en f.

car rental, n. Autovermietung f.

carriage, n. (vehicle) Wagen, - m.; (posture) Haltung, -en f.

carrier, n. Träger, - m.

carrot, n. Mohr'rübe, -n f.

carry, vb. tragen*; (c. on, intr.) fort-fahren*; (c. on, tr.) fortsetzen; (c. out) ausführen; (c. through) durch-führen.

cart, n. Karren, - m.

cartage, n. Transport', -e m.

cartel, n. Kartell', -e m.

cartilage, n. Knorpel, - m.

carton, n. Karton', -s m.

cartoon, n. Karikatur', -en f.

cartridge, n. Patro'ne, -n f.

carve, vb. schneiden*; (wood) schnitzen; (meat) zerle'gen, tranchie'ren.

carving, n. Schnitzwerk, -e nt.

car wash, n. Autowaschanlage, -n f.

case, n. Fall, -̈e m.

cash, 1. n. Bargeld, -er nt. 2. vb. ein·lösen. 3. adj. bar.

cashier, n. Kassie'rer, - m., Kassie'rerin, -nen f.

cashmere, n. Kaschmir, -e m.

casing, n. Hülle, -n f.

casino, n. Kasi'no, -s nt.

cask, n. Tonne, -n f., Faß, -̈sser nt.

casket, n. Sarg, -̈e m.

casserole, n. Schmorpfanne, -n f.

cassette, n. Kasset'te, -n f.

cast, 1. n. (theater) Rollenverteilung, -en f. 2. vb. (throw) werfen*; (metal) gießen*.

caste, n. Kaste, -n f.

castigate, vb. züchtigen.

castle, n. Schloß, -̈sser, nt.

castoff, adj. abgelegt.

castor oil, n. Rizinusöl, -e m.

casual, adj. (accidental) zufällig; (nonchalant) zwanglos.

casualness, n. Zwanglosigkeit, -en f.

casualty, n. Opfer, - nt.; (casualties) Verlus'te pl.

cat, n. Katze, -n f.; (tomcat) Kater, - m.

cataclysm, n. Sündflut, -en f.

catacomb, n. Katakom'be, -n f.

catalogue, n. Katalog', -e m.

catapult, n. Katapult', -e m.

cataract, n. (eye) Katarakt', -e m., grauer Star, -e m.

catarrh, n. Katarrh', -e m.

catastrophe, n. Katastro'phe, -n f.

catch, vb. fangen*; (sickness, train) bekom'men*.

catcher, n. Fänger, - m.

catechism, n. Katechis'mus, -men m.

categorical, adj. katego'risch.

category, n. Kategorie', -i'en f.

cater, vb. versor'gen.

caterpillar, n. Raupe, -n f.

cathartic, 1. n. Abführmittel, - nt. 2. adj. abführend.

cathedral, n. Kathedra'le, -n f.; Dom, -e m.; Münster nt.

cathode, n. Katho'de, -n f.

Catholic, 1. n. Katholik', -en, -en m. 2. adj. katho'lisch.

Catholicism, n. Katholizis'mus, -men m.

catsup, n. Ketchup nt.

cattle, n. Vieh nt.

cauliflower, n. Blumenkohl, -e m.

cause, 1. n. (origin) Ursache, -n f.; (idea) Sache, -n f. **2.** vb. verur'sachen.

caustic, adj. beißend.

cauterize, vb. aus·brennen*.

cautery, n. Ausbrennen nt.

caution, 1. n. Vorsicht, -en f. **2.** vb. warnen.

cautious, adj. vorsichtig.

cavalcade, n. Kavalka'de, -n f.

cavalier, n. Kavalier', -e m.

cavalry, n. Kavallerie, -i'en f.

cave, n. Höhle, -n f.

cavern, n. Höhle, -n f.

caviar, n. Kaviar m.

cavity, n. Loch, ⁻er nt., Höhle, -n f.

cease, vb. (intr.) auf·hören, (tr.) ein·stellen.

cedar, n. Zeder, -n f.

cede, vb. ab·treten*.

ceiling, n. Zimmerdecke, -n f.; (fig.) Höchstgrenze, -n f.

celebrate, vb. feiern.

celebrated, adj. berühmt'.

celebration, n. Feier, -n f.

celebrity, n. Berühmt'heit, -en f.

celery, n. Sellerie m.

celestial, adj. himmlisch.

celibacy, n. Zölibat' nt., Ehelosigkeit f.

celibate, adj. ehelos.

cell, n. Zelle, -n f.

cellar, n. Keller, - m.

cellist, n. Cellist', -en, -en m., Cellis'tin, -nen f.

cello, n. Cello, -s nt.

cellophane, n. Zellophan' nt.

celluloid, n. Zelluloid' nt.

cellulose, n. Zellstoff, -e m.

Celtic, adj. keltisch.

cement, 1. n. Zement', -e m. **2.** vb. zementie'ren.

cemetery, n. Friedhof, ⁻e m.

censor, 1. n. Zensor, -o'ren m. **2.** vb. zensie'ren.

censorship, n. Zensur', -en f.

censure, n. Tadel, - m., Verweis', -e m.

census, n. Volkszählung, -en f., Zensus, - m.

cent, n. Cent, -s m.

centenary, n. Hundertjahr'feier, -n f.

centennial, 1. n. Hundertjahr'feier, -n f. **2.** adj. hundertjährig.

center, n. Mitte, -n f.; Mittelpunkt, -e m.; Zentrum, -tren nt.

centerfold, n. Mittelfaltblatt, ⁻er nt.

centigrade, n. (c. thermometer) Celsiusthermometer, - nt.; (10 degrees c.) 10 Grad Celsius.

central, adj. zentral'.

centralize, vb. zentralisie'ren.

century, n. Jahrhun'dert, -e nt.

ceramic, adj. kera'misch.

ceramics, n. Kera'mik, -en f.

cereal, n. Getrei'de, - nt., Getrei'despeise, -n f.

cerebral, adj. Gehirn- (cpds.).

ceremonial, adj. zeremoniell'.

ceremonious, adj. feierlich.

ceremony, n. Zeremonie', -i'en f.; Feierlichkeit, -en f.

certain, adj. sicher.

certainty, n. Gewißheit, -en f.

certificate, n. Beschei'nigung, -en f.; Urkunde, -n f.

certification, n. Beschei'nigung, -en f.

certify, vb. beschei'nigen, beglau'bigen, bezeu'gen.

cervix, n. Gebär'mutterhals m.

cessation, n. Aufhören nt.

cesspool, n. Senkgrube, -n f.

chafe, vb. reiben*.

chagrin, n. Kummer, - m.

chain, 1. n. Kette, -n f. **2.** vb. an·ketten, fesseln.

chain reaction, n. Kettenreaktion, -en f.

chair, n. Stuhl, ⁻e m.

chairman, n. Vorsitzend- m.

chairperson, n. Vorsitzend- m. & f.

chalice, n. Kelch, -e m.

chalk, n. Kreide, -n f.

chalky, adj. kreidig.

challenge, 1. n. Heraus'forderung, -en f. **2.** vb. heraus·fordern, auf·fordern.

challenger, n. Heraus'forderer, - m.

chamber, n. Kammer, -n f.; (pol.) Haus, ⁻er nt.

chambermaid, n. Zimmermädchen, - nt.

chamber music, n. Kammermusik f.

chamois, n. (animal) Gemse, -n f.; (leather) Wildleder nt.

champagne, n. Sekt, -e m., Champag'ner, - m.

champion, n. Kämpfer, - m.; (sport) Meister, - m., Meisterin, -nen f.

championship, n. Meisterschaft, -en f.

chance, 1. n. Zufall, ∹e m.; (expectation) Aussicht, -en f.; (occasion) Gele'genheit, -en f. 2. vb. wagen. 3. adj. zufällig.

chancel, n. Altar'platz, ∹e m.

chancellery, n. Kanzlei', -en f.

chancellor, n. Kanzler, - m.

chandelier, n. Kronleuchter, - m.

change, 1. n. Verän'derung, -en f.; (alteration) Änderung, -en f.; (variety) Abwechslung, -en f.; (small coins) Kleingeld nt.; (money due) Rest m. 2. vb. verän'dern; (alter) ändern; (money) wechseln.

changeability, n. Unbeständigkeit, -en f.

changeable, adj. unbeständig.

channel, n. Fahrwasser nt., Kanal', ∹e m.; (radio) Frequenz'band,∹er nt.

chant, 1. n. Gesang, ∹e m. 2. vb. singen*.

chaos, n. Chaos, nt.

chaotic, adj. chao'tisch.

chap, 1. n. Bursche, -n, -n m., Kerl, -e m. 2. vb. (become chapped) auf'springen*.

chapel, n. Kapel'le, -n f.

chaplain, n. Geistlich- m.; (mil.) Feldgeistlich- m.

chapter, n. Kapi'tel, - nt.

char, vb. verkoh'len.

character, n. Charak'ter, -te're m., Person', -en f.

characteristic, adj. charakteri'stisch.

characterization, n. Charakterisie'rung, -en f.

characterize, vb. charakteri'sie'ren.

charcoal, n. Holzkohle, -n f.

charge, 1. n. (load) Ladung, -en f.; (attack) Angriff, -e m.; (price)

Preis, -e m.; (custody) Obhut, -en f. 2. vb. (load) laden*; (set a price) berech'nen; (put on one's account) an'schreiben* lassen*.

chariot, n. Wagen, - m.

charisma, n. Charis'ma nt.

charitable, adj. wohltätig, nachsichtig.

charity, n. Wohltätigkeit, -en f., Nächstenliebe f.

charlatan, n. Scharlatan, -e m.

charm, 1. n. Charme m.; Liebreiz, -e m.; (magic saying) Zauberspruch, ∹e m. 2. vb. bezau'bern.

charming, adj. bezau'bernd, reizend.

chart, n. (map) Karte, -n f.; (graph) Tabel'le, -n f.

charter, n. Urkunde, -n f.

charter flight, n. Charterflug, ∹e m.

charwoman, n. Putzfrau, -en f.

chase, 1. n. Jagd, -en f. 2. vb. jagen.

chasm, n. Abgrund, ∹e m.

chassis, n. Fahrgestell, -e nt.

chaste, adj. züchtig, keusch.

chasten, vb. züchtigen.

chastise, vb. züchtigen.

chastity, n. Keuschheit f.

chat, 1. n. Plauderei', -en f. 2. vb. plaudern.

chateau, n. Chateau', -s nt.

chatter, 1. n. Geschwätz' nt. 2. vb. schwatzen; (teeth) klappern.

chauffeur, n. Fahrer, - m., Chauffeur', -e m.

cheap, adj. billig, (fig.) ordinär'.

cheapen, vb. im Wert herab'setzen.

cheapness, n. Billigkeit, -en f.

cheat, vb. betrü'gen*; (harmless) schummeln.

check, 1. n. (restraint) Hemmnis, -se nt.; (verification) Kontrol'le, -n f.; (Überprü'fung, -en f.; (clothes, luggage) Kontroll'marke, -n f.; (bank) Scheck, -s m.; (bill) Rechnung, -en f. 2. vb. (verify) kontrollie'ren, überprü'fen; (luggage) auf'geben*, ab'geben*; (mark) ab'hacken.

checkerboard, n. Damebrett, -er nt.

checkers, n. Damespiel nt.

cheek, *n.* Backe, -n *f.;* Wange, -n *f.*

cheer, 1. *n.* Beifallsruf, -e *m.* **2.** *vb.* Beifall rufen*; **(c. up)** auf-muntern.

cheerful, *adj.* fröhlich.

cheerfulness, *n.* Fröhlichkeit *f.*

cheery, *adj.* heiter.

cheese, *n.* Käse *m.*

cheesecloth, *n.* grobe Gaze, -n *f.*

chef, *n.* Küchenchef, -s *m.*

chemical, 1. *n.* chemisches Präpa-rat', -e *nt.;* **(c. s)** Chemikal'ien *pl.* **2.** *adj.* chemisch.

chemist, *n.* Chemiker, -m., Che-mikerin, -nen *f.*

chemistry, *n.* Chemie' *f.*

chemotherapy, *n.* Chemotherapie' *f.*

chenille, *n.* Chenille', -n *f.*

cherish, *vb.* schätzen.

cherry, *n.* Kirsche, -n *f.*

cherub, *n.* Cherub, -s *or* -im *or* -i'nen *m.*

chess, *n.* Schach *nt.,* Schachspiel *nt.*

chessboard, *n.* Schachbrett, -er *nt.*

chessman, *n.* Schachfigur, -en *f.*

chest, *n.* *(box)* Kiste, -n *f.,* Truhe, -n *f.; (body)* Brust *f.*

chestnut, *n.* Kasta'nie, -n *f.*

chevron, *n.* Dienstgradabzeichen, - *nt.*

chew, *vb.* kauen.

chic, *adj.* schick; elegant'.

chick, *n.* Küken - *nt.*

chicken, *n.* Huhn, ⸚er *nt.*

chicken pox, *n.* Windpocken *pl.*

chicory, *n.* Zicho'rie, -n *f.*

chide, *vb.* schelten*.

chief, 1. *n.* Oberhaupt, ⸚er *nt.* **2.** *adj.* hauptsächlich; Haupt- *(cpds.).*

chiefly, *adv.* vorwiegend.

chieftain, *n.* Häuptling, -e *m.*

child, *n.* Kind, -er *nt.*

childbirth, *n.* Geburt' *f.*

childhood, *n.* Kindheit, -en *f.*

childish, *adj.* kindisch.

childishness, *n.* Kindhaftigkeit, -en *f.*

childless, *adj.* kinderlos.

childlike, *adj.* kindlich.

chill, 1. *n.* Frost, ⸚e *m.; (fever)* Schauer, - *m.* **2.** *vb.* auf Eis stellen.

chilliness, *n.* Kühle *f.*

chilly, *adj.* kühl.

chime, 1. *n.* *(chimes)* Glocken-spiel, -e *nt.* **2.** *vb.* läuten.

chimney, *n.* Schornstein, -e *m.*

chimpanzee, *n.* Schimpan'se, -n, -n *m.*

chin, *n.* Kinn, -e *nt.*

china, *n.* Porzellan', -e *nt.*

China, *n.* China *nt.*

Chinchilla, *n.* Chinchil'la, -s *m.*

Chinese, 1. *n.* Chine'se, -n, -n *m.;* Chine'sin, -nen *f.* **2.** *adj.* chine'-sisch.

chintz, *n.* Chintz, -e *m.*

chip, 1. *n.* Splitter, - *m.* **2.** *vb.* ab-brechen*; ab'splittern.

chiropodist, *n.* Fußpfleger, - *m.*

chiropractor, *n.* Chiroprak'tiker, - *m.,* Chiroprak'tikerin, -nen *f.*

chirp, 1. *n.* Gezirp' *nt.* **2.** *vb.* zir-pen.

chisel, 1. *n.* *(stone, metal)* Meißel, - *m.; (wood)* Beitel, - *m.* **2.** *vb.* meißeln.

chivalrous, *adj.* ritterlich.

chivalry, *n.* Ritterlichkeit, -en *f.*

chive, *n.* Schnittlauch, -e *m.*

chloride, *n.* Chlorid', -e *nt.*

chlorine, *n.* Chlor, -s *nt.*

chloroform, *n.* Chloroform' *nt.*

chocolate, *n.* Schokola'de, -n *f.*

choice, *n.* Wahl, -en *f.; (selection)* Auswahl, -en *f.*

choir, *n.* Chor, ⸚e *m.*

choke, *vb.* erwür'gen, ersticke'en.

choker, *n.* Halsband, ⸚er *nt.*

cholera, *n.* Cholera *f.*

choose, *vb.* wählen.

chop, 1. *n.* *(meat)* Kotelett', -s *nt.* **2.** *vb.* hacken.

choppy, *adj.* *(sea)* unruhig.

chopsticks, *n.* Eßstäbchen *pl.*

choral, *adj.* Chor- *(cpds.).*

chord, *n.* *(string)* Saite, -n *f.; (harmony)* Akkord', -e *m.*

chore, *n.* Alltagsarbeit, -en *f.*

choreographer, *n.* Choreo-graph', -en, -en *m.*

choreography, *n.* Choreogra-phie', -i'en *f.*

chorus, *n.* Chor, ⸚e *m.;* Refrain', -s *m.*

Christ, *n.* Christus *m.*

christen, *vb.* taufen.

Christendom, *n.* Christenheit *f.*

christening, *n.* Taufe, -n *f.*

Christian, 1. *n.* Christ, -en, -en *m.* **2.** *adj.* christlich.

Christianity, *n.* Christentum *nt.*

Christmas, *n.* Weihnachten *nt.*

Christmas Eve, *n.* Heiligabend *m.*

chrome, chromium, *n.* Chrom *nt.*

chronic, *adj.* chronisch.

chronicle, *n.* Chronik, -en *f.*

chronological, *adj.* chronolo'gisch.

chronology, *n.* Chronologie', -i'en *f.*

chrysanthemum, *n.* Chrysan-the'me, -n *f.*

chubby, *adj.* dicklich.

chuckle, *vb.* vergnügt'lachen.

chug, *vb.* daher'keuchen.

chunk, *n.* Stück, -e *nt.*

church, *n.* Kirche, -n *f.*

churchyard, *n.* Kirchhof, ⸗e *m.*

churn, 1. *n.* Butterfaß, ⸗sser *nt.* **2.** *vb.* buttern; *(fig.)* auf·wühlen.

chute, *n. (mail)* Postschacht, ⸗e *m.; (laundry)* Wäscheschacht, ⸗e *m.*

cider, *n.* Apfelwein, -e *m.*

cigar, *n.* Zigar're, -n *f.*

cigarette, *n.* Zigaret'te, -n *f.*

cinch, *n.* Sattelgurt, -e *m; (fam.)* Kleinigkeit, -en *f.*

cinder, *n.* Asche, -n *f.*

cinema, *n.* Kino, -s *nt.*

cinnamon, *n.* Zimt *m.*

cipher, *n. (number)* Ziffer, -n *f.; (zero)* Null, -en *f.; (code)* Chiffre, -n *f.*

circle, *n.* Kreis, -en *m.*

circuit, *n. (course)* Umkreis, -e *m.; (elec.)* Stromkreis, -e *m.; (short c.)* Kurzschluß, ⸗sse *m.*

circuitous, *adj.* umwegig.

circular, 1. *n.* Rundschreiben, - *nt.* **2.** *adj.* kreisförmig.

circulate, *vb.* zirkulie'ren.

circulation, *n. (blood)* Kreislauf, ⸗e *m.; (paper)* Auflage, -n *f.; (money)* Umlauf, ⸗e *m.*

circulatory, *adj.* zirkulie'rend.

circumcise, *vb.* beschnei'den*.

circumcision, *n.* Beschnei'dung, -en *f.*

circumference, *n.* Umfang, ⸗e *m.*

circumlocution, *n.* Ums-chrei'bung, -en *f.*

circumscribe, *vb. (geom.)* um-schrei'ben*; *(delimit)* begren'zen.

circumspect, *adj.* umsichtig.

circumstance, *n.* Umstand, ⸗e *m.; (pl.)* Verhält'nisse *pl.*

circumstantial, *adj.* eingehend; **(c. evidence)** Indi'zienbeweis, -e *m.*

circumvent, *vb.* umge'hen*.

circumvention, *n.* Umge'hung, -en *f.*

circus, *n.* Zirkus, -se *m.*

cirrhosis, *n.* Zirrho'se, -n *f.*

cistern, *n.* Zister'ne, -n *f.*

citadel, *n.* Zitadel'le, -n *f.*

citation, *n.* Auszeichnung, -en *f.; (law)* Vorladung, -en *f.*

cite, *vb.* an·führen, zitie'ren; *(law)* vor·laden*.

citizen, *n.* Bürger, - *m.,* Bürgerin, -nen *f.*

citizenship, *n.* Staatsangehörig-keit, -en *f.*

city, *n.* Stadt, ⸗e *f.*

city map, *n.* Stadtplan, ⸗e *m.*

civic, *adj.* Bürger- *(cpds.)*.

civil, *adj.* bürgerlich; *(law)* zivil'-rechtlich; *(polite)* höflich.

civilian, 1. *n.* Zivilist', -en, -en *m.* **2.** *adj.* bürgerlich.

civility, *n.* Höflichkeit, -en *f.*

civilization, *n.* Zivilisation', -en *f.*

civilize, *vb.* zivilisie'ren.

civilized, *adj.* zivilisiert'.

civil rights, *n.* Bürgerrechte *pl.*

clad, *adj.* geklei'det.

claim, 1. *n.* Anspruch, ⸗e *m.* **2.** *vb.* bean·spruchen, fordern.

claimant, *n.* Bean'spruchende *m.&f.*

clairvoyance, *n.* Hellsehen *nt.*

clairvoyant, 1. *n.* Hellseher, - *m.,* Hellseherin, -nen *f.* **2.** *adj.* hell-seherisch.

clammy, *adj.* feuchtkalt.

clamor, 1. *n.* Geschrei' *nt.* **2.** *vb.* schreien*.

clamp, 1. *n.* Klammer, -n *f.* **2.** *vb.* fest·klammern.

clandestine, *adj.* heimlich.

clap, *vb.* klatschen.

claret, n. Rotwein, -e m.

clarification, n. Klarstellung, -en f.

clarify, vb. klar-stellen.

clarinet, n. Klarinet'te, -n f.

clarity, n. Klarheit, -en f.

clash, 1. n. Zusam'menstoß, -̈ m. **2.** vb. zusam'men-stoßen*; (fig.) sich nicht vertra'gen*.

clasp, 1. n. Schnalle, -n f.; (hands) Händedruck m. **2.** vb. fest-schnallen; (grasp) umfas'sen; (embrace) umar'men.

class, n. Klasse, -n f.; (period of instruction) Stunde, -n f.

classic, classical, adj. klassisch.

classicism, n. Klassizis'mus, -men m.

classification, n. Klassifizie'rung, -en f.

classify, vb. klassifizie'ren.

classmate, n. Klassenkamerad, -en, -en m., Klassenkameradin, -nen f.

classroom, n. Klassenzimmer, - nt.

clatter, 1. n. Geklap'per nt. **2.** vb. klappern.

clause, n. Satzteil, -e m.; (main c.) Hauptsatz, -̈e m.; (subordinate c.) Nebensatz, -̈e m.; (law) Klausel, -n f.

claw, 1. n. Kralle, -n f., Klaue, -n f. **2.** vb. krallen.

clay, n. Ton, -e m., Lehm, -e m.

clean, 1. vb. sauber machen, reinigen. **2.** adj. sauber.

clean-cut, adj. sauber.

cleaner, n. (the c.s) Reinigung, -en f.

cleanliness, cleanness, n. Sauberkeit f.

cleanse, vb. reinigen.

clear, 1. vb. klären; (profit) rein verdie'nen; (weather) sich aufklären. **2.** adj. klar.

clearance, n. (enough space) Raum m.; (sale) Räumung, -en f.; (approval) Gutheißung f.

clearing, n. Lichtung, -en f.

clearness, n. Klarheit, -en f.

cleat, n. (naut.) Klampe, -n f.; (on boots) Krampe, -n f.

cleavage, n. Spaltung, -en f.

cleave, vb. spalten*.

cleaver, n. Fleischerbeil, -e nt.

clef, n. Notenschlüssel, - m.

cleft, 1. n. Spalte, -n f. **2.** adj. gespal'ten.

clemency, n. Milde f.

clench, vb. zusam'men-pressen; (fist) ballen.

clergy, n. Geistlichkeit f.

clergyman, n. Geistlich-, - m.

clerical, adj. (eccles.) geistlich, klerikal'; (writing) Schreib-(cpds.).

clerk, n. Schreiber, - m., Schreibkraft, -̈e f.; (salesc.) Verkäu'fer, - m., Verkäu'ferin, -nen f.

clever, adj. klug (-̈), geschickt', schlau.

cleverness, n. Klugheit, -en f., Geschick'lichkeit, -en f.

clew, n. (object) Knäuel, - nt.

cliché, n. Klischee', -s nt.

click, n. Klicken nt.; (language) Schnalzlaut, -e m. **2.** vb. klicken, knacken.

client, n. Kunde, -n, -n m., Kundin, -nen f. Klient', -en, -en m., Klien'tin, -nen f.

clientele, n. Kundschaft, -en f.

cliff, n. Klippe, -n f.

climate, n. Klima, -s or a'te nt.

climatic, adj. klima'tisch.

climax, n. Höhepunkt, -e m.

climb, vb. (intr.) steigen*, klettern; (tr.) erstei'gen*.

climber, n. Kletterer, - m.

clinch, vb. fest-machen; (fig.) den Ausschlag geben*.

cling, vb. sich an-klammern.

clinic, n. Klinik, -en f.

clinical, adj. klinisch.

clip, 1. n. Klammer, -n f.; (jewelry) Schmucknadel, -n f. **2.** vb. beschnei'den*.

clippers, n.pl. Schere, -n f.; (barber) Haarschneidemaschine, -n, -f.

clipping, n. (newspaper) Zeitungsausschnitt, -e m.

clique, n. Clique, -n f.

cloak, n. Mantel, -̈ m.

cloakroom, n. Gardero'be, -n f.

clock, n. Uhr, -en f.

clod, n. Klumpen, - m.

clog, 1. n. Holzschuh, -e m. **2.** vb. verstop'fen.

cloister, n. Kloster, - nt.; (arch.) Kreuzgang, -̈e m.

clone, n. Klon, -s m.

close, 1. adj. (narrow) eng. knapp; (near) nah (-). **2.** vb. schließen; zu-machen.

closeness, n. Enge, -n f., Nähe, -n f.

closet, n. Wandschrank, -̈e m.

clot, 1. n. Klumpen, - m. **2.** vb. gerin'nen*.

cloth, n. Tuch, -̈er nt., Stoff, -e m.

clothe, vb. kleiden.

clothes, n.pl. Kleider pl.

clothing, n. Kleidung, -en f.

cloud, n. Wolke, -n f.

cloudburst, n. Wolkenbruch, -̈e m.

cloudiness, n. Bewölkt'heit f.

cloudy, adj. bewölkt', trübe.

clove, n. Gewürz'nelke, -n f.

clover, n. Klee m.

clown, n. Clown, -s m.

cloy, vb. übersät'tigen.

club, n. (group) Klub, -s m.; (stick) Keule, -n f.

clubs, n. (cards) Treff nt.

clue, n. Anhaltspunkt, -e m., Schlüssel, - m.

clump, n. Klumpen, - m.

clumsiness, n. Ungeschicklichkeit, -en f.

clumsy, adj. ungeschickt.

cluster, 1. n. Büschel, - m. **2.** vb. sich zusam'men-scharen.

clutch, 1. n. (auto) Kuppelung, -en f. **2.** vb. packen.

clutter, vb. umher'-streuen.

coach, 1. n. Kutsche, -n f.; (train) Eisenbahnwagen, - m.; (sports) Trainer, - m., Trainerin, -nen f.; (tutor) Privat'lehrer, - m. **2.** vb. (sports) trainie'ren; (tutor) Privat'stunden geben*.

coagulate, vb. gerin'nen*.

coagulation, n. Gerin'nen nt.

coal, n. Kohle, -n f.

coalesce, vb. verschmel'zen*.

coalition, n. Koaliti'on, -en f.

coarse, adj. grob (-̈).

coarsen, vb. vergrö'bern.

coarseness, n. Grobheit, -en f.

coast, n. Küste, -n f.

coastal, adj. Küsten- (cpds.).

coaster, n. Küstenfahrer, - m.

coat, n. (suit) Jacke, -n f.; (overcoat) Mantel, -̈ m.

coating, n. Überzug, -̈e m.

coat of arms, n. Wappen, - nt.

coax, vb. überre'den.

cobalt, n. Kobalt m.

cobblestone, n. Kopfstein, -e m.

cobweb, n. Spinngewebe, - nt.

cocaine, n. Kokain' nt.

cock, 1. n. Hahn, -̈e m. **2.** vb. (gun) spannen.

cockeyed, adj. schielend; (crazy) verrückt'.

cockpit, n. Führersitz, -e m.

cockroach, n. Küchenschabe, -n f.

cocktail, n. Cocktail, -s m.

cocky, adj. frech.

cocoa, n. Kaka'o, -s m.

coconut, n. Kokosnuß, -̈sse f.

cocoon, n. Kokon', -s m.

cod, n. Kabeljau, -e m.

C. O. D., adv. per Nachnahme.

coddle, vb. verpäp'peln.

code, n. (law) Kodex, -dizes m.; (secret) Kode, -s m.

codeine, n. Kodein' nt.

codfish, n. Kabeljau, -e m.

codify, vb. kodifizie'ren.

cod-liver oil, n. Lebertran m.

coeducation, n. Koedukation' f.

coerce, vb. zwingen*.

coercion, n. Zwang m.

coexist, vb. koexistie'ren.

coffee, n. Kaffee m.

coffin, n. Sarg, -̈e m.

cog, n. Zahn, -̈e m.; (c. railway) Zahnradbahn, -en f.

cogent, adj. zwingend.

cogitate, vb. nach-denken*.

cognizance, n. Kenntnis, -se f.

cognizant, adj. bewußt'.

cogwheel, n. Zahnrad, -̈er nt.

cohere, vb. zusam'men-hängen*.

coherent, adj. zusam'menhängend.

cohesion, n. Kohäsion' f.

cohesive, adj. kohärent'.

cohort, n. Kohor'te, -n f.

coiffure, n. Frisur', -en f.

coil, 1. n. Rolle, -n f.; (elec.) Spule, -n f. **2.** vb. auf-rollen; (rope) auf-schießen.

coin, 1. n. Münze, -n f. **2.** vb. prägen.

coinage, n. Prägung, -en f.

coincide, vb. zusam'men·treffen*.

coincidence, n. Zufall, =e m.

coincident, adj. gleichzeitig.

coincidental, adj. zufällig.

cold, 1. n. Kälte, -n f.; (med.) Erkäl'tung, -en f. **2.** adj. kalt (-).

cold-blooded, adj. kaltblütig.

collaborate, vb. zusam'men·arbeiten, mit·arbeiten.

collaboration, n. Mitarbeit f.

collaborator, n. Mitarbeiter, - m., Mitarbeiterin, -nen f.

collapse, 1. n. Zusam'menbruch =e m. **2.** vb. zusam'men·brechen*.

collar, n. Kragen, - m.

collarbone, n. Schlüsselbein, -e nt.

collate, vb. verglei'chen*.

collateral, 1. n. (econ.) Deckung f. **2.** adj. kollateral'.

colleague, n. Kolle'ge, -n, -n m., Kolle'gin, -nen f.

collect, vb. sammeln; (money) ein·kassieren.

collection, n. Sammlung, -en f.; (church) Kollek'te, -n f.

collective, adj. kollektiv'.

collector, n. (art.) Sammler, - m., Sammlerin, -nen f.; (tickets) Schaffner, - m.; (tax) Steuereinnehmer, - m.

college, n. College, -s nt.

collegiate, adj. College- (cpds.)

collide, vb. zusam'men·stoßen*.

collision, n. Zusam'menstoß, =e m.

colloquial, adj. umgangssprachlich.

colloquialism, n. umgangssprachlicher Ausdruck, =e m.

collusion, n. Kollusion', -en f.

Cologne, n. Köln nt.

colon, n. (typogr.) Doppelpunkt, -e m., Kolon, -s or Kola nt.; (med.) Dickdarm, =e m., Kolon, -s or Kola nt.

colonel, n. Oberst, -en, -en m.

colonial, adj. kolonial'.

colonist, n. Siedler, - m., Kolonist', -en, -en m.

colonization, n. Kolonisation', -en f.

colonize, vb. kolonisie'ren.

colony, n. Kolonie', -i'en f.

color, 1. n. Farbe, -n f. **2.** vb. färben.

colored, adj. farbig.

colorful, adj. farbenreich.

coloring, n. Färbung, -en f.

colorless, adj. farblos.

colossal, adj. kolossal'.

colt, n. Fohlen, -.

column, n. (arch.) Säule, -n f.; (typogr.) Spalte, -n f.; (mil.) Kolon'ne, -n f.

columnist, n. Zeitungsartikelschreiber, - m.

coma, n. Koma nt.

comb, 1. n. Kamm, =e m. **2.** vb. kämmen.

combat, 1. n. Kampf, =e m. **2.** vb. bekäm'pfen.

combatant, n. Kämpfer, - m.

combination, n. Kombination', -en f.

combine, vb. verbin'den*, verei'nigen, zusam'men·setzen, kombinie'ren.

combustible, adj. (ver)brenn'bar.

combustion, n. Verbren'nung f.

come, vb. kommen*.

comedian, n. Komiker, - m.

comedienne, n. Komikerin, -nen f.

comedy, n. Komö'die, -n f.

come in, interj. herein'!

comely, adj. hübsch.

comet, n. Komet', -en, -en m.

comfort, 1. n. Behag'lichkeit, -en f., Bequem'lichkeit, -en f. **2.** vb. trösten.

comfortable, adj. behag'lich, bequem'.

comforter, n. Steppdecke, -n f.

comic, comical, adj. komisch.

comma, n. Komma, -s or -ta nt.

command, 1. n. Befehl', -e m. **2.** vb. befeh'len*.

commandeer, vb. requirie'ren.

commander, n. Befehls'haber, - m.; (navy) Fregat'tenkapitän, -e m.

commander in chief, n. Oberbefehlshaber, - m.

commandment, n. Gebot', -e nt.

commemorate, vb. geden'ken*.

commemoration, n. Gedächt'nisfeier, -n f.

commemorative, *adj.* Gedächt'nis- *(cpds.).*

commence, *vb.* begin'nen*.

commencement, *n.* Anfang, ⸚e *m.; (college)* akade'mische Abschlußfeier, -n *f.*

commend, *vb. (praise)* loben; *(recommend)* empfeh'len*.

commendable, *adj.* lobenswert.

commendation, *n.* Lob *nt.,* Auszeichnung, -en *f.*

commensurate, *adj.* angemessen.

comment, 1. *n.* Bemerkung, -en *f.* **2.** *vb.* bemer'ken.

commentary, *n.* Kommentar', -e *m.*

commentator, *n.* Kommenta'tor, -o'ren *m.*

commerce, *n.* Handel *m.*

commercial, *adj.* kommerziell', kaufmännisch; *(cpds.)* Handels-.

commercialism, *n.* Handelsgeist *m.*

commercialize, *vb.* in den Handel bringen*.

commiserate, *vb.* bemit'leiden.

commissary, *n.* Kommissar', -e *m.,* Kommissa'rin, -nen *f.; (store)* Militärversor'gungsstelle, -n *f.*

commission, 1. *n. (committee)* Kommission', -en *f.; (percentage)* Provision', -en *f.; (assignment)* Auftrag, ⸚e *m.* **2.** *vb.* beauf'tragen; *(mil.)* das Offiziers'patent verlei'hen*.

commissioner, *n.* Beauf'tragt-*m.*

commit, *vb. (give over)* an'vertrauen; *(crime)* bege'hen*; *(oneself)* sich verpflich'ten.

commitment, *n.* Verpflich'tung, -en *f.*

committee, *n.* Ausschuß, ⸚sse *m.*

commodity, *n.* Ware, -n *f.*

common, *adj.* allgemein, gewöhn'lich; *(vulgar)* ordinär'.

commonness, *n.* Häufigkeit *f.*

commonplace, 1. *n.* Gemein'platz, ⸚e *m.* **2.** *adj.* abgedroschen.

commonwealth, *n.* Commonwealth *nt.*

commotion, *n.* Aufruhr *m.*

communal, *adj.* Gemein'de- *(cpds.).*

commune, 1. *n.* Gemein'de, -n *f.* **2.** *vb.* kommunizie'ren.

communicable, *adj.* mitteilbar; *(med.)* ansteckbar.

communicant, *n.* Kommunikant', -en, -en *m.*

communicate, *vb.* mit'teilen.

communication, *n.* Mitteilung, -en *f.*

communicative, *adj.* mitteilsam.

communion, *n.* Gemein'schaft *f.; (eccl.)* Abendmahl *nt.; (Catholic)* Kommunion', -en *f.*

communiqué, *n.* Kommuniqué'-s *nt.*

communism, *n.* Kommunis'mus *m.*

communist, 1. *n.* Kommunist', -en, -en *m.,* Kommunis'tin, -nen *f.* **2.** *adj.* kommuni'stisch.

communistic, *adj.* kommuni'stisch.

community, *n.* Gemein'de, -n *f.,* Gemein'schaft, -en *f.*

commutation, *n.* Austausch *m.; (law)* Milderung *f.*

commute, *vb.* pendeln; *(jur)* herab'setzen.

commuter, *n.* Pendler, - *m.,* Pendlerin, -nen *f.*

compact, 1. *n. (cosmetics)* Puderdose, -n *f.* **2.** *adj.* kompakt'.

compactness, *n.* Kompakt'heit *f.*

companion, *n.* Beglei'ter *m.,* Beglei'terin, -nen *f.*

companionable, *adj.* gesel'lig.

companionship, *n.* Kamerad'schaft, -en *f.*

company, *n.* Gesell'schaft, -en *f.,* Firma, -men *f.*

comparable, *adj.* vergleich'bar.

comparative, 1. *n. (gram.)* Komparativ, -e *m.* **2.** *adj.* verhält'nismäßig.

compare, *vb.* verglei'chen*.

comparison, *n.* Vergleich', -e *m.*

compartment, *n.* Abtei'lung, -en *f.,* Fach, ⸚er *nt.; (train)* Abteil -en *nt.*

compass, *n. (naut.)* Kompaß, ⸚sse *m.; (geom.)* Zirkel, - *m.*

compassion, *n.* Mitleid *nt.,* Erbar'men *nt.*

compassionate, *adj.* mitleidig.

compatible, *adj.* verträg'lich.

compatriot, *n.* Landsmann, -leute *m.,* Landsmännin, -nen *f.*

compel, vb. zwingen*.

compensate, vb. entschä'digen, kompensie'ren.

compensation, n. Entschä'digung, -en f., Kompensation', -en f.

compete, vb. wetteifern, konkurrie'ren.

competence, n. (ability) Fähigkeit, -en f.; (field of responsibility) Zuständigkeit, -en f.

competent, adj. (able) fähig; (responsible) zuständig.

competition, n. Wettbewerb, -e m., Konkurrenz', -en f.

competitive, adj. auf Konkurrenz' eingestellt.

competitor, n. Mitbewerber, -m., Mitbewerberin, -nen f. Konkurrent', -en, -en m., Konkurren'tin, -nen f.

compile, vb. zusam'mentragen*.

complacency, n. Selbstzufriedenheit f.

complacent, adj. selbstzufrieden.

complain, vb. sich bekla'gen, sich beschwe'ren.

complaint, n. Klage, -n f., Beschwer'de, -n f.

complement, 1. n. Ergän'zung, -en f. 2. vb. ergän'zen.

complete, 1. vb. vollen'den. 2. adj. vollständig, fertig.

completely, adv. völlig.

completion, n. Vollen'dung, -en f.

complex, 1. n. Komplex', -e m. 2. adj. komplex', weitläufig.

complexion, n. (type) Natur' f.; (skin) Teint, -s m.

complexity, n. Weitläufigkeit, -en f.

compliance, n. Bereit'willigkeit f., Einwilligen nt.

compliant, adj. bereit'willig, nachgiebig.

complicate, vb. (make more complex) verwi'ckeln; (make harder) erschwe'ren.

complicated, adj. kompliziert', verwi'ckelt.

complication, n. Komplikation', -en f.

compliment, 1. n. Kompliment', -e nt. 2. vb. beglück'wünschen.

complimentary, adj. schmeichelhaft; (free) Frei- (cpds.).

comply, vb. ein'willigen, sich fügen.

component, n. Bestand'teil, -e m.

compose, vb. zusam'mensetzen; (music) komponie'ren.

composer, n. Komponist', -en, -en m., Komponis'tin, -nen f.

composite, adj. zusam'mengesetzt.

composition, n. Zusam'mensetzung, -en f.; (school) Aufsatz, -̈e m.; (mus.) Komposition', -en f.

composure, n. Fassung f.

compote, n. Kompott', -e nt.

compound, 1. n. Mischung, -en f.; (gram.) Kompo'situm, -ta nt.; (chem.) Verbin'dung, -en f.; (mil.) eingezäunte Lagerabteilung, -en f. 2. adj. zusam'mengesetzt; (c. interest) Zinseszins m. 3. vb. zusam'men·setzen*.

comprehend, vb. verste'hen*, begrei'fen*.

comprehensible, adj. verständ'lich.

comprehension, n. Fassungsvermögen, -nt.

comprehensive, adj. umfas'send.

compress, 1. n. Kompres'se, -n f. 2 vb. zusam'men·pressen.

compressed, adj. Preß- (cpds.).

compression, n. Kompression', -en f.

comprise, vb. umfas'sen, enthal'ten*.

compromise, 1. n. Kompromiß', -sse m. 2. vb. einen Kompromiß schließen*; (embarrass) kompromittie'ren.

compulsion, n. Zwang m.

compulsive, adj. Zwangs- (cpds.).

compulsory, adj. obligato'risch.

compunction, n. Beden'ken, - nt.

computation, n. Berech'nung, -en f.

compute, vb. rechnen, berech'nen.

computer, n. Komputer, - m.; Elektro'nenrechner, - m.

computerize, vb. auf Komputer umstellen.

computer science, n. Kompu'terwissenschaft f.

comrade, n. Kamerad', -en, -en m., Kamera'din, -nen f.

concave, adj. konkav'.

conceal, vb. verste'cken, verheim'lichen.

concealment, n. Versteck', -e nt., Verheim'lichung, -en f.

concede, vb. zu'gestehen*.

conceit, n. Einbildung, -en f.

conceited, adj. eingebildet.

conceivable, adj. vorstellbar.

conceivably, adv. unter Umständen.

conceive, vb. begrei'fen*, sich vor'stellen; (child) empfan'gen*.

concentrate, vb. konzentrie'ren.

concentration camp, n. Konzentrations'lager, - nt.

concept, n. Begriff', -e m.

concern, 1. n. (affair) Angelegenheit, -en f.; (interest) Interes'se, -n nt.; (firm) Konzern', -e m.; (worry) Sorge, -n f. **2.** vb. an'gehen*.

concerning, prep. hinsichtlich.

concert, n. Konzert', -e nt.

concession, n. Konzession', -en f.

concierge, n. Portier', -s m.

conciliate, vb. versöh'nen, schlichten.

conciliation, n. Versöh'nung, -en f., Schlichtung, -en f.

conciliator, n. Schlichter, - m.

conciliatory, adj. versöh'nend.

concise, adj. knapp, gedrängt'.

conciseness, n. Gedrängt'heit f.

conclude, vb. schließen*.

conclusion, n. Abschluß, ⸗sse m., Schluß, ⸗sse m.

conclusive, adj. entschei'dend.

concoct, vb. zusam'menbrauen.

concoction, n. Gebräu', -e nt.

concomitant, adj. beglei'tend.

concord, n. Eintracht f.

concourse, n. Sammelplatz, ⸗e m.

concrete, 1. n. Zement' m. **2.** adj. konkret'.

concubine, n. Konkubi'ne, -n f.

concur, vb. überein'stimmen.

concurrence, n. Zustimmung, -en f.

concurrent, adj. (simultaneous) gleichzeitig; (agreeing) überein'stimmend.

concussion, n. Erschüt'terung, -en f.; (brain) Gehirn'erschütterung, -en f.

condemn, vb. verur'teilen; (disapprove) mißbil'ligen.

condemnable, adj. strafbar; nichtswürdig.

condemnation, n. Verur'teilung f.; Mißbilligung f.

condensation, n. Kondensation', -en f.; (summary) Zusam'menfassung, -en f.

condense, vb. kondensie'ren; (summarize) zusam'menfassen.

condenser, n. Kondensa'tor, -o'ren m.

condescend, vb. sich herab'lassen*.

condescending, adj. herab'lassend.

condescension, n. Herab'lassung, -en f.

condiment, n. Gewürz', -e nt.

condition, 1. n. (stipulation) Bedin'gung, -en f.; (state) Zustand, ⸗e m. **2.** vb. bedin'gen; (training) in Form bringen*.

conditional, adj. abhängig.

conditionally, adv. unter gewissen Bedingungen.

condolence, n. Beileid nt.

condom, n. Kondom, -s m.

condominium, n. Eigentumswohnung, -en f.

condone, vb. entschul'digen.

conducive, adj. förderlich.

conduct, 1. n. Betra'gen nt. **2.** vb. leiten; (behave) sich betra'gen*; (music) dirigie'ren.

conductor, n. Leiter, - m., Leiterin, -nen f.; (train) Schaffner, - m., Schaffnerin, -nen f.; (music) Dirigent', -en, -en m., Dirigen'tin, -nen f.

conduit, n. Leitungsrohr, -e nt.

cone, n. Kegel, - m.; (pine) Tannenzapfen, - m.

confection, n. Konfekt', -e nt.

confectioner, n. Zuckerbäcker, - m.

confectionery, n. Zuckerwerk nt.

confederacy, n. Bündnis, -se nt.; (conspiracy) Verschwö'rung, -en f.

confederate, 1. n. Helfershelfer, - m. **2.** adj. verbün'det.

confederation, n. Staatenbund, -̈e m.

confer, vb. (bestow) verlei'hen*; (counsel) berat'schlagen.

conference, n. Bespre'chung, -en f., Konferenz', -en f.

confess, vb. zu•gestehen*; (eccles.) beichten.

confession, n. Geständ'nis, -se nt.; (eccles.) Beichte, -n f.

confessional, n. Beichtstuhl, -̈e m.

confessor, n. Beken'ner, - m.; (father c.) Beichtvater, -̈ m.

confidant, n. Vertraut'- m.

confidante, n. Vertraut'- f.

confide, vb. vertrau'en; sich an•vertrauen.

confidence, n. (trust) Vertrau'en nt.; (assurance) Zuversicht f.

confident, adj. zuversichtlich.

confidential, adj. vertrau'lich.

confidentially, adv. unter uns.

confine, vb. beschrän'ken; (imprison) ein•sperren.

confirm, vb. bestä'tigen; (church) konfirmie'ren.

confirmation, n. Bestä'tigung, -en f.; (church) Konfirmation', -en f.

confiscate, vb. beschlag'nahmen, konfiszie'ren.

confiscation, n. Beschlag'nahme, -n f.

conflagration, n. Brand, -̈e m., Feuersbrunst f.

conflict, 1. n. Konflikt', -e m. **2.** vb. in Widerspruch stehen*, nicht überein'stimmen.

conform, vb. sich an•passen.

conformation, n. Anpassung, -en f.; (shape) Gestal'tung, -en f.

conformer, conformist, n. Mitmacher, - m.

conformity, n. Überein'stimmung, -en f.

confound, vb. (make confused) verwir'ren; (c. A with B) A mit B

verwech'seln; **(c. it!)** zum Donnerwetter!

confront, vb. gegenü'ber•stellen, konfrontie'ren.

confuse, vb. (make confused) verwir'ren; **(c. A with B)** A mit B verwech'seln.

confusion, n. Verwir'rung, -en f.; Durcheinan'der nt.; Verwechs'lung, -en f.

congeal, vb. erstar'ren.

congenial, adj. sympa'thisch.

congenital, adj. angeboren.

congestion, n. Stauung, -en f.

conglomerate, 1. n. Anhäufung, -en f. **2.** vb. zusam'men•ballen.

conglomeration, n. Anhäufung, -en f.

congratulate, vb. gratulie'ren, beglück'wünschen.

congratulation, n. Glückwunsch, -̈e m.

congratulatory, adj. Glückwunsch- (cpds.).

congregate, vb. sich versam'meln.

congregation, n. (church) Gemein'de, -n f.

congress, n. Kongreß', -sse m.

congressional, adj. Kongreß'- (cpds.).

conjecture, 1. n. Mutmaßung, -en f. **2.** vb. mutmaßen.

conjugal, adj. ehelich.

conjugate, vb. konjugie'ren.

conjugation, n. Konjugation', -en f.

conjunction, n. Zusam'mentreffen, - nt.; (gram.) Bindewort, -̈er nt., Konjunktion', -en f.

conjunctive, adj. verbin'dend.

conjunctivitis, n. Bindehautentzündung, -en f.

conjure, vb. zaubern.

connect, vb. verbin'den*.

connection, n. Verbin'dung, -en f.

connive, vb. in heimlichem Einverständnis stehen*.

connoisseur, n. Kenner, - m.

connotation, n. Nebenbedeutung, -en f., Beiklang, -̈e m.

connote, vb. in sich schließen*.

conquer, vb. ero'bern.

conqueror, n. Ero'berer, - m.

conquest, n. Ero'berung, -en f.

conscience, n. Gewis'sen, - nt.

conscientious, adj. gewis'senhaft.

conscious, adj. bewußt', bei Bewußt'sein.

consciousness, n. Bewußt'sein nt.

conscript, n. Dienstpflichtig- m.

conscription, n. Militär'dienstpflicht f.

consecrate, vb. weihen.

consecration, n. Weihung, -en f.

consecutive, adj. aufeinan'derfolgend.

consensus, n. allgemeine Meinung, -en f.

consent, 1. n. Zustimmung, -en f. 2. vb. zu-stimmen.

consequence, n. Folge, -n f.

consequent, adj. folgend.

consequential, adj. folgenreich.

consequently, adv. folglich.

conservation, n. Bewah'rung, -en f.; Konservie'rung, -en f.

conservatism, n. Konservatis'mus m.

conservative, adj. konservativ'.

conservatory, n. (music) Konservato'rium, -rien nt.; (plants) Treibhaus, -̈er nt.

conserve, vb. bewah'ren.

consider, vb. betrach'ten; (take into account) berück'sichtigen.

considerable, adj. beträcht'lich.

considerate, adj. rücksichtsvoll.

consideration, n. (thought) Erwä'gung, -en f.; (kindness) Rücksicht, -en f.; (in c. of) in Anbetracht.

consign, vb. übersen'den*.

consignment, n. Übersen'dung, -en f.

consist, vb. beste'hen*.

consistency, n. Folgerichtigkeit f.; (substance) Konsistenz' f.

consistent, adj. folgerichtig, konsequent'.

consolation, n. Trost m.

console, vb. trösten.

consolidate, vb. festigen, konsolidie'ren.

consommé, n. Bouillon', -s f.

consonant, n. Konsonant', -en, -en m.

consort, 1. n. Gemahl', -e m.; Gemah'lin, -nen f. 2. vb. verkeh'ren.

conspicuous, adj. auffällig.

conspiracy, n. Verschwö'rung, -en f.

conspirator, n. Verschwö'rer, - m.; Verschwö'rerin, -nen f.

conspire, vb. sich verschwö'ren*.

constancy, n. Standhaftigkeit f.

constant, adj. bestän'dig, konstant'.

constantly, adv. dauernd.

constellation, n. Konstellation', -en f.

consternation, n. Bestür'zung, -en f.

constipated, adj. verstopft'.

constipation, n. Verstop'fung, -en f.

constituency, n. (people) Wählerschaft, -en f.; (place) Wahlbezirk, -e m.

constituent, n. Bestand'teil, -e m.; (voter) Wähler, - m., Wählerin, -nen f.

constitute, vb. (make up) ausmachen; (found) gründen.

constitution, n. Konstitution', -en f.; (government) Verfas'sung, -en f.

constitutional, adj. konstitutionell'.

constrain, vb. zwingen*.

constrict, vb. zusam'men-ziehen*.

construct, vb. konstruie'ren.

construction, n. Konstruktion', -en f.

constructive, adj. positiv.

construe, vb. aus-legen.

consul, n. Konsul, -n, m.

consular, adj. konsula'risch.

consulate, n. Konsulat', -e nt.

consult, vb. zu Rate ziehen*; konsultie'ren.

consultant, n. Bera'ter, - m., Bera'terin, -nen f.

consultation, n. Konferenz', -en f.; (med.) Konsultation', -en f.

consume, vb. verzeh'ren, verbrau'chen.

consumer, n. Verbrau'cher, - m.

consummate, 1. vb. vollen'den. 2. adj. vollen'det.

consummation, *n.* Vollzie'hung, -en *f.*

consumption, *n.* Verbrauch' *m.;* *(med.)* Schwindsucht *f.*

consumptive, *adj.* schwindsüchtig.

contact, 1. *n.* Kontakt', -e *m.* **2.** *vb.* sich in Verbin'dung setzen mit.

contagion, *n.* Ansteckung, -en *f.*

contagious, *adj.* ansteckend.

contain, *vb.* enthal'ten*.

container, *n.* Behäl'ter, - *m.*

contaminate, *vb.* verun'reinigen.

contemplate, *vb.* betrach'ten.

contemplation, *n.* Betrach'tung, -en *f.*

contemplative, *adj.* nachdenklich.

contemporary, 1. *n.* Zeitgenosse, -n, -n, *m.,* Zeitgenossin, -nen *f.* **2.** *adj.* zeitgenössisch.

contempt, *n.* Verach'tung, -en *f.*

contemptible, *adj.* verach'tenswert.

contemptuous, *adj.* veräcit'lich.

contend, *vb. (assert)* behaup'ten; *(fight)* streiten*.

contender, *n.* Streiter, - *m.*

content, 1. *n.* Inhalt *m.* **2.** *adj.* zufrie'den.

contented, *adj.* zufrie'den.

contention, *n. (assertion)* Behaup'tung, -en *f.; (fight)* Streit, -e *m.*

contentment, *n.* Zufrie'denheit *f.*

contest, 1. *n.* Wettstreit, -e *m.; (advertising)* Preisausschreiben, -nt. **2.** *vb.* bestrei'ten*.

contestant, *n.* Bewer'ber, - *m.,* Bewer'berin, -nen *f.*

context, *n.* Zusam'menhang, -e *m.*

continent, 1. *n.* Kontinent, -e *m.* **2.** *adj.* enthalt'sam.

continental, *adj.* kontinental'.

contingency, *n.* Eventualität', -en *f.*

continual, *adj.* dauernd.

continuation, *n.* Fortsetzung, -en *f.*

continue, *vb. (tr.)* fort'setzen; *(intr.)* fort'fahren*.

continuity, *n.* Fortdauer *f.*

continuous, *adj.* fortdauernd.

contort, *vb.* verdre'hen.

contortion, *n.* Verdre'hung, -en *f.*

contour, *n.* Umriß', -sse *m.*

contraband, *n.* Schmuggelware, -n *f.*

contraception, *n.* Empfängnisverhütung *f.*

contraceptive device, *n.* Verhütungsmittel, -nt.

contract, 1. *n.* Vertrag', -e *m.* **2.** *vb.* vertrag'lich ab'schließen*; *(disease)* sich zu'ziehen*.

contraction, *n.* Zusam'menziehung, -en *f.*

contractor, *n.* Bauunternehmer, - *m.*

contradict, *vb.* widerspre'chen*.

contradiction, *n.* Widerspruch, -e *m.*

contradictory, *adj.* widerspre'chend.

contralto, *n.* Altstimme, -n *f.*

contraption, *n.* Vorrichtung, -en *f.*

contrary, 1. *n.* Gegenteil, -e *nt.* **2.** *adj. (opposite)* entge'gengesetzt; *(obstinate)* widerspenstig.

contrast, 1. *n.* Gegensatz, -e *m.* **2.** *vb.* entge'gensetzen.

contribute, *vb.* bei'tragen*.

contribution, *n.* Beitrag, -e *m.,* Beiträgerin, -nen *f.*

contributor, *n.* Beiträger, - *m.,* Beiträgerin, -nen *f.*

contributory, *adj.* mitwirkend.

contrite, *adj.* zerknirscht'.

contrivance, *n.* Vorrichtung, -en *f.*

contrive, *vb.* fertig bringen*, erfin'den*.

control, 1. *n.* Kontrol'le, -n *f.* **2.** *vb.* beherr'schen.

controllable, *adj.* kontrollier'bar.

controller, *n.* Überprü'fer, - *m.*

controversial, *adj.* strittig.

controversy, *n.* Streitfrage, -n *f.*

contusion, *n.* Quetschung, -en *f.*

convalesce, *vb.* gene'sen*.

convalescence, *n.* Konvaleszenz' *f.*

convalescent, *adj.* gene'send.

convene, *vb.* zusam'men-kommen*.

convenience, *n.* Annehmlichkeit, -en *f.*

convenient, *adj.* bequem', geeig'-net.

convent, *n.* Nonnenkloster, ⸚ *nt.*

convention, *n.* Versamm'lung, -en *f.,* Tagung, -en *f.; (contract)* Abkommen, - *nt.; (tradition)* Konvention', -en *f.*

conventional, *adj.* konven-tionell'.

converge, *vb.* zusam'men-laufen*.

convergence, *n.* Konvergenz', -en *f.*

convergent, *adj.* konvergie'rend.

conversant with, *adj.* bewan'dert in.

conversational, *adj.* Gesprächs'- *(cpds.).*

converse, 1. *n.* Kehrseite, -n *f.* 2. *vb.* sich unterhal'ten*. 3. *adj.* um-gekehrt.

convert, 1. *n.* Konvertit', -en, -en *m.* 2. *vb. (belief, goods, money)* konvertie'ren; *(missionary)* be-keh'ren.

converter, *n.* Bekeh'rer, - *m.; (elec.)* Transforma'tor, -o'ren *m.*

convertible, 1. *n. (auto)* Kabri-olett', -s *nt.* 2. *adj.* konvertier'bar.

convex, *adj.* konvex'.

convey, *vb.* beför'dern, übermit'-teln.

conveyance, *n. (vehicle)* Beför'-derungsmittel, - *nt.; (law)* Übermitt'-lung, -en *f.*

conveyor, *n.* Beför'derer, - *m.*

convict, 1. *n.* Sträfling, -e *m.* 2. *vb.* überfüh'ren.

conviction, *n.* Schuldigspre-chung, -en *f.; (belief)* Über-zeu'gung, -en *f.*

convince, *vb.* überzeu'gen.

convincing, *adj.* überzeu'gend.

convivial, *adj.* gesel'lig.

convocation, *n.* Versamm'lung, -en *f.*

convoy, 1. *n.* Geleit'zug, ⸚e *m.* 2. *vb.* gelei'ten.

convulse, *vb.* in Zuckungen ver-setzen; **(be c.d)** sich krümmen.

convulsion, *n.* Krampf, ⸚e *m.*

convulsive, *adj.* krampfhaft.

cook, 1. *n.* Koch, ⸚e *m.;* Köchin, -nen *f.* 2. *vb.* kochen.

cookbook, *n.* Kochbuch, ⸚er *nt.*

cookie, *n.* Keks, -e *m.*

cool, 1. *adj.* kühl. 2. *vb.* ab-kühlen.

coolness, *n.* Kühle, *f.*

coop, *n.* Hühnerkorb, ⸚e *m.*

cooperate, *vb.* zusam'men-ar-beiten.

cooperation, *n.* Zusam'menar-beit, -en *f.*

cooperative, 1. *n.* Konsum'-verein, -e *m.* 2. *adj.* hilfsbereit.

coordinate, 1. *adj.* beigeordnet, koordiniert'. 2. *vb.* bei-orden, koordinie'ren.

coordination, *n.* Beiordnung, -en *f.;* Koordination', -en *f.*

coordinator, *n.* Organisations'-planer, - *m.*

cop, *n.* Schupo, -s *m.*

cope, *vb.* sich ab-mühen.

copier, *n.* Kopier'maschine, -n *f.*

copious, *adj.* reichlich.

copper, *n.* Kupfer *nt.*

copy, 1. *n.* Abschrift, -en *f.,* Kopie', -i'en *f.; (book)* Exem-plar', -e *nt.* 2. *vb.* ab-schreiben*, kopie'ren.

copyright, *n.* Urheberrecht, -e *nt.*

coquette, 1. *n.* Koket'te, -n *f.* 2. *adj.* kokett'.

coral, *n.* Koral'le, -n *f.*

cord, *n.* Schnur, ⸚e *f.*

cordial, *adj.* herzlich.

cordiality, *n.* Herzlichkeit *f.*

cordovan, *n.* Korduanleder, *nt.*

core, *n. (fruit)* Kernhaus, ⸚er *nt.; (heart)* Kern, -e *m.*

cork, *n. (material)* Kork *m.; (stopper)* Korken, - *m.*

corkscrew, *n.* Korkenzieher, - *m.*

corn, *n. (grain)* Getrei'de *nt.; (maize)* Mais *m.; (foot)* Hühner-auge, -n *nt.*

cornea, *n.* Hornhaut, ⸚e *f.*

corner, *n.* Ecke, -n *f.*

cornet, *n.* Kornett', -e *nt.*

cornice, *n.* Gesims', -e *nt.*

corn-plaster, *n.* Hühneraugen-pflaster, - *nt.*

cornstarch, *n.* Maize'na *nt.*

coronation, *n.* Krönung, -en *f.*

coronet, *n.* Adelskrone, -n *f.*

corporal, 1. *n. (mil.)* Gefreit- *m.* 2. *adj.* körperlich.

corporate, *adj.* körperschaftlich.

corporation, *n.* Körperschaft, -en

f.; (comm.) Aktiengesellschaft, -en *f.*

corps, *n.* Korps, - *nt.*

corpse, *n.* Leichnam, -e *m.*

corpulent, *adj.* korpulent'.

corpuscle, *n.* Körperchen, - *nt.*

correct, 1. *adj.* richtig, korrekt'. **2.** *vb.* verbes'sern, berich'tigen, korrigie'ren.

correction, *n.* Verbes'serung, -en *f.*, Berich'tigung, -en *f.*

corrective, *adj.* korrektiv'.

correctness, *n.* Korrekt'heit, -en *f.*

correlate, *vb.* aufeinan'der bezie'hen*.

correlation, *n.* Korrelation', -en *f.*

correspond, *vb.* entspre'chen*; *(agree)* überein'stimmen; *(letters)* korrespondie'ren.

correspondence, *n.* Entspre'chung, -en *f.; (agreement)* Überein'stimmung, -en *f.; (letters)* Korrespondenz', -en *f.*

correspondent, *n.* Korrespondent', -en,-en *m.*, Korresponden'tin, -nen *f.*

corridor, *n.* Korridor, -e *m.*

corroborate, *vb.* bestä'tigen.

corroboration, *n.* Bestä'tigung, -en *f.*

corrode, *vb.* korrodie'ren.

corrosion, *n.* Korrosion', -en *f.*

corrugate, *vb.* wellen.

corrupt, 1. *vb.* korrumpie'ren. **2.** *adj.* korrupt'.

corrupter, *n.* Verfüh'rer, *m.* Verfüh'rerin, -nen *f.*

corruptible, *adj.* verführ'bar.

corruption, *n.* Korruption', -en *f.*

corsage, *n.* Ansteckblume, -n *f.*

corset, *n.* Korsett', -s *nt.*

cortège, *n.* Leichenzug, -̈e *m.*

cosmetic, 1. *n.* kosme'tisches Mittel, - *nt.* **2.** *adj.* kosme'tisch.

cosmic, *adj.* kosmisch.

cosmopolitan, *adj.* kosmopoli'tisch.

cosmos, *n.* Kosmos *m.*

cost, 1. *n.* Preis, -e *m.;* Kosten *pl.* **2.** *vb.* kosten.

costliness, *n.* Kostspieligkeit, -en *f.*

costly, *adj.* kostspielig.

costume, *n. (fancy)* Kostüm, -e *nt.; (native)* Tracht, -en *f.*

cot, *n.* Feldbett, -en *nt.*

cottage, *n.* Häuschen, - *nt.; Landhaus, -̈er *nt.*

cotton, *n.* Baumwolle *f.;* Watte *f.*

couch, *n.* Couch, -es *f.*

cough, 1. *n.* Husten *m.* **2.** *vb.* husten.

could, *vb. (was able)* konnte; *(would be able)* könnte.

council, *n.* Rat, -̈e *m.*

counsel, 1. *n.* Rat, -̈e *m.; (lawyer)* Anwalt, -̈e *m.*, Anwältin, -nen *f.* **2.** *vb.* bera'ten*, raten*.

counselor, *n.* Bera'ter, - *m.*, Bera'terin, -nen *f.*

count, 1. *n.* Gesamt'zahl, -en *f.; (noble)* Graf, -en, -en *m.* **2.** *vb.* zählen.

countenance, *n.* Gesicht', -er *nt.*

counter, 1. *n.* Zähler, - *m.; (store)* Ladentisch, -e *m.* **2.** *adv.* (c. to) entge'gen.

counteract, *vb.* entge'gen·arbeiten.

counterattack, 1. *n.* Gegenangriff, -e *m.* **2.** *vb.* einen Gegenangriff machen.

counterbalance, 1. *n.* Gegengewicht, -e *nt.* **2.** *vb.* auf·wiegen*.

counterfeit, 1. *n.* Falschgeld, -er *nt.* **2.** *adj.* gefälscht*. **3.** *vb.* fälschen.

countermand, *vb.* widerru'fen*.

counteroffensive, *n.* Gegenoffensive, -n *f.*

counterpart, *n.* Gegenstück, -e *nt.*

countess, *n.* Gräfin, -nen *f.*

countless, *adj.* zahllos.

country, *n.* Land, -̈er *nt.*

countryman, *n.* Landsmann, -leute *m.*

countryside, *n.* Landschaft, -en *f.*

county, *n.* Grafschaft, -en *f.*

coupé, *n.* geschlossenes Zweisitzer-Auto, -s *nt.*

couple, 1. *n.* Paar, -e *nt.* **2.** *vb.* koppeln.

coupon, *n.* Coupon', -s *m.*

courage, *n.* Mut *m.*

courageous, *adj.* mutig.

courier, *n.* Kurier', -e *m.*

course, *n.* Lauf, -̈e *m.; (race)*

Rennbahn, -en *f.; (nautical)* Kurs, -e *m.; (school)* Kursus, Kurse *m.; (food)* Gang, ⸚e *m.; (of c.)* natür'lich.

court, 1. *n.* Hof, ⸚e *m.* 2. *vb.* den Hof machen.

courteous, *adj.* höflich.

courtesan, *n.* Kurtisa'ne, -n *f.*

courtesy, *n.* Höflichkeit, -en *f.*

courthouse, *n.* Gerichts'gebäude, - *nt.*

courtier, *n.* Höfling, -e *m.*

courtly, *adj.* höfisch.

court-martial, *n.* Kriegsgericht, -e *nt.*

courtroom, *n.* Gerichts'saal, -säle *m.*

courtship, *n.* Freien *nt.*

courtyard, *n.* Hof, ⸚e *m.*

cousin, *n.* Vetter, -n *m.;* Cousi'ne, -n *f.*

covenant, *n.* Vertrag', ⸚e *m.*

cover, 1. *n.* Deckel, - *m.* 2. *vb.* bede'cken; (c. up) zu'decken.

covering, *n.* Bede'ckung, -en *f.*

covet, *vb.* begeh'ren.

covetous, *adj.* begie'rig.

cow, *n.* Kuh, ⸚e *f.*

coward, *n.* Feigling, -e *m.*

cowardice, *n.* Feigheit, -en *f.*

cowardly, *adj.* feige.

cowboy, *n.* Cowboy, -s *m.*

cower, *vb.* kauern.

cowhide, *n.* Rindsleder, - *nt.*

coy, *adj.* spröde.

cozy, *adj.* behag'lich.

crab, *n.* Taschenkrebs, -e *m.*

crack, 1. *n.* Spalt, -e *m.*, Sprung, ⸚e *m.*, Riß, -sse *m.* 2. *vb.* brechen*, springen*.

cracker, *n.* Salzkeks, -e *m.*

cradle, *n.* Wiege, -n *f.*

craft, *n.* Kunstfertigkeit, -en *f.; (ship)* Schiff, -e *nt.*

craftsman, *n.* Handwerker, - *m.*

craftsmanship, *n.* Kunstfertigkeit, -en *f.*

crafty, *adj.* gewiegt'.

cram, *vb.* voll'stopfen; *(exam)* pauken.

cramp, *n.* Krampf, ⸚e *m.*

crane, *n.* Kran, ⸚e *m.; (bird)* Kranich, -e *m.*

crank, 1. *n. (handle)* Kurbel, -n *f.; (crackpot)* Sonderling, -e *m.* 2. *vb.* an'kurbeln.

cranky, *adj.* mißvergnügt, grantig

cranny, *n.* Ritze, -n *f.*

crash, 1. *n.* Krach *m.; (collision)* Zusam'menstoß, ⸚e *m.; (plane)* Absturz, ⸚e *m.* 2. *vb.* krachen; zusam'men·stoßen*; ab'stürzen.

crate, *n.* Kiste, -n *f.*

crater, *n.* Krater, - *m.*

crave, *vb.* verlan'gen nach.

craving, *adj.* gieriges Verlan'gen, - *nt.*

crawl, *vb.* kriechen*; *(swimming)* kraulen.

crayon, *n.* Buntstift, -e *m.*

crazed, *adj.* wahnsinnig.

crazy, *adj.* verrückt'.

creak, *vb.* knarren.

cream, *n.* Sahne *f.*, Rahm *m.; (cosmetic)* Creme, -s *f.*, Krem, -s *m.*

creamery, *n.* Molkerei', -en *f.*

creamy, *adj.* sahnig.

crease, 1. *n.* Falte, -n *f.* 2. *vb.* falten.

create, *vb.* schaffen*, erschaf'fen*; erzeu'gen.

creation, *n.* Erschaf'fung, -en *f.;* Schöpfung, -en *f.*

creative, *adj.* schöpferisch.

creator, *n.* Schöpfer, - *m.*

creature, *n.* Geschöpf', -e *nt.;* Wesen, - *nt.*

credentials, *n.pl.* Beglau'bigungsschreiben, - *nt.*

credibility, *n.* Glaubwürdigkeit *f.*

credible, *adj.* glaubwürdig.

credit, 1. *n.* Verdienst', *nt.; (comm.)* Kredit', -e *m.* 2. *vb.* gut·schreiben*.

creditable, *adj.* anerkennenswert.

credit card, *n.* Kredit'karte, -n *f.*

creditor, *n.* Gläubig- *m.*

credo, *n.* Glaubensbekenntnis, -se *nt.*

credulity, *n.* Leichtgläubigkeit *f.*

credulous, *adj.* leichtgläubig.

creed, *n.* Glaubensbekenntnis, -se *nt.*

creek, *n.* Bach, ⸚e *m.*

creep, *vb.* kriechen*.

cremate, *vb.* ein·äschern.

cremation, *n.* Einäscherung, -en *f.*

crematory, *n.* Krema'to'rium, -rien *nt.*

crepe, *n.* Krepp *m.*

crescent, *n.* Mondsichel, -n *f.*

crest, *n.* Kamm, -̈e *m.*

crestfallen, *adj.* geknickt'.

cretonne, *n.* Kretonn'e, -s *m.*

crevasse, *n.* Gletscherspalte, -n *f.*

crevice, *n.* Riß, -sse *m.*

crew, *n.* Mannschaft, -en *f.*

crib, *n.* Krippe, -n *f.; (bed)* Kinderbett, -en *nt.*

cricket, *n.* Grille, -n *f.*

crime, *n.* Verbre'chen, - *nt.*

criminal, 1. *n.* Verbre'cher, - *m.,* Verbre'cherin, -nen *f.* **2.** *adj.* verbre'cherisch.

criminology, *n.* Kriminalis'tik *f.*

crimson, *adj.* karmin'rot.

cringe, *vb.* sich krümmen.

cripple, 1. *n.* Krüppel - *m.* **2.** *vb.* zum Krüppel machen; lähmen.

crippled, *adj.* verkrüp'pelt, gelähmt'.

crisis, *n.* Krise, -n *f.*

crisp, *adj. (weather, vegetables)* frisch; *(bread, etc.)* knusprig.

criterion, *n.* Krite'rium, -rien *nt.*

critic, *n.* Kritiker, - *m.,* Kritikerin, -nen *f.*

critical, *adj.* kritisch.

criticism, *n.* Kritik', -en *f.*

criticize, *vb.* kritisie'ren.

croak, *vb.* krächzen.

crochet, *vb.* häkeln.

crock, *n.* Steintopf, -̈e *m.*

crockery, *n.* Steingut *nt.*

crocodile, *n.* Krokodil', -e *nt.*

crook, *n. (bend)* Biegung, -en *f.; (cheater)* Schwindler, - *m.,* Schwindlerin, -nen *f.*

crooked, *adj. (not straight)* krumm, schief; *(dishonest)* unehrlich, betrü'gerisch.

croon, *vb.* summen; *(jazz)* Schlager singen*.

crop, *n.* Ernte, -n *f.; (riding)* Peitsche, -n *f.*

croquet, *n.* Kroket'spiel *nt.*

croquette, *n.* Kroket'te, -n *f.*

cross, 1. *n.* Kreuz, -e *nt.; (mixture)* Kreuzung, -en *f.* **2.** *vb.* kreuzen.

cross-eyed, *adj.* (be c.) schielen.

crossing, *n.* Kreuzung, -en *f.*

crossroads, *n.pl.* Scheideweg, -e *m.;* Kreuzung, -en *f.*

cross section, *n.* Querschnitt, -e *m.*

crossword puzzle, *n.* Kreuzworträtsel, - *nt.*

crotch, *n. (trousers)* Schritt, - *m.; (tree)* Gabelung, -en *f.*

crouch, *vb.* kauern.

croup, *n.* Krupp *m.*

crouton, *n.* Crouton', -s *m.*

crow, 1. *n.* Krähe, -n *f.* **2.** *vb.* krähen.

crowd, 1. *n.* Menge, -n *f.* **2.** *vb.* drängeln.

crown, 1. *n.* Krone, -n *f.* **2.** *vb.* krönen.

crucial, *adj.* entschei'dend.

crucible, *n.* Schmelztiegel, - *m.*

crucifix, *n.* Kruzifix, -e *nt.*

crucifixion, *n.* Kreuzigung, -en *f.*

crucify, *vb.* kreuzigen.

crude, *adj.* roh, grob (-).

crudeness, *n.* Grobheit, -en *f.,* Unfeinheit, -en *f.*

crudity, *n.* Roheit, -en *f.,* Unfeinheit, -en *f.*

cruel, *adj.* grausam.

cruelty, *n.* Grausamkeit, -en *f.*

cruise, 1. *n.* Seereise, -n *f.* **2.** *vb.* kreuzen.

cruiser, *n.* Kreuzer, - *m.*

crumb, *n.* Krümel, - *m.*

crumble, *vb.* zerbrö'ckeln.

crumple, *vb.* zerknül'len.

crusade, *n.* Kreuzzug, -̈e *m.*

crusader, *n.* Kreuzzügler - *m.*

crush, 1. *n. (crowd)* Gedrän'ge *nt.* **2.** *vb.* zerdrü'cken.

crust, *n.* Kruste, -n *f.*

crustacean, *n.* Krustentier, -e *nt.*

crusty, *adj.* knusprig.

crutch, *n.* Krücke, -n *f.*

cry, 1. *n.* Schrei, -e *m.* **2.** *vb.* schreien*; *(weep)* weinen.

crying, *adj. (urgent)* dringend.

cryosurgery, *n.* Kryochirurgie' *f.*

cryptic, *adj.* geheim'.

cryptography, *n.* Geheim'schrift, -en *f.*

crystal, 1. *n.* Kristall', -e *nt.* **2.** *adj.* kristal'len.

crystalline, *adj.* kristal'len.

crystallize, *vb.* kristallisie'ren.

cub, *n.* Jung- *nt.*

cube, n. Würfel - m.

cubic, adj. würfelförmig, kubisch; Kubik'- (cpds.).

cubicle, n. kleiner Schlafraum, ‑e m.

cuckoo, n. Kuckuck - m.

cucumber, n. Gurke, -n f.

cud, n. Widergekäut- nt.; (chew the c.) wieder-käuen.

cuddle, vb. herzen.

cudgel, n. Keule, -n f.

cue, n. Stichwort, ‑er nt.

cuff, n. (sleeve) Manschet'te, -n f.; (trousers) Hosenaufschlag, ‑e m.

cuisine, n. Küche, -n f.

culinary, adj. kulina'risch.

cull, vb. pflücken.

culminate, vb. gipfeln.

culmination, n. Höhepunkt, -e m.

culpable, adj. schuldhaft.

culprit, n. Täter - m., Täterin, -nen f.

cult, n. Kult, -e m.

cultivate, vb. kultivie'ren.

cultivated, adj. kultiviert'.

cultivation, n. Kultivie'rung f.

cultural, adj. kulturell'.

culture, n. Kultur', -ren f.

cultured, adj. kultiviert'.

cumbersome, adj. schwerfällig.

cumulative, adj. kumulativ'.

cunning, 1. n. List, -en f. 2. adj. listig; (sweet) goldig.

cup, n. Tasse, -n f.

cupboard, n. Schrank, ‑e m.

cupidity, n. Begier'de, -n f.

cupola, n. Kuppel, -n f.

curable, adj. heilbar.

curator, n. Kura'tor, -o'ren m.

curb, 1. n. (sidewalk) Bordstein, -e m.; (harness) Zügel, - m. 2. vb. zügeln.

curdle, vb. gerin'nen*.

cure, 1. n. Kur, -en f.; (medicine) Heilmittel, - nt. 2. vb. heilen.

curfew, n. Polizei'stunde, -n f.

curio, n. Kuriosität', -en f.

curiosity, n. Neugier'de f.

curious, adj. neugierig.

curl, 1. n. Locke, -n f. 2. vb. locken, kräuseln.

curly, adj. lockig, kraus.

currant, n. Johan'nisbeere, -n f.; (dried) Korin'the, -n f.

currency, n. Währung, -en f.

current, 1. n. Strom, ‑e m. 2. adj. laufend; aktuell'.

currently, adv. zur Zeit.

curriculum, n. Lehrplan, ‑e m.

curry, n. Curry nt.

curse, 1. n. Fluch, ‑e m. 2. vb. (intr.) fluchen, (tr.) verflu'chen.

cursed, adj. verflucht'.

curse-word, n. Schimpfwort, ‑er nt.

cursory, adj. flüchtig.

curt, adj. kurz angebunden.

curtail, vb. ein-schränken.

curtain, n. Gardi'ne, -n f.; (drapes) Vorhang, ‑e m.

curtsy, n. Knicks, -e m.

curvature, n. Krümmung, -en f.

curve, n. Kurve, -n f.

cushion, n. Kissen, - nt.

custard, n. Eierpudding, -s m.

custodian, n. Hausmeister, - m.

custody, n. Verwah'rung f.

custom, n. Sitte, -n f., Brauch, ‑e m.; (habit) Gewohn'heit, -en f.

customary, adj. gebräuch'lich.

customer, n. Kunde, -n, -n m., Kundin, -nen f.

custom house, n. Zollamt, ‑er nt.

customs, n. Zoll, ‑e m.

customs officer, n. Zollbeamt', m., Zollbeamtin, -nen f.

cut, 1. n. Schnitt, -e m.; (wound) Schnittwunde, -n f.; (salary) Kürzung, -en f.; (taxes) Senkung, -en f. 2. vb. schneiden*; kürzen; senken; (class) schwänzen.

cute, adj. niedlich, süß, goldig.

cut glass, n. geschlif'fenes Glas nt.

cuticle, n. Nagelhaut, ‑e f.

cutlery, n. Stahlwaren pl.

cutlet, n. Kotelett', -s nt.

cutter, n. Zuschneider, - m.; (boat) Kutter, - m.

cyclamate, n. Zyklamat', -e nt.

cycle, 1. n. Kreislauf, ‑e m.; Zyklus, -klen m. 2. vb. radeln.

cyclist, n. Radfahrer - m., Radfahrerin, -nen f.

cyclone, n. Wirbelsturm, ‑e m.

cyclotron, n. Zyklotron, -e nt.

cylinder, n. Zylin'der, - m.

cylindrical, *adj.* zylin'drisch.
cymbal, *n.* Zimbel, -n *f.*
cynic, *n.* Zyniker, - *m.*, Zynikerin, -nen, *f.*

cynical, *adj.* zynisch.
cynicism, *n.* Zynis'mus, -men *m.*
cypress, *n.* Zypres'se, -n *f.*
cyst, *n.* Zyste, -n *f.*

D

dab, *vb.* tupfen.
dabble, *vb.* sich dilettan'tenhaft mit einer Sache ab·geben*.
daffodil, *n.* Narzis'se, -n *f.*
dagger, *n.* Dolch, -e *m.*
dahlia, *n.* Dahlie, -n *f.*
daily, 1. *n. (newspaper)* Tageszeitung, -en *f.* **2.** *adj.* täglich.
daintiness, *n.* Zartheit, -en *f.*
dainty, *adj.* zart, delikat', zierlich.
dairy, *n.* Milchwirtschaft, -en *f.*, Molkerei' -en *f.*
dairyman, *m.* Milchhändler, - *m.*
dais, *n.* Podium, -ien *nt.*
daisy, *n.* Margeri'te, -n *f.*
dale, *n.* Tal, ⸚er *nt.*
dally, *vb.* tändeln; *(dawdle)* trödeln.
dam, 1. *n.* Damm, ⸚e *m.* **2.** *vb.* ein·dämmen.
damage, 1. *n.* Schaden, ⸚ *m.*; *(damages, law)* Schadenersatz *m.* **2.** *vb.* schädigen; beschä'digen.
damask, *n.* Damast, -e *m.*
damn, *vb.* verdam'men; *(curse)* verflu'chen.
damnation, *n.* Verdam'mung, -en *f.*
damp, *adj.* feucht.
dampen, *vb. (moisten)* ein·feuchten; *(quiet)* dämpfen; *(fig.)* nieder·schlagen*.
dampness, *n.* Feuchtigkeit, -en *f.*
dance, 1. *n.* Tanz, ⸚e *m.* **2.** *vb.* tanzen.
dancer, *n.* Tänzer, - *m.*, Tänzerin, -nen *f.*
dancing, *n.* Tanzen *nt.*
dandelion, *n.* Löwenzahn *m.*
dandruff, *n.* Kopfschuppen *pl.*
dandy, 1. *n.* Geck, -en, -en *m.* **2.** *adj.* prima.
Dane, *n.* Däne, -n, -n *m.* Dänin, -nen *f.*
danger, *n.* Gefahr', -en *f.*
dangerous, *adj.* gefähr'lich.

dangle, *vb.* baumeln; baumeln lassen*.
Danish, *adj.* dänisch.
dapper, *adj.* klein und elegant'.
dare, *vb.* wagen.
daredevil, *n.* Draufgänger, - *m.*
daring, *adj.* gewagt'.
dark, 1. *n.* Dunkel *nt.*; Dunkelheit, -en *f.* **2.** *adj.* dunkel.
darken, *vb.* verdun'keln.
darkness, *n.* Dunkel *nt.*; Dunkelheit, -en *f.*
darling, 1. *n.* Liebling, -e *m.* **2.** *adj.* goldig.
darn, *vb. (socks)* stopfen.
dart, 1. *n.* Wurfpfeil, -e *m.* **2.** *vb.* fliezen*.
dash, 1. *n. (pen)* Strich, -e *m*; *(sport)* Lauf, ⸚e *m.* **2.** *vb. (intr.)* sich stürzen; *(tr.)* stoßen*, schleudern.
dashboard, *n.* Armatu'renbrett, -er *nt.*
dashing, *adj.* schneidig.
data, *n.pl.* Angaben *pl.*
data processing, *n.* Datenverarbeitung, -en *f.*
date, 1. *n.* Datum, -ten *nt.*; *(appointment)* Verab'redung, -en *f.* *(fruit)* Dattel, -n *f.* **2.** *vb.* datie'ren; aus·gehen* mit.
daub, *vb.* schmieren.
daughter, *n.* Tochter, ⸚ *f.*
daughter-in-law, *n.* Schwiegertochter, ⸚ *f.*
daunt, *vb.* entmu'tigen.
dauntless, *adj.* kühn.
dawdle, *vb.* trödeln.
dawn, 1. *n.* Morgendämmerung, -en *f.* **2.** *vb.* dämmern.
day, *n.* Tag, -e *m.*
daybreak, *n.* Tagesanbruch *m.*
daydream, 1. *n.* Träumerei', -en *f.* **2.** *vb.* vor sich hin träumen; sinnie'ren.
daylight, *n.* Tageslicht *nt.*

daze, 1. *n.* Benom'menheit *f.* **2.** *vb.* betäu'ben.

dazzle, *vb.* blenden.

deacon, *n.* Diakon', -e *m.*

dead, *adj.* tot.

deaden, *vb.* dämpfen.

dead end, *n.* Sackgasse, -n *f.*

deadline, *n.* Termin', -e *m.,* Frist, -en *f.*

deadlock, *n.* Stockung, -en *f.*

deadly, *adj.* tötlich.

deaf, *adj.* taub.

deafen, *vb.* betäu'ben.

deafness, *n.* Taubheit *f.*

deal, 1. *n.* Anzahl *f.; (business)* Geschäft', -e *nt.* **2.** *vb. (cards)* geben*; **(d. with)** behan'deln; **(d. in)** handeln mit.

dealer, *n.* Händler, - *m.,* Händlerin, -nen *f.; (cards)* Geber, - *m.*

dean, *n.* Dekan', -e *m.*

dear, *adj.* lieb, teuer.

dearly, *adv.* sehr.

dearth, *n.* Mangel, ⁼ *m.*

death, *n.* Tod *m.;* Todesfall, ⁼e *m.*

deathless, *adj.* unsterblich.

debase, *vb.* ernie'drigen.

debatable, *adj.* bestreit'bar.

debate, 1. *n.* Debat'te, -n *f.* **2.** *vb.* debattie'ren.

debauch, 1. *n.* Orgie, -n *f.* **2.** *vb.* verfüh'ren.

debenture, *n.* Obligation', -en *f.*

debilitate, *vb.* entkräf'ten.

debit, *n.* Debet, -s *nt.*

debonair, *adj.* zuvor'kommend; heiter und sorglos.

debris, *n.* Trümmer *pl.*

debt, *n.* Schuld, -en *f.*

debtor, *n.* Schuldner, - *m.,* Schuldnerin, -nen *f.*

debunk, *vb.* mit etwas aufräumen, den Nimbus rauben.

debut, *n.* Debüt', -s *nt.*

debutante, *n.* Debütan'tin, -nen *f.*

decade, *n.* Jahrzehnt', -e *nt.*

decadence, *n.* Dekadenz' *f.*

decadent, *adj.* dekadent'.

decaffeinated, *adj.* koffein'frei.

decanter, *n.* Karaf'fe, -n *f.*

decapitate, *vb.* enthaup'ten.

decay, 1. *n.* Verfall' *m.;* Verwe'sung, -en *f.* **2.** *vb.* verfal'len*; verwe'sen.

deceased, *adj.* verstor'ben.

deceit, *n.* Täuschung, -en *f.;* Betrug', ⁼e *m.*

deceitful, *adj.* falsch; betrü'gerisch.

deceive, *vb.* täuschen; betrü'gen*.

December, *n.* Dezem'ber *m.*

decency, *n.* Anständigkeit, -en *f.*

decent, *adj.* anständig.

decentralization, *n.* Dezentralisation', -en *f.*

decentralize, *vb.* dezentralisie'ren.

deception, *n.* Täuschung, -en *f.*

deceptive, *adj.* irreführend, täuschend.

decibel, *n.* Dezi'bel, -n *f.*

decide, *vb.* entschei'den*; sich entschlie'ßen*.

decimal, 1. *n.* Dezimal'bruch, ⁼e *m.* **2.** *adj.* Dezimal'- *(cpds.).*

decimate, *vb.* dezimie'ren.

decipher, *vb.* entzif'fern.

decision, *n.* Entschei'dung, -en *f.;* Beschluß', ⁼sse *m.*

decisive, *adj.* entschei'dend.

deck, *n. (ship)* Deck, -s *nt.; (cards)* Spiel, -e *nt.*

declaration, *n.* Erklä'rung, -en *f.*

declarative, *adj.* erklä'rend; **(d. sentence)** Aussagesatz, ⁼e *m.*

declare, *vb.* erklä'ren, behaup'ten; *(customs)* deklarie'ren.

declension, *n.* Deklination', -en *f.*

decline, 1. *n.* Niedergang *m.* **2.** *vb.* neigen; *(refuse)* ablehnen; *(gram.)* deklinie'ren.

décolleté, *n.* Dekolleté', -s *nt.*

decompose, *vb. (tr.)* zerset'zen; *(intr.)* verwe'sen.

decomposition, *n.* Zerset'zung, -en *f.;* Verwe'sung, -en *f.*

decongestant, *n.* schleimlösendes Mittel *nt.*

décor, *n.* Ausstattung, -en *f.*

decorate, *vb.* schmücken, dekorie'ren.

decoration, *n.* Dekoration', -en *f.*

decorative, *adj.* dekorativ'.

decorator, *n.* Dekorateur', -e *m.,* Dekorateu'rin, -nen *f.;* **(interior d.)** Innenarchitekt, -en, -en *m.,* Innenarchitektin, -nen *f.*

decorous, *adj.* schicklich.

decorum, *n.* Schicklichkeit *f.*

decoy, 1. n. Lockvogel, ⸗ m. **2.** vb. locken.

decrease, 1. n. Abnahme, -n f. **2.** vb. (tr.) verrin'gern; (intr.) abnehmen*.

decree, 1. n. Erlaß', -sse m. **2.** vb. verord'nen.

decrepit, adj. gebrech'lich, klapprig.

decry, vb. mißbil'ligen, tadeln.

dedicate, vb. widmen.

dedication, n. Widmung, -en f.

deduce, vb. folgern.

deduct, vb. abziehen*.

deduction, n. Abzug, ⸗e m.; (logic) Folgerung, -en f.

deductive, adj. deduktiv'.

deed, n. Tat, -en f.; (document) Urkunde, -n f.

deem, vb. denken*; halten* für.

deep, adj. tief.

deepen, vb. vertie'fen.

deep freeze, n. Tiefkühltruhe, -n f.

deer, n. Reh, -e nt.; Hirsch, -e m.

deerskin, n. Rehleder, - nt.; Hirschleder, - nt.

deface, vb. entstel'len.

defamation, n. Verleum'dung, -en f.

defame, vb. in schlechten Ruf bringen*.

default, 1. n. Versäum'nis, -se nt.; Unterlas'sung, -en f. **2.** vb. im Verzug' sein*.

defeat, 1. n. Niederlage, -n f. **2.** vb. besie'gen.

defect, 1. n. Fehler, - m., Defekt', -e m. **2.** vb. überlau'fen*.

defection, n. Versa'gen nt.; Treubruch, ⸗e m.

defective, adj. fehlerhaft.

defend, vb. vertei'digen.

defendant, n. Angeklagt- m.&f.

defender, n. Vertei'diger, - m., Vertei'digerin, -nen f., Beschüt'zer, - m. Beschüt'zerin, -nen f.

defense, n. Vertei'digung, -en f.

defenseless, adj. wehrlos.

defensible, adj. verfecht'bar, zu vertei'digen.

defensive, 1. n. Defensi've, -n f. **2.** adj. defensiv'.

defer, vb. (put off) aufschieben*; (yield) nachgeben*.

deference, n. Achtung f.

deferential, adj. ehrerbietig.

defiance, n. Heraus'forderung, -en f.; Trotz m.

defiant, adj. trotzig, heraus'fordernd.

deficiency, n. Mangel, ⸗ m.

deficient, adj. unzureichend.

deficit, n. Defizit, -e nt.

defile, 1. n. Engpaß, ⸗sse m. **2.** vb. (march) defilie'ren; (soil) besudeln.

definite, adj. bestimmt'.

definition, n. Definition', -en f.

definitive, adj. definitiv'.

deflate, vb. die Luft heraus'lassen*.

deflation, n. Deflation', -en f.

deflect, vb. abwenden*.

deform, vb. entstel'len.

deformity, n. Verwachs'ung, -en f.

defraud, vb. betrü'gen*.

defray, vb. bestrei'ten*.

defrost, vb. entfros'ten.

deft, adj. geschickt'.

defy, vb. trotzen.

degenerate, 1. adj. degeneriert'. **2.** vb. entar'ten.

degeneration, n. Degeneration' f.

degradation, n. Ernie'drigung, -en f.

degrade, vb. ernie'drigen.

degree, n. Grad, -e m.

deify, vb. vergött'lichen.

deign, vb. geru'hen.

deity, n. Gottheit, -en f.

dejected, adj. niedergeschlagen.

dejection, n. Trübsinn m.

delay, 1. n. Verzö'gerung, -en f. **2.** vb. aufschieben*, verzö'gern.

delectable, adj. ergötz'lich.

delegate, 1. n. Delegiert- m.&f. **2.** vb. delegie'ren.

delegation, n. Abordnung, -en f., Delegation', -en f.

delete, vb. ausstreichen*.

deletion, n. Streichung f.

deliberate, 1. vb. erwä'gen*. **2.** adj. bedäch'tig; (on purpose) absichtlich.

deliberation, n. Überle'gung, -en f., Erwä'gung, -en f.

delicacy, n. (food) Delikates'se, -n f.; (fig.) Feinheit, -en f.

delicate, adj. delikat'.

delicious, adj. köstlich.

delight, 1. n. Entzü'cken, - nt. **2.** vb. entzü'cken.

delightful, adj. entzü'ckend.

delineate, vb. darstellen.

delinquency, n. Verge'hen, - nt.; Unterlas'sung, -en f.

delinquent, 1. n. Kriminell'- m.&f.; **(juvenile d.)** Jugendverbrecher, - m. **2.** adj. verbre'cherisch, kriminell'; (in default) säumig.

delirious, adj. im Fieberwahnsinn; wahnsinnig.

delirium, n. Deli'rium, -rien nt.

deliver, vb. (set free) erlö'sen; (hand over) überge'ben*, ab-liefern.

deliverance, n. Erlö'sung, -en f.; Befrei'ung, -en f.

delivery, n. Lieferung, -en f.; (childbirth) Entbin'dung, -en f.

delude, vb. täuschen, verlei'ten.

deluge, 1. n. Überschwem'mung, -en f.; (Bible) Sintflut f. **2.** vb. überflu'ten.

delusion, n. Täuschung, -en f.; Wahn m.

de luxe, adj. Luxus- (cpds.)

delve, vb. graben*; (fig.) sich vertie'fen.

demand, 1. n. Forderung, -en f.; (claim) Anspruch, ˮe m.; (econ.) Nachfrage f. **2.** vb. fordern, verlan'gen; fragen.

demean (oneself), vb. sich erniedur'digen.

demeanor, n. Betra'gen nt.

demerit, n. (school) Tadel, - m.

demilitarize, vb. entmilitarisie'ren.

demobilization, n. Demobilisie'rung, -en f.

demobilize, vb. demobilisie'ren.

democracy, n. Demokratie', -n f.

democrat, n. Demokrat', -en, -en m.

democratic, adj. demokra'tisch.

demolish, vb. ab-reißen*, zerstö'ren.

demolition, n. Zerstö'rung, -en f.

demon, n. Dämon, -o'nen m.

demonstrable, adj. nachweisbar.

demonstrate, vb. zeigen, vorführen, demonstrie'ren.

demonstration, n. Beweis' -e m., Darlegung, -en f.; Kundgebung, -en f.

demonstrative, adj. demonstrativ'.

demonstrator, n. Demonstrie'rend- m.&f.

demoralize, vb. demoralisie'ren.

demote, vb. degradie'ren.

demur, vb. Einwendungen machen.

demure, adj. züchtig.

den, n. Höhle, -n f.

denaturalize, vb. denaturalisie'ren.

denial, n. Vernei'nung, -en f.

denim, n. Jeansstoff, -e m.

Denmark, n. Dänemark nt.

denomination, n. (money) Nennwert, -e m.; (church) Sekte, -n f.

denominator, n. Nenner, - m.

denote, vb. kennzeichnen.

dense, adj. dicht.

density, n. Dichte f.

dent, n. Einbuchtung, -en f.

dental, adj. Zahn- (cpds.)

dental floss, n. Zahnseide f.

dentifrice, n. Zahnputzmittel, - nt.

dentist, n. Zahnarzt, ˮe m., Zahnärztin, -nen, f.

dentistry, n. Zahnheilkunde f.

denture, n. künstliches Gebiß', -sse nt.

denunciation, n. Denunzie'rung, -en f.

deny, vb. leugnen, vernei'nen.

deodorant, n. Desodorisie'rungsmittel, - nt., Deodorant' nt.

depart, vb. ab-fahren*; (deviate) ab-weichen*.

department, n. Abtei'lung, -en f.; (government) Ministe'rium, -rien nt.

departmental, adj. Abtei'lungs- (cpds.).

departure, n. Abfahrt, -en f.; (deviation) Abweichung, -en f.

depend, vb. ab'hängen*; (rely) sich verlas'sen*.
dependability, n. Verläß'lichkeit f.
dependable, adj. zuverlässig.
dependence, n. Abhängigkeit f.
dependent, 1. n. Angehörig- m.&f. **2.** adj. abhängig; angewiesen.
depict, vb. dar'stellen.
depiction, n. Darstellung, -en f.
deplete, vb. erschöp'fen.
deplorable, adj. bekla'genswert.
deplore, vb. bekla'gen.
deport, vb. deportie'ren.
deportation, n. Deportation', -en f.
deportment, n. Betra'gen nt.
depose, vb. ab'setzen.
deposit, 1. n. Anzahlung, -en f.; (bank) Einzahlung, -en f.; (ore, etc.) Lager, - nt. **2.** vb. ein'zahlen; hinterle'gen.
deposition, n. (eidesstattliche) schriftliche Aussage, -n f.
depositor, n. Einzahler, - m.; Bankkunde, -n, -n m.
depot, n. Lager, -̈ nt.; Depot' -s nt.; (railroad) Kleinbahnhof, -̈e m.
depravity, n. Verwor'fenheit f.
deprecate, vb. mißbilligen.
depreciate, vb. (tr.) entwer'ten, den Wert mindern; (intr.) im Wert sinken*.
depreciation, n. Wertminderung f.
depress, vb. deprimie'ren.
depression, n. Depression', -en f.
deprivation, n. Berau'bung, -en f.
deprive, vb. berau'ben.
depth, n. Tiefe, -n f.
deputy, n. (substitute) Stellvertreter, - m., Stellvertreterin, -nen f.; (parliament) Abgeordnet- m.&f.
derail, vb. entglei'sen lassen*; (be d.ed) entglei'sen.
deranged, adj. geistesgestört.
derelict, 1. n. Wrack, -s or -e nt. 2. adj. nachlässig.
dereliction, n. Vernach'lässigung, -en f.
deride, vb. verspot'ten, verhöhnen.

derision, n. Hohn m.
derisive, adj. spöttisch.
derivation, n. Ableitung, -en f.
derivative, adj. abgeleitet.
derive, vb. ab'leiten.
derogatory, adj. abfällig.
derrick, n. Ladebaum, -̈e m.; (oil) Bohrturm, -̈e m.
descend, vb. herab'steigen*; (ancestry) ab'stammen.
descendant, n. Nachkomme, -n, -n m.
descent, n. Abstieg, -e m.
describe, vb. beschrei'ben*.
description, n. Beschrei'bung, -en f.
descriptive, adj. beschrei'bend.
desecrate, vb. entwei'hen.
desert, 1. n. Wüste, -n f.; (merit) Verdienst', -e nt. **2.** vb. verlas'sen*.
deserter, n. Fahnenflüchtig- m.&f., Deserteur', -e m.
desertion, n. (law) böswilliges Verlas'sen nt.; (army) Desertion', -en f., Fahnenflucht f.
deserve, vb. verdie'nen.
deserving, adj. verdienst'voll.
design, 1. n. Entwurf', -̈e m., Muster, - nt.; (aim) Absicht, -en f. **2.** vb. entwer'fen*; beab'sichtigen.
designate, vb. bezeich'nen, bestim'men.
designation, n. Bezeich'nung, -en f., Bestim'mung, -en f.
designer, n. Konstrukteur', -e m.; (fashion) Modeschöpfer, - m., Modeschöpferin, -nen f.
desirability, n. Erwünscht'heit, -en f.
desirable, adj. wünschenswert.
desire, 1. n. Verlan'gen, - nt., Wunsch, -̈e m. **2.** vb. verlan'gen, wünschen.
desirous, adj. begie'rig.
desist, vb. ab'lassen*.
desk, n. Schreibtisch, -e m.
desolate, 1. adj. trostlos. **2.** vb. verhee'ren.
desolation, n. Verwüs'tung, -en f.; Trostlosigkeit f.
despair, 1. n. Verzweif'lung, -en f. **2.** vb. verzwei'feln.
despatch, 1. n. Absendung, -en f.

2. *vb.* ab·senden*, eilig weg·schicken.

desperado, *n.* Bandit', -en, -en *m.;* Despera'do, -s *m.*

desperate, *adj.* verzwei'felt.

desperation, *n.* Verzweif'lung, -en *f.*

despicable, *adj.* verach'tenswert, gemein'.

despise, *vb.* verach'ten.

despite, *prep.* trotz.

despondent, *adj.* verzagt'.

despot, *n.* Despot', -en, -en *m.*

despotic, *adj.* despo'tisch.

despotism, *n.* Gewalt'herrschaft *f.*

dessert, *n.* Nachtisch, -e *m.*

destination, *n.* Bestim'mung *f.;* Bestim'mungsort, -e *m.*

destine, *vb.* bestim'men.

destiny, *n.* Schicksal, -e *nt.*

destitute, *adj.* mittellos.

destitution, *n.* Armut *f.,* Not, -e *f.*

destroy, *vb.* zerstö'ren.

destroyer, *n.* Zerstö'rer, - *m.*

destruction, *n.* Zerstö'rung, -en *f.*

destructive, *adj.* zerstö'rend.

desultory, *adj.* flüchtig.

detach, *vb.* ab·trennen; *(mil.)* ab·kommandieren.

detachment, *n.* *(mil.)* Ab·teil'ung, -en *f.;* Objektivität' *f.*

detail, *n.* Einzelheit, -en *f.*

detain, *vb.* ab·halten*; fest·halten*; auf·halten*.

detect, *vb.* entde'cken, ermit'teln.

detection, *n.* Entde'cken *nt.;* Ermitt'lung, -en *f.*

detective, *n.* Detektiv' -e *m.*

détente, *n.* Entspan'nung *f.*

detention, *n.* Haft *f.*

deter, *v.* ab·halten*, hindern.

detergent, *n.* Waschmittel, - *nt,* Reinigungsmittel, - *nt.*

deteriorate, *vb.* sich verschlech'tern.

deterioration, *n.* Verschlech'terung, -en *f.*

determination, *n.* Bestim'mung, -en *f.;* *(resolve)* Entschlos'senheit *f.*

determine, *vb.* bestim'men.

determined, *adj.* entschlos'sen.

deterrence, *n.* Abschreckung *f.*

detest, *vb.* verab'scheuen.

detonate, *vb.* explodie'ren.

detonation, *n.* Explosion', -en *f.*

detour, *n.* Umweg, -e *m.;* *(traffic)* Umleitung, -en *f.*

detract, *vb.* ab·ziehen*; **(d. from)** schmälern.

detriment, *n.* Nachteil, -e *m,* Schaden, - *m.*

detrimental, *adj.* nachteilig.

devaluate, *vb.* ab·werten.

devastate, *vb.* verwüs'ten.

devastation, *n.* Verwüs'tung, -en *f.*

develop, *vb.* entwi'ckeln.

developer, *n.* Entwick'ler, - *m.*

developing nation, *n.* Entwick'lungsland, -er *nt.*

development, *n.* Entwick'lung, -en *f.*

deviate, *vb.* ab·weichen*.

deviation, *n.* Abweichung, -en *f.*

device, *n.* Vorrichtung, -en *f.*

devil, *n.* Teufel, - *m.*

devilish, *adj.* teuflisch.

devious, *adj.* abweichend.

devise, *vb.* ersin'nen*.

devoid, *adj.* **(d. of)** leer an, ohne.

devote, *vb.* widmen.

devoted, *adj.* erge'ben.

devotee, *n.* Verfech'ter, - *m.*

devotion, *n.* Hingebung *f.;* *(religious)* Andacht, -en *f.*

devour, *vb.* verschlin'gen*.

devout, *adj.* andächtig, fromm.

dew, *n.* Tau *m.*

dewy, *adj.* betaut.

dexterity, *n.* Gewandt'heit, -en *f.*

dexterous, *adj.* gewandt'.

diabetes, *n.* Zuckerkrankheit *f.*

diabolic, *adj.* teuflisch.

diadem, *n.* Diadem', -e *nt.*

diagnose, *vb.* diagnostizie'ren.

diagnosis, *n.* Diagno'se, -n *f.*

diagnostic, *adj.* diagnos'tisch.

diagonal, 1. *n.* Diagona'le, -n *f.* **2.** *adj.* diagonal', schräg.

diagram, *n.* graphische Darstel·lung, -en *f.*

dial, 1. *n.* Zifferblatt, -er *nt.;* *(telephone)* Wählscheibe, -n *f.* **2.** *vb.* *(telephone)* wählen.

dialect, *n.* Dialekt', -e *m,* Mund·art, -en *f.*

dialogue, n. Dialog', -e m.
diameter, n. Durchmesser, -m.
diametrical, adj. diametral'.
diamond, n. Diamant', -en, -en m.; (cards) Karo nt.
diaper, n. Windel, -n f.
diaphragm, n. Zwerchfell, -e nt.
diarrhea, n. Durchfall m.
diary, n. Tagebuch, -̈er nt.
diathermy, n. Diathermie' f.
diatribe, n. Schmähschrift f.
dice, n.pl. Würfel, - m.
dicker, vb. feilschen.
dictate, vb. diktie'ren.
dictation, n. Diktat', -e nt.
dictator, n. Dikta'tor, -o'ren m.
dictatorial, adj. diktato'risch.
dictatorship, n. Diktatur', -en f.
diction, n. Aussprache, -n f.
dictionary, n. Wörterbuch, -̈er nt., Lexikon, -ka nt.
didactic, adj. didak'tisch.
die, 1. n. (gaming cube) Würfel, - m.; (stamper) Prägestempel, - m. 2. vb. sterben*.
diet, n. Diät', -en f.; (government) Parlament', -e nt.
dietary, adj. diät'gemäß.
dietetic, adj. diäte'tisch.
dietitian, n. Diät'planer, - m.
differ, vb. sich unterschei'den*, ab•weichen*, verschiedener Meinung sein*.
difference, n. Unterschied, -e m.
different, adj. verschie'den, ander-.
differential, 1. n. Unterschied, - m.; (d. gear) Differential', -e nt., Ausgleichsgetriebe, - nt. 2. adj. differential'.
differentiate, vb. unterschei'den*.
difficult, adj. schwer, mühsam, schwierig.
difficulty, n. Schwierigkeit, -en f.
diffident, adj. zurück'haltend, schüchtern.
diffuse, 1. adj. weitverbreitet, diffus'. 2. vb. verbrei'ten.
diffusion, n. Diffusion', -en f.
dig, vb. graben*.
digest, vb. verdau'en.
digestible, adj. verdau'lich.
digestion, n. Verdau'ung f.

digestive, adj. Verdau'ungs- (cpds.).
digital, adj. digital'.
digitalis, n. Digita'lis nt.
dignified, adj. würdig.
dignify, vb. ehren, aus•zeichnen.
dignitary, n. Würdenträger, - m.
dignity, n. Würde f.
digress, vb. ab•schweifen.
digression, n. Abschweifung, -en f.
dike, n. Deich, -e m.
dilapidated, adj. baufällig.
dilate, vb. aus•dehnen.
dilemma, n. Dilem'ma, -s nt.
dilettante, n. Dilettant', -en, -en m.
diligence, n. Fleiß m.
diligent, adj. fleißig.
dill, n. Dill m.
dilute, vb. verdün'nen.
dilution, n. Verdün'nung, -en f.
dim, 1. adj. trübe, dunkel. 2. vb. trüben; (auto lights) ab•blenden.
dimension, n. Ausmaß, -e nt., Dimension', -en f.
diminish, vb. vermin'dern.
diminution, n. Vermin'derung, f.
diminutive, 1. n. Diminutiv', -e nt. 2. adj. winzig.
dimness, n. Dunkelheit f.
dimple, n. Grübchen, - nt.
din, n. Lärm m.
dine, vb. speisen.
diner, dining-car, n. Speisewagen, - m.
dingy, adj. schäbig.
dining room, n. Eßzimmer, - nt.; (in hotel) Speiseraum, -̈e m.
dinner, n. (noon) Mittagessen, - nt.; (evening) Abendessen, - nt.
dinosaur, n. Dinosau'rier, - m.
diocese, n. Diöze'se, -n f.
dip, vb. tauchen, ein•tauchen.
diphtheria, n. Diphtherie' f.
diploma, n. Diplom', -e nt.
diplomacy, n. Diplomatie', -en f.
diplomat, n. Diplomat', -en, -en m.
diplomatic, adj. diploma'tisch.
dipper, n. Schöpflöffel, - m., Schöpfkelle, -n f.; (Big D.) Großer Bär m.; (Little D.) Kleiner Bär m.
dire, adj. gräßlich.

direct, 1. *adj.* direkt'. 2. *vb.* führen; an·weisen*; leiten.

direct current, *n.* Gleichstrom, ⁻e *m.*

direction, *n.* (leadership) Leitung, -en *f.*, Führung, -en *f.*; (instruction) Anweisung, -en *f.*; (course) Richtung, -en *f.*

directional, *adj.* Leitungs-, Richtungs- (cpds.).

directive, 1. *adj.* leitend; Richtung gebend. 2. *n.* Direkti've, -n *f.*

directness, *n.* Gerad'heit *f.*, Offenheit *f.*

director, *n.* Leiter, - *m.*, Leiterin, -nen *f.*, Direk'tor, -o'ren *m.*, Direkto'rin, -nen *f.*

directory, *n.* (addresses) Adreß'buch, ⁻er *nt.*; (telephone d.) Telephon'buch, ⁻er *nt.*

dirigible, *n.* Luftschiff, -e *nt.*

dirt, *n.* Schmutz *m.*

dirty, *adj.* schmutzig.

disability, *n.* Unfähigkeit *f.*; Körperbehinderung, -en *f.*

disable, *vb.* untauglich machen.

disabled, *adj.* untauglich; kriegsversehrt.

disadvantage, *n.* Nachteil, -e *m.*

disagree, *vb.* anderer Meinung sein*; (food) nicht bekom'men*.

disagreeable, *adj.* unangenehm, unsympathisch.

disagreement, *n.* Uneinigkeit, -en *f.*, Widerspruch, ⁻e *m.*

disappear, *vb.* verschwin'den*.

disappearance, *n.* Verschwin'den *nt.*

disappoint, *vb.* enttäu'schen.

disappointment, *n.* Enttäu'schung, -en *f.*

disapproval, *n.* Mißbilligung, -en *f.*

disapprove, *vb.* mißbilligen.

disarm, *vb.* entwaff'nen, ab·rüsten.

disarmament, *n.* Abrüstung, -en *f.*

disarray, *n.* Unordnung *f.*

disaster, *n.* Unglück, -e *nt.*, Katastro'phe, -n *f.*

disastrous, *adj.* verhee'rend.

disavow, *vb.* ab·leugnen.

disband, *vb.* auf·lösen.

disburse, *vb.* aus·zahlen.

discard, *vb.* ab·legen.

discern, *vb.* unterschei'den*.

discerning, *adj.* scharfsinnig.

discernment, *n.* Scharfsinn *m.*, Einsicht *f.*

discharge, 1. *n.* Entlas'sung, -en *f.*; (medicine) Ausscheidung, -en *f.* 2. *vb.* entlas'sen*, ausscheiden*; (gun) ab·feuern.

disciple, *n.* Jünger, - *m.*

disciplinary, *adj.* maßregelnd.

discipline, 1. *n.* Disziplin' *f.* 2. *vb.* schulen, diszipline'ren.

disclaim, *vb.* ab·leugnen; verzich'ten.

disclose, *vb.* enthül'len.

disclosure, *n.* Enthül'lung, -en *f.*

discomfort, *n.* Unbehagen *nt.*

disconcert, *vb.* in Verwir'rung bringen*.

disconnect, *vb.* los·lösen; (elec.) aus·schalten.

discontent, 1. *n.* Unzufriedenheit *f.* 2. *adj.* unzufrieden.

discontinue, *vb.* ein·stellen.

discord, *n.* Mißklang ⁻e *m.*; (fig.) Uneinigkeit, -en *f.*

discotheque, *n.* Diskothek', -en *f.*

discount, 1. *n.* Rabatt' *m.* 2. *vb.* ab·ziehen*.

discourage, *vb.* entmu'tigen.

discouragement, *n.* Entmu'tigung, -en *f.*

discourse, 1. *n.* Gespräch', -e *nt.*; Abhandlung, -en *f.* 2. *vb.* sprechen*.

discourteous, *adj.* unhöflich.

discourtesy, *n.* Unhöflichkeit, -en *f.*

discover, *vb.* entde'cken.

discovery, *n.* Entde'ckung, -en *f.*

discredit, 1. *n.* Nichtachtung *f.* 2. *vb.* nicht glauben; in schlechten Ruf bringen*.

discreet, *adj.* diskret'.

discrepancy, *n.* Zwiespalt, -e *m.*

discretion, *n.* Diskretion' *f.*; Beson'nenheit *f.*

discriminate, *vb.* unterschei'den*; diskrimi'nie'ren.

discrimination, *n.* Diskrimi'nie'rung, -en *f.*

discuss, *vb.* diskutie'ren.

discussion, *n.* Diskussion', -en *f.*

disdain, vb. verach'ten.

disdainful, adj. veräch'tlich.

disease, n. Krankheit, -en f.

disembark, vb. landen.

disembarkation, n. Landung, -en f.

disenchantment, n. Enttäu'schung, -en f.; Ernüch'terung f.

disengage, vb. los•lösen.

disentangle, vb. entwir'ren.

disfavor, n. Mißfallen nt.; Ungnade f.

disfigure, vb. entstel'len.

disgrace, 1. n. Schande, -n f.; Unehre f. 2. vb. schänden, blamie'ren.

disgraceful, adj. schändlich.

disgruntled, adj. mürrisch.

disguise, 1. n. Verklei'dung, -en f. 2. vb. verklei'den.

disgust, 1. n. Ekel m. 2. vb. anekeln.

disgusting, adj. ekelhaft, widerlich.

dish, n. Schüssel, -n f.; (food) Gericht', -e nt.

dishcloth, n. Abwaschtuch, ̈er nt.

dishearten, vb. entmu'tigen.

dishonest, adj. unehrlich.

dishonesty, n. Unehrlichkeit, -en f.

dishonor, 1. n. Schande, -n f. 2. vb. enteh'ren.

dishonorable, adj. unehrenhaft.

dishtowel, n. Geschirr'handtuch, ̈er nt.

disillusion, 1. n. Enttäu'schung, -en f. 2. vb. enttäu'schen.

disinfect, vb. desinfizie'ren.

disinfectant, n. Desinfizie'rungsmittel, - nt.

disinherit, vb. enter'ben.

disintegrate, vb. zerfal'len*.

disinterested, adj. gleichgültig.

disjointed, adj. unzusammenhängend.

disk, n. Scheibe, -n f.; Diskette, -n f.

dislike, 1. n. Abneigung, -en f. 2. vb. nicht mögen*.

dislocate, vb. aus•renken.

dislodge, vb. los•reißen*, vertrei'ben*.

disloyal, adj. treulos.

disloyalty, n. Untreue, -n f.

dismal, adj. jämmerlich.

dismantle, vb. demontie'ren.

dismay, 1. n. Bestür'zung, -en f. 2. vb. erschre'cken.

dismember, vb. zerstü'ckeln.

dismiss, vb. entlas'sen*; fallen lassen*.

dismissal, n. Entlas'sung, -en f.

dismount, vb. ab•steigen*.

disobedience, n. Ungehorsam m.

disobedient, adj. ungehorsam.

disobey, vb. nicht gehor'chen.

disorder, n. Unordnung f.

disorderly, adj. unordentlich, liederlich.

disorganize, vb. in Unordnung bringen*.

disown, vb. verleug'nen.

disparage, vb. herab'•setzen.

disparity, n. Ungleichheit, -en f.

dispassionate, adj. leidenschaftslos.

dispatch, 1. n. Absendung, -en f. 2. vb. ab•senden*, eilig weg•schicken.

dispatcher, n. Absender, - m.

dispel, vb. vertrei'ben*.

dispensable, adj. entbehr'lich.

dispensary, n. Arznei'ausgabestelle, -n f.

dispensation, n. Befrei'ung, -en f.

dispense, vb. aus•geben*; (d. with) verzich'ten auf.

dispersal, n. Vertei'lung, -en f.

disperse, vb. vertei'len.

displace, vb. verdrän'gen.

displaced person, n. Zwangsverschleppt- m.&f.

display, 1. n. Aufwand m.; (window) Schaufensterauslage, -n f. 2. vb. entfal'ten, zeigen.

displease, vb. mißfal'len*.

displeasure, n. Mißfallen nt.

disposable, adj. verfüg'bar.

disposal, n. Verfü'gung, -en f.

dispose, vb. bestim'men.

disposition, n. Verfü'gung, -en f.; (character) Anlage f.

dispossess, vb. enteig'nen.

disproof, n. Widerle'gung, -en f.

disproportion, n. Mißverhältnis, -se nt.

disproportionate, adj. unverhältnismäßig.

disprove, *vb.* widerle'gen.

disputable, *adj.* bestreit'bar.

dispute, 1. *n.* Streit, -e *m.* **2.** *vb.* bestrei'ten*.

disqualification, *n.* Disqualifizie'rung, -en *f.*

disqualify, *vb.* disqualifizie'ren.

disregard, 1. *n.* Nichtbeachtung *f.* **2.** *vb.* nicht beach'ten.

disrepair, *n.* Verfall' *m.*

disreputable, *adj.* verru'fen.

disrespect, *n.* Nichtachtung *f.,* Mißachtung *f.*

disrespectful, *adj.* unehrerbietig, unhöflich.

disrobe, *vb.* entklei'den.

disrupt, *vb.* stören.

dissatisfaction, *n.* Unzufriedenheit, -en *f.*

dissatisfy, *vb.* nicht befrie'digen.

dissect, *vb.* zerglie'dern; *(med.)* sezie'ren.

disseminate, *vb.* verbrei'ten.

dissension, *n.* Uneinigkeit, -en *f.*

dissent, 1. *n.* Meinungsverschiedenheit, -en *f.* **2.** *vb.* anderer Meinung sein*.

dissertation, *n.* Dissertation', -en *f.*

dissimilar, *adj.* unähnlich.

dissipated, *adj.* ausschweifend, verlebt'.

dissipation, *n.* Ausschweifung, -en *f.*

dissociate, *vb.* trennen.

dissolute, *adj.* verkom'men.

dissolution, *n.* Auflösung, -en *f.*

dissolve, *vb.* auf'lösen.

dissonance, *n.* Dissonanz', -en *f.*

dissonant, *adj.* dissonant'.

dissuade, *vb.* ab'raten*.

distance, *n.* Entfer'nung, -en *f.,* Abstand, -e *m.*

distant, *adj.* entfernt'; *(fig.)* zurück'haltend.

distaste, *n.* Widerwille(n), - *m.,* Abneigung, -en *f.*

distasteful, *adj.* widerwärtig, widerlich.

distemper, *n. (dog)* Staupe *f.*

distend, *vb.* aus'dehnen.

distill, *vb.* destillie'ren.

distillation, *n.* Destillation', -en *f.*

distiller, *n.* Destillateur', -e *m.*

distillery, *n.* Branntweinbrennerei, -en *f.*

distinct, *adj.* deutlich; *(different)* verschie'den.

distinction, *n. (difference)* Unterscheidung, -en *f.,* Unterschied, -e *m.; (elegance)* Vornehmheit *f.; (honor)* Auszeichnung, -en *f.*

distinctive, *adj.* kennzeichnend.

distinctness, *n.* Deutlichkeit *f.*

distinguish, *vb. (differentiate)* unterscheiden*; *(honor)* aus'zeichnen.

distinguished, *adj. (famous)* berühmt'; *(elegant)* vornehm.

distort, *vb.* verzer'ren.

distract, *vb.* ab'lenken.

distraction, *n.* Ablenkung, -en *f.*

distress, 1. *n.* Not, -e *f.* **2.** *vb.* betrü'ben.

distribute, *vb.* vertei'len.

distribution, *n.* Vertei'lung, -en *f.*

distributor, *n.* Vertei'ler, - *m.; (agent)* Vertriebs'stelle, -en *f.*

district, *n.* Bezirk', -e *m.*

distrust, 1. *n.* Mißtrauen *nt.* **2.** *vb.* mißtrau'en.

distrustful, *adj.* mißtrauisch.

disturb, *vb.* stören, beun'ruhigen.

disturbance, *n.* Störung, -en *f.,* Unruhe, -n *f.*

ditch, *n.* Graben, - *m.*

diva, *n.* Diva, -s *f.*

divan, *n.* Diwan, -e *m.*

dive, 1. *n.* Kopfsprung, -e *m.* **2.** *vb.* tauchen.

diver, *n.* Taucher, - *m.,* Taucherin, -nen *m.*

diverge, *vb.* auseinan'der•gehen*.

divergence, *n.* Divergenz', -en *f.*

divergent, *adj.* divergie'rend.

diverse, *adj.* verschie'den.

diversion, *n.* Ablenkung, -en *f.; (pastime)* Zeitvertreib, -e *m.*

diversity, *n.* Mannigfaltigkeit, -en *f.*

divert, *vb.* ab'lenken, um'leiten.

divest, *vb.* entle'digen, entklei'den.

divide, *vb.* teilen.

dividend, *n.* Dividen'de, -n *f.*

divine, *adj.* göttlich.

divinity, *n.* Gottheit, -en *f.; (study)* Theologie, -i'en *f.*

divisible, *adj.* teilbar.

division, n. Teilung, -en f.; (mil.) Division', -en f.

divorce, 1. n. Scheidung, -en f. **2.** vb. **(get d.d)** sich scheiden lassen*. **(d. a person)** sich von einem Menschen scheiden lassen*.

divorcée, n. geschie'dene Frau, -en f.

divulge, vb. enthül'len.

dizziness, n. Schwindel m.

dizzy, adj. schwindlig.

do, vb. tun*, machen.

docile, adj. fügsam.

dock, n. Dock, -s m.

docket, n. Gerichts'kalender, - m.; Geschäfts'ordnung, -en f.

doctor, n. Doktor, -o'ren m.; (physician) Arzt, -̈e m.; Ärztin, -nen f.

doctorate, n. Doktorat', -e nt.

doctrine, n. Lehre, -n f.; Grundsatz, -̈e m.

document, n. Urkunde, -n f.; Dokument', -e nt.

documentary, adj. urkundlich, dokumenta'risch.

documentation, n. Dokumentation', -en f.

dodge, vb. aus·weichen*.

doe, n. Reh, -e nt.

doeskin, n. Rehleder nt.

dog, n. Hund, -e m.

dogma, n. Dogma, -men nt.

dogmatic, adj. dogma'tisch.

dogmatism, n. Dogma'tik f.

dole, vb. **(d. out)** vertei'len.

doleful, adj. kummervoll.

doll, n. Puppe, -n f.

dollar, n. Dollar, -s m.

domain, n. Bereich', -e m.

dome, n. Dom, -e m.; Kuppel, -n f.

domestic, adj. häuslich; **(d. policy)** Innenpolitik f.

domesticate, vb. zähmen.

domicile, n. Wohnort, -e m.

dominance, n. Herrschaft, -en f.

dominant, adj. vorherrschend.

dominate, vb. beherr'schen.

domination, n. Herrschaft, -en f.

domineer, vb. tyrannisie'ren.

dominion, n. Domi'nion, -s nt.

domino, n. Domino f.

don, vb. an·ziehen*; (hat) auf·setzen.

donate, vb. stiften.

donation, n. Gabe, -n f., Schenkung, -en f.

done, adj. (food) gar.

donkey, n. Esel, - m.

doom, n. Verder'ben nt.

door, n. Tür, -en f.

doorman, n. Portier', -s m.

doorway, n. Türeingang, -̈e m.

dope, n. (drug) Rauschgift, -e nt.; (fool) Trottel, - m.

dormant, adj. ruhend, latent'.

dormitory, n. (room) Schlafsaal, -säle m.; (building) Studentenheim, -e nt.

dosage, n. Dosie'rung, -en f.

dose, n. Dosis, -sen f.

dossier, n. Akte, -n f.

dot, n. Punkt, -e m.

double, 1. n. Doppelgänger, - m. **2.** adj. doppelt.

double-breasted, adj. zweireihig.

double-cross, vb. hinterge'hen*.

doubt, 1. n. Zweifel, - m. **2.** vb. zweifeln, bezwei'feln.

doubtful, adj. zweifelhaft.

doubtless, adj. zweifellos.

dough, n. Teig, -e m.

douse, vb. begie'ßen; (fire) löschen.

dove, n. Taube, -n f.

dowdy, adj. unschick.

down, 1. n. Flaum m.; (material) Daune, -n f. **2.** vb. nieder·werfen*, (fig.) besie'gen. **3.** adv. unten, nieder, ab; hin·, herun'ter; hin·, herab'

downcast, adj. niedergeschlagen.

downfall, n. Untergang, -̈e m.

downhearted, adj. betrübt'.

downhill, adv. bergab'.

down payment, n. Anzahlung, -en f.

downpour, n. Regenguß, -̈sse m.

downstairs, adv. unten.

downtown, 1. n. Geschäfts'viertel, - nt. **2.** adv. (direction) in die Stadt; (location) in der Stadt.

downward, adv. nach unten.

dowry, n. Mitgift, -en f.

doze, vb. dösen.

dozen, n. Dutzend, -e nt.

drab, adj. (color) bräunlich gelb; (dull) farblos.

draft, 1. n. (plan) Entwurf', -̈e m.; (money) Wechsel, - m.; (air) Zug,

̈e *m.; (military service)* militä'rische Dienstpflicht *f.* **2.** *vb.* entwer'fen*; *(mil.)* ein•zie'hen*.

draftee, *n.* Rekrut', -en, -en *m.*

draftsman, *n.* Zeichner, - *m.,* Zeichnerin, -nen *f.*

drafty, *adj.* zugig.

drag, *vb.* schleppen, schleifen.

dragon, *n.* Drache, -n, -n *m.*

drain, **1.** *n.* Abfluß, ̈sse *m.* **2.** *vb.* ab•laufen lassen*; entwäs'sern.

drainage, *n.* Abfluß, ̈sse *m.;* Entwäs'serung, -en *f.*

dram, *n.* Drachme, -n *f.*

drama, *n.* Drama, -men *nt.;* Schauspiel, -e *nt.*

dramatic, *adj.* drama'tisch.

dramatist, *n.* Drama'tiker, - *m.*

dramatize, *vb.* dramatisie'ren.

dramaturgy, *n.* Thea'terwissenschaft, -en *f.*

drape, **1.** *n.* Vorhang, ̈e *m.* **2.** *vb.* drapie'ren.

drapery, *n.* Vorhang, ̈e *m.;* Behang', ̈e *m.*

drastic, *adj.* drastisch.

draught, see draft.

draw, *vb.* *(pull)* ziehen*; *(picture)* zeichnen; *(d. up)* ab•fassen.

drawback, *n.* Nachteil, -e *m.;* Schattenseite, -n *f.*

drawbridge, *n.* Zugbrücke, -n *f.*

drawer, *n.* Schublade, -n *f.*

drawing, *n.* *(picture)* Zeichnung, -en *f.;* *(lottery)* Ziehung, -en *f.*

drawl, *vb.* langsam und ausgedehnt sprechen*.

dread, **1.** *n.* Furcht *f.,* Angst, ̈e *f.* **2.** *vb.* fürchten.

dreadful, *adj.* furchtbar.

dream, **1.** *n.* Traum, ̈e *m.* **2.** *vb.* träumen.

dreamy, *adj.* träumerisch, verträumt'.

dreary, *adj.* trostlos.

dredge, **1.** *n.* Bagger, - *m.* **2.** *vb.* baggern.

dregs, *n.pl.* Bodensatz, ̈e *m.; (fig.)* Abschaum, ̈e *m.*

drench, *vb.* durchnäs'sen.

dress, **1.** *n.* Kleid, -er *nt.* **2.** *vb.* an•ziehen*, kleiden.

dresser, *n.* Kommo'de, -n *f.*

dressing, *n.* *(food)* Soße, -n *f.;* *(med.)* Verband', ̈e *m.*

dressing gown, *n.* Schlafrock, ̈e *m.,* Morgenrock, ̈e *m.*

dressmaker, *n.* Schneiderin, -nen.

drier, *n.* *(hair)* Trockenhaube, -n *f.;* *(clothes)* Trockner, - *m.*

drift, **1.** *n.* *(snow)* Schneewehe, -n *f.;* *(tendency)* Richtung, -en *f.,* Strömung, -en *f.* **2.** *vb.* treiben*.

drill, **1.** *n.* *(tool)* Drillbohrer, - *m.; (practice)* Schulung, -en *f.; (mil.)* Exerzie'ren *nt.* **2.** *vb.* bohren; schulen; exerzie'ren.

drink, **1.** *n.* Getränk', -e *nt.* **2.** *vb.* trinken*.

drinkable, *adj.* trinkbar.

drip, *vb.* tropfen.

drive, **1.** *n.* *(ride)* Spazier'fahrt, -en *f.; (energy)* Schwungkraft *f.* **2.** *vb.* treiben*; *(auto)* fahren*.

driver, *n.* Fahrer, - *m.,* Fahrerin, -nen *f.;* *(d.'s license)* Führerschein *m.*

driveway, *n.* Auffahrt, -en *f.*

drizzle, **1.** *n.* Sprühregen, - *m.* **2.** *vb.* nieseln.

drone, **1.** *n.* *(bee)* Drohne, -n *f.; (hum)* Gesum'me, -n *nt.* **2.** *vb.* summen.

droop, *vb.* herab'•hängen*.

drop, **1.** *n.* Tropfen, - *m.* **2.** *vb.* *(fall)* fallen*; *(let fall)* fallen* lassen*.

dropout, *n.* jemand, der absichtlich seine ordnungsgemäße Tätigkeit, Ausbildung, Lebensart, aufgibt.

dropper, *n.* Tropfer, - *m.*

dropsy, *n.* Wassersucht *f.*

drought, *n.* Dürre, -n *f.,* Trockenheit, -en *f.*

drown, *vb.* *(intr.)* ertrin'ken*; *(tr.)* erträn'ken.

drowsiness, *n.* Schläfrigkeit *f.*

drowsy, *adj.* schläfrig.

drudgery, *n.* Plackerei', -en *f.*

drug, *n.* Droge, -n *f.,* Medikament', -e *nt.*

druggist, *n.* Drogist', -en, -en *m.,* Drogistin, -nen *f.,* Apothe'ker, - *m.,* Apothe'kerin, -nen *f.*

drug store, *n.* Drogerie', -i'en *f.,* Apothe'ke, -n *f.*

drum, *n.* Trommel, -n *f.*

drummer, *n.* Trommler, *m.*

drumstick, n. Trommelschlegel, - m.; (fowl) Geflü'gelschlegel, - m.

drunk, adj. betrun'ken; **(get d.)** sich betrin'ken*.

drunkard, n. Trinker, - m.; Trunkenbold, -e m.

drunken, adj. betrun'ken.

drunkenness, n. Trunkenheit f.

dry, 1. adj. trocken. **2.** vb. trocknen.

dry cell, n. Trockenelement, -e nt.

dry-cleaner, n. Reinigung, -en f.

dry-cleaning, n. chemische Reinigung, -en f.

dry goods, n.pl. Texti'lien pl.

dryness, n. Trockenheit, -en f.

dual, adj. Doppel- (cpds.).

dubious, adj. zweifelhaft.

duchess, n. Herzogin, -nen f.

duchy, n. Herzogtum, ⸚er nt.

duck, 1. n. Ente, -n f. **2.** vb. sich ducken.

duct, n. Rohr, -e nt.; Kanal', ⸚e nt.

due, adj. schuldig; fällig.

duel, n. Duell', -e nt.

dues, n.pl. Gebüh'ren pl., Beitrag, ⸚e m.

duet, n. Duett', -e nt.

duffle bag, n. Seesack, ⸚e m.

duke, n. Herzog, ⸚e m.

dull, adj. (not sharp) stumpf; (boring) langweilig.

dullness, n. Stumpfheit f.; Langweiligkeit f.

duly, adv. gebüh'rend.

dumb, adj. stumm; (stupid) dumm (⸚), blöde.

dumbwaiter, n. Drehaufzug, ⸚e m.

dumfound, vb. verblüf'fen.

dummy, n. (posing as someone) Strohmann, ⸚er m.; (window-display) Schaufensterpuppe, -n f.; (bridge) Tisch m.; (theater) Statist', -en, -en m.

dump, 1. n. Abladeplatz, ⸚e m.; (refuse) Schuttablade, -n f. **2.** vb. ab-laden*.

dumpling, n. Kloß, ⸚e m.

dun, 1. adj. graubraun. **2.** vb. zur Zahlung mahnen.

dunce, n. Schafskopf, ⸚e m., Dummkopf, ⸚e m.

dune, n. Düne, -n f.

dung, n. Dung m.

dungarees, n.pl. Arbeitshose, -n f.

dungeon, n. Kerker, - m.

dunk, vb. tunken.

dupe, 1. vb. düpie'ren. **2.** n. Düpiert'- m.&f.

duplex, adj. Doppelt- (cpds.).

duplicate, vb. verdop'peln, kopie'ren.

duplication, n. Verdop'pelung, -en f.

duplicity, n. Duplizität', -en f.

durability, n. Dauerhaftigkeit f.

durable, adj. dauerhaft; strapazierfähig.

duration, n. Dauer f.

duress, n. Zwang m.

during, prep. während.

dusk, n. Abenddämmerung, -en f.

dust, 1. n. Staub m. **2.** vb. ab-stauben.

dusty, adj. staubig.

Dutch, adj. holländisch.

Dutchman, n. Holländer, - m.

Dutchwoman, n. Holländerin, -nen f.

dutiful, adj. pflichtgetreu.

duty, n. Pflicht, -en f.; (tax) Zoll, ⸚e m.

duty-free, adj. zollfrei.

dwarf, n. Zwerg, -e m.

dwell, vb. wohnen.

dweller, n. Bewoh'ner, - m.

dwelling, n. Wohnung, -en f.; Wohnsitz, -e m.

dwindle, vb. schrumpfen.

dye, 1. n. Farbe, -n f.; Farbstoff, -e m. **2.** vb. färben.

dyer, n. Färber, - m.

dyestuff, n. Farbstoff, -e m.

dynamic, adj. dyna'misch.

dynamite, n. Dynamit' nt.

dynamo, n. Dyna'mo, -s m.

dynasty, n. Dynastie', -i'en f.

dysentery, n. Ruhr f.

dyslexia, n. Dyslexie' f.

dyspepsia, n. Dyspepsie' f.

each, *adj.* jeder, -es, -e.

each other, *pron.* einan'der.

eager, *adj.* eifrig.

eagerness, *n.* Eifer *m.*

eagle, *n.* Adler, - *m.*

ear, *n.* Ohr, -en *nt.*

earache, *n.* Ohrenschmerzen *pl.*

eardrum, *n.* Trommelfell, -e *nt.*

earl, *n.* Graf, -en, -en *m.*

early, *adj.* früh.

earmark, 1. *n.* Anzeichen, - *nt.* **2.** *vb.* bestim'men *f.* **(be e.ed)** vorgesehen sein*.

earn, *vb.* verdie'nen.

earnest, *adj.* ernst.

earnestness, *n.* Ernst *m.*

earnings, *n.pl.* Einnahmen *pl.*

earring, *n.* Ohrring, -e *m.*

earth, *n.* Erde, -n *f.*

earthenware, *n.* Steingut *nt.*

earthly, *adj.* irdisch.

earthquake, *n.* Erdbeben, - *nt.*

earthy, *adj.* erdig; *(fig.)* derb.

ease, 1. *n.* Leichtigkeit, -en *f.; (comfort)* Behag'lichkeit, -en *f.* **2.** *vb.* erleich'tern, lindern.

easel, *n.* Staffelei', -en *f.*

easiness, *n.* Leichtigkeit, -en *f.*

east, 1. *n.* Osten *m.,* Orient *m.* **2.** *adj.* östlich; Ost *(cpds.).*

Easter, *n.* Ostern *nt.*

easterly, *adj.* östlich.

eastern, *adj.* östlich.

eastward, *adv.* ostwärts.

easy, *adj.* leicht.

easygoing, *adj.* gutmütig, ungezwungen.

eat, *vb.* essen*.

eatable, *adj.* eßbar.

eaves, *n.pl.* Dachrinne, -n *f.*

ebb, 1. *n.* Ebbe, -n *f.* **2.** *vb.* ab·neh·men*.

ebony, *n.* Ebenholz, ⁻er *nt.*

eccentric, *adj.* exzen'trisch.

eccentricity, *n.* Exzentrizität', -en *f.*

ecclesiastic, *adj.* kirchlich, geistlich.

ecclesiastical, *adj.* kirchlich, geistlich.

echelon, *n.* Staffel, -n *f.*

echo, 1. *n.* Echo, -s *nt.* **2.** *vb.* wider·hallen.

eclipse, *n.* Finsternis, -se *f.*

ecological, *adj.* ökologisch.

ecology, *n.* Ökologie' *f.*

economic, *adj.* wirtschaftlich.

economical, *adj.* sparsam.

economics, *n.* Volkswirtschaft *f.,* National'ökonomie *f.*

economist, *n.* Volkswirtschaftler, - *m.*

economize, *vb.* haus·halten*.

economy, *n.* Wirtschaft *f.;* Sparsamkeit *f.*

ecstasy, *n.* Verzü'ckung, -en *f.*

ecumenical, *adj.* ökume'nisch.

eczema, *n.* Ekzem', -e *nt.*

eddy, *n.* Strudel, - *m.*

edge, *n.* Rand, ⁻er *m.; (knife, etc.)* Schneide, -n *f.*

edible, *adj.* eßbar.

edict, *n.* Verord'nung, -en *f.,* Edikt', -e *nt.*

edifice, *n.* Gebäu'de, - *nt.*

edify, *vb.* erbau'en.

edit, *vb.* heraus'·geben*.

edition, *n.* Ausgabe, -n *f.,* Auflage, -n *f.*

editor, *n.* Heraus'geber, - *m.,* Heraus'geberin, -nen *f.*

editorial, 1. *n.* Leitartikel, - *m.* **2.** *adj.* Redaktions'- *(cpds.).*

educate, *vb. (bring up)* erzie'hen*; *(train)* aus·bilden.

education, *n. (upbringing)* Erzie'hung *f.; (training)* Ausbildung *f.; (culture)* Bildung *f.*

educational, *adj.* erzie'herisch.

educator, *n.* Erzie'her, - *m.,* Erzie'herin, -nen *f.;* Pädago'ge, -n, -n *m.* Pädago'gin, -nen *f.*

eel, *n.* Aal, -e *m.*

effect, *n.* Wirkung, -en *f.*

effective, *adj.* wirkungsvoll.

effectiveness, *n.* Wirksamkeit *f.*

effectual, *adj.* wirksam.

effeminate, *adj.* verweich'licht.

effervescence, *n.* Sprudeln *nt.*

effete, *adj.* entkräf'tet.

efficiency, *n.* Leistungsfähigkeit *f.,* Tüchtigkeit *f.,* Wirksamkeit *f.*

efficient, *adj.* leistungsfähig, tüchtig, wirksam.

effigy, *n.* Abbild, -er *nt.*

effort, *n.* Mühe, -n *f.; (exertion)* Anstrengung, -en *f.; (attempt)* Versuch, -e *m.*

effusive, *adj.* überschwenglich.

egg, *n.* Ei, -er *nt.*

eggplant, *n.* Aubergi'ne, -n *f.*

ego, *n.* Ich *nt.*

egoism, *n.* Egois'mus *m.*

egotism, *n.* Egotis'mus *m.*

egotist, *n.* Egoist', -en, -en *m.*

Egypt, *n.* Ägyp'ten *nt.*

Egyptian, 1. *n.* Ägyp'ter, - *m.,* Ägyp'terin, -nen *f.* **2.** *adj.* ägyp'tisch.

eight, *num.* acht.

eighteen, *num.* achtzehn.

eighteenth, 1. *adj.* achtzehnt- **2.** *n.* Achzehntel, -nt.

eighth, 1. *adj.* acht-. **2.** *n.* Achtel, - *nt.*

eightieth, 1. *adj.* achtzigst-. **2.** *n.* Achtzigstel, - *nt.*

eighty, *num.* achtzig.

either, 1. *pron.&adj.* jeder, -es, -e; beides, *pl.* beide **2.** *conj.* (e. . . . or) entweder . . . oder. **3.** *adv.* (not . . . e.) auch nicht, auch kein, -, -e.

ejaculation, *n.* Ausruf, -e *m.*

eject, *vb.* hinaus'werfen*; vertrei'ben*.

ejection, *n.* Hinaus'werfen *nt.*

eke out, *vb.* sich durch·helfen*.

elaborate, 1. *adj.* weitläufig; kunstvoll. **2.** *vb.* ins einzelne gehen*.

elapse, *vb.* verge'hen*.

elastic, 1. *n.* Gummiband, "er *nt.* **2.** *adj.* elas'tisch.

elasticity, *n.* Elastizität' *f.*

elate, *vb.* erfreu'en.

elated, *adj.* hocherfreut.

elation, *n.* Freude, -n *f.*

elbow, *n.* Ellbogen, - *m.*

elder, 1. *n. (tree)* Holun'der, - *m.; (church)* Ältest- *m.* **2.** *adj.* älter.

elderly, *adj.* ältlich.

eldest, *adj.* ältest-.

elect, *vb.* wählen.

election, *n.* Wahl, -en *f.*

elective, *adj.* Wahl- *(cpds.).*

electorate, *n.* Wählerschaft, -en *f.*

electric, electrical, *adj.* elek'trisch.

electrician, *n.* Elek'triker, - *m.*

electricity, *n.* Elektrizität' *f.*

electrocardiogram, *n.* EKG, -s *nt.;* Elektrokardiogramm', -e *nt.*

electrocution, *n.* Tötung durch elektrischen Strom.

electrode, *n.* Elektro'de, -n *f.*

electrolysis, *n.* Elektroly'se *f.*

electron, *n.* Elektron, -o'nen *nt.*

electronic, *adj.* Elektro'nen- *(cpds.).*

electronics, *n.* Elektro'nenwissenschaft *f.*

elegance, *n.* Eleganz' *f.*

elegant, *adj.* elegant'.

elegy, *n.* Elegie', -i'en *f.*

element, *n.* Element', -e *nt.*

elemental, elementary, *adj.* elementar'.

elephant, *n.* Elefant', -en, -en *m.*

elephantine, *adj.* elefan'tenartig.

elevate, *vb.* erhö'hen.

elevation, *n.* Erhö'hung, -en *f.;* Höhe, -n *f.*

elevator, *n.* Fahrstuhl, "e *m.*

eleven, *num.* elf.

eleventh, 1. *adj.* elft-. **2.** *n.* Elftel, - *nt.*

elf, *n.* Kobold, -e *m.*

elfin, *adj.* koboldartig.

elicit, *vb.* heraus'·holen.

eligibility, *n.* Qualifiziert'heit *f.*

eligible, *adj.* qualifiziert'.

eliminate, *vb.* besei'tigen, aus·scheiden*.

elimination, *n.* Besei'tigung, -en *f.;* Ausscheidung, -en *f.*

elixir, *n.* Elixier', -e *nt.*

elk, *n.* Elch, -e *m.*

elm, *n.* Ulme, -n *f.*

elocution, *n.* Redekunst, "e *f.*

elongate, *vb.* verlän'gern.

elope, *vb.* mit einem Mädchen oder einem Jungen durchbrennen*.

eloquence, *n.* Bered'samkeit *f.*

eloquent, *adj.* redegewandt.

else, *adv.* anders, sonst.

elsewhere, *adv.* anderswo.

elucidate, *vb.* erläu'tern.

elude, *vb.* entge'hen*.

elusive, *adj.* nicht greifbar; aalglatt.

emaciated, adj. abgezehrt.

emanate, vb. aus'strömen.

emancipate, vb. emanzipie'ren.

emancipation, n. Emanzipation', -en f.

emancipator, n. Befrei'er, - m.

emasculate, vb. entman'nen.

embalm, vb. ein'balsamieren.

embankment, n. Uferanlage, -n f.

embargo, n. Embar'go, -s nt.

embark, vb. (sich) ein'schiffen.

embarrass, vb. in Verle'genheit bringen*.

embarrassed, adj. verle'gen.

embarrassment, n. Verle'genheit, -en f.

embassy, n. Botschaft, -en f.

embellish, vb. aus'schmücken.

embellishment, n. Ausschmück-ung, -en f.

embezzle, vb. unterschla'gen*.

embitter, vb. verbit'tern.

emblem, n. Wahrzeichen, - nt., Emblem', -e nt.

embody, vb. verkör'pern.

embrace, vb. umar'men.

embroider, vb. sticken.

embroidery, n. Stickerei', -en f.

embroil, vb. verwi'ckeln.

embryo, n. Embryo, -s m.

emerald, n. Smaragd', -e m.

emerge, vb. hervor'treten*, auf'tauchen.

emergency, n. Notfall, ̈-e m. (e. exit) Notausgang m.

emery, n. Schmirgel m.

emetic, n. Brechmittel, - nt.

emigrant, n. Auswanderer, - m.

emigrate, vb. aus'wandern.

emigration, n. Auswanderung, -en f.

eminence, n. (hill) Anhöhe, -n f.; (distinction) Auszeichnung, -en f.; (title) Eminenz', -en f.

eminent, adj. erha'ben.

emissary, n. Gesandt'- m.&f.

emission controls, n.pl. Abgasbestimmungen f.pl.

emit, vb. von sich geben*.

emotion, n. Gefühl', -e nt.; Erre'gung, -en f.

emotional, adj. gefühls'mäßig; erreg'bar.

emperor, n. Kaiser, - m.

emphasis, n. Nachdruck m., Schwerpunkt m.

emphasize, vb. beto'nen, hervor'heben*.

emphatic, adj. nachdrücklich.

empire, n. Kaiserreich, -e nt.

empirical, adj. empi'risch.

employ, vb. an'stellen, beschäf'tigen.

employee, n. Arbeitnehmer, - m., Arbeitnehmerin, -nen f., Angestellt- m.&f.

employer, n. Arbeitgeber, - m., Arbeitgeberin, -nen f.

employment, n. Anstellung, -en f.; Beschäf'tigung, -en f.

employment office, n. Arbeitsamt nt.

empower, vb. ermäch'tigen.

empress, n. Kaiserin, -nen f.

emptiness, n. Leere f.

empty, 1. vb. leeren. **2.** adj. leer.

emulate, vb. nach'eifern.

emulsion, n. Emulsion', -en f.

enable, vb. ermög'lichen; (enabling act) Ermäch'tigungsgesetz, -e nt.

enact, vb. (law) erlas'sen; (role) spielen.

enactment, n. Verord'nung, -en f.

enamel, n. Emai'lle f.

enamor, vb. (be e.ed of) in jemand verliebt' sein*; (become e.ed of) sich in jemand verlie'ben.

encamp, vb. sich lagern.

encampment, n. Lager, - nt.

encephalitis, n. Gehirn'entzündung, -en f.

enchant, vb. entzü'cken; bezau'bern.

enchantment, n. Bezau'berung f.; Zauber m.

encircle, vb. umrin'gen.

enclose, vb. ein'schließen*; (letter) bei'fügen.

enclosure, n. Einzäunung, -en f.; (letter) Beilage, -n f.

encompass, vb. umschlie'ßen*, ein'schließen*.

encounter, vb. treffen*, bege'gnen.

encourage, vb. ermu'tigen.

encouragement, n. Ermu'tigung, -en f.

encroach upon, vb. sich ein·drän-
gen.

encyclical, n. Enzy'klika, -ken f.

encyclopedia, n. Konversa-
tions'lexikon, -ka nt.; Enzyklopädie', -i'en f.

end, 1. n. Ende, -n nt.; (purpose)
Zweck, -e m.; (goal) Ziel, -e nt. **2.**
vb. been'den, vollen'den, been'digen.

endanger, vb. gefähr'den.

endear, vb. lieb, teuer, wert machen.

endearment, n. Zärtlichkeit, -en
f.

endeavor, vb. sich bemü'hen,
streben.

ending, n. Ende, -n nt., Schluß,
-̈sse m.

endless, adj. endlos.

endocrine, adj. endokrin'.

endorse, vb. gut·heißen*; (check)
girie'ren.

endorsement, n. Billigung, -en f.;
(check) Giro nt.

endow, vb. aus·statten; stiften.

endowment, n. Ausstattung, -en
f.; Stiftung, -en f.

endurance, n. Ausdauer f.

endure, vb. (last) dauern; (bear)
ertra'gen*.

enema, n. Klistier', -e nt.

enemy, n. Feind, -e m., Feindin,
-nen f.

energetic, adj. ener'gisch, tatkräftig.

energy, n. Tatkraft, -̈e f., Energie', -n f.

enfold, vb. ein·hüllen.

enforce, vb. durch·setzen.

enforcement, n. Durchführung,
-en f., Durchsetzung, -en f.

engage, vb. (hire) an·stellen;
(affiance) verlo'ben; (rent) mieten.

engaged, adj. (busy) beschäf'tigt;
(affianced) verlobt'.

engagement, n. (date) Vera-
b'redung, -en f.; (betrothal) Verlo'bung, -en f.

engaging, adj. anziehend.

engender, vb. hervor'·bringen*.

engine, n. Maschi'ne, - f.; Motor,
-o'ren m.; Lokomoti've, -n f.

engineer, n. Ingenieur', -e m., In-

genieu'rin, -nen f.; (locomotive)
Lokomotiv'führer, - m.; (mil.)
Pionier', -e m.

engineering, n. Ingenieur'wesen
nt.

England, n. England nt.

English, adj. englisch.

Englishman, n. Engländer, - m.

Englishwoman, n. Engländerin,
-en f.

engrave, vb. gravie'ren.

engraver, n. Graveur', -e m.
Graveu'rin, -nen f.

engraving, n. Kupferstich, -e m.

engross, vb. in Anspruch nehmen*.

enhance, vb. erhö'hen.

enigma, n. Rätsel, - nt.

enigmatic, adj. rätselhaft, dunkel.

enjoin, vb. (command) befeh'len*; (forbid) verbie'ten*.

enjoy, vb. genie'ßen*, sich erfreu'en.

enjoyable, adj. erfreu'lich, angenehm, nett.

enjoyment, n. Freude, -n f.,
Genuß', -̈sse m.

enlarge, vb. vergrö'ßern.

enlargement, n. Vergrö'ßerung,
-en f.

enlarger, n. Vergrö'ßerungsapparat, -e m.

enlighten, vb. auf·klären.

enlightenment, n. Aufklärung f.

enlist, vb. ein·spannen; (mil.) sich
freiwillig melden.

enlisted man, n. Soldat', -en, -en
m.

enlistment, n. freiwillige Meldung zum Militärdienst.

enliven, vb. bele'ben.

enmity, n. Feindschaft, -en f.

ennui, n. Langeweile f.

enormity, n. Ungeheuerlichkeit,
-en f.

enormous, adj. ungeheuer,
enorm'.

enough, adv. genug', genü'gend.

enrage, vb. rasend machen.

enrapture, vb. entzü'cken.

enrich, vb. berei'chern.

enroll, vb. als Mitglied ein·tra-
gen.*

enrollment, *n.* Eintragung *(f.)* als Mitglied; Mitgliederzahl, -en *f.*

ensemble, *n.* Ensem'ble, -s *nt.*

enshrine, *vb.* als Heiligtum verwah'ren.

ensign, *n. (rank)* Fähnrich, -e *m.; (flag)* Fahne, -n *f.*

enslave, *vb.* verskla'ven, knechten.

enslavement, *n.* Versklavung *f.*

ensnare, *vb.* verstri'cken.

ensue, *vb.* folgen.

entail, *vb.* ein·schließen*.

entangle, *vb.* verwi'ckeln.

enter, *vb.* ein·treten*, ein·dringen*.

enterprise, *n.* Unterneh'men, - *nt.*

enterprising, *adj.* unterneh'mend.

entertain, *vb.* unterhal'ten*.

entertainer, *n.* Unterhal'ter, - *m.,* Unterhal'terin, - nen *f.*

entertainment, *n.* Unterhal'tung, -en *f.*

enthrall, *vb.* bezau'bern.

enthuse, *vb.* schwärmen.

enthusiasm, *n.* Begeis'terung, *f.*

enthusiastic, *adj.* begeis'tert, enthusiastisch.

entice, *vb.* verlo'cken.

entire, *adj.* ganz, gesamt'.

entirety, *n.* Ganz- *nt.,* Ganzheit *f.,* Gesamt'heit *f.*

entitle, *vb.* berech'tigen; *(name)* beti'teln.

entity, *n.* Wesenheit *f.*

entrails, *n.pl.* Eingeweide *pl.*

entrain, *vb.* den Zug bestei'gen*.

entrance, *n.* Eingang, *-e m.*

entrant, *n.* Teilnehmer, - *m.,* Teilnehmerin, -nen *f.*

entrap, *vb.* in einer Falle fangen*; verstri'cken.

entreat, *vb.* an·flehen.

entreaty, *n.* Gesuch', -e *nt.*

entree, *n.* Haupgericht, -e *nt.*

entrench, *vb.* verschan'zen.

entrepreneur, *n.* Unterneh'mer, - *m.,* Unterneh'merin, -nen *f.*

entrust, *vb.* an·vertrauen.

entry, *n.* Eintritt, -e *m.; (writing)* Eintragung, -en *f.*

enumerate, *vb.* auf·zählen.

enumeration, *n.* Aufzählung, -en *f.*

enunciate, *vb.* aus·sprechen*.

enunciation, *n.* Aussprache, -n *f.*

envelop, *vb.* ein·hüllen.

envelope, *n.* Umschlag, *-e m.,* Kuvert', -s *nt.*

enviable, *adj.* benei'denswert.

envious, *adj.* neidisch.

environment, *n.* Umge'bung, -en *f.,* Umwelt *f.*

environmentalist, *n.* Umweltschützer, - *m.*

environmental protection, *n.* Umweltschutz *m.*

environs, *n.* Umge'bung, -en *f.*

envisage, *vb.* vergegenwär'tigen.

envoy, *n.* Gesandt'- *m&f.*

envy, *n.* Neid *m.*

eon, *n.* Äon', -en *m.*

ephemeral, *adj.* vergäng'lich.

epic, **1.** *n.* Epos, -pen *nt.* **2.** *adj.* episch.

epicure, *n.* Feinschmecker, - *m.*

epidemic, **1.** *n.* Epidemie', -i'en *f.* **2.** *adj.* epide'misch.

epidermis, *n.* Epider'mis *f.*

epigram, *n.* Epigramm', -e *nt.*

epilepsy, *n.* Epilepsie' *f.*

epilogue, *n.* Epilog, -e *m.*

episode, *n.* Episo'de, -n *f.*

epistle, *n.* Schreiben, - *nt.*

epitaph, *n.* Epitaph', -e *nt.*

epithet, *n.* Beiwort, *-er nt.*

epitome, *n.* Kurzfassung, -en *f.; (fig.)* Verkör'perung, -en *f.*

epitomize, *vb.* zusam'men·fassen; bezeich'nend sein* für*.

epoch, *n.* Epo'che, -n *f.*

equal, **1.** *adj.* gleich. **2.** *vb.* gleichen*.

equality, *n.* Gleichheit *f.*

equalize, *vb.* gleich·machen; aus·gleichen*.

equanimity, *n.* Gleichmut *m.*

equate, *vb.* gleich·setzen.

equation, *n.* Gleichung, -en *f.*

equator, *n.* Äqua'tor *m.*

equatorial, *adj.* äquatorial'.

equestrian, *n.* Reiter, - *m.*

equilateral, *adj.* gleichseitig.

equilibrium, *n.* Gleichgewicht *nt.*

equinox, *n.* Tag- und Nachtgleiche, -n *f.*

equip, *vb.* aus·rüsten.

equipment, *n.* Ausrüstung, -en *f.*

equitable, *adj.* gerecht', billig.

equity, n. Billigkeit f.; Billigkeitsrecht nt.; (mortgage, etc.) Rückkaufswert, -e m.

equivalent, adj. gleichwertig.

equivocal, adj. zweideutig.

equivocate, vb. zweideutig sein*.

era, n. Zeitalter, - nt.

eradicate, vb. aus·rotten.

erase, vb. aus·radieren.

erasure, n. Ausradierung, -en f.

erect, 1. adj. gera'de. **2.** vb. er·rich'ten.

erection, n. Errich'tung, -en f.

erectness, n. Gerad'heit f.

ermine, n. Hermelin' m.

erode, vb. erodie'ren, zerfres'sen*.

erosion, n. Erosion', -en f.

erotic, adj. ero'tisch.

err, vb. irren.

errand, n. Besor'gung, -en f.

errant, adj. wandernd; abwegig.

erratic, adj. verirrt'; ziellos.

erroneous, adj. irrtümlich.

error, n. Fehler, - m.; Irrtum, =er m.

erudite, adj. gelehrt'.

erudition, n. Gelehr'samkeit f.

erupt, vb. hervor'·brechen*, aus·brechen*.

eruption, n. Ausbruch, =e m.

escalate, vb. steigern.

escalator, n. Rolltreppe, -n f.

escapade, n. Streich, -e m.

escape, 1. n. Flucht f. **2.** vb. entkom'men*, entge'hen*.

escapism, n. Wirklichkeitsflucht f.

escort, 1. n. Beglei'ter, - m., Beglei'terin, -nen f. **2.** vb. beglei'ten.

escutcheon, n. Wappenschild, -er nt.

esophagus, n. Speiseröhre, -n f.

esoteric, adj. esote'risch.

especial, adj. beson'der-.

especially, adv. beson'ders.

espionage, n. Spiona'ge f.

espousal, n. Vermäh'lung, -en f.; (e. of) Eintreten für nt.

espouse, vb. vermäh'len; (e. a cause) ein·treten* für.

essay, 1. n. Essay, -s m. **2.** vb. versu'chen.

essence, nt. Wesen nt., Wesentlich- nt.

essential, adj. wesentlich.

establish, vb. fest·setzen; er·rich'ten; ein·richten.

establishment, n. Einrichtung, -en f.; Betrieb', -e m.

estate, n. (inheritance) Nachlaß, =sse m.; (possessions) Vermö'gen nt.; (condition) Zustand, =e m., Stand, =e m.

esteem, 1. n. Achtung f. **2.** vb. achten, schätzen.

estimable, adj. schätzenswert.

estimate, 1. n. Kostenanschlag, =e m. **2.** vb. schätzen.

estimation, n. Achtung f.; (view) Ansicht, -en f.

Estonia, n. Estland nt.

estrange, vb. entfrem'den.

etch, vb. ätzen.

etching, n. Radie'rung, -en f.

eternal, adj. ewig.

eternity, n. Ewigkeit, -en f.

ether, n. Äther m.

ethereal, adj. äthe'risch.

ethical, adj. ethisch, sittlich, mora'lisch.

ethics, n. Ethik f.

ethnic, adj. ethnisch.

etiquette, n. Etiket'te f.

etymology, n. Etymologie', -i'en f.

eucalyptus, n. Eukalyp'tus, -ten m.

eugenic, adj. euge'nisch.

eugenics, n. Eugene'tik f.

eulogize, vb. lobpreisen*.

eulogy, n. Lobrede, -n f.

eunuch, n. Eunuch', -en, -en m.

euphonious, adj. wohlklingend.

Europe, n. Euro'pa nt.

European, 1. n. Europä'er, - m. Europä'erin, -nen f. **2.** adj. europä'isch.

European Community, n. Europäische Gemeinschaft f.

euthanasia, n. Gnadentod m., Euthanasie' f.

evacuate, vb. evakuie'ren.

evade, vb. aus·weichen*, vermei'den*.

evaluate, vb. ab·schätzen, den Wert berech'nen.

evaluation, n. Abschätzung, -en f., Wertbestimmung, -en f.

evangelist, n. Evangelist', -en, -en m.

evaporate, vb. verdam'pfen.

evaporation, n. Verdam'pfung f.

evasion, n. Umge'hen, - nt.

evasive, adj. ausweichend.

eve, n. Vorabend, -e m.

even, 1. adj. gleich, gera'de, eben. **2.** adv. eben, sogar', selbst.

evening, n. Abend, -e m.

evenness, n. Ebenheit, -en f.; Gleichheit, -en f.; Gleichmut m.

event, n. Ereig'nis, -se nt.

eventful, adj. ereig'nisreich.

eventual, adj. (approximate) etwaig; (final) schließlich.

ever, adv. je, jemals.

evergreen, adj. immergrün.

everlasting, adj. ewig.

every, adj. jeder, -es, -e.

everybody, pron. jeder m.; alle pl.

everyday, adj. Alltags- (cpds.).

everyone, pron. jeder m.; alle pl.

everything, pron. alles.

everywhere, adv. überall'.

evict, vb. aus'weisen; zwangsräumen.

eviction, n. Ausweisung, -en f.; Zwangsräumung, -en f.

evidence, n. Beweis, -e m.; Augenschein, m.; (law) Beweismaterial, -ien nt.; (give e.) aus'sagen.

evident, adj. klar, deutlich.

evidently, adv. offenbar.

evil, 1. n. Bös- nt. **2.** adj. böse, übel.

evince, vb. offenba'ren.

evoke, vb. hervor'rufen*.

evolution, n. Evolution', -en f.

evolve, vb. entwi'ckeln.

ewe, n. Mutterschaf, -e nt.

exact, 1. adj. genau'. **2.** vb. erzwin'gen*.

exaggerate, vb. übertrei'ben*.

exaggeration, n. Übertrei'bung, -en f.

exalt, vb. erhö'hen, verherr'lichen.

exaltation, n. Erhö'hung f.; Erre'gung, -en f.

examination, n. Prüfung, -en f.; Exa'men, - nt.; Untersu'chung, -en f.

examine, vb. prüfen; untersu'chen.

example, n. Beispiel, -e nt.

exasperate, vb. reizen, verär'gern.

exasperation, n. Gereizt'heit f.

excavate, vb. aus'graben*.

excavation, n. Ausgrabung, -en f.; Aushöhlung, -en f.

exceed, vb. übertref'fen*.

exceedingly, adv. außerordentlich.

excel, vb. sich aus'zeichnen.

excellence, n. Vorzüg'lichkeit, -en f.

Excellency, n. Exzellenz', -en f.

excellent, adj. ausgezeich'net.

except, 1. vb. aus'schließen*. **2.** prep. außer, ausgenommen; (e. for) außer.

exception, n. Ausnahme, -n f.

exceptional, adj. außergewöhnlich.

excerpt, n. Auszug, ⁼e m.

excess, n. Übermaß nt.

excessive, adj. übermäßig.

exchange, 1. n. Tausch m.; (rate of e.) Wechselkurs m.; (foreign e.) Valu'ta f.; (student) Austausch m.; (stock e.) Börse, -n f. **2.** vb. tauschen; wechseln; aus'tauschen; (goods) um'tauschen.

exchangeable, adj. austauschbar; umtauschbar.

excise, 1. n. Verbrauchs'steuer, -n f. **2.** vb. heraus'schneiden*.

excite, vb. auf'regen, erre'gen; (get e.d) sich auf'regen.

excitement, n. Erre'gung, -en f.; Aufregung, -en f.

exclaim, vb. aus'rufen*.

exclamation, n. Ausruf, -e m.

exclamation point or **mark,** n. Ausrufungszeichen, - nt.

exclude, vb. aus'schließen*.

exclusion, n. Ausschluß, ⁼sse m.

exclusive, adj. ausschließlich; (e. of) abgesehen von; (select) exklusiv'.

excommunicate, vb. exkommunizie'ren.

excommunication, n. Exkommunikation', -en f.

excrement, n. Exkrement', -e nt.

excruciating, adj. qualvoll.

excursion, *n.* Ausflug, -̈e *m.*
excusable, *adj.* entschuld'bar.
excuse, *vb.* entschul'digen, verzei'hen*.
execute, *vb.* aus•führen; *(legal killing)* hin•richten.
execution, *n.* Ausführung, -en *f.; (legal killing)* Hinrichtung, -en *f.*
executioner, *n.* Scharfrichter, - *m.*
executive, 1. *n.* leitender Angestellter *m.,* leitende Angestellte *f. (gov't.)* Exekuti've *f.* **2.** *adj.* vollzie'hend, ausübend.
executor, *n.* Testaments'vollstrecker, - *m.*
exemplary, *adj.* musterhaft.
exemplify, *vb.* als Beispiel dienen.
exempt, 1. *adj.* befreit'. **2.** *vb.* befrei'en.
exercise, 1. *n.* Übung, -en *f.; (carrying out)* Ausübung, -en *f.; (physical)* Bewe'gung, -en *f.* **2.** *vb.* üben; aus•üben; bewe'gen.
exert, *vb.* aus•üben; *(e. oneself)* sich an•strengen.
exertion, *n.* Anstrengung, -en *f.*
exhale, *vb.* aus•atmen.
exhaust, 1. *n. (auto.)* Auspuff, -e *m.* **2.** *vb.* erschöp'fen.
exhaustion, *n.* Erschöp'fung, -en *f.*
exhaustive, *adj.* erschöp'fend.
exhibit, 1. *n.* Ausstellung, -en *f.* **2.** *vb.* aus•stellen; zeigen.
exhibition, *n.* Ausstellung, -en *f.*
exhibitionism, *n.* Exhibitionis'mus *m.*
exhilarate, *vb.* auf•heitern.
exhort, *vb.* ermah'nen.
exhortation, *n.* Ermah'nung, -en *f.*
exhume, *vb.* aus•graben*.
exigency, *n.* Dringlichkeit, -en *f.*
exile, 1. *n.* Verban'nung, -en *f.* **2.** *vb.* verban'nen.
exist, *vb.* beste'hen*, existie'ren.
exodus, *n.* Auszug, -̈e *m.;* Auswanderung, -en *f.*
exonerate, *vb.* entlas'ten.
exorbitant, *adj.* übermäßig.
exotic, *adj.* exo'tisch.
expand, *vb.* aus•dehnen, aus•breiten, erwei'tern.

expanse, *n.* Ausdehnung, -en *f.,* Weite, -n *f.*
expansion, *n.* Ausdehnung, -en *f.,* Ausbreitung, -en *f.;* Expansion', -en *f.*
expansive, *adj.* umfas'send.
expatriate, *n.* Emigrant', -en, -en *m.*
expect, *vb.* erwar'ten.
expectancy, *n.* Erwar'tung, -en *f.*
expectation, *n.* Erwar'tung, -en *f.*
expectorate, *vb.* (aus)spucken.
expediency, *n.* Zweckmäßigkeit, -en *f.*
expedient, *adj.* zweckmäßig.
expedite, *vb.* beschleu'nigen.
expedition, *n.* Expedition', -en *f.*
expel, *vb.* vertrei'ben*.
expend, *vb. (money)* aus•geben*; *(energy)* auf•wenden*.
expenditure, *n.* Ausgabe, -n *f.,* Aufwand *m.*
expense, *n.* Ausgabe, -n *f.;* Kosten *pl.,* Unkosten *pl.;* **(on an e. account)** auf Spesen.
expensive, *adj.* teuer, kostspielig.
experience, 1. *n.* Erfah'rung, -en *f.* **2.** *vb.* erfah'ren*.
experienced, *adj.* erfah'ren.
experiment, 1. *n.* Versuch' -e *m.,* Experiment', -e *nt.* **2.** *vb.* experimentie'ren.
experimental, *adj.* Versuchs'- *(cpds.).*
experimentally, *adv.* versuchs'weise.
expert, 1. *n.* Sachverständig-m&*f.,* Exper'te, -n, -n *m.,* Exper'tin, -nen *f.* **2.** *adj.* erfah'ren.
expiate, *vb.* büßen.
expiration, *n. (breath)* Ausatmung, -en *f.; (end)* Ablauf *m.*
expire, *vb. (breathe out)* aus•atmen; *(die)* verschei'den; *(end)* ab•laufen*.
explain, *vb.* erklä'ren.
explanation, *n.* Erklä'rung, -en *f.*
explanatory, *adj.* erklä'rend.
expletive, 1. *n.* Füllwort, -̈er *nt.;* Ausruf, -e *m.* **2.** *adj.* ausfüllend.
explicit, *adj.* ausdrücklich.
explode, *vb.* explodie'ren.
exploit, *vb.* aus•beuten, aus•nutzen.
exploitation, *n.* Ausbeutung, -en *f.,* Ausnutzung, -en *f.*

exploration, n. Erfor'schung, -en f.

exploratory, adj. untersu'chend, erkun'dend.

explore, vb. erfor'schen, untersu'chen.

explorer, n. Forscher, - m., Forschungsreisend-e m.

explosion, n. Explosion', -en f.

explosive, 1. n. Sprengstoff, -e m. **2.** adj. explosiv'.

exponent, n. Exponent', -en, -en m.

export, 1. n. Export', -e m., Ausfuhr f. **2.** vb. exportie' ren, ausführen.

exportation, n. Ausfuhr f.

expose, vb. aus·setzen; (photo) belich'ten; (disclose) enthül'len.

exposé, n. Darlegung, -en f.; (disclosure) Enthül'lung, -en f.

exposition, n. Darlegung, -en f.; (exhibit) Ausstellung, -en f.

expository, adj. erklä'rend.

exposure, n. Aussetzung, -en f.; (photo) Belich'tung, -en f.; Bloßstellung, -en f.

expound, vb. aus·legen, erklä'ren.

express, 1. n. (train) Schnellzug, ⁻e m. **2.** vb. aus·drücken. **3.** adj. ausdrücklich.

expression, n. Ausdruck, ⁻e m.

expressive, adj. ausdrucksvoll.

expropriate, vb. enteig'nen.

expulsion, n. Vertrei'bung, -en f., Entlas'sung, -en f.

expurgate, vb. reinigen.

exquisite, adj. vorzüg'lich.

extant, adj. vorhan'den.

extemporaneous, adj. aus dem Stegreif.

extend, vb. (intr.) sich erstre'cken, reichen; (tr.) aus·dehnen.

extension, n. Ausdehnung, -en f.; Verlän'gerung, -en f.

extensive, adj. umfangreich.

extent, n. Umfang, ⁻e m.

exterior, adj. äußer-, äußerlich.

exterminate, vb. aus·rotten. vernich'ten.

extermination, n. Ausrottung, -en f.; Vernich'tung, -en f.

external, adj. äußer-; auswärtig.

extinct, adj. ausgestorben.

extinction, n. Aussterben nt.

extinguish, vb. aus·löschen.

extol, vb. loben, preisen*.

extort, vb. ab·zwingen*.

extortion, n. Erpres'sung, -en f.

extra, adj. extra, beson'der-.

extra-, (cpds.) außer-.

extract, 1. n. Auszug, ⁻e m., Extrakt', -e m. **2.** vb. heraus'·ziehen*, heraus'·holen.

extraction, n. Ausziehen nt.; (ethnic) Herkunft -¨e f., Abstammung, -en f.

extradite, vb. aus·liefern.

extradition, n. Auslieferung, -en f.

extraneous, adj. fremd.

extraordinary, adj. außergewöhnlich.

extravagance, n. Verschwen'dung, -en f., Extravaganz', -en f.

extravagant, adj. verschwen'derisch; übertrie'ben.

extravaganza, n. phantas'tische, überspann'te Komposition', -en f.

extreme, adj. äußerst-.

extremely, adv. äußerst, höchst.

extremity, n. Äußerst- nt.; (limbs) Gliedmaßen pl.

extricate, vb. heraus'·winden*.

exuberant, adj. überschwenglich.

exult, vb. frohlo'cken.

exultant, adj. frohlo'ckend.

eye, n. Auge, -n nt.

eyeball, n. Augapfel, ⁻ m.

eyebrow, n. Augenbraue, -n f.

eyeglasses, n.pl. Brille, -n f.

eyelash, n. Augenwimper, -n f.

eyelet, n. Öse, -n f.

eyelid, n. Augenlid -er nt.

eyesight, n. Augensicht f.; Augen pl.

F

fable, n. Fabel, -n f.

fabric, n. Stoff, -e m.

fabricate, vb. her·stellen; (lie) erdich'ten.

fabrication, n. Herstellung, -en f.; (lie) Erdich'tung, -en f.

fabulous, adj. sagenhaft.

façade, n. Fassa'de, -n f.

face, 1. n. Gesicht', -er nt.; (surface) Oberfläche, -n f. **2.** vb. ins Gesicht' sehen*; (be opposite) gegenü'ber·lie·gen*.

facet, n. Facet'te, -n f.

facetious, adj. scherzhaft.

face value, n. Nennwert, -e m.

facial, 1. n. Gesichts'massage, -n f. **2.** adj. Gesichts'- (cpds.).

facile, adj. gewandt'.

facilitate, vb. erleich'tern.

facility, n. (ease) Leichtigkeit f.; (skill) Geschick'lichkeit f.; (possibility) Möglichkeit, -en f.

facing, n. (clothing) Besatz' m.

facsimile, n. Faksi'mile, -s nt.

fact, n. Tatsache, -n f.

faction, n. Gruppe, -n f.

factor, n. Faktor, -o'ren m.

factory, n. Fabrik', -en f.

factual, adj. auf Tatsachen beschränkt'; Tatsachen- (cpds.).

faculty, n. Fähigkeit, -en f.; Gabe, -n f.; (college) Fakultät', -en f.

fad, n. Mode, -n f.

fade, vb. verblas'sen.

fail, vb. versa'gen; (school) durch·fal·len*; (f. to do) nicht tun*.

failure, n. Versa'gen nt., Mißerfolg, -e m.; (bankruptcy) Bankrott', -e m.

faint, 1. adj. schwach. **2.** vb. in Ohnmacht fallen*.

fair, 1. n. Messe, -n f., Jahrmarkt, -̈e m., Rummelplatz, -̈e m. **2.** adj. (weather) heiter; (blond) blond; (just) gerecht'.

fairness, n. Gerech'tigkeit, -en f.

fairy, n. Fee, Fe'en f.

fairy tale, n. Märchen, - nt.

faith, n. (trust) Vertrau'en nt.; (belief) Glaube(n), m.

faithful, adj. treu.

faithfulness, n. Treue f.

faithless, adj. treulos.

fake, 1. adj. falsch. **2.** vb. vortäuschen.

faker, n. Schwindler, - m., Schwindlerin, -nen f.

falcon, n. Falke, -n, -n m.

fall, 1. n. Fall, -̈e m., Sturz -̈e m.;

(autumn) Herbst, -e m. **2.** vb. fallen*.

fallacious, adj. trügerisch.

fallacy, n. Trugschluß, -̈sse m.

fallible, adj. fehlbar.

fallout, n. (radioaktiver) Niederschlag, -̈e m.

fallow, adj. brach.

false, adj. falsch.

falsehood, n. Lüge, -n f.

falseness, n. Falschheit, -en f.

falsetto, n. Falsett', -e nt.

falsification, n. Verfäl'schung, -en f.

falsify, vb. verfäl'schen.

falter, vb. straucheln, stocken.

fame, n. Ruhm m.

famed, adj. berühmt'.

familiar, adj. vertraut'.

familiarity, n. Vertraut'heit, -en f.; Vertrau'lichkeit, -en f.

familiarize, vb. vertraut'machen.

family, n. Fami'lie, -n f.

famine, n. Hungersnot, -̈e f.

famished, adj. ausgehungert.

famous, adj. berühmt'.

fan, 1. n. Fächer, - m.; Ventila'tor, -o'ren m.; (enthusiast) Vereh'rer, - m., Vereh'rerin, -nen f., Anhänger, - m., Anhängerin, -nen f. **2.** vb. fächern.

fanatic, n. Fana'tiker, - m., Fana'tikerin, -nen f. **2.** adj. fana'tisch.

fanatical, adj. fana'tisch.

fanaticism, n. Fanatis'mus m.

fanciful, adj. phantas'tisch.

fancy, 1. n. (imagination) Einbildung, -en f.; (mood) Laune, -n f.; (liking) Vorliebe f. **2.** adj. apart', ausgefallen; Luxus- (cpds.). **3.** vb. sich ein·bilden.

fanfare, n. Fanfa're, -n f.; (fig.) Getu'e nt.

fang, n. Fang, -̈e, m.

fantastic, adj. phantas'tisch.

fantasy, n. Phantasie', -i'en f.

far, adj. weit, fern.

faraway, adj. entfernt'; (fig.) träumerisch.

farce, n. Farce, -n f.

fare, 1. n. (passenger) Fahrgeld, -er nt.; (price) Fahrpreis, -e m.; (food) Kost f. vb. gehen*.

farewell, 1. n. Abschied, -e m.;

Abschieds- *(cpds.).* 2. *interj.* lebe wohl! leben Sie wohl!

far-fetched, *adj.* gesucht'.

farina, *n.* Grießmehl *nt.*

farm, 1. *n.* landwirtschaftlicher Betrieb', -e *m.,* Farm, -en *f.* 2. *vb.* Landwirtschaft betrei'ben*, Landwirt sein*.

farmer, *n.* Landwirt, -e *m.,* Landwirtin, -nen *f.* Farmer, - *m.,* Bauer, (-n), -n *m.*

farmhouse, *n.* Farmhaus, ̈er *nt.;* Bauernhaus, ̈er *nt.*

farming, *n.* Landwirtschaft *f.;* Ackerbau *m.*

farmyard, *n.* Bauernhof, ̈e *m.*

far-sighted, *adj.* weitsichtig.

farther, *adj.* weiter.

farthest, *adj.* weitest-.

fascinate, *vb.* faszinie'ren, bezau'bern.

fascination, *n.* Faszination *f.,* Zauber *m.*

fascism, *n.* Faschis'mus *m.*

fascist, 1. *n.* Faschist', -en, -en *m.* 2. *adj.* faschis'tisch.

fashion, *n.* Mode, -n *f.; (manner)* Art, -en *f.*

fashionable, *adj.* modern', schick.

fast, 1. *n.* Fasten *nt.* 2. *adj. (speedy)* schnell; **(be f.,** *of a clock)* vor'gehen*; *(firm)* fest. 3. *vb.* fasten.

fasten, *vb.* fest'machen.

fastener, fastening, *n.* Verschluß', ̈sse *m.*

fastidious, *adj.* wählerisch; eigen.

fat, 1. *n.* Fett, -e *nt.* 2. *adj.* fett, dick.

fatal, *adj.* tötlich; verhäng'nisvoll.

fatality, *n.* Verhäng'nis, -se *nt.;* Todesfall, ̈e *m.*

fate, *n.* Schicksal, -e *nt.*

fateful, *adj.* schicksalsschwer; verhäng'nisvoll.

father, *n.* Vater, - *m.*

fatherhood, *n.* Vaterschaft, -en *f.*

father-in-law, *n.* Schwiegervater, ̈ *m.*

fatherland, *n.* Vaterland *nt.*

fatherless, *adj.* vaterlos.

fatherly, *adj.* väterlich.

fathom, 1. *n.* Klafter, -n *f.* 2. *vb.* loten; *(fig.)* ergrün'den.

fatigue, 1. *n.* Ermü'dung *f.* ermü'den. 2. *vb.*

fatten, *vb.* mästen.

fatty, *adj.* fettig.

faucet, *n.* Wasserhahn, ̈e *m.*

fault, *n.* Fehler, - *m.; (it's my f.)* es ist meine Schuld.

faultless, *adj.* fehlerlos, makellos.

faulty, *adj.* fehlerhaft.

favor, 1. *n.* Gunst, -en *f.; (do a f.)* einen Gefallen tun*. 2. *vb.* begün'stigen, bevor'zugen; *(a sore limb)* schonen.

favorable, *adj.* günstig.

favorite, 1. *n.* Liebling, -e *m.; (sport)* Favorit', -en, -en *m.;* Favori'tin, -nen *f.* 2. *adj.* Lieblings- *(cpds.).*

favoritism, *n.* Begün'stigung *f.*

fawn, *n.* Rehkalb, -er *nt.*

fax, *vb.* faxen.

faze, *vb.* in Verle'genheit bringen*.

fear, 1. *n.* Furcht *f.,* Angst, ̈e *f.* 2. *vb.* fürchten.

fearful, *adj. (afraid)* furchtsam; *(terrible)* furchtbar.

fearless, *adj.* furchtlos.

fearlessness, *n.* Furchtlosigkeit *f.*

feasible, *adj.* durchführbar, machbar.

feast, *n.* Fest, -e *nt.,* Festmahl, -e *nt.*

feat, *n.* Tat, -en *f.;* Kunststück, -e *nt.*

feather, *n.* Feder, -n *f.*

feature, *n. (quality)* Eigenschaft, -en *f.; (face)* Gesichtszug, ̈e *m.; (distinguishing mark)* Kennzeichen, - *nt.*

February, *n.* Februar *m.*

feces, *n. pl.* Exkremen'te *pl.*

federal, *adj.* bundesstaatlich; Bundes- *(cpds.).*

federation, *n.* Staatenbund, -e *m.,* Föderation', -en *f.;* Bundesstaat, -en *m.*

fee, *n.* Gebühr', -en *f.*

feeble, *adj.* schwach (̈).

feeble-minded, *adj.* schwachsinnig.

feebleness, *n.* Schwäche, -n *f.*

feed, 1. *n.* Futter, - *nt.* 2. *vb.* füttern.

feedback, n. Feedback m., Rückkopplung f.
feel, vb. fühlen.
feeling, n. Gefühl', -e nt.
feign, vb. vor'geben*, heucheln.
felicitate, vb. beglück'wünschen.
felicity, n. Glück nt.
fell, vb. fällen.
fellow, n. Kerl, -e m., Bursche, -n, -n m.; (member) Mitglied, -er nt.
fellowship, n. Gemein'schaft, -en f.
felony, n. Gewalt'verbrechen, - nt.
felt, n. Filz, -e m.
female, 1. n. (human) Frau, -en f.; (animal) Weibchen, - nt. 2. adj. weiblich.
feminine, adj. weiblich, feminin'.
femininity, n. Weiblichkeit f.
feminist, n. Frauenrechtlerin, -nen f., Frauenrechtler, -m.; Feminist', -en, -en m., Feminist'tin, -nen f.
fence, 1. n. Zaun, ⸚e m. 2. vb. ein'zäunen; (sport) fechten*.
fencing, n. Fechten nt.
fender, n. (auto) Kotflügel, - m.
ferment, vb. gären*.
fermentation, n. Gärung, -en f.
fern, n. Farnkraut, ⸚er nt.
ferocious, adj. wild.
ferocity, n. Wildheit f.
ferry, n. Fähre, -n f.
fertile, adj. fruchtbar.
fertility, n. Fruchtbarkeit f.
fertilization, n. Befruch'tung, -en f.
fertilize, vb. befruch'ten; düngen.
fertilizer, n. Dünger m., Kunstdünger m.
fervent, adj. inbrünstig.
fervid, adj. brennend.
fervor, n. Inbrunst f., Eifer m.
fester, vb. eitern.
festival, n. Fest, -e nt.
festive, adj. festlich.
festivity, n. Festlichkeit, -en f.
festoon, n. Girlan'de, -n f.
fetch, vb. holen.
fetching, adj. reizend.
fête, n. Fest, -e nt.
fetid, adj. stinkend.
fetish, n. Fetisch, -e m.
fetters, n.pl. Fesseln pl.
fetus, n. Foetus, -se m.

feud, n. Feindschaft, -en f.; (historical) Fehde, -n f.
feudal, adj. feudal'.
feudalism, n. Feudalis'mus m.
fever, n. Fieber, - nt.
feverish, adj. fieberhaft.
few, adj. wenig; (a f.) ein paar.
fiancé, n. Verlobt'-e m.
fiancée, n. Verlobt'- f.
fiasco, n. Fias'ko, -s nt.
fib, n. Lüge, -n f.
fiber, n. Faser, -n f.
fickle, adj. wankelmütig.
fickleness, n. Wankelmütigkeit f.
fiction, n. Erdich'tung, -en f.; (novel writing) Prosadichtung, -en f.
fictional, adj. erdich'tet.
fictitious, adj. fingiert'.
fiddle, 1. n. Geige, -n f. 2. vb. geigen.
fidelity, n. Treue f.
fidget, vb. zappeln.
field, n. Feld, -er nt.
fiend, n. Teufel, - m.
fiendish, adj. teuflisch.
fierce, adj. wild.
fiery, adj. feurig.
fife, n. Querpfeife, -n f.
fifteen, num. fünfzehn.
fifteenth, 1. adj. fünfzehnt-. 2. n. Fünfzehntel, - nt.
fifth, 1. adj. fünft-. 2. n. Fünftel, - nt.
fiftieth, 1. adj. fünfzigst-. 2. n. Fünfzigstel, - nt.
fifty, num. fünfzig.
fig, n. Feige, -n f.
fight, 1. n. Kampf, ⸚e m.; (brawl) Schlägerei, -en f.; (quarrel) Streit, -e m. 2. vb. kämpfen; bekämp'fen.
fighter, n. Kämpfer, - m.
figment, n. Fiktion', -en f.
figurative, adj. bildlich; (f. meaning) übertra'gene Bedeu'tung, -en f.
figure, 1. n. Figur', -en f., Gestalt', -en f.; (number) Zahl, -en f. 2. vb. rechnen; berech'nen.
figurehead, n. Galionsfigur, -en f.; (fig.) Repräsentations'figur, -en f.
figure of speech, n. Redewendung, -en f.
figurine, n. Porzellan'figur, -en f.

filament, *n.* Faser, -n *f.*; Faden, ⁼
m.

file, 1. *n. (tool)* Feile, -n *f.*; *(row)*
Reihe, -n *f.*; *(papers, etc.)* Akte,
-n *f.*; *(cards)* Kartothek', -en *f.* **2.**
vb. (tool) feilen; *(papers)* ein·ord-
nen.

filigree, *n.* Filigran', -e *nt.*

fill, *vb.* füllen.

fillet, *n.* Filet', -s *nt.*

filling, *n. (tooth)* Plombe, -n *f.*

filling station, *n.* Tankstelle, -n *f.*

film, 1. *n.* Film, -e *m.* **2.** *vb.* filmen.

filmy, *adj.* mit einem Häutchen
bedeckt; duftig.

filter, 1. *n.* Filter, - *m.* **2.** *vb.* filtrie'ren.

filth, *n.* Dreck *m.*

filthy, *adj.* dreckig; *(fig.)* unanständig.

fin, *n.* Flosse, -n *f.*

final, *adj.* endgültig.

finale, *n.* Fina'le, -s *nt.*

finalist, *n.* Teilnehmer (-, *m.*),
Teilnehmerin (-nen, *f.*) in der
Schlußrunde.

finality, *n.* Endgültigkeit *f.*

finance, 1. *n.* Finanz', -en *f.*;
(study) Finanz'wesen *nt.*; **(f.s.)**
Finan'zen *pl.* **2.** *vb.* financie'ren.

financial, *adj.* finanziell'.

financier, *n.* Finanz'mann, ⁼er *m.*

find, *vb.* finden*.

findings, *n.pl.* Tatbestand, ⁼e *m.*

fine, 1. *n.* Geldstrafe, -n *f.* **2.** *adj.*
fein. **3.** *vb.* zu einer Geldstrafe
verur'teilen.

fine arts, *n.* Kunstwissenschaft *f.*

finery, *n.* Putz *m.*

finesse, *n.* Fines'se, -n *f.*

finger, *n.* Finger, - *m.*

fingernail, *n.* Fingernagel, ⁼ *m.*

fingerprint, *n.* Fingerabdruck, ⁼e
m.

finicky, *adj.* zimperlich.

finish, 1. *n.* Ende, -n *nt.*; Abschluß. ⁼sse *m.* **2.** *vb.* been'den,
vollen'den.

finite, *adj.* endlich.

fir, *n.* Fichte, -n *f.*

fire, 1. *n.* Feuer, - *nt.* **2.** *vb. (shoot)*
feuern; *(dismiss)* entlas'sen*.

fire alarm, *n.* Feueralarm, -e *m.*

fire-alarm box, *n.* Feuermelder, -
m.

firearm, *n.* Feuerwaffe, -n *f.*

fire engine, *n.* Feuerspritze, -n *f.*

fire escape, *n.* Feuerleiter, -n *f.*

fire extinguisher, *n.* Feuer-
löscher, - *m.*

fireman, *n.* Feuerwehrmann, ⁼er
m.

fireplace, *n.* Kamin', -e *m.*

fireproof, *adj.* feuerfest.

fireworks, *n.* Feuerwerk, -e *nt.*

firm, 1. *n.* Firma, -men *f.* **2.** *adj.*
fest.

firmness, *n.* Festigkeit *f.*

first, 1. *adj.* erst. **2.** *adv.* zuerst'.

first aid, *n.* erste Hilfe *f.*

first-class, *adj.* erstklassig, erster
Klasse.

fiscal, *adj.* fiska'lisch.

fish, 1. *n.* Fisch, -e *m.* **2.** *vb.* fischen, angeln.

fisherman, *n.* Fischer, - *m.*, Angler, - *m.*

fishing, *n.* Angeln *nt.*

fission, *n.* Spaltung, -en *f.*; **(nuclear f.)** Kernspaltung *f.*

fissure, *n.* Spalt, -e *m.*

fist, *n.* Faust, ⁼e *f.*

fit, 1. *(attack)* Anfall, ⁼e *m.* **2.** *adj.*
in Form. **3.** *vb.* passen; *(adapt)*
an·passen.

fitful, *adj.* unregelmäßig.

fitness, *n.* Tauglichkeit *f.*; Gesund'heit *f.*

fitting, 1. *n.* Anprobe, -n *f.* **2.** *adj.*
passend.

five, *num.* fünf.

fix, 1. *n. (predicament)* Verle'genheit, -en *f.* **2.** *vb.* fest·setzen; *(prepare)* zubereiten; *(repair)* repa-
rie'ren.

fixation, *n.* Fixie'rung, -en *f.*

fixed, *adj. (repaired)* heil; *(set)*
fest.

fixture, *n.* Vorrichtung, -en *f.*;
Zubehör *nt.*

flabby, *adj.* schlaff.

flag, *n.* Fahne, -n *f.*, Flagge, -n *f.*

flagpole, *n.* Fahnenstange, -n *f.*

flagrant, *adj.* schreiend.

flagship, *n.* Flaggschiff, -e *nt.*

flair, *n.* Flair *nt.*

flake, *n.* Flocke, -n *f.*

flamboyant, *adj.* flammend;
(fig.) überla'den.

flame, 1. n. Flamme, -n f. **2.** vb. flammen.

flank, 1. n. Flanke, -n f. **2.** vb. flankie'ren.

flannel, n. Flanell', -e m.

flap, 1. n. Klappe, -n f.; (wings) Flügelschlag, -e m. **2.** vb. flattern.

flare, 1. n. Leuchtsignal, -e nt. **2.** vb. flackern.

flash, 1. n. Lichtstrahl, -en m. **2.** vb. auf-flammen.

flashcube, n. Blitzwürfel, - m.

flashlight, n. Taschenlampe, -n f.

flashy, adj. auffällig; (clothes, etc.) laut.

flask, n. Flasche, -n f.

flat, 1. n. Mietswohnung, -en f. **2.** adj. flach, platt.

flatcar, n. offener Güterwagen, - m.

flatness, n. Flachheit, -en f.

flatten, vb. flach machen.

flatter, vb. schmeicheln.

flattering, adj. schmeichelhaft.

flattery, n. Schmeichelei', -en f.

flaunt, vb. zur Schau stellen.

flavor, 1. n. (taste) Geschmack', -e m.; (odor) Geruch', -e m. **2.** vb. würzen.

flavoring, n. Geschmack', -e m.; Essenz', -en f.

flavorless, adj. fade.

flaw, n. Fehler, - m., Makel, - m.

flawless, adj. fehlerfrei, makellos.

flax, n. Flachs m.

flay, vb. schinden*.

flea, n. Floh, -e m.

fleck, n. Fleck, -e m.

flee, vb. fliehen*, flüchten.

fleece, n. Vlies, -e nt.

fleecy, adj. wollig.

fleet, n. Flotte, -n f.

fleeting, adj. flüchtig.

Fleming, n. Flame, -n, -n m.

Flemish, adj. flämisch.

flesh, n. Fleisch nt.

fleshy, adj. fleischig.

flex, vb. biegen*; beugen.

flexibility, n. Biegsamkeit f.

flexible, adj. biegsam, flexi'bel.

flicker, vb. flackern.

flier, n. Flieger, - m.

flight, n. Flug, -e m.; (escape) Flucht, -en f.

flight attendants, n.pl. Flugpersonal nt.

flimsy, adj. dünn; lose.

flinch, vb. zurück'-zucken.

fling, vb. schleudern.

flint, n. Feuerstein, -e m.

flip, vb. schnellen.

flippant, adj. vorlaut.

flirt, 1. n. Flirt, -s m. **2.** vb. flirten, kokettie'ren.

flirtation, n. Flirt, -s m.

float, 1. n. Floß, -e nt. **2.** vb. treiben*, schwimmen*.

flock, n. Herde, - f., Schar, -en f.

flog, vb. peitschen.

flood, 1. n. Flut, -en f.; Überschwem'mung, -en f. **2.** vb. überschwem'men.

floodlight, n. Scheinwerfer, - m.

floor, n. Fußboden, - m.; (story) Stockwerk, -e nt.

floorwalker, n. Abteilungsaufseher (, - m.) in einem Warenhaus.

flop, 1. n. (thud) Plumps m.; (failure) Reinfall, -e m. **2.** vb. plumpsen: rein-gallen*.

floral, adj. Blumen- (cpds.).

florid, adj. gerö'tet.

florist, n. Blumenhändler, - m., Blumenhändlerin, -nen f.

flounce, 1. n. Volant', -s m. **2.** vb. tänzeln.

flounder, 1. n. Flunder, -n f. **2.** vb. taumeln.

flour, n. Mehl nt.

flourish, vb. (grow) gedei'hen*, blühen; (shake) schwenken.

flow, vb. fließen*.

flower, 1. n. Blume, -n f. **2.** vb. blühen.

flowerpot, n. Blumentopf, -e m.

flowery, adj. blumig.

fluctuate, vb. schwanken.

fluctuation, n. Schwankung, -en f.

flue, n. Rauchfang, -e m.

fluency, n. Geläu'figkeit f.

fluent, adj. fließend.

fluffy, adj. flaumig, wollig.

fluid, 1. n. Flüssigkeit, -en f. **2.** adj. flüssig.

fluidity, n. flüssiger Aggregat'zustand m.; Flüssigsein nt.

fluorescent, adj. fluoresziie'rend.

fluoroscope, n. Leuchtschirm, -e m., Fluroskop', -e nt.

flurry, n. Wirbel, - m.

flush, 1. n. Röte f.; (fig.) Flut f. 2. vb. errö'ten; (wash out) ausspülen; (toilet) aufzie'hen*.

flute, n. Flöte, -n f.

flutter, vb. flattern.

flux, n. Fluß m.; Strömen nt.

fly, 1. n. Fliege, -n f. 2. vb. fliegen*.

foam, 1. n. Schaum, -̈e m. 2. vb. schäumen.

focal, adj. fokal'.

focus, 1. n. Brennpunkt, -e m. 2. vb. (scharf, richtig) ein·stellen.

fodder, n. Futter nt.

foe, n. Feind, -e m.

fog, n. Nebel m.

foggy, adj. neblig.

foil, 1. n. Rapier', -e nt. 2. vb. verei'teln.

foist, vb. unterschie'ben*.

fold, 1. n. Falte, -n f. 2. vb. falten.

folder, n. (for papers) Mappe, -n f., Hefter, - m.; (brochure) Broschü're, -n f., Prospekt', -e m.

foliage, n. Laub nt.

folio, n. Folio, -lien nt.

folk, n. Volk, -̈er nt.

folklore, n. Volkskunde f.

folks, n.pl. Leute pl.

follow, vb. folgen.

follower, n. Anhänger, - m., Anhängerin, -nen f.

folly, n. Torheit, -en f., Verrückt'heit, -en f.

foment, vb. schüren.

fond, adj. (be f. of) gern haben*.

fondle, vb. liebkosen.

fondness, n. Vorliebe f.

food, n. Nahrung, f., Essen nt.

foodstuffs, n. Nahrungsmittel pl.

fool, 1. n. Narr, -en, -en m. 2. vb. täuschen, zum Narren halten*.

foolhardiness, n. Tollkühnheit, -en f.

foolhardy, adj. tollkühn.

foolish, adj. dumm, närrisch.

foolproof, adj. narrensicher.

foot, n. Fuß, -̈e m.

footage, n. Länge in Fuß gemessen.

football, n. Fußball, -̈e m.

foothills, n.pl. Vorgebirge nt.

foothold, n. Halt m.

footing, n. Stand m.; Boden m.

footlights, n.pl. Rampenlicht, -er nt.

footnote, n. Fußnote, -n f.

footprint, n. Fußstapfe, -n f.

footstep, n. Fußstapfe, -n f.

for, 1. prep. für. 2. conj. denn.

forage, 1. n. Futter nt. 2. vb. furagie'ren.

foray, n. Überfall, -̈e m.

forbearance, n. Enthal'tung f.; Nachsicht f.

forbid, vb. verbie'ten*.

forbidding, adj. abschreckend.

force, 1. n. Kraft, -̈e f., Gewalt', -en f. 2. vb. zwingen*.

forceful, adj. kräftig, wirkungsvoll.

forcefulness, n. Überzeu'gungskraft f.

forceps, n. Zange, -n f.

forcible, adj. kräftig, heftig, mit Gewalt'.

ford, n. Furt, -en f.

fore, adv. vorn.

forearm, n. Unterarm, -e m.

forebears, n.pl. Vorfahren pl.

foreboding, n. Vorahnung, -en f.

forecast, 1. n. Voraus'sage, -n f. 2. vb. voraus'·sagen.

forecaster, n. Wetterprophet, -en, -en m.

foreclosure, n. Zwangsvollstreckung, -en f.

forefather, n. Vorfahr, -en, -en m.

forefinger, n. Zeigefinger, - m.

forefront, n. Vorderseite f.

foreground, n. Vordergrund m.

forehead, n. Stirn, -en f.

foreign, adj. fremd, ausländisch.

foreign aid, n. Entwick'lungshilfe f.

foreigner, n. Ausländer, - m., Ausländerin, -nen f.

foreman, n. Vorarbeiter, - m.

foremost, adj. vorderst-.

forenoon, n. Vormittag, -e m.

forerunner, n. Vorläufer, - m.

foresee, vb. vorher'·sehen*.

foreshadow, vb. ahnen lassen*.

foresight, n. Voraus'sicht f.

forest, n. Wald, -̈er m.

forestall, vb. verhin'dern, vorweg'·nehmen*.

forester, n. Förster, - m.

forestry, n. Forstwirtschaft f.
foretaste, n. Vorgeschmack, ⸚e m.
foretell, vb. vorher'sagen, prophezei'en.
forever, adv. ewig.
forevermore, adv. für, auf immer und ewig.
forewarn, vb. vorher warnen.
foreword, n. Vorwort, -e nt.
forfeit, vb. verwir'ken, ein-büßen.
forfeiture, n. Verwir'kung f., Einbuße f.
forgather, vb. sich versam'meln.
forge, 1. n. Schmiede, -n f. **2.** vb. schmieden; (falsify) fälschen.
forger, vb. Fälscher, - m., Fälscherin, -nen f.
forgery, n. Fälschung, -en f.
forget, vb. verges'sen*.
forgetful, adj. vergeß'lich.
forgive, vb. verge'ben*, verzei'hen*.
forgiveness, n. Verge'bung f.
forgo, vb. verzich'ten auf.
fork, n. Gabel, -n f.
forlorn, adj. verlas'sen.
form, 1. n. Form, -en f.; (blank) Formular', -e nt. **2.** vb. bilden, formen.
formal, adj. formell'; offiziell'.
formaldehyde, n. Formaldehyd', -e nt.
formality, n. Formalität', -en f.; Förmlichkeit, -en f.
format, n. Format', -e nt.
formation, n. Gestal'tung, -en f.; (mil.) Formation', -en f.
former, adj. ehemalig, früher; (the f.) jener, -es, -e.
formerly, adv. früher.
formidable, adj. beacht'lich.
formless, adj. formlos.
formula, n. Formel, -n f.
formulate, vb. formulie'ren.
formulation, n. Formulie'rung, -en f.
forsake, vb. verlas'sen*.
fort, n. Feste, -n f.
forte, n. Stärke, -n f.
forth, adv. fort; (and so f.) und so weiter.
forthcoming, adj. angekündigt.
forthright, adj. offen, ehrlich.
fortieth, 1. adj. vierzigst-. **2.** n. Vierzigstel, - nt.

fortification, n. Befes'tigungswerk, -e nt.
fortify, vb. stärken, befes'tigen.
fortissimo, adj. fortis'simo.
fortitude, n. seelische Stärke f., Mut m.
fortnight, n. vierzehn Tage pl.
fortress, n. Festung, -en f.
fortuitous, adj. zufällig.
fortunate, adj. glücklich.
fortune, n. Glück nt.; (money) Vermö'gen, - nt.
fortune-teller, n. Wahrsager, - m., Wahrsagerin, -nen f.
forty, adj. vierzig.
forum, n. Forum, -ra nt.
forward, adv. vorwärts.
forwardness, n. Dreistigkeit f.
fossil, n. Fossil', -e nt.
foster, vb. (nourish) nähren; (raise) auf'ziehen*; Pflege- (cpds.).
foul, adj. schmutzig.
found, vb. gründen.
foundation, n. (building) Fundament', -e nt.; (fund) Stiftung, -en f.
founder, n. Gründer, - m.
foundling, n. Findling, -e m.
foundry, n. Gießerei', -en f.
fountain, n. Springbrunnen, - m.
fountainhead, n. Urquell, -e m.
fountain pen, n. Füllfederhalter, - m.
four, num. vier.
fourteen, num. vierzehn.
fourteenth, 1. adj. vierzehnt-. **2.** n. Vierzehntel, - nt.
fourth, 1. adj. viert-. **2.** n. Viertel, - nt.
fowl, n. Geflü'gel nt.; Huhn, ⸚er nt.
fox, n. Fuchs, ⸚e m.
foxglove, n. Fingerhut, ⸚e m.
foxhole, n. Schüt'zenloch, ⸚er nt.
foxy, adj. schlau.
foyer, n. Foyer', -s nt.
fracas, n. Keilerei', -en f.
fraction, n. (number) Bruchstück, -e nt.; (part) Bruchteil, -e m.; (f.s.) Bruchrechnung f.
fracture, 1. n. Bruch, ⸚e m. **2.** vb. brechen*.
fragile, adj. zerbrech'lich.
fragment, n. Bruchstück, -e nt.

fragmentary, *adj.* fragmenta'risch.
fragrance, *n.* Duft, ̈-e *m.*
fragrant, *adj.* wohlriechend.
frail, *adj.* zerbrech'lich, schwach
(̈).
frailty, *n.* Schwachheit, -en *f.*
frame, 1. *n.* Rahmen, - *m.* **2.** *vb.*
(shape) formen; *(enclose)* ein-
rahmen.
framework, *n.* Rahmen, - *m.*
France, *n.* Frankreich *nt.*
franchise, *n.* Wahlrecht, -e *nt.*
frank, *adj.* frei, offen.
frankfurter, *n.* Frankfurter
Würstchen, - *nt.*
frankly, *adv.* ehrlich gesagt.
frankness, *n.* Offenheit *f.*
frantic, *adj.* wahnsinnig.
fraternal, *adj.* brüderlich.
fraternity, *n.* Brüderlichkeit *f.;*
(students) Studen'tenverbindung,
-en *f.*
fraternize, *vb.* fraterni'sie'ren.
fraud, *n.* Betrug' *m.*
fraudulent, *adj.* betrügerisch.
fraught, *adj.* voll.
fray, *n.* Tumult', -e *m.;*
Schlägerei', -en *f.*
freak, 1. *n.* Mißgeburt, -en *f.;*
Kurio'sum, -sa *nt.* **2.** *adj.* monströs', bizarr'.
freckle, *n.* Sommersprosse, -n *f.*
freckled, *adj.* sommersprossig.
free, 1. *adj.* frei; kostenlos. **2.** *vb.*
befrei'en; frei-lassen*.
freedom, *n.* Freiheit, -en *f.*
freeze, *vb.* *(be cold)* frieren*;
(turn to ice) (intr.) gefrie'ren*
(tr.) gefrie'ren lassen*; *(food)*
tief kühlen; *(wages)* stoppen
(Löhne).
freezer, *n.* Tiefkühler, - *m.; (in refrigerator)* Gefrier'fach, ̈er *nt.*
freezing, *adj.* eisig.
freight, *n.* Fracht, -en *f.;* Fracht-
gut *nt.*
freightage, *n.* Frachtspesen *pl.*
freighter, *n.* Frachter, - *m.*
French, *adj.* franzö'sisch.
Frenchman, *n.* Franzo'se, -n, -n
m.
Frenchwoman, *n.* Franzö'sin,
-nen *f.*
frenzied, *adj.* rasend.

frenzy, *n.* Raserei', -en *f.*
frequency, *n.* Häufigkeit, -en *f.;*
(physics) Frequenz', -en *f.*
frequent, *adj.* häufig.
fresh, *adj.* frisch; *(impudent)*
frech.
freshen, *vb.* erfri'schen.
freshman, *n.* Student' im ersten
College-Jahr.
freshness, *n.* Frische *f.*
fresh water, *n.* Süßwasser *nt.*
fret, *vb.* nervös' sein*, nervös'
werden*.
fretful, *adj.* nervös', unruhig.
fretfulness, *n.* Reizbarkeit, *f.*
friar, *n.* Bettelmönch, -e *m.*
fricassee, *n.* Frikassee', -s *nt.*
friction, *n.* Reibung, -en *f.*
Friday, *n.* Freitag, -e *m.*
friend, *n.* Freund, -e *m.;* Freundin, -nen *f.*
friendless, *adj.* freundlos.
friendliness, *n.* Freundlichkeit, *f.*
-en *f.*
friendly, *adj.* freundlich.
friendship, *n.* Freundschaft, -en *f.*
frigate, *n.* Frega'tte, -n *f.*
fright, *n.* Angst, ̈-e *f.,* Schreck *m.*
frighten, *vb.* ängstigen, erschre'-
cken; *(be f.ed)* erschre'cken*.
frightful, *adj.* schrecklich.
frigid, *adj.* kalt (̈); *(sexual)*
frigid'.
frill, *n.* Krause, -n *f.*
fringe, *n.* Franse, -n *f.;* Rand, ̈er
m.
frisky, *adj.* lebhaft.
fritter, *n.* eine Art Pfannkuchen.
frivolity, *n.* Frivolität', -en *f.*
frivolous, *adj.* leichtsinnig, frivol'.
frivolousness, *n.* Leichtsinnig-
keit, -en *f.*
frock, *n.* Kleid, -er *nt.; (monk)*
Kutte, -n *f.*
frog, *n.* Frosch, ̈-e *m.*
frolic, *vb.* ausgelassen sein*.
from, *prep.* von, aus.
front, *n.* Vorderseite, -n *f.; (mil.)*
Front, -en *f.; (in f.)* vorn; *(in f. of)*
vor.
frontage, *n.* Vorderfront, -en *f.*
frontal, *adj.* frontal'.
frontier, *n.* Grenze, -n *f.*

frost, n. Frost, ⸚e m.
frostbite, n. Frostbeule, -n f.
frosting, n. Kuchenglasur, -en f.
frosty, adj. frostig.
froth, n. Schaum, ⸚e m.
frown, vb. die Stirn runzeln.
frugal, adv. sparsam, frugal*.
frugality, n. Sparsamkeit f.
fruit, n. Frucht, ⸚e f., Obst nt.
fruitful, adj. fruchtbar.
fruition, n. Reife f.
fruitless, adj. unfruchtbar; (fig.)
  vergeb'lich.
frustrate, vb. verdrän'gen; (nullify) verei'teln.
frustration, n. Verdrän'gung, -en f.; Verei'telung, -en f.
fry, vb. braten*.
fryer, n. junges Brathuhn, ⸚er nt.
frying pan, n. Bratpfanne, -n f.
fuchsia, n. Fuchsie, -n f.
fuel, n. Brennstoff, -e m; Treibstoff m.
fugitive, n. Flüchtling, -e m.
fugue, n. Fuge, -n f.
fulcrum, n. Drehpunkt, -e m.
fulfill, vb. erfül'len.
fulfillment, n. Erfül'lung, -en f.
full, adj. voll.
full dress, n. Frack, ⸚e m.; Gala-Uniform, -en f.
fullness, n. Fülle f.
fully, adv. völlig.
fumble, vb. umher'tappen.
fume, 1. n. Dampf, ⸚e m., Dunst, ⸚e m. 2. vb. dampfen, dunsten; (fig.) wüten.
fumigate, vb. aus'räuchern.
fumigator, n. Räucherapparat, -e m.
fun, n. Vergnü'gen nt., Spaß m., Jux m.
function, 1. n. Funktion', -en f. 2. vb. funktionie'ren.
functional, adj. sachlich.
fund, n. Fond, -s m.
fundamental, adj. grundlegend.

funeral, n. Begräb'nis, -se nt., Beer'digung, -en f.
funereal, adj. düster.
fungicide, n. Pilzvernichtungsmittel, - nt.
fungus, n. Fungus - m.
funnel, n. Trichter, - m.; (smokestack) Schornstein, -e m.
funny, adj. komisch, drollig.
fur, n. Pelz, -e m.
furious, adj. wütend.
furlough, n. Urlaub, -e m.
furnace, n. Ofen, ⸚ m.
furnish, vb. möblie'ren.
furnishings, n.pl. Ausstattung, -en f.
furniture, n. Möbel pl.
furor, n. Aufsehen nt.
furrier, n. Pelzhändler, - m.
furrow, n. Furche, -n f.
furry, adj. pelzartig.
further, 1. vb. fördern. 2. adj. weiter, ferner.
furtherance, n. Förderung, -en f.
furthermore, adv. außerdem, überdies.
fury, n. Wut f.; Zorn m.; (mythology) Furie, -n f.
fuse, 1. n. (elec.) Sicherung, -en f.; (explosives) Zünder, - m. 2. vb. verschmel'zen*.
fuselage, n. Rumpf, ⸚e m.
fusillade, n. Gewehr'feuer nt.
fusion, n. Verschmel'zung, -en f.; Fusion', -en f.
fuss, n. Aufheben nt, Umstand, ⸚e m.
fussy, adj. umständlich, genau', betu'lich.
futile, adj. vergeb'lich, nutzlos.
futility, n. Nutzlosigkeit f.
future, 1. n. Zukunft f. 2. adj. zukünftig.
futurity, n. Zukunft f.
futurology, n. Futurologie' f.
fuzz, n. Flaum m.
fuzzy, adj. flaumig.

G

gab, vb. schwatzen.
gabardine, n. Gabardine m.

gable, n. Giebel, - m.
gadget, n. Vorrichtung, -en f.

gag, 1. *n.* Knebel, - *m.; (joke)* Witz, -e *m.* **2.** *vb.* knebeln.

gaiety, *n.* Ausgelassenheit *f.*

gain, 1. *n.* Gewinn', -e *m.* **2.** *vb.* gewin'nen*.

gainful, *adj.* einträglich.

gait, *n.* Gang, ⸚e *m.*

gala, *adj.* festlich.

galaxy, *n.* Milchstraße, -n *f.*

gale, *n.* Sturm, ⸚e *m.*

gall, 1. *n. (bile)* Galle, -n *f.; (insolence)* Unverschämtheit, -en *f.* **2.** *vb.* ärgern.

gallant, *adj.* aufmerksam, galant'.

gallantry, *n.* Höflichkeit, -en *f.,* Galanterie', -i'en *f.*

gall bladder, *n.* Gallenblase, -n *f.*

gallery, *n.* Galerie', -i'en *f.*

galley, *n. (ship)* Galee're, -n *f.; (kitchen)* Kombü'se, -n *f.; (typogr.)* Setzschiff, -e *nt.*

Gallic, *adj.* gallisch.

gallivant, *vb.* bummeln.

gallon, *n.* Gallo'ne, -n *f.*

gallop, 1. *n.* Galopp', -s *m.* **2.** *vb.* galoppie'ren.

gallows, *n.pl.* Galgen, - *m.*

gallstone, *n.* Gallenstein, -e *m.*

galore, *adv.* in Hülle und Fülle.

galosh, *n.* Überschuh, -e *m.*

gamble, 1. *n. (game)* Glücksspiel, -e *nt.; (risk)* Risiko, -s *nt.* **2.** *vb.* um Geld spielen; riskie'ren.

gambler, *n.* Glücksspieler,- *m.,* Glücksspielerin, -nen *f.*

gambling, *n.* Glücksspiel, -e *nt.*

game, 1. *n.* Spiel, -e *nt.; (hunting)* Wild *nt.,* Wildbret *nt.* **2.** *adj.* beherzt'; *(lame)* lahm.

gander, *n.* Gänserich, -e *m.*

gang, *n.* Bande, -n *f.*

gangplank, *n.* Laufplanke, -n *f.*

gangrene, *n.* Gangrän', -e *nt.*

gangrenous, *adj.* gangränös', brandig.

gangster, *n.* Gangster, - *m.*

gangway, *n.* Laufplanke, -n *f.*

gap, *n.* Lücke, -n *f.; Spalte, -n *f.*

gape, *vb.* gaffen.

garage, *n.* Gara'ge, -n *f.*

garb, *n.* Gewand', -⸚er *nt.*

garbage, *n.* Abfall, ⸚e *m.,* Müll *m.*

garble, *vb.* entstel'len, verzer'ren.

garden, *n.* Garten, - *m.*

gardener, *n.* Gärtner, - *m.,* Gärtnerin, -nen *f.*

gardenia, *n.* Garde'nia, -ien *f.*

gargle, *vb.* gurgeln.

gargoyle, *n.* Wasserspeier, - *m.*

garish, *adj.* grell.

garland, *n.* Girlan'de, -n *f.*

garlic, *n.* Knoblauch *m.*

garment, *n.* Kleidungsstück, -e *nt.*

garner, *vb.* aufspeichern.

garnet, *n.* Granat', -e *m.*

garnish, *vb.* garnie'ren.

garret, *n.* Dachstube, -n *f.*

garrison, *n.* Garnison', -en *f.*

garrulous, *adj.* schwatzhaft.

garter, *n.* Strumpfband, ⸚er *nt.; Hosenband, ⸚er *nt.; Sockenhalter, - *m.*

gas, *n.* Gas, -e *nt.; (gasoline)* Benzin' *nt; (g. station)* Tankstelle, -n *f.*

gaseous, *adj.* gasförmig.

gash, 1. *n.* klaffende Wunde, -n *f.* **2.** *vb.* eine tiefe Wunde schlagen*.

gasket, *n.* Dichtung *f.*

gas mask, *n.* Gasmaske, -n *f.*

gasohol, *n.* Benzin-AlkoholGech' *nt.*

gasoline, *n.* Benzin' *nt.*

gasp, *vb.* keuchen; nach Luft schnappen.

gastric, *adj.* gastrisch.

gastritis, *n.* Magenschleimhautentzündung, -en *f.*

gastronomical, *adj.* gastrono'misch.

gate, *n.* Tor, -e *nt.,* Pforte, -n *f.*

gateway, *n.* Einfahrt, -en *f.,* Tor, -e *nt.*

gather, *vb.* sammeln, pflücken; *(infer)* schließen*.

gathering, *n.* Versamm'lung, -en *f.*

gaudiness, *n.* auffälliger Protz *m.*

gaudy, *adj.* protzig.

gauge, 1. *n. (measurement)* Maß, -e *nt.; (instrument)* Messer, - *m.,* Zeiger, - *m.; (railway)* Spurweite, -n *f.* **2.** *vb.* abmes'sen*.

gaunt, *adj.* hager.

gauntlet, *n.* Handschuh, -e *m.*

gauze, *n.* Gaze, -n *f.*

gavel, *n.* Hammer, ⸚ *m.*

gawky, *adj.* linkisch.

gay, *adj.* fröhlich, heiter; *(homosexual)* homosexuell, schwul.

gaze, vb. starren.
gazelle, n. Gazel'le, -n f.
gazette, n. Zeitung, -en f.
gazetteer, n. geogra'phisches Namenverzeichnis, -se nt.
gear, n. Zahnrad, ̈-er nt.; (auto) Gang, ̈-e m.; (equipment) Zeug nt.
gearing, n. Getrie'be, - nt.
gearshift, n. Schalthebel, m.
gelatin, n. Gelati'ne, - f.
gelatinous, adj. gallertartig.
geld, vb. kastrie'ren.
gelding, n. Wallach, -e m.
gem, n. Edelstein, -e m.
gender, n. Geschlecht', -er nt., Genus, -nera nt.
gene, n. Gen, -e nt.
genealogical, adj. genealo'gisch.
genealogy, n. Genealogie', -i'en f.
general, 1. n. General', ̈-e m. **2.** adj. allgemein.
generality, n. Allgemein'heit, -en f.
generalization, n. Verallgemei'nerung, -en f.
generalize, vb. verallgemei'nern.
generally, adv. (in general) im allgemei'nen; (usually) gewöhn'lich, meistens.
generate, vb. erzeu'gen.
generation, n. Generation', -en f.
generator, n. Genera'tor, -o'ren m.
generic, adj. Gattungs- (cpds.).
generosity, n. Großzügigkeit f.
generous, adj. großzügig, freigebig.
genetic, adj. gene'tisch.
genetics, n. Verer'bungslehre f.
Geneva, n. Genf nt.
genial, adj. freundlich, froh.
geniality, n. Freundlichkeit f.
genital, adj. genital'.
genitals, n. Geschlechts'organe pl.
genitive, n. Genitiv, -e m.
genius, n. Genie', -s nt.
genocide, n. Völkermord m.
genre, n. Genre, -s nt.
genteel, adj. vornehm.
gentile, 1. n. Nichtjude, -n, -n m. **2.** adj. nichtjüdisch.
gentility, n. Vornehmheit f.
gentle, adj. sanft, mild.

gentleman, n. Herr, -n, -en m.
gentleness, n. Sanftheit f.
gentry, n. niederer Adel m.
genuflect, vb. das Knie beugen.
genuine, adj. echt.
genuineness, n. Echtheit f.
genus, n. Geschlecht', -er nt., Gattung, -en f.
geographer, n. Geograph', -en, -en m.
geographical, adj. geogra'phisch.
geography, n. Geographie' f., Erdkunde f.
geometric, adj. geome'trisch.
geometry, n. Geometrie' f.
geopolitics, n. Geopolitik' f.
geranium, n. Gera'nie, -n f.
germ, n. Keim, -e m.; Bakte'rie, -n f.
German, 1. n. Deutsch- -e m.&f. **2.** adj. deutsch.
germane, adj. zur Sache gehö'rig.
Germanic, adj. germa'nisch.
German measles, n. Röteln pl.
Germany, n. Deutschland nt.; Bundesrepublik' f.; (former East G.) Deutsche Demokratische Republik' f.; Ostdeutschland nt.
germicide, n. keimtötendes Mittel, - nt.
germinal, adj. Keim- (cpds.).
germinate, vb. keimen.
gestate, vb. aus'tragen*.
gestation, n. Gestation', -en f.
gesticulate, vb. gestikulie'ren.
gesticulation, n. Gebär'de, -n f.
gesture, n. Gebär'de, -n f., Geste, -n f.
get, vb. (receive) bekom'men*, kriegen; (fetch) holen; (become) werden*; (arrive) ankommen*; (g. to) hin'kommen*; (g. up) auf'stehen*; (g. in) ein'steigen*; (g. out) aus'steigen*.
geyser, n. Geiser, - m.
ghastly, adj. grauenhaft.
ghost, n. Geist, -er m., Gespenst', -er nt.
giant, 1. n. Riese, -n, -n m. **2.** adj. riesenhaft.
gibberish, n. Kauderwelsch nt.
gibbon, n. Gibbon, -s m.
giblets, n. Geflü'gelklein nt.
giddy, adj. schwindlig.

gift, n. Gabe, -n f.; Geschenk', -e nt.

gifted, adj. begabt'.

gigantic, adj. riesenhaft.

giggle, vb. kichern.

gigolo, n. Gigolo, -s m.

gild, vb. vergol'den.

gill, n. Kieme, -n f.

gilt, n. Vergol'dung, -en f.

gimlet, n. Handbohrer, - m.

gin, n. Gin, -s m.; (cotton) Entker'nungsmaschine, -n f.

ginger, n. Ingwer m.

gingerly, adv. sachte.

gingham, n. Kattun', -e m.

giraffe, n. Giraf'fe, -n f.

gird, vb. gürten.

girder, n. Träger, - m.

girdle, n. Gürtel, - m.; Strumpfbandgürtel, - m.

girl, n. Mädchen, - nt.

girlish, adj. mädchenhaft.

girth, n. Umfang, -̈e m.

gist, n. Kern, -e m.

give, vb. geben*.

given name, n. Vorname(n), - m.

gizzard, n. Geflü'gelmagen, -̈ m.

glacé, adj. glaciert'.

glacial, adj. Eis- (cpds.).

glad, adj. froh.

gladden, vb. erfreu'en.

gladiolus, n. Schwertlilie, -n f.

gladly, adv. gern.

gladness, n. Freude, -n f.

glamor, n. äußerer Glanz m.; beste'chende Schönheit f.

glamorous, adj. äußerlich beste'chend, blendend.

glance, 1. n. Blick, -e m. 2. vb. blicken.

gland, n. Drüse, -n f.

glandular, adj. Drüsen- (cpds.).

glare, 1. n. blendendes Licht nt. 2. vb. blenden; (look) starren; (g. at) an'starren.

glaring, adj. grell.

glass, n. Glas, -̈er nt.

glasses, n.pl. Brille, -n f.

glassware, n. Glasware, -n f.

glassy, adj. glasig.

glaucoma, n. Glaukom', -e nt.

glaze, 1. n. Glasur', -en f. 2. vb. glasie'ren.

glazier, n. Glaser, - m.

gleam, 1. n. Lichtstrahl, -en m. 2. vb. strahlen, glänzen.

glee, n. Freude, -n f.

gleeful, adj. fröhlich.

glen, n. enges Tal, -̈er nt.

glib, adj. zungenfertig.

glide, 1. n. Gleitflug, -̈e m. 2. vb. gleiten*.

glider, n. Segelflugzeug, -e nt.

glimmer, 1. n. Schimmer, - m. 2. vb. schimmern.

glimpse, n. flüchtiger Blick, -e m.

glint, n. Lichtschimmer, - m.

glisten, vb. glänzen.

glitter, 1. n. Glanz m. 2. vb. glitzern.

gloat, vb. sich weiden; schadenfroh sein*.

global, adj. global'.

globe, n. Erdkugel, -n f.; Globus, -se m.

globular, adj. kugelförmig.

globule, n. Kügelchen, - nt.

gloom, n. Düsterheit f.; (fig.) Trübsinn m.

gloomy, adj. düster; trübsinnig.

glorification, n. Verherr'lichung f.

glorify, vb. verherr'lichen.

glorious, adj. ruhmvoll, glorreich.

glory, n. Ruhm m.; Herrlichkeit f.

gloss, n. Glanz m.

glossary, n. Glossar', -e nt.

glossy, adj. glänzend.

glove, n. Handschuh, -e m.

glow, 1. n. Glühen nt. 2. vb. glühen.

glucose, n. Traubenzucker m.

glue, 1. n. Leim m.; Klebstoff, -e m. 2. vb. leimen, kleben.

glum, adj. mürrisch.

glumness, n. Mürrischkeit f.

glut, 1. n. Überfluß m. 2. vb. übersät'tigen.

glutinous, adj. leimig.

glutton, n. Vielfraß, -e m.

gluttonous, adj. gefrä'ßig.

glycerine, n. Glyzerin' nt.

gnarled, adj. knorrig.

gnash, vb. knirschen.

gnat, n. Schnake, -n f.

gnaw, vb. knabbern.

go, vb. gehen*; (become) werden*; (g. without) entbeh'ren.

goad, 1. *n.* Treibstock, ⸗e *m.* **2.** *vb.* an·stacheln.

goal, *n.* Ziel, -e *nt.; (soccer)* Tor, -e *nt.*

goal-keeper, *n.* Torwart, ⸗er *m.*

goat, *n.* Ziege, -n *f.; (billy g.)* Ziegenbock, ⸗e *m.*

goatee, *n.* Spitzbart, ⸗e *m.*

goatskin, *n.* Ziegenleder *nt.*

gobble, *vb.* verschlin'gen*.

go-between, *n.* Vermitt'ler, - *m.,* Vermitt'lerin, -nen *f.*

goblet, *n.* Kelchglas, ⸗er *nt.*

goblin, *n.* Kobold, -e *m.*

god, *n.* Gott, ⸗er *m.*

godchild, *n.* Patenkind, -er *nt.*

goddess, *n.* Göttin, -nen *f.*

godfather, *n.* Patenonkel *m.*

godless, *adj.* gottlos.

godlike, *adj.* gottähnlich.

godly, *adj.* göttlich.

godmother, *n.* Patentante, -n *f.*

godsend, *n.* Gottesgabe, -n *f.*

Godspeed, *n.* Lebewohl' *nt.*

go-getter, *n.* Draufgänger, - *m.*

goiter, *n.* Kropf, ⸗e *m.*

gold, *n.* Gold *nt.*

golden, *adj.* golden.

goldfinch, *n.* Stieglitz, -e *m.*

goldfish, *n.* Goldfisch, -e *m.*

goldsmith, *n.* Goldschmied, -e *m.*

golf, *n.* Golf *nt.*

gondola, *n.* Gondel, -n *f.*

gondolier, *n.* Gondelführer, - *m.*

gone, *adv.* weg.

gong, *n.* Gong -s *m.*

gonorrhea, *n.* Tripper *m.*

good, *adj.* gut (besser, best-).

good-by, *interj.* auf Wiedersehen.

Good Friday, *n.* Karfrei'tag *m.*

good-hearted, *adj.* gutherzig.

good-humored, *adj.* gutmütig.

good-looking, *adj.* gutaussehend.

good-natured, *adj.* gutmütig.

goodness, *n.* Güte *f.*

goods, *n.pl.* Waren *pl.*

good will, *n.* Wohlwollen *nt.*

goose, *n.* Gans, ⸗e *f.*

gooseberry, *n.* Stachelbeere, -n *f.*

gooseneck, *n.* Gänsehals, ⸗e *m.*

goose step, *n.* Stechschritt *m.*

gore, 1. *n.* Blut *nt.* **2.** *vb.* auf·spießen.

gorge, *n. (anatomical)* Gurgel, -n *f.; (ravine)* Schlucht, -en *f.*

gorgeous, *adj.* prachtvoll.

gorilla, *n.* Goril'la, -s *m.*

gory, *adj.* blutig.

gospel, *n.* Evange'lium, -ien *nt.*

gossamer, 1. *n.* hauchdünner Stoff *m.* **2.** *adj.* hauchdünn.

gossip, 1. *n.* Klatsch *m.* **2.** *vb.* klatschen.

Gothic, 1. *n.* Gotik *f.* **2.** *adj.* gotisch.

gouge, 1. *n.* Hohleisen, - *nt.* **2.** *vb.* aus·höhlen.

gourd, *n.* Kürbis, -se *m.*

gourmand, *n.* Schlemmer, - *m.,* Schlemmerin, -nen *f.*

gourmet, *n.* Feinschmecker, - *m.,* Feinschmeckerin, -nen *f.*

govern, *vb.* regie'ren.

governess, *n.* Erzie'herin, -nen *f.*

government, *n.* Regie'rung, -en *f.*

governmental, *adj.* Regie'rungs-(*cpds.*).

governor, *n.* Gouverneur', -e *m.,* Gouverneu'rin, -nen *f.*

governorship, *n.* Gouverneurs'-amt, ⸗er *nt.*

gown, *n.* Kleid, -er *nt.*

grab, *vb.* greifen*.

grace, *n.* Anmut *f.; (mercy)* Gnade *f.*

graceful, *adj.* anmutig.

graceless, *adj.* unbeholfen.

gracious, *adj.* gnädig, gütig.

grade, 1. *n.* Grad, -e *m.,* Rang, ⸗e *m.; (mark)* Zensur', -en *f.; (class)* Klasse, -n *f.; (rise)* Steigung, -en *f.* **2.** *vb.* bewer'ten; *(smooth)* ebnen.

grade crossing, *n.* Bahnüber-gang, ⸗e *m.*

gradual, *adj.* allmäh'lich.

graduate, *vb.* graduie'ren.

graft, 1. *n.* Beste'chung, -en *f.,* Korruption' *f.* **2.** *vb. (bot.)* propfen.

grail, *n.* Gral *m.*

grain, *n.* Körnchen, - *nt.; (wheat, etc.)* Getrei'de *nt.; (wood)* Maserung, -en *f.*

gram, *n.* Gramm, - *nt.*

grammar, *n.* Gramma'tik, -en *f.*

grammar school, *n.* Grund-schule, -n *f.*

grammatical, *adj.* gramma'tisch.

gramophone, n. Grammophon', -e nt.

granary, n. Kornspeicher, - m.

grand, adj. großartig.

grandchild, n. Enkelkind, -er nt.

granddaughter, n. Enkelin, -nen f.

grandeur, n. Erha'benheit f.

grandfather, n. Großvater, ⸚ m.

grandiloquent, adj. schwülstig.

grandiose, adj. grandios'.

grandmother, n. Großmutter, ⸚ f.

grandparents, n.pl. Großeltern pl.

grandson, n. Enkel, - m.

grandstand, n. Tribü'ne, -n f.

granite, n. Granit' m.

grant, 1. n. finanziel'le Beihilfe, -n f.; Stipen'dium, -en nt. **2.** vb. gewäh'ren.

granular, adj. körnig.

granulated sugar, n. Streuzucker m.

granulation, n. Körnung f.

granule, n. Körnchen, - nt.

grape, n. Weintraube, -n f.

grapefruit, n. Pampelmu'se, -n f.

grapevine, n. Weinstock, ⸚e m.; (rumor) Gerücht n.

graph, n. graphische Darstellung, -en f., Diagramm', -e nt.

graphic, adj. graphisch.

graphite, n. Graphit', -e m.

graphology, n. Graphologie' f.

grapple, 1. n. Enterhaken, - m. **2.** vb. packen; ringen*.

grasp, 1. n. Griff, -e m.; (mental) Fassungsvermögen, - nt. **2.** vb. ergrei'fen*.

grasping, adj. habgierig.

grass, n. Gras, ⸚er nt.; (lawn) Rasen, - m.; (marijuana) Hasch m.

grasshopper, n. Heuschrecke, -n f.

grassy, adj. grasartig.

grate, 1. n. Rost m. **2.** vb. (cheese, etc.) reiben*, (irritate) irritie'ren.

grateful, adj. dankbar.

grater, n. Reibe, -n f.

gratify, vb. befrie'digen.

grating, n. Gitter, - nt.

gratis, adj. gratis.

gratitude, n. Dankbarkeit, -en f.

gratuitous, adj. unentgeltlich.

gratuity, n. Geschenk', -e nt.; (tip) Trinkgeld, -er nt.

grave, 1. n. Grab, ⸚er nt. **2.** adj. schwerwiegend.

gravel, n. Kies m.

graveyard, n. Friedhof, ⸚e m.

gravitate, vb. angezogen werden*; gravitie'ren.

gravity, n. Schwerkraft f.; Ernst m.

gravure, n. Gravü're, -n f.

gravy, n. Soße, -n f.

gray, adj. grau.

graze, vb. grasen, weiden.

grease, 1. n. Fett, -e nt. **2.** vb. fetten; schmieren.

greasy, adj. fettig, schmierig.

great, adj. groß (größer, größt-).

greatness, n. Größe, -n f.

Greece, n. Griechenland nt.

greed, n. Gier f., Habsucht f.

greediness, n. Gier f., Habsucht f.

greedy, adj. gierig, habsüchtig.

Greek, 1. n. Grieche, -n m., Griechin, -nen f. **2.** adj. griechisch.

green, adj. grün.

greenery, n. Grün nt.

greenhouse, n. Gewächs'haus, ⸚er nt., Treibhaus, ⸚er nt.

greet, vb. begrü'ßen.

greeting, n. Gruß, ⸚e m.

gregarious, adj. gesel'lig.

grenade, n. Grana'te, -n f.

grenadine, n. Granat'apfellikör m.

greyhound, n. Windhund, -e m.

grid, n. Gitter, - nt.; (elec.) Stromnetz, -e nt.

griddle, n. Bratpfanne, -n f.

grief, n. Kummer m.

grievance, n. Beschwer'de, -n f.

grieve, vb. (intr.) trauern; (tr.) betrü'ben.

grievous, adj. schmerzlich; (serious) schwerwiegend.

grill, n. Grill, -s m.

grim, adj. grimmig.

grimace, n. Grimas'se, -n f., Fratze, -n f.

grime, n. Ruß m.

grimy, adj. schmutzig.

grin, 1. *n.* Grinsen *nt.* 2. *vb.* grinsen.

grind, *vb.* mahlen*.

grindstone, *n.* Schleifstein, -e *m.*

grip, 1. *n.* Griff, -e *m.; (suitcase)* Koffer, - *m.* 2. *vb.* fassen.

gripe, 1. *n. (complaint)* Ärgernis, -se *nt.* 2. *vb. (complain)* nörgeln.

grippe, *n.* Grippe, -n *f.*

gristle, *n.* Knorpel, - *m.*

grit, 1. *n.* Kies *m.; (courage)* Mut *m.* 2. *vb.* (g. one's teeth) die Zähne zusam'men•beißen*.

grizzled, *adj.* grau.

groan, 1. *n.* Stöhnen *nt.* 2. *vb.* stöhnen.

grocer, *n.* Kolonial'warenhändler, - *m.*

groceries, *n.pl.* Kolonial'waren *pl.*

grocery store, *n.* Kolonial'warengeschäft, -e *nt.,* Lebensmittelgeschäft, -e *nt.*

grog, *n.* Grog, -s *m.*

groggy, *adj.* benom'men; (be g.) taumeln.

groin, *n.* Leistengegend *f.*

groom, *n.* Reitknecht, -e *m.; (footman)* Diener, - *m.; (bridegroom)* Bräutigam -e *m.*

groove, *n.* Rinne, -n *f.*

grope, *vb.* tappen.

gross, 1. *n.* Gros, -se *nt.* 2. *adj.* grob (-); *(weight)* brutto.

grossness, *n.* Kraßheit, -en *f.*

grotesque, *adj.* grotesk'.

grotto, *n.* Grotte, -n *f.*

grouch, 1. *n.* Griesgram, -e *m.* 2. *vb.* verdrieß'lich sein*.

ground, 1. *n.* Grund, *̈-e m.,* Boden *m.; Gebiet',* -e *nt.* 2. *vb. (elec.)* erden.

groundless, *adj.* grundlos.

groundwork, *n.* Grundlage, -n *f.*

group, 1. *n.* Gruppe, -n *f.* 2. *vb.* gruppie'ren.

groupie *n.* Mitläufer im Gefolge Prominenter, besonders Rockmusikstars.

grouse, *n.* schottisches Schneehuhn, *̈-er nt.*

grove, *n.* Hain, -e *m.*

grovel, *vb.* kriechen*, speichelleckerisch sein*.

grow, *vb.* wachsen*.

grow up, *vb.* auf•wachsen*, heran•wachsen*.

growl, *vb.* knurren.

grown, *adj.* erwach'sen.

grown-up, 1. *n.* Erwach'senm.&f.* 2. *adj.* erwach'sen.

growth, *n.* Wachstum *nt.; (med.)* Gewächs', -e *nt.*

grub, 1. *n.* Larve, -n *f.; (food)* Fressa'lien *pl.* 2. *vb.* wühlen.

grudge, *n.* Groll *m.*

gruel, *n.* dünne Hafergrütze *f.*

gruesome, *adj.* schauerlich.

gruff, *adj.* bärbeißig.

grumble, *vb.* murren.

grumpy, *adj.* mürrisch.

grunt, 1. *n.* Grunzen, - *nt.* 2. *vb.* grunzen.

guarantee, 1. *n.* Garantie', -i'en *f.* 2. *vb.* garantie'ren.

guarantor, *n.* Bürge, -n, -n *m.*

guaranty, *n.* Sicherheit, -en *f.;* Bürgschaft, -en *f.*

guard, 1. *n.* Wache, -n *f.;* 2. *vb.* bewa'chen.

guarded, *adj.* vorsichtig.

guardian, *n.* Vormund, -e *m.*

guerrilla, *n.* Partisan', (-en,) -en *m.*

guess, *vb.* raten*.

guesswork, *n.* Raterei *f.*

guest, *n.* Gast, *̈-e m.*

guidance, *n.* Leitung *f.,* Führung *f.*

guide, 1. *n.* Führer, - *m.,* Führerin, -nen *f.* 2. *vb.* führen, leiten.

guidebook, *n.* Reiseführer, - *m.*

guidepost, *n.* Wegweiser, - *m.*

guild, *n.* Gilde, -n *f.*

guile, *n.* Arglist *f.*

guillotine, *n.* Guilloti'ne, -n *f.*

guilt, *n.* Schuld *f.*

guiltless, *adj.* schuldlos.

guilty, *adj.* schuldig.

guinea fowl, *n.* Perlhuhn, *̈-er nt.*

guinea pig, *n.* Meerschweinchen, - *nt.*

guise, *n.* Art, -en *f.; (clothes)* Aussehen *nt.*

guitar, *n.* Gitar're, -n *f.*

gulf, *n.* Golf, -e *m.*

gull, *n.* Möwe, -n *f.*

gullet, *n.* Kehle, -n *f.*

gullible, *adj.* leichtgläubig.

gully, *n.* Wasserrinne, -n *f.*

gulp, *vb.* schlucken.

gum, *n.* Gummi, -s *nt.; (teeth)* Zahnfleisch *nt.; (chewing g.)* Kaugummi, -s *m.*

gummy, *adj.* gummiartig, klebrig.

gun, *n. (small)* Gewehr', -e *nt.; (large)* Geschütz', -e *nt.*

gunboat, *n.* Kano'nenboot, -e *nt.*

gunner, *n.* Kanonier', -e *m.*

gunpowder, *n.* Schießpulver *nt.*

gunshot, *n.* Schuß, -sse *m.*

gurgle, *vb.* gluckern.

guru, *n.* Guru, -s *m.*

gush, *vb.* hervor'quellen*.

gusher, *n.* sprudelnde Petroleumquelle, -n *f.*

gusset, *n.* Zwickel, - *m.*

gust, *n.* Windstoß, -e *m.*

gustatory, *adj.* Geschmacks'- *(cpds.).*

gusto, *n.* Schwung *m.*

gusty, *adj.* windig.

guts, *n.* Eingeweide *pl.; (courage)* Mumm *m.*

gutter, *n. (street)* Rinnstein, -e *m.,* Gosse, -n *f.; (house)* Dachtraufe, -n *f.*

guttural, *adj.* guttural'.

guy, *n.* Kerl, -e *m.*

guzzle, *vb.* saufen*.

gymnasium, *n.* Turnhalle, -n *f.*

gymnast, *n.* Turner, - *m.,* Turnerin, -nen *f.*

gymnastic, *adj.* gymnas'tisch.

gymnastics, *n.* Gymnas'tik *f.*

gynecologist, *n.* Frauenarzt, -e *m.,* Frauenärztin, -nen *f.* Gynäkolo'ge, -n, -n *m.,* Gynäkolo'gin, -nen *f.*

gynecology, *n.* Gynäkologie' *f.*

gypsum, *n.* Gips *m.*

gypsy, *n.* Zigeu'ner, - *m.,* Zigeu'nerin, -nen *f.*

gyrate, *vb.* kreiseln.

gyroscope, *n.* Kreiselkompaß, -sse *m.*

H

haberdashery, *n.* Geschäft' für Herrenartikel.

habit, *n.* Gewohn'heit, -en *f.;* Kleidung, -en *f.*

habitable, *adj.* bewohn'bar.

habitat, *n.* Wohnbereich, -e *m.*

habitual, *adj.* gewöhn'lich; Gewohn'heits- *(cpds.).*

habitué, *n.* Stammgast, -e *m.*

hack, 1. *n.* Droschke, -n *f.; (horse)* Klepper, - *m.* 2. *vb.* hacken.

hacksaw, *n.* Metall'säge, -n *f.*

hag, *n.* Vettel, -n *f.*

haggard, *adj.* abgehärmt.

haggle, *vb.* feilschen.

Hague, *n.* Den Haag *m.*

hail, 1. *n.* Hagel *m.* 2. *vb.* hageln; *(greet)* begrü'ßen. 3. *interj.* heil!

hailstone, *n.* Hagelkorn, -er *nt.*

hailstorm, *n.* Hagelwetter, - *nt.*

hair, *n.* Haar, -e *nt.*

haircut, *n.* Haarschnitt, -e *m.; (get a h.)* sich die Haare schneiden lassen*.

hairdo, *n.* Frisur', -en *f.*

hairdresser, *n.* Friseur', - *m.,* Friseu'se, -n *f.*

hair drier, *n.* Fön *m.,* Haartrockner *m.*

hairline, *n.* Haaransatz, -e *m.;* Haarstrich, -e *m.*

hairpin, *n.* Haarnadel, -n *f.*

hair-raising, *adj.* haarsträubend.

hairspray, *n.* Haarspray *m.*

hairy, *adj.* haarig.

hale, *adj.* kräftig.

half, 1. *n.* Hälfte, -n *f.* 2. *adj.* halb.

half-breed, *n.* Mischling, -e *m.*

half-brother, *n.* Stiefbruder, - *m.*

half-hearted, *adj.* lauwarm.

half-mast, *n.* Halbmast *m.*

halfway, *adv.* halbwegs.

half-wit, *n.* Narr, -en, -en *m.*

halibut, *n.* Heilbutt, -e *m.*

hall, *n. (auditorium)* Halle, -n *f.; (large room)* Saal, Säle *m.; (corridor)* Gang, -e *m.,* Korridor, -e *m.; (front h.)* Diele, -n *f.*

hallmark, *n.* Stempel der Echtheit *m.*

hallow, *vb.* heiligen.

Halloween, n. Abend (m.) vor Allerhei'ligen.

hallucination, n. Wahnvorstellung, -en f.; Halluzination', -en f.

hallway, n. Gang, ⁒e m.; Korridor, -e m.

halo, n. Heiligenschein, -e m.

halt, 1. n. Halt, -e m.; (fig.) Stillstand m. **2.** vb. an'halten*. **3.** interj. halt!

halter, n. (horse) Halfter, - nt.; (female clothing) Oberteil eines Bade- oder Luftanzuges.

halve, vb. halbie'ren.

ham, n. Schinken, - m.

Hamburg, n. Hamburg nt.

hamlet, n. Flecken, - m.

hammer, 1. n. Hammer, ⁒ m. **2.** vb. hämmern.

hammock, n. Hängematte, -n f.

hamper, 1. n. Korb, ⁒e m. **2.** vb. hemmen.

hamstring, vb. lähmen.

hand, 1. n. Hand, ⁒e f. **2.** vb. reichen.

handbag, n. Handtasche, -n f.

handbook, n. Handbuch, ⁒er nt.

handcuffs, n.pl. Handschellen pl.

handful, n. Handvoll f.

handicap 1. n. Handikap, -s nt.; Hindernis, -se nt. **2.** vb. hemmen.

handicraft, n. Handwerk nt.

handiwork, n. Handarbeit, -en f.; Handwerk nt.

handkerchief, n. Taschentuch, ⁒er nt.

handle, 1. n. Henkel, - m., Griff, -e m. **2.** vb. handhaben.

hand-made, adj. handgearbeitet.

handout, n. Almosen, - nt.

hand-rail, n. Gelän'der, - nt.

handsome, adj. gutaussehend; ansehnlich.

handwriting, n. Handschrift, -en f.

handy, adj. handlich; (skilled) geschickt'.

handyman, n. Fakto'tum, -s nt.

hangar, n. Schuppen, - m.

hanger, n. Aufhänger, - m.; (clothes) Kleiderbügel, - m.

hanger-on, n. Schmarot'zer, - m.

hang glider, n. Drachenflieger, - m.

hanging, n. Hinrichtung (-en f.) durch Hängen.

hangman, n. Henker, - m.

hangnail, n. Niednagel, ⁒ m.

hangout, n. Stammlokal, -e nt.

hangover, n. Kater, - m., Katzenjammer m.

hangup, n. (to have a h.) einen Komplex haben, verklemmt sein.

haphazardly, adv. aufs Geratewohl'.

happen, vb. sich ereig'nen, geschie'hen*, passie'ren.

happening, n. Ereig'nis, -se nt.

happiness, n. Glück nt.

happy, adj. glücklich.

happy-go-lucky, adj. sorglos.

harangue, 1. n. marktschreierische Ansprache, -n f. **2.** vb. eine marktschreierische Ansprache halten*.

harass, vb. plagen.

harbinger, n. Vorbote, -n, -n m.

harbor, n. Hafen, ⁒ m.

hard, adj. (not soft) hart (⁒); (not easy) schwer, schwierig.

hard-boiled, adj. hartgekocht; (fig.) abgebrüht.

hard coal, n. Anthrazit', -e m.

harden, vb. (intr.) hart werden*; (tr.) ab'härten.

hard-headed, adj. praktisch, realis'tisch.

hard-hearted, adj. hartherzig.

hardiness, n. Rüstigkeit f.

hardly, adv. kaum.

hardness, n. Härte, -n f.

hardship, n. Not, (⁒e f.; (exertion) Anstrengung, -en f.

hardware, n. Eisenwaren pl.

hardwood, n. Hartholz nt.

hardy, adj. rüstig.

hare, n. Hase, -n, -n m.

harem, n. Harem, -s m.

hark, vb. horchen.

Harlequin, n. Harlekin, -e m.

harm, 1. n. Schaden, ⁒ m.; Unrecht, -e nt. **2.** vb. schaden; Unrecht zu'fügen.

harmful, adj. schädlich.

harmless, adj. harmlos.

harmonic, adj. harmo'nisch.

harmonica, n. Harmo'nika, -s f.

harmonious, adj. harmo'nisch.

harmonize, vb. harmonisie'ren.

harmony, n. Harmonie', -i'en f.; (fig.) Eintracht f.

harness, 1. n. Geschirr', -e nt. **2.** vb. ein·spannen.

harp, n. Harfe, -n f.

harpoon, 1. n. Harpu'ne, -n f. **2.** vb. harpunie'ren.

harpsichord, n. Spinett', -e nt.

harrow, 1. n. Egge, -n f. **2.** vb. eggen.

harry, vb. plündern; plagen.

harsh, adj. rauh; streng.

harshness, n. Rauheit f.; Strenge f.

harvest, 1. n. Ernte, -n f. **2.** vb. ernten.

hassle, n. Hetze f.

hassock, n. gepolsterter Hocker, - m.

haste, n. Eile f.

hasten, vb. eilen; sich beei'len.

hat, n. Hut, ⸚e m.; Mütze, -n f.

hatch, 1. n. Luke, -n f. **2.** vb. aus·brüten.

hatchet, n. Beil, -e nt.

hate, 1. n. Haß m. **2.** vb. hassen.

hateful, adj. verhaßt'; widerlich.

hatred, n. Haß m.

haughtiness, n. Hochmut m.

haughty, adj. hochmütig.

haul, vb. schleppen.

haunch, n. Keule, -n f.

haunt, vb. verfol'gen.

have, vb. haben*; **(I h. it made)** ich lasse* es machen; **(I h. him make it)** ich lasse* ihn es machen.

haven, n. Hafen, ⸚ m.; Zufluchtsort, -e m.

havoc, n. Verwüs'tung, -en f.

hawk, n. Habicht, -e m.

hawser, n. Trosse, -n f.

hay, n. Heu nt.

hay fever, n. Heuschnupfen, - m.

hayloft, n. Heuboden, ⸚ m.

haystack, n. Heuhaufen, - m.

hazard, 1. n. Risiko, -s or -en nt. **2.** vb. riskie'ren.

hazardous, adj. gewagt'.

haze, n. Dunst, ⸚e m.

hazel, adj. haselnußbraun.

hazelnut, n. Haselnuß, ⸚sse f.

hazy, adj. dunstig, unklar.

he, pron. er.

head, n. Kopf, ⸚e m., Haupt, ⸚er nt.

headache, n. Kopfschmerzen pl.

headfirst, adv. Hals über Kopf.

headgear, n. Kopfbedeckung, -en f.

heading, n. Überschrift, -en f., Rubrik', -en f.

headlight, n. Scheinwerfer, - m.

headline, n. Überschrift, -en f.; (newspaper) Schlagzeile, -n f.

headlong, adj. überstürzt'.

headmaster, n. Schuldirektor, -en m.

headmistress, n. Schuldirektorin, -nen f.

head-on, adv. direkt von vorn.

headquarters, n.pl. Hauptquartier, -e nt.

headstone, n. (grave) Grabstein, -e m.; (arch.) Eckstein, -e m.

headstrong, adj. dickköpfig.

headwaters, n.pl. Quelle, -n f.

headway, n. **(make h.)** vorwärts kommen*.

heal, vb. heilen.

health, n. Gesund'heit, -en f.

healthful, adj. gesund (⸚).

health insurance, -nen, n. Krankenkasse f.

healthy, adj. gesund'(⸚).

heap, 1. n. Haufen, - m. **2.** vb. häufen.

hear, vb. hören.

hearing, n. Gehör' nt.; (jur.) Verhör', -e nt.

hearsay, n. Hörensagen nt.

hearse, n. Leichenwagen, - m.

heart, n. Herz(en), -e nt.

heartache, n. Herzenskummer m.

heartbreaking, adj. herzzerbrechend.

heartbroken, adv. tieftraurig.

heartburn, n. Sodbrennen, - nt.

heartfelt, adj. aufrichtig.

hearth, n. Kamin', -e m.

heartless, adj. herzlos.

heartrending, adj. herzzerreißend.

heartsick, adj. niedergeschlagen.

heart-to-heart, adj. freimütig.

hearty, adj. herzhaft.

heat, 1. n. Hitze f., Wärme f.; (house) Heizung f. **2.** vb. heiß machen, erhit'zen; (house) heizen.

heated, adj. geheizt'; (fig.) hitzig.

heater, n. Heizvorrichtung, -en f.
heathen, 1. n. Heide, -n, -n m. **2.** adj. heidnisch.
heather, n. Heidekraut nt.
heat-stroke, n. Hitzschlag, -̈e m.
heat up, vb. auf•wärmen.
heat wave, n. Hitzewelle, -n f.
heave, vb. heben*; wogen; (utter) aus•stoßen*.
heaven, n. Himmel, - m.
heavenly, adj. himmlisch.
heavy, adj. schwer; (fig.) heftig.
heavyweight, n. Schwergewicht nt.
Hebrew, 1. n. Hebrä'er, - m. Hebrä'erin, -nen f. **2.** adj. hebrä'isch.
heckle, vb. hecheln.
hectic, adj. hektisch.
hedge, n. Hecke, -n f.
hedgehog, n. Igel, - m.
hedge-hop, vb. (mil.) im Tiefflug an•fliegen*.
hedgerow, n. Baumhecke, -n f.
hedonism, n. Hedonis'mus m.
heed, vb. beach'ten.
heedless, adj. achtlos.
heel, n. (shoes) Absatz, -̈e m.; (foot) Ferse, -n f.; (scoundrel) Schuft, -e m.
heifer, n. junge Kuh, -̈e f.
height, n. Höhe, -n f.; (person) Größe, -n f.
heighten, vb. erhö'hen.
heinous, adj. abscheu'lich, verrucht'.
heir, n. Erbe, -n, -n m.
heiress, n. Erbin, -nen f.
heirloom, n. Erbstück, -e nt.
helicopter, n. Hubschrauber, - m.
heliotrope, n. Heliotrop', -e nt.
helium, n. Helium nt.
hell, n. Hölle, -n f.
Hellenic, adj. helle'nisch.
Hellenism, n. Hellenis'mus m.
hello, interj. guten Tag (Morgen, Abend); (call for attention) hallo.
helm, n. Steuerruder, - nt.
helmet, n. Helm, -e m.
helmsman, n. Steuermann, -̈er m.
help, 1. n. Hilfe f. **2.** vb. helfen*.
helper, n. Helfer, - m., Helferin, -nen f.
helpful, adj. hilfreich, hilfsbereit.
helpfulness, n. Hilfsbereitschaft f.

helping, n. Portion', -en f.
helpless, adj. hilflos.
helter-skelter, adv. hol'ter-diepol'ter.
hem, 1. n. Saum, -̈e m. **2.** vb. säumen.
hematite, n. Hematit', -e m.
hemisphere, n. Halbkugel, -n f.
hemlock, n. Schierling m.
hemoglobin, n. Hämoglobin' nt.
hemophilia, n. Bluterkrankheit f.
hemorrhage, n. Bluterguß, -̈sse m.
hemorrhoid, n. Hämorrhoi'de, -n f.
hemp, n. Hanf m.
hemstitch, n. Hohlsaum, -̈e m.
hen, n. Henne, -n f.
hence, adv. (time) von nun an; (place) von hier aus; (therefore) daher, deshalb, deswegen, also.
henceforth, adv. von nun an.
henchman, n. Trabant', -en, -en m.
henna, n. Henna f.
henpecked, adj. unter dem Pantof'fel stehend.
hepatic, adj. Leber- (cpds.).
hepatica, n. Hepa'tika, -ken f.
her, 1. pron. sie, ihr. **2.** adj. ihr, -, -e.
heraldic, adj. heral'disch.
heraldry, n. Wappenkunde f.
herb, n. Kraut, -̈er nt., Gewürz'-kraut, -̈er nt.
herculean, adj. herku'lisch.
herd, n. Herde, -n f.
here, adv. (in this place) hier; (to this place) hierher; (from h.) hierhin'.
hereabout, adv. hier.
hereafter, 1. n. Leben (nt.) nach dem Tode. **2.** adv. in Zukunft.
hereby, adv. hiermit.
hereditary, adj. erblich.
heredity, n. Erblichkeit f.; Vererbung, -en f.
herein, adv. hierbei, hiermit.
heresy, n. Ketzerei', -en f.
heretic, 1. n. Ketzer, - m. **2.** adj. ketzerisch.
heritage, n. Erbe nt.
hermetic, adj. herme'tisch.
hermit, n. Einsiedler, - m.
hernia, n. Bruch, -̈e m.

hero, n. Held, -en, -en m.
heroic, adj. heldenhaft.
heroin, n. Heroin' nt.
heroine, n. Heldin, -nen f.
heroism, n. Heldenmut m.
heron, n. Reiher, - m.
herring, n. Hering, -e m.
herringbone, n. Heringsgräte, -n f.
hers, pron. ihrer, -es, -e.
hertz, n. Hertz nt.
hesitancy, n. Zögern nt.
hesitant, adj. zögernd.
hesitate, vb. zögern.
hesitation, n. Zögern nt.
heterodox, adj. heterodox'.
heterogeneous, adj. heterogen'.
heterosexual, adj. heterosexuell'.
hew, vb. hauen*.
hexagon, n. Sechseck, -e nt.
heyday, n. Blütezeit, -en f.
hi, interj. hallo.
hibernate, vb. überwin'tern.
hibernation, n. Überwin'terung, -en f.
hibiscus, n. Hibis'kus, -ken m.
hiccup, n. Schluckauf m.
hickory, n. Hickoryholz, ⁻er nt.
hide, 1. n. Haut, ⁻e f.; Fell, -e nt. 2. vb. verber'gen*, verste'cken; verheim'lichen.
hideous, adj. gräßlich.
hide-out, n. Schlupfwinkel, - m.
hierarchy, n. Rangordnung, -en f., Hierarchie', -i'en f.
hieroglyphic, adj. hierogly'phisch.
high, adj. hoch, hoh- (höher, höchst); (tipsy) beschwipst'.
highbrow, adj. intellektuell'.
high fidelity, n. Hifi nt.
high-handed, adj. anmaßend.
highland, n. Hochland, ⁻er nt.
highlight, n. Höhepunkt, -e m.
highly, adv. höchst.
high-minded, adj. edelmütig.
Highness, n. Hoheit, -en f.
high school, n. höhere Schule, -n f.
high seas, n. hohe See f.
high-strung, adj. nervös, kribbelig.
high tide, n. Flut, -en f.
highway, n. Landstraße, -n f., Chaussee', -n f.

hijacker, n. Flugzeugentführer, - m.; Luftpirat, -en, -en m.
hike, 1. n. Wanderung, -en f. 2. vb. wandern.
hilarious, adj. ausgelassen.
hilarity, n. Ausgelassenheit f.
hill, n. Hügel, - m.
hilt, n. Heft, -e nt.
him, pron. ihn; ihm.
hind, adj. hinter-.
hinder, vb. hindern; verhin'dern.
hindmost, adj. letzt-, hinterst-.
hindrance, n. Hindernis, -se nt.; (disadvantage) Nachteil, -e m.
hinge, n. Scharnier, -e nt.
hint, 1. n. Wink, -e m. 2. vb. andeuten.
hinterland, n. Hinterland nt.
hip, n. Hüfte, -n f.
hippopotamus, n. Nilpferd, -e nt.
hire, vb. mieten; (persons) an-stellen.
his, 1. adj. sein, -, -e. 2. pron. seiner, -es, -e.
Hispanic, n. erste oder zweite Generation Amerikaner spanisch sprechender Herkunft.
hiss, vb. zischen.
historian, n. Histo'riker, - m., Histo'rikerin, -nen f.
historic, historical, adj. historisch.
history, n. Geschich'te, -n f.
hit, 1. n. Stoß, ⁻e m., Schlag, ⁻e m.; (success) Treffer, - m. 2. vb. stoßen*, schlagen*, treffen*.
hitch, 1. n. (knot) Knoten, - m.; (obstacle) Hindernis, -se nt. 2. vb. festmachen.
hitchhike, vb. per Anhalter fahren*.
hive, n. Bienenstock, ⁻e m.
hives, n. Nesselsucht f.
hoard, 1. n. Vorrat, ⁻e m. 2. vb. hamstern.
hoarse, adj. heiser.
hoax, n. Schabernack, -e m.
hobble, vb. humpeln.
hobby, n. Hobby, -s nt., Liebhaberei', -en f.
hobgoblin, n. Kobold, -e m.
hobnob with, vb. mit jemand auf vertrau'tem Füße stehen*.
hobo, n. Landstreicher, - m.
hockey, n. Hockey nt.

hocus-pocus, n. Ho'kuspo'kus m.

hod, n. Traggestell, -e nt.

hodgepodge, n. Mischmasch, -e m.

hoe, 1. n. Hacke, -n f. 2. vb. hacken.

hog, n. Schwein, -e nt.

hoist, vb. hoch•ziehen*, hissen.

hold, 1. n. Halt m.; (ship) Laderaum, ⸚e m. 2. vb. halten*; (contain) enthal'ten*; (h. up) auf•halten*.

holder, n. Halter, - m.

holdup, n. Überfall, ⸚e m.

hole, n. Loch, ⸚er nt.

holiday, n. Feiertag, -e m., Festtag, -e m.

holiness, n. Heiligkeit f.

Holland, n. Holland nt.

hollow, adj. hohl.

holly, n. Stechpalme, -n f.

hollyhock, n. Malve, -n f.

holocaust, n. Brandopfer, - nt., Großfeuer, - nt.

hologram, n. Hologramm', -e nt.

holography, n. Holografie' f.

holster, n. Pisto'lenhalter, - m.

holy, adj. heilig.

holy day, n. Kirchenfeiertag, -e m.

Holy Spirit, n. der Heilige Geist m.

Holy Week, n. Karwoche f.

homage, n. Huldigung, -en f.

home, 1. n. Heim, -e nt.; (h. town) Heimat, -en f.; (place of residence) Wohnort, -e m.; (house) Haus, ⸚er nt.; (institution) Heim, -e nt. 2. adv. (location) zu Hause, daheim'; (direction) nach Hause, heim.

homeland, n. Heimatland, ⸚er nt.

homeless, adj. heimatlos; obdachlos.

homelike, adj. behag'lich.

homely, adj. häßlich.

home-made, adj. selbstgefertigt.

home rule, n. Selbstverwaltung f.

homesick, be, vb. Heimweh haben*.

homesickness, n. Heimweh nt.

homestead, n. Fami'liensitz, -e m.

homeward, adv. heimwärts.

homework, n. Hausaufgabe, -n f., Schularbeiten pl.

homicide, n. Mord, -e m.

homogeneous, adj. homogen'.

homogenize, vb. homogeni•sie'ren.

homonym, n. Homonym', -e nt.

homosexual, adj. homosexuell'.

hone, n. Wetzstein, -e m.

honest, adj. ehrlich, aufrichtig.

honesty, n. Ehrlichkeit, -en f.

honey, n. Honig m.

honey-bee, n. Honigbiene, -n f.

honeycomb, n. Honigwabe, -n f.

honeymoon, n. Hochzeitsreise, -n f., Flitterwochen pl.

honeysuckle, n. Geißblatt nt.

honor, 1. n. Ehre, -n f. 2. vb. ehren; honorie'ren.

honorable, adj. ehrbar, ehrenvoll.

honorary, adj. Ehren- (cpds.).

honored, adj geehrt'.

hood, n. Haube, -n f., (monk) Kapu'ze, -n f.

hoodlum, n. Rowdy, -s m.

hoodwink, vb. übertöl'peln.

hoof, n. Huf, -e nt.

hook, 1. n. Haken, - m. 2. vb. zu•haken; (catch) fangen*.

hoop, n. Reifen, - m.

hoot, vb. schreien*.

hop, 1. n. (plant) Hopfen m.; (jump) Sprung, ⸚e m. 2. vb. hüpfen, springen*.

hope, 1. n. Hoffnung, -en f. 2. vb. hoffen.

hopeful, adj. hoffnungsvoll.

hopeless, adj. hoffnungslos.

hopelessness, n. Hoffnungslosigkeit f.

horde, n. Horde, -n f.

horizon, n. Horizont', -e m.

horizontal, adj. waagerecht, horizontal'.

hormone, n. Hormon', -e nt.

horn, n. Horn, ⸚er nt.

hornet, n. Hornis'se, -n f.

horny, adj. hornig, hörnern.

horoscope, n. Horoskop', -e nt.

horrible, adj. grauenhaft.

horrid, adj. gräßlich.

horrify, vb. entset'zen.

horror, n. Grauen nt.

horse, n. Pferd, -e nt.

horseback, on, adv. zu Pferde.

horsehair, n. Roßhaar, -e nt.

horseman, n. Reiter, - m.

horsemanship, n. Reitkunst f.

horse-power, n. Pferdestärke, -n f.

horseradish, n. Meerrettich, -e m.

horseshoe, n. Hufeisen, - nt.

horticulture, n. Gartenbau m.

hose, n. (tube) Schlauch, ⸚e m.; (stocking) Strumpf, ⸚e m.

hosiery, n. Strumpfwaren pl.

hospitable, adj. gastfreundlich, gastfrei.

hospital, n. Krankenhaus, ⸚er nt.

hospitality, n. Gastfreundschaft, Gastfreiheit f.

hospitalization, n. Krankenhausaufenthalt m.

hospitalize, vb. ins Krankenhaus einweisen; (be h.d) im Krankenhaus liegen müssen*.

host, n. Gastgeber, - m.; (innkeeper) Wirt, - e m.; (crowd) Menge, -n f.; (Eucharist) Hostie f.

hostage, n. Geisel, -n m.

hostel, n. Herberge, -n f.; (youth h.) Jugendherberge, -n f.

hostess, n. Gastgeberin, -nen f.

hostile, adj. feindlich.

hostility, n. Feindseligkeit, -en f., Krieg, -e m.

hot, adj. heiß.

hotbed, n. Mistbeet, -e nt.; (fig.) Brutstätte, -n f.

hot dog, n. Bockwurst, ⸚e f.

hotel, n. Hotel', -s nt.

hothouse, n. Treibhaus, ⸚er nt.

hound, n. Hund, -e m.

hour, n. Stunde, -n f.

hourglass, n. Stundenglas, ⸚er nt.

hourly, adj. stündlich.

house, n. Haus, ⸚er nt.

housefly, n. Stubenfliege, -n f.

household, n. Haushalt, -e m.

housekeeper, n. Haushälterin, -nen f.

housekeeping, n. Haushaltung f.

housemaid, n. Hausmädchen, - nt.

housewife, n. Hausfrau, -en f.

housework, n. Hausarbeit, -en f.

hovel, n. Hütte, -n f.

hover, vb. schweben.

hovercraft, n. Hovercraft m. & nt.; Luftkissenboot, -e nt.

how, adv. wie.

however, 1. conj. aber, doch, jedoch'. 2. adv. wie . . . auch.

howitzer, n. Haubit'ze, -n f.

howl, 1. n. Gebrüll' nt. 2. vb. brüllen.

hub, n. Nabe, -n f.; (fig.) Mittelpunkt, -e m.

hubbub, n. Tumult', -e m.

huckleberry, n. Heidelbeere, -n f.

huddle, vb. zusam'men-kauern, sich zusam'men-drängen.

hue, n. Färbung, -en f.

hug, 1. n. Umar'mung, -en f. 2. vb. umar'men.

huge, adj. sehr groß, ungeheuer.

hull, n. Hülse, -n f.; (fruit) Schale, -n f.; (ship) Rumpf, ⸚e m.

hum, n. (people) Gemur'mel nt.; (insects) Summen nt. 2. vb. murmeln; summen.

human, adj. menschlich.

humane, adj. human', menschlich.

humanism, n. Humanis'mus m.

humanitarian, adj. menschenfreundlich.

humanity, n. (mankind) Menschheit f.; (humaneness) Menschlichkeit f.

humble, adj. demütig, bescheiden.

humbug, n. Schwindel m., Quatsch m.

humdrum, adj. langweilig, eintönig.

humid, adj. feucht.

humidity, n. Feuchtigkeit f.

humidor, n. Tabakstopf, ⸚e m.

humiliate, vb. demütigen.

humiliation, n. Demütigung, -en f.

humility, n. Demut f.

humor, n. Humor' m.; (mood) Laune, -n f.

humorist, n. Humorist', -en, -en m.

humorous, adj. humor'voll, witzig.

hump, n. Buckel, - m., Höcker, - m.

hunch, 1. n. Höcker, - m., Buckel, - m.; (suspicion) Ahnung, -en f., Riecher, - m. 2. vb. krümmen.

hunchback, 1. n. Buckel, - m.; (person) Bucklig- m.&f. 2. adj. bucklig.

hundred, num. hundert.

hundredth, 1. adj. hundertst-. 2. n. Hundertstel, -nt.

Hungarian, 1. n. Ungar, -n, -n m., Ungarin, -nen f. 2. adj. ungarisch.

Hungary, n. Ungarn nt.

hunger, n. Hunger m.

hungry, adj. hungrig.

hunt, 1. n. Jagd, -en f. 2. vb. jagen.

hunter, n. Jäger, - m.

hunting, n. Jagd, -en f.

hurdle, 1. n. Hürde, -n f. 2. vb. hinü'ber·springen*.

hurl, vb. schleudern.

hurrah, interj. (h. for him) er lebe hoch!

hurricane, n. Orkan', -e m.

hurry, vb. eilen, sich beei'len.

hurt, vb. weh tun*, verlet'zen.

hurtful, adj. schädlich.

husband, n. Mann, ¨er m., Gatte, -n, -n m.

husbandry, n. Landwirtschaft f.; (management) Wirtschaften nt.

hush, 1. n. Stille f. 2. vb. zum Schweigen bringen*. 3. interj. still!

husk, 1. n. Hülse, -n f. 2. vb. enthül'sen.

husky, adj. (hoarse) rauh; (strong) stark (¨).

hustle, vb. rührig sein*.

hut, n. Hütte, -n f.

hyacinth, n. Hyazin'the, -n f.

hybrid, adj. hybrid'.

hydrangea, n. Horten'sie, -n f.

hydrant, n. Hydrant', -en, -en m.

hydraulic, adj. hydrau'lisch.

hydrochloric acid, n. Salzsäure f.

hydroelectric, adj. hydroelek'trisch.

hydrogen, n. Wasserstoff m.

hydrogen bomb, n. Wasserstoffbombe, -n f.

hydrophobia, n. krankhafte Wasserscheu f.

hydroplane, n. Wasserflugzeug, -e nt.

hydrotherapy, n. Hydrotherapie' f.

hyena, n. Hyä'ne, -n f.

hygiene, n. Hygie'ne f., Körperpflege f.

hygienic, adj. hygie'nisch.

hymn, n. Hymne, -n f., Choral', -e m., Kirchenlied, -er nt.

hymnal, n. Gesang'buch, ¨er nt.

hyperacidity, n. Hyperacidität', f.

hyperbole, n. Hyper'bel, -n f.

hypercritical, adj. überkritisch.

hypersensitive, adj. überempfindlich.

hypertension, n. übernormaler Blutdruck m.

hyphen, n. Bindestrich, -e m.

hyphenate, vb. trennen.

hypnosis, n. Hypno'se, -n f.

hypnotic, adj. hypno'tisch.

hypnotism, n. Hypnotis'mus m.

hypnotize, vb. hypnotisie'ren.

hypochondria, n. Schwermut f.

hypochondriac, 1. n. Hypochon'der, - m. 2. adj. schwermütig.

hypocrisy, n. Heuchelei', -en f.

hypocrite, n. Heuchler, - m., Heuchlerin, -nen f.

hypocritical, adj. heuchlerisch.

hypodermic, n. Spritze, -n f.

hypothesis, n. Hypothe'se, -n f.

hypothetical, adj. hypothe'tisch.

hysterectomy, n. Hysterek'tomie f.

hysteria, hysterics, n. Hysterie' f.

hysterical, adj. hyste'risch.

I

I, pron. ich.

ice, n. Eis nt.

iceberg, n. Eisberg, -e m.

ice-box, n. Eisschrank, ¨e m.

ice cream, n. Eis nt., Sahneneis nt.

ice cream parlor, n. Eisdiele, -n f.

ice skate, 1, n. Schlittschuh, -e m.
2. vb. Schlittschuh laufen*.
icing, n. Zuckerguß, ¨sse m.
icon, n. Iko'ne, -n f.
icy, adj. eisig.
idea, n. Idee', -n f., Gedan'-ke(n), - m.
ideal, 1. n. Ideal', -e nt. **2.** adj. ideal'.
idealism, n. Idealis'mus m.
idealist, n. Idealist', -en, -en m.
idealistic, adj. idealis'tisch.
idealize, vb. idealisie'ren.
identical, adj. iden'tisch.
identifiable, adj. identifizier'bar.
identification, n. Iden-tifizie'rung, -en f.; (card) Aus-weis, -e m.
identify, vb. identifizie'ren.
identity, n. Identität', -en f.
ideology, n. Ideologie', -i'en f.
idiocy, n. Blödsinn m.
idiom, n. Idiom', -e nt., Redewen-dung, -en f.
idiot, n. Idiot', -en, -en m.
idiotic, adj. idio'tisch, blödsinnig.
idle, adj. müßig; arbeitslos; un-tätig.
idleness, n. Müßigkeit f.
idol, n. Götzenbild, -er nt.
idolatry, n. Abgötterrei', -en f.
idolize, vb. vergöt'tern.
if, conj. wenn; (as if) als ob.
ignite, vb. an·zünden.
ignition, n. Zündung f.
ignition key, n. Zündschlüssel, - m.
ignominious, adj. schmachvoll.
ignoramus, n. Nichtswisser, - m.
ignorance, n. Unwissenheit f.
ignorant, adj. unwissend.
ignore, vb. überse'hen*, unbeach-tet lassen*.
ill, adj. krank (¨).
illegal, adj. illegal, ungesetzlich.
illegible, adj. unleserlich.
illegitimate, adj. ungesetzlich; (unmarried) unehelich.
illicit, adj. unerlaubt.
illiteracy, n. Analphabe'tentum, nt.
illiterate, 1. n. Analphabet', -en, -en m. **2.** adj. des Lesens und Schreibens unkundig.
illness, n. Krankheit, -en f.

illogical, adj. unlogisch.
illuminate, vb. beleuch'ten, er-leuch'ten.
illumination, n. Beleuch'tung, -en f.
illusion, n. Illusion', -en f.
illusive, illusory, adj. trügerisch, illuso'risch.
illustrate, vb. erläu'tern; (with pictures) illustrie'ren.
illustration, n. Erläu'terung, -en f.; (picture) Illustration', -en f.
illustrative, adj. erläu'ternd.
illustrious, adj. berühmt.
image, n. Abbild, -er nt.
imaginable, adj. denkbar.
imaginary, adj. scheinbar, imagi-när'.
imagination, n. Einbildung, -en f., Vorstellung, -en f.
imaginative, adj. phantasievoll.
imagine, vb. sich ein·bilden, sich vor·stellen.
imam, n. Imam, -e m.
imbecile, adj. schwachsinnig.
imitate, vb. nach·ahmen, imi-tie'ren.
imitation, n. Nachahmung, -en f., Imitation', -en f.
immaculate, adj. unbefleckt, makellos, blitzsauber; (i. conception) unbefleckte Empfäng'nis f.
immaterial, adj. unwesentlich.
immature, adj. unreif.
immediate, adj. unmittelbar.
immediately, adv. sofort'.
immense, adj. unermeßlich.
immerse, vb. unter·tauchen, ver-sen'ken.
immigrant, n. Einwanderer, - m., Einwanderin, -nen f.
immigrate, vb. ein·wandern.
imminent, adj. bevor'stehend.
immobile, adj. unbeweglich.
immobilize, vb. unbeweglich machen.
immoderate, adj. maßlos, un-mäßige.
immodest, adj. unbescheiden, an-stößig.
immoral, adj. unsittlich, un-moralisch.
immorality, n. Unsittlichkeit, -en f.
immortal, adj. unsterblich.

immortality, *n.* Unsterblichkeit *f.*

immortalize, *vb.* unsterblich machen.

immune, *adj.* immun'.

immune system, *n.* Abwehrsystem, *nt.*

immunity, *n.* Immunität', -en *f.*

immunize, *vb.* immunisie'ren.

impact, *n.* Zusam'menprall *m.;* (*fig.*) Auswirkung, -en *f.*

impair, *vb.* verrin'gern, verschlechtern.

impart, *vb.* zu•kommen lassen*.

impartial, *adj.* unparteiisch.

impatience, *n.* Ungeduld *f.*

impatient, *adj.* ungeduldig.

impeach, *vb.* an•klagen, beschul'digen.

impeachment, *n.* Anklage, -n *f.;* Beschul'digung, -en *f.*

impede, *vb.* behin'dern.

impediment, *n.* Behin'derung, -en *f.;* (**speech i.**) Sprachfehler, - *m.*

impel, *vb.* an•treiben*, zwingen*.

impenetrable, *adj.* undurchdringlich.

imperative, 1. *n.* Imperativ, -e *m.* **2.** *adj.* zwingend.

imperceptible, *adj.* unmerklich, unwahrnehmbar.

imperfect, 1. *n.* Imperfekt, -e *nt.* **2.** *adj.* unvollkommen, fehlerhaft.

imperfection, *n.* Unvollkommenheit, -en *f.,* Fehler, - *m.*

imperial, *adj.* kaiserlich.

imperialism, *n.* Imperialis'mus *m.*

impersonal, *adj.* unpersönlich.

impersonate, *vb.* verkör'pern; (*theater*) dar•stellen.

impersonation, *n.* Verkör'perung, -en *f.;* (*theater*) Darstellung, -en *f.*

impersonator, *n.* Imita'tor, -o'ren *m.;* (*swindler*) Hochstapler, - *m.*

impertinence, *n.* Frechheit, -en *f.,* Unverschämtheit, -en *f.*

impertinent, *adj.* frech, unverschämt.

impervious, *adj.* unzugänglich; (*fig.*) gefühl'los.

impetuous, *adj.* ungestüm.

impetus, *n.* Anstoß *m.,* Antrieb *m.*

implement, 1. *n.* Werkzeug, -e *nt.* **2.** *vb.* durch•führen.

implicate, *vb.* verwi'ckeln.

implication, *n.* implizier'ter Gedan'ke(n), - *m.;* Verwick'lung, -en *f.;* (**by i.**) impli'zite.

implicit, *adj.* inbegriffen, stillschweigend.

implied, *adj.* miteinbegriffen.

implore, *vb.* an•flehen.

imply, *vb.* in sich schliessen*, impli'zite sagen, an•deuten.

impolite, *adj.* unhöflich.

import, 1. *n.* Einfuhr *f.,* Import', -e *m.;* (*meaning*) Bedeu'tung, -en *f.* **2.** *vb.* ein•führen, importie'ren.

importance, *n.* Wichtigkeit *f.*

important, *adj.* wichtig, bedeu'tend.

importation, *n.* Einfuhr *f.*

impose, *vb.* auf•erlegen.

imposition, *n.* Belas'tung, -en *f.*

impossibility, *n.* Unmöglichkeit, -en *f.*

impossible, *adj.* unmöglich.

impotence, *n.* Unfähigkeit, -en *f.;* (*med.*) Impotenz, -en *f.*

impotent, *adj.* unfähig; (*med.*) impotent.

impoverish, *vb.* arm machen; (*fig.*) aus•saugen.

impregnable, *adj.* uneinnehmbar.

impregnate, *vb.* durchdrin'gen*; (*make pregnant*) schwängern.

impresario, *n.* Impresa'rio, -s *m.*

impress, *vb.* (*imprint*) prägen, ein•prägen; (*affect*) beein'drucken, imponie'ren.

impression, *n.* Druck, -e *m.;* (*copy*) Abdruck, -e *m.;* (*fig.*) Eindruck, ⁀e *m.*

impressive, *adj.* eindrucksvoll.

imprison, *vb.* ein•sperren.

imprisonment, *n.* Haft *f.*

improbable, *adj.* unwahrscheinlich.

impromptu, *adv.* aus dem Stegreif.

improper, *adj.* unrichtig; unschicklich.

improve, *vb.* verbes'sern.

improvement, *n.* Verbes'serung, -en *f.;* Besserung *f.*

improvise, *vb.* improvisie'ren.
impudent, *adj.* frech.
impulse, *n.* Impuls', -e *m.*
impulsive, *adj.* impulsiv'.
impunity, *n.* **(with i.)** ungestraft.
impure, *adj.* unrein.
impurity, *n.* Unreinheit, -en *f.*
in, *prep.* in.
inadvertent, *adj.* achtlos, unaufmerksam.
inalienable, *adj.* unveräußerlich.
inane, *adj.* leer, geistlos.
inaugural, *adj.* Antritts- *(cpds.).*
inaugurate, *vb.* ins Amt einführen.
inauguration, *n.* Einweihung, -en *f.*; Amtseinführung, -en *f.*
incandescence, *n.* Glühen *nt.*
incandescent, *adj.* glühend; Glüh- *(cpds.).*
incantation, *n.* Beschwö'rung *f.,* Zauberspruch, =e *m.*
incapacitate, *vb.* unfähig machen.
incapacity, *n.* Unfähigkeit, -en *f.*
incarcerate, *vb.* ein-kerkern.
incarnate, *adj.* verkör'pert, fleischgeworden.
incarnation, *n.* Verkör'perung, -en *f.,* Fleischwerdung *f.*
incendiary, *adj.* Brand- *(cpds.);* aufwieglerisch.
incense, *n.* Weihrauch *m.*
incentive, *n.* Anreiz, -e *m.,* Antrieb, -e *m.*
inception, *n.* Begin'nen *nt.*
incessant, *adj.* unaufhörlich.
incest, *n.* Blutschande *f.*
inch, *n.* Zoll, - *m.*
incidence, *n.* Vorkommen *nt.*
incident, *n.* Vorfall, =e *m.*
incidental, *adj.* zufällig.
incidentally, *adv.* übrigens.
incision, *n.* Einschnitt, -e *m.*
incisor, *n.* Schneidezahn, =e *m.*
incite, *vb.* an-regen, an-stacheln.
inclination, *n.* Neigung, -en *f.*
incline, *vb.* neigen; **(be i.d)** geneigt sein*.
include, *vb.* ein-schließen*.
including, *prep.* einschließlich.
inclusive, *adj.* einschließlich.
incognito, *adv.* inkog'nito.
income, *n.* Einkommen, - *nt.*

incomparable, *adj.* unvergleichlich.
inconsiderate, *adj.* unüberlegt, rücksichtslos.
inconvenience, *n.* Mühe, -n *f.,* Belas'tung, -en *f.*
inconvenient, *adj.* mühsam, ungelegen.
incorporate, *vb.* verei'nigen; auf-nehmen*.
incorrigible, *adj.* unverbesserlich.
increase, **1.** *n.* Zunahme, -n *f.* **2.** *vb.* zu-nehmen*, wachsen*.
incredible, *adj.* unglaublich.
incredulity, *n.* Zweifel, - *m.*
incredulous, *adj.* zweifelnd.
increment, *n.* Zunahme, -n *f.*
incriminate, *vb.* belas'ten, beschul'digen.
incrimination, *n.* Beschul'digung, -en *f.,* Belas'tung, -en *f.*
incrust, *vb.* überkrus'ten.
incubator, *n.* Brutapparat, -e *m.*
incumbent, **1.** *n.* Amtsinhaber, - *m.* **2.** *adj.* verpflich'tend.
incur, *vb.* auf sich laden*.
incurable, *adj.* unheilbar.
indebted, *adj.* verschul'det.
indeed, *adv.* in der Tat.
indefatigable, *adj.* unermüdlich.
indefinite, *adj.* unbestimmt.
indefinitely, *adv.* endlos.
indelible, *adj.* unauslöschlich.
indemnify, *vb.* sicher-stellen; entschä'digen.
indemnity, *n.* Sicherstellung, -en *f.*; Entschä'digung, -en *f.*
indent, *vb.* zacken; *(paragraph)* ein-rücken; *(damage)* verbeu'len.
indentation, *n.* Einkerbung, -en *f.*; *(paragraph)* Einrückung, -en *f.*; *(damage)* Verbeu'lung, -en *f.*
independence, *n.* Unabhängigkeit *f.*
independent, *adj.* unabhängig.
in-depth, *adj.* gründlich, Tiefen- *(cpds.).*
index, *n.* Verzeich'nis, -se *nt.,* Regis'ter, - *nt.;* **(i. finger)** Zeigefinger, - *m.*
India, *n.* Indien *nt.*
Indian, **1.** *n.* Inder, - *m.,* Inderin, -nen *f.;* **(American I.)** India'ner, - *m.,* India'nerin, -nen *f.* **2.** *adj.* indisch; india'nisch.

indicate, *vb.* zeigen, an'deuten.
indication, *n.* Hinweis, -e *m.*, Anzeichen, -*nt.*
indicative, 1. *n.* Indikativ, -e *m.* **2.** *adj.* bezeich'nend.
indicator, *n.* Zeiger, - *m.*, Indika'tor, -o'ren *m.*; (sign) Zeichen, -*nt.*
indict, *vb.* an'klagen.
indictment, *n.* Anklage, -n *f.*
indifference, *n.* Gleichgültigkeit.
indifferent, *adj.* gleichgültig.
indigent, *adj.* bedürftig.
indigestible, *adj.* unverdaulich.
indigestion, *n.* Verdau'ungsstörung, -en *f.*
indignant, *adj.* entrüs'tet.
indignation, *n.* Entrüs'tung, -en *f.*
indignity, *n.* Unwürdigkeit, -en *f.*; (insult) Belei'digung, -en *f.*
indirect, *adj.* indirekt.
indiscreet, *adj.* indiskret.
indiscretion, *n.* Indiskretion', -en *f.*
indispensable, *adj.* unabkömmlich.
indisposed, *adj.* unpäßlich; (disinclined) abgeneigt.
indisposition, *n.* Unpäßlichkeit, -en *f.*; Abneigung, -en *f.*
individual, 1. *n.* Einzeln- *m.*, Indivi'duum, -duen *nt.* **2.** *adj.* einzeln, individuell'.
individuality, *n.* Individualität', -en *f.*
indivisible, *adj.* unteilbar.
indoctrinate, *vb.* schulen.
indolent, *adj.* träge.
Indonesia, *n.* Indone'sien *nt.*
indoor, *adj.* Haus-, Zimmer- (cpds.).
indoors, *adv.* zu Hause, drinnen.
induce, *vb.* veran'lassen; (elec.) induzie'ren.
induct, *vb.* ein'führen; (physics) induzie'ren; (mil.) verei'digen.
induction, *n.* Einführung, -en *f.*; (physics) Induktion', -en *f.*; (mil.) Verei'digung, -en *f.*
inductive, *adj.* induktiv'.
indulge, *vb.* nach'sehen*; frönen.
indulgence, *n.* Nachsicht, -en *f.*, Langmut *m.*, Frönen *nt.*; (eccles.) Ablaß, -sse *m.*

indulgent, *adj.* nachsichtig, langmütig.
industrial, *adj.* industriell', Industrie'- (cpds.).
industrialist, *n.* Industriell' *m.*
industrious, *adj.* fleißig.
industry, *n.* Industrie', -i'en *f.*; (hard work) Fleiß *m.*
ineligible, *adj.* unwählbar; nicht in Frage kommend.
inept, *adj.* ungeschickt, unfähig.
inert, *adj.* träge.
inertia, *n.* Trägheit, -en *f.*
inevitable, *adj.* unvermeidlich.
infallible, *adj.* unfehlbar.
infamous, *adj.* berüch'tigt.
infamy, *n.* Niedertracht, -en *f.*, Schande, -n *f.*
infancy, *n.* Kindheit, -en *f.*; (fig.) Anfang, -̈e *m.*
infant, *n.* Säugling, -e *m.*
infantile, *adj.* kindlich, kindisch.
infantry, *n.* Infanterie', -i'en *f.*
infantryman, *n.* Infanterist', -en, -en *m.*
infatuate, *vb.* betö'ren, hinreißen*.
infect, *vb.* an'stecken.
infected, *adj.* infiziert.
infection, *n.* Entzün'dung, -en *f.*
infectious, *adj.* ansteckend.
infer, *vb.* folgern, an'nehmen*.
inference, *n.* Folgerung, -en *f.*, Annahme, -n *f.*
inferior, *adj.* minderwertig, unterle'gen.
inferiority, *n.* Minderwertigkeit, -en *f.*, Unterle'genheit *f.*
infernal, *adj.* höllisch.
inferno, *n.* Hölle *f.*; Fegefeuer *nt.*
infest, *vb.* heim'suchen.
infidel, *n.* Ungläubig- *m. & f.*
infidelity, *n.* Untreue *f.*
infiltrate, *vb.* ein'dringen*, infiltrie'ren.
infinite, *adj.* unendlich.
infinitesimal, *adj.* unendlich klein; winzig.
infinitive, *n.* Infinitiv, -e *m.*
infinity, *n.* Unendlichkeit, -en *f.*
infirm, *adj.* schwach (-̈).
infirmary, *n.* Schul- oder Studen'tenkrankenhaus, -̈er *nt.*
infirmity, *n.* Schwachheit, -en *f.*
inflame, *vb.* entzün'den.

inflammable, *adj.* entzünd'bar, feuergefährlich.

inflammation, *n.* Entzün'dung, -en *f.*

inflate, *vb.* auf•blasen*; *(tires)* auf•pumpen

inflation, *n.* Inflation', -en *f.*

inflection, *n.* Biegung, -en *f.; (voice)* Tonfall, -̈e *m.; (gram.)* Beugung, -en *f.*

inflict, *vb.* zu•fügen.

infliction, *n.* Last, -en *f.*

influence, 1. *n.* Einfluß, -̈sse *m.* **2.** *vb.* beein'flussen.

influential, *adj.* einflußreich.

influenza, *n.* Grippe, -n *f.*

inform, *vb.* benach'richtigen, mit•teilen; **(i. on)** denunzie'ren.

informal, *adj.* zwanglos, nicht for-mell'.

information, *n.* Auskunft, -̈e *f.,* Information', *f.*

infringe, *vb.* übertre'ten*; *(jur.)* verlet'zen.

infuriate, *vb.* wütend machen, ra-send machen, erbo'sen.

ingenious, *adj.* erfin'derisch, ge-nial'.

ingenuity, *n.* Findigkeit *f.,* Genialität' *f.*

ingredient, *n.* Bestand'teil, -e *m.; (cooking)* Zutat, -en *f.*

inhabit, *vb.* bewoh'nen.

inhabitant, *n.* Bewoh'ner, - *m.,* Bewoh'nerin, -nen *f.,* Einwohner, - *m.* Einwohnerin, -nen *f.*

inhale, *vb.* ein•atmen.

inherent, *adj.* angeboren, eigen.

inherit, *vb.* erben.

inheritance, *n.* Erbe *nt.;* Erb-schaft, -en *f.*

inhibit, *vb.* hindern, ab•halten*.

inhibited, *adj.* gehemmt'.

inhibition, *n.* Hemmung, -en *f.*

inhuman, *adj.* unmenschlich.

inimitable, *adj.* unnachahmlich.

iniquity, *n.* Ungerechtigkeit, -en *f.;* Schändlichkeit, -en *f.*

initial, 1. *n.* Anfangsbuchstabe, -n, -n *m.* **2.** *adj.* anfänglich; An-fangs- *(cpds.).*

initiate, *vb.* ein•führen, ein•wei-hen.

initiation, *n.* Einführung, -en *f.,* Einweihung, -en *f.*

initiative, *n.* Initiati've, -n *f.*

inject, *vb.* ein•spritzen.

injection, *n.* Einspritzung, -en *f.*

injunction, *n.* gerichtlicher Un-terlas'sungsbefehl, -e *m.*

injure, *vb.* verlet'zen.

injurious, *adj.* schädlich; *(fig.)* nachteilig.

injury, *n.* Verlet'zung, -en *f.;* Schaden, -̈ *m.*

injustice, *n.* Ungerechtigkeit, -en *f.*

ink, *n.* Tinte, -n *f.*

inland, 1. *n.* Binnenland, -̈er *nt.* **2.** *adj.* inländisch.

inlet, *n.* kleine Bucht, -en *f.*

inmate, *n.* Insasse, -n, -n *m.,* In-sassin, -nen *f.*

inn, *n.* Gasthaus, -̈er *nt.,* Wirt-shaus, -̈er *nt.*

inner, *adj.* inner-.

innermost, *adj.* innerst-.

innocence, *n.* Unschuld *f.*

innocent, *adj.* unschuldig.

innovation, *n.* Neuerung, -en *f.*

innuendo, *n.* Unterstel'lung, -en *f.*

innumerable, *adj.* zahllos.

inoculate, *vb.* ein•impfen.

inoculation, *n.* Einimpfung, -en *f.*

input, *n.* Input, -s *m.;* Eingabe, -n *f.*

inquest, *n.* gerichtliche Untersu-chung, -en *f.*

inquire, *vb.* fragen, sich erkun'di-gen.

inquiry, *n.* Nachfrage, -n *f.,* Er-kun'digung, -en *f.*

inquisition, *n.* Untersu'chung, -en *f.; (eccles.)* Inquisition', -en *f.*

inquisitive, *adj.* neugierig.

insane, *adj.* wahnsinnig, un-zurechnungsfähig.

insanity, *n.* Wahnsinn *m.*

insatiable, *adj.* unersättlich.

inscribe, *vb.* ein•zeichnen, ein•schreiben*.

inscription, *n.* Inschrift, -en *f.*

insect, *n.* Insekt', -en *nt.*

insecticide, *n.* Insek'tenpulver, - *nt.*

insensible, *adj.* gefühl'los.

insensitive, *adj.* unempfindlich.

inseparable, *adj.* unzertrennlich.

insert, 1. *n.* Beilage, -n *f.* 2. *vb.* ein·fügen, ein·setzen.

insertion, *n.* Einsatz, ⸚e *m.*

inside, 1. *n.* Innenseite, -n *f.,* Inner- *nt.* 2. *adj.* inner-. 3. *adv.* innen, drinnen.

insidious, *adj.* hinterlistig.

insight, *n.* Einsicht, *-en f.*

insignia, *n.pl.* Abzeichen, - *nt.;* Insig'nien *pl.*

insignificance, *n.* Bedeu'tungslosigkeit *f.*

insignificant, *adj.* bedeu'tungslos.

insinuate, *vb.* an·spielen auf; (i. oneself) sich ein·schmeicheln.

insinuation, *n.* Anspielung, -en *f.*

insipid, *adj.* fade.

insist, *vb.* beste'hen*, behar'ren.

insistence, *n.* Beste'hen *nt.,* Behar'ren *nt.*

insistent, *adj.* beharr'lich, hartnäckig.

insolence, *n.* Unverschämt'heit, -en *f.*

insolent, *adj.* unverschämt.

insomnia, *n.* Schlaflosigkeit *f.*

inspect, *vb.* besich'tigen.

inspection, *n.* Besich'tigung, -en *f.*

inspector, *n.* Inspek'tor, -o'ren *m.,* Inspekto'rin, -nen *f.*

inspiration, *n.* Eingebung, -en *f.,* Inspiration', -en *f.*

inspire, *vb.* an·feuern, begei'stern.

install, *vb.* ein·bauen; *(fig.)* ein·führen.

installation, *n.* Installation', -en *f.*

installment, *n.* Rate, -n *f.;* (i. plan) Ratenzahlung, -en *f.*

instance, *n. (case)* Fall, ⸚e *m.; (example)* Beispiel, -e *nt.; (law)* Instanz', -en *f.;* (for i.) zum Beispiel.

instant, 1. *n.* Augenblick, -e *m.* 2. *adj.* augenblicklich.

instantaneous, *adj.* sofor'tig.

instantly, *adv.* sofort', auf der Stelle.

instead, *adv.* statt dessen, dafür; (i. of) statt, anstatt'.

instigate, *vb.* veran'lassen, an·stacheln.

instill, *vb.* ein·flößen.

instinct, *n.* Instinkt', -e *m.*

instinctive, *adj.* unwillkürlich, instinktiv'.

institute, 1. *n.* Institut', -e *nt.* 2. *vb.* ein·leiten, an·ordnen.

institution, *n.* Einrichtung, -en *f.;* Institut', -e *nt.,* Anstalt, -en *f.*

instruct, *vb.* unterrich'ten, an·weisen*.

instruction, *n.* Anweisung, -en *f.; (school)* Unterricht *m.*

instructive, *adj.* lehrreich.

instructor, *n.* Lehrer, - *m.*

instructress, *n.* Lehrerin, -nen *f.*

instrument, *n.* Werkzeug, -e *nt.,* Instrument', -e *nt.*

instrumental, *adj.* behilf'lich; *(music)* Instrumental'- *(cpds.).*

insufferable, *adj.* unerträglich.

insufficient, *adj.* ungenügend.

insulate, *vb.* isolie'ren.

insulation, *n.* Isolie'rung, -en *f.*

insulator, *n.* Isola'tor, -o'ren *m.*

insulin, *n.* Insulin' *nt.*

insult, 1. *n.* Belei'digung, -en *f.* 2. *vb.* belei'digen.

insurance, *n.* Versi'cherung, -en *f.*

insure, *vb.* versi'chern.

insurgent, 1. *n.* Aufständisch - *m.* 2. *adj.* aufständisch.

insurrection, *n.* Aufstand, ⸚e *m.*

intact, *adj.* intakt'.

intangible, *adj.* nicht greifbar.

integral, 1. *n. (math.)* Integral', -e *nt.* 2. *adj.* unerläßlich.

integrate, *vb.* integrie'ren.

integrity, *n.* Unbescholtenheit *f.*

intellect, *n.* Verstand' *m.,* Intellekt' *m.*

intellectual, 1. *n.* Intellektuell- *m.& f.* 2. *adj.* intellektuell'.

intelligence, *n.* Intelligenz' *f.*

intelligent, *adj.* intelligent'.

intelligentsia, *n.* geistige Oberschicht *f.*

intelligible, *adj.* verständ'lich.

intend, *vb.* beab'sichtigen.

intense, *adj.* angespannt, intensiv'.

intensify, *vb.* verstär'ken.

intensive, *adj.* intensiv'.

intent, 1. *n.* Absicht, -en *f.* 2. *adj.* erpicht'.

intention, *n.* Absicht, -en *f.*

intentional, *adj.* absichtlich.

inter, vb. beer'digen.

intercede, vb. dazwi'schentreten*.

intercept, vb. ab'fangen*.

intercourse, n. Verkehr' m., Umgang m.

interest, 1. n. Interes'se, -n nt.; (comm.) Zins, -en m. **2.** vb. interessie'ren.

interesting, adj. interessant'.

interface, n. Schnittstelle, -n f.

interfere, vb. sich ein'mischen; ein'greifen*.

interference, n. Einmischung, -en f.; (radio) Störung, -en f.

interim, 1. n. Zwischenzeit, -en f. **2.** adj. Interims- (cpds.).

interior, 1. n. Inner- nt. **2.** adj. inner-; Innen- (cpds.).

interject, vb. dazwi'schenwerfen*.

interjection, n. Ausruf, -e m.; (gram.) Interjektion', -en f.

interlude, n. Zwischenspiel, -e nt.

intermarry, vb. untereinander heiraten.

intermediary, 1. n. Vermitt'ler, -m., Vermitt'lerin, -nen f. **2.** adj. Zwischen- (cpds.).

intermediate, adj. Zwischen- (cpds.).

interment, n. Begräb'nis, -se nt.

intermission, n. Unterbre'chung, -en f.; (theater) Pause, -n f.

intermittent, adj. wechselnd, perio'disch.

intern, vb. internie'ren.

intern, n. Volontär'arzt, -̈e m., Volontär'ärztin, -nen f.

internal, adj. inner-, innerlich.

international, adj. international'.

internationalism, n. Internationalis'mus m.

interne, n. Volontär'arzt, -̈e m.

interpose, vb. ein'fügen.

interpret, vb. interpretie'ren; (language) dolmetschen.

interpretation, n. Interpretation', -en f., Auslegung, -en f.

interpreter, n. Dolmetscher, - m., Dolmetscherin, -nen f.

interrogate, vb. aus'fragen; (law) verneh'men*, verhö'ren.

interrogation, n. Verhör', -e nt.

interrogative, 1. n. Fragewort, -̈er nt. **2.** adj. fragend, Frage- (cpds.).

interrupt, vb. unterbre'chen*.

interruption, n. Unterbre'chung, -en f.

intersect, vb. (intr.) sich schneiden*, sich kreuzen; (tr.) durchschnei'den, durchkreu'zen.

intersection, n. Kreuzung, -en f.

intersperse, vb. durchset'zen.

interval, n. Abstand, -̈e m.

intervene, vb. dazwi'schenkommen*, sich ein'mischen.

intervention, n. Dazwi'schentreten nt., Einmischung, -en f.

interview, 1. n. Interview' -s nt., Vorstellungsgespräch, -e nt. **2.** vb. interview'en.

intestine, n. Darm, -̈e m.

intimacy, n. Vertrau'lichkeit, -en f.

intimate, adj. vertraut', innig.

intimidate, vb. ein'schüchtern.

intimidation, n. Einschüchterung, -en f.

into, prep. in.

intolerant, adj. intolerant.

intonation, n. Tonfall, -̈e m.

intoxicate, vb. berau'schen.

intoxication, n. Rausch, -̈e m.

intravenous, adj. intravenös'.

intrepid, adj. furchtlos.

intricacy, n. Kompliziert'heit, -en f.

intricate, adj. verwi'ckelt; kompliziert'.

intrigue, 1. n. Intri'ge, -n f. **2.** vb. intrigie'ren.

intrinsic, adj. innerlich; wahr.

introduce, vb. ein'führen, ein'leiten; (persons) vor'stellen.

introduction, n. Einführung, -en f., Einleitung, -en f.; Vorstellung, -en f.

introductory, adj. einleitend.

introvert, n. nach innen gekehr'ter Mensch, -en m.

intrude, vb. ein'dringen*.

intruder, n. Eindringling, -e m.

intuition, n. Intuition', -en f.

inundate, vb. überschwem'men.

invade, *vb.* ein·dringen*, ein·fallen*.

invader, *n.* Angreifer - *m.*

invalid, **1.** *n.* Invali'de, -n, -n *m.* **2.** *adj.* ungültig.

invariable, *adj.* unveränderlich.

invasion, *n.* Invasion', -en *f.*

inveigle, *vb.* verlei'ten.

invent, *vb.* erfin'den*.

invention, *n.* Erfin'dung, -en *f.*

inventive, *adj.* erfin'derisch.

inventor, *n.* Erfin'der - *m.*, Erfin'derin, -nen *f.*

inventory, *n.* Inventar', -e *nt.*; Inventur', -en *f.*

inverse, *adj.* umgekehrt.

invertebrate, *adj.* ohne Wirbelsäule.

invest, *vb.* investie'ren, an·legen.

investigate, *vb.* untersu'chen.

investigation, *n.* Untersu'chung, -en *f.*

investment, *n.* Kapitals'anlage, -n *f.*

inveterate, *adj.* eingefleischt.

invigorate, *vb.* bele'ben, erfri'schen.

invincible, *adj.* unbesiegbar.

invisible, *adj.* unsichtbar.

invitation, *n.* Einladung, -en *f.*; Aufforderung, -en *f.*

invite, *vb.* ein·laden*, auf·fordern.

invocation, *n.* Anrufung, -en *f.*; *(eccles.)* Bittgebet, -en *nt.*

invoice, *n.* Warenrechnung, -en *f.*

invoke, *vb.* an·rufen*; erbit'ten.

involuntary, *adj.* unfreiwillig.

involve, *vb.* ein·schließen*; verwi'ckeln.

involved, *adj.* verwi'ckelt.

invulnerable, *adj.* unverletzlich; uneinnehmbar.

inward, *adj.* inner-, innerlich.

inwardly, *adv.* innerlich.

iodine, *n.* Jod *nt.*

Iran, *n.* Iran' *nt.*

Iraq, *n.* Irak' *m.*

irate, *adj.* zornig.

Ireland, *n.* Irland *nt.*

iridium, *n.* Iri'dium *nt.*

iris, *n.* Iris *f.*; *(flower)* Schwertlilie, -n *f.*

Irish, *adj.* irisch.

Irishman, *n.* Irländer - *m.*, Ire, -n, -n *m.*

Irishwoman, *n.* Irländerin, -nen *f.*

irk, *vb.* ärgern.

iron, **1.** *n.* Eisen *nt.*; **(flati.)** Bügeleisen, - *nt.* **2.** *adj.* eisern. **3.** *vb.* bügeln.

ironical, *adj.* spöttisch, iro'nisch.

irony, *n.* Spott *m.*, Ironie' *f.*

irrational, *adj.* irrational'.

irrefutable, *adj.* unwiderlegbar.

irregular, *adj.* unregelmäßig.

irregularity, *n.* Unregelmäßigkeit, -en *f.*

irrelevant, *adj.* belang'los; unanwendbar.

irresistible, *adj.* unwiderstehlich.

irresponsible, *adj.* unverantwortlich.

irreverent, *adj.* unehrerbietig.

irrevocable, *adj.* unwiderruflich.

irrigate, *vb.* bewäs'sern.

irrigation, *n.* Bewäs'serung, -en *f.*

irritability, *n.* Reizbarkeit *f.*

irritable, *adj.* reizbar.

irritant, *n.* Reizfaktor, -en *m.*

irritate, *vb.* reizen, irritie'ren.

irritation, *n.* Reizung, -en *f.*; Ärger *m.*

island, *n.* Insel, -n *f.*

isolate, *vb.* isolie'ren.

isolation, *n.* Isolie'rung, -en *f.*

isolationist, *n.* Isolationist', -en, -en *m.*

Israel, *n.* Israel *nt.*

Israeli, **1.** *n.* Israe'li, -s *m&f.* **2.** *adj.* israe'lisch.

Israelite, **1.** *n.* Israelit', -en, -en *m.* **2.** *adj.* israeli'tisch.

issuance, *n.* Ausgabe, -n *f.*

issue, **1.** *n.* Ausgabe, -n *f.*; Problem', -e *nt.*; *(result)* Ergeb'nis, -se *nt.* **2.** *vb.* aus·geben*, aus·stellen.

isthmus, *n.* Isthmus, -men *m.*

it, *pron.* es.

Italian, **1.** *n.* Italie'ner, - *m.*, Italie'nerin, -nen *f.* **2.** *adj.* italie'nisch.

italic, *adj.* ita'lisch.

italics, *n.* Kursiv'schrift *f.*

Italy, *n.* Ita'lien *nt.*

itch, **1.** *n.* Jucken *nt.* **2.** *vb.* jucken.

item, *n.* Arti'kel, - *m.*, Posten, - *m.*

itemize, *vb.* auf·zählen.

itinerary, *n.* Reiseroute, -n *f.*

ivory, *n.* Elfenbein *nt.*

ivy, *n.* Efeu *m.*

jab, 1. n. Stoß, ∺e m., Stich, -e m. **2.** vb. stoßen*, stechen*.

jack, n. (auto) Wagenheber, - m.; (card) Bube, -n, -n m.

jackal, n. Schakal, -e m.

jackass, n. Esel, - m.

jacket, n. Jacke, -n f.

jack-knife, n. Klappmesser, - nt.

jack-of-all-trades, n. Hansdampf in allen Gassen m.

jade, n. Jade m.

jaded, adj. ermat'tet.

jagged, adj. zackig.

jail, n. Gefäng'nis, -se nt.

jailer, n. Gefäng'niswärter, - m., Gefäng'niswärterin, -nen f.

jam, 1. n. Marmela'de, -n f., Konfitüre, -n f.; (trouble) Klemme, -n f. **2.** vb. klemmen.

jangle, vb. rasseln.

janitor, n. Pförtner, - m., Hausmeister, - m.

January, n. Januar m.

Japan, n. Japan nt.

Japanese, 1. n. Japa'ner, - m., Japa'nerin, -nen f. **2.** adj. japa'nisch.

jar, 1. n. Krug, ∺e m., Glas, ∺er nt. **2.** vb. rütteln.

jargon, n. Jargon', -s m.

jasmine, n. Jasmin', -s m.

jaundice, n. Gelbsucht f.

jaunt, n. kurze Reise, -n f.

javelin, n. Speer, -e m.

jaw, n. Kiefer, - m.

jay, n. Eichelhäher, - m.

jaywalk, vb. quer über eine Straßenkreuzung gehen*.

jazz, n. Jazz m.

jealous, adj. eifersüchtig.

jealousy, n. Eifersucht f.

jeans, n. Jeans pl.

jeer, vb. spotten.

jelly, n. Gelee, -s nt.

jeopardize, vb. gefähr'den.

jeopardy, n. Gefahr', -en f.

jerk, 1. n. Ruck, -e m. **2.** vb. ruckartig bewe'gen.

jerky, adj. ruckartig.

jersey, n. Jersey, -s f.

Jerusalem, n. Jeru'salem nt.

jest, 1. n. Scherz, -e m. **2.** vb. scherzen.

jester, n. Spaßmacher, - m.; (court j.) Hofnarr, -en, -en m.

Jesuit, 1. n. Jesuit', -en, -en m. **2.** adj. jesui'tisch; Jesui'ten- (cpds.).

Jesus Christ, n. Jesus Christus m.

jet, n. Strahl, -en m.; (tech.) Düse, -n f.; (plane) Düsenflugzeug, -e nt.; (mineral) Pechkohle, -n f.

jet lag, n. Jet-lag m.; körperliches Unbehagen durch Zeitverschiebung.

jetsam, n. Strandgut nt.; über Bord gewor'fenes Gut nt.

jetty, n. Mole, -n f.

Jew, n. Jude, -n, -n m., Jüdin, -nen f.

jewel, n. Juwel', -en nt., Edelstein, -e m.

jeweler, n. Juwelier', -e m., Juwelie'rin, -nen f.

jewelry, n. Schmucksachen pl., Schmuck m.

Jewish, adj. jüdisch.

jib, n. Klüver, - m.

jibe, vb. (sailing) halsen; (agree) sich decken.

jiffy, n. Nu m.

jig, n. Gigue f.

jilt, vb. sitzen lassen*.

jingle, vb. klingeln.

job, n. Stellung, -en f.; Aufgabe, -n f.

jobber, n. Zwischenhändler, - m., Zwischenhändlerin, -nen f.

jockey, n. Jockey, -s m.

jocular, adj. scherzhaft.

jog, vb. (push) schubsen; (run) joggen.

joggle, vb. (tr.) stubsen; (intr.) wackeln.

join, vb. verbin'den*; (club, etc.) bei'treten*.

joint, 1. n. Gelenk', -e nt. **2.** adj. gemein'sam.

joist, n. Querbalken, - m.

joke, 1. n. Witz, -e m., Scherz, -e m., Spaß, ∺e m. **2.** vb. einen Witz machen, scherzen.

joker, n. Witzbold, -e m.; (cards) Joker, - m.

jolly, adj. heiter.

jolt, 1. *n.* Stoß, ⁼e *m.* **2.** *vb.* rütteln.
jonquil, *n.* gelbe Narzis'se, -n *f.*
jostle, *vb.* stoßen*.
journal, *n.* Journal', -e *nt.;* *(diary)* Tagebuch, ⁼er *nt.; (newspaper)* Zeitung, -en *f.; (periodical)* Zeitschrift, -en *f.*
journalism, *n.* Zeitungswesen *nt.*
journalist, *n.* Journalist', -en, -en *m.,* Journali'stin, -nen *f.*
journey, *n.* Reise, -n *f.*
journeyman, *n.* Gesel'le, -n, -n *m.*
jovial, *adj.* jovial'.
jowl, *n.* Backe, -n *f.*
joy, *n.* Freude, -n *f.*
joyful, *adj.* freudig.
joyous, *adj.* freudig.
jubilant, *adj.* frohlockend.
jubilee, *n.* Jubilä'um, -ä'en *nt.*
Judaism, *n.* Judentum *nt.*
judge, 1. *n.* Kenner, - *m.; (law)* Richter, - *m.,* Richterin, -nen *f.* **2.** *vb.* beur'teilen; *(law)* richten, Recht sprechen*.
judgment, *n.* Urteil, -e *nt.; (law also:)* Rechtsspruch, ⁼e *m.*
judicial, *adj.* richterlich; Gerichts'- *(cpds.).*
judiciary, 1. *n.* Justiz'gewalt *f.;* Richterstand *m.* **2.** *adj.* richterlich.
judicious, *adj.* weise, klug.
jug, *n.* Krug, ⁼e *m.*
juggle, *vb.* jonglie'ren.
juggler, *n.* Jongleur', -e *m.*
juice, *n.* Saft, ⁼e *m.*

juicy, *adj.* saftig.
July, *n.* Juli *m.*
jumble, *n.* Durcheinan'der *nt.*
jump, 1. *n.* Sprung, ⁼e *m.* **2.** *vb.* springen*.
junction, *n.* Verbin'dung, -en *f.; (railroad)* Knotenpunkt, -e *m.*
juncture, *n.* Zusam'mentreffen, - *nt.*
June, *n.* Juni *m.*
jungle, *n.* Dschungel, - *m. or nt. (or* -n *f.).*
junior, *adj.* jünger.
juniper, *n.* Wachol'der, - *m.*
junk, *n.* Altwaren *pl.; (fig.)* Kram *m.*
junket, *n. (food)* Milchpudding *m.; (trip)* Reise, -n *f.*
jurisdiction, *n.* Rechtsprechung, -en *f.;* Gerichts'barkeit *f.;* Zuständigkeit *f.*
jurisprudence, *n.* Rechtswissenschaft *f.*
jurist, *n.* Rechtsgelehrt- *m. & f.*
juror, *n.* Geschwo'ren- *m. & f.*
jury, *n.* Geschwo'ren- *pl.*
just, 1. *adj.* gerecht'. **2.** *adv.* gera'de, eben.
justice, *n.* Gerech'tigkeit *f.*
justifiable, *adj.* berech'tigt.
justification, *n.* Rechtfertigung, -en *f.;* Berech'tigung, -en *f.*
justify, *vb.* rechtfertigen.
jut, *vb.* hervor'stehen*.
jute, *n.* Jute *f.*
juvenile, *adj.* jugendlich.

K

kale, *n.* Grünkohl *m.*
kaleidoscope, *n.* Kaleidoskop', -e *nt.*
kangaroo, *n.* Känguruh', -s *nt.*
karat, *n.* Karat, -e *nt.*
karate, *n.* Kara'te *nt.*
keel, *n.* Kiel, -e *m.*
keen, *adj.* scharf; *(fig.)* eifrig.
keep, 1. *n. (lodging)* Unterhalt *m.* **2.** *vb.* behal'ten*, bewah'ren; *(animals, etc.)* halten*; **(k. doing something)** etwas immer wieder tun*; **(k. on doing something)** etwas weiter tun*.

keeper, *n.* Wärter, - *m.,* Wärterin, -nen *f.,* Wächter, - *m.,* Wächterin, -nen *f.*
keepsake, *n.* Andenken, - *nt.*
keg, *n.* Faß, ⁼sser *nt.*
kennel, *n.* Hundezwinger, - *m.*
kerchief, *n.* Halstuch, ⁼er *nt.;* Kopftuch, ⁼er *nt.*
kernel, *n.* Kern, -e *m.; (grain)* Korn, ⁼er *nt.*
kerosene, *n.* Kerosin' *nt.*
ketchup, *n.* Ketchup *nt.*
kettle, *n.* Kessel, - *m.*

kettledrum, *n.* Kesselpauke, -n *f.*

key, *n.* Schlüssel, - *m.; (piano)* Taste, -n *f.; (musical structure)* Tonart, -en *f.*

keyhole, *n.* Schlüsselloch, ᵉer *nt.*

khaki, *n.* Khaki *nt.*

kick, 1. *n.* Stoß, ᵉe *m.,* Tritt, -e *m.* **2.** *vb.* stoßen*, treten*.

kid, 1. *n. (goat)* Zicklein, - *nt.; (child)* Kind, -er *nt.* **2.** *vb.* necken, rein·legen.

kidnap, *vb.* gewalt'sam entfüh'ren.

kidnaper, *n.* Kinderräuber, - *m.,* Kinderräuberin, -nen *f.*

kidnaping, *n.* Kinderraub *m.*

kidney, *n.* Niere, -n *f.*

kidney bean, *n.* Schminkbohne, -n *f.*

kill, *vb.* töten, um·bringen*.

killer, *n.* Mörder, - *m.*

kiln, *n.* Brennofen, ᵉ *m.*

kilocycle, *n.* Kilohertz, - *nt.*

kilogram, *n.* Kilo, -s *nt.*

kilohertz, *n.* Kilohertz, - *nt.*

kilometer, *n.* Kilome'ter, - *nt.*

kilowatt, *n.* Kilowatt, - *nt.*

kilt, *n.* Kilt, -s *m.*

kimono, *n.* Kimo'no, -s *m.*

kin, *n.* Verwandt'schaft, -en *f.*

kind, 1. *n.* Art, -en *f.,* Sorte, -n *f.* **2.** *adj.* gütig, freundlich.

kindergarten, *n.* Kindergarten, - *m.*

kindle, *vb.* an·zünden, entzün'den.

kindly, *adj.* freundlich.

kindness, *n.* Güte *f.,* Freundlichkeit *f.*

kindred, *adj.* verwandt'.

king, *n.* König, -e *m.*

kingdom, *n.* Königreich, -e *nt.*

kink, *n.* Knoten, - *m.*

kiosk, *n.* Kiosk, -e *m.*

kiss, 1. *n.* Kuß, ᵉsse *m.* **2.** *vb.* küssen.

kitchen, *n.* Küche, -n *f.*

kite, *n.* Drachen, - *m.; (bird)* Milan, -e *m.*

kitten, *n.* Kätzchen, - *nt.*

kleptomaniac, *n.* Kleptoma'ne, -n, -n *m.*

knack, *n.* Talent', -e *nt.*

knapsack, *n.* Rucksack, ᵉe *m.*

knead, *vb.* kneten.

knee, *n.* Knie, Kni'e *nt.*

kneel, *vb.* knien.

knickers, *n.pl.* Kniehose, -n *f.*

knife, *n.* Messer, - *nt.*

knight, *nn.* Ritter, - *m.; (chess)* Springer, - *m.*

knit, *vb.* stricken; *(fig.)* verknüp'fen.

knock, 1. *n.* Klopfen *nt.* **2.** *vb.* klopfen.

knot, 1. *n.* Knoten, - *m.; (wood)* Knorren, - *m.* **2.** *vb.* knoten.

knotty, *adj.* knotig; *(wood)* knorrig; *(fig.)* schwierig.

know, *vb. (facts)* wissen*; *(people, places, things)* kennen'*.

knowledge, *n.* Kenntnis, -se *f.;* Wissen *nt.*

knuckle, *n.* Knöchel, - *m.*

Korea, *n.* Kore'a *nt.*

L

label, *n.* Etiket'te, -n *f.*

labor, 1. *n.* Arbeit, -en *f.; (workers)* Arbeiterschaft *f.; (birth)* Wehen *pl.* **2.** *vb.* arbeiten.

laboratory, *n.* Laborato'rium, -rien *nt.*

laborer, *n.* Arbeiter, - *m.*

laborious, *adj.* arbeitsam, mühselig.

labor union, *n.* Gewerk'schaft, -en *f.*

labyrinth, *n.* Labyrinth', -e *nt.*

lace, *n.* Spitze, -n *f.*

lacerate, *vb.* auf·reißen*.

laceration, *n.* Riß, -sse *m.*

lack, 1. *n.* Mangel, ᵉ *m.* **2.** *vb.* Mangel leiden* an; **(I l. something)** es fehlt, mangelt mir an etwas.

lackadaisical, *adj.* schwunglos, unlustig.

laconic, *adj.* lako'nisch.

lacquer, 1. *n.* Lack, -e *m.* **2.** *vb.* lackie'ren.

lacy, *adj.* spitzenartig; Spitzen- *(cpds.).*

lad, n. Knabe, -n, -n m.
ladder, n. Leiter, -n f.
ladle, n. Schöpflöffel, - m.
lady, n. Dame, -n f.
ladybug, n. Mari'enkäfer, - m.
lag, n. Verzö'gerung, -en f.
lag behind, vb. zurück'bleiben*.
lagoon, n. Lagu'ne, -n f.
laid-back, adj. entspannt, unverkrampft.
lair, n. Lagerstätte, -n f.; Höhle, -n f.
laity, n. Laienstand m., Laien pl.
lake, n. See, Se'en m.
lamb, n. Lamm, ¨er nt.
lame, adj. lahm.
lament, 1. n. Wehklage, -n f. 2. vb. bekla'gen.
lamentable, adj. bekla'genswert.
lamentation, n. Wehklage, -n f.
laminate, vb. (metal) aus·walzen, plattie'ren; (l.d wood) Furnier'holz nt.
lamp, n. Lampe, -n f.
lance, 1. n. Lanze, -n f. 2. vb. durchsto'ßen*; (med.) mit der Lanzet'te öffnen.
land, 1. n. (country) Land, ¨er nt.; (ground) Grund und Boden m. 2. vb. landen.
landing, n. Landung, -en f.; (stairs) Treppenabsatz, ¨e m.
landlady, n. Wirtin, -nen f.; Hausbesitzerin, -nen f.
landlord, n. Wirt, -e m.; Hausbesitzer, - m.
landmark, n. Markstein, -e m.
landscape, n. Landschaft, -en f.
landslide, n. Erdrutsch, -e m.; (election) überwäl'tigender Wahlsieg, -e m.
lane, n. Pfad, -e m.; (boat) Fahrrinne, -n f.; (auto) Fahrbahn, -en f.
language, n. Sprache, -n f.
languid, adj. energie'los, schlaff.
languish, vb. schmachten.
lanky, adj. baumlang.
lanolin, n. Lanolin' nt.
lantern, n. Later'ne, -n f.
lap, 1. n. Schoß, ¨e m.; (sport) Runde, -n f. 2. vb. übereinan'der·legen.

lapel, n. Revers', - m.
lapin, n. Kanin'chenpelz m.
lapse, 1. n. (error) Lapsus, - m., Verse'hen, - nt.; (time) Zwischenzeit, -en f. 2. vb. verstrei'chen*.
larceny, n. Diebstahl, ¨e m.
lard, n. Schweinefett m.
large, adj. groß (größer, größt-); weit; umfangreich.
largely, adv. größtenteils.
largo, n. Largo, -s nt.
lariat, n. Lasso, -s nt.
lark, n. Lerche, -n f.; (fun) Vergnü'gen nt.
larkspur, n. Rittersporn m.
larva, n. Larve, -n f.
laryngitis, n. Kehlkopfentzündung, -en f.
larynx, n. Kehlkopf, ¨e m.
lascivious, adj. wollüstig.
laser, n. Laser m.
lash, 1. n. Peitsche, -n f.; Peitschenhieb, -e m.; (eye) Wimper, -n f. 2. vb. peitschen.
lass, n. Mädchen, - nt.
lasso, n. Lasso, -s nt.
last, 1. n. Leisten, - m. 2. adj. letzt-, 3. vb. dauern.
lasting, adj. dauernd, anhaltend, bestän'dig.
latch, 1. n. Klinke, -n f. 2. vb. ein·klinken.
late, adj. spät, verspä'tet; (dead) verstor'ben.
lately, adv. in letzter Zeit.
latent, adj. latent.
lateral, adj. seitlich.
lath, n. Latte, -n f.
lathe, n. Drehbank, ¨e f.
lather, n. Schaum m.
Latin, 1. n. (language) Latein' nt.; (person) Roma'ne, -n, -n m. 2. adj. latei'nisch; roma'nisch.
latitude, n. Breite, -n f.
latrine, n. Latri'ne, -n f.
latter, 1. adj. letzter-. 2. pron. (the l.) dieser, -es, -e.
lattice, n. Gitterwerk nt.
laud, vb. loben, preisen*.
laudable, adj. lobenswert.
laudanum, n. Laudanum nt.
laudatory, adj. Lob- (cpds.).
laugh, 1. n. Lachen nt. 2. vb. lachen.
laughable, adj. lächerlich.

laughter, n. Gelächter nt.

launch, 1. n. Barkasse, -n f. **2.** vb. *(throw)* schleudern; *(boat)* vom Stapel lassen*.

launching, n. Stapellauf, -e m.

launder, vb. waschen*.

laundress, n. Waschfrau, -en f.

laundry, n. *(clothes)* Wäsche f.; *(establishment)* Wäscherei, -en f.

laundryman, n. Wäscherei'angestellt- m.

laurel, n. Lorbeer, -en m.

lava, n. Lava f.

lavatory, n. Waschraum, -e m.

lavender, n. Laven'del m.

lavish, adj. üppig.

law, n. *(individual)* Gesetz' -e nt.; *(system)* Recht nt.

lawful, adj. gesetz'lich, rechtmäßig.

lawless, adj. gesetz'los; *(fig.)* zügellos.

lawn, n. Rasen m.

lawsuit, n. Prozeß', -sse m.

lawyer, n. Rechtsanwalt, -e m., Rechtsanwältin, -nen f.; Jurist', -en, -en m., Juris'tin, -nen f.

lax, adj. lax.

laxative, n. Abführmittel, - nt.

laxity, n. Laxheit f.

lay, 1. adj. Laien- *(cpds.)* **2.** vb. legen.

layer, n. Schicht, -en f.

layman, n. Laie, -n, -n m.

lazy, adj. faul.

lead, 1. n. Führung f., Leitung f.; *(metal)* Blei nt. **2.** vb. führen, leiten.

leaden, adj. bleiern.

leader, n. Führer, - m., Führerin, -nen f., Leiter, - m., Leiterin, -nen f.

leadership, n. Führung f.

lead pencil, n. Bleistift, -e m.

leaf, n. Blatt, -er nt.

leaflet, n. Broschü're, -n f., Flugblatt, -er nt.

league, n. Bund, -e m., Bündnis, -se nt.

League of Nations, n. Völkerbund m.

leak, 1. n. Leck, -e nt. **2.** vb. lecken.

leakage, n. Durchsickern nt.

leaky, adj. leck, undicht.

lean, 1. adj. mager. **2.** vb. lehnen.

leap, 1. n. Sprung, -e m. **2.** vb. springen*.

leap year, n. Schaltjahr, -e nt.

learn, vb. lernen; erfah'ren*.

learned, adj. gelehrt'.

learning, n. Wissen nt., Bildung f.

lease, 1. n. Mietvertrag, -e m., Pacht, -en f. **2.** vb. mieten, pachten.

leash, n. Leine, -n f.

least, adj. *(slightest)* geringst'-; *(smallest)* kleinst'-; (at l., *in any case*) wenigstens; (at l., *surely this much*) mindestens, zum mindesten.

leather, 1. n. Leder, - nt. **2.** adj. ledern.

leathery, adj. ledern.

leave, 1. n. *(farewell)* Abschied, -e m.; *(permission)* Erlaub'nis, -e f.; *(furlough)* Urlaub, -e m. **2.** vb. *(depart)* ab-fahren*; *(go away)* fort-gehen*; *(abandon)* verlas'sen*; *(let)* lassen*.

leaven, n. Sauerteig, -e m.

lecherous, adj. lüstern.

lecture, 1. n. Vortrag, -e m.; *(academic)* Vorlesung, -en f. **2.** vb. einen Vortrag halten*; eine Vorlesung halten*.

lecturer, n. Vortragend-e m. & f.

ledge, n. Felsvorsprung, -e m.; Sims, -e m.

ledger, n. Hauptbuch, -er nt.

lee, n. Lee f.

leech, n. Blutegel, - m.

leek, n. Lauch, -e m.

leer, vb. begehr'lich schielen.

leeward, adv. leewärts.

left, 1. n. *(pol.)* Link- f. **2.** adj. link-; **(l. over)** übriggeblieben. **3.** adv. links.

leftist, adj. links orientiert'.

left-over, n. Überbleibsel, - nt., Rest, -e m.

leg, n. Bein, -e nt.

legacy, n. Vermächt'nis, -se nt., Erbschaft, -en f.

legal, adj. gesetz'lich, gesetz'mäßig.

legalize, vb. legalisie'ren.

legation, n. Gesandt'schaft, -en f.

legend, n. Legen'de, -n f.

legendary, adj. legendär'.

legible, adj. leserlich.

legion, *n.* Legion', -e *f.*

legislate, *vb.* Gesetze geben*.

legislation, *n.* Gesetz'gebung *f.*

legislator, *n.* Gesetz'geber - *m.,* Gesetz'geberin, -nen *f.*

legislature, *n.* gesetz'gebende Gewalt' *f.;* gesetz'gebende Versamm'lung, -en *f.*

legitimate, *adj.* legitim'.

leisure, *n.* Muße *f.*

leisurely, *adj.* gemäch'lich.

lemon, *n.* Zitro'ne, -n *f.*

lemonade, *n.* Limona'de, -n *f.*

lend, *vb.* leihen*.

length, *n.* Länge, -n *f.; (time)* Dauer *f.*

lengthen, *vb.* verlän'gern.

lengthwise, *adv.* der Länge nach.

lengthy, *adj.* langwierig.

lenient, *adj.* mild, nachsichtig.

lens, *n.* Linse, -n *f.; (photo)* Objektiv', -e *nt.*

Lent, *n.* Fastenzeit *f.*

Lenten, *adj.* Fasten- *(cpds.).*

lentil, *n.* Linse, -n *f.*

leopard, *n.* Leopard', -en, -en *m.*

leper, *n.* Aussätzige- *m.&f.*

leprosy, *n.* Aussatz *m.*

lesbian, *adj.* lesbisch.

lesion, *n.* Verlet'zung, -en *f.*

less, *adj.* weniger.

lessen, *vb. (tr.)* vermin'dern; *(intr.)* nach·lassen*.

lesser, *adj. (size)* kleiner; *(degree)* gerin'ger.

lesson, *n.* Lehre, -n *f.; (school)* Lehrstunde, -n *f.; (assignment)* Aufgabe, -n *f.*

lest, *conj.* damit' . . . nicht.

let, *vb. (allow)* lassen*; *(lease)* vermie'ten.

letdown, *n.* Enttäu'schung, -en *f.*

lethal, *adj.* tödlich.

lethargic, *adj.* teilnahmslos, lethar'gisch.

lethargy, *n.* Teilnahmslosigkeit *f.,* Lethargie' *f.*

letter, *n. (alphabet)* Buchstabe(n), - *(or* -n, -n) *m.; (communication)* Brief, -e *m.*

letterhead, *n.* Briefkopf, ̈-e *m.*

lettuce, *n.* Kopfsalat, -e *m.*

leukemia, *n.* Leukämie' *f.*

levee, *n.* Damm, ̈-e *m.*

level, 1. *n.* Stand, ̈-e *m.,* Niveau',

-s *nt.* **2.** *adj.* eben, gera'de; flach. **3.** *vb.* ebnen; gleich·machen.

lever, *n.* Hebel, - *m.*

levity, *n.* Leichtsinn *m.*

levy, 1. *n.* Abgabe, -n *f.,* Steuer, -n *f.*

lewd, *adj.* unzüchtig.

lexicon, *n.* Lexikon, -ka *nt.*

liability, *n.* Verant'wortlichkeit, -en *f.;* Verpflich'tung, -en *f.*

liable, *adj.* verant'wortlich; *(law)* haftbar.

liaison, *n.* Verbin'dung, -en *f.;* Liaison', -s *f.*

liar, *n.* Lügner, - *m.,* Lügnerin, -nen *f.*

libel, *n.* Verleum'dung, -en *f.*

libelous, *adj.* verleum'derisch.

liberal, 1. *n.* Liberal'- *m.* **2.** *adj.* liberal'.

liberalism, *n.* Liberalis'mus *m.*

liberality, *n.* Freigebigkeit *f.;* Freisinnigkeit *f.*

liberate, *vb.* befrei'en.

liberation, *n.* Befrei'ung, -en *f.*

libertine, *n.* Lüstling, -e *m.*

liberty, *n.* Freiheit, -en *f.*

libido, *n.* Libido *f.*

librarian, *n.* Bibliothekar', -e *m.;* Bibliotheka'rin, -nen *f.*

library, *n.* Bibliothek', -en *f.,* Bücherei', -en *f.*

libretto, *n.* Libret'to, -s *nt.*

license, *n.* Erlaub'nis, -se *f.;* Geneh'migung, -en *f.* **(driver's l.)** Führerschein, -e *m.*

lick, *vb.* lecken.

licorice, *n.* Lakrit'ze, -n *f.*

lid, *n.* Deckel, - *m.; (eye)* Lid, -er *nt.*

lie, 1. *n.* Lüge, -n *f.* **2.** *vb. (tell untruths)* lügen*; *(recline)* liegen*; **(l. down)** sich (hin·)legen.

lien, *n.* dinglich gesi'chertes Anrecht *nt.*

lieutenant, *n.* Leutnant, -s *m.*

life, *n.* Leben, - *nt.*

lifeboat, *n.* Rettungsboot, -e *nt.*

lifeguard, *n.* Bademeister, - *m.,* Bademeisterin, -nen *f.*

life insurance, *n.* Lebensversicherung, -en *f.*

lifeless, *adj.* leblos.

life preserver, *n.* Rettungsring, -e *m.; (vest)* Schwimmweste, -n *f.*

life style, *n.* Lebensstil *m.*

lifetime, *n.* Lebenszeit, -en *f.*

lift, 1. *n.* Fahrstuhl, ⸚e *m.* **2.** *vb.* heben*.

ligament, *n.* Sehne, -n *f.*

ligature, *n.* Ligatur', -en *f.*

light, 1. *n.* Licht, -er *nt.* **2.** *adj. (color)* hell; *(weight)* leicht. **3.** *vb. (fire)* an'zünden; *(illuminate)* beleuch'ten.

lighten, *vb.* leichter machen; *(fig.)* erleich'tern; *(lightning)* blitzen.

lighter, *n. (cigar, cigarette)* Feuerzeug, -e *nt.*

lighthouse, *n.* Leuchtturm, ⸚e *m.*

lightness, *n. (color)* Helligkeit *f.; (ease)* Leichtfertigkeit *f.*

lightning, *n.* Blitz, -e *m.*

like, 1. *adj.* gleich. **2.** *vb.* gern haben*, (gern) mögen*; (I l. it) es gefällt* mir; (I l. to do it) ich tue(*) es gern. **3.** *prep.* wie; (l. this, l. that) so.

likeable, *adj.* angenehm, liebenswert.

likelihood, *n.* Wahrschein'lichkeit, -en *f.*

likely, *adj.* wahrschein'lich.

liken, *vb.* verglei'chen*.

likeness, *n.* Ähnlichkeit, -en *f.*

likewise, *adv.* ebenso.

lilac, *n.* Flieder *m.*

lilt, *n.* wiegender Rhythmus *m.*

lily, *n.* Lilie, -n *f.*

lily of the valley, *n.* Maiglöckchen, - *nt.*

limb, *n.* Glied, -er *nt.*

limber, *adj.* biegsam.

limbo, *n.* Vorhölle *f.*

lime, *n.* Kalk *m.; (fruit)* Limo'ne, -n *f.*

limelight, *n.* Rampenlicht, -er *nt.*

limestone, *n.* Kalkstein *m.*

limit, 1. *n.* Grenze, -n *f.;* Höchstgrenze, -n *f.* **2.** *vb.* begren'zen, beschrän'ken.

limitation, *n.* Begren'zung, -en *f.,* Beschrän'kung, -en *f.*

limited, *adj.* begrenzt', beschränkt'.

limitless, *adj.* unbegrenzt.

limousine, *n.* Limousi'ne -n *f.*

limp, 1. *adj.* schlaff. **2.** *vb.* hinken.

linden, *n.* Linde, -n *f.*

line, *n.* Linie, -n *f.; (mark)* Strich, -e *m.; (row)* Reihe, -n *f.; (writing)* Zeile, -n *f.; (rope)* Leine, -n *f.*

lineage, *n.* Geschlecht', -er *nt.*

lineal, *adj.* in gerader Linie.

linear, *adj.* linear'.

linen, 1. *n.* Leinen, - *nt.; (household)* Wäsche *f.* **2.** *adj.* leinen.

liner, *n. (boat)* Ozeandampfer, - *m.*

linger, *vb.* verwei'len.

lingerie, *n.* Damenunterwäsche *f.*

linguist, *n.* Sprachwissenschaftler, - *m.,* Sprachwissenschaftlerin, -nen *f.;* Linguist', -en, -en *m.,* Linguis'tin, -nen *f.*

linguistic, *adj.* sprachlich; sprachwissenschaftlich, lingui'stisch.

linguistics, *n.* Sprachwissenschaft, -en *f.,* Linguis'tik *f.*

liniment, *n.* Einreibemittel, - *nt.*

lining, *n.* Futter, - *nt.*

link, 1. *n. (bond)* Band, -e *nt.; (chain)* Glied, -er *nt.* **2.** *vb.* verbin'den; verket'ten.

linoleum, *n.* Lino'leum *nt.*

linseed oil, *n.* Leinöl *nt.*

lint, *n.* Fussel, -n *f.*

lion, *n.* Löwe, -n, -n *m.*

lip, *n.* Lippe, -n *f.*

lip-stick, *n.* Lippenstift, -e *m.*

liquefy, *vb.* flüssig machen.

liqueur, *n.* Likör', -e *m.*

liquid, 1. *n.* Flüssigkeit, -en *f.* **2.** *adj.* flüssig.

liquidate, *vb.* liquidie'ren.

liquidation, *n.* Liquidation', -en *f.*

liquor, *n.* Alkohol *m.,* Spirituo'sen *pl.*

lira, *n.* Lira, -re *f.*

lisp, *vb.* lispeln.

lisle, *n.* Baumwollfaden *m.*

list, 1. *n.* Liste, -n *f.,* Verzeich'nis, -se *nt.; (ship)* Schlagseite *f.* **2.** *vb.* verzeich'nen.

listen, *vb.* zu'hören, horchen.

listless, *adj.* lustlos.

litany, *n.* Litanei' *f.*

liter, *n.* Liter, - *m.*

literacy, *n.* Lesen und Schreiben Können *nt.*

literal, *adj.* buchstäblich, wörtlich.

literary, *adj.* litera'risch.

literate, adj. des Lesens und Schreibens kundig.

literature, n. Literatur, -en f.

lithe, adj. geschmei'dig.

lithograph, 1. n. Lithographie', -i'en f. **2.** vb. lithographie'ren.

litigant, n. Rechtsstreitführer, -m.

litigation, n. Rechtsstreit, -e m.

litter, 1. n. (rubbish) Abfall, -¨e m.; (stretcher) Tragbahre, -n f.; (puppies, kittens, etc.) Wurf, -¨e m. **2.** vb. Sachen herum'liegen lassen*.

little, adj. (size) klein; (amount) wenig; **(a l.)** ein bißchen, ein wenig.

liturgical, adj. litur'gisch.

liturgy, n. Liturgie', -i'en f.

live, 1. adj. leben'dig. **2.** vb. (be alive) leben; (dwell) wohnen.

livelihood, n. Lebensunterhalt m.

lively, adj. lebhaft.

liver, n. Leber, -n f.

livery, n. Livree', -n f.

livestock, n. Viehbestand m.

livid, adj. aschfahl.

living, 1. n. Leben nt.; Lebensweise f. **2.** adj. lebend.

lizard, n. Eidechse, -n f.

lo, interj. siehe!

load, 1. n. Ladung, -en f., (burden) Last, -en f. **2.** vb. laden*.

loaf, 1. n. Laib, -e m. **2.** vb. faulenzen.

loafer, n. Faulenzer, - m. Faulenzerin, -nen f.

loam, n. Lehm m.

loan, 1. n. Anleihe, -n f. **2.** vb. leihen*.

loath, adj. abgeneigt.

loathe, vb. verab'scheuen.

loathing, n. Abscheu f.

loathsome, adj. widerlich, ekelhaft.

lobby, n. Wandelhalle, -n f.; (political) Interes'sengruppe, -n f.

lobe, n. Lappen, - m.

lobster, n. Hummer, - m.

local, 1. n. (train) Vorortzug, -¨e m. **2.** adj. örtlich, lokal'.

locale, n. Schauplatz, -¨e m.

locality, n. Ort, -e m.

localize, vb. lokalisie'ren.

locate, vb. finden*; **(be l.d)** liegen*.

location, n. Lage, -n f.

lock, 1. n. Schloß, -¨sser nt.; (canal) Schleuse, -n f.; (hair) Locke, -n f. **2.** vb. ab'schließen*.

locker, n. Schrank, -¨e m.; (baggage) Schließfach, -¨er nt.

locket, n. Medaillon', -s nt.

lockjaw, n. Kieferkrampf.

locksmith, n. Schlosser, - m.

locomotion, n. Fortbewegung, -en f.

locomotive, n. Lokomoti've, -n f.

locust, n. Heuschrecke, -n f.

lode, n. Erzader, -n f.

lodge, 1. n. Häuschen, - nt.; (fraternal) Loge, -n f. **2.** vb. (intr.) logie'ren; (tr.) beherbergen.

lodger, n. Untermieter, - m., Untermieterin, -nen f.

lodging, n. Unterkunft, -¨e f.

loft, n. Boden, -¨ m.; (warehouse) Speicher, - m.

lofty, adj. erha'ben.

log, n. Holzklotz, -¨e m.; (tree trunk) Baumstamm, -¨e m.; (ship's l.) Logbuch, -¨er nt.

loge, n. Loge, -n f.

logic, n. Logik f.

logical, adj. logisch.

loin, n. Lende, -n f.

loiter, vb. herum'stehen*.

London, n. London nt.

lone, lonely, lonesome, adj. einsam.

loneliness, n. Einsamkeit f.

long, 1. adj. lang (-). **2.** vb. sich sehnen.

longevity, n. Langlebigkeit f.

longing, 1. n. Sehnsucht f. **2.** adj. sehnsüchtig.

longitude, n. Länge f.

longitudinal, adj. Längen- (cpds.).

long-lived, adj. langlebig.

long playing record, n. Langspielplatte, -n f.

look, 1. n. Blick, -e m.; (appearance, l.s) Aussehen nt. **2.** vb. sehen*, schauen, blicken, gucken; **(l. at)** an'sehen*, schauen, blicken, gucken; **(l. good, etc.)** gut (etc.) aus'sehen*; **(l. out, be careful)** auf'passen.

looking glass, n. Spiegel, - m.
loom, n. Webstuhl, ¨-e m.
loop, n. Schlaufe, -n f.
loophole, n. Schlupfloch, ¨-er nt.
loose, adj. lose, locker.
loosen, vb. lockern.
loot, 1. n. Beute f. 2. vb. plündern.
lop off, vb. ab•schlagen*.
lopsided, adj. schief.
loquacious, adj. schwatzhaft.
lord, n. Herr, -n, -en m.; (title) Lord, -s m.
lordship, n. Herrschaft, -en f.
lose, vb. verlie'ren*.
loss, n. Verlust', -e m.
lot, n. Los, -e nt.; (quantity) Menge, -n f.; (ground) Grundstück, -e nt.
lotion, n. Lotion', -en f.
lottery, n. Lotterie', -i'en f.
lotus, n. Lotosblume, -n f.
loud, adj. laut; (color) grell.
loudspeaker, n. Lautsprecher, - m.
lounge, 1. n. Vorhalle, -n f. 2. vb. herum'•lungern.
louse, n. Laus, ¨-e f.
lout, n. Lümmel, - m.
louver, n. Lattenfenster, - nt.
lovable, adj. liebenswert.
love, 1. n. Liebe, -n f. 2. vb. lieben; (fall in l.) sich verlie'ben.
lovely, adj. lieblich, reizend.
lover, n. Liebhaber, - m., Liebhaberin, -nen f.
low, adj. niedrig, tief; (nasty) gemein'.
lowbrow, adj. unintellektuell, ungeistig.
lower, 1. adj. tiefer, niedriger; gemei'ner. 2. vb. herun'ter•lassen*; herab•'setzen, senken.
lowly, adj. beschei'den.
loyal, adj. treu.
loyalist, n. Loyalist', -en
loyalty, n. Treue f., Loyalität' f.
lozenge, n. Pastil'le, -n f.
lubricant, n. Schmiermittel, - nt.
lubricate, vb. schmieren.
lucid, adj. klar.
luck, n. Glück nt., Zufall, ¨-e m.

lucky, adj. glücklich; (be l.) Glück haben*.
lucrative, adj. gewinn'bringend.
ludicrous, adj. lächerlich.
lug, vb. schleppen.
luggage, n. Gepäck' nt.
lukewarm, adj. lauwarm.
lull, 1. n. Pause, -n f. 2. vb. beru'higen; (l. to sleep) ein•schläfern.
lullaby, n. Wiegenlied, -er nt.
lumbago, n. Hexenschuß m.
lumber, n. Holz nt.
luminous, adj. leuchtend.
lump, n. Klumpen, - m., (skin) Beule, -n f.
lumpy, adj. klumpig.
lunacy, n. Irrsinn m.
lunar, adj. Mond- (cpds.).
lunatic, 1. n. Irrsinnig- m. 2. adj. irrsinnig.
lunch, 1. n. leichtes Mittagessen, - nt. 2. vb. zu Mittag essen*.
luncheon, n. leichtes Mittagessen, - nt.
lung, n. Lunge, -n f.
lunge, vb. vor•stoßen*.
lurch, vb. torkeln; (leave in the l.) sitzen lassen*.
lure, vb. locken.
lurid, adj. grell; (fig.) grausig.
lurk, vb. lauren.
luscious, adj. saftig, lecker.
lush, adj. saftig, üppig.
lust, 1. n. Wollust f. 2. vb. gelü'sten.
luster, n. Glanz m.
lustful, adj. lüstern.
lustrous, adj. glänzend.
lusty, adj. munter; kräftig.
lute, n. Laute, -n f.
Lutheran, 1. n. Luthera'ner, - m. 2. adj. luthe'risch.
luxuriant, adj. üppig.
luxurious, adj. verschwen'derisch, luxuriös.
luxury, n. Luxus m.
lying, adn. lügnerisch.
lymph, n. Lymphe, -n f.
lynch, vb. lynchen.
lyre, n. Leier, -n f.
lyric, adj. lyrisch.
lyricism, n. Lyrik f.

macabre, *adj.* maka′ber.

macaroni, *n.* Makkaro′ni *pl.*

machine, *n.* Maschi′ne, -n *f.*

machine gun, *n.* Maschi′nengewehr, -e *nt.*

machinery, *n.* Mechanis′mus *m.*; Maschi′nen *pl.*

machinist, *n.* Maschinist′, -en, -en *m.*

machismo, *n.* Männlichkeit *f.*, Virilität′ *f.*

macho, *adj.* protzig männlich.

mackerel, *n.* Makre′le, -n *f.*

mackinaw, *n.* kurzer wollener Mantel, ⁼ *m.*

mad, *adj.* verrückt′; *(angry)* böse.

madam, *n.* gnädige Frau *f.*

madden, *vb.* verrückt′ machen.

mafia, *n.* Mafia *f.*

magazine, *n.* Magazin′, -e *nt.*, Zeitschrift, -en *f.*

magic, 1. *n.* Zauberkunst, ⁼e *f.* **2.** *adj.* magisch.

magician, *n.* Zauberer, - *m.*

magistrate, *n.* Polizei′richter, - *m.*

magnanimous, *adj.* großzügig.

magnate, *n.* Magnat′, -en, -en *m.*

magnesium, *n.* Magne′sium *nt.*

magnet, *n.* Magnet′, (-en), -en *m.*

magnetic, *adj.* magne′tisch.

magnificence, *n.* Herrlichkeit *f.*, Pracht *f.*

magnificent, *adj.* großartig, prächtig.

magnify, *vb.* vergrö′ßern.

magnitude, *n.* Größe, -n *f.*

mahogany, *n.* Mahago′ni *nt.*

maid, *n.* Dienstmädchen, - *nt.*; **(old m.)** alte Jungfer, -n *f.*

maiden, *adj.* Jungfern- *(cpds.)*; **(m. name)** Mädchenname(n), - *m.*

mail, **1.** *n.* Post *f.* **2.** *vb.* mit der Post schicken; zur Post bringen*.

mailbox, *n.* Briefkasten, ⁼ *m.*

mail carrier, *n.* Postbote, -n, -n *m.*, Postbotin, -nen *f.*; Briefträger, - *m.*, Briefträgerin, -nen *f.*

maim, *vb.* verstüm′meln.

main, *adj.* hauptsächlich.

mainframe, *n.* Großrechenanlage, -n *f.*

mainland, *n.* Festland *nt.*

mainspring, *n.* Triebfeder, -n *f.*

maintain, *vb.* aufrecht∙erhalten*; *(assert)* behaup′ten.

maintenance, *n.* Aufrechterhaltung *f.*, Instand′haltung *f.*

maize, *n.* Mais *m.*

majestic, *adj.* majestä′tisch.

majesty, *n.* Majestät′, -en *f.*

major, 1. *n.* Major′, -e *m.* **2.** *adj.* größer; Haupt- *(cpds.)*; *(music)* Dur *nt.*, **(A-major)** A-dur.

majority, *n.* Mehrzahl, -en *f.*, Mehrheit, -en *f.*, Majorität′, -en *f.*

make, *vb.* machen; *(manufacture)* her∙stellen; *(compel)* zwingen*.

make-believe, 1. *n.* Vorspiegelung, -en *f.* **2.** *adj.* vorgetäuscht. **3.** *vb.* vor∙täuschen.

maker, *n.* Hersteller, - *m.*

makeshift, *n.* Notbehelf *m.*

makeup, *n.* Struktur′, -en *f.*; *(face)* Schminke *f.*, Make-up *nt.*

malady, *n.* Krankheit, -en *f.*

malaria, *n.* Mala′ria *f.*

male, 1. *n.* *(human)* Mann, ⁼er *m.*; *(animal)* Männchen, - *nt.* **2.** *adj.* männlich.

malevolent, *adj.* böswillig.

malice, *n.* Bosheit, -en *f.*

malicious, *adj.* boshaft.

malignant, *adj.* bösartig.

malnutrition, *n.* Unterernährung *f.*

malt, *n.* Malz *nt.*

maltreat, *vb.* mißhan′deln.

mammal, *n.* Säugetier, -e *nt.*

man, *n.* Mann, ⁼er *m.*; *(human being)* Mensch, -en, -en *m.*

manage, *vb.* handhaben; *(administer)* verwal′ten; *(direct)* leiten.

management, *n.* Verwal′tung, -en *f.*; Leitung, -en *f.*

manager, *n.* Leiter, - *m.* Leiterin, -nen *f.*; Unterneh′mer, - *m.* Unterneh′merin, -nen *f.*

mandate, *n.* Mandat′, -e *nt.*

mandatory, *adj.* unerläßlich.

mandolin, *n.* Mandoli′ne, -n *f.*

mane, *n.* Mähne, -n *f.*

maneuver, 1. *n.* Manö′ver, - *nt.* **2.** *vb.* manövrie′ren.

manganese, *n.* Mangan' *nt.*

manger, *n.* Krippe, -n *f.*

mangle, *vb.* zerflei'schen; *(laundry)* mangeln.

manhood, *n.* Mannesalter *nt.;* Mannhaftigkeit *f.*

mania, *n.* Manie', -i'en *f.*

maniac, *n.* Wahnsinnig- *m.*

manicure, 1. *n.* Manikü're, -n *f.* 2. *vb.* maniku'ren.

manifest, 1. *adj.* offenkundig. 2. *vb.* bekun'den.

manifesto, *n.* Manifest', -e *nt.*

manifold, *adj.* mannigfaltig.

manipulate, *vb.* manipulie'ren.

mankind, *n.* Menschheit *f.*

manly, *adj.* mannhaft.

manner, *n.* Art, -en *f.;* Weise, -n *f.;* Manier', -en *f.*

mannerism, *n.* Manieris'mus *m.*

mansion, *n.* Haus, ‑er *nt.*

manslaughter, *n.* Totschlag, ‑e *m.*

mantelpiece, *n.* Kamin'sims, -e *m.*

mantle, *n.* Mantel, ‑ *m.*

manual, 1. *n.* Handbuch, ‑er *nt.* 2. *adj.* Hand- *(cpds.).*

manufacture, 1. *n.* Herstellung, -en *f.* 2. *vb.* her'stellen.

manufacturer, *n.* Fabrikant', -en, -en *m.*

manure, *n.* Mist *m.*

manuscript, *n.* Handschrift, -en *f.,* Manuskript', -e *nt.*

many, *adj.* pl. viele.

map, *n.* Landkarte, -n *f.; (of a small area)* Plan, ‑e *m.*

maple, *n.* Ahorn, -e *m.*

mar, *vb.* verun'zieren.

marble, *n.* Marmor, -e *m.*

march, 1. *n.* Marsch, ‑e *m.* 2. *vb.* marschie'ren.

March, *n.* März *m.*

mare, *n.* Stute, -n *f.*

margarine, *n.* Margari'ne *f.*

margin, *n. (edge)* Rand, ‑er *m.; (latitude)* Spielraum, ‑e *m.*

marginal, *adj.* Rand- *(cpds.).*

marijuana, *n.* Marihua'na *nt.*

marinate, *vb.* marinie'ren.

marine, *adj.* Meeres-, See- *(cpds.).*

mariner, *n.* Seemann, -leute *m.*

marionette, *n.* Marionet'te, -n *f.*

marital, *adj.* ehelich.

maritime, *adj.* Schiffahrts-, Seemanns- *(cpds.).*

mark, 1. *n.* Zeichen, - *nt.; (school)* Zensur', -en *f.,* Note, -n *f.* 2. *vb.* kennzeichnen.

market, *n.* Markt, ‑e *m.*

market place, *n.* Marktplatz, -e *m.*

marmalade, *n.* Marmelade, -n *f.*

maroon, 1. *adj.* rotbraun. 2. *vb.* aus'setzen.

marquee, *n.* Überda'chung, -en *f.*

marquis, *n.* Marquis', - *m.*

marriage, *n.* Heirat, -en *f.; (ceremony)* Trauung, -en *f.; (institution)* Ehe, -n *f., (matrimony)* Ehestand *f.*

marrow, *n.* Mark *nt.*

marry, *vb.* heiraten; *(join in marriage)* trauen; **(get married)** heiraten, sich verhei'raten; **(m. off)** verhei'raten.

marsh, *n.* Marsch, -en *f.*

marshal, *n.* Marschall, ‑e *m.*

martial, *adj.* kriegerisch; Kriegs- *(cpds.).*

martyr, *n.* Märtyrer, - *m.* Märtyrerin, -nen

martyrdom, *n.* Märtyrertum *nt.*

marvel, 1. *n.* Wunder, - *nt.* 2. *vb.* **(m. at)** bewun'dern.

marvelous, *adj.* wunderbar.

mascara, *n.* Augenwimperntusche *f.*

mascot, *n.* Maskot'te, -n *f.*

masculine, *adj.* männlich, maskulin.

mash, 1. *n.* Brei, -e *m.* 2. *vb.* zersto'ßen*.

mask, 1. *n.* Maske, -n *f.* 2. *vb.* maskie'ren.

mason, *n.* Maurer, - *m.*

masquerade, *n.* Maskera'de, -n *f.*

mass, *n.* Masse, -n *f., (church)* Messe, -n *f.*

massacre, 1. *n.* Gemet'zel, - *nt.* 2. *vb.* nieder'metzeln.

massage, 1. *n.* Massa'ge, -n *f.* 2. *vb.* massie'ren.

masseur, *n.* Masseur', -e *m.*

masseuse, *n.* Masseuse, -n *f.*

massive, *adj.* massiv'.

mass meeting, *n.* Massenversammlung, -en *f.*

mast, *n.* Mast, -en *m.*

master, 1. *n.* Meister, - *m.*; Herr, -n, -en *m.* **2.** *vb.* beherr'schen.

masterpiece, *n.* Meisterstück, -e *nt.*

mastery, *n.* Beherr'schung *f.*; Herrschaft *f.*

mat, *n.* Matte, -n *f.*

match, 1. *n. (light)* Streichholz, ⁼er *nt.*; *(contest)* Wettkampf, ⁼e *m.*; *(marriage)* Heirat, -en *f.*, Partie', -i'en *f.* **2.** *vb.* passen zu; sich messen* mit.

mate, 1. *n. (spouse)* Ehemann, ⁼er *m.*; Ehefrau, -en *f.*; *(naut.)* Maat, -e *m.* **2.** *vb.* sich paaren.

material, 1. *n.* Material', -ien *nt.*; *(cloth)* Stoff, -e *m.* **2.** *adj.* materiell'; wesentlich.

materialism, *n.* Materialis'mus *m.*

materialize, *vb.* sich verwirk'lichen.

maternal, *adj.* mütterlich.

maternity, *n.* Mutterschaft *f.*

mathematical, *adj.* mathema'tisch.

mathematics, *n.* Mathematik' *f.*

matinée, *n.* Nachmittagsvorstellung, -en *f.*

matrimony, *n.* Ehestand *m.*

matron, *n.* Matro'ne, -n *f.*

matter, 1. *n.* Stoff, -e *m.*, Mate'rie, -n *f.*; *(fig.)* Sache, -n *f.*, Angelegenheit, -en *f.* **2.** *vb.* von Bedeu'tung sein*; aus•machen; **(it doesn't m.)** es macht nichts.

mattress, *n.* Matrat'ze, -n *f.*

mature, 1. *adj.* reif. **2.** *vb.* reifen; *(fall due)* fällig werden*.

maturity, *n.* Reife *f.*; Fälligkeit *f.*

maul, *vb.* übel zu•richten.

mausoleum, *n.* Mausole'um, -le'en *nt.*

maxim, *n.* Grundsatz, ⁼e *m.*

maximum, 1. *n.* Maximum, -ma *nt.* **2.** *adj.* höchst- *(cpds.).*

may, *vb. (be permitted)* dürfen*; **(he m. come)** er wird vielleicht kommen*; **(that m. be)** das kann *or* mag sein*.

May, *n.* Mai *m.*

maybe, *adv.* vielleicht'.

mayhem, *n.* Mord und Totschlag *m.*

mayonnaise, *n.* Mayonnai'se, -n *f.*

mayor, *n.* Bürgermeister, - *m.*, Bürgermeisterin, -nen *f.*

maze, *n.* Wirrwarr *nt.*

me, *pron.* mir; mich.

meadow, *n.* Wiese, -n *f.*

meager, *adj.* dürftig.

meal, *n.* Mahlzeit, -en *f.*; *(flour)* Mehl *nt.*

mean, 1. *n. (average)* Durchschnitt, -e *m.* **2.** *adj.* mittler-, durchschnittlich; Mittel-, Durchschnitts- *(cpds.)*; *(nasty)* gemein'. **3.** *vb. (signify)* bedeu'ten; *(intend to say)* meinen.

meaning, *n.* Bedeu'tung, -en *f.*, *(sense)* Sinn, -e *m.*

means, *n.* Mittel *pl.*

meantime, meanwhile, *n.* Zwischenzeit *f.*; **(in the m.)** inzwi'schen, unterdes'sen.

measles, *n.* Masern *pl.*

measure, 1. *n.* Maß -e *nt.*; *(fig.)* Maßnahme, -n *f.* **2.** *vb.* messen*.

measurement, *n.* Maß, -e *nt.*

measuring, *n.* Messen *nt.*

meat, *n.* Fleisch *nt.*

mechanic, *n.* Mecha'niker, - *m.*, Mecha'nikerin, -nen *f.*

mechanical, *adj.* mecha'nisch.

mechanism, *n.* Mechanis'mus, -men *m.*

mechanize, *vb.* mechanisie'ren.

medal, *n.* Orden, - *m.*

meddle, *vb.* sich ein•mischen.

mediaeval, *adj.* mittelalterlich.

median, *n.* Mittelwert, -e *m.*

mediate, *vb.* vermit'teln.

mediator, *n.* Vermitt'ler, - *m.*, Vermitt'lerin, -nen *f.*

medical, *adj.* ärztlich, medizi'nisch.

medicate, *vb.* medizi'nisch behan'deln.

medicine, *n.* Medizin', -en *f.*

mediocre, *adj.* mittelmäßig.

mediocrity, *n.* Mittelmäßigkeit *f.*

meditate, *vb.* nach•denken*.

meditation, *n.* Nachdenken *nt.*

Mediterranean, *adj.* Mittelmeer- *(cpds.).*

Mediterranean Sea, *n.* Mittelmeer *nt.*

medium, 1. n. Mittel, - nt.; Medium, -ien nt. **2.** adj. mittler-.

medley, n. (music) Potpourri, -s nt.

meek, adj. sanft.

meekness, n. Sanftmut f.

meet, vb. treffen*; sich treffen*; begeg'nen.

meeting, n. Versamm'lung, -en f., Zusam'menkunft, ¨e f., Tagung, -en f.; (encounter) Begeg'nung, -en f.

melancholy, 1. n. Schwermut f., Melancholie' f. **2.** adj. schwermütig, melancho'lisch.

megahertz, n. Megahertz nt.

mellow, adj. gereift'.

melodious, adj. wohlklingend, melo'disch.

melodrama, n. Melodrama, -men nt.

melody, n. Melodie', -'i en f.

melon, n. Melo'ne, -n f.

melt, vb. schmelzen*.

meltdown, n. (atomic power plant) Zerschmel'zen nt.

member, n. Mitglied, -er nt.

membership, n. Mitgliedschaft f.

membrane, n. Membra'ne, -n f.

memento, n. Andenken, - nt.

memoirs, n.pl. Memoi'ren pl.

memorable, adj. denkwürdig.

memorandum, n. Memoran'dum, -den nt.

memorial, 1. n. Denkmal, ¨er nt.; Andenken, - nt. **2.** adj. Gedenk- (cpds.).

memorize, vb. auswendig lernen.

memory, n. (retentiveness) Gedächt'nis, -se nt.; (remembrance) Erin'nerung, -en f.

menace, 1. n. drohende Gefahr', -en f. **2.** vb. drohen, bedro'hen.

menagerie, n. Menage'rie, -'i en f.

mend, vb. aus·bessern.

menial, adj. niedrig.

menopause, n. Wechseljahre pl.

menstruation, n. Regel f., Menstruation' f.

menswear, n. Herrenbekleidung f.

mental, adj. geistig.

mentality, n. Mentalität', -en f.

menthol, n. Menthol' nt.

mention, 1. n. Erwäh'nung, -en f. **2.** vb. erwäh'nen.

menu, n. Menü', -s nt.; Speisekarte, -n f.

mercantile, adj. kaufmännisch.

mercenary, adj. gewinnsüchtig.

merchandise, n. Ware, -n f.

merchant, n. Kaufmann, -leute m.; Geschäfts'mann, -leute m.

merchant marine, n. Handelsmarine, -n f.

merciful, adj. barmher'zig, gütig, gnädig.

merciless, adj. unbarmherzig, schonungslos.

mercury, n. Quecksilber nt.

mercy, n. Gnade f., Mitleid nt. Erbar'men nt.

mere, adj. bloß, nichts als.

merely, adv. nur, bloß.

merge, vb. verschmel'zen*.

merger, n. Zusam'menschluß, -¨sse m.; Fusion', -en f.

meringue, n. Baiser', -s nt.

merit, 1. n. Verdienst', -e nt.; Wert, -e nt.; Vorzug, ¨e m. **2.** vb. verdie'nen.

meritorious, adj. verdienst'lich.

mermaid, n. Nixe, -n f.

merriment, n. Fröhlichkeit, -en f.

merry, adj. fröhlich, lustig.

merry-go-round, n. Karussell', -s nt.

mesh, n. Netz, -e nt.

mess, n. Durcheinan'der nt.; Unordnung, -en f.; Schlamas'sel nt.; (mil.) Eßsaal, -säle m.

message, n. Botschaft, -en f., Nachricht, -en f.

messenger, n. Bote, -n, -n m., Botin, -nen f.

messy, adj. unordentlich, schlampig.

metabolism, n. Stoffwechsel m.

metal, n. Metall', -e nt.

metallic, adj. metal'len.

metamorphosis, n. Metamorpho'se, -n f.

metaphysics, n. Metaphysik' f.

meteor, n. Meteor', -e nt.

meteorite, n. Meteorit', -e m.

meteorology, n. Meteorologie' f.

meter, n. (unit of measure) Meter, - nt. or m.; (recording device) Zähler, - m.

method, n. Metho'de, -n f.
meticulous, adj. sorgfältig.
metric, adj. metrisch.
metropolis, n. Großstadt, ⸚e f.
metropolitan, adj. zur Großstadt gehö'rend.
mettle, n. Mut m.
Mexican, 1. n. Mexika'ner, - m., Mexika'nerin, -nen f. **2.** adj. mexika'nisch.
Mexico, n. Mexiko nt.
mezzanine, n. Zwischenstock m.
microbe, n. Mikro'be, -n f.
microfiche, n. Mikrofiche m.
microfilm, n. Mikrofilm, -e m.
microform, n. Mikroform' f.
microphone, n. Mikrophon', -e nt.
microscope, n. Mikroskop', -e nt.
mid, adj. Mittel- (cpds.); **(in m. air)** mitten in der Luft.
middle, 1. n. Mitte, -n f. **2.** adj. mittler-.
middle-aged, adj. in mittlerem Alter.
Middle Ages, n. Mittelalter nt.
middle class, n. Mittelstand, ⸚e m.
Middle East, n. Mittlerer Osten m.; Nahost- (cpds.).
midget, n. Lilliputa'ner, - m.
midnight, n. Mitternacht f.
midwife, n. Hebamme, -n f.
mien, n. Miene, -n f.
might, n. Macht, ⸚e f.
mighty, adj. mächtig.
migraine, n. Migrä'ne f.
migrate, vb. wandern.
migration, n. Wanderung f.
migratory, adj. wandernd, Zug-
(cpds.).
mildew, n. Schimmel m.
mildness, n. Milde f.
mile, n. Meile, -n f.
mileage, n. Meilenzahl f.
militant, adj. kriegerisch.
militarism, n. Militaris'mus m.
military, 1. n. Militär', -s nt. **2.** adj. militä'risch.
militia, n. Miliz', -en f.
milk, 1. n. Milch f. **2.** vb. melken*.
milkman, n. Milchmann, ⸚er m.
milky, adj. milchig.

mill, 1. n. Mühle, -n f.; (factory) Fabrik', -en f. **2.** vb. mahlen*.
miller, n. Müller, - m., Müllerin, -nen f.
millimeter, n. Millime'ter, - nt.
millinery, n. Putzwaren pl.
million, n. Million', -en f.
millionaire, n. Millionär', -e m., Millionärin, -nen f.
mimic, 1. n. Schauspieler, - m. **2.** vb. nach•ahmen.
mince, vb. klein schneiden*; **(he doesn't m. his words)** er nimmt kein Blatt vor den Mund.
mind, 1. n. Geist m., Verstand' m., Sinn m. **2.** vb. (obey) gehor'chen; (watch over) auf•passen auf; **(never m.)** das macht nichts.
mindful, adj. eingedenk.
mine, 1. n. Bergwerk, -e nt.; (mil.) Mine, -n f. **2.** pron. meiner, -es, -e. **3.** vb. ab•bauen; (mil.) Minen legen.
miner, n. Bergarbeiter, - m.
mineral, 1. n. Mineral', -e nt. **2.** adj. minera'lisch.
mingle, vb. mischen.
miniature, n. Miniatur', -en f.
miniaturize, vb. miniaturisie'ren.
minimal, adj. minimal'; Mindest-, Minimal'- (cpds.).
minimize, vb. herab'•setzen.
minimum, n. Minimum, -ma nt.
mining, n. Bergbau m.
minister, n. (government) Mini'ster, - m., Mini'sterin, -nen f.; (church) Pfarrer, - m., Pastor, -o'ren m., Geistlich- m.
ministry, n. (government) Ministe'rium, -rien nt.; (church) Geistlicher Stand m.
mink, n. Nerz, -e m.
minnow, n. Elritze, -n f.
minor, 1. n. Minderjährig m.&f. **2.** adj. gering'; minderjährig; (music) Moll nt., **(A-minor)** a-Moll.
minority, n. Minderzahl, -en f., Minderheit, -en f., Minorität', -en f.
minstrel, n. Spielmann, -leute m.
mint, 1. n. (plant) Minze, -n f.; (coin factory) Münze, -n f. **2.** vb. münzen.
minus, prep. minus, weniger.

minute, 1. n. Minu'te, -n f. **2.** adj. winzig.

miracle, n. Wunder, -nt.

miraculous, adj. wie ein Wunder.

mirage, n. Luftspiegelung, -en f.

mire, n. Sumpf, ⸚e m.; Schlamm m.

mirror, n. Spiegel, - m.

mirth, n. Fröhlichkeit f.

misappropriate, vb. verun'-treuen.

misbehave, vb. sich schlecht beneh'men*.

miscellaneous, adj. divers'.

mischief, n. Unfug m.

mischievous, adj. schelmisch.

misconstrue, vb. mißdeu'ten.

misdemeanor, n. Verge'hen, - nt.

miser, n. Geizhals, ⸚e m.

miserable, adj. jämmerlich, kläglich.

miserly, adj. geizig.

misery, n. Elend nt., Jammer m.

misfit, n. Blindgänger, - m.

misfortune, n. Unglück, -e nt., Pech m.

misgiving, n. Beden'ken, - nt.

mishap, n. Unglück, -e nt.

mislay, vb. verle'gen.

mislead, vb. irre-führen.

misplace, vb. verle'gen.

mispronounce, vb. falsch aussprechen*.

miss, 1. n. Fehlschlag, ⸚e m. **2.** vb. verfeh'len; *(feel the lack of)* vermis'sen; *(fail to obtain)* verpas'sen.

Miss, n. Fräulein, - nt.

missile, n. Wurfgeschoß, -sse nt.; **(guided m.)** ferngesteuertes Rake'-tengeschoß, -sse nt.

mission, n. Mission', -en f.

missionary, 1. n. Missionar', -e m., Missiona'rin, -nen f. **2.** adj. Missionars'- (cpds.).

misspell, vb. falsch buchstabie'ren.

mist, n. *(fog)* Nebel, - m.; *(haze)* Dunst, ⸚e m.

mistake, 1. n. Fehler, - m., Irrtum, ⸚er m. **2.** vb. verken'nen*; **(be m.)** sich irren.

mister, n. Herr, -n, -en m.

mistletoe, n. Mistel, -n f.

mistreat, vb. mißhan'deln.

mistress, n. Herrin, -nen f.; *(of the house)* Hausfrau, ⸚en f.; *(of a pet)* Frauchen, - nt.; *(lover)* Geliebt'- f.

mistrust, 1. n. Mißtrauen nt. **2.** vb. mißtrau'en.

misty, adj. neblig; dunstig.

misunderstand, vb. mißverste-hen*.

misuse, 1. n. Mißbrauch, ⸚e m. **2.** vb. mißbrau'chen.

mite, n. Bißchen n.; *(bug)* Milbe, -n f.

mitigate, vb. mildern.

mitten, n. Fausthandschuh, -e m.

mix, vb. mischen.

mixture, n. Mischung, -en f.

mix-up, n. Verwir'rung, -en f.; Verwechs'lung, -en f.

moan, n. stöhnen.

mob, n. Menschenmenge, -n f.; Pöbel m.

mobile, adj. beweg'lich; mobilisi-ert'.

mobilization, n. Mobil'machung, -en f.

mobilize, vb. mobilisie'ren.

mock, vb. *(tr.)* verspot'ten; *(intr.)* spotten.

mockery, n. Spott m., Hohn m.

mod, adj. auffällig modern in Kleidung, Benehmen.

mode, n. *(way)* Art und Weise f.; *(fashion)* Mode, -n f.

model, 1. n. Vorbild, -er nt., Muster, - nt.; Modell', -e nt. **2.** vb. modellie'ren.

moderate, 1. adj. mäßig, gemä'ßigt. **2.** vb. mäßigen; vermit'-teln.

moderation, n. Mäßigung f.

modern, adj. modern'.

modernize, vb. modernisie'ren.

modest, adj. beschei'den.

modesty, n. Beschei'denheit f.

modify, vb. modifizie'ren.

modish, adj. modisch.

modulate, vb. modulie'ren.

moist, adj. feucht.

moisten, vb. befeuch'ten.

moisture, n. Feuchtigkeit f.

molar, n. Backenzahn ⸚e m.

molasses, n. Melas'se f.; Sirup m.

mold, 1. n. Form, -en f.; *(mildew)*

Schimmel *m.* 2. *vb.* formen; schimmelig werden*.

moldy, *adj.* schimmelig.

mole, *n. (animal)* Maulwurf, ∹e *m.; (mark)* Muttermal, -e *nt.*

molecule, *n.* Molekül´, -e *nt.*

molest, *vb.* beläs´tigen.

molten, *adj.* flüssig.

moment, *n.* Augenblick, -e *m.,* Moment´, -e *m.; (factor)* Moment´, -e *nt.*

momentary, *adj.* augenblick´lich, momentan´.

momentous, *adj.* folgenschwer.

monarch, *n.* Monarch´, -en, -en *m.*

monarchy, *n.* Monarchie´, -i´en *f.*

monastery, *n.* Kloster, ∹ *nt.*

Monday, *n.* Montag, -e *m.*

monetary, *adj.* Geld- *(cpds.).*

money, *n.* Geld, -er *nt.*

money changer, *n.* Geldwechsler, - *m.*

money order, *n.* Postanweisung, -en *f.*

mongrel, *n.* Bastard, -e *m.*

monitor, *n. (man)* Abhörer, - *m.; (apparatus)* Kontroll´gerät, -e *nt.*

monk, *n.* Mönch, -e *m.*

monkey, *n.* Affe, -n, -n *m.*

monocle, *n.* Mono´kel, - *nt.*

monologue, *n.* Monolog´, -e *m.*

monopolize, *vb.* monopolizie´ren.

monopoly, *n.* Monopol´, -e *nt.*

monotone, *n.* einförmiger Ton, ∹e *m.*

monotonous, *adj.* eintönig, monoton´.

monotony, *n.* Eintönigkeit *f.,* Monotonie´ *f.*

monster, *n.* Ungeheuer, - *nt.*

monstrosity, *n.* Ungeheuerlichkeit, -en *f.*

monstrous, *adj.* ungeheuerlich, haarsträubend.

month, *n.* Monat, -e *m.*

monthly, 1. *n.* Monatsschrift, -en *f.* 2. *adj.* monatlich.

monument, *n.* Denkmal, ∹er *nt.*

monumental, *adj.* monumental´.

mood, *n.* Stimmung, -en *f.;* Laune, -n *f.*

moody, *adj.* launisch; schwermütig.

moon, *n.* Mond, -e *m.*

moonlight, *n.* Mondschein *m.*

moor, 1. *n.* Moor, -e *nt.* 2. *vb.* veran´kern.

mooring, *n.* Ankerplatz, ∹e *m.*

moot, *adj.* strittig.

mop, *n.* Mop, -s *m.*

moped, *n.* Mofa, -s *nt.*

moral, 1. *n.* Moral´, -en *f.* 2. *adj.* sittlich, mora´lisch.

morale, *n.* Stimmung, -en *f.,* Moral´ *f.*

moralist, *n.* Moralist´, -en, -en *m.*

morality, *n.* Sittlichkeit *f.,* Moral´ *f.;* Sittenlehre *f.*

morbid, *adj.* morbid´.

more, *adv.* mehr.

moreover, *adv.* außerdem.

morgue, *n.* Leichenhaus, ∹er *nt.*

morning, *n.* Morgen, - *m.,* Vormittag, -e *m.*

moron, *n.* Schwachsinni- ge *m.&f.*

morose, *adj.* verdrieß´lich.

morphine, *n.* Morphium *nt.*

morsel, *n.* Bissen, - *m.*

mortal, *adj.* sterblich; tödlich.

mortality, *n.* Sterblichkeit *f.*

mortar, *n. (vessel)* Mörser, - *m.; (building material)* Mörtel *m.*

mortgage, *n.* Hypothek´, -en *f.*

mortician, *n.* Leichenbestatter, - *m.*

mortify, *vb.* kastei´en; demütigen.

mortuary, *n.* Leichenhalle, -n *f.*

mosaic, *n.* Mosaik´, -e *nt.*

Moscow, *n.* Moskau *nt.*

Moslem, *n.* Moslem *m.*

mosque, *n.* Moschee´ *f.*

mosquito, *n.* Mücke, -n *f.*

moss, *n.* Moos, -e *nt.*

most, *adj.* meist-.

mostly, *adv.* meistens, hauptsächlich.

moth, *n.* Motte, -n *f.*

mother, *n.* Mutter, ∹ *f.*

mother-in-law, *n.* Schwiegermutter, ∹ *f.*

motif, *n.* Motiv´, -e *nt.*

motion, *n.* Bewe´gung, -en *f.; (parliament)* Antrag, ∹e *m.*

motionless, *adj.* bewe´gungslos.

motion picture, *n.* Film, -e *m.*

motivate, *vb.* veran´lassen, motivie´ren.

motivation, *n.* Motivie'rung, -en *f.*

motive, *n.* Beweg'grund, ̈-e *m.*

motor, *n.* Motor, -o'ren *m.*

motorboat, *n.* Motorboot, -e *nt.*

motorcycle, *n.* Motorrad, ̈er *nt.*

motorist, *n.* Kraftfahrer, - *m.*, Kraftfahrerin, -nen *f.*

motto, *n.* Motto, -s *nt.*

mound, *n.* Erdhügel, - *m.*

mount, 1. *vb. (get on)* bestei'gen*; *(put on)* montie'ren.

mountain, *n.* Berg, -e *m.*

mountaineer, *n.* Bergbewohner, - *m.*; Bergsteiger, - *m.* Bergsteigerin, -nen *f.*

mountainous, *adj.* bergig, gebirgig.

mourn, *vb. (intr.)* trauern; *(tr.)* betrau'ern.

mournful, *adj.* trauervoll.

mourning, *n.* Trauer *f.*

mouse, *n.* Maus, ̈e *f.*

mouth, *n.* Mund, ̈er *m.*; *(river)* Mündung, -en *f.*

mouthpiece, *n.* *(instrument)* Mundstück, -e *nt.*; *(spokesman)* Wortführer, - *m.*

movable, *adj.* beweg'lich.

move, 1. *n. (household goods)* Umzug, ̈e *m.*; *(motion)* Bewe'gung, -en *f.*; *(games)* Zug, ̈e *m.* 2. *vb.* um·ziehen*; bewe'gen, sich bewe'gen; ziehen*; *(parliamentary)* bean'tragen.

movement, *n.* Bewe'gung, -en *f.*; *(music)* Satz, ̈e *m.*

movie, *n.* Kino, -s *nt.*; Film, -e *m.*

moving, 1. *n.* Umzug, ̈e *m.* 2. *adj.* ergrei'fend.

mow, *vb.* mähen.

Mr., *n.* Herr *m.*

Mrs., *n.* Frau *f.*

much, *adj.* viel.

mucilage, *n.* Klebstoff, -e *m.*

muck, *n.* Schlamm *m.*

mucous, *adj.* schleimig.

mucus, *n.* Nasenschleim *m.*

mud, *n.* Schlamm *m.*; Dreck *m.*

muddy, *adj.* schlammig, trübe.

muff, 1. *n.* Muff, -e *m.* 2. *vb.* vermas'seln.

muffle, *vb. (wrap up)* ein·hüllen; *(silence)* dämpfen.

muffler, *n. (scarf)* Schal, -s *m.*; *(auto)* Auspufftopf, ̈-e *m.*

mug, *n.* Krug, ̈e *m.*

mulatto, *n.* Mulat'te, -n, -n *m.*

mule, *n.* Esel, - *m.*

mullah, *n.* Mullah, -s *m.*

multinational, *adj.* multinatio-nal'.

multiple, *adj.* vielfältig.

multiplication, *n.* Multiplika-tion', -en *f.*

multiply, *vb. (math.)* multiplizi-e'ren; *(increase)* verviel'fältigen.

multitude, *n.* Menge, -n *f.*

mummy, *n.* Mumie, -n *f.*

mumps, *n.* Ziegenpeter *m.*

Munich, *n.* München *nt.*

municipal, *adj.* städtisch.

munificent, *adj.* freigebig.

munition, *n.* Munition', -en *f.*

mural, *n.* Wandgemälde, - *nt.*

murder, 1. *n.* Mord, -e *m.* 2. *vb.* morden, ermor'den.

murderer, *n.* Mörder, - *m.*, Mörderin, -nen *f.*

murmur, 1. *n.* Gemur'mel, - *nt.* 2. *vb.* murmeln.

muscle, *n.* Muskel, -n *m.*

muscular, *adj.* muskulös; Muskel- *(cpds.)*.

muse, 1. *n.* Muse, -n *f.* 2. *vb.* nach·denken*.

museum, *n.* Muse'um, -se'en *nt.*

mushroom, *n.* Pilz, -e *m.*

music, *n.* Musik' *f.*

musical, *adj.* musika'lisch.

musical comedy, *n.* Operet'te, -n *f.*

musician, *n.* Musiker, - *m.*, Musikerin, -nen *f.*

muslin, *n.* Musselin', -e *m.*

must, *vb.* müssen*.

mustache, *n.* Schnurrbart, ̈e *m.*

mustard, *n.* Senf *m.*, Mostrich *m.*

muster, 1. *n.* Musterung, -en *f.* 2. *vb.* mustern.

musty, *adj.* muffig.

mutation, *n.* Mutation', -en *f.*

mute, *adj.* stumm.

mutilate, *vb.* verstüm'meln.

mutiny, 1. *n.* Meuterei', -en *f.* 2. *vb.* meutern.

mutter, *vb.* murmeln.

mutton, *n.* Hammelfleisch *nt.*

mutual, *adj.* gegenseitig, gemein'sam.

muzzle, *n.* (gun) Mündung, -en *f.*; (animal's mouth) Maul, -er *nt.*; (mouth covering) Maulkorb, -e *m.*

my, *adj.* mein, -, -e.

myopia, *n.* Kurzsichtigkeit *f.*

myriad, 1. *n.* Myria'de, -n *f.*; (fig.) Unzahl, -en *f.* 2. *adj.* unzählig.

myrtle, *n.* Myrte, -n *f.*

mysterious, *adj.* geheim'nisvoll.

mystery, *n.* Geheim'nis, -se *nt.*; Rätsel, - *nt.*

mystic, 1. *n.* Mystiker. - *m.* 2. *adj.* mystisch; Geheim'- (cpds.).

mystify, *vb.* verwir'ren; verdun'keln.

myth, *n.* Sage, -n *f.*; Mythus, -then *m.*

mythical, *adj.* sagenhaft, mythisch.

mythology, *n.* Mythologie', -i'en *f.*

N

nag, 1. *n.* Gaul, -e *m.* 2. *vb.* herum'nörgeln; keifen.

nail, 1. *n.* Nagel, - *m.*; (n. polish) Nagellack *m.* 2. *vb.* nageln.

naive, *adj.* naiv', unbefangen.

naked, *adj.* nackt.

name, 1. *n.* Name(n), - *m.* 2. *vb.* nennen*.

namely, *adv.* nämlich.

namesake, 1. *n.* Namensvetter, -n *m.*

nap, 1. *n.* (sleep) Nickerchen, - *nt.*, Nachmittagsschläfchen, - *nt.*; (cloth) Noppe, -n *f.* 2. *vb.* einnicken.

naphtha, *n.* Naphtha *nt.*

napkin, *n.* Serviet'te, -n *f.*; (sanitary n.) Binde, -n *f.*

narcissus, *n.* Narzis'se, -n *f.*

narcotic, 1. *n.* Rauschgift, -e *nt.* 2. *adj.* narko'tisch.

narrate, *vb.* erzäh'len.

narration, *n.* Erzäh'lung, -en *f.*

narrative, 1. *n.* Erzäh'lung, -en *f.* 2. *adj.* erzäh'lend.

narrow, *adj.* (tight, confined) eng; (not broad) schmal (-, -).

nasal, *adj.* nasal'.

nasty, *adj.* häßlich.

natal, *adj.* Geburts'- (cpds.).

nation, *n.* Nation', -en *f.*; Volk, -er *nt.*

national, 1. *n.* Staatsangehörig- *m.&f.* 2. *adj.* national'.

nationalism, *n.* Nationalis'mus *m.*

nationality, *n.* Staatsangehörigkeit, -en *f.*, Nationalität', -en *f.*

nationalization, *n.* Verstaat'lichung, -en *f.*

nationalize, *vb.* verstaat'lichen.

native, 1. *n.* Eingeboren- *m.&f.*, Einheimisch- *m.&f.* 2. *adj.* gebür'tig, einheimisch.

Native American, *n.* India'ner, -*m.*, Indian'nerin, -nen *f.*

natural, *adj.* natür'lich.

naturalist, *n.* Natur'forscher, - *m.*, Natur'forscherin, -nen *f.*, Naturalist', -en, -en *m.*

naturalize, *vb.* naturalisie'ren.

naturalness, *n.* Natür'lichkeit *f.*

nature, *n.* Natur', -en *f.*; (essence) Wesen *nt.*

naughty, *adj.* unartig.

nausea, *n.* Übelkeit *f.*

nauseating, *adj.* ekelerregend.

nautical, *adj.* nautisch.

naval, *adj.* See-, Schiffs-, Mari'ne- (cpds.).

nave, *n.* Kirchenschiff, -e *nt.*

navel, *n.* Nabel, - *m.*

navigable, *adj.* schiffbar.

navigate, *vb.* schiffen, steuern.

navigation, *n.* Schiffahrt *f.*, Naviga'tion' *f.*

navigator, *n.* Seefahrer, - *m.*; (airplane) Orter, - *m.*

navy, *n.* Mari'ne *f.*; Flotte, -n *f.*

navy yard, *n.* Mari'newerft, -en *f.*

near, 1. *prep.* in der Nähe von. 2. *adj.* nahe (näher, nächst-).

nearby, 1. *adj.* naheliegend, nahe gele'gen. 2. *adv.* in der Nähe.

nearly, *adv.* beinahe, fast.

near-sighted, *adj.* kurzsichtig.

neat, *adj.* ordentlich, sauber.

neatness, *n.* Sauberkeit *f.*

nebula, *n.* Nebelfleck, -e *m.*

nebulous, *adj.* nebelhaft.

necessary, *adj.* nötig, notwendig.

necessity, *n.* Notwendigkeit, -en *f.*

neck, *n.* Hals, ∸e *m.*

necklace, *n.* Halskette, -n *f.*

necktie, *n.* Schlips, -e *m.,* Krawat'te, -n *f.*

nectar, *n.* Nektar *m.*

need, 1. *n.* Not, ∸e *f.;* Bedürf'nis, -se *nt.* **2.** *vb.* benö'tigen, brauchen.

needful, *adj.* notwendig.

needle, *n.* Nadel, -n *f.*

needless, *adj.* unnötig.

needy, *adj.* notleidend.

negative, 1. *n. (photo)* Negativ, -e *nt.* **2.** *adj.* vernei'nend, negativ.

neglect, 1. *n.* Vernach'lässigung, -en *f.* **2.** *vb.* vernach'lässigen.

negligee, *n.* Negligé', -s *nt.*

negligent, *adj.* nachlässig, fahrlässig.

negligible, *adj.* gering'fügig.

negotiate, *vb.* verhan'deln.

negotiation, *n.* Verhand'lung, -en *f.*

neighbor, *n.* Nachbar, (-n,) -n *m.,* Nachbarin, -nen *f.*

neighborhood, *n.* Nachbarschaft, -en *f.*

neither, 1. *pron.* keiner, -es, -e (von beiden). **2.** *conj.* **(n. . . . nor)** weder . . . noch.

neon, *n.* Neon *nt.*

nephew, *n.* Neffe, -n, -n *m.*

nepotism, *n.* Nepotis'mus *m.*

nerve, *n.* Nerv, -en *m.; (effrontery)* Dreistigkeit *f.*

nervous, *adj.* nervös'.

nest, *n.* Nest, -er *n.*

nestle, *vb.* nisten; *(fig.)* sich an·schmiegen.

net, 1. *n.* Netz *f.* **2.** *adj.* netto.

network, *n.* Netz, -e *nt.*

neuralgia, *n.* Neuralgie' *f.*

neurology, *n.* Neurologie' *f.*

neurotic, *adj.* neuro'tisch.

neutral, *adj.* neutral', unparteiisch.

neutrality, *n.* Neutralität' *f.*

neutron, *n.* Neutron, -o'nen *nt.*

neutron bomb, *n.* Neutro'nenbombe, -n *f.*

never, *adv.* nie, niemals.

nevertheless, *adv.* dennoch, trotzdem.

new, *adj.* neu.

news, *n.* Nachrichten *pl.; (item of n.)* Nachricht, -en *f.*

newsboy, *n.* Zeitungsjunge, -n, -n *m.*

newscast, *n.* Nachrichtensendung, -en *f.*

newspaper, *n.* Zeitung, -en *f.*

newsreel, *n.* Wochenschau *f.*

next, *adj.* nächst-.

nibble, *vb.* knabbern.

nice, *adj.* nett, hübsch.

nick, *n.* Kerbe, -n *f.*

nickel, *n.* Nickel *nt.*

nickname, *n.* Spitzname(n), - *m.*

nicotine, *n.* Nikotin' *f.*

niece, *n.* Nichte, -n *f.*

niggardly, *adj.* knauserig.

night, *n.* Nacht, ∸e *f.*

night club, *n.* Nachtlokal, -e *nt.*

nightgown, *n.* Nachthemd, -en *nt.*

nightingale, *n.* Nachtigall, -en *f.*

nightly, *adj.* nächtlich, jede Nacht.

nightmare, *n.* Alptraum, ∸e *m.,* böser Traum, ∸e *m.,* Alpdruck *m.*

nimble, *adj.* flink.

nine, *num.* neun.

nineteen, *num.* neunzehn.

nineteenth, 1. *adj.* neunzehnt-. **2.** *n.* Neunzehntel, - *nt.*

ninetieth, 1. *adj.* neunzigst-. **2.** *n.* Neunzigstel, - *nt.*

ninety, *num.* neunzig.

ninth, 1. *adj.* neunt-. **2.** *n.* Neuntel, - *nt.*

nip, 1. *n.* Zwick, -e *m.; (drink)* Schlückchen, - *nt.* **2.** *vb.* zwicken.

nipple, *n.* Brustwarze, -n *f.; (baby's bottle)* Sauger, - *m.*

nitrate, *n.* Nitrat', -e *nt.*

nitrogen, *n.* Stickstoff *m.*

no, 1. *adj.* kein, -, -e. **2.** *interj.* nein.

nobility, *n.* Adel *m.*

noble, *adj. (rank)* adlig; *(character)* edel.

nobleman, *n.* Adlig- *m.*

nobody, *pron.* niemand, keiner.

nocturnal, *adj.* nächtlich.

nocturne, *n.* Noktur'ne, -n *f.*

nod, *vb.* nicken.

no-frills, *adj.* einfach, ohne Verschönerung.

noise, *n.* Geräusch, -e *nt.*; Lärm *m.*

noiseless, *adj.* geräusch'los.

noisy, *adj.* laut.

nomad, *n.* Noma'de, -n, -n *m.*

nominal, *adj.* nominal'.

nominate, *vb.* ernen'nen*; *(candidate)* auf'stellen.

nomination, *vb.* Ernen'nung, -en *f.*; Kandidatur', -en *f.*

nominee, *n.* Kandidat', -en, -en *m.*

non-aligned, *adj.* blockfrei.

nonchalant, *adj.* zwanglos, nonchalant'.

noncombatant, *n.* Nichtkämpfer, - *m.*

non-commissioned officer, *n.* Unteroffizier, -e *m.*

noncommittal, *adj.* nichtverpflich'tend.

nondescript, *adj.* unbestimmbar.

none, *pron.* keiner, -es, -e.

nonpartisan, *adj.* unparteiisch.

nonsense, *n.* Unsinn *m.*

nonstop, *adj.* durchgehend.

noodle, *n.* Nudel, -n *f.*

nook, *n.* Ecke, -n *f.*, Winkel, - *m.*

noon, *n.* Mittag *m.*

noose, *n.* Schlinge, -n *f.*

nor, *conj.* noch.

normal, *adj.* normal', gewöhn'lich.

north, 1. *n.* Norden *m.* 2. *adj.* nördlich; Nord- *(cpds.)*.

northeast, 1. *n.* Nordos'ten *m.* 2. *adj.* nordöst'lich; Nordost- *(cpds.)*.

northeastern, *adj.* nordöst'lich.

northern, *adj.* nördlich.

North Pole, *n.* Nordpol *m.*

North Sea, *n.* Nordsee *f.*

northwest, 1. *n.* Nordwes'ten *m.* 2. *adj.* nordwest'lich; Nordwest- *(cpds.)*.

Norway, *n.* Norwegen *nt.*

Norwegian, 1. *n.* Norweger, - *m.*, Norwegerin, -nen *f.* 2. *adj.* norwegisch.

nose, *n.* Nase, -n *f.*

nosebleed, *n.* Nasenbluten *nt.*

nose dive, *n.* Sturz, -̈e *m.*; *(airplane)* Sturzflug, -̈e *m.*

nostalgia, *n.* Heimweh *nt.*; Sehnsucht *f.*

nostril, *n.* Nasenloch, -̈er *nt.*, Nüster, -n *f.*

not, *adv.* nicht; *(n. a, n. any)* kein, -, -e.

notable, *adj.* bemer'kenswert.

notary, *n.* Notar', -e *m.*

notation, *n.* Aufzeichnung, -en *f.*

notch, 1. *n.* Kerbe, -n *f.* 2. *vb.* ein'-kerben.

note, 1. *n.* Notiz', -en *f.*; *(comment)* Anmerkung, -en *f.*; *(music)* Note, -n *f.*; *(letter)* kurzer Brief, -e *m.* 2. *vb.* bemer'ken.

note-book, *n.* Notiz'buch, -̈er *nt.*, Heft, -e *nt.*

noted, *adj.* bekannt'.

notepaper, *n.* Notiz'block, -̈e *m.*; Schreibblock, -̈e *m.*

noteworthy, *adj.* beach'tenswert.

nothing, *pron.* nichts.

notice, 1. *n.* *(attention)* Beach'-tung, -en *f.*; *(poster)* Bekannt'-machung, -en *f.*; *(announcement)* Anzeige, -n *f.*; *(give n.)* kündigen. 2. *vb.* beach'ten; bemer'ken.

noticeable, *adj.* bemer'kenswert; *(conspicuous)* auffällig.

notification, *n.* Benach'richtigung, -en *f.*

notify, *vb.* benach'richtigen.

notion, *n.* Vorstellung, -en *f.*, Idee', -de'en *f.*; *(n.s)* articles) Kurzwaren *pl.*

notoriety, *n.* Verruf' *m.*, Verru'fenheit *f.*

notorious, *adj.* berüch'tigt.

notwithstanding, 1. *prep.* ungeachtet, trotz. 2. *adv.* nichtsdestoweniger.

noun, *n.* Hauptwort, -̈er *nt.*, Substantiv, -e *nt.*

nourish, *vb.* nähren; ernäh'ren.

nourishment, *n.* Nahrung, -en *f.*

novel, 1. *n.* Roman', -e *m.* 2. *adj.* neu.

novelist, *n.* Roman'schriftsteller, - *m.*, Roman'schriftstellerin, -nen *f.*

novelty, *n.* Neuheit, -en *f.*

November, *n.* Novem'ber *m.*

novena, n. Nove'ne, -n f.

novice, n. Neuling, -e m.

novocaine, n. Novocain' nt.

now, adv. jetzt, nun.

nowadays, adv. heutzutage.

nowhere, adv. nirgends.

nozzle, n. Düse, -n f.; (gun) Mündung, -en f.

nuance, n. Nuan'ce, -n f.

nuclear, adj. Kern- (cpds.); nuklear'.

nuclear power plant, n. Kernkraftwerk, -e nt.

nuclear warhead, n. nuklea'rer Sprengkopf m.

nuclear waste, n. Atom'müll m.

nucleus, n. Kern, -e m.

nude, adj. nackt.

nugget, n. Klumpen, - m.

nuisance, n. Ärgernis, -se nt.; (be a n.) ärgerlich, lästig sein*.

nuke, n. Rakete mit nuklearem Sprengkopf.

nullify, vb. annullie'ren, aufheben*.

number, 1. n. Zahl, -en f.; (figure) Ziffer, -n f.; (magazine, telephone, house) Nummer, -n f.; (amount) Anzahl, -en f. **2.** vb. numerie'ren; (amount to) sich belau'fen auf.

numerical, adj. zahlenmäßig.

numerous, adj. zahlreich.

nun, n. Nonne, -n f.

nuptial, adj. Hochzeits-, Ehe- (cpds.).

nurse, 1. n. Krankenschwester, -n f. **2.** vb. pflegen; (suckle) stillen.

nursery, n. Kinderzimmer, - nt.; (plants) Pflanzschule, -n f.

nursing home, n. Altersheim, -e nt.

nurture, vb. ernäh'ren, nähren; (fig.) hegen.

nut, n. Nuß, ⁺sse f.

nutcracker, n. Nußknacker, - m.

nutrition, n. Ernäh'rung f.

nutritious, adj. nahrhaft.

nylon, n. Nylon nt.

nymph, n. Nymphe, -n f.

O

oak, n. Eiche, -n f.

oar, n. Ruder, - nt.

oasis, n. Oa'se, -n f.

oath, n. (pledge) Eid, -e m., Schwur, ⁺e m.; (curse) Fluch, ⁺e m.

oatmeal, n. Hafergrütze f.

oats, n. Hafer m.; Haferflocken pl.

obedience, n. Gehor'sam m.

obedient, adj. gehor'sam.

obeisance, n. Ehrerbietung, -en f.

obese, adj. fettleibig.

obey, vb. gehor'chen, befol'gen.

obituary, n. Nachruf, -e m.

object, 1. n. Gegenstand, ⁺e m.; (aim) Ziel, -e nt.; (purpose) Zweck, -e m.; (gram.) Objekt', -e nt. **2.** vb. ein·wenden*, Einspruch erhe'ben*.

objection, n. Einwand, ⁺e m., Einspruch, ⁺e m.

objectionable, adj. widerwärtig.

objective, 1. n. Ziel, -e nt.; (photo) Objektiv', -e nt. **2.** adj. sachlich, objektiv'.

obligation, n. Verpflich'tung, -en f.

obligatory, adj. obligato'risch.

oblige, vb. verpflich'ten; jemandem gefäl'lig sein*.

obliging, adj. gefäl'lig.

oblique, adj. schief, schräg.

obliterate, vb. aus·radieren, vernich'ten.

oblivion, n. Verges'senheit f.

oblong, adj. länglich; rechteckig.

obnoxious, adj. widerlich.

obscene, adj. unanständig, obszön'.

obscure, adj. dunkel.

obsequious, adj. unterwürfig.

observance, n. Beach'tung, -en f.; (celebration) Feier f.

observation, n. Beob'achtung, -en f.

observatory, n. Sternwarte, -n f.

observe, vb. beob'achten; befol'gen.

observer, n. Beo'bachter, - m., Beo'bachterin, -nen f.

obsession, n. fixe Idee', -de'en f.

obsolete, *adj.* veral'tet, überholt'.
obstacle, *n.* Hindernis, -se *nt.*
obstetrical, *adj.* geburts'hilflich.
obstetrician, *n.* Geburts'helfer, - *m.*, Geburts'helferin, -nen *f.*
obstinate, *adj.* hartnäckig.
obstreperous, *adj.* lautmäulig.
obstruct, *vb.* versper'ren, hindern.
obstruction, *n.* Hindernis, -se *nt.*
obtain, *vb.* erhal'ten*, bekom'men*.
obviate, *vb.* besei'tigen.
obvious, *adj.* selbstverständlich, offensichtlich.
occasion, *n.* Gele'genheit, -en *f.*
occasional, *adj.* gele'gentlich.
Occident, *n.* Abendland *nt.*
occidental, *adj.* abendländisch.
occult, *adj.* verbor'gen, okkult'.
occupant, *n.* Inhaber, - *m.*, Inhaberin, -nen *f.*; Insasse, -n -n *m.*, Insassin, -nen *f.*, Bewoh'ner, - *m.*, Bewoh'nerin, -nen *f.*
occupation, *n.* (profession) Beruf', -e *m.*; (mil.) Beset'zung, -en *f.*; (o. forces) Besat'zung, -en *f.*
occupy, *vb.* (take up) ein'nehmen*; (keep busy) beschäf'tigen; (mil.) beset'zen.
occur, *vb.* vor'kommen*, gesche'hen*, passie'ren.
occurrence, *n.* Ereig'nis, -se *nt.*
ocean, *n.* Ozean, -e *m.*
o'clock, *n.* Uhr *f.*
octagon, *n.* Achteck, -e *nt.*
octave, *n.* Okta've, -n *f.*
October, *n.* Okto'ber *m.*
octopus, *n.* Tintenfisch, -e *m.*
ocular, *adj.* Augen- (cpds.).
oculist, *n.* Augenarzt, ∹e *m.*, Augenärztin, -nen *f.*
odd, *adj.* (numbers) ungerade; (queer) merkwürdig.
oddity, *n.* Merkwürdigkeit, -en *f.*
odds, *n.pl.* Chance, -n *f.*; (probability) Wahrschein'lichkeit, -en *f.*; (advantage) Vorteil, -e *m.*
odious, *adj.* verhaßt'.
odor, *n.* Geruch', ∹e *m.*
of, *prep.* von.
off, *adv.* ab.
offend, *vb.* verlet'zen, belei'digen.
offender, *n.* Missetäter, - *m.*, Missetäterin, -nen *f.*

offense, *n.* (crime) Verge'hen, - *nt.*; (offensive) Offensi've, -n *f.*; (insult) Kränkung, -en *f.*
offensive, **1.** *n.* Offensi've, -n *f.* **2.** *adj.* anstößig.
offer, **1.** *n.* Angebot, -e *nt.* **2.** *vb.* an'bieten*.
offering, *n.* Opfer, - *nt.*, Spende, -n *f.*
offhand, *adj.* un'verhofft.
office, *n.* Amt, ∹er *nt.*; (room) Büro', -s *nt.*; (doctor's, dentist's o.) Praxis *f.*
officer, *n.* Offizier', -e *m.*; (police) Polizist', -en, -en *m.* Polizis'tin, -nen *f.*
official, **1.** *n.* Beamt'er - *m.*, Beam'tin, -nen *f.* **2.** *adj.* amtlich, offiziell'.
officiate, *vb.* amtie'ren.
offspring, *n.* Abkömmling, -e *m.*
often, *adv.* oft, häufig.
oil, **1.** *n.* Öl, -e *nt.*; Petro'leum *nt.* **2.** *vb.* ölen.
oily, *adj.* ölig, fettig.
ointment, *n.* Salbe, -n *f.*
okay, *adv.* okay.
old, *adj.* alt (∹).
old-fashioned, *adj.* altmodisch.
olive, *n.* Oli've, -n *f.*
ombudsman, *n.* Ombudsmann, ∹er *m.*
omelet, *n.* Omelett', -e *nt.*
omen, *n.* Omen *nt.*
ominous, *adj.* unheilvoll.
omission, *n.* Versäum'nis, -se *nt.*, Überse'hen, - *nt.*
omit, *vb.* aus'lassen*, unter'lassen*.
omnibus, *n.* Omnibus, -se *m.*
omnipotent, *adj.* allmäch'tig.
on, *prep.* auf, an.
once, *adv.* einmal.
one, **1.** *pron.* man; einer, -es, -e. **2.** *adj.* ein, -, -e. **3.** *num.* eins.
one-sided, *adj.* einseitig.
one-way, *adj.* Einbahn- (cpds.).
onion, *n.* Zwiebel, -n *f.*
only, **1.** *adj.* einzig. **2.** *adv.* nur.
onslaught, *n.* Angriff, -e *m.*
onward, *adv.* vorwärts.
ooze, *vb.* hervor'-quellen*.
opacity, *n.* Undurchsichtigkeit *f.*
opal, *n.* Opal', -e *m.*
opaque, *adj.* undurchsichtig.

open, 1. *adj.* offen. **2.** *adv.* offen, auf. **3.** *vb.* öffnen, auf•machen; *(inaugurate)* eröff′nen.

opening, 1. *n. (hole)* Öffnung, -en *f.; (inauguration)* Eröff′nung, -en *f.* **2.** *adj.* eröff′nend.

opera, *n.* Oper, -n *f.*

opera-glasses, *n.-pl.* Opernglas, -̈er *nt.*

operate, *vb.* operie′ren.

operatic, *adj.* Opern- *(cpds.).*

operation, *n.* Verfah′ren, - *nt.;* Unterneh′men, - *nt.; (med.)* Operation′, -en *f.*

operator, *n. (of a machine)* Bedie′ner, - *m.; (telephone)* Telefonist′, -en *m.,* Telephonis′tin, -en *f.,* Vermitt′lung *f.; (manager)* Manager, - *m.*

operetta, *n.* Operet′te, -n *f.*

ophthalmic, *adj.* Augen- *(cpds.).*

opinion, *n.* Meinung, -en *f.,* Ansicht, -en *f.*

opponent, *n.* Gegner, - *m.,* Gegnerin, -nen *f.*

opportunism, *n.* Opportunis′mus *m.*

opportunity, *n.* günstige Gele′genheit, -en *f.,* Chance, -n *f.*

oppose, *vb.* sich widerset′zen.

opposite, 1. *n.* Gegenteil, -e *nt.; (contrast)* Gegensatz, -̈e *m.* **2.** *adj.* entge′gengesetzt. **3.** *adv.* gegenü′ber.

opposition, *n.* Opposition′, -en *f.*

oppress, *vb.* unterdrü′cken.

oppression, *n.* Unterdrü′ckung, -en *f.*

oppressive, *adj.* tyran′nisch; bedrü′ckend, drü′ckend.

oppressor, *n.* Unterdrü′cker, - *m.*

optic, *adj.* optisch.

optician, *n.* Optiker, - *m.,* Optikerin, -nen *f.*

optics, *n.* Optik *f.*

optimism, *n.* Optimis′mus *m.*

optimistic, *adj.* optimis′tisch.

option, *n.* Wahl, -en *f.; (privilege of buying)* Vorkaufsrecht, -e *nt.*

optional, *adj.* freigestellt, fakultativ′.

optometry, *n.* praktische Augenheilkunde *f.*

opulence, *n.* Üppigkeit *f.*

opulent, *adj.* üppig.

or, *conj.* oder.

oracle, *n.* Ora′kel, - *nt.*

oral, *adj.* mündlich.

orange, 1. *n.* Apfelsi′ne, -n *f.,* Oran′ge, -n *f.* **2.** *adj.* orange′farbig; *(pred. adj. only)* orange′.

oration, *n.* Rede, -n *f.*

orator, *n.* Redner, - *m.,* Rednerin, -nen *f.*

oratory, *n.* Redekunst *f.*

orbit, *n.* Bahn, -en *f.;* Gestirns′-, Plane′tenbahn, -en *f.*

orchard, *n.* Obstgarten, -̈ *m.*

orchestra, *n. (large)* Orches′ter, - *nt.; (small)* Kapel′le, -n *f.*

orchid, *n.* Orchide′e, -n *f.*

ordain, *vb.* bestimm′en, *(eccles.)* ordinier′en.

ordeal, *n.* Qual, -en *f.*

order, 1. *n. (command)* Befehl′, -e *m.; (neatness)* Ordnung *f.; (decree)* Erlaß, -sse *m.,* Verord′nung, -en *f.; (fraternity, medal)* Orden, -*m.* **2.** *vb. (command)* befeh′len*; **m. 2.** *vb. (command)* befeh′len*; **(put in o.)** ordnen; *(decree)* verord′nen.

orderly, *adj.* ordentlich; geord′net.

ordinance, *n.* Verord′nung, -en *f.*

ordinary, *adj.* gewöhn′lich.

ore, *n.* Erz, -e *nt.*

organ, *n.* Organ′, -e *nt.; (music)* Orgel, -n *f.*

organdy, *n.* Organ′dy *m.*

organic, *adj.* orga′nisch.

organism, *n.* Organis′mus, -men *m.*

organist, *n.* Organist′, -en, -en *m.,* Organis′tin, -nen *f.*

organization, *n.* Organisation′, -en *f.*

organize, *vb.* organisie′ren.

orgy, *n.* Orgie, -n *f.*

orient, *vb.* orientie′ren.

Orient, *n.* Orient *m.*

Oriental, *adj.* orienta′lisch.

orientation, *n.* Orientie′rung, -en *f.*

origin, *n.* Ursprung, -̈e *m.*

original, *adj.* ursprünglich; *(novel)* originell′.

originality, *n.* Originalität′ -en *f.*

ornament, 1. *n.* Verzie′rung, -en *f.,* Schmuck *m.* **2.** *vb.* verzie′ren, schmücken.

ornamental, *adj.* dekorativ'.

ornate, *adj.* überla'den.

ornithology, *n.* Vogelkunde *f.*

orphan, *n.* Waise, -n *f.*

orphanage, *n.* Waisenhaus, ̈-er *nt.*

orthodox, *adj.* orthodox'.

orthography, *n.* Rechtschrei-bung, -en *f.*, Orthographie', -i'en *f.*

orthopedic, *adj.* orthopä'disch.

oscillate, *vb.* schwingen*.

osmosis, *n.* Osmo'se *f.*

ostensible, *adj.* augenscheinlich.

ostentation, *n.* Schaustellung *f.*

ostentatious, *adj.* ostentativ'.

ostracize, *vb.* ächten.

ostrich, *n.* Strauß, -e *m.*

other, *adj.* ander-.

otherwise, *adv.* sonst.

ouch, *interj.* au!

ought, *vb.* sollte; **(o. to have)** hätte . . . sollen.

ounce, *n.* Unze, -n *f.*

our, *adj.* unser, -, -e.

ours, *pron.* unserer, -es, -e.

oust, *vb.* enthe'ben* (eines Amtes).

out, *adv.* aus, hin-, heraus'.

outbreak, *n.* Ausbruch, ̈-e *m.*

outburst, *n.* Ausbruch, ̈-e *m.*

outcast, *n.* Ausgestoßen -en *m.&f.*

outcome, *n.* Ergeb'nis, -se *nt.*

outdoors, *adv.* draußen, im Freien.

outer, *adj.* äußer-.

outfit, **1.** *n.* Ausrüstung, -en *f.*; **(mil.)** Einheit, -en *f.* **2.** *vb.* aus'rüsten.

outgrowth, *n.* Folge, -n *f.*

outing, *n.* Ausflug, ̈-e *m.*

outlandish, *adj.* bizarr'.

outlaw, **1.** *n.* Gesetz'los- *m.* **2.** *vb.* verbie'ten*.

outlet, *n.* Abfluß, ̈-sse *m.*; **(fig.)** Ventil', -e *nt.*; **(elec.)** Steckdose, -n *f.*

outline, **1.** *n.* Umriß, -sse *m.*, Kon-tur', -en *f.*; **(summary)** Übersicht, -en *f.* **2.** *vb.* umrei'ßen*.

outlive, *vb.* überle'ben, überdau'-ern.

out of, *prep.* aus.

out-of-date, *adj.* veral'tet, über-holt'.

outpost, *n.* Vorposten, - *m.*

output, *n.* Leistung, -en *f.*, Pro-duktion', -en *f.*; **(computer)** Out-put, -s *m.*; Ausgabe, -n *f.*

outrage, *n.* Frevel, - *m.*

outrageous, *adj.* unerhört.

outrank, *vb.* einen höheren Rang bekleiden.

outright, *adj.* uneingeschränkt.

outrun, *vb.* hinter sich lassen*.

outside, **1.** *n.* Außenseite, -n *f.*; Außenwelt *f.* **2.** *adj.* äußer-. **3.** *adv.* draußen. **4.** *prep.* außer, außer-halb.

outskirts, *n.* Außenbezirke *pl.*

outward, *adj.* äußerlich.

oval, *adj.* oval'.

ovary, *n.* Eierstock, ̈-e *m.*

ovation, *n.* Huldigung, -en *f.*

oven, *n.* Ofen, ̈- *m.*

over, **1.** *prep.* über. **2.** *adv.* über; hin-, herü'ber; **(past)** vorbei'.

overbearing, *adj.* anmaßend.

overcoat, *n.* Mantel, ̈- *m.*, Über-zieher, - *m.*

overcome, *vb.* überwin'den*.

overdue, *adj.* überfällig.

overflow, **1.** *n.* Überfluß, -sse *m.* **2.** *vb.* über-fließen*.

overhaul, *vb.* überho'len.

overhead, **1.** *n.* laufende Unkos-ten *pl.* **2.** *adv.* oben.

overkill, *n.* Overkill *m.*; übertrie-benes Vernichtungsvermögen *nt.*

overlook, *vb.* überse'hen*.

overnight, *adv.* über Nacht.

overpass, *n.* Unterfüh'rung, -en *f.*

overpower, *vb.* überwäl'tigen.

overrule, *vb.* überstim'men.

overrun, *vb.* überlau'fen*, **(flood)** überflu'ten.

oversee, *vb.* beauf'sichtigen.

oversight, *n.* Überse'hen *f.*

overt, *adj.* offen.

overtake, *vb.* ein-holen.

overthrow, **1.** *n.* Sturz *m.* **2.** *vb.* stürzen; um-werfen*.

overtime, *n.* Überstunden *pl.*

overture, *n.* **(music)** Ouvertü're, -n *f.*; Annäherung, -en *f.*

overturn, *vb.* um-stürzen.

overview, *n.* Übersicht *f.*

overweight, *n.* Übergewicht *nt.*

overwhelm, *vb.* überwäl'tigen.

overwork, *vb.* überar'beiten.

owe, vb. schulden.
owing, adj. schuldig; (o. to) dank.
owl, n. Eule, -n f.
own, 1. adj. eigen. **2.** vb. besit'zen*.
owner, n. Besit'zer, - m., Besit'-

zerin, -nen f.; Eigentümer, - m.,
Eigentümerin, -nen f.; Inhaber, -
m. Inhaberin, -nen f.
ox, n. Ochse, -n, -n m.
oxygen, n. Sauerstoff m.
oyster, n. Auster, -n f.

P

pace, n. Schritt, -e m.; (fig.)
Tempo, -pi nt.
pacific, adj. friedlich.
Pacific Ocean, n. Pazi'fischer
Ozean m.
pacifier, n. (baby's) Schnuller, -
m.
pacifism, n. Pazifis'mus m.
pacifist, n. Pazifist', -en, -en m.
pacify, vb. beschwich'tigen.
pack, 1. n. Bündel, - nt.; (gang)
Bande, -n f.; (cards) Kartenspiel,
-e nt.; (animals) Rudel, - nt. **2.** vb.
packen.
package, n. Paket', -e nt.
packing, n. Dichtung, -en f.
pact, n. Pakt, -e m.
pad, 1. n. Polster, - nt.; (paper)
Block, -s m. **2.** vb. polstern.
padding, n. Polsterung, -en f.
paddle, 1. n. Paddel, - nt. **2.** vb.
paddeln.
padlock, n. Vorlegeschloß, ⁻sser
nt.
pagan, adj. heidnisch.
page, 1. n. (book) Seite, -n f.;
(servant) Page, -n, -n m. **2.** vb.
suchen lassen.
pageant, n. prunkvoller Aufzug,
⁻e m.
pail, n. Eimer, - m.
pain, 1. n. Schmerz, -en m. **2.** vb.
schmerzen.
painful, adj. schmerzlich,
schmerzhaft.
painless, adj. schmerzlos.
painstaking, adj. sorgfältig.
paint, 1. n. Farbe, -n f. **2.** vb.
malen.
painter, n. Maler, - m., Malerin,
-nen f.
painting, n. Bild, -er nt., Malerei',
-en f.

pair, n. Paar, -e nt.
palace, n. Schloß, ⁻sser nt., Palast', ⁻e m.
palatable, adj. schmackhaft.
palate, n. Gaumen, - m.
palatial, adj. palast'artig.
pale, adj. blaß (⁻, -).
paleness, n. Blässe f.
palette, n. Palet'te, -n f.
pall, vb. schal werden*.
pallbearer, n. Sargträger, - m.
palm, n. (tree) Palme, -n f.;
(hand) Handfläche, -n f.
palpitate, vb. klopfen.
paltry, adj. armselig.
pamper, vb. verzär'teln.
pamphlet, n. Broschü're, -n f.
pan, 1. n. Pfanne, -n f. **2.** vb.
herun'termachen.
panacea, n. Universal'mittel, - nt.
pancake, n. Pfannkuchen, - m.
pane, n. Glasscheibe, -n f.
panel, n. (wood) Einsatzstück, -e
nt., Täfelung f.; (group of men)
Diskussionsgruppe, -n f.; (dashboard) Armatu'renbrett, -e nt.
pang, n. plötzlicher Schmerz, -en
m.
panic, n. Panik f.
panorama, n. Panora'ma, -men
nt.
pant, vb. keuchen, schnaufen.
panther, n. Panther, - m.
pantomime, n. Pantomi'me, -n f.
pantry, n. Speisekammer, - f.
pants, n. Hose, -n f.
panty hose, n. Strumpfhose, -n f.
papal, adj. päpstlich.
paper, 1. n. Papier', -e nt.; (news)
Zeitung, -en f. **2.** adj. papieren;
Papier'- (cpds.).
paperback, n. Taschenausgabe,
-n f.
paper-hanger, n. Tapezie'rer, -
m.

par, n. Pari nt.
parachute, n. Fallschrim, -e m.
parade, n. Para'de, -n f.
paradise, n. Paradies' nt.
paradox, n. Paradox', -e m.
paraffin, n. Paraffin', -e m.
paragraph, n. Paragraph', -en, -en m.; (typing) Absatz, ⁼e m.
parallel, 1. n. Paralle'le, -n f. **2.** adj. parallel'.
paralysis, n. Lähmung, -en f.
paralyze, vb. lähmen.
paramedic, n. jemand, der Erste Hilfe bei Unglücksfällen leistet.
parameter, n. Para'meter, -m.
paramount, adj. oberst-.
paraphrase, vb. umschrei'ben*.
parasite, n. Schmarot'zer, -m.
parcel, n. Päckchen, -nt.; Paket', -e nt.
parch, vb. dörren.
parchment, n. Pergament', -e nt.
pardon, 1. n. Verzei'hung, -en f.; (legal) Begna'digung, -en f. **2.** vb. verzei'hen*; begna'digen.
pare, vb. schälen.
parentage, n. Herkunft. ⁼e f.
parenthesis, n. Klammer, -n f.
parents, n.pl. Eltern pl.
Paris, n. Paris' nt.
parish, n. Kirchspiel, -e nt., Gemein'de, -n f.
Parisian, 1. n. Pari'ser, -m.; Pa-ri'serin, -nen f. **2.** adj. pari'sisch.
park, 1. n. Park, -s m. **2.** vb. parken.
parking meter, n. Parkuhr, -en f.
parkway, n. Ausfallstrasse, -n f.
parliament, n. Parlament', -e nt.
parliamentary, adj. parlamenta'risch.
parlor, n. gute Stube, -n f.; Salon', -s m.
parochial, adj. Pfarr-, Gemein'de- (cpds.); (fig.) beschränkt'.
parody, n. Parodie', -i'en f.
parrot, n. Papagei', -en m.
parsimony, n. Geiz m.
parsley, n. Petersi'lie f.
parson, n. Geistlich-m.
part, 1. n. Teil, -e m.; (hair) Scheitel, -m.; (theater) Rolle -n f. **2.** vb. trennen.
partake, vb. teil-nehmen*.

partial, adj. Teil- (cpds.); partei'isch.
partiality, n. Voreingenommenheit f.
participant, n. Teilnehmer, - m., Teilnehmerin, -nen f.
participate, vb. teil-nehmen*.
participation, n. Teilnahme f.
participle, n. Partizip', -ien nt.
particle, n. Teilchen, -m.
particular, adj. beson'der-.
parting, n. Abschied, -e m.
partisan, 1. n. Anhänger, -m., Partisan', (-en), -en m. **2.** adj. partei'isch.
partition, n. Teilung, -en f.; (wall) Scheidewand, -⁼e f.
partly, adv. teilweise, teils.
partner, n. Teilhaber, - m.; Teilhaberin, -nen f.; (games) Partner, - m., Partnerin, -nen f.
part of speech, n. Redeteil, -e m., Wortart, -en f.
party, n. (pol.) Partei', -en f.; (social) Gesell'schaft, -en f.
pass, 1. n. (mountain) Paß, ⁼sse m.; (identification) Ausweis, -e m. **2.** vb. vorü'ber-gehen*; (car) überho'len; (exam) beste'hen*; (to hand) reichen.
passable, adj. (roads) befahr'bar; (fig.) erträg'lich, passa'bel.
passage, n. Durchgang, ⁼e m., Durchfahrt, -en f.; (steamer) Überfahrt, -en f.; (law) Annahme, -n f.
passenger, n. Passagier', -e m.
passer-by, n. Passant', -en, -en m.
passion, n. Leidenschaft, -en f.; (Christ) Passion' f.
passionate, adj. leidenschaftlich.
passive, 1. n. Passiv nt. **2.** adj. passiv.
passport, n. Paß, ⁼sse m.
past, 1. n. Vergan'genheit f. **2.** adj. vergan'gen, früher. **3.** adv. vorbei', vorü'ber.
paste, 1. n. Paste, -n f.; (mucilage) Klebstoff, -e m. **2.** vb. kleben.
pasteurize, vb. pasteurisie'ren.
pastime, n. Zeitvertreib m.
pastor, n. Pfarrer, -m.
pastry, n. Gebäck' nt.
pastry shop, n. Bäckerei', -en f., Konditorei', -en f.

pasture, n. Weide, -n f.
pat, 1. n. Klaps, -e m. **2.** vb. einen leichten Schlag geben*.
patch, 1. n. Flicken, - m. **2.** vb. flicken.
patchwork, n. Flickwerk nt.
patent, n. Patent', -e nt.
patent leather, n. Lackleder nt.
paternal, adj. väterlich.
path, n. Weg, -e m., Pfad, -e m.
pathetic, adj. rührend, armselig.
pathology, n. Pathologie' f.
patience, n. Geduld' f.
patient, 1. n. Patient', -en, -en m., Patien'tin, -nen f. **2.** adj. gedul'dig.
patio, n. Patio, -s m.
patriarch, n. Patriarch', -en, -en m.
patriot, n. Patriot', -en, -en m.
patriotic, adj. patrio'tisch.
patriotism, n. Patriotis'mus m.
patrol, 1. n. Streife, -n f. **2.** vb. patrouille'ren.
patrolman, n. Polizist', -en, -en m.
patron, n. Schutzherr, -n, -en m.; (client) Kunde, -n, -n m.
patronage, n. Schirmherrschaft f.
patronize, vb. begün'stigen.
pattern, n. Muster, -nt.; (sewing) Schnittmuster, - nt.
pauper, n. Arm- m.&f.
pause, n. Pause, -n f.
pave, vb. pflastern.
pavement, n. Pflaster, - nt.
pavillion, n. Pavillon, -s m.
paw, n. Pfote, -n f.
pawn, 1. n. Pfand, ⁼er m.; (chess) Bauer, -(n), -n m. **2.** vb. pfänden.
pay, 1. n. Bezah'lung f., Gehalt', ⁼er nt. **2.** vb. bezah'len.
payment, n. Bezah'lung f.; (installment) Rate, -n f.
pea, n. Erbse, -n f.
peace, n. Friede(n), -n m.
peaceful, adj. friedlich.
peach, n. Pfirsich, -e m.
peacock, n. Pfau, -e m.
peak, n. Gipfel, - m.
peal, vb. läuten, dröhnen.
peanut, n. Erdnuß, ⁼sse f.
pear, n. Birne, -n f.
pearl, n. Perle, -n f.

peasant, n. Bauer, -(n), -n m., Bäuerin, -nen f.
pebble, n. Kieselstein, -e m.
peck, vb. picken.
peculiar, adj. merkwürdig, beson'der-.
peculiarity, n. Beson'derheit, -en f.
pedal, n. Pedal', -e nt.
pedant, n. Pedant', -en, -en m.
peddler, n. Hausie'rer, - m.
pedestal, n. Sockel, - m.
pedestrian, n. Fußgänger, - m.
pediatrician, n. Kinderarzt, ⁼e m., Kinderärztin, -nen f.
pedigree, n. Stammbaum, ⁼e m.
peek, n. gucken.
peel, 1. n. Schale, -n f. **2.** vb. schälen.
peep, vb. (look) lugen; (chirp) piepsen.
peer, n. Ebenbürtig- m.&f.
peg, n. Pflock, ⁼e m.; Stift, -e m.
pelt, 1. n. Fell, -e nt. **2.** vb. bewer'fen*; nieder'prasseln.
pelvis, n. Becken, - m.
pen, 1. n. Feder, -n f.; (sty) Stall, ⁼e m. **2.** vb. schreiben*.
penalty, n. Strafe, -n f.
penchant, n. Hang m.
pencil, n. Bleistift, -e m.
pendant, n. Anhänger, - m.
penetrate, vb. (tr.) durchdrin'gen*; (intr.) ein•dringen*.
penetration, n. Eindringen nt., Durchdrin'gung f.
penicillin, n. Penicillin' nt.
peninsula, n. Halbinsel, -n f.
penis, n. Penis, -se m.
penitent, adj. reuig.
penitentiary, n. Zuchthaus, ⁼er nt.
penknife, n. Federmesser, - nt.
penniless, adj. mittellos.
penny, n. Pfennig, -e m.
pension, n. Pension', -en f.
pensive, adj. nachdenklich.
people, n. Leute pl., Menschen pl.; (nation) Volk, ⁼er nt.
pepper, n. Pfeffer m.
per, prep. pro.
perambulator, n. Kinderwagen, - m.
perceive, vb. wahr•nehmen*.
percent, n. Prozent', -e nt.

percentage, n. Prozent'satz, -̈e m.; Provision', -en f.

perceptible, adj. wahrnehmbar.

perception, n. Wahrnehmung, -en f.

perch, 1. n. (fish) Barsch, -e m.; (pole) Stange, -n f. **2.** vb. sich nieder·setzen.

peremptory, adj. endgültig, diktato'risch.

perennial, 1. n. (plant) Staude, -n f. **2.** adj. alljähr'lich.

perfect, 1. n. (gram.) Perfekt, -e nt. **2.** adj. vollkom'men, perfekt'. **3.** vb. vervoll'kommnen.

perfection, n. Vollkom'menheit f.

perforate, vb. durchlö'chern.

perforation, n. Durchlö'cherung, -en f.

perform, vb. aus·führen; (drama) auf·führen.

performance, n. Ausführung, -en f.; (accomplishment) Leistung, -en f.; (drama) Aufführung, -en f., Vorstellung, -en f.

perfume, n. Parfüm', -s nt.

perfunctory, adj. oberflächlich, mecha'nisch.

perhaps, adv. vielleicht'.

peril, n. Gefahr', -en f.

perimeter, n. Umfang, -̈e m.

period, n. Zeitraum, -̈e m., Perio'de, -n f.; (punctuation) Punkt, -e m.

periodic, adj. perio'disch.

periphery, n. Umkreis, -e m., Peripherie', -i'en f.

perish, vb. unter·gehen*; verder'ben*.

perishable, adj. verderb'lich.

perjure oneself, vb. Meineid bege'hen*.

perjury, n. Meineid, -e m.

permanent, 1. n. (hair) Dauerwelle, -n f. **2.** adj. bestän'dig.

permissible, adj. zulässig.

permission, n. Erlaub'nis, -se f.

permit, 1. n. Erlaub'nisschein, -e m. **2.** vb. erlau'ben, zu·lassen*.

perpendicular, adj. senkrecht.

perpetrate, vb. bege'hen*.

perpetual, adj. ewig.

perplex, vb. verwir'ren.

perplexity, n. Verwir'rung, -en f.

persecute, vb. verfol'gen.

persecution, n. Verfol'gung, -en f.

perseverance, n. Beharr'lichkeit f.

persevere, vb. behar'ren.

persist, n. behar'ren, beste'hen*.

persistent, adj. beharr'lich.

person, n. Mensch, -en, -en m., Person', -en f.

personal, adj. persön'lich.

personality, n. Persön'lichkeit, -en f.

personnel, n. Personal' nt.

perspective, n. Perspekti've, -n f.

perspiration, n. Schweiß m.

perspire, vb. schwitzen.

persuade, vb. überre'den.

persuasive, adj. überzeu'gend.

pertain, vb. betref'fen*.

pertinent, adj. zugehörig.

perturb, vb. beun'ruhigen.

perverse, adj. verkehrt', widernatürlich; pervers'.

perversion, n. Verdre'hung, -en f.

pervert, 1. n. perver'ser Mensch, -en, -en m. **2.** vb. verdre'hen; verfüh'ren.

pessimism, n. Pessimis'mus m.

pestilence, n. Pest f.

pet, 1. n. Liebling, -e m.; (animal) Haustier, -e nt. **2.** vb. streicheln.

petal, n. Blütenblatt, -̈er nt.

petition, n. Eingabe, -n f., Antrag, -̈e m.

petrify, vb. verstei'nern; (be petrified) wie gelähmt' sein*.

petrol, n. Benzin' nt.

petroleum, n. Petro'leum nt.

petticoat, n. steifer Unterrock, -̈e m.

petty, adj. gering'fügig; kleinlich.

petulant, adj. mürrisch.

pew, n. Kirchenstuhl, -̈e m.

phantom, n. Phantom', -e nt.

pharmacist, n. Apothe'ker, - m., Apothe'kerin, -nen f.

pharmacy, n. Apothe'ke, -n f.

phase, n. Phase, -n f.

pheasant, n. Fasan', -e(n) m.

phenomenal, adj. erstaun'lich.

phenomenon, n. Erschei'nung, -en f., Phänomen', -e nt.

philanthropy, n. Menschenliebe f., Wohltätigkeit, -en f.

philately, n. Briefmarkenkunde f.
philosopher, n. Philosoph', -en, -en m., Philoso'phin, -nen f.
philosophical, adj. philoso'phisch.
philosophy, n. Philosophie', -i'en f.
phlegm, n. Phlegma nt.; (med.) Schleim m.
phlegmatic, adj. phlegma'tisch.
phobia, n. krankhafte Angst f., Phobie', -i'en f.
phonetic, adj. phone'tisch.
phonetics, n. Phone'tik f.
phonograph, n. Grammophon', -e nt.
phosphorus, n. Phosphor m.
photocopier, n. Photokopier'-maschine, -n f.
photocopy, n. Photokopie', -i'en f.; Ablichtung, -en f.
photocopy, vb. photokopie'ren.
photogenic, adj. photogen'.
photograph, n. Photographie', -i'en f., Lichtbild, -er nt.
photographer, n. Photograph', -en, -en m., Photogra'phin, -nen f.
photography, n. Photographie' f.
photostat, n. Photokopie', -i'en f. 2. vb. photokopie'ren.
phrase, 1. n. Satz, -e m., Redewendung, -en f. 2. vb. ausdrücken.
physical, adj. körperlich, physisch.
physician, n. Arzt, -e m., Ärztin, -nen f.
physicist, n. Physiker, - m., Physikerin, -nen f.
physics, n. Physik f.
physiology, n. Physiologie' f.
physiotherapy, n. Physiotherapie' f.
physique, n. Körperbau m.
pianist, n. Klavier'spieler, - m., Klavier'spielerin, -nen f., Pianist', -en, -en m., Pianis'tin, -nen f.
piano, n. Klavier', -e nt.
piccolo, n. Piccoloflöte, -n f.
pick, 1. n. Spitzhacke, -n f. 2. vb. (gather) pflücken; (select) auswählen.
picket, 1. n. Holzpfahl, -e m.; (striker) Streikposten, - m. 2. vb. Streikposten stehen*.

pickle, n. saure Gurke f.
pickpocket, n. Taschendieb, -e m.
picnic, n. Picknick, -s nt.
picture, 1. n. Bild, -er nt.; (fig.) Vorstellung, -en f. 2. vb. dar·stellen; sich vor·stellen.
picturesque, adj. malerisch.
pie, n. eine Art Backwerk.
piece, n. Stück, -e nt.
pier, n. Pier, -s m.
pierce, vb. durchboh'ren.
piety, n. Frömmigkeit f.
pig, n. Schwein, -e nt.; (young) Ferkel, -e nt.
pigeon, n. Taube, -n f.
pigment, n. Pigment, -e nt.
pile, 1. n. (heap) Haufen, m.; (post) Pfahl, -e m. 2. vb. auf·häufen.
pilfer, vb. stehlen*.
pilgrim, n. Pilger, - m., Pilgerin, -nen, f.
pilgrimage, n. Wallfahrt, -en f.
pillage, 1. n. Plünderung, -en f. 2. vb. plündern.
pillar, n. Säule, -n f.
pillow, n. Kissen, - nt.
pillowcase, n. Kissenbezug, -e m.
pilot, n. Pilot', -en, -en m., Pilo'tin, -nen f.; (ship) Lotse, -n, -n m.
pimple, n. Pickel, - m.
pin, 1. n. Stecknadel, -n f. 2. vb. stecken.
pinch, 1. n. (of salt, etc.) Prise, -n f. 2. vb. kneifen*, zwicken.
pine, 1. n. Fichte, -n f.; Keifer, -n f. 2. vb. sich sehnen.
pineapple, n. Ananas, -se f.
ping-pong, n. Tischtennis nt.
pink, adj. rosa.
pinnacle, n. Gipfel, - m.
pint, n. etwa ein halber Liter.
pioneer, n. Pionier', -e m.
pious, adj. fromm(-, -).
pipe, n. Rohr, -e nt.; Röhre, -n f.; (smoking) Pfeife, -n f.
piquant, adj. pikant'.
pirate, n. Seeräuber, - m.
pistol, n. Pisto'le, -n f.
piston, n. Kolben, - m.
pit, n. (stone) Kern, -e m; (hole) Grube, -n f.
pitch, 1. n. (tar) Pech nt.; (resin) Harz, -e nt.; (throw) Wurf, -e m.;

(music) Tonhöhe, -n f. **2.** vb.
(throw) werfen*; *(a tent)* auf-
schlagen*.
pitcher, n. *(jug)* Krug, -̈e m.;
(thrower) Ballwerfer beim Baseball m.
pitchfork, n. Heugabel, -n f.,
Mistgabel, -n f.; *(music)* Stimm-
gabel, -n f.
pitfall, n. Falle, -n f.
pitiful, adj. erbärm'lich.
pitiless, adj. erbar'mungslos.
pity, n. Mitleid nt., Erbar'men nt.
pivot, n. Drehpunkt, -e m.
pizza, n. Pizza, -s f.
placard, n. Plakat', -e nt.
placate, vb. beschwich'tigen.
place, **1.** n. Platz, -̈e m., Ort, -e m.
2. vb. setzen, stellen, legen; unter-
bringen*.
placid, adj. gelas'sen.
plagiarism, n. Plagiat' nt.
plague, **1.** n. Seuche, -n f. **2.** vb.
plagen.
plain, **1.** n. Ebene, -n f. **2.** adj.
eben; *(fig.)* einfach, schlicht.
plaintiff, n. Kläger, - m., Klägerin, -nen f.
plan, **1.** n. Plan, -̈e m. **2.** vb. planen.
plane, **1.** n. *(geom.)* Fläche, -n f.;
(tool) Hobel, - m.; *(airplane)*
Flugzeug, -e nt. **2.** vb. hobeln.
planet, n. Planet', -en, -en m.
planetarium, Planeta'rium, -ien
nt.
plank, n. Brett, -er nt., Planke, -n
f.
plant, **1.** n. Pflanze, -n f.; *(factory)*
Fabrik', -en f.; *(installation)*
Werk, -e nt. **2.** vb. pflanzen.
planter, n. Pflanzer, - m.
plasma, n. Plasma, -men nt.
plaster, n. Gips m.; *(med.)*
Pflaster, - nt.; *(walls)* Verputz' m.
plastic, **1.** n. Kunststoff, -e m. **2.**
adj. plastisch.
plate, n. Platte, -n f.; *(dish)* Teller,
- m.
plateau, n. Hochebene, -n f., Plateau', -s nt.
platform, n. Plattform, -en f.;
(train) Bahnsteig, -e m.
platinum, n. Platin nt.
platitude, n. Plattheit, -en f.
platoon, n. Zug, -̈e m.

platter, n. Servier'platte, -n f.
plausible, adj. einleuchtend.
play, **1.** n. Spiel, -e nt.; *(theater)*
Thea'terstück, -e nt. **2.** vb. spielen.
player, n. *(game)* Mitspieler, - m.,
Mitspielerin, -nen f.; *(theater)*
Schauspieler, - m., Schauspielerin,
-nen f.; *(music)* Spieler, - m., Spielerin, -nen f.
playful, adj. spielerisch.
playground, n. Spielplatz, -̈e m.
playmate, n. Spielgefährte, -n, -n
m., Spielgefährtin, -nen f.
playwright, n. Drama'tiker, - m.
plea, n. Bitte, -n f.; *(excuse)* Vorwand, -̈e m.; *(jur.)* Plädoyer', -s
nt.
plead, vb. bitten*, plädie'ren.
pleasant, adj. angenehm.
please, **1.** vb. gefal'len*. **2.** interj.
bitte.
pleasing, adj. angenehm.
pleasure, n. Vergnü'gen nt.,
Freude, -n f.
pleat, n. Falte, -n f.
plebiscite, n. Volksabstimmung,
-en f.
pledge, **1.** n. Gelüb'de, -nt. **2.** vb.
gelo'ben.
plentiful, adj. reichlich.
plenty, n. Fülle f.; **(p. of)** reichlich,
genug'.
pleurisy, n. Rippenfellentzündung, -en f.
pliable, pliant, adj. biegsam.
pliers, n. Zange, -n f., Kneifzange,
-n f.
plight, n. schwierige Lage, -n f.
plot, **1.** n. Stück Land nt.; *(story)*
Handlung, -en f.; *(intrigue)*
Komplott', -e nt. **2.** vb. intrigie'-
ren; *(plan)* entwer'fen*.
plow, **1.** n. Pflug, -̈e m. **2.** vb. pflügen.
pluck, **1.** n. Mut m. **2.** vb. rupfen.
plug, **1.** n. Stöpsel, - m., Pfropfen,
- m.; **(spark p.)** Zündkerze, -n f.;
(fire p.) Feuerhydrant, -en, -en m.
2. vb. zu'stopfen.
plum, n. Pflaume, -n f.
plumage, n. Gefie'der nt.
plumber, n. Klempner, - m.
plume, n. Feder, -n f.
plump, adj. dicklich.

plunder, 1. *n.* Beute *f.*, Raub *m.* **2.** *vb.* plündern.
plunge, *vb.* rauchen, stürzen.
plural, 1. *n.* Mehrzahl, -en *f.*, Plural, -e *m.*
plus, *prep.* plus.
plutocrat, *n.* Plutokrat', -en, -en *m.*
pneumatic, *adj.* pneuma'tisch.
pneumonia, *n.* Lungenentzün'dung, -en *f.*
poach, *vb. (hunt illegally)* wildern; *(eggs)* pochie'ren.
pocket, *n.* Tasche, -n *f.*
pocketbook, *n.* Handtasche, -n *f.*
pod, *n.* Schote, -n *f.*
podiatry, *n.* Fußheilkunde *f.*
poem, *n.* Gedicht', -e *nt.*
poet, *n.* Dichter, - *m.*, Dichterin, -nen *f.*
poetic, *adj.* dichterisch, poe'tisch.
poetry, *n.* Dichtung, -en *f.*, Poesie' *f.*
poignant, *adj.* treffend.
point, 1. *n.* Punkt, -e *m.* **2.** *vb.* zeigen, hin'weisen*.
pointed, *adj.* spitz.
pointless, *adj.* sinnlos, witzlos.
poise, *n.* Schwebe *f.*; *(assuredness)* sicheres Auftreten *nt.*
poison, 1. *n.* Gift, -e *nt.* **2.** *vb.* vergif'ten.
poisonous, *adj.* giftig.
poke, *vb.* stoßen*.
Poland, *n.* Polen *nt.*
polar, *adj.* polar'.
pole, *n. (post)* Pfahl, -̈e *m.*; *(rod)* Stange, -n *f.*; *(electrical, geographic)* Pol, -e *m.*
Pole, *n.* Pole, -n, -n *m.*, Polin, -nen *f.*
police, *n.* Polizei' *f.*
police officer, *n.* Polizist', -en, -en *m.*, Polizis'tin, -nen *f.*
policy, *n.* Politik' *f.*; *(insurance)* Poli'ce, -n *f.*
polish, 1. *n.* Politur', -en *f.*; *(shoe p.)* Schuhkrem, -s *f.* **2.** *vb.* polie'ren, putzen.
Polish, *adj.* polnisch.
polite, *adj.* höflich.
politeness, *n.* Höflichkeit, -en *f.*
politic, political, *adj.* poli'tisch.
politician, *n.* Poli'tiker, - *m.*, Poli'tikerin, -nen *f.*

politics, *n.* Politik' *f.*
poll, 1. *n.* Wahl, -en *f.*, Abstimmung, -en *f.*; Meinungsumfrage, -n *f.* **2.** *vb.* befra'gen.
pollen, *n.* Blütenstaub *m.*
pollute, *vb.* verun'reinigen.
pollution, *n.* Umweltverschmut'zung *f.*
polonaise, *n.* Poloña'se, -n *f.*
polygamy, *n.* Polygamie' *f.*
pomp, *n.* Pomp *m.*
pompous, *adj.* prunkvoll; *(fig.)* hochtrabend.
poncho, *n.* Poncho, -s *m.*
pond, *n.* Teich, -e *m.*
ponder, *vb. (tr.)* erwä'gen; *(intr.)* nach'denken*.
ponderous, *adj.* schwerfällig.
pontiff, *n.* Papst, -̈e *m.*
pontoon, *n.* Schwimmer, - *m.*
pony, *n.* Pony, -s *nt.*
pool, 1. *n. (pond)* Tümpel, - *m.*; *(swimming pool)* Schwimmbad, -̈er, *nt.*; *(group)* Interes'sengemeinschaft, -en *f.* **2.** *vb.* zusam'men·legen.
poor, *adj.* arm (-).
pop, 1. *n.* Knall, -e *m.*; *(father)* Papi, -s *m.* **2.** *vb.* knallen.
pope, *n.* Papst, -̈e *m.*
popular, *adj.* volkstümlich; beliebt'.
popularity, *n.* Beliebt'heit *f.*
population, *n.* Bevöl'kerung, -en *f.*
porcelain, *n.* Porzellan', -e *nt.*
porch, *n.* Veran'da, -den *f.*
pore, *n.* Pore, -n *f.*
pork, *n.* Schweinefleisch *nt.*
pornography, *n.* Pornographie' *f.*
porous, *adj.* porös'.
port, *n.* Hafen, -̈ *m.*; *(wine)* Port *m.*
portable, *adj.* tragbar.
portal, *n.* Portal', -e *nt.*
portend, *vb.* Unheil verkün'den.
porter, *n.* Gepäck'träger, - *m.*
portfolio, *n.* Mappe, -n *f.*; Portefeuille' *nt.*
porthole, *n.* Luke, -n *f.*
portion, *n.* Teil, -e *m.*; *(serving)* Portion', -en *f.*
portrait, *n.* Porträt', -s *nt.*
portray, *vb.* schildern.
Portugal, *n.* Portugal *nt.*

Portuguese, 1. n. Portugie'se, -n, -n m., Portugie'sin, -nen f. **2.** adj. portugie'sisch.
pose, 1. n. Haltung, -en f., Pose, -n f. **2.** vb. stellen; **(p. as)** sich ausgeben* für.
position, n. Stellung, -en f.
positive, adj. positiv.
possess, vb. besit'zen*.
possession, n. Besitz, -e m., Eigentum, -̈er nt.
possessive, adj. besitz'gierig.
possessor, n. Besit'zer, - m., Besit'zerin, -nen f., Eigentümer, - m., Eigentümerin, -nen f.
possibility, n. Möglichkeit, -en f.
possible, adj. möglich.
possibly, adv. möglicherweise.
post, 1. n. **(pole)** Pfahl, -̈e m.; **(place)** Posten, - m.; **(mail)** Post f. **2.** vb. auf·stellen; zur Post geben*.
postage, n. Porto nt.
postal, adj. Post- (cpds.).
postcard, n. Postkarte, -n f.
poster, n. Plakat, -e nt.
posterior, adj. hinter-; Hinter- (cpds.).
posterity, n. Nachwelt f.
postman, n. Postbote, -n, -n m., Briefträger, - m.
post office, n. Post f., Postamt, -̈er nt.
postpone, vb. auf·schieben*, verschie'ben*.
postscript, n. Nachschrift, -en f.
posture, n. Haltung, -en f.
pot, n. Topf, -̈e m.; **(marijuana)** Hasch m.
potassium, n. Kalium nt.
potato, n. Kartof'fel, -n f.
potent, adj. stark (-).
potential, 1. n. Möglichkeit, -en f. **2.** adj. möglich.
potion, n. Trank, -̈e m.
pottery, n. Töpferware, -n f.
pouch, n. Tasche, -n f., Beutel, - m.
poultry, n. Geflü'gel nt.
pound, 1. n. Pfund, -e nt. **2.** vb. hämmern, schlagen*.
pour, vb. gießen*.
poverty, n. Armut f.

powder, 1. n. Pulver, - nt.; **(cosmetic)** Puder, - m. **2.** vb. pudern.
power, n. Macht, -̈e f.
powerful, adj. mächtig.
powerless, adj. machtlos.
practicable, adj. durchführbar.
practical, adj. praktisch.
practice, n. Übung, -en f.; **(carrying out)** Ausübung f.; **(custom)** Gewohn'heit, -en f.; **(doctor)** Praxis, -xen f. **2.** vb. üben; **(carry out)** aus·üben.
practitioner, n. Vertre'ter, - m., Vertre'terin, -nen f.; **(med.)** praktischer Arzt, -̈e m.
prairie, n. Prairie, -'i'en f.
praise, 1. n. Lob, -e nt. **2.** vb. loben.
prank, n. Streich, -e m.
pray, vb. beten.
prayer, n. Gebet', -e nt.
preach, vb. predigen.
preacher, n. Prediger, - m.
precarious, adj. heikel.
precaution, n. Vorsichtsmaßregel, -n f.
precede, vb. voran'·gehen*.
precedence, n. Vorrang m.
precedent, n. Präzedenz'fall, -̈e m.
precept, n. Vorschrift, -en f.
precinct, n. Bezirk', -e m.
precious, adj. kostbar.
precipice, n. Abgrund, -̈e m.
precipitate, 1. adj. überstürzt'. **2.** vb. überstür'zen.
precise, adj. genau.
precision, n. Genau'igkeit f., Präzision' f.
preclude, vb. aus·schließen*.
precocious, adj. frühreif, altklug (-).
predecessor, n. Vorgänger, - m., Vorgängerin, -nen f.
predestination, n. Prädestination' f.
predicament, n. Dilem'ma, -s nt.
predicate, n. Prädikat', -e nt. **2.** vb. begrün'den.
predict, vb. voraus'·sagen.
predisposed, adj. geneigt'; **(med.)** anfällig.
predominant, adj. vorherrschend.

prefabricated, *adj.* Fertig-(cpds.).

preface, *n.* Vorwort, -e *nt.*

prefer, *vb.* vor•ziehen*.

preferable, *adj.* vorzuziehend; **(is p.)** ist vorzuziehen.

preferably, *adv.* vorzugsweise.

preference, *n.* Vorzug *m.,* Vorliebe *f.*

prefix, *n.* Vorsilbe, -n *f.,* Präfix, -e *nt.*

pregnancy, *n.* Schwangerschaft, -en *f.*

pregnant, *adj.* schwanger.

prehistoric, *adj.* vorgeschichtlich, prähisto'risch.

prejudice, *n.* Vorurteil, -e *nt.*

prejudiced, *adj.* voreingenommen.

preliminary, *adj.* einleitend.

prelude, *n.* Einleitung, -en *f.,* Vorspiel, -e *nt.*

premature, *adj.* vorzeitig.

premeditate, *vb.* vorher überle'gen.

premeditated, *adj.* vorbedacht; mit Vorbedacht.

premier, *n.* Minis'terpräsident, -en, -en *m.*

première, *n.* Urauffführung, -en *f.*

premise, *n.* Prämis'se, -n *f.*

premium, *n.* Prämie, -n *f.*

premonition, *n.* Vorahnung, -en *f.*

prenatal, *adj.* vorgeburtlich.

preparation, *n.* Vorbereitung, -en *f.; (of food)* Zubereitung *f.*

preparatory, *adj.* vorbereitend; Vorbereitungs-(cpds.).

prepare, *vb.* vor•bereiten; *(food)* zu•bereiten.

preponderant, *adj.* überwie'gend.

preposition, *n.* Präposition', -en *f.*

preposterous, *adj.* widersinnig.

prerequisite, *n.* Vorbedingung, -en *f.*

prerogative, *n.* Vorrecht, -e *nt.*

prescribe, *vb.* vor•schreiben*; *(med.)* verschrei'ben*.

prescription, *n.* Rezept', -e *nt.*

presence, *n.* Anwesenheit *f.,* Gegenwart *f.*

present, 1. *n. (time)* Gegenwart *f.; (gram.)* Präsens *nt.; (gift)* Geschenk', -e *nt.* **2.** *adj.* anwesend, gegenwärtig. **3.** *vb.* dar•bieten*; *(introduce)* vor•stellen; *(arms)* präsentie'ren.

presentable, *adj.* präsenta'bel.

presentation, *n.* Darstellung, -en *f.;* Vorstellung, -en *f.*

presently, *adv.* gleich.

preservation, *n.* Erhal'tung *f.*

preservative, *n.* Konservie'rungsmittel, - *nt.*

preserve, *vb.* bewah'ren, erhal'ten*; *(food)* konservie'ren, ein•machen.

preside, *vb.* den Vorsitz führen.

presidency, *n.* Vorsitz, -e *m.;* Präsi'dentschaft *f.*

president, *n.* Präsident', -en, -en *m.,* Präsi'dentin, -nen *f.*

press, 1. *n.* Presse *f.* **2.** *vb.* pressen, drücken; *(iron)* bügeln.

pressing, *adj.* dringend.

pressure, *n.* Druck *m.*

pressure cooker, *n.* Dampfkochtopf, -̈e *m.*

prestige, *n.* Prestige' *nt.*

presume, *vb.* an•nehmen*; voraus'•setzen.

presumptuous, *adj.* anmaßend.

presuppose, *vb.* voraus'•setzen.

pretend, *vb.* vor•geben*.

pretense, *n.* Vorwand, -̈e *m.*

pretentious, *adj.* prätentiös'.

pretext, *n.* Vorwand, -̈e *m.*

pretty, 1. *adj.* hübsch, niedlich. **2.** *adv.* ziemlich.

prevail, *vb.* vor•herrschen; *(win)* siegen; **(p. upon)** überre'den.

prevalent, *adj.* vorherrschend.

prevent, *vb.* verhin'dern, verhü'ten.

prevention, *n.* Verhin'derung *f.,* Verhü'tung, -en *f.*

preventive, *adj.* Verhü'tungs-, Präventiv'-(cpds.).

preview, *n.* Vorschau *f.,* Voranzeige, -n *f.*

previous, *adj.* vorher'gehend.

prey, *n.* Raub *m.,* Beute *f.*

price, *n.* Preis, -e *m.*

priceless, *adj.* unbezahl'bar.

prick, *vb.* stechen*.

pride, *n.* Stolz *m.,* Hochmut *m.*

priest, *n.* Priester, - *m.*, Pfarrer, - *m.*

prim, *adj.* spröde, prüde.

primary, *adj.* primär'.

prime, 1. *n.* Blüte *f.* **2.** *adj.* Haupt- (*cpds.*); erstklassig; **(p. number)** Primzahl, -en *f.*

prime minister, *n.* Premier'minister, - *m.*, Premier'ministerin, -nen *f.*

primitive, *adj.* primitiv'.

prince, *n.* (*king's son*) Prinz, -en, -en *m.*; (*other ruler*) Fürst, -en, -en *m.*

princess, *n.* Prinzes'sin, -nen *f.*

principal, 1. *n.* (*school*) Schuldirektor, -o'ren *m.*, Schuldirektorin, -nen *f.* **2.** *adj.* hauptsächlich, Haupt- (*cpds.*).

principle, *n.* Prinzip', -ien *nt.*, Grundsatz, ⁓e *m.*

print, 1. *n.* Druck, -e *m.* **2.** *vb.* drucken.

printing, *n.* Buchdruck *m.*

printing press, *n.* Druckerpresse, -n *f.*

printout, *n.* Printout, -s *m.*

priority, *n.* Vorrang *m.*, Priorität', -en *f.*

prism, *n.* Prisma, -men *nt.*

prison, *n.* Gefäng'nis, -se *nt.*

prisoner, *n.* Gefan'gene *m.&f.*

privacy, *n.* ungestörtes Allein'sein *nt.*

private, 1. *n.* (*mil.*) Soldat', -en, -en *m.* **2.** *adj.* privat'.

privation, *n.* Berau'bung, -en *f.*; Not, ⁓e *f.*

privilege, *n.* Vorrecht, -e *nt.*, Privileg', -ien *nt.*

privy, 1. *n.* Abort, -e *m.* **2.** *adj.* geheim'.

prize, 1. *n.* Preis, -e *m.* **2.** *vb.* schätzen.

probability, *n.* Wahrschein'lichkeit, -en *f.*

probable, *adj.* wahrschein'lich.

probation, *n.* Probezeit, -en *f.*; (*jur.*) Bewäh'rungsfrist *f.*

probe, *vb.* sondie'ren.

problem, *n.* Problem', -e *nt.*

procedure, *n.* Verfah'ren *nt.*

proceed, *vb.* (*go on*) fort·fahren*; (*act*) verfah'ren*.

process, *n.* Verfah'ren, - *nt.*

procession, *n.* Prozession', -en *f.*

proclaim, *vb.* aus·rufen*, verkün'den.

proclamation, *n.* Bekannt'machung, -en *f.*, Proklamation', -en *f.*

procrastinate, *vb.* zögern.

procure, *vb.* besor'gen, verschaf'fen.

prodigy, *n.* Wunder, - *nt.*; **(infant p.)** Wunderkind, -er *nt.*

produce, *vb.* (*show*) vor·legen, vor·führen; (*create*) erzeu'gen, her·stellen, produzie'ren.

product, *n.* Erzeug'nis, -se *nt.*, Produkt', -e *nt.*

production, *n.* Herstellung, -en *f.*, Produktion', -en *f.*

productive, *adj.* produktiv'.

profane, *adj.* profan'.

profanity, *n.* Fluchen *nt.*

profess, *vb.* beken'nen*; (*pretend*) vor·geben*.

profession, *n.* Bekennt'nis, -se *nt.*; (*calling*) Beruf', -e *m.*

professional, *adj.* berufs'mäßig.

professor, *n.* Profes'sor, -o'ren *m.*, Profes'sorin, -nen *f.*

proficient, *adj.* erfah'ren, beschla'gen.

profile, *n.* Profil', -e *nt.*

profit, 1. *n.* Gewinn' *m.* **2.** *vb.* profitie'ren.

profitable, *adj.* einträglich; (*fig.*) vorteilhaft.

profiteer, *n.* Schieber, - *m.*

profound, *adj.* tief, tiefsinnig.

profundity, *n.* Tiefe *f.*; Tiefgründigkeit *f.*

profuse, *adj.* überreich.

program, *n.* Programm', -e *nt.*

progress, 1. *n.* Fortschritt, -e *m.* **2.** *vb.* fort·schreiten*.

progressive, *adj.* fortschrittlich.

prohibit, *vb.* verbie'ten*; verhin'dern.

prohibition, *n.* Verbot', -e *nt.*

prohibitive, *adj.* verbie'terisch.

project, 1. *n.* Projekt', -e *nt.* **2.** *vb.* (*plan*) projizie'ren; (*stick out*) vor·springen*.

projectile, *n.* Geschoß', -sse *nt.*

projection, *n.* Projektion', -en *f.*

projector, *n.* Projek'tor, -o'ren *m.*

proliferation, n. Verbreitung f.

prolific, adj. fruchtbar.

prologue, n. Prolog, -e m.

prolong, vb. verlän'gern, aus-dehnen.

prominent, adj. prominent'.

promiscuous, adj. unterschieds-los; sexuell' zügellos.

promise, 1. n. Verspre'chen, - nt. **2.** vb. verspre'chen*.

promote, vb. fördern; (in rank) beför'dern.

promotion, n. Förderung f.; Beför'derung, -en f.

prompt, adj. prompt.

promulgate, vb. verkün'den.

pronoun, n. Fürwort, ⸚er nt., Prono'men, -mina nt.

pronounce, vb. aus'sprechen*.

pronunciation, n. Aussprache, -n f.

proof, n. Beweis, -e m.; (printing) Korrektur'bogen, - m.; (photo) Abzug, ⸚e m.

prop, 1. n. Stütze, -n f. **2.** vb. stützen.

propaganda, n. Propagan'da f.

propagate, vb. fort'pflanzen; ver-brei'ten.

propel, vb. an'treiben*.

propeller, n. Propel'ler, - m.

proper, adj. passend, angebracht.

property, n. Besitz' m., Eigentum nt.

prophecy, n. Prophezei'ung, -en f.

prophesy, vb. prophezei'en.

prophet, n. Prophet', -en, -en m.

prophetic, adj. prophe'tisch.

propitious, adj. günstig.

proponent, n. Verfech'ter, - m.

proportion, n. Verhält'nis, -se nt., Proportion', -en f.; Ausmaß, -e nt.

proportionate, adj. angemessen.

proposal, n. Vorschlag, ⸚e m.; (marriage) Heiratsantrag, ⸚e m.

propose, vb. vor'schlagen*; (in-tend) beab'sichtigen; einen Hei-ratsantrag machen.

proposition, n. Vorschlag, ⸚e m.; (logic) Lehrsatz, ⸚e m.

proprietor, n. Inhaber, - m., Inha-berin, -nen f., Eigentümer, - m., Eigentümerin, -nen f.

propriety, n. Anstand m.

prosaic, adj. prosa'isch.

prose, n. Prosa f.

prosecute, vb. verfol'gen; (jur.) an'klagen.

prospect, n. Aussicht, -en f.

prospective, adj. voraus'sicht-lich.

prosper, vb. gedei'hen*.

prosperity, n. Wohlstand m.

prosperous, adj. blühend, wohl-habend.

prostitute, n. Prostituiert'- f.

prostrate, 1. adj. hingestreckt. **2.** vb. zu Boden werfen*.

protect, vb. schützen, be-schüt'zen.

protection, n. Schutz m.

protective, adj. Schutz- (cpds.).

protector, n. Beschüt'zer, - m.

protégé, n. Protegé', -s m.

protein, n. Protein' nt.

protest, 1. n. Einspruch, ⸚e m., Protest', -e m. **2.** vb. Einspruch er-he'ben*, protestie'ren.

Protestant, 1. n. Protestant', -en, -en m. **2.** adj. protestan'tisch.

Protestantism, n. Protestantis'-mus m.

protocol, n. Protokoll', -e nt.

proton, n. Proton, -o'nen nt.

protrude, vb. hervor'stehen*.

protuberance, n. Auswuchs, ⸚e m., Buckel, - m.

proud, adj. stolz.

prove, vb. bewei'sen*.

proverb, n. Sprichwort, ⸚er nt.

proverbial, adj. sprichwörtlich.

provide, vb. (p. for) sorgen für; (p. with) versor'gen mit, verse'hen* mit.

provided, adv. voraus'gesetzt daß.

providence, n. Vorsehung f.; Vorsorge f.

province, n. Provinz', -en f.

provincial, adj. provinziell'.

provision, n. (stipulation) Be-stim'mung, -en f.; (food) Provi-ant' m.; (stock) Vorrat, ⸚e m.

provocation, n. Provokation', -en f.

provoke, vb. provozie'ren; (call forth) hervor'rufen*.

prowess, n. Tüchtigkeit f.

prowl, vb. umher'schleichen*.

proximity, n. Nähe f.

proxy, n. *(thing)* Vollmacht, -en f.; *(person)* Stellvertreter, - m.

prudence, n. Vorsicht f.; Klugheit f.

prudent, adj. klug (-); umsichtig.

prune, n. Backpflaume, -n f.

Prussia, n. Preußen nt.

pry, vb. *(break open)* auf·bre'chen*; *(peer about)* herum'·schnüffeln.

psalm, n. Psalm, -en m.

pseudonym, n. Pseudonym', -e nt.

psychedelic, adj. psyche'lisch, halluzine'rend.

psychiatrist, n. Psychia'ter, - m., Psychia'terin, -nen f.

psychiatry, n. Psychiatrie' f.

psychoanalysis, n. Psycho-analy'se, -n f.

psychological, adj. psycholo'gisch.

psychology, n. Psychologie' f.

psychosis, n. Psycho'se, -n f.

ptomaine, n. Ptomain', -e nt.

puberty, n. Pubertät' f.

public, 1. n. Öffentlichkeit f. **2.** adj. öffentlich.

publication, n. Veröf'fentlichung, -en f., Publikation', -en f.

publicity, n. Rekla'me f., Propagan'da f.

publish, vb. veröf'fentlichen, publizie'ren; *(make known)* be-kannt'·machen.

publisher, n. Heraus'geber, - m., Heraus'geberin, -nen f., Verle'ger, - m., Verle'gerin, -nen f.

pudding, n. Pudding, -s m.

puddle, n. Pfütze, -n f.

puff, 1. n. *(wind)* Windstoß, -̈e m.; *(smoke)* Rauchwolke, -n f.; *(powder)* Puderquaste, -n f. **2.** vb. blasen*; paffen.

pull, 1. n. Zugkraft f., Anziehungskraft f.; *(influence)* Bezie'hung, -en f. **2.** vb. ziehen*.

pulley, n. Flaschenzug, -̈e m.

pulmonary, adj. Lungen- *(cpds.)*.

pulp, n. Brei m.; *(fruit)* Fruchtfleisch nt.

pulpit, n. Kanzel, -n f.

pulsar, n. Pulsar m.

pulsate, vb. pulsie'ren.

pulse, n. Puls, -e m.

pump, 1. n. Pumpe, -n f.; *(shoe)* Pump -s m. **2.** vb. pumpen.

pumpkin, n. Kürbis, -se m.

pun, n. Wortspiel, -e nt.

punch, 1. n. Schlag, -̈e m., Stoß, -̈e m.; *(drink)* Punsch m. **2.** vb. schlagen*, stoßen*; *(make holes)* lochen.

punctual, adj. pünktlich.

punctuate, vb. interpunktie'ren.

punctuation, n. Interpunktion' f.

puncture, 1. n. Loch, -̈er nt.; *(tire)* Reifenpanne, -n f.; *(med.)* Punktion', -en f. **2.** vb. durchste'chen*.

pungent, adj. stechend, beißend.

punish, vb. strafen, bestra'fen.

punishment, n. Strafe, -n f.

puny, adj. mickrig.

pupil, n. Schüler, - m.; Schülerin, -nen f.

puppet, n. Marionet'te, -n f.

puppy, n. junger Hund, -e m.

purchase, 1. n. Kauf, -̈e m., Einkauf, -̈e m. **2.** vb. kaufen, erwer'ben*.

pure, adj. rein.

purée, n. Püree', -s nt.

purgative, n. Abführmittel, - nt.

purge, 1. n. Säuberungsaktion, -en f. **2.** vb. säubern.

purify, vb. reinigen, läutern.

puritanical, adj. purita'nisch.

purity, n. Reinheit f., Echtheit f.

purple, adj. purpurn; lila.

purport, 1. n. Sinn m.; *(fig.)* Energie', -i'en f. **2.** vb. den Anschein erwecken als ob.

purpose, n. Zweck m.; Absicht, -en f.

purposely, adv. absichtlich.

purse, n. *(handbag)* Handtasche, -n f.; Geldbeutel, - m.

pursue, vb. verfol'gen.

pursuit, n. Verfol'gung, -en f.

push, 1. n. Stoß, -̈e m.; *(fig.)* Energie', -i'en f. **2.** vb. stoßen*, schieben*.

put, vb. setzen; stellen; legen.

putrid, adj. faul, verfault'.

puzzle, 1. n. Rätsel, - nt.; *(game)* Puzzle, -s nt. **2.** vb. verwir'ren, zu denken geben*.

pyjamas, n.pl. Pyja'ma, -s m.

pyramid, n. Pyrami'de, -n f.

Q

quadrangle, n. Viereck, -e nt.

quadraphonic, adj. quadraphon'.

quadruped, n. Vierfüßler, -m.

quail, n. Wachtel, -n f.

quaint, adj. seltsam; altmodisch.

quake, 1. n. Beben nt. 2. vb. beben, zittern.

qualification, n. Befä'higung, -en f., Qualifikation', -en f.; (reservation) Einschränkung, -en f.

qualified, adj. geeig'net; (limited) eingeschränkt.

qualify, vb. qualifizie'ren; (limit) ein•schränken.

quality, n. (characteristic) Eigenschaft, -en f.; (grade) Qualität, -en f.

qualm, n. Beden'ken nt.

quandary, n. Dilem'ma nt.

quantity, n. Menge, -n f., Quantität', -en f.

quarantine, n. Quarantä'ne f.

quarrel, 1. n. Streit m., Zank m. 2. vb. streiten*, sich streiten*, sich zanken.

quarry, n. Steinbruch, -̈e m.

quarter, 1. n. Viertel, - nt. 2. vb. ein•quartieren.

quarterly, 1. n. Vierteljah'resschrift, -en f. 2. adj. vierteljähr'lich.

quartet, n. Quartett', -e nt.

quasar, n. Quasar m.

queen, n. Königin, -nen f.

queer, adj. merkwürdig, sonderbar.

quell, vb. unterdrü'cken.

quench, vb. löschen, stillen.

query, 1. n. Frage, -n f. 2. vb. fragen.

quest, n. Suche, -n f.

question, 1. n. Frage, -n f. 2. vb. fragen, befra'gen; an•zweifeln.

questionable, adj. fraglich, fragwürdig.

question mark, n. Fragezeichen, - nt.

questionnaire, n. Fragebogen, -̈

quick, adj. schnell, rasch.

quiet, 1. adj. leise, ruhig, still. 2. vb. beru'higen.

quilt, n. Steppdecke, -n f.

quinine, n. Chinin' nt.

quintet, n. Quintett', -e nt.

quip, 1. n. witziger Seitenhieb, -e m.; spitze Bemer'kung, -en f. 2. vb. witzeln.

quit, vb. (leave) verlas'sen*; (stop) auf•hören; (resign) kündigen.

quite, adj. ziemlich; (completely) ganz, völlig.

quiver, 1. n. Köcher, - m. 2. vb. beben, zittern.

quiz, 1. n. Quiz m.; (school) Klassenarbeit, -en f. 2. vb. aus•fragen.

quorum, n. beschluß'fähige Versamm'lung f.

quota, n. Quote, -n f.

quotation, n. Zitat', -e nt.; (price) Notie'rung, -en f.

quotation mark, n. Anführungsstrich, -e m., Anführungszeichen, - nt.

quote, vb. an•führen, zitie'ren.

R

rabbi, n. Rabbi'ner, - m.

rabbit, n. Kanin'chen, - nt.

rabble, n. Volksmenge f., Pöbel m.

rabid, adj. fana'tisch.

rabies, n. Tollwut f.

race, 1. n. (contest) Rennen, - nt., Wettrennen, - nt.; (breed) Rasse, -n f. 2. vb. rennen*, um die Wette rennen*.

race-track, n. Rennbahn, -en f.

rack, 1. n. (torture) Folterbank, -̈e f.; (feed) Futtergestell, -e nt.; (luggage) Ständer, - m.; (train) Gepäcknetz, -e nt. 2. vb. foltern.

racket, n. (tennis) Schläger, - m.; (uproar) Krach m.; (crime) Schiebung, -en f.

radar, n. Radar nt.

radiance, n. Glanz m., Strahlen nt.
radiant, adj. strahlend.
radiate, vb. aus·strahlen.
radiation, n. Ausstrahlung, -en f.
radiator, n. Heizkörper, - m.; (auto) Kühler, - m.
radical, adj. radikal'.
radio, n. Rundfunk m.; Rundfunkgerät, -e nt.; Radio, -s nt.
radioactive, adj. radioaktiv'; (r. fall-out) radioakti'ver Niederschlag, -̈e m.
radish, n. Radies'chen, - nt.; (white) Rettich, -e m.; (horser.) Meerrettich, -e m.
radium, n. Radium nt.
radius, n. Radius, -ien m.
raffle, 1. n. Lotterie, -i'en f. 2. vb. (r. off) aus·losen.
raft, n. Floß, -̈e m.
rag, n. Lumpen, - m., Lappen, - m.
rage, 1. n. Wut f.; (fashion) Schrei m. 2. vb. wüten, rasen.
ragged, adj. zerlumpt'; (jagged) zackig.
raid, 1. n. Überfall, -̈e m., Razzia, -ien f. 2. vb. überfal'len*, plündern.
rail, n. Schiene, -n f.
railing, n. Gelän'der, - nt.
railroad, n. Eisenbahn, -en f.
rain, 1. n. Regen m. 2. vb. regnen.
rainbow, n. Regenbogen, -̈ m.
raincoat, n. Regenmantel, -̈ m.
rainy, adj. regnerisch.
raise, 1. n. (pay) Gehalts'erhöhung, -en f. 2. vb. (increase) erhö'hen; (lift) heben*; (erect) auf·stellen; (collect) auf·treiben*; (bring up) groß·ziehen*.
raisin, n. Rosi'ne, -n f.
rake, 1. n. (tool) Harke, -n f., Rechen, - m.; (person) Roué -̇, -s m. 2. vb. harken.
rally, 1. n. (recovery) Erho'lung, -en f.; (meeting) Kundgebung, -en f., Massenversammlung, -en f. 2. vb. sich erho'len; sich sammeln.
ram, 1. n. Widder, - m. 2. vb. rammen.
ramble, vb. umher'·schweifen.

ramp, n. Rampe, -n f.
rampart, n. Burgwall, -̈e m.
ranch, n. Ranch, -es f.
rancid, adj. ranzig.
rancor, n. Groll m.
random, n. (at r.) aufs Geratewohl'.
range, 1. n. (distance) Entfer'nung, -en f.; (scope) Spielraum, -̈e m.; (mountains) Bergkette, -n f.; (stove) Herd, -e m. 2. vb. (extend) sich erstre'cken.
rank, 1. n. Rang, -̈e m. 2. vb. ein·reihen.
ransack, vb. durchwüh'len.
ransom, n. Lösegeld, -er nt.
rap, vb. schlagen*, klopfen.
rape, 1. n. Vergewal'tigung, -en f. 2. vb. vergewal'tigen.
rapid, adj. schnell.
rare, adj. selten; (meat) roh; blutig.
rascal, n. Schlingel, - m.
rash, adj. übereilt', waghalsig.
raspberry, n. Himbeere, -n f.
rat, n. Ratte, -n f.
rate, 1. n. (proportion) Maßstab, -̈e m.; (price) Preis, -e m.; (exchange r.) Kurs, -e m.; (speed) Geschwin'digkeit, -en f. 2. vb. ein·schätzen.
rather, adv. (preferably) lieber; (on the other hand) vielmehr.
ratify, vb. ratifizie'ren.
ratio, n. Verhält'nis, -se nt.
ration, 1. n. Ration', -en f. 2. vb. rationie'ren.
rational, adj. vernunft'gemäß.
rattle, vb. klappern.
ravage, 1. n. Verwüs'tung, -en f. 2. vb. verwüs'ten.
rave, vb. (fury) toben; (enthusiasm) schwärmen.
raven, 1. n. Rabe, -n m. 2. adj. rabenschwarz.
raw, adj. rauh; (uncooked) roh.
ray, n. Strahl, -en m.
rayon, n. Kunstseide, -n f.
razor, n. Rasier'messer, - nt.; (safety) Rasier'apparat, -e m.
reach, 1. n. Reichweite f. 2. vb. (tr.) errei'chen; (intr.) reichen.
react, vb. reagie'ren.
reaction, n. Wirkung, -en f., Reaktion', -en f.

reactionary, 1. n. Reaktionär', -e m. **2.** adj. reaktionär'.

reactor, n. Reak'tor, -o'ren m.

read, vb. lesen*.

reader, n. (person) Leser, - m., Leserin, -nen f.; (book) Lesebuch, -̈er nt.

readily, adv. gern; (easily) leicht.

reading, n. Lesen nt.

ready, adj. (prepared) bereit'; (finished) fertig.

real, adj. wirklich, tatsächlich; (genuine) echt.

realist, n. Realist', -en m.

reality, n. Wirklichkeit f.

realization, n. (understanding) Erkennt'nis, -se f.; (making real) Verwirk'lichung, -en f., Realisie'rung, -en f.

realize, vb. (understand) erken'nen, begrei'fen; (I r. it) ich bin mir darüber im klaren; (make real, attain) verwirk'lichen, realisie'ren.

realm, n. Reich, -e nt.; (fig.) Be-reich', -e m.

reap, vb. ernten.

rear, 1. n. (back) Rückseite, -n f.; (r.-guard) Nachhut, -en f. **2.** vb. (bring up) erzie'hen*; (erect) er-rich'ten; (of horses) sich bäumen.

rear-view mirror, n. Rückspiegel, - m.

reason, 1. n. Vernunft' f.; (cause) Grund, -̈e m. **2.** vb. überle'gen, denken*; (r. with) vernünf'tig reden mit.

reasonable, adj. vernünf'tig.

reassure, vb. versi'chern; beru'hi-gen.

rebate, n. Rabatt', -e m.

rebel, 1. n. Rebell', -en, -en m. **2.** vb. rebellie'ren.

rebellion, n. Aufstand, -̈e m., Re-bellion', -en f.

rebellious, adj. rebel'lisch.

rebound, vb. zurück'prallen.

rebuild, vb. wieder auf bauen.

rebuke, 1. n. Tadel, - m. **2.** vb. ta-deln.

rebuttal, n. Widerle'gung, -en f.

recalcitrant, adj. starrköpfig.

recall, vb. zurück'rufen*; (re-member) sich erin'nern an, (re-voke) widerru'fen*.

recapitulate, vb. zusam'men-fassen.

recede, vb. zurück'weichen*.

receipt, n. Quittung, -en f.; (rec-ipe) Rezept', -e nt.

receiver, n. Empfän'ger, - m., Empfängerin, -nen f.; (telephone) Hörer, - m.

recent, adj. neu.

recently, adv. neulich, kürzlich.

receptacle, n. Behäl'ter, - m.

reception, n. Aufnahme, -n f.; (ceremony) Empfang', -̈e m.

receptive, adj. empfäng'lich.

recess, n. (in wall) Nische, -n f.; (intermission) Pause, -n f.

recipe, n. Rezept', -e nt.

recipient, n. Empfän'ger m., Empfängerin, -nen f.

reciprocate, vb. aus'tauschen; er-wi'dern.

recitation, n. Rezitation', -en f.

recite, vb. auf'sagen, vor'tragen*.

reckless, adj. rücksichtslos; leichtsinnig.

reclaim, vb. ein'fordern; (land) urbar machen; (waste product) aus'werten.

reclamation, n. (land) Urbar-machung f.

recline, vb. sich zurück'lehnen.

recognition, n. (acknowledg-ment) Anerkennung, -en f.; (know again) Wiedererkennung, -en f.

recognize, vb. (acknowledge) an'erkennen*; (know again) wieder'erkennen*.

recoil, vb. zurück'prallen.

recollect, vb. sich erin'nern an.

recommend, vb. empfeh'len*.

recommendation, n. Empfeh'-lung, -en f.

recompense, 1. n. Erstat'tung, -en f. **2.** vb. wieder'erstatten.

reconcile, vb. versöh'nen.

reconsider, vb. wieder erwä'gen.

reconstruct, vb. rekonstruie'ren.

record, 1. n. (document) Ur-kunde, -n f.; (top achievement) Rekord', -e m.; (phonograph) Schallplatte, -n f.; (r. player) Plat-tenspieler, - m. **2.** vb. ein'tragen*; auf'zeichnen; (phonograph, tape) auf'nehmen*.

recording, n. (phonograph, tape) Aufnahme, -n f.

recourse, n. Zuflucht f.

recover, vb. wieder•gewinnen*; (health) sich erho'len, gene'sen.

recovery, n. Wiedergewinnung, -en f.; (health) Erho'lung, -en f., Gene'sung, -en f.

recruit, 1. n. Rekrut', -en, -en m. 2. vb. an•werben*.

rectangle, n. Rechteck, -e nt.

rectifier, n. Gleichrichter, - m.

rectify, vb. berich'tigen.

recuperate, vb. sich erho'len.

recur, vb. wieder•kommen*, zurück'•kommen*.

recycle, vb. wieder auf•bereiten.

red, adj. rot (-).

Red Cross, n. Rotes Kreuz nt.

redeem, vb. ein•lösen; (eccles.) erlö'sen.

redeemer, n. (eccles.) Erlö'ser m., Heiland m.

redemption, n. Einlösung, -en f.; (eccles.) Erlö'sung f.

reduce, vb. verrin'gern, mindern, reduzie'ren; (prices) herab'•setzen; (weight) ab•nehmen*.

reduction, n. Vermin'derung, -en f.; Herab•setzung, -en f.; Ermäßigung, -en f.; Reduktion', -en f.

reed, n. Schilf nt.; (music) Rohr-flöte, -n f.

reef, 1. n. Riff, -e nt.; (sail) Reff, -e nt. 2. vb. reffen.

reel, 1. n. Winde, -n f., Spule, -n f., Rolle, -n f. 2. vb. wickeln, spulen, drehen.

refer, vb. (r. to) sich bezie'hen* auf; sich beru'fen* auf; verwei'sen* auf.

referee, n. Schiedsrichter, - m.

reference, n. Bezug'nahme, -n f., Hinweis, -e m.; (recommendation) Zeugnis, -se nt.; (cross-r.) Querverweis, -e m.; (r. library) Handbibliothek, -en f.

refill, vb. wiederfüllen, nach•füllen.

refine, vb. verfei'nern; (tech.) raffinie'ren.

refinement, n. Verfei'nerung, -en f.; (culture) Bildung f.

reflect, vb. zurück'strahlen;

wider•spiegeln; (think) nach•denken*.

reflection, n. Widerspiegelung, -en f., Reflexion', -en f.

reflex, n. Reflex', -e m.

reform, 1. n. Reform', -en f. 2. vb. verbes'sern, reformie'ren.

reformation, n. Reformation' f.

refrain, 1. n. Refrain', -s m. 2. vb. sich enthal'ten*.

refresh, vb. auf•frischen; erfri'schen.

refreshment, n. Erfri'schung, -en f.

refrigerator, n. Kühlschrank, ⸚e m.

refuge, n. Zuflucht f.

refugee, n. Flüchtling, -e m.

refund, n. Rückzahlung, -en f. 2. vb. zurück'•zahlen.

refusal, n. Verwei'gerung, -en f.

refuse, 1. n. (waste matter) Abfall, ⸚e m. 2. vb. verwei'gern; ab•schlagen*.

refute, vb. widerle'gen.

regain, vb. wieder•gewinnen*.

regal, adj. königlich.

regard, 1. n. Achtung, f.; (greetings) Grüße pl.; (in r. to) hinsichtlich. 2. vb. betrach'ten.

regarding, prep. hinsichtlich.

regardless, adv. (r. of) ohne Rücksicht auf.

regime, n. Regi'me, -s nt.

regiment, n. Regiment', ⸚er nt.

region, n. Gebiet', -e nt., Gegend, -en f.

register, 1. n. Verzeich'nis, -se nt.; (music) Regis'ter, - nt. 2. vb. verzeich'nen; ein•tragen*, an•melden; (letter) ein•schreiben*.

registration, n. Registrie'rung, -en f.

regret, 1. n. Bedau'ern nt. 2. vb. bedau'ern, bereu'en.

regular, adj. regelmäßig; ordentlich; gewöhn'lich.

regularity, n. Regelmäßigkeit f.

regulate, vb. regeln, ordnen, regulie'ren.

regulation, n. Regelung, -en f., Vorschrift, -en f.

rehabilitate, vb. rehabilitie'ren.

rehearsal, n. Probe, -n f.

rehearse, vb. proben.

reign, 1. n. Herrschaft f. 2. vb. herrschen.

reimburse, vb. zurück'erstatten.

rein, n. Zügel - m.

reindeer, n. Renntier, -e nt.

reinforce, vb. verstär'ken.

reinforcement, n. Verstär'kung, -en f.

reinstate, vb. wiederein'setzen.

reiterate, vb. wiederhol'en.

reject, vb. ab·lehnen, verwer'fen*.

rejoice, vb. frohlo'cken.

rejuvenate, vb. verjün'gen.

relapse, 1. n. Rückfall, =e m. 2. vb. zurück'fallen*.

relate, vb. (tell) berich'ten erzäh'len; (connect) verknüp'fen; (be connected with) sich bezie'hen*; (r. to) gemein haben (mit), zurechtkommen* (mit).

related, adj. verwandt'.

relation, n. (story) Erzäh'lung, -en f.; (connection) Bezie'hung, -en f.; (person) Verwandt'- m.&f.

relationship, n. Bezie'hung, -en f.; (kinship) Verwandt'schaft, -en f.

relative, 1. n. Verwandt'- m.&f. 2. adj. relativ'.

relativity, n. Relativität' f.

relax, vb. sich entspan'nen; lockern.

relay, 1. n. Relais', - nt. 2. vb. übermit'teln.

release, 1. n. Entlas'sung, -en f.; Befrei'ung, -en f. 1. vb. entlas'sen*; frei'lassen*.

relent, vb. sich erwei'chen lassen*.

relevant, adj. einschlägig.

reliable, adj. zuverlässig.

relic, n. Reli'quie, -n f.; Überrest -e m.

relief, n. Erleich'terung, -en f.; (social work) Unterstüt'zung, -en f.; (replacement) Ablösung, -en f.; (art) Relief', -s nt.

relieve, vb. erleich'tern; ab·lösen.

religion, n. Religion', -en f.

religious, adj. religiös', fromm.

relinquish, vb. auf·geben*.

relish, 1. n. Genuß', =se m. 2. vb. genie'ßen*.

reluctance, n. Widerstre'ben nt.

reluctant, adj. widerstre'bend.

rely, vb. (r. on) sich verlas'sen* auf.

remain, vb. bleiben*; übrig bleiben*.

remainder, n. Rest, -e m.

remark, 1. n. Bemer'kung, -en f. 2. vb. bemer'ken.

remarkable, adj. bemer'kenswert, beacht'lich.

remedy, 1. n. Heilmittel, - nt. 2. vb. heilen; ab·helfen*.

remember, vb. sich erin'nern an.

remind, vb. erin'nern; ermah'nen.

reminiscence, n. Erin'nerung, -en f.

remiss, adj. nachlässig.

remit, vb. (send) übersen'den*; (send money) überwei'sen*; (forgive) verzei'hen*.

remittance, n. Überwei'sung, -en f.

remnant, n. Rest, -e m.

remorse, n. Gewis'senbiß, -sse m.

remote, adj. entle'gen.

removable, adj. abnehmbar, entfern'bar.

removal, n. Entfer'nung f., Besei'tigung f.

remove, vb. entfer'nen, weg·räumen, besei'tigen.

renaissance, n. Renaissance' f.

rend, vb. zerrei'ßen*.

render, vb. geben*; erwei'sen*.

rendezvous, n. Stelldichein, - nt., Rendezvous', - nt.

rendition, n. Wiedergabe, -n f.

renew, vb. erneu'ern; (subscription) verlän'gern.

renewal, n. Erneu'erung, -en f.; (subscription) Verlän'gerung, -en f.

renounce, vb. entsa'gen, verzich'ten auf.

renovate, vb. renovie'ren.

renowned, adj. berühmt', namhaft.

rent, 1. n. Miete, -n f. 2. vb. (from someone) mieten; (to someone) vermie'ten.

rental, n. Miete, -n f.

repair, 1. n. Ausbesserung, -en f.; Reparatur', -en f. 2. vb. aus·bessern, reparie'ren.

reparation, n. Reparation', -en f.

repatriate, 1. *n.* Repatriiert'- *m.&f.* 2. *vb.* repatriie'ren.

repay, *vb.* zurück'·zahlen.

repeat, *vb.* wiederho'len.

repel, *vb.* zurück'·treiben*; abschlagen*.

repent, *vb.* bereu'en.

repentance, *n.* Reue *f.*

repercussion, *n.* Auswirkung, -en *f.*

repertoire, *n.* Repertoire', -s *nt.*

repetition, *n.* Wiederho'lung, -en *f.*

replace, *vb.* erset'zen.

replenish, *vb.* wieder auf·füllen.

reply, 1. *n.* Antwort, -en *f.* 2. *vb.* antworten, erwi'dern.

report, 1. *n.* Bericht', -e *m.; (bang)* Knall, -e *m.; (rumor)* Gerücht', -e *nt.* 2. *vb.* berich'ten; *(complain of)* an·zeigen.

reporter, *n.* Bericht'erstatter, - *m.,* Berichterstatterin, -nen *f.;* Repor'ter, - *m.,* Repor'terin, -nen *f.*

repose, 1. *n.* Ruhe *f.* 2. *vb.* ruhen.

represent, *vb.* dar·stellen; vertre'ten*.

representation, *n.* Darstellung, -en *f.;* Vertre'tung, -en *f.*

representative, 1. *n.* Vertre'ter, - *m.,* Vertre'terin, -nen *f.; (pol.)* Abgeordnet- *m.&f.* 2. *adj.* bezeich'nend, typisch.

repress, *vb.* unterdrü'cken.

repression, *n.* Unterdrü'ckung, -en *f.,* Repression', -en *f.*

reprimand, 1. *n.* Tadel, - *m.,* Verweis', -e *m.* 2. *vb.* einen Verweis' ertei'len.

reprisal, *n.* Vergel'tungsmaßnahme, -n *f.*

reproach, 1. *n.* Vorwurf, ⸚e *m.* 2. *vb.* vor·werfen*.

reproduce, *vb.* reproduzie'ren.

reproduction, *n.* Wiedergabe, -n *f.,* Reproduktion', -en *f.*

reptile, *n.* Reptil', -e *nt.*

republic, *n.* Republik', -en *f.*

republican, 1. *n.* Republika'ner, - *m.* 2. *adj.* republika'nisch.

repudiate, *vb.* ab·leugnen.

repudiation, *n.* Zurück'weisung, -en *f.,* Nichtanerkennung, -en *f.*

repulse, *vb.* zurück'·schlagen*.

repulsive, *adj.* widerwärtig.

reputation, *n.* Ruf *m.,* Ansehen *nt.*

repute, *n.* Ansehen *nt.*

request, 1. *n.* Bitte, -n *f.,* Gesuch', -e *nt.* 2. *vb.* bitten*, ersu'chen.

require, *vb.* verlan'gen, erfor'dern.

requirement, *n.* Erfor'dernis, -se *nt.;* Bedin'gung, -en *f.*

requisite, 1. *n.* Erfor'dernis, -se *nt.* 2. *adj.* erfor'derlich.

requisition, 1. *n.* Forderung, -en *f.,* Requisition', -en *f.* 2. *vb.* an·fordern; beschlag'nahmen.

rescind, *vb.* rückgängig machen, auf·heben*.

rescue, 1. *n.* Rettung, -en *f.* 2. *vb.* retten.

research, *n.* Forschung, -en *f.*

resemble, *vb.* gleichen*, ähneln.

resent, *vb.* übel·nehmen*.

reservation, *n.* vorbehalt *m.; (tickets)* Vorbestellung, -en *f.; (Indian r.)* Reservation', -en *f.*

reserve, 1. *n.* Reser've, -n *f.* 2. *vb.* vor·behalten*; *(seats)* reservie'ren.

reservoir, *n.* Reservoir', -s *nt.*

reside, *vb.* wohnen.

residence, *n.* Wohnsitz, -e *m.*

resident, *n.* Einwohner, - *m.,* Einwohnerin, -nen *f.* 2. *adj.* wohnhaft.

residue, *n.* Rest, -e *m.,* Restbestand, ⸚e *m.*

resign, *vb.* zurück'·treten*; *(r. oneself)* sich ab·finden* mit, resignie'ren.

resignation, *n.* Rücktritt, -e *m.;* Resignation', -en *f.*

resist, *vb.* widerste'hen*.

resistance, *n.* Widerstand, ⸚e *m.*

resolute, *adj.* entschlos'sen.

resolution, *n.* Beschluß', ⸚sse *m.;* Entschlos'senheit *f.*

resolve, *vb.* entschei'den*; beschlie'ßen*.

resonance, *n.* Resonanz', -en *f.*

resonant, *adj.* resonant'.

resort, *n.* Ferienort, -e *m.;* Kurort, -e *m.*

resound, *vb.* wider·hallen, schallen*.

resources, n.pl. Hilfsquellen pl.; **(natural r.)** Bodenschätze pl.

respect, 1. n. (esteem) Achtung f.; (reference) Hinsicht, -en f. **2.** vb. achten.

respectable, adj. angesehen, ansehnlich.

respectful, adj. ehrerbietig, höflich.

respective, adj. entspre'chend.

respiration, n. Atmung f.

respite, n. Frist, -en f.; Atempause, -n f.

respond, vb. (answer) antworten; (react) reagie'ren.

response, n. Antwort, -en f.; Reaktion', -en f.

responsibility, n. Verant'wortung, -en f.

responsible, adj. verant'wortlich.

responsive, adj. zugänglich.

rest, 1. n. (remainder) Rest, -e m.; (repose) Ruhe f. **2.** vb. ruhen; (be based on) beru'hen auf.

restaurant, n. Restaurant', -s nt.

restful, adj. ausruhsam.

restitution, n. Wiedergut'machung, -en f.

restless, adj. unruhig.

restoration, n. Wiederher'stellung, -en f.

restore, vb. wiederher'stellen.

restrain, vb. zurück'halten*.

restraint, n. Zurück'haltung f.

restrict, vb. beschrän'ken, einschränken.

restriction, n. Einschränkung, -en f.; Beschrän'kung, -en f.

result, 1. n. Ergeb'nis, -se nt., Resultat', -e nt. **2.** vb. erge'ben*; zur Folge haben*.

resume, vb. wieder auf•nehmen*.

résumé, n. Resümee', -s nt.

resurrect, vb. wiedererwecken; wieder hervor'•holen.

resurrection, n. (eccles.) Auferstehung f.

retail, 1. n. Einzelhandel m. **2.** vb. im Einzelhandel vertrei'ben*.

retain, vb. bei•behalten*; zurück'halten*; auf•halten*.

retaliate, vb. vergel'ten*.

retaliation, n. Vergel'tung, -en f.

retard, vb. verzö'gern, zurück'halten*.

retention, n. Beibehaltung, -en f.

reticence, n. Zurück'haltung f.; Verschwie'genheit f.

reticent, adj. zurück'haltend, schweigsam.

retina, n. Netzhaut, -̈e f.

retinue, n. Gefol'ge nt.

retire, vb. sich zurück'•ziehen*; (from office) sich pensionie'ren lassen*, in den Ruhestand treten*.

retort, 1. n. Retor'te, -n f.; (answer) Erwi'derung, -en f. **2.** vb. erwi'dern.

retract, vb. (pull back) zurück'•ziehen*; (recant) widerru'fen*.

retreat, 1. n. (withdrawal) Rückzug, -̈e m.; (refuge) Zuflucht f.; (privacy) Zurück'gezogenheit f. **2.** vb. zurück'•weichen*.

retribution, n. Strafe, -n f., Vergel'tung f.

retrieve, vb. wiedererlangen.

retroactive, adj. rückwirkend.

retrospect, n. Rückblick m.

return, 1. n. Rückkehr f., Heimkehr f.; Rückgabe f. **2.** vb. zurück'•kehren, zurück'•kommen*; zurück'•geben*.

reunion, n. Wiederzusam'menkommen nt.

reunite, vb. wieder verei'nigen.

reveal, vb. offenba'ren; zeigen.

revel, vb. schwelgen.

revelation, n. Offenba'rung, -en f.

revelry, n. Schwiegerei'*, -en f.

revenge, 1. n. Rache f. **2.** vb. rächen.

revenue, n. Einkommen, -̈ nt.

reverberate, vb. wider•hallen.

revere, vb. vereh'ren.

reverence, n. Vereh'rung, -en f.; Ehrfurcht f.

reverend, adj. ehrwürdig.

reverent, adj. ehrerbietig.

reverie, n. Träumerei', -en f.

reverse, 1. n. (opposite) Gegenteil nt.; (back) Rückseite, -n f.; (misfortune) Rückschlag, -̈e m.; (auto) Rückwärtsgang, -̈e m. **2.** vb. um•drehen; (auto) rückwärts fahren*; (tech.) um•steuern.

revert, vb. zurück'•kehren.

review, 1. n. nochmalige Durchsicht, -en f.; Überblick, -e m.; (book r.) Kritik', -en f.; Besprechung, -en f. **2.** vb. überbli'cken, revidie'ren; bespre'chen*.

revise, vb. ab'ändern, revidie'ren.

revision, n. Revision', -en f.

revival, n. Wiederbelebung, -en f.; Neubelebung, -en f.

revive, vb. (person) wieder zu Bewußt'sein bringen*; (fashion) wieder auf'leben lassen*.

revocation, n. Aufhebung, -en f.

revoke, vb. widerru'fen*, auf'heben*.

revolt, 1. n. Aufstand, ⸗e m. **2.** vb. revoltie'ren.

revolution, n. Revolution', -en f.; (turn) Umdre'hung, -en f.

revolutionary, adj. revolutionär'.

revolve, vb. sich drehen.

revolver, n. Revol'ver, - m.

reward, 1. n. Beloh'nung, -en f. **2.** vb. beloh'nen.

rhetorical, adj. rheto'risch.

rheumatic, adj. rheuma'tisch.

rheumatism, n. Rheumatis'mus m.

rhinoceros, n. Nashorn, ⸗er nt.

rhubarb, n. Rhabar'ber m.

rhyme, n. Reim, -e m.

rhythm, n. Rhythmus, -men m.

rhythmical, adj. rhythmisch.

rib, n. Rippe, -n f.

ribbon, n. Band, ⸗er nt.

rice, n. Reis m.

rich, adj. reich.

rid, vb. los'werden*; sich los'machen.

riddle, n. Rätsel, - nt.

ride, 1. n. (horse) Ritt, -e m.; (vehicle) Fahrt, -en f. **1.** vb. reiten*; fahren*.

rider, n. Reiter, - m., Reiterin, -nen f.

ridge, n. (mountain) Grat, -e m.; (mountain range) Bergrücken, - m.

ridicule, 1. n. Spott m. **2.** vb. lächerlich machen, bespöt'teln.

ridiculous, adj. lächerlich.

rifle, n. Gewehr', -e nt.

rig, 1. n. (gear) Ausrüstung, -en f.; (ship) Takela'ge, -n f.; (oil) Ölbohrer, - m. **2.** vb. auf'takeln.

right, 1. n. Recht, -e nt. **2.** adj. (side) recht-; (just) gerecht'; (be r.) recht haben*. **3.** adv. rechts. **4.** vb. (set upright) auf'richten; (correct) wiedergut'machen.

righteous, adj. rechtschaffen; (smug) selbstgerecht.

righteousness, n. Rechtschaffenheit f.; Selbstgerechtigkeit f.

right of way, n. Vorfahrtsrecht, -e nt.

rigid, adj. steif; starr.

rigidity, n. Starrheit f.

rigor, n. Härte, -n f.

rigorous, adj. hart (⸗), streng.

rim, n. Rand, ⸗er m.

ring, 1. n. Ring, -e m.; (circle) Kreis, -e m.; (of bell) Klingeln nt. **2.** vb. klingeln.

rinse, vb. spülen.

riot, 1. n. Aufruhr, -e m. **2.** vb. in Aufruhr gera'ten*.

rip, vb. reißen*; auf'trennen.

ripe, adj. reif.

ripen, vb. reifen.

ripoff, n. Übervor'teilung f.

rip off, vb. jemand reinlegen.

ripple, 1. n. leichte Welle, -n f. **2.** vb. leichte Wellen schlagen*.

rise, 1. n. (increase) Zuwachs m.; (emergence) Aufgang, ⸗e m.; (advance) Aufstieg, -e m. **2.** vb. an'steigen*; auf'gehen*; (get up) auf'stehen*.

risk, 1. n. Risiko, -s nt. **2.** vb. wagen.

rite, n. Ritus, -ten m.

ritual, 1. n. Rituell', -e nt. **2.** adj. rituell'.

rival, 1. n. Riva'le, -n, -n m., Riva'lin, -nen f., Konkurrenz', -en f. **2.** adj. Konkurrenz'- (cpds.). **3.** vb. wetteifern, rivalisie'ren.

rivalry, n. Konkurrenz', -en f., Wettstreit m.

river, n. Fluß, ⸗sse m.

rivet, 1. n. Niete, -n f. **2.** vb. nieten.

road, n. Straße, -n f., Landstraße, -n f.

roam, vb. umher'schweifen.

roar, 1. n. Gebrüll' nt. **2.** vb. brüllen; brausen.

roast, 1. n. Braten, - m. **2.** vb. braten*; rösten.

rob, vb. rauben; berau'ben.

robber, n. Räuber, - m.; Dieb, -e m., Diebin, -nen f.

robbery, n. Raub m.

robe, n. Gewand', -̈er nt.

robin, n. Rotkehlchen, - nt.

robot, n. Roboter, - m.

robust, adj. robust'.

rock, 1. n. Stein, -e m.; Felsen, - m.; (music) Rock m., Rockmusik f. **2.** vb. schaukeln.

rocker, n. Schaukelstuhl, -̈e m.

rocket, n. Rake'te, -n f.

rocky, adj. felsig; (shaky) wackelig.

rod, n. Stab, -̈e m., Stange, -n f.

rodent, n. Nagetier, -e nt.

roe, n. Rogen, - m.; (deer) Reh, -e nt.

role, n. Rolle, -n f.

roll, 1. n. Rolle, -n f.; Walze, -n f.; (bread) Brötchen, - nt. **2.** vb. rollen; (ship) schlingern.

roller, n. Rolle, -n f.; Walze, -n f.; Römerin, -nen f.

Roman, 1. n. Römer, - m. **2.** adj. römisch.

romance, n. Roman'ze, -n f.; Liebesaffäre, -n f.

Romance, adj. roma'nisch.

romantic, adj. roman'tisch.

romanticism, n. Roman'tik f.

Rome, n. Rom nt.

roof, n. Dach, -̈er nt.

room, n. Zimmer, - nt., Raum, -̈e m.; (space) Raum m.

roommate, n. Zimmergenosse, -n, -n m., Zimmergenossin, -nen f.

rooster, n. Hahn, -̈e m.

root, 1. n. Wurzel, -n f. **2.** vb. (be rooted) wurzeln.

rope, n. Tau, -e nt., Seil, -e nt., Strick, -e m.

rosary, n. Rosenkranz, -̈e m.

rose, n. Rose, -n f.

rosy, adj. rosig.

rot, vb. verfau'len, verwe'sen.

rotate, vb. rotie'ren; sich ab·wechseln.

rotation, n. Umdre'hung, -en f., Rotation', -en f.; Wechsel, - m.

rotten, adj. faul; (base) niederträchtig.

rouge, n. Rouge nt.

rough, adj. rauh; (coarse) grob(-̈); (sea) stürmisch.

round, 1. n. Runde, -n f. **2.** adj. rund. **3.** prep. um, um . . . herum'.

rout, 1. n. wilde Flucht f. **2.** vb. in die Flucht schlagen*.

route, n. Weg, -e m. Route, -n f.

routine, 1. n. Routi'ne, -n f. **2.** adj. alltäg'lich.

rove, vb. umher'·streifen.

row, 1. n. (line, series) Reihe, -n f.; (fight) Krach m. **2.** vb. rudern.

rowboat, n. Ruderboot, -e nt.

royal, adj. königlich.

royalty, n. Königstum nt.; Mitglied eines Königshauses; (share of profit) Gewinn'anteil, -e m.

rub, vb. reiben*.

rubber, n. Gummi nt.

rubbish, n. Abfall, -̈e m.; (nonsense) Quatsch m.

ruby, n. Rubin', -e m.

rudder, n. Steuerruder, - nt.

rude, adj. rauh, unhöflich.

rudiment, n. erster Anfang, -̈e m.; Anfangsgrund m.

ruffle, 1. n. Rüsche, -n f. **2.** vb. kräuseln.

rug, n. Teppich, -e m.

rugged, adj. rauh, hart (-̈).

ruin, 1. n. Untergang m.; Rui'ne, -n f.; (r.s) Trümmer pl. **2.** vb. ruinie'ren.

ruinous, adj. verderb'lich, katastrophal'.

rule, 1. n. (reign) Herrschaft f.; (regulation) Regel, -n f. **2.** vb. herrschen; entschei'den*.

ruler, n. Herrscher, - m. Herrscherin, -nen f.; (measuring stick) Lineal', -e nt.

rum, n. Rum m.

rumor, 1. n. Gerücht', -e nt. **2.** vb. munkeln.

run, 1. n. Lauf m.; (stocking) Laufmasche, -n f. **2.** vb. laufen*; (flow) fließen*.

rung, n. Sprosse, -n f.

runner, n. Läufer, - m., Läuferin, -nen f.

runway, n. Startbahn, -en f.

rupture, 1. n. Bruch, -̈e m. **2.** vb. brechen*; reißen*.

rural, adj. ländlich.

rush, 1. n. Andrang m.; (hurry) Eile f. **2.** vb. drängen; eilen, sich stürzen.

Russia, *n.* Rußland *nt.*
Russian, 1. *n.* Russe, -n, -n *m.;* Russin, -nen *f.* 2. *adj.* russisch.
rust, 1. *n.* Rost *m.* 2. *vb.* rosten.
rustic, *adj.* bäurisch.
rustle, *vb.* rascheln.

rusty, *adj.* rostig.
rut, *n.* Rinne, -n *f.;* Radspur, -en *f.*
ruthless, *adj.* erbar'mungslos, rücksichtslos.
rye, *n.* Roggen *m.*

S

Sabbath, *n.* Sabbat, -e *m.*
saber, *n.* Säbel, - *m.*
sable, *n.* Zobel *m.*
sabotage, 1. *n.* Sabota'ge *f.* 2. *vb.* sabotie'ren.
saboteur, *n.* Saboteur', -e *m.*
saccharine, *n.* Sacharin' *nt.*
sack, 1. *n.* Sack, ⁼e *m.* 2. *vb.* (*plunder*) plündern; (*discharge*) auf der Stelle entlas'sen*.
sacrament, *n.* Sakrament', -e *nt.*
sacred, *adj.* heilig.
sacrifice, 1. *n.* Opfer, - *nt.* 2. *vb.* opfern.
sacrilege, *n.* Sakrileg', -e *nt.*
sacrilegious, *adj.* gotteslästerlich.
sad, *adj.* traurig.
sadden, *vb.* betrü'ben.
saddle, 1. *n.* Sattel, - *m.* 2. *vb.* satteln.
sadism, *n.* Sadis'mus *m.*
safe, 1. *n.* Geldschrank, ⁼e *m.* 2. *adj.* sicher.
safeguard, 1. *n.* Schutz *m.* 2. *vb.* schützen; sichern.
safety, *n.* Sicherheit *f.*
safety-pin, *n.* Sicherheitsnadel, -n *f.*
sage, *adj.* weise.
sail, 1. *n.* Segel, - *nt.* 2. *vb.* segeln.
sailboat, *n.* Segelboot, -e *nt.*
sailor, *n.* Matro'se, -n, -n *m.*
saint, 1. *n.* Heilig- *m.&f.* 2. *adj.* heilig.
sake, *n.* (for the s. of) um . . . willen.
salad, *n.* Salat', -e *m.*
salary, *n.* Gehalt', ⁼er *nt.*
sale, *n.* Verkauf' *m.;* (**bargain s.**) Ausverkauf *m.*
salesperson, *n.* Verkäu'fer, - *m.;* Verkäu'ferin, -nen *f.;* (**traveling s.**) Handelsreisend- *m.&f.*
sales tax, *n.* Umsatzsteuer, -n *f.*
saliva, *n.* Speichel *m.*

salmon, *n.* Lachs *m.*
salon, *n.* Salon', -s *m.*
salt, 1. *n.* Salz, -e *nt.* 2. *vb.* salzen.
salty, *adj.* salzig.
salutation, *n.* Gruß, ⁼e *m.;* Begrü'ßung, -en *f.*
salute, 1. *n.* Gruß, ⁼e *m.* 2. *vb.* salutie'ren.
salvage, 1. *n.* (*act*) Bergung *f.;* (*material*) Bergegut *nt.* 2. *vb.* bergen*, retten.
salvation, *n.* Rettung *f.,* Heil *nt.*
salve, *n.* Salbe, -n *f.*
same, *adj.* selb-; (**the s.**) derselbe, dasselbe, dieselbe.
sample, 1. *n.* Probe, -n *f.,* Muster, - *nt.* 2. *vb.* probie'ren.
sanatorium, *n.* Sanato'rium, -rien *nt.*
sanctify, *vb.* heiligen.
sanction, 1. *n.* Sanktion', -en *f.* 2. *vb.* sanktionie'ren.
sanctity, *n.* Heiligkeit *f.*
sanctuary, *n.* Heiligtum, ⁼er *nt.;* (*refuge*) Zufluchtsort, -e *m.*
sand, *n.* Sand, -e *m.*
sandal, *n.* Sanda'le, -n *f.*
sandwich, *n.* belegtes Brot, -e *nt.*
sandy, *adj.* sandig.
sane, *adj.* vernünf'tig; geistig gesund'.
sanitary, *adj.* Gesund'heits-(*cpds.*); hygie'nisch; (**s. napkin**) Damenbinde, -n *f.*
sanitation, *n.* Gesund'heitswesen *nt.*
sanity, *n.* geistige Gesund'heit *f.*
Santa Claus, *n.* Weihnachtsmann, ⁼er *m.*
sap, 1. *n.* Saft, ⁼e *m.* 2. *vb.* schwächen.
sapphire, *n.* Saphir', -e *m.*
sarcasm, *n.* Sarkas'mus *m.*
sarcastic, *adj.* sarkas'tisch.
sardine, *n.* Sardi'ne, -n *f.*

sash, n. Schärpe, -n f.; (window) Fensterrahmen, - m.

satellite, n. Satellit', -en, -en m.

satin, n. Satin', -s m.

satire, n. Sati're, -n f.

satirize, vb. verspot'ten.

satisfaction, n. Genug'tuung, -en f.; Befrie'digung, -en f.

satisfactory, adj. befrie'digend, genü'gend.

satisfy, vb. befrie'digen, genü'gen.

saturate, vb. sättigen.

saturation, n. Sättigung f.

Saturday, n. Sonnabend, -e m., Samstag, -e m.

sauce, n. Soße, -n f.

saucer, n. Untertasse, -n f.

sausage, n. Wurst, ⸚e f.

savage, 1. n. Wild- m.&f. **2.** adj. wild.

save, 1. vb. (preserve) bewah'ren; (rescue) retten; (economize) sparen. **2.** prep. außer.

savings, n.pl. Erspar'nisse pl.

savior, n. Retter, - m.; (eccles.) Heiland m.

savor, 1. n. Geschmack', ⸚e m. **2.** vb. aus·kosten.

saw, 1. n. Säge, -n f.; (proverb) Sprichwort, ⸚er nt. **2.** vb. sägen.

say, vb. sagen.

saying, n. Redensart, -en f.

scab, n. Schorf m.; (strike breaker) Streikbrecher, - m.

scaffold, n. Gerüst', -e nt.; (execution) Schafott', -e nt.

scald, vb. brühen; verbrü'hen.

scale, 1. n. Maßstab, ⸚e m, Skala, -len f.; (music) Tonleiter, -n f.; (weight measuring) Waage, -n f.; (fish) Schuppe, -n f. **2.** vb. (climb) erklet'tern.

scalp, n. Kopfhaut, ⸚e f.; (Indian) Skalp, -e m.

scan, vb. überflie'gen*; (verse) skandie'ren.

scandal, n. Skandal', -e m.

scandalous, adj. schimpflich, unerhört'.

scant, adj. knapp.

scape goat, n. Sündenbock m.

scar, n. Narbe, -n f.

scarce, adj. selten; knapp.

scarcely, adv. kaum.

scarcity, n. Knappheit f., Mangel m.

scare, 1. n. Schreck m. **2.** vb. erschre'cken; (be s.d) erschre'cken*.

scarf, n. Schal, -s m., Halstuch, ⸚er nt.

scarlet, adj. scharlachrot.

scarlet fever, n. Scharlach m.

scatter, vb. zerstreu'en.

scenario, n. Inszenie'rung, -en f.; (film) Drehbuch, ⸚er nt.

scene, n. Szene, -n f.

scenery, n. Landschaft, -en f.; (stage) Bühnenausstattung, -en f.

scent, n. Geruch', ⸚e m.; (track) Spur, -en f.

schedule, n. Liste, -n f.; Programm', -e nt.; (timetable) Fahrplan, ⸚e m.; (school) Stundenplan, ⸚e m. an·setzen.

scheme, 1. n. Plan, ⸚e m.; Schema, -s nt. **2.** vb. intrigie'ren.

scholar, n. Gelehrt'- m.&f.

scholarship, n. (knowledge) Gelehr'samkeit f.; (stipend) Stipen'dium, -dien nt.

school, n. Schule, -n f.

science, n. Wissenschaft, -en f.

science fiction, n. Science fiction f.

scientific, adj. wissenschaftlich.

scientist, n. Natur'wissenschaftler, - m., Natur'wissenschaftlerin, -nen f.

scissors, n.pl. Schere, -n f.

scold, vb. schelten.

scolding, n. Schelte f.

scoop, n. (ladle) Schöpfkelle, -n f.; (newspaper) Erstmeldung, -en f.

scope, n. Reichweite f., Bereich', -e m.

scorch, vb. sengen, brennen*.

score, 1. n. (points) Punktzahl, -en f.; (what's the s.?) wie steht das Spiel?; (music) Partitur', -en f. **2.** vb. an·schreiben*; (mark) markie'ren.

scorn, 1. n. Verach'tung f. **2.** vb. verach'ten.

scornful, adj. veräc'htlich.

Scotland, n. Schottland nt.

Scotsman, n. Schotte, -n, -n m.

Scotswoman, n. Schottin, -nen f.

Scottish, adj. schottisch.

scour, vb. scheuern.

scout, 1. n. Kundschafter, - m.; (boy s.) Pfadfinder, - m. **2.** vb. erkun'den.

scowl, vb. finster blicken.

scramble, vb. (tr.) durcheinan'der-werfen*; (intr.) klettern.

scrambled eggs, n. Rührei, -er nt.

scrap, 1. n. Fetzen, - m.; (fight) Streit m. **2.** vb. aus-rangieren; (fight) streiten*.

scrape, vb. kratzen.

scratch, 1. n. Schramme, -n f. **2.** vb. kratzen; streichen*; (start from s.) von Anfang an begin'nen*.

scream, 1. n. Schrei, -e m. **2.** vb. schreien*, brüllen.

screen, 1. n. (furniture) Wandschirm, -e m.; (window) Fliegengitter, - nt.; (movie) Leinwand, ⁼e f.; (TV, radar) Schirm, -e m.; (camouflage) Tarnung, -en f. **2.** vb. (sift) sieben; (hide) tarnen.

screw, 1. n. Schraube, -n f. **2.** vb. schrauben.

scribble, vb. kritzeln, schmieren.

scripture, n. (eccles.) Heilige Schrift, -en f.

scroll, n. Schriftrolle, -n f.

scrub, vb. scheuern.

scruple, n. Skrupel, - m., Beden'ken, - nt.

scrupulous, adj. gewis'senhaft.

scrutinize, vb. genau' betrach'ten.

sculptor, n. Bildhauer, - m., Bildhauerin, -nen f.

sculpture, 1. n. Skulptur', -en f. **2.** vb. bildhauern.

scythe, n. Sense, -n f.

sea, n. See, Se'en f., Meer, -e nt.

seabed, n. Meeresboden m.

seal, 1. n. Siegel, - nt.; (animal) Seehund, -e m., Robbe, -n f. **2.** vb. siegeln, versie'geln.

seam, 1. n. Saum, ⁼e m. **2.** vb. säumen.

seaport, n. Hafen, ⁼ m.

search, 1. n. Suche f.; Durchsu'chung, -en f. **2.** vb. suchen; durch-su'chen.

seasick, adj. seekrank (⁻).

seasickness, n. Seekrankheit f.

season, 1. n. Jahreszeit, -en f.; Saison', -s f. **2.** vb. würzen.

seasoning, n. Gewürz', -e nt.

seat, 1. n. Platz, ⁼e m., Sitzplatz, ⁼e m.; (headquarters) Sitz, -e m. **2.** vb. Sitzplätze haben* für.

seat belt, n. Sicherheitsgurt, -e m.

second, 1. n. Sekun'de, -n f. **2.** adj. zweit-. **3.** vb. (s. a motion) einen Antrag unterstüt'zen.

secondary, adj. sekundär'.

secret, 1. n. Geheim'nis, -se nt. **2.** adj. geheim', heimlich.

secretary, n. Sekretär', -e m.; Sekretä'rin, -nen f.; (organization) Schriftführer, - m.

sect, n. Sekte, -n f.

section, n. Schnitt, -e m.; Teil, -e m.; Abschnitt, -e m.; Abtei'lung, -en f.

secular, adj. weltlich.

secure, 1. adj. sicher. **2.** vb. sichern.

security, n. Sicherheit, -en f.

sedative, n. Beru'higungsmittel, - nt.

seduce, vb. verfüh'ren.

seductive, adj. verfüh'rerisch.

see, vb. sehen*, schauen.

seed, n. (individual) Samen, - m.; (collective & fig.) Saat, -en f.

seek, vb. suchen.

seem, vb. scheinen*.

seep, vb. sickern.

seesaw, n. Wippe, -n f.

segment, n. Segment', -e nt.

segregate, vb. ab-sondern.

seize, vb. fassen, ergrei'fen*; (confiscate) beschlag'nahmen.

seldom, adv. selten.

select, 1. adj. ausgesucht. **2.** vb. aus-wählen, aus-suchen.

selection, n. Auswahl, f.

selective, adj. auswählend.

self, adv. selbst, selber.

selfish, adj. selbstsüchtig.

selfishness, n. Selbstsucht f.

sell, vb. verkau'fen.

semantic, adj. seman'tisch.

semantics, n. Seman'tik f.

semester, n. Semes'ter, - nt.

semicircle, n. Halbkreis, -e m.

semicolon, n. Strichpunkt, -e m., Semiko'lon nt.

seminary, n. Seminar', -e nt.

senate, n. Senat', -e m.

senator, n. Sena'tor, -o'ren m., Senato'rin, -nen f.

send, vb. senden*, schicken.

senile, adj. senil'.

senior, adj. älter-.

senior citizen, n. Senior, -o'ren m.; Senio'rin, -nen f.

sensation, n. Sensation', -en f.; (feeling) Gefühl', -e nt.

sensational, adj. sensationell'.

sense, 1. n. Sinn, -e m.; (feeling) Gefühl', -e nt.; (meaning) Bedeu'tung, -en f. **2.** vb. fühlen, empfin'den*.

sensible, adj. vernünf'tig.

sensitive, adj. empfind'lich; sen-si'bel.

sensual, adj. sinnlich.

sentence, 1. n. Satz, ̈e m.; (judg-ment) Urteil, -e nt. **2.** vb. verur'-teilen.

sentiment, n. Gefühl', -e nt., Empfin'dung, -en f.

sentimental, adj. gefühl'voll, sen-timental'.

separate, 1. adj. getrennt'. **2.** vb. trennen.

separation, n. Trennung, -en f.

September, n. Septem'ber, - m.

sequence, n. Reihenfolge, -n f.

serenade, n. Ständchen, - nt.

serene, adj. klar, ruhig.

sergeant, n. Unteroffizier, -e m.; (police) Wachtmeister, - m.

serial, 1. n. fortlaufende Erzäh'-lung, -en f. **2.** adj. Reihen- (cpds.).

series, n. Reihe, -n f.

serious, adj. ernst.

seriousness, n. Ernst m.

sermon, n. Predigt, -en f.

serpent, n. Schlange, -n f.

serum, n. Serum, -ra nt.

servant, n. Diener, - m., Dienerin, -nen f.; (domestic) Hausanges-tellt- m.&f.

serve, vb. dienen; (offer food) ser-vie'ren.

service, n. Dienst, -e m.; (hotel, etc.) Bedie'nung f.; (china, etc.) Servi'ce, -s nt.; (church) Gottes-dienst, -e m.

session, n. Sitzung, -en f.

set, 1. n. (dishes, tennis) Satz, ̈e m.; (articles belonging together)

Garnitur', -en f. **2.** adj. bestimmt'. **3.** adj. setzen; stellen; legen; (sun) unter'gehen*.

settle, vb. (dwell) sich nieder-lassen*; (conclude) erle'digen; (decide) entschei'den*.

settlement, n. Niederlassung, -en f.; Siedlung, -en f.; (decision) Überein'kommen, - nt.

settler, n. Siedler, - m., Siedlerin, -nen f.

seven, num. sieben.

seventeen, num. siebzehn.

seventeenth, 1. adj. siebzehnt-. **2.** n. Siebzehntel, - nt.

seventh, 1. adj. sieb(en)t-. **2.** n. Sieb(en)tel, - nt.

seventieth, 1. adj. siebzigst-. **2.** n. Siebzigstel, - nt.

seventy, num. siebzig.

sever, vb. ab'trennen, ab'brec-hen*.

several, adj. mehrer-.

severe, adj. streng; hart (-); ernst.

severity, n. Strenge f.; Härte f.; Ernst m.

sew, vb. nähen.

sewer, n. Kanalisation' f.

sex, n. Geschlecht', -er nt.; Sexus m.

sexism, n. Sexis'mus m.

sexist, n. Sexist', -en m.

sexton, n. Küster, - m.

sexual, adj. geschlecht'lich, sex-uell'.

shabby, adj. schäbig.

shack, n. Bretterbude, -n f.

shade, 1. n. Schatten, - m; (color) Farbton, ̈e m. **2.** vb. beschat'ten; schattie'ren.

shadow, n. Schatten, - m.

shady, adj. schattig; (dubious) zwielechtig.

shaft, n. Schaft, ̈e m.; (mine) Schacht, ̈e m.; (transmission) Welle, -n f.; (wagon) Deichsel, -n f.

shaggy, adj. zottig.

shake, vb. schütteln.

shall, vb. (we s. do it) wir werden* es tun; (what s. we do?) was sollen* wir tun?

shallow, adj. flach.

shame, 1. n. Schande f.; (what a s.) wie schade. **2.** vb. beschä'men.

shameful, *adj.* schandbar.

shameless, *adj.* schamlos.

shampoo, 1. *n.* Schampun', -s *nt.* **2.** *vb.* die Haare waschen*.

shape, 1. *n.* Form, -en *f.;* Gestalt', -en *f.* **2.** *vb.* formen, gestal'ten.

share, 1. *n.* Anteil, - *m.; (stock)* Aktie, -n *f.* **2.** *vb.* teilen; teil'haben*.

shark, *n.* Haifisch, -e *m.*

sharp, 1. *n. (music)* Kreuz, -e *nt.* **2.** *adj.* scharf (-); *(clever)* schlau.

sharpen, *vb.* schärfen.

sharpness, *n.* Schärfe *f.*

shatter, *vb.* zerbre'chen*.

shave, 1. *vb.* rasie'ren. **2.** *n.* Rasie'ren *nt.; (get a s.)* sich rasie'ren lassen.

shawl, *n.* Schal, -s *m.*

she, *pron.* sie.

shear, *vb.* scheren*.

shears, *n.pl.* Schere, -n *f.*

sheath, *n.* Scheide, -n *f.; (dress)* körperenges Kleid, -er *nt.*

shed, 1. *n.* Schuppen, - *m.* **2.** *vb.* ab'werfen*; *(tears, blood)* vergie'ßen*.

sheep, *n.* Schaf, -e *nt.*

sheet, *n. (bed)* Laken, - *nt.; (paper)* Bogen, - *m.; (metal)* Platte, -n *f.*

shelf, *n.* Bord, -e *nt.*

shell, 1. *n.* Schale, -n *f.; (conch)* Muschel, -n *f.; (explosive)* Grana'te, -n *f.* **2.** *vb.* beschie'ßen*.

shellac, *n.* Schellack, -e *m.*

shelter, 1. *n.* Schutz *m.,* Obdach *nt.* **2.** *vb.* beschir'men; beher'bergen.

shepherd, *n.* Schäfer, - *m.,* Hirt, -en, -en *m.*

sherbet, *n.* Sorbett, -e *nt.*

sherry, *n.* Sherry, -s *m.*

shield, 1. *n.* Schild, -e *m.* **2.** *vb.* schützen.

shift, 1. *n.* Wechsel, - *m.; (workers)* Schicht, -en *f.; (auto)* Schalthebel, - *m.* **2.** *vb.* wechseln; schalten; verschie'ben*.

shin, *n.* Schienbein, -e *nt.*

shine, *vb.* scheinen*, glänzen; *(shoes)* putzen.

shingle, *n.* Schindel, -n *f.,* Dachschindel, -n *f.*

shiny, *adj.* glänzend.

ship, 1. *n.* Schiff, -e *nt.* **2.** *vb.* senden*.

shipment, *n.* Ladung, -en *f.,* Sendung, -en *f.*

shipper, *n.* Verfrach'ter, - *m.,* Verla'der, - *m.*

shipping agent, *n.* Spediteur', -e *m.*

shipwreck, *n.* Schiffbruch, -̈e *m.*

shirk, *vb.* sich drücken vor.

shirt, *n.* Hemd, -en *nt.*

shiver, *vb.* zittern.

shock, 1. *n.* Schock, -s *m.* **2.** *vb.* schockie'ren.

shoe, *n.* Schuh, -e *m.*

shoelace, *n.* Schnürsenkel, - *m.*

shoemaker, *n.* Schuhmacher, - *m.,* Schuster, -*m.*

shoot, 1. *n. (sprout)* Schößling, -e *m.* **2.** *vb. (gun)* schießen*; *(person)* erschie'ßen*.

shop, 1. *n.* Laden, -̈ *m.,* Geschäft', -e *nt.; (factory)* Werkstatt, -̈en *f.* **2.** *vb.* Einkäufe machen.

shopping, *n.* Einkaufen *nt.*

shore, *n.* Küste, -n *f.; (beach)* Strand, -e *m.*

short, *adj.* kurz (-); *(scarce)* knapp.

shortage, *n.* Knappheit, -en *f.*

short circuit, *n.* Kurzschluß, -̈sse *m.*

short cut, *n.* Abkürzung, -en *f.*

shorten, *vb.* kürzen.

shorthand, *n.* Stenographie' *f.*

shortly, *adv.* bald (-).

shorts, *n.pl.* Shorts, *pl.*

shot, *n.* Schuß, -̈sse *m.; (photo)* Aufnahme, -n *f.*

should, *vb.* sollte; *(s. have)* hätte . . . sollen.

shoulder, 1. *n.* Schulter, -n *f.* **2.** *vb.* schultern.

shout, *vb.* schreien*.

shovel, *n.* Schaufel, -n *f.*

show, 1. *n. (theater, film)* Vorstellung, -en *f.; (spectacle)* Thea'ter, - *nt.; (exhibit)* Ausstellung, -en *f.* **2.** *vb.* zeigen; vor'führen; aus'stellen.

shower, *n. (rain)* Schauer, - *m.; (bath)* Dusche, -n *f.*

shrapnel, *n.* Schrapnell', -s *nt.*

shrewd, *adj.* scharfsinnig; *(derogatory)* geris'sen.

shriek, vb. kreischen.

shrill, adj. schrill, gellend.

shrimp, n. Garne'le, -n f.; Krabbe, -n f.; *(small person)* Dreikä'sehoch, -s m.

shrine, n. Schrein, -e m.

shrink, vb. schrumpfen; *(cloth)* ein·laufen*.

shroud, n. Leichentuch, ⁻er nt.

shrub, n. Strauch, ⁻er m., Busch, ⁻e m.

shudder, vb. schaudern.

shun, vb. vermei'den*.

shut, 1. vb. schließen*, zu·machen. **2.** adj. geschlos·sen. **3.** adv. zu.

shutter, n. Fensterladen, - m.; *(camera)* Verschluß', ⁻sse m.

shy, 1. adj. scheu, schüchtern. **2.** vb. scheuen.

Sicily, n. Sizi'lien nt.

sick, adj. krank (-); **(be s. of)** satt·haben*.

sickness, n. Krankheit, -en f.

side, n. Seite, -n f.; *(edge)* Rand, ⁻er m.

sidewalk, n. Bürgersteig, -e m.

siege, n. Bela'gerung, -en f.

sieve, n. Sieb, -e nt.

sift, vb. sieben; sichten.

sigh, 1. n. Seufzer, - m. **2.** vb. seufzen.

sight, 1. n. Sicht f.; *(vision)* Sehkraft f.; *(view)* Anblick, -e m.; *(sights)* Sehenswürdigkeit, -en f. **2.** vb. sichten.

sightseeing, n. Besich'tigung *(f.)* von Sehenswürdigkeiten.

sign, 1. n. Zeichen, - nt.; Schild, -er nt. **2.** vb. unterzeich'nen, unter·schrei'ben*.

signal, 1. n. Signal', -e nt. **2.** vb. signali·sie'ren.

signature, n. Unterschrift, -en f.

significance, n. Bedeu'tung, -en f., Wichtigkeit f.

significant, adj. bezeich'nend, bedeu'tend.

signify, vb. bezeich'nen, bedeu'ten.

silence, 1. n. Schweigen nt., Ruhe f. **2.** vb. zum Schweigen bringen*.

silent, adj. still, schweigsam.

silk, 1. n. Seide f. **2.** adj. seiden.

silken, silky, adj. seidig.

sill, n. *(door)* Schwelle, -n f.; *(window)* Fensterbrett, -er nt.

silly, adj. albern.

silo, n. Silo, -s m.

silver, 1. n. Silber nt. **2.** adj. silbern.

silverware, n. (silbernes) Besteck', -e nt.

similar, adj. ähnlich.

similarity, n. Ähnlichkeit, -en f.

simple, adj. einfach, schlicht; *(ignorant)* einfältig.

simplicity, n. Einfachheit f., Schlichtheit f.

simplify, vb. verein'fachen.

simulate, vb. vor·geben*; nach·ahmen.

simultaneous, adj. gleichzeitig.

sin, 1. n. Sünde, -n f. **2.** vb. sündigen.

since, 1. prep. seit. **2.** conj. seit, seitdem'; *(because)* da. **3.** adv. seitdem'.

sincere, adj. aufrichtig, ehrlich.

sincerely, adv. *(s. yours)* Ihr ergeˈbener, Ihre ergeˈbene.

sincerity, n. Aufrichtigkeit f.

sinful, adj. sündhaft.

sing, vb. singen*.

singe, vb. sengen.

singer, n. Sänger, - m., Sängerin, -nen f.

single, adj. einzeln; *(unmarried)* ledig.

singular, 1. n. *(gram.)* Einzahl f., Singular m. **2.** adj. einzig; *(unusual)* eigentümlich.

sinister, adj. düster, unheimlich.

sink, 1. n. Ausguß, ⁻sse m., Spülstein, -e m. **2.** vb. *(tr.)* versen'ken; *(intr.)* sinken*.

sinner, n. Sünder, - m., Sünderin, -nen f.

sinus, n. Stirnhöhle, -n f.

sinusitis, n. Stirnhöhlenentzündung, -en f.

sip, 1. n. Schluck, -e m. **2.** vb. schlürfen.

siphon, n. Siphon, -s m.

sir, n. **(yes, s.)** jawohl'!

siren, n. Sire'ne, -n f.

sirloin, n. Lendenstück, -e nt.

sister, n. Schwester, - f.

sister-in-law, n. Schwägerin, -nen f.

sit, *vb.* sitzen*; **(s. down)** sich (hin·)setzen.

site, *n.* Lage, -n *f.*

sitting, *n.* Sitzung, -en *f.*

situated, *adj.* gele'gen.

situation, *n.* Lage, -n *f.,* Situation', -en *f.*

six, *num.* sechs.

sixteen, *num.* sechzehn.

sixteenth, 1. *adj.* sechzehnt-. **2.** *n.* Sechzehntel, - *nt.*

sixth, 1. *adj.* sechst-. **2.** *n.* Sechstel, - *nt.*

sixtieth, 1. *adj.* sechzigst-. **2.** *n.* Sechzigstel, - *nt.*

sixty, *num.* sechzig.

size, *n.* Größe, -n *f.,* Ausmaß, -e *nt.*

skate, 1. *n.* Schlittschuh, -e *m.* **2.** *vb.* Schlittschuh laufen*.

skateboard, *n.* Skatebord *nt.;* Rollbrett *nt.*

skeleton, *n.* Skelett', -e *nt.*

skeptic, *n.* Skeptiker, - *m.*

skeptical, *adj.* skeptisch.

sketch, 1. *n.* Skizze, -n *f.;* Sketch, -e *m.* **2.** *vb.* skizzie'ren.

ski, 1. *n.* Ski, -er *m.* **2.** *vb.* Ski'-laufen*.

skid, 1. *n.* Hemmschuh, -e *m.* **2.** *vb.* rutschen.

skill, *n.* Geschick', *nt.,* Fertigkeit, -en *f.*

skillful, *adj.* geschickt'.

skim, *vb. (remove cream)* entrah'-men; *(go lightly)* flüchtig lesen*.

skim milk, *n.* Magermilch *f.*

skin, 1. *n.* Haut, ⸚e *f.; (fur)* Fell, -e *nt.; (of fruit)* Schale, -n *f.* **2.** *vb.* häuten.

skip, 1. *vb.* springen*; *(omit)* überschla'gen*.

skirt, 1. *n.* Rock, ⸚e *m.* **2.** *vb.* umge'hen*.

skull, *n.* Schädel, - *m.*

skunk, *n.* Stinktier, -e *nt.; (person)* Schuft, -e *m.*

sky, *n.* Himmel, - *m.*

skyscraper, *n.* Wolkenkratzer, - *m.*

slab, *n.* Platte, -n *f.*

slack, *adj.* schlaff, flau.

slacken, *vb.* nach·lassen*.

slacks, *n.pl.* Slacks *pl.*

slam, *vb.* knallen, zu·knallen.

slander, 1. *n.* Verleum'dung, -en *f.* **2.** *vb.* verleum'den.

slang, *n.* Slang *m.,* Jargon', -s *m.*

slant, 1. *n.* Neigung, -en *f.;* schiefe Ebene, -n *f.;* Aspekt', -e *m.* **2.** *vb.* neigen.

slap, 1. *n.* Klaps, -e *m.,* Ohrfeige, -n *f.* **2.** *vb.* schlagen*.

slash, 1. *n.* Schlitz, -e *m.;* Schnittwunde, -n *f.* **2.** *vb.* schlitzen

slat, *n.* Latte, -n *f.*

slate, *n.* Schiefer *m.; (list)* Liste, -n *f.*

slaughter, 1. *n.* Schlachten *nt.;* Gemet'zel, - *nt.* **2.** *vb.* schlachten; nieder·metzeln.

Slav, *n.* Slawe, -n, -n *m.,* Slawin, -nen *f.*

slave, *n.* Sklave, -n, -n *m.,* Sklavin, -nen *f.*

slavery, *n.* Sklaverei' *f.*

Slavic, *adj.* slawisch.

slay, *vb.* erschla'gen*.

sled, *n.* Schlitten, - *m.; (go sledding)* Schlitten fahren*, rodeln.

sleek, *adj.* glatt (⸚, -); geschniegelt.

sleep, 1. *n.* Schlaf *m.* **2.** *vb.* schlafen*; **(go to s.)** ein·schlafen*.

sleeper, sleeping car, *n.* Schlafwagen, - *m.*

sleeping pill, *n.* Schlaftablette, -n *f.*

sleepy, *adj.* schläfrig, müde.

sleet, *n.* Eisregen *m.*

sleeve, *n.* Ärmel, - *m.*

sleigh, *n.* Schlitten, - *m.*

slender, *adj.* schlank; *(slight)* schwach (⸚).

slice, 1. *n.* Scheibe, -n *f.* **2.** *vb.* in Scheiben schneiden*.

slide, *vb.* gleiten*, rutschen.

slight, *adj.* leicht, gering'; *(thin)* schmächtig.

slim, *adj.* schlank; gering'.

slime, *n.* Schlamm *m.;* Schleim.

slip, 1. *n. (plant)* Steckling, -e *m.; (error)* Verse'hen, - *nt.; (underwear)* Unterrock, ⸚e *m.; (paper)* Zettel, - *m.; (bedding)* Bezug', ⸚e *m.* **2.** *vb.* gleiten*, aus·gleiten*.

slipper, *n.* Hausschuh, -e *m.,* Pantof'fel, -n *m.*

slippery, *adj.* glatt (⸚, -), schlüpf-rig.

slit, 1. n. Schlitz, -e m. **2.** vb. schlitzen.
slogan, n. Schlagwort, -e or ‑er nt.; (election s.) Wahlspruch, ‑e m.
slope, n. Abhang, ‑e m.; Neigung, -en f.
sloppy, adj. schlampig.
slot, n. Schlitz, -e m.
slovenly, adj. liederlich.
slow, adj. langsam; (be s., of a clock) nach‑gehen*.
slowness, n. Langsamkeit f.
sluggish, adj. träge.
slum, n. Elendsviertel, - nt.
slur, 1. n. Anwurf, ‑e m. **2.** vb. (speech) nuscheln.
slush, n. Matsch m.
sly, adj. schlau, verschla'gen.
small, adj. klein.
smallpox, n. Blattern, pl.
smart, adj. intelligent'; elegant'.
smash, 1. n. zerschla'gen*, zerschmei'ßen*.
smear, vb. schmieren, beschmie'ren.
smell, 1. n. Geruch', ‑e m. **2.** vb. riechen*.
smelt, 1. n. Stint, -e m. **2.** vb. schmelzen, ein‑schmelzen.
smile, 1. n. Lächeln nt. **2.** vb. lächeln.
smock, n. Kittel, - m.
smoke, 1. n. Rauch f. **2.** vb. rauchen; (meat, fish) räuchern.
smooth, 1. adj. glatt (‑, ‑). **2.** vb. glätten.
smother, vb. ersti'cken.
smug, adj. selbstgefällig.
smuggle, vb. schmuggeln.
snack, n. Imbiß, -sse m.
snag, n. (stocking) Zugmasche, -n f.; (obstacle) Hindernis, -se nt.
snail, n. Schnecke, -n f.
snake, n. Schlange, -n f.
snap, 1. n. Druckknopf, ‑e m. **2.** vb. schnappen; (break) zerrei'ßen*.
snapshot, n. Schnappschuß, ‑sse m.
snare, n. Falle, -n f.
snarl, vb. (growl) drohend knurren.
snatch, vb. erha'schen, weg‑schnappen.
sneak, vb. schleichen*.

sneakers, n.pl. Freizeitschuhe m.pl., Turnschuhe m.pl.
sneer, vb. höhnisch grinsen.
sneeze, vb. niesen.
snob, n. Snob, -s m.
snore, vb. schnarchen.
snow, 1. n. Schnee m. **2.** vb. schneien.
snub, 1. n. Affront', -s m. **2.** vb. schneiden*.
snug, adj. eng; (fig.) mollig.
so, adv. so.
soak, vb. durchnäs'sen; ein‑weichen.
soap, n. Seife, -n f.
soar, vb. sich empor'schwingen*.
sob, vb. schluchzen.
sober, adj. nüchtern.
sociable, adj. gesel'lig.
social, adj. gesell'schaftlich, sozial'.
socialism, n. Sozialis'mus f.
socialist, n. Sozialist', -en, -en m.; Sozialis'tin, -nen f.
society, n. Gesell'schaft, -en f.
sociology, n. Soziologie' f.
sock, n. Socke, -n f. **2.** vb. schlagen*.
socket, n. (eye) Augenhöhle, -n f.; (elec.) Steckdose, -n f.
sod, n. Sode, -n f.
soda, n. Soda nt.
sofa, n. Sofa, -s nt.
soft, adj. weich; (not loud) leise; (not rough) sanft, sacht.
soft drink, n. alkoholfreies Getränk'; -e m.
soften, vb. weich machen*; (fig.) mildern.
soil, 1. n. Boden, ‑ m. **2.** vb. beschmut'zen.
soiled, adj. schmutzig.
sojourn, 1. n. Aufenthalt, -e m. **2.** vb. sich auf‑halten*.
solace, n. Trost m.
solar, adj. Sonnen- (cpds.).
soldier, n. Soldat', -en, -en m.
sole, 1. n. Sohle, -n f.; (fish) Seezunge, -n f. **2.** adj. allei'nig, einzig.
solemn, adj. feierlich.
solicit, vb. an‑halten* um.
solicitous, adj. besorgt'; eifrig.
solid, adj. fest; solid'; kompakt'.
solidify, vb. festigen; verdich'ten.
solitary, adj. einzeln.

solitude, n. Einsamkeit, -en f.
solo, n. Solo, -s nt.
soloist, n. Solist', -en, -en m., Solis'tin, -nen f.
so long, interj. Wiedersehen.
solution, n. Lösung, -en f.
solve, vb. lösen.
solvent, 1. n. Lösungsmittel, - nt. 2. adj. (financially capable) zahlungsfähig.
somber, adj. düster.
some, pron. & adj. (with singulars) etwas; (with plurals) einig-, ein paar.
somebody, pron. jemand.
somehow, adv. irgendwie.
someone, pron. jemand.
somersault, n. Purzelbaum, -̈e m.
something, pron. etwas.
sometime, adv. irgendwann.
sometimes, adv. manchmal.
somewhat, adv. etwas.
somewhere, adv. irgendwo.
son, n. Sohn, -̈e m.
song, n. Lied, -er nt.
son-in-law, n. Schwiegersohn, -̈e m.
soon, adv. bald.
soot, n. Ruß m.
soothe, vb. beschwich'tigen.
soothing, adj. wohltuend.
sophisticated, adj. anspruchsvoll, verfei'nert, weltgewandt; (tech.) hochentwickelt.
soprano, n. Sopran', -e m.
sorcery, n. Zauberei' f.
sordid, adj. dreckig; gemein'.
sore, 1. n. wunde Stelle, -n f., offene Wunde, -n f. 2. adj. wund; schmerzhaft; (angry) eingeschnappt; (be s.) weh•tun*.
sorrow, n. Kummer, - m.
sorrowful, adj. kummervoll.
sorry, adj. traurig, betrübt'; (I am s.) es tut* mir leid.
sort, 1. n. Sorte, -n f., Art, -en f. 2. vb. sortie'ren.
soul, n. Seele, -n f.
sound, 1. n. Ton, -̈e m., Laut, -e m., Klang, -̈e m. 2. adj. gesund(-, -); (valid) einwandfrei. 3. vb. klingen*; (take soundings) loten.
soup, n. Suppe, -n f.
sour, adj. sauer.
source, n. Quelle, -n f.

south, 1. n. Süden m. 2. adj. südlich; Süd- (cpds.).
southeast, 1. n. Südos'ten m. 2. adj. südöst'lich; Südöst'- (cpds.).
southeastern, adj. südöst'lich.
southern, adj. südlich.
South Pole, n. Südpol m.
southwest, 1. n. Südwes'ten m. 2. adj. südwest'lich; Südwest'- (cpds.).
southwestern, adj. südwest'lich.
souvenir, n. Andenken, - nt.; Reiseandenken, - nt.
Soviet, 1. n. Sowjet, -s m. 2. adj. sowje'tisch.
sow, 1. n. Sau, -̈e f. 2. vb. säen.
space, n. Raum, -̈e m.
space shuttle, n. Raumtransporter, - m.
spacious, adj. geräu'mig.
spade, n. Spaten, - m.; (cards) Pik nt.
spaghetti, n. Spaghet'ti pl.
Spain, n. Spanien nt.
span, 1. n. Spanne, -n f. 2. vb. überspan'nen.
Spaniard, n. Spanier, - m., Spanierin, -nen f.
Spanish, adj. spanisch.
spank, vb. hauen*.
spanking, n. Haue f.
spar, 1. n. Sparren, - m. 2. vb. boxen.
spare, 1. adj. Ersatz'-, Reser've- (cpds.). 2. vb. sparen, scheuen.
spark, n. Funke(n), - m.
sparkle, vb. funkeln.
spark-plug, n. Zündkerze, -n f.
sparrow, n. Sperling, -e m.
sparse, adj. spärlich.
spasm, n. Krampf, -̈e m.
spasmodic, adj. krampfhaft; sprunghaft.
spatter, vb. spritzen, besprit'zen.
speak, vb. sprechen*, reden.
speaker, n. Redner, - m.; (presiding officer) Präsident', -en, -en m.
spear, 1. n. Speer, -e m.; Spieß, -e m. 2. vb. auf•spießen.
special, adj. beson'der-.
specialist, n. Spezialist', -en, -en m., Spezialis'tin, -nen f.
specially, adv. beson'ders.
specialty, n. Spezialität', -en f.

species, n. Art, -en f.; Gattung, -en f.
specific, adj. spezi'fisch.
specify, vb. spezifizie'ren; (stipulate) bestim'men.
specimen, n. Muster, - nt., Exemplar', -e nt., Probe, -n f.
spectacle, n. Schauspiel, -e nt.; Anblick, -e m.; (s.s) Brille, -n f.
spectacular, adj. aufsehenerregend.
spectator, n. Zuschauer, - m., Zuschauerin, -nen f.
spectrum, n. Spektrum, -tren nt.
speculate, vb. spekulie'ren.
speculation, n. Spekulation, -en f.
speech, n. Sprache, -n f.; (address) Rede, -n.
speechless, adj. sprachlos.
speed, 1. n. Geschwin'digkeit, -en f., Tempo nt. 2. vb. hasten; (s. up) beschleu'nigt erle'digen; (auto) die Geschwin'digkeitsgrenze überschrei'ten*.
speedometer, n. Geschwin'digkeitsmesser, - m.
speedy, adj. schnell; unverzüglich.
spell, 1. n. Zauber, - m. 2. vb. buchstabie'ren.
spelling, n. Rechtschreibung f.
spend, vb. (money) aus-geben*; (time) verwen'den*, verbrin'gen*.
sphere, n. Kugel, -n f., Sphäre, -n f.
spice, n. Gewürz', -e nt.
spider, n. Spinne, -n f.
spike, n. langer Nagel, = m.; (thorn) Dorn, -en m., Stachel, -n m.
spill, vb. verschüt'ten; (make a spot) kleckern.
spin, vb. spinnen*.
spinach, n. Spinat' m.
spine, n. Rückgrat, -e nt.
spiral, 1. n. Spira'le, -n f. 2. adj. spiral'förmig.
spire, n. spitzer Turm, =e m.
spirit, n. Geist, m.; (ghost) Gespenst', -er nt.; (vivacity) Schwung m.; (s.s) Spiritou'sen pl.
spiritual, 1. n. Spiritual, -e m. 2. adj. geistig, seelisch.

spiritualism, n. Spiritualis'mus m.; Spiritis'mus m.
spit, 1. n. (saliva) Speichel m.; (roasting) Spieß, -e m. 2. vb. spucken.
spite, 1. n. Trotz m.; (in s. of) trotz. 2. vb. ärgern.
splash, vb. spritzen; planschen.
splendid, adj. prächtig.
splendor, n. Pracht f.
splice, vb. spleißen*.
splint, n. Schiene, -n f.
splinter, n. Splitter, - m.
split, 1. n. Spalt, -e m. 2. vb. spalten.
spoil, vb. verder'ben*; schlecht werden*; (child) verwöh'nen, verzie'hen*.
spoke, n. Speiche, -n f.
spokesperson, n. Sprecher, - m., Sprecherin, -nen f.
sponge, 1. n. Schwamm, =e m. 2. vb. (live off) nassauern.
sponsor, 1. n. Bürge, -n, -n m.; Förderer, - m.; (radio, TV, etc.) Rekla'meauftraggeber, - m. 2. vb. fördern; (advertising) in Auftrag geben*.
spontaneity, n. Impulsivität' f.
spontaneous, adj. spontan'.
spool, n. Spule, -n f.
spoon, n. Löffel, - m.
sport, n. Sport m.; Vergnü'gen, - nt.
spot, n. (place) Stelle, -n f.; (blot) Fleck, -en m.
spouse, n. Gatte, -n, -n m.; Gattin, -nen f.
spout, 1. n. Tülle, -n f.; (water) Strahl, -en m. 2. vb. hervor'-sprudeln; speien*.
sprain, 1. n. Verren'kung, -en f., Verstau'chung, -en f. 2. vb. verren'ken, verstau'chen.
sprawl, vb. sich aus-breiten; alle Viere aus-strecken.
spray, vb. spritzen; zerstäu'ben.
spread, 1. n. Spanne, -n f.; Umfang, =e m. 2. vb. aus-breiten.
spree, n. Bummel, - m. Ausflug, =e m.
sprightly, adj. munter.
spring, 1. n. (season) Frühling, -e m., Frühjahr, -e nt.; (source) Quelle, -n f.; (leap) Sprung, =e m.

(metal) Feder, -n *f.* 2. *vb.* springen*.

sprinkle, *vb.* sprengen; streuen.

sprint, 1. *n.* Kurzstreckenlauf, *:e m.* 2. *vb.* sprinten.

sprout, 1. *n.* Sproß, -sse *m.* 2. *vb.* sprießen*.

spry, *adj.* flink.

spur, 1. *n.* Sporn, Sporen *m.* 2. *vb.* an·spornen.

spurn, *vb.* verschmä'hen.

spurt, *vb.* hervor'schießen*.

spy, 1. *n.* Spion', -e *m.,* Spio'nin, -nen *f.* 2. *vb.* spionie'ren.

squabble, 1. *n.* Zank *m.* 2. *vb.* zanken.

squad, *n.* Trupp, -s *m.;* *(sport)* Mannschaft *f.*

squadron, *n.* *(air)* Staffel, -n *f.;* *(navy)* Geschwa'der, - *nt.*

squall, *n.* Bö, -en *f.*

squalor, *n.* Schmutz *m.*

squander, *vb.* vergeu'den.

square, 1. *n.* Viereck, -e *nt.,* Quadrat', -e *nt.;* *(open place)* Platz, *:e m.* 2. *adj.* viereckig, quadra'tisch. 3. *vb.* quadrie'ren.

squash, 1. *n.* Kürbis, -se *m.* 2. *vb.* quetschen, zerquet'schen.

squat, 1. *adj.* kurz und dick. 2. *vb.* hocken, kauern.

squeak, *vb.* quietschen.

squeamish, *adj.* zimperlich.

squeeze, *vb.* drücken; *(juice)* aus·pressen.

squirrel, *n.* Eichhörnchen, - *nt.*

squirt, *vb.* spritzen.

stab, 1. *n.* Stich, -e *m.* 2. *vb.* stechen*; erste'chen*.

stability, *n.* Bestän'digkeit *f.,* Stabilität' *f.*

stabilize, *vb.* stabilisie'ren.

stable, 1. *n.* Stall, *:e m.* 2. *adj.* bestän'dig; stabil'.

stack, 1. *n.* Haufen, - *m.* 2. *vb.* auf·stapeln.

stadium, *n.* Stadion, -dien *nt.*

staff, *n.* Stab, *:e m.;* *(personnel)* Personal' *nt.;* *(music)* Notenlinien *pl.*

stag, *n.* Hirsch, -e *m.*

stage, 1. *n.* *(theater)* Bühne, -n *f.;* *(phase)* Stadium, -dien *nt.* 2. *vb.* inszenie'ren.

stagflation, *n.* Stagflation' *f.*

stagger, *vb.* taumeln; *(amaze)* verblüf'fen; *(alternate)* staffeln.

stagnant, *adj.* stagnie'rend.

stagnate, *vb.* stagnie'ren.

stain, 1. *n.* Fleck, -e *m.;* *(color)* Färbstoff, -e *m.;* *(paint)* Beize *f.* 2. *vb.* befle'cken, färben; beizen.

staircase, stairs, *n.* Treppe, -n *f.*

stake, 1. *n.* *(post)* Pfahl, *:e m.;* *(sum, bet)* Einsatz, *:e m.* 2. *vb.* aufs Spiel setzen.

stale, *adj.* alt (-), schal.

stalk, *n.* Stiel, -e *m.,* Halm, -e *m.*

stall, 1. *n.* Stall, *:e m.;* *(vendor's)* Bude, -n *f.* 2. *vb.* *(hesitate)* Zeit schinden*; *(engine)* ab·würgen.

stamina, *n.* Energie' *f.,* Ausdauer *f.*

stammer, *vb.* stammeln.

stamp, 1. *n.* Stempel, - *m.;* *(mark)* Geprä'ge *nt.;* *(postal)* Freimarke, -n *f.,* Briefmarke, -n *f.* 2. *vb.* stempeln; prägen.

stand, 1. *n.* Stellung, -en *f.;* *(vendor's)* Bude, -n *f.;* *(grandstand)* Tribü'ne, -n *f.* 2. *vb.* stehen*; *(endure)* ertra'gen*.

standard, 1. *n.* Norm, -en *f.,* Standard, -s *m.* 2. *adj.* Standard- *(cpds.).*

standardize, *vb.* standardisie'ren.

standing, *n.* Bestand' *m.;* *(reputation)* Ruf *m.*

standpoint, *n.* Standpunkt, -e *m.*

star, *n.* Stern, -e *m.;* *(movie)* Star, -s *m.*

starch, 1. *n.* Stärke *f.* 2. *vb.* stärken.

stare, *vb.* starren, glotzen.

stark, *adj.* kraß; *(bare)* kahl.

start, 1. *n.* Anfang, *:e m.,* Start, -s *m.* 2. *vb.* an·fangen, starten.

startle, *vb.* erschre'cken, auf·schrecken.

starvation, *n.* Verhun'gern *n.;* Hungertod *m.*

starve, *vb.* hungern; *(s. to death)* verhun'gern.

state, 1. *n.* Staat, -en *m.;* *(condition)* Zustand, *:e m.* 2. *vb.* dar·legen, erklä'ren*.

statement, *n.* Erklä'rung, -en *f.,* Behaup'tung, -en *f.*

stateroom, *n.* Kabi'ne, -n *f.*

statesman, *n.* Staatsmann, *:er m.*

static, 1. n. atmosphä'rische Störung, -en f. **2.** adj. statisch.

station, n. Station', -en f.; (position) Stellung, -en f.; (R.R.) Bahnhof, ⸚e m.

stationary, adj. feststehend, stationär'.

stationer, n. Schreibwarenhändler, - m.

stationery, n. Schreibwaren pl.; Briefpapier nt.

station wagon, n. Kombiwagen, - m.

statistics, n.pl. Statis'tik f.

statue, n. Statue, -n f.

stature, n. Wuchs m., Statur' f.; (fig.) Format', -e nt.

status, n. Stand, ⸚e m.

statute, n. Statut', -e nt., Satzung, -en f.

staunch, adj. treu, wacker.

stay, 1. n. (sojourn) Aufenthalt m.; (delay) Einstellung, -en f. **2.** vb. bleiben*; (hold back) zurück'halten*.

steady, adj. fest; sicher; bestän'dig.

steak, n. Beefsteak, -s nt.

steal, vb. stehlen*.

stealth, n. Verstoh'lenheit f.

stealthy, adj. verstoh'len.

steam, 1. n. Dampf, ⸚e m. **2.** vb. dampfen.

steamboat, n. Dampfboot, -e nt.

steamship, n. Dampfer, - m.

steel, 1. n. Stahl, ⸚e m. **2.** vb. stählern; Stahl- (cpds.).

steep, adj. steil; (price) hoch (hoh-, höher, höchst-).

steeple, n. Kirchturm, ⸚e m.

steer, 1. n. Stier, -e m. **2.** vb. steuern.

stellar, adj. Sternen- (cpds.).

stem, 1. n. Stiel, -e m. **2.** vb. stammen.

stenographer, n. Stenotypis'tin, -nen f.

stenography, n. Kurzschrift, -en f.; Stenographie', -i'en f.

step, 1. n. Schritt, -e m.; (stair) Stufe, -n f. **2.** vb. treten*.

stepfather, n. Stiefvater, ⸚ m.

stepladder, n. Trittleiter, -n f.

stepmother, n. Stiefmutter, ⸚ f.

stereophonic, adj. stereophon'.

sterile, adj. unfruchtbar; steril'.

sterility, n. Sterilität' f.

sterilize, vb. sterilisie'ren.

sterling, adj. münzecht; (silver) echt; (pound s.) Pfund Sterling nt.

stern, adj. streng.

stethoscope, n. Stethoskop', -e nt.

stew, 1. n. Eintopf, ⸚e m. **2.** vb. dämpfen.

steward, n. Steward, -s m.

stewardess, n. Stewardess', -en f.

stick, 1. n. Stock, ⸚e m. **2.** vb. (adhere) kleben; (pin) stecken.

sticker, n. Etikett', -e nt.; Ankleber, - m.

sticky, adj. klebrig.

stiff, adj. steif.

stiffen, vb. steif werden*; (fig.) verhär'ten.

stiffness, n. Steifheit, -en f.

stifle, vb. ersti'cken.

stigma, n. Stigma, -men nt., Schandfleck, -e m.

still, 1. n. Destillier'apparat, -e m. **2.** adj. still. **3.** vb. stillen. **4.** adv. noch; doch; dennoch.

stillness, n. Stille f.

stimulant, n. Reizmittel, - nt.

stimulate, vb. an'regen.

stimulus, n. Anreiz, -e m.

sting, 1. n. Stache. - m.; (bite) Stich, -e m. **2.** vb. stechen*; (burn) brennen.

stingy, adj. geizig.

stink, vb. stinken*.

stipulate, vb. bestim'men.

stir, 1. n. Aufregung, -en f. **2.** vb. rühren; erre'gen.

stitch, 1. n. Stich, -e m.; (knitting) Masche, -n f. **2.** vb. steppen.

stock, 1. n. (supply) Vorrat, ⸚e m., Lager, - nt.; (lineage) Fami'lie, -n f.; (livestock) Viehbestand, ⸚e m.; (gun) Schaft, ⸚e m. **2.** vb. versor'gen; auf Lager haben*.

stockbroker, n. Börsenmakler, - m.

stock exchange, n. Börse, -n f.

stocking, n. Strumpf, ⸚e m.

stodgy, adj. schwerfällig; untersetzt'.

stole, n. Stola, -len f.

stomach, 1. n. Magen, ⸚ m. **2.** vb. (fig.) schlucken.

stone, 1. n. Stein, -e m.; (fruit) Kern, -e m. **2.** vb. steinigen.

stool, n. Schemel. - m.

stoop, vb. sich bücken; (demean oneself) sich ernied'rigen.

stop, 1. n. Haltestelle, -n f. **2.** vb. halten*; stoppen; (cease) aufhören.

stopover, n. Fahrtunterbrechung, -en f.

storage, n. Lagern nt.; Lagerhaus, -"er nt.

store, 1. n. Laden, -" m., Geschäft', -e nt.; (supplies) Vorräte pl. **2.** vb. lagern.

storehouse, n. Lagerhaus, -"er nt.

storm, n. Sturm, -"e m. **2.** vb. stürmen.

stormy, adj. stürmisch.

story, n. Erzäh'lung, -en f., Geschich'te, -n f.

stout, adj. dick; (strong) wacker.

stove, n. (cooking) Herd, -e m.; (heating) Ofen, -" m.

straight, adj. gera'de; (honest) ehrlich.

straighten, vb. gera'de machen; in Ordnung bringen*.

straightforward, adj. offen.

strain, 1. n. Anstrengung, -en f.; Belas'tung, -en f. **2.** vb. anstrengen; belas'ten; (filter) seihen.

strait, n. Meeresenge, -n f.

strand, 1. n. Strähne, -n f. **2.** vb. stranden.

strange, adj. merkwürdig; (foreign) fremd.

stranger, n. Fremd- m.&f.

strangle, vb. erwür'gen.

strap, n. Riemen, - m.

stratagem, n. Kriegslist, -en f.

strategic, adj. strate'gisch.

strategy, n. Strategie' f.

stratosphere, n. Stratosphä're f.

stratum, n. Schicht, -en f.

straw, n. Stroh nt.; (for drinking) Strohalm, -e m.

strawberry, n. Erdbeere, -n f.

stray, 1. adj. verein'zelt. **2.** vb. abweichen; abschweifen.

streak, n. Strähne, -n f.

stream, n. Strom, -"e m.; (small) Bach, -"e m.

streamlined, adj. stromlinienförmig.

street, n. Straße, -n f.

streetcar, n. Straßenbahn, -en f.

strength, n. Kraft, -"e f., Stärke, -n f.

strengthen, vb. stärken.

strenuous, adj. anstrengend.

stress, 1. n. Belas'tung, -en f.; (accent) Beto'nung f. **2.** vb. belas'ten; beto'nen.

stretch, 1. n. Strecke, -n f.; Spanne, -n f. **2.** vb. strecken; spannen.

stretcher, n. Tragbahre, -n f.

strew, vb. streuen.

stricken, adj. getrof'fen.

strict, adj. streng.

stride, 1. n. Schritt, -e m. **2.** vb. schreiten*.

strife, n. Streit m.

strike, 1. n. (workers') Streik, -s m. **2.** vb. streiken; (hit) schlagen*.

string, 1. n. Bindfaden, -" m., Schnur, -"e f.; (music) Saite, -n f. **2.** vb. aufreihen.

string bean, n. grüne Bohne, -n f.

strip, 1. n. Streifen, - m. **2.** vb. abstreifen; entklei'den.

stripe, n. Streifen, - m.

strive, vb. streben.

stroke, 1. n. Schlag, -"e m.; (pen, brush, etc.) Strich, -e m.; (med.) Schlaganfall, -"e m. **2.** vb. streicheln.

stroll, 1. n. kleiner Spazier'gang, -"e m. **2.** vb. spazie'rengehen*.

stroller, n. Spazier'gänger, m.; (baby-carriage) Kindersportwagen, - m.

strong, adj. stark (-), kräftig.

stronghold, n. Feste, -n f.

structure, n. Struktur', -en f.

struggle, 1. n. Ringen nt. **2.** vb. ringen*.

strut, vb. stolzie'ren.

stub, 1. n. Kontroll'abschnitt, -e m. **2.** vb. anstoßen*.

stubborn, adj. hartnäckig; (person) dickköpfig.

student, n. Student', -en, -en m., Studen'tin, -nen f.

studio, n. Atelier', -s nt.

studious, adj. eifrig.

study, 1. n. Studium, -dien nt.; (room) Arbeitszimmer, - nt. **2.** vb. studie'ren; (do homework) arbeiten.

stuff, 1. n. Zeug nt. **2.** vb. stopfen.

stuffing, n. Füllung, -en f.

stumble, vb. stolpern.

stump, n. Stumpf, ⸚e m.

stun, vb. betäu'ben; verblüffen.

stunt, n. Kunststück, -e nt.

stupid, adj. dumm (⸚), blöde.

stupidity, n. Dummheit, -en f.

stupor, n. Betäu'bungszustand m.

sturdy, adj. stark (⸚), stämmig.

stutter, vb. stottern.

sty, n. Schweinestall, ⸚e m.; (eye) Gerstenkorn, ⸚er nt.

style, n. Stil, -e m.

stylish, adj. elegant'.

suave, adj. verbind'lich.

subconscious, adj. unterbewußt.

subdue, vb. unterdrü'cken.

subject, 1. n. (gram.) Subjekt, -e nt.; (topic) Thema, -men nt.; (of king) Untertan, -en, -en m. **2.** adj. unterwor'fen. **3.** vb. unterwer'fen*; aus•setzen.

subjugate, vb. unterjo'chen.

subjunctive, n. Konjunktiv, -e m.

sublime, adj. erha'ben.

submarine, n. Unterseeboot, -e nt., U-Boot, -e nt.

submerge, vb. unter•tauchen.

submission, n. Unterwer'fung, -en f.

submit, vb. (lay before) unterbrei'ten; (offer opinion) anheim'stellen; (yield) sich fügen; (surrender) sich unterwer'fen*.

subnormal, adj. unternormal.

subordinate, 1. n. Unterge'ben m.&f. **2.** adj. untergeordnet; (s. clause) Nebensatz, ⸚e m.

subscribe, vb. (underwrite) zeichnen; (take regularly) abonnie'ren; (approve) billigen.

subscription, n. Abonnement', -s nt.; Zeichnung, -en f.

subsequent, adj. folgend.

subside, vb. nach•lassen*.

subsidy, n. Zuschuß, ⸚sse m.

substance, n. Substanz', -en f.

substantial, adj. wesentlich; beträcht'lich.

substitute, 1. n. Ersatz' m.; Ver-

tre'tung, -en f. **2.** vb. erset'zen; als Ersatz' geben*; die Vertre'tung überneh'men*.

substitution, n. Erset'zung, -en f.

subtle, adj. subtil', fein.

subtract, vb. ab•ziehen*.

suburb, n. Vorort, -e m.

subversive, adj. zerset'zend, staatsfeindlich.

subway, n. Untergrundbahn, -en f., U-Bahn, -en f.

succeed, vb. erfolg'reich sein*, gelin'gen*; (come after) folgen.

success, n. Erfolg', -e m.

successful, adj. erfolg'reich.

succession, n. (to throne) Erbfolge, -n f.; (sequence) Reihenfolge, -n f.

successive, adj. aufeinan'derfolgend.

successor, n. Nachfolger, - m., Nachfolgerin, -nen f.

succumb, vb. erlie'gen*.

such, adj. solch.

suck, vb. saugen, lutschen.

suction, n. Saugen nt.; Saug- (cpds.).

sudden, adj. plötzlich, jäh.

sue, vb. verkla'gen, gericht'lich belan'gen.

suffer, vb. leiden*.

suffice, vb. genü'gen, aus•reichen.

sufficient, adj. genü'gend.

suffocate, vb. ersti'cken.

sugar, n. Zucker m.

suggest, vb. vor•schlagen*.

suggestion, n. Vorschlag, ⸚e m.

suicide, n. Selbstmord, -e m.

suit, 1. n. (man's clothing) Anzug, ⸚e m.; (woman's clothing) Kostüm', -e nt.; (cards) Farbe, -n f.; (law) Prozeß', -sse m. **2.** vb. passen; (be becoming) stehen*.

suitable, adj. passend; angemessen.

suitcase, n. Koffer, - m.

suitor, n. Freier, - m.

sullen, adj. griesgrämig.

sum, n. Summe, -n f.

summarize, vb. zusam'menfassen.

summary, 1. n. Übersicht, -en f. **2.** adj. summa'risch.

summer, n. Sommer, - m.

summit, n. Gipfel, - m.; Gipfelkonferenz f.

summon, vb. zusam'men·rufen*, ein·berufen*; (law) vor·laden*.

sun, n. Sonne, -n f.

sunburn, n. Sonnenbrand, ̈e m.

sunburned, adj. sonnenverbrannt.

Sunday, n. Sonntag, -e m.

sunken, adj. versun'ken.

sunny, adj. sonnig.

sunshine, n. Sonnenschein m.

superb, adj. hervor'ragend.

superficial, adj. oberflächlich.

superfluous, adj. überflüssig.

super-highway, n. Autobahn, -en f.

superior, 1. n. Vorgesetzt- m.& f. **2.** adj. höher; überle'gen.

superiority, n. Überle'genheit f.

superlative, 1. n. Superlativ, -e m. **2.** adj. überra'gend.

supernatural, adj. übernatürlich.

supersede, vb. verdrän'gen; erset'zen.

supersonic, adj. Überschall- (cpds.).

superstar, n. Superstar, -s m.

superstition, n. Aberglaube(n), - m.

superstitious, adj. abergläubisch.

supervise, vb. beauf'sichtigen.

supervisor, n. Aufseher, - m., Aufseherin, -nen f.

supper, n. Abendbrot, -e nt., Abendessen, - nt.; (Lord's S.) Abendmahl, -̈e nt.

supplement, n. Ergän'zung, -en f., Nachtrag, -̈e m.

supply, 1. n. Versor'gung f.; Vorrat, -̈e m.; (s. and demand) Angebot (nt.) und Nachfrage (f.). **2.** vb. versor'gen, liefern.

support, 1. n. Stütze, -n f.; Unterstüt'zung, -en f. **2.** vb. stützen; unterstüt'zen.

suppose, vb. an·nehmen*, vermu'ten.

suppress, vb. unterdrü'cken.

suppression, n. Unterdrü'ckung, -en f.

supreme, adj. oberst-, höchst-; Ober- (cpds.).

sure, adj. sicher.

surely, adv. sicherlich, gewiß'.

surf, n. Brandung, -en f.

surface, n. Oberfläche, -n f.

surge, vb. wogen, branden.

surgeon, n. Chirurg', -en, -en m., Chirur'gin, -nen f.

surgery, n. Chirurgie' f.; Operation', -en f.

surmise, 1. n. Vermu'tung, -en f. **2.** vb. vermu'ten.

surmount, vb. überwin'den*.

surname, n. Zuname(n), - m., Fami'liennamme(n), - m.

surpass, vb. überstei'gen*, übertref'fen*.

surplus, 1. n. Überschuß, -̈sse m. **2.** adj. überschüssig; Über- (cpds.).

surprise, 1. n. Überra'schung, -en f. **2.** vb. überra'schen.

surrender, 1. n. Übergabe f., Erge'bung, -en f.

surround, vb. umge'ben*; umzin'geln.

surroundings, n.pl. Umge'bung, -en f.

survey, 1. n. Überblick, -e m.; (measuring) Vermes'sung, -en f. **2.** vb. überbli'cken; vermes'sen*.

survival, n. Überle'ben nt.

survive, vb. überle'ben.

susceptible, adj. empfäng'lich, zugänglich.

suspend, vb. (debar) suspendie'ren; (stop temporarily) zeitweilig auf·heben*; (payment) ein·stellen; (sentence) aus·setzen; (hang) auf·hängen.

suspense, n. Schwebe f.; Spannung, -en f.

suspension, n. Schwebe f.; Suspension', -en f.

suspicion, n. Verdacht' m., Argwohn m.

suspicious, adj. (doubting) misstrauisch; (doubtful looking) verdäch'tig.

sustain, vb. aufrecht·erhalten*; (suffer) erlei'den*.

swallow, 1. n. (bird) Schwalbe, -n f.; (gulp) Schluck, -e m. **2.** vb. schlucken.

swamp, 1. n. Sumpf, -̈e m. **2.** vb. überschwem'men.

swan, n. Schwan, -̈e m.
swarm, 1. n. Schwarm, -̈e m. 2. vb. schwärmen; (fig.) wimmeln.
sway, vb. schwingen*; schwanken.
swear, vb. schwören; (curse) fluchen.
sweat, 1. n. Schweiß m. 2. vb. schwitzen.
sweater, n. Pullo'ver, - m., Strickjacke, -n f.
Swede, n. Schwede, -n, -n m., Schwedin, -nen f.
Sweden, n. Schweden nt.
Swedish, adj. schwedisch.
sweet, adj. süß.
sweetheart, n. Liebst- m.&f.
sweetness, n. Süße f.; (fig.) Anmut f.
swell, 1. adj. prima. 2. vb. schwellen*.
swift, adj. rasch, geschwind'.
swim, vb. schwimmen*.
swindle, vb. schwindeln.
swindler, n. Schwindler, - m.
swine, n. Schwein, - e nt.
swing, 1. n. Schaukel, -n f. 2. vb. schwingen*, schaukeln.
Swiss, n. Schweizer, - m., Schweizerin, -nen f. 2. adj. schweizerisch; Schweizer- (cpds.).
switch, 1. n. (whip) Gerte, -n f.; (railway) Weiche, -n f.; (elec.)

Schalter, - m. 2. vb. (railway) rangie'ren; um'schalten; (exchange) vertau'schen.
Switzerland, n. die Schweiz f.
sword, n. Schwert, -er nt.
syllabic, adj. silbisch.
syllable, n. Silbe, -n f.
symbol, n. Symbol', -e nt.
symbolic, adj. symbo'lisch.
sympathetic, adj. mitfühlend; (med.) sympa'thisch.
sympathize, vb. mit'fühlen.
sympathy, n. Sympathie', -i'en f.
symphonic, adj. sympho'nisch.
symphony, n. Symphonie', -i'en f.
symptom, n. Anzeichen, - nt., Symptom', -e nt.
symptomatic, adj. symptoma'tisch; charakteris'tisch.
syndicate, n. Syndikat', -e nt.
syndrome, n. Syndrom', -e nt.
synonym, n. Synonym', -e nt.
synonymous, adj. sinnverwandt, synonym').
synthetic, adj. synthe'tisch, künstlich; Kunst- (cpds.).
syphilis, n. Syphilis f.
syringe, n. Spritze, -n f.
syrup, n. Sirup m.
system, n. System', -e nt.
systematic, adj. systema'tisch.

T

table, n. Tisch, -e m.; (list) Verzeich'nis, -se nt.
tablecloth, n. Tischdecke, -n f., Tischtuch, -̈er nt.
tablespoon, n. Eßlöffel, - m.
tablet, n. Tafel, -n f.; (pill) Tablet'te, -n f.
tack, 1. n. Stift, -e m.; (thumb t.) Heftzwecke, -n f. 2. vb. (sew) heften; (sail) kreuzen.
tact, n. Takt m.
tag, n. Etikett, -e nt.; (play t.) Fangen spielen.
tail, n. Schwanz, -̈e m.
tailor, n. Schneider, - m.
take, vb. nehmen*; (carry) bringen*; (need) erfor'dern.
tale, n. Geschich'te, -n f., Erzäh'lung, -en f.

talent, n. Bega'bung, -en f., Talent', -e nt.
talk, 1. n. Gespräch', -e nt.; (lecture) Vortrag, -̈e m. 2. vb. reden, sprechen*.
talkative, adj. gesprä'chig.
tall, adj. groß (-̈); hoch (hoh-, höher, höchst-); lang (-̈).
tame, 1. adj. zahm. 2. vb. zähmen.
tamper, vb. herum'pfuschen.
tan, 1. n. (sun) Sonnenbräune f. 2. adj. gelbbraun. 3. vb. bräunen; (leather) gerben.
tangle, 1. n. Gewirr' nt. 2. vb. sich zu schaffen machen mit.
tank, n. Tank, -s m.; (mil.) Panzer, - m.

tap, 1. n. (blow) Taps, -e m.; (faucet) Hahn, ⁼e m. **2.** vb. leicht schlagen*; (wire) an'zapfen.

tape, n. Band, ⁼er nt.

tape recorder, n. Tonbandgerät, -e nt., Magnetophon', -e nt.

tapestry, n. Wandteppich, -e m.; Tapisserie', -i'en f.

tar, 1. n. Teer m. **2.** vb. teeren.

target, n. Ziel, -e nt.; Zielscheibe, -n f.

tariff, n. Zolltarif, -e m.

tarnish, vb. (fig.) befle'cken; (silver) sich beschla'gen*.

tart, 1. n. Törtchen, - nt. **2.** adj. sauer, herb.

task, n. Aufgabe, -n f.

taste, 1. n. Geschmack', ⁼e m. **2.** vb. schmecken, kosten.

tasty, adj. schmackhaft.

taut, adj. straff.

tavern, n. Bierlokal, -e nt.

tax, 1. n. Steuer, -n f. **2.** vb. besteu'ern, belas'ten.

taxi, n. Taxe, -n f., Taxi, -s nt.

taxpayer, n. Steuerzahler, - m.

tea, n. Tee, -s m.

teach, vb. lehren, unterrich'ten.

teacher, n. Lehrer, - m., Lehrerin, -nen f.

tea-pot, n. Teekanne, -n f.

tear, 1. n. Träne, -n f.; (rip) Riß, -sse m. **2.** vb. reißen*.

tease, vb. necken.

teaspoon, n. Teelöffel, - m.

technical, adj. technisch.

technique, n. Technik, -en f., Kunstfertigkeit f.

tedious, adj. langweilig, mühsam.

telegram, n. Telegramm', -e nt.

telegraph, 1. n. Telegraph', -en, -en m. **2.** vb. telegraphie'ren.

telephone, 1. n. Telephon', -e nt., Fernsprecher, - m. **2.** vb. telephonie'ren.

telescope, n. Fernrohr, -e nt.

televise, vb. im Fernsehen übertra'gen*.

television, n. Fernsehen nt.

television set, n. Fernsehapparat, -e m.

tell, vb. erzäh'len, berich'ten, sagen.

teller, n. Kassie'rer, - m.

temper, 1. n. Laune, -n f.; Temperament' nt.; (anger) Zorn m. **2.** vb. mäßigen; (steel) härten.

temperament, n. Gemüts'art, -en f.

temperamental, adj. Gemüts'- (cpds.); temperament'voll.

temperate, adj. mäßig.

temperature, n. Temperatur', -en f.

tempest, n. Sturm, ⁼e m.

temple, n. Tempel, - m.

temporary, adj. zeitweilig, vorü'bergehend, proviso'risch.

tempt, vb. versu'chen; reizen.

temptation, n. Versu'chung, -en f.

ten, num. zehn.

tenant, n. Mieter, - m., Mieterin, -nen f.; Pächter, -, Pächterin, -nen f.

tend, vb. pflegen, hüten; (incline) neigen zu.

tendency, n. Neigung, -en f., Tendenz', -en f.

tender, 1. n. (money) Zahlungsmittel, - nt.; (train, boat) Tender, - m. **2.** adj. zart; zärtlich. **3.** vb. bieten*.

tenderness, n. Zartheit, -en f., Zärtlichkeit, -en f.

tendon, n. Sehne, -n f.

tennis, n. Tennis nt.

tenor, n. Tenor', -e m.

tense, adj. gespannt'; kribbelig.

tension, n. Spannung, -en f.

tent, n. Zelt, -e nt.

tentative, adj. probeweise.

tenth, 1. adj. zehnt-. **2.** n. Zehntel, - nt.

term, n. (rail) Perio'de, -n f.; (of office) Amtszeit, -en f.; (college) Semester, - nt.; (expression) Ausdruck, ⁼e m.; (condition) Bedin'gung, -en f.

terminal, n. (rail) Endbahnhof, ⁼e m.; (air) Terminal, -e m.

terminate, vb. been'den; begren'zen.

terrace, n. Terras'se, -n f.

terrible, adj. schrecklich, furchtbar.

terrify, vb. erschre'cken.

territory, n. Gebiet', -e nt.

terror, n. Schrecken, - m., Terror m.

terrorism, n. Terroris'mus m.

terrorist, n. Terrorist' m.; Terroris'tin f.

test, 1. n. Prüfung, -en f.; Probe, -n f.; Test, -s m.; Versuch', -e m. 2. vb. prüfen.

testify, vb. bezeu'gen; (court) aus'sagen.

testimony, n. Zeugnis, -se nt.; Zeugenaussage, -n f.

text, n. Text, -e m.

textile, 1. n. Textil'ware, -n f. 2. adj. Textil'- (cpds.).

texture, n. Gewe'be, -nt.; Aufbau m.; Beschaf'fenheit, -en f.

than, conj. als.

thank, vb. danken.

thankful, adj. dankbar.

that, 1. pron.&adj. der, das, die; jener, -es, -e. 2. conj. daß.

thaw, vb. tauen.

the, art. der, das, die.

theater, n. Thea'ter, - nt.; (fig.) Schauplatz, -̈e m.

thee, pron. dich; dir.

theft, n. Diebstahl, -̈e m.

their, adj. ihr, -, -e.

theirs, pron. ihrer, -es, -e.

them, pron. sie; ihnen.

theme, n. Thema, -men nt.

then, adv. (after that) dann; (at that time) damals; (therefore) dann, also.

thence, adv. von da, von dort.

theology, n. Theologie' f.

theoretical, adj. theore'tisch.

theory, n. Theorie', -i'en f.

therapy, n. Therapie' f.

there, adv. (in that place) da, dort; (to that place) dahin', dorthin'; (from t.) dort'her, dorther'.

therefore, adv. daher, darum, deshalb, deswegen, also.

thermometer, n. Thermome'ter, - nt.

thermonuclear, adj. kernphysikalisch.

these, adj. diese.

they, pron. sie.

thick, adj. dick; (dense) dicht.

thicken, vb. dicken, verdi'cken.

thickness, n. Dicke f.; Dichtheit f.; (layer) Schicht, -en f.

thief, n. Dieb, -e m.

thigh, n. Schenkel, - m.

thimble, n. Fingerhut, -̈e m.

thin, adj. dünn; mager.

thing, n. Ding, -e nt.; Sache, -n f.

think, vb. meinen, glauben; denken*, nach'denken*.

thinker, n. Denker, -.

third, 1. adj. dritt-. 2. n. Drittel, - nt.

Third World, n. Dritte Welt f.

thirst, 1. n. Durst m. 2. vb. dürsten.

thirsty, adj. durstig.

thirteen, num. dreizehn.

thirteenth, 1. adj. dreizehnt-. 2. n. Dreizehntel, - nt.

thirtieth, 1. adj. dreißigst-. 2. n. Dreißigstel, - nt.

thirty, num. dreißig.

this, pron.&adj. dieser, -es, -e.

thorough, adj. gründlich.

thou, pron. du.

though, 1. adv. doch. 2. conj. obwohl', obgleich'.

thought, n. Gedan'ke(n), -(n).

thoughtful, adj. gedan'kenvoll; (considerate) rücksichtsvoll.

thousand, num. tausend.

thousandth, 1. adj. tausendst-. 2. n. Tausendstel, - nt.

thread, n. Faden, -̈ m.; Garn, -e nt.

threat, n. Drohung, -en f.

threaten, vb. drohen.

three, num. drei.

thrift, n. Sparsamkeit f.

thrill, 1. n. Aufregung, -en f.; Sensa'tion', -en f.; Nervenkitzel, - m. 2. vb. erre'gen, packen.

throat, n. Hals, -̈e m., Kehle, -n f.

throb, vb. pochen, pulsie'ren.

throne, n. Thron, -e m.

through, 1. prep. durch. 2. adj. fertig.

throughout, 1. adv. überall; völlig. 2. prep. durch.

throw, 1. n. Wurf, -̈e m. 2. vb. werfen*, schleudern.

thrust, 1. n. Stoß, -̈e m.; (tech.) Schub m. 2. vb. stoßen*.

thumb, n. Daumen, - m.

thunder, 1. n. Donner, - m. 2. vb. donnern.

thunderstorm, n. Gewit'ter, - nt.

Thursday, n. Donnerstag, -e m.

thus, adv. so.

ticket, n. Karte, -n f.; Billett', -s or -e nt.; (admission) Eintrittskarte, -n f.; (travel) Fahrkarte, -n f., Fahrschein, -e m.; (traffic) Strafmandat, -e nt.
tickle, vb. kitzeln.
ticklish, adj. kitzlig; (delicate, risky) heikel.
tide, n. Gezei'ten pl.; (low t.) Ebbe f.; (high t.) Flut f.
tidy, adj. sauber, ordentlich.
tie, 1. n. (bond) Band, -e nt.; (necktie) Krawat'te, -n f., Schlips, -e m.; (equal score) Punktgleichheit f., Stimmengleichheit f. **2.** vb. binden*, knüpfen.
tiger, n. Tiger, - m.
tight, adj. eng; (taut) straff; (firm) fest; (drunk) beschwipst'.
tighten, vb. straffen, enger machen.
tile, n. (wall, stove) Kachel, - f.; (floor) Fliese, -n f.; (roof) Ziegel, - m.
till, 1. n. Ladenkasse, -n f. **2.** vb. bebau'en, bestel'len. **3.** adv., conj. bis.
tilt, 1. n. Neigung, -en f. **2.** vb. neigen, kippen.
timber, n. Holz nt.
time, 1. n. Zeit, -en f.; (o'clock) Uhr f. **2.** vb. die Zeit nehmen*.
timetable, n. Fahrplan, ⸗e m., Kursbuch, ⸗er nt.
timid, adj. ängstlich, schüchtern.
timidity, n. Ängstlichkeit f., Schüchternheit f.
tin, n. (metal) Zinn nt.; (t. plate) Blech nt.; (t. can) Konser'vendose, -n f.
tint, n. Farbtönung, -en f.
tiny, adj. winzig.
tip, 1. n. (end) Spitze, -n f.; (gratuity) Trinkgeld, -er nt. **2.** vb. (tilt) kippen; (give gratuity) ein Trinkgeld geben*.
tire, 1. n. Reifen, - m. **2.** vb. ermü'den.
tired, adj. müde.
tissue, n. Gewe'be, - nt.; (facial t.) Papier'taschentuch, ⸗er nt.
title, n. Titel, - m.; (heading) Überschrift, -en f.
to, prep. zu.

toast, 1. n. Toast m.; (drink to health) Trinkspruch, ⸗e m. **2.** vb. rösten; auf Wohl trinken*.
tobacco, n. Tabak m.
today, adv. heute.
toe, n. Zehe, -n f.
together, adv. zusam'men.
toil, 1. n. Arbeit, -en f., Mühe, -n f. **2.** vb. arbeiten, sich ab•mühen.
toilet, n. Toilet'te, -n f.; (t. paper) Toilettenpapier nt.
token, n. Zeichen, - nt.; Symbol', -e nt.
tolerance, n. Duldsamkeit f., Toleranz' f.
tolerant, adj. duldsam, tolerant'.
tolerate, vb. dulden.
toll, 1. n. Zoll m.; (highway) Wegegeld, -er nt., (bridge) Brückengeld, -er nt. **2.** vb. läuten.
tomato, n. Toma'te, -n f.
tomb, n. Grab, ⸗er nt., Grabmal, ⸗er nt.
tomorrow, adv. morgen.
ton, n. Tonne, -n f.
tone, n. Ton, ⸗e m.
tongue, n. Zunge, -n f.
tonic, 1. n. Stärkungsmittel nt. **2.** adj. tonisch.
tonight, adv. heute abend.
tonsil, n. Mandel, -n f.
too, adv. zu; (also) auch.
tool, n. Werkzeug, -e nt.
tooth, n. Zahn, ⸗e m.
toothache, n. Zahnschmerzen pl.
toothbrush, n. Zahnbürste, -n f.
toothpaste, n. Zahnpaste, -n f.
top, 1. n. Spitze, -n f., oberstes Ende, -n nt.; (surface) Oberfläche, -n f.; (on t. of all) auf. **2.** vb. (fig.) krönen.
topcoat, n. Mantel, ⸗ m.
topic, n. Thema, -men nt.
torch, n. Fackel, -n f.
torment, 1. n. Qual, -en f. **2.** vb. quälen.
torrent, n. reißender Strom, ⸗e m.
torture, 1. n. Folter, -n f., Qual, -en f. **2.** vb. foltern, quälen.
toss, vb. werfen*, schleudern.
total, 1. n. Summe, -n f. **2.** adj. gesamt'; total'.
totalitarian, adj. totalitär'.
touch, 1. n. Berüh'rung, -en f.; (sense of t.) Tastsinn m.; (final t.)

letzter Schliff, -e f. **2.** vb. berüh'ren.
touching, adj. rührend.
tough, 1. n. Rabau'ke, -n, -n m. **2.**
adj. zäh; (hard) hart (-).
tour, 1. n. Reise, -n f., Tour, -en f.
2. vb. berei'sen.
tourist, n. Tourist', -en, -en m.,
Touris'tin, -nen f.
tourist office, n. Fremdenverkehrsbüro, -s nt.
tow, vb. schleppen.
toward, prep. nach; gegen; zu.
towel, n. Handtuch, ⸚er nt.
tower, n. Turm, ⸚e m.
town, n. Stadt, ⸚e f., Ort, -e m.
toy, 1. n. Spielzeug, -e nt. **2.** vb.
spielen.
trace, 1. n. Spur, -en f. **2.** vb. (delineate) nach'zeichnen; (track)
zurück'verfolgen.
track, 1. n. Spur, -en f., Fährte, -n
f.; (sports) Leichtathletik f.;
(R.R.) Gelei'se, -, nt., Gleis, -e nt.
2. vb. (t. down) nach'spüren.
tract, n. (land) Gebiet', -e nt.;
(pamphlet) Traktat', -e m.
tractor, n. Trecker, - m.
trade, 1. n. Handel m.; (exchange) Tausch m. **2.** vb. Handel
treiben*; aus'tauschen.
trader, n. Händler, - m.
tradition, n. Tradition', -en f.
traditional, adj. traditionell'.
traffic, n. Verkehr' m.; (trade)
Handel m.
traffic light, n. Verkehrs'licht, -er
nt., Verkehrs'ampel, -n f.
tragedy, n. Tragö'die, -n f.
tragic, adj. tragisch.
trail, n. Fährte, -n f.
trailer, n. Anhänger, - m.; (for living) Wohnwagen, - m.
train, 1. n. Zug, ⸚e m.; (of dress)
Schleppe, -n f. **2.** vb. aus'bilden.
traitor, n. Verrä'ter, - m., Verrä'-
terin, -nen f.
tramp, n. Landstreicher, - m.
tranquil, adj. ruhig.
tranquillity, n. Ruhe f.
tranquilizer, n. Beruhigungsmit-
tel, -, nt.
transaction, n. Transaktion', -en
f.
transfer, 1. n. (ticket) Um-

steigefahrschein, - em. **2.** vb.
(change cars) um'steigen*;
(money) überwei'sen*; (owner-
ship) übertra'gen*; (move) verset'zen.
transfix, vb. durchboh'ren.
transform, vb. um'wandeln, um-
formen.
transfusion, n. Transfusion', -en
f.
transition, n. Übergang, ⸚e m.
translate, vb. überset'zen.
translation, n. Überset'zung, -en
f.
transmit, vb. übertra'gen*; übersen'den.
transparent, adj. durchsichtig.
transport, 1. n. Beför'derung, -en
f., Transport', -e m. **2.** vb. beför'-
dern, transportie'ren.
transportation, n. Beför'derung,
-en f.
transsexual, adj. transsexuell'.
transvestite, n. Transvestit', -en,
-en m.
trap, n. Falle, -n f.
trash, n. Abfall, ⸚e m.; (fig.)
Kitsch m.
travel, 1. n. Reise, -n f. **2.** vb.
reisen.
travel agency, n. Reisebüro, -s nt.
traveler, n. Reisend - m & f.
traveler's check, n. Reisescheck,
-s m.
tray, n. Tablett', -e nt.
treacherous, adj. verrä'terisch;
tückisch.
tread, 1. n. Schritt, -e m. **2.** vb.
treten*.
treason, n. Verrat' m.
treasure, 1. n. Schatz, ⸚e m. **2.** vb.
hoch'schätzen.
treasurer, n. Schatzmeister, - m.
treasury, n. Finanz'ministerium,
-rien nt.
treat, 1. n. Extragenuß, ⸚sse m. **2.**
vb. gehandeln; (pay for) frei-
halten*.
treatment, n. Behand'lung, -en f.
treaty, n. Vertrag', ⸚e m.
tree, n. Baum, ⸚e m.
tremble, vb. zittern.
tremendous, adj. ungeheuer.
trench, n. Graben, ⸚ m.
trend, n. Trend, -s m.

trespass, vb. widerrechtlich betre'ten*; übertre'ten*.

triage, n. Einteilung je nach Priorität f.

trial, n. Versuch', -e m.; (jur.) Prozeß', -sse m.

triangle, n. Dreieck, -e nt.

tribute, n. Tribut', -e m.; (fig.) Ehrung, -en f.

trick, 1. n. Kniff, -e m., Trick, -s m. 2. vb. rein'legen.

tricky, adj. knifflig; heikel.

trifle, n. Kleinigkeit, -en f., Lappa'lie, -n f.

trigger, n. (gun) Abzug, ⸚e m.

trim, 1. adj. adrett'. 2. vb. (clip) stutzen; (adorn) besetzen.

trip, 1. n. Reise, -n f. 2. vb. stolpern; (tr.) einem ein Bein stellen.

triple, 1. adj. dreifach. 2. vb. verdrei'fachen.

trite, adj. abgedroschen.

triumph, 1. n. Triumph', -e m. 2. vb. triumphie'ren.

triumphant, adj. triumphie'rend.

trivial, adj. trivial'.

trolley-bus, n. Obus, -se m.

trolley-car, n. Straßenbahn, -en f.

troop, n. Trupp, -s m.

troops, n.pl. Truppen pl.

trophy, n. Trophä'e, -n f.

tropic, n. Wendekreis, -e m.

tropical, adj. tropisch.

tropics, n.pl. Tropen pl.

trot, 1. n. Trab m. 2. vb. traben.

trouble, 1. n. Mühe, -n f.; (difficulty) Schwierigkeit, -en f.; (unpleasantness) Unannehmlichkeit, -en f.; (jam) Klemme, -n f. 2. vb. bemü'hen; beun'ruhigen.

troublesome, adj. lästig.

trough, n. Trog, ⸚e m.

trousers, n.pl. Hose, -n f.

trousseau, n. Aussteuer, -n f.

trout, n. Forel'le, -n f.

truce, n. Waffenstillstand, ⸚e m.

truck, n. Lastauto, -s nt., Lastwagen, - m., Lastkraftwagen, - m.

true, adj. wahr; wahrhaf'tig; (faithful) treu.

truly, adv. wahrhaf'tig; (yours t.) Ihr erge'bener, Ihre erge'bene.

trumpet, n. Trompe'te, -n f.

trunk, n. (tree) Stamm, ⸚e m.; (luggage) Koffer, - m.

trust, 1. n. Zuversicht f., Vertrau'en nt.; (comm.) Trust, -s m.; (in t.) zu treuen Händen. 2. vb. vertrau'en.

trustworthy, adj. zuverlässig.

truth, n. Wahrheit, -en f.

truthful, adj. wahr; ehrlich.

try, 1. n. Versuch', -e m. 2. vb. versu'chen, probie'ren.

T-shirt, n. T-shirt, -s nt.

tub, n. Wanne, -n f.

tube, n. Röhre, -n f.; (container) Tube, -n f.

tuberculosis, n. Tuberkulo'se f.

tuck, n. Falte, -n f. 2. vb. falten.

Tuesday, n. Dienstag, -e m.

tuft, n. Büschel, - nt., Quaste, -n f.

tug, vb. ziehen*.

tuition, n. Schulgeld, -er nt.; (university) Studiengeld, -er nt.

tulip, n. Tulpe, -n f.

tumor, n. Tumor, -o'ren m.

tumult, n. Tumult', -e m.

tuna, n. Thunfisch, -e m.

tune, 1. n. Melodie', -i'en f. 2. vb. stimmen.

tuneful, adj. melo'disch.

tunnel, n. Tunnel, - m.

turbine, n. Turbi'ne, -n f.

turbojet, n. (plane) Turbi'nenjäger, - m.

turboprop, n. Propel'lerturbine f.

Turk, n. Türke, -n, -n m., Türkin, -nen f.

turkey, n. Truthahn, ⸚e m., Puter, - m.

Turkey, n. die Türkei' f.

Turkish, adj. türkisch.

turmoil, n. Durcheinan'der nt.

turn, 1. n. Umdre'hung, -en f.; Wendung, -en f., Kurve, -n f.; (to take t.s) sich ab'wechseln; (it's my t.) ich bin dran. 2. vb. drehen, wenden*; (t. around) um'drehen.

turning point, n. Wendepunkt m.

turnip, n. Steckrübe, -n f.

turret, n. Turm, ⸚e m.

turtle, n. Schildkröte, -n f.

tutor, 1. n. Lehrer, - m., Lehrerin,

-nen *f.*; Nachhilfelehrer, - *m.*, Nachhilfelehrerin, -nen *f.* *vb.* Nachhilfeunterricht geben*.

twelfth, 1. *adj.* zwölft-. 2. *n.* Zwölftel, -*nt.*

twelve, *num.* zwölf.

twentieth, 1. *adj.* zwanzigst-. 2. *n.* Zwanzigstel, -*nt.*

twenty, *num.* zwanzig.

twice, *adv.* zweimal.

twig, *n.* Zweig, -e *m.*

twilight, *n.* Dämmerung, -en *f.*; Zwielicht *nt.*

twin, *n.* Zwilling, -e *m.*

twine, 1. *n.* (*thread*) Zwirn, -e *m.*; (*rope*) Tau, -e *nt.* 2. *vb.* winden*.

twist, 1. *n.* Drehung, -en *f.*; (*distortion*) Verdre'hung, -en *f.* 2. *vb.* drehen; verdre'hen.

two, *num.* zwei.

type, 1. *n.* Typ, -en *m.*, Typus, -pen *m.*; (*printing*) Schriftsatz, ⁻e *m.*; (*letter*) Type, -n *f.* 2. *vb.* kennzeichnen; (*write on typewriter*) tippen.

typewriter, *n.* Schreibmaschine, -n *f.*

typhoid fever, *n.* Typhus *m.*

typical, *adj.* typisch.

typist, *n.* Schreibkraft, ⁻e *f.*

tyranny, *n.* Tyrannei' *f.*

tyrant, *n.* Tyrann', -en, -en *m.*

U

ugliness, *n.* Häßlichkeit *f.*

ugly, *adj.* häßlich.

ulcer, *n.* Geschwür', -e *nt.*

ulterior, *adj.* höher; weiter; (**u. motives**) Hintergedanken *pl.*

ultimate, *adj.* äußerst-.

umbrella, *n.* Regenschirm, -e *m.*

umpire, *n.* Schiedsrichter, - *m.*

un-, *prefix* un-.

unable, *adj.* unfähig.

unanimous, *adj.* einstimmig.

unbecoming, *adj.* unschicklich; (*of clothes*) unkleidsam.

uncertain, *adj.* ungewiß.

uncertainty, *n.* Ungewißheit, -en *f.*

uncle, *n.* Onkel, - *m.*

unconscious, *adj.* bewußt'los; (*unaware*) unbewußt.

uncover, *vb.* auf·decken; entblö'ßen.

under, *prep.* unter.

underground, 1. *n.* Untergrundbahn, -en *f.* 2. *adj.* unter der Erde gelegen; Untergrund- (*cpds.*).

underline, *vb.* unterstrei'chen*.

underneath, 1. *adv.* unter, drunter. 2. *prep.* unter.

undershirt, *n.* Unterhemd, -en *nt.*

undersign, *vb.* unterzeich'nen.

understand, *vb.* verste'hen*, begrei'fen*.

understanding, *n.* Verständ'nis *nt.*; (*agreement*) Einvernehmen, - *nt.*

undertake, *vb.* unterneh'men*.

undertaker, *n.* Leichenbestatter, - *m.*

underwear, *n.* Unterwäsche *f.*

underworld, *n.* Unterwelt *f.*

undo, *vb.* auf·machen, lösen; ungeschehen machen.

undress, *vb.* entklei'den, (sich) aus·ziehen*.

uneasy, *adj.* unruhig, unbehaglich.

unemployed, *adj.* arbeitslos.

unemployment, *n.* Arbeitslosigkeit *f.*

unemployment insurance, *n.* Arbeitslosenunterstützung *f.*

unequal, *adj.* ungleich.

uneven, *adj.* uneben; ungleich; (*numbers*) ungerade.

unexpected, *adj.* unerwartet.

unfair, *adj.* ungerecht.

unfamiliar, *adj.* unbekannt; ungeläufig.

unfavorable, *adj.* ungünstig.

unfit, *adj.* untauglich.

unfold, *vb.* entfal'ten.

unforgettable, *adj.* unvergeßlich.

unfortunate, *adj.* unglücklich; bedau'erlich.

unhappy, *adj.* unglücklich.
uniform, 1. *n.* Uniform', -en *f.* **2.** *adj.* einheitlich.
unify, *vb.* verei'nigen; verein'heitlichen.
union, *n.* Verei'nigung, -en *f.;* **(labor u.)** Gewerk'schaft, -en *f.*
unique, *adj.* einzigartig.
unisex, *adj.* unisex.
unit, *n.* Einheit, -en *f.*
unite, *vb.* verei'nigen.
United Nations, *n.* Verein'te Natio'nen *pl.*
United States, *n.* Verein'igte Staaten *pl.*
unity, *n.* Einigkeit *f.*
universal, *adj.* universal'.
universe, *n.* Weltall *nt.*
university, *n.* Universität', -en *f.*
unjust, *adj.* ungerecht.
unknown, *adj.* unbekannt.
unleaded, *adj.* bleifrei.
unless, *conj.* wenn nicht; es sei denn, daß.
unlike, *adj.* ungleich.
unlikely, *adj.* unwahrscheinlich.
unload, *vb.* ab·laden*, aus·laden*.
unlock, *vb.* auf·schließen*.
unlucky, *adj.* **(be u.)** kein Glück haben*, Pech haben*.
unmarried, *adj.* unverheiratet, ledig.
unpack, *vb.* aus·packen.
unpleasant, *adj.* unangenehm.
unqualified, *adj.* **(unfit)** ungeeignet; **(unreserved)** uneingeschränkt.
unsettled, *adj.* unsicher, in der Schwebe.
unsteady, *adj.* unstet.
unsuccessful, *adj.* erfolg'los.
untie, *vb.* auf·knüpfen.
until, 1. *prep.* bis; **(not u.)** erst. **2.** *conj.* bis; **(not u.)** erst wenn; erst als.
untruth, *n.* Unwahrheit, -en *f.*
untruthful, *adj.* unwahr.
unusual, *adj.* ungewöhnlich.
unwell, *adj.* unpäßlich, nicht wohl.
up, 1. *prep.* auf. **2.** *adv.* auf, hinauf', herauf'.

upbraid, *vb.* schelten*.
uphill, 1. *adj.* (*fig.*) mühsam. **2.** *adv.* bergan', bergauf'.
uphold, *vb.* aufrecht·erhalten*.
upholster, *vb.* bezie'hen*.
upholsterer, *n.* Tapezie'rer, - *m.*
upon, *prep.* auf.
upper, *adj.* ober-.
upright, *adj.* aufrecht.
uprising, *n.* Aufstand, ‒e *m.*
uproar, *n.* Getö'se *nt.*
uproot, *vb.* entwur'zeln.
upset, 1. *n.* Rückschlag, ‒e *m.;* **(stomach u.)** Magenverstimmung, -en *f.* **2.** *vb.* (*overturn*) um·werfen*; (*disturb*) über den Haufen werfen, verstim'men; (*discompose*) aus der Fassung bringen*.
upside down, *adv.* umgekehrt, verkehrt' herum'.
upstairs, *adv.* oben; nach oben.
uptight, *adj.* unsicher, verklemmt.
urban, *adj.* städtisch.
urge, 1. *n.* Drang, ‒e *m.;* (*sex*) Trieb, -e *m.* **2.** *vb.* drängen, nötigen.
urgency, *n.* Dringlichkeit *f.*
urgent, *adj.* dringend.
urinal, *n.* Harnglas, ‒er *nt.;* (*public*) Bedürf'nisanstalt, -en *f.*
urinate, *vb.* urinie'ren.
urine, *n.* Urin', -e *nt.*
us, *pron.* uns.
usage, *n.* Gebrauch', ‒e *m.*
use, 1. *n.* Gebrauch', ‒e *m.,* Benut'zung, -en *f.* **2.** *vb.* gebrau'chen, verwen'den, benut'zen.
useful, *adj.* nützlich.
useless, *adj.* nutzlos.
user, *n.* Benut'zer, - *m.*
usher, *n.* (*theater, etc.*) Platzanweiser, - *m.;* (*wedding*) Brautführer, - *m.*
usual, *adj.* gewöhn'lich.
usury, *n.* Wucher *m.*
utensil, *n.* Gerät', -e *nt.*
uterus, *n.* Gebär'mutter, ‒ *f.*
utility, *n.* Nutzbarkeit *f.*
utilize, *vb.* aus·nutzen.
utmost, *adj.* äußerst.
utter, 1. *adj.* völlig. **2.** *vb.* äußern.
utterance, *n.* Äußerung, -en *f.*

vacancy, n. (position) freie Stellung, -en f.; (hotel, etc.) unvermietetes Zimmer, - nt.

vacant, adj. frei; (empty) leer.

vacate, vb. räumen.

vacation, n. Ferien pl.

vacationer, n. Urlauber, - m., Urlauberin, -nen f.

vaccinate, vb. impfen.

vaccination, n. Impfung, -en f.

vaccine, n. Impfstoff, -e m.

vacuum, n. Vakuum, -kua nt.

vacuum cleaner, n. Staubsauger, - m.

vagina, n. Vagi'na, -nen f.

vagrant, 1. n. Landstreicher, m.; (worker) Saison'arbeiter, - m. 2. adj. vagabundie'rend.

vague, adj. unbestimmt, vage.

vain, 1. adj. (conceited) eitel; (useless) vergeb'lich. 2. n. (in v.) umsonst', verge'bens.

valet, n. Diener, - m.

valiant, adj. tapfer.

valid, adj. gültig.

valise, n. Reisetasche, -n f.

valley, n. Tal, =er nt.

valor, n. Tapferkeit f.

valuable, adj. wertvoll.

value, n. Wert, -e m.

valve, n. Ventil', -e nt.; (med.) Klappe, -n f.

van, n. (delivery truck) Lieferwagen, - m.; (moving v.) Möbelwagen, - m.

vandal, n. Vanda'le, -n, -n m.

vanguard, n. Vorhut f.; (person) Vorkämpfer, - m.

vanilla, n. Vanil'le f.

vanish, vb. verschwin'den*.

vanity, n. Eitelkeit f.

vanquish, vb. besie'gen.

vapor, n. Dampf, =e m.

variance, n. Widerstreit m.

variation, n. Abwechslung, -en f.; Abänderung, -en f., Variation', -en f.

varied, adj. verschie'den; mannigfaltig.

variety, n. Mannigfaltigkeit f.; (choice) Auswahl f.; (theater) Varieté nt.

various, adj. verschie'den.

varnish, 1. n. Firnis, -se m. 2. vb. firnissen.

vary, vb. variie'ren, verän'dern.

vase, n. Vase, -n f.

vasectomy, n. Vasektomie' f.

vast, adj. riesig.

vat, n. Faß, Fässer nt.

vaudeville, n. Varieté nt.

vault, n. Gewöl'be, - nt.; (burial chamber) Gruft, =e f.; (bank) Tresor', -e m.; (jump) Sprung, =e m. 2. vb. springen*.

veal, n. Kalbfleisch nt.

vegetable, n. Gemü'se, - nt.

vehement, adj. heftig.

vehicle, n. Fahrzeug, -e nt.

veil, 1. n. Schleier, - m. 2. vb. verschlei'ern.

vein, n. Vene, -n f.; Ader, -n f.

velocity, n. Geschwin'digkeit, -en f.

velvet, n. Samt m.

veneer, n. Furnier', -e nt.

vengeance, n. Rache f.

venom, n. Gift, -e nt.

vent, 1. n. Öffnung, -en f.; (escape passage) Abzugsröhre, -n f. 2. vb. freien Lauf lassen*.

ventilate, vb. lüften, ventilie'ren.

ventilation, n. Lüftung f., Ventilation' f.

venture, 1. n. Wagnis, -se nt. 2. vb. wagen.

verb, n. Verb, -en nt., Zeitwort, =er nt.

verbal, adj. verbal'; (oral) mündlich.

verdict, n. Urteil, -e nt.

verge, 1. n. (fig.) Rand, =er m. 2. vb. (v. on) grenzen an.

verification, n. Bestä'tigung, -en f.

verify, vb. bestä'tigen.

vernacular, 1. n. Umgangssprache, -n f. 2. adj. umgangssprachlich.

versatile, adj. vielseitig.

verse, n. Vers, -e m.

versify, vb. in Verse bringen*.

version, n. Fassung, -en f.; Ver'sion', -en f.

versus, prep. gegen.

vertebrate, 1. n. Wirbeltier, -e nt. **2.** adj. Wirbel- (cpds.).

vertical, adj. senkrecht.

very, adv. sehr.

vespers, n. Vesper, -n f.

vessel, n. Schiff, -e nt.; (container) Gefäß', -e nt.

vest, n. Weste, -n f.

vestige, n. Spur, -en f.

veteran, n. Veteran', -en, -en m.

veterinarian, n. Tierarzt, -̈e m., Tierärztin, -nen f.

veterinary, adj. tierärztlich.

veto, 1. n. Veto, -s nt. **2.** vb. das Veto ein|legen.

vex, vb. ärgern; verblüf'fen.

via, prep. über.

viaduct, n. Viadukt', -e m.

vibrate, vb. vibrie'ren, schwingen*.

vibration, n. Vibration', -en f., Schwingung, -en f.; (tremor) Erschüt'terung, -en f.

vice, n. Laster, - nt.

vicinity, n. Nähe f., Umge'bung, -en f.

vicious, adj. gemein', heimtückisch.

victim, n. Opfer, - nt.

victor, n. Sieger, - m.

victorious, adj. siegreich.

victory, n. Sieg, -e m.

videodisc, n. Videoscheibe, -n f.

Vienna, n. Wien nt.

view, 1. n. Aussicht, -en f. **2.** vb. bese'hen*, betrach'ten.

vigil, n. Nachtwache, -n f.

vigilant, adj. wachsam.

vigor, n. Kraft, -̈e f., Energie', -i'en f.

vigorous, adj. kräftig, kraftstrotzend.

vile, adj. gemein', niederträchtig.

village, n. Dorf, -̈er nt.

villain, n. Bösewicht, -e m. Schurke, -n, -n m.

vindicate, vb. rechtfertigen.

vine, n. Rebstock, -̈e m.; (creeper) Ranke, -n f.

vinegar, n. Essig m.

vineyard, n. Weingarten, -̈ m., Weinberg, -e m.

vintage, n. (gathering) Weinlese f.; (year) Jahrgang, -̈e m.

viol, viola, n. Bratsche, -n f.

violate, vb. verlet'zen; (oath) brechen*; (law, territory) übertre'ten*.

violation, n. Verlet'zung, -en f.; Bruch, -̈e m.; Übertre'tung, -en f.

violator, n. Verlet'zer, - m.; Übertre'ter, - m.

violence, n. Gewalt'tätigkeit, -en f.; (vehemence) Gewalt'samkeit f., Heftigkeit f.

violent, adj. gewalt'tätig; gewalt'sam, heftig.

violet, 1. n. Veilchen, - nt. **2.** adj. violett', veilchenblau.

violin, n. Geige, -n f.

virgin, n. Jungfrau, -en f.

virile, adj. männlich.

virtue, n. Tugend, -en f.

virtuous, adj. tugendhaft, tugendsam.

virus, n. Virus, -ren m.

visa, n. Visum, -sa nt.

vise, n. Schraubstock, -̈e m.

visible, adj. sichtbar.

vision, n. Sehkraft, -̈e f.; (visual image) Vision', -en f.

visit, 1. n. Besuch', -e m. **2.** vb. besu'chen.

visitor, n. Besu'cher, - m., Besu'cherin, -nen f.

visual, adj. visuell'.

vital, adj. (essential) wesentlich; (strong) vital'.

vitality, n. Lebenskraft f., Vitalität' f.

vitamin, n. Vitamin', -e nt.

vivacious, adj. lebhaft, temperament'voll.

vivid, adj. leben'dig, lebhaft.

vocabulary, n. Wortschatz, -̈e m.; (list of words) Wörterverzeichnis, -se nt.

vocal, adj. Stimm-, Gesang'- (cpds.); lautstark.

vogue, n. Mode, -n f.

voice, n. Stimme, -n f.

void, adj. ungültig.

volcano, n. Vulkan', -e m.

volt, n. Volt, - nt.

voltage, n. Stromspannung, -en f.

volume, n. Volu'men, - nt.;

Useful Words and Phrases

How do I get to the station?	Wie komme ich zum Bahnhof?
Where can I check my baggage?	Wo ist die Gepäckauf'bewahrung?
Is this a non-stop flight?	Ist dies ein direkt'er Flug?
I'm sick.	Ich bin krank.
I need a doctor.	Ich brauche einen Arzt.
Where is the nearest drugstore?	Wo ist die nächste Drogerie'?
Where is the next pharmacy?	Wo ist die nächste Apotheke?
Is there any mail for me?	Ist Post für mich da?
Where can I mail this letter?	Wo kann ich diesen Brief einstecken?
I want to send a fax.	Ich möchte gern ein Fax schicken.
Where is the nearest bank?	Wo ist die nächste Bank?
Where can I change money?	Wo kann ich hier Geld wechseln?
Do you accept travelers checks?	Nehmen Sie Reiseschecks?
May I have the bill, please?	Könnte ich bitte die Rechnung haben?

Right away.	Sofort'.
Help!	Hilfe!
Please call the police.	Rufen Sie bitte die Polizei'.
Who is it?	Wer ist dort?
Come in.	Herein'.
Just a minute!	Einen Augenblick, bitte!
Hello *(on telephone)*.	Hier . . . *(say your name)*.
Look out!	Vorsicht! Achtung!
Stop.	Halt.
Hurry.	Schnell.
As soon as possible.	So bald wie möglich.
To the right.	Rechts.
To the left.	Links.
Straight ahead.	Gera'de aus.

Useful Words and Phrases

What time is it?	Wieviel Uhr ist es?
How much does that cost?	Wie viel kostet das?
I would like . . .	Ich möchte gern . . . ; Ich hätte gern . . .
May I see something better?	Könnten Sie mir etwas Besseres zeigen?
May I see something cheaper?	Könnten Sie mir etwas Billigeres zeigen?
It is not exactly what I want.	Es ist nicht ganz das, was ich suche.
I'd like to buy . . .	Ich möchte gern . . . kaufen.
I'd like to eat.	Ich möchte gern essen.
Where is there a good restaurant?	Wo ist hier ein gutes Restaurant?
I'm hungry (thirsty).	Ich habe Hunger (Durst).
Please give me . . .	Bitte geben Sie mir . . .
Please bring me . . .	Bitte bringen Sie mir . . .
May I see the menu?	Ich hätte gern die Speisekarte.
The check, please.	Bitte zahlen.
Is service included in the bill?	Ist das mit Bedie'nung?
Where is there a good hotel?	Wo ist hier ein gutes Hotel'?
Please help me with my luggage.	Helfen Sie mir bitte mit meinem Gepäck'.
Where can I get a taxi?	Wo bekom'me (finde) ich eine Taxe?
What is the fare to . . . ?	Was kostet die Fahrt nach (bis) . . . ?
Please take me to this address.	Bitte bringen (fahren) Sie mich zu dieser Adres'se.
Please let me off at . . .	Bitte halten Sie . . .
I am lost.	Ich habe mich verlau'fen (verfah'ren).
I have a reservation.	Ich habe . . . reserviert'.
Where is the men's (ladies') room?	Wo ist die Toilet'te, bitte?

Food Terms

apple	Apfel	**lobster**	Hummer
artichoke	Artischo'cken	**meat**	Fleisch
asparagus	Spargel	**melon**	Melo'ne
bacon	Speck	**milk**	Milch
banana	Bana'ne	**mushroom**	Pilz
beans	Bohnen	**noodle**	Nudel
beer	Bier	**nuts**	Nüsse
beet	Bete	**omelet**	Omelett'
bread	Brot	**onion**	Zwiebel
butter	Butter	**orange**	Apfelsi'ne
cake	Kuchen	**pastry**	Gebäck'
carrot	Mohrrübe	**peach**	Pfirsich
cauliflower	Blumenkohl	**pear**	Birne
celery	Sellerie	**pepper**	Pfeffer
cheese	Käse	**pie**	Obstkuchen
chicken	Huhn	**pineapple**	Ananas
chocolate	Schokola'de	**pork**	Schweinefleisc
coffee	Kaffee	**potato**	Kartof'fel
cookie	Keks	**rice**	Reis
crab	Taschenkrebs	**roast beef**	Roastbeef
cream	Sahne	**salad**	Salat'
cucumber	Gurke	**salmon**	Lachs
dessert	Nachtisch	**salt**	Salz
duck	Ente	**sandwich**	beleg'tes Brot
egg	Ei	**shrimp**	Garne'le
fish	Fisch	**soup**	Suppe
fowl	Geflü'gel	**spinach**	Spinat'
fruit	Frucht, Obst	**steak**	Beefsteak
goose	Gans	**strawberry**	Erdbeere
grape	Weintraube	**sugar**	Zucker
grapefruit	Pampelmu'se	**tea**	Tee
ham	Schinken	**tomato**	Toma'te
ice cream	Sahneneis	**trout**	Forel'le
juice	Saft	**turkey**	Truthahn
lamb	Lammfleisch	**veal**	Kalbfleisch
lemonade	Limona'de	**vegetable**	Gemü'se
lettuce	Kopfsalat	**water**	Wasser
liver	Leber	**wine**	Wein

zap, *vb. (lit.)* töten; *(slang)* fertig
  machen, zerschmettern.
zeal, *n.* Eifer *m.*
zebra, *n.* Zebra, -s *nt.*
zero, *n.* Null, -en *f.*
zest, *n. (zeal)* Eifer *m.; (relish)*
  Genuß' *m.*

zinc, *n.* Zink *nt.*
zip code, *n.* Postleitzahl, -en *f.*
zipper, *n.* Reißverschluß, -sse *m.*
zone, *n.* Zone, -n *f.*
zoo, *n.* Zoo, -s *m.*
zoological, *adj.* zoolo'gisch.
zoology, *n.* Zoologie' *f.*

worse, adj. schlimmer, schlechter.
worship, 1. n. Vereh'rung, -en f.; (church) Gottesdienst, -e m. **2.** vb. vereh'ren, an'beten.
worst, adj. schlimmst-, schlechtest-.
worth, 1. n. Wert, -e m. **2.** adj. wert.
worthless, adj. wertlos.
worthy, adj. würdig, ehrenwert.
wound, 1. n. Wunde, -n f. **2.** vb. verwun'den.
wrap, 1. n. Umhang, ⁼e m. **2.** vb. wickeln.
wrapping, n. Verpa'ckung, -en f.
wrath, n. Zorn m.
wreath, n. Kranz, ⁼e m.
wreck, 1. n. Wrack, -s nt. **2.** vb. demolie'ren, kaputt'machen.
wrench, 1. n. Ruck m.; (tool) Schraubenschlüssel, - m. **2.** vb. verren'ken.

wrestle, vb. ringen*.
wretched, adj. erbärm'lich.
wring, vb. (hands) ringen*; (laundry) wringen*; (neck) ab'drehen.
wrinkle, 1. n. Falte, -n f., Runzel, -n f. **2.** vb. runzeln; (cloth) knittern.
wrist, n. Handgelenk, -e nt.
wrist-watch, n. Armbanduhr, -en f.
write, vb. schreiben*.
writer, n. Schreiber, - m., Schreiberin, -nen f.; (by profession) Schriftsteller, - m. Schriftstellerin, -nen f.; (author) Verfas'ser, - m., Verfas'serin, -nen f.
writing, n. Schrift, -en f.; (in w.) schriftlich.
wrong, 1. n. Unrecht nt. **2.** adj. falsch; unrecht; (be w.) unrecht haben*, sich irren. **3.** vb. Unrecht tun*.

X

x-ray, 1. n. Röntgenaufnahme, -n f. **2.** vb. röntgen.

x-rays, n.pl. Röntgenstrahlen pl.
xylophone, n. Xylophon', -e nt.

Y

yacht, n. Jacht, -en f.
yard, n. (garden) Garten, ⁼ m.; (railroad) Verschie'bebahnhof, ⁼e m.; (measure) Yard, -s nt.
yarn, n. Garn, -e nt.; (story) Geschich'te, -n f.
yawn, vb. gähnen.
year, n. Jahr, -e nt.
yearly, adj. jährlich.
yearn, vb. sich sehnen.
yell, 1. n. Schrei, -e m. **2.** vb. schreien*, brüllen.
yellow, adj. gelb.
yes, interj. ja.
yesterday, adv. gestern.
yet, 1. adv. (still) noch; (already) schon; (not y.) noch nicht. **2.** conj. doch.

yield, 1. n. Ertrag', ⁼e m. **2.** vb. ein'bringen*; (cede) nach'geben*.
yoke, n. Joch, -e nt.
yolk, n. Eigelb, - nt.
you, pron. du, Sie.
young, adj. jung (-).
youth, n. junger Mann, ⁼er m., Jüngling, -e m.; (young people; time of life) Jugend, -en f.
youthful, adj. jugendlich.
Yugoslav, 1. n. Jugosla'we, -n, -n m., Jugoslawin, -nen f.
Yugoslavia, n. Jugosla'wien nt.
Yugoslavian, 1. n. Jugosla'we, -n, -n m. **2.** adj. jugosla'wisch.

whoever, *pron.* wer . . . auch.
whole, 1. *n.* Ganz-e *nt.* **2.** *adj.* ganz; *(unbroken)* heil.
wholesale, 1. *n.* Großhandel *m.* **2.** *adv.* en gros.
wholesome, *adj.* gesund' (-, -).
why, *adv.* warum', wieso', weshalb.
wicked, *adj.* böse, verrucht'.
wickedness, *n.* Verrucht'heit *f.*
wide, *adj.* weit; breit.
widen, *vb.* erwei'tern.
widespread, *adj.* weit verbrei'tet.
widow, *n.* Witwe, -n *f.*
widower, *n.* Witwer, - *m.*
width, *n.* Weite, -n *f.;* Breite, -n *f.*
wield, *vb.* handhaben*; *(fig.)* aus'üben.
wife, *n.* Frau, -en *f.*
wig, *n.* Perü'cke, -n *f.*
wild, *adj.* wild.
wilderness, *n.* Wildnis, -se *f.*
wildlife, *n.* Tierwelt *f.*
will, 1. *n.* Wille(n) *m.; (testament)* Testament' (die, -e) *nt.* **2.** *vb. (future)* werden*; *(want to)* wollen*; *(bequeath)* verma'chen.
willful, *adj.* eigensinnig; *(intentional)* vorsätzlich.
willing, *adj.* willig; gewillt'; **(be w.)** wollen*.
willow, *n.* Weide, -n *f.*
wilt, *vb.* welken, verwel'ken.
wilted, *adj.* welk.
win, *vb.* gewin'nen*.
wind, 1. *n.* Wind, -e *m.* **2.** *vb.* winden*, wickeln; *(watch)* auf'ziehen*.
window, *n.* Fenster, - *nt.*
windshield, *n.* Windschutzscheibe, -n *f.*
windy, *adj.* windig.
wine, *n.* Wein, -e *m.*
wing, *n.* Flügel, - *m.*
wink, *vb.* blinzeln.
winner, *n.* Gewin'ner, - *m.,* Gewin'nerin, -nen *f.,* Sieger, - *m.,* Siegerin, -nen *f.*
winter, *n.* Winter, - *m.*
wintry, *adj.* winterlich.
wipe, *vb.* wischen.
wire, 1. *n.* Draht, -e *m.; (telegram)* Telegramm', -e *nt.* **2.** *vb.* telegrafie'ren.

wire recorder, *n.* Drahtaufnahmegerät, -e *nt.*
wisdom, *n.* Weisheit, -en *f.*
wise, *adj.* weise, klug (-).
wish, 1. *n.* Wunsch, -e *m.;* **2.** *vb.* wünschen.
wit, *n.* Verstand' *m.; (humor)* Humor' *m.*
witch, *n.* Hexe, -n *f.*
with, *prep.* mit.
withdraw, *vb.* zurück'-ziehen*.
wither, *vb.* verdor'ren.
withhold, *vb.* zurück'-halten*; ein'behalten*.
within, 1. *adv.* drinnen. **2.** *prep.* innerhalb.
without, 1. *adv.* draußen. **2.** *prep.* ohne.
witness, 1. *n.* Zeuge, -n, -n *m.,* Zeugin, -nen *f.* **2.** *vb.* Zeuge sein* von.
witty, *adj.* witzig; geistreich.
woe, *n.* Leid *nt.*
wolf, *n.* Wolf, -e *m.*
woman, *n.* Frau, -en *f.*
womb, *n.* Mutterleib *m.*
wonder, 1. *n.* Wunder, - *nt.* **2.** *vb.* **(I w.)** ich möchte gern wissen.
wonderful, *adj.* wunderbar, herrlich.
woo, *vb.* umwer'ben*.
wood, *n.* Holz, -er *nt.; (forest)* Wald, -er *m.*
wooden, *adj.* hölzern.
wool, *n.* Wolle *f.*
woolen, *adj.* wollen.
word, *n. (single)* Wort, -er *nt.; (connected)* Wort, -e *nt.*
wordy, *adj. (fig.)* langatmig.
work, 1. *n. (labor)* Arbeit, -en *f.; (thing produced)* Werk, -e *nt.* **2.** *vb.* arbeiten; *(function)* gehen*, funktionie'ren.
worker, *n.* Arbeiter, - *m.,* Arbeiterin, -nen *f.*
workman, *n.* Arbeiter, - *m.*
work permit, *n.* Arbeitserlaubnis *f.,* Arbeitsgenehmigung *f.*
world, *n.* Welt, -en *f.*
worldly, *adj.* weltlich.
worm, *n.* Wurm, -er *m.*
worn-out, *adj.* abgenutzt.
worry, 1. *n.* Sorge, -n *f.* **2.** *vb.* sich sorgen.

(book) Band, ⁼e m.; *(quantity)* Umfang, ⁼e m.
voluntary, *adj.* freiwillig.
volunteer, 1. *n.* Freiwillig- m.&f. 2. *vb.* sich freiwillig melden.
vomit, *vb.* erbre'chen*.
vote, 1. *n.* *(individual ballot)* Wahlstimme, -n f.; *(quantity)* Stimmabgabe, -n f.; *(v. of confidence)* Vertrau'ensvotum nt. 2. *vb.* wählen, stimmen, ab·stimmen.

voter, *n.* Wähler, - m., Wählerin, -nen f.
vouch for, *vb.* verbür'gen für.
vow, 1. *n.* Gelüb'de - nt. 2. *vb.* gelo'ben.
vowel, *n.* Vokal', -e m.
voyage, *n.* Reise, -n f.
vulgar, *adj.* vulgär', ordinär'.
vulgarity, *n.* Ordinär'heit, -en f.
vulnerable, *adj.* verletz'bar; angreifbar.

W

wad, *n.* Bündel, - nt.; *(of cotton)* Wattebausch, ⁼e m.; *(roll)* Rolle, -n f.
wade, *vb.* waten.
wag, 1. *n.* Spaßvogel, ⁼ m. 2. *vb.* wedeln.
wage, 1. *n.* Lohn, ⁼e m. 2. *vb.* **(w. war)** Krieg führen.
wager, 1. *n.* Wette, -n f. 2. *vb.* wetten.
wagon, *n.* Wagen, - m.
wail, *vb.* wehklagen.
waist, *n.* Taille, -n f.
waistcoat, *n.* Weste, -n f.
wait, 1. *n.* Wartezeit, -en f. 2. *vb.* warten; **(w. for)** warten auf.
waiter, *n.* Kellner, - m.
waitress, *n.* Kellnerin, -nen f.
waiver, *n.* Verzicht'leistung, -en f.
wake, 1. *n.* *(vigil)* Totenwache, -n f.; *(of boat)* Kielwasser nt. 2. *vb.* *(tr.)* wecken; *(intr.)* erwa'chen.
walk, 1. *n.* Spazier'gang, ⁼e m. 2. *vb.* gehen*, laufen*.
wall, *n.* Wand, ⁼e f.; *(of stone or brick)* Mauer, -n f.
wallcovering, *n.* Wandverkleidung f.
wallet, *n.* Brieftasche, -n f.
wallpaper, *n.* Tape'te, -n f.
walnut, *n.* Walnuß, -sse f.
walrus, *n.* Walroß, -sse nt.
waltz, 1. *n.* Walzer, - m. 2. *vb.* Walzer tanzen.
wander, *vb.* wandern; **(w. around)** umher'·wandern.
want, 1. *n.* Mangel, ⁼ m.; *(needs)* Bedarf' m.; *(poverty)* Armut f. 2. *vb.* wollen, wünschen.
war, *n.* Krieg, -e m.

ward, *n.* Mündel, - nt.; *(city)* Bezirk', -e m.; *(hospital, prison)* Abtei'lung, -en f.
ware, *n.* Ware, -n f.
warlike, *adj.* kriegerisch.
warm, 1. *adj.* warm (⁼). 2. *vb.* wärmen.
warmth, *n.* Wärme f.
warn, *vb.* warnen.
warning, *n.* Warnung, -en f.
warp, *vb.* krümmen; *(fig.)* verdre'hen, entstel'len.
warrant, 1. *n.* *(authorization)* Vollmacht, -en f.; *(writ of arrest)* Haftbefehl, -e m. 2. *vb.* gewähr'-leisten, garantie'ren.
warrior, *n.* Krieger, - m.
warship, *n.* Kriegsschiff, -e nt.
wash, 1. *n.* Wäsche, -n f. 2. *vb.* waschen*.
wash-basin, *n.* Waschbecken, - nt.
washroom, *n.* Waschraum, ⁼e m.
wasp, *n.* Wespe, -n f.
waste, 1. *n.* Abfall, ⁼e m. 2. *adj.* *(superfluous)* überflüssig; *(bare)* öde. 3. *vb.* verschwen'den, vergeu'den.
watch, 1. *n.* *(guard)* Wache, -n f.; *(timepiece)* Uhr, -en f.; *(wrist w.)* Armbanduhr, -en f.; *(pocket w.)* Taschenuhr, -en f. 2. *vb.* *(guard)* bewa'chen, passen auf; *(observe)* beob'achten, acht·geben; **(w. out)** auf·passen; **(w. out!)** Vorsicht!
watchful, *adj.* wachsam.
watchmaker, *n.* Uhrmacher, - m.
water, 1. *n.* Wasser, - nt. 2. *vb.* wässern, begie'ßen*.

waterbed, *n.* Matratze mit Wasser gefüllt *f.*

waterfall, *n.* Wasserfall, ⸗e *m.*

waterproof, *adj.* wasserdicht.

wave, 1. *n.* Welle, -n *f.* **2.** *vb.* wellen, wogen; *(flag)* wehen; *(hand)* winken.

waver, *vb.* schwanken.

wax, **1.** *n.* Wachs, -e *nt.* **2.** *vb.* wachsen; *(moon)* zu·nehmen*.

way, *n.* Weg, -e *m.*

we, *pron.* wir.

weak, *adj.* schwach (⸗).

weaken, *vb. (tr.)* schwächen; *(intr.)* schwach werden*.

weakness, *n.* Schwäche, -n *f.*

wealth, *n.* Reichtum, ⸗er *m.;* *(possessions)* Vermö'gen, - *nt.;* *(abundance)* Fülle *f.*

wealthy, *adj.* reich, vermö'gend.

weapon, *n.* Waffe, -n *f.*

wear, *vb.* tragen*, an·haben*, *(hat)* auf·haben*; **(w. out)** ab·tragen*, *(fig.)* erschöp'fen; **(w. away)** aus·höhlen.

weary, *adj.* müde, erschöpft*.

weasel, *n.* Wiesel, - *nt.*

weather, 1. *n.* Wetter *nt.* **2.** *vb.* *(fig.)* durch·stehen*.

weather forecast, *n.* Wetter-vorher'sage *f.*

weave, *vb.* weben(*).

weaver, *n.* Weber, - *m.*

web, *n.* Netz, -e *nt.,* Gewe'be *nt.;* **(spider w.)** Spinngewebe *nt.*

wedding, *n.* Hochzeit, -en *f.*

wedge, *n.* Keil, -e *m.*

Wednesday, *n.* Mittwoch, -e *m.*

weed, 1. *n.* Unkraut *nt.* **2.** *vb.* jäten.

week, *n.* Woche, -n *f.*

weekday, *n.* Wochentag, -e *m.*

weekend, *n.* Wochenende, -n *nt.*

weekly, 1. *n.* Wochenschrift, -en *f.* **2.** *adj.* wöchentlich.

weep, *vb.* weinen.

weigh, *vb.* wiegen*; *(ponder)* wägen.

weight, *n.* Gewicht', -e *nt.;* *(burden)* Last, -en *f.*

weird, *adj.* unheimlich.

welcome, 1. *n.* Willkom'men *nt.* **2.** *vb.* bewill'kommnen, be-

grü'ßen. **3.** *adj.* willkom'men; **(you're w.)** bitte.

welfare, *n.* Wohlergehen *nt.;* *(social)* Wohlfahrt *f.*

well, 1. *n.* Brunnen, - *m.* **2.** *vb.* quellen*. **3.** *adv.* gut; *(health)* gesund' (⸗, -), wohl.

well-done, *adj.* gut gemacht; *(meat)* durchgebraten.

well-known, *adj.* bekannt'.

west, 1. *n.* Westen *m.* **2.** *adj.* westlich; West- *(cpds.)*.

western, *adj.* westlich.

westward, *adv.* nach Westen.

wet, 1. *adj.* naß (⸗, -). **2.** *vb.* nässen, naß machen.

whale, *n.* Walfisch, -e *m.*

what, 1. *pron.* was. **2.** *adj.* welcher, -es, -e.

whatever, 1. *pron.* was . . . auch. **2.** *adj.* welcher, -es, -e . . . auch.

wheat, *n.* Weizen *m.*

wheel, 1. *n.* Rad, ⸗er *nt.;* **(w. chair)** Rollstuhl, ⸗e *m.* **2.** *vb.* rollen.

when, 1. *adv.* *(question)* wann. **2.** *conj.* *(once in the past)* als; *(future; whenever)* wenn; *(indirect question)* wann.

whence, *adv.* woher', von wo.

whenever, 1. *conj.* wenn. **2.** *adv.* wann . . . auch.

where, *adv.* *(in what place)* wo; *(to what place)* wohin'; **(w. . . . from)** woher'.

wherever, *adv.* wo(hin) . . . auch.

whether, *conj.* ob.

which, *pron.&adj.* welcher, -es, -e.

whichever, *pron.&adj.* welcher, -es, -e . . . auch.

while, 1. *n.* Weile *f.* **2.** *conj.* während.

whim, *n.* Laune, -n *f.*

whip, 1. *n.* Peitsche, -n *f.* **2.** *vb.* peitschen, schlagen*.

whirl, *vb.* wirbeln.

whirlpool, *n.* Strudel, - *m.*

whirlwind, *n.* Wirbelwind, -e *m.*

whisker, *n.* Barthaar, -e *nt.*

whiskey, *n.* Whisky, -s *m.*

whisper, *vb.* flüstern.

whistle, 1. *n.* Flöte, -n *f.,* Pfeife, -n *f.* **2.** *vb.* flöten, pfeifen*.

white, *adj.* weiß.

who, *pron.* *(interrogative)* wer; *(relative)* der, das, die.